With gratitude to

Furthermore:
a program of the J.M. Kaplan Fund
©

for the generous support of the publication of this volume

DESIGNING
DETROIT

Great Lakes Books

A complete listing of the books in this series can be found online
at wsupress.wayne.edu

Editor

Thomas Klug
Marygrove College

Advisory Editors

Fredric C. Bohm
DeWitt, Michigan

Sandra Sageser Clark
Michigan Historical Center

Thomas R. Dilley
Grand Rapids, Michigan

Brian Leigh Dunnigan
Clements Library

De Witt Dykes
Oakland University

Joe Grimm
Michigan State University

Laurie Harris
Pleasant Ridge, Michigan

Charles K. Hyde
Pittsfield, Massachusetts

Susan Higman Larsen
Detroit Institute of Arts

Philip P. Mason
Prescott, Arizona and Eagle Harbor, Michigan

Dennis Moore
Consulate General of Canada

Erik C. Nordberg
Walter P. Reuther Library

Deborah Smith Pollard
University of Michigan–Dearborn

Michael O. Smith
Bentley Historical Library

Arthur M. Woodford
Harsens Island, Michigan

DESIGNING
DETROIT

WIRT ROWLAND AND THE RISE OF
MODERN AMERICAN ARCHITECTURE

MICHAEL G. SMITH

WAYNE STATE UNIVERSITY PRESS
DETROIT

ISBN 978-0-8143-3979-4 (jacketed cloth); ISBN 978-0-8143-3980-0 (ebook)

Library of Congress Cataloging Number: 2017933001

Designed and typeset by Rachel Ross
Composed in Adobe Garamond Pro

Wayne State University Press
Leonard N. Simons Building
4809 Woodward Avenue
Detroit, Michigan 48201-1309

Visit us online at wsupress.wayne.edu

All photographs by Michael G. Smith unless otherwise indicated.

CONTENTS

ARCHITECTURAL TERMS ILLUSTRATED

MODERN STRUCTURAL ELEMENTS

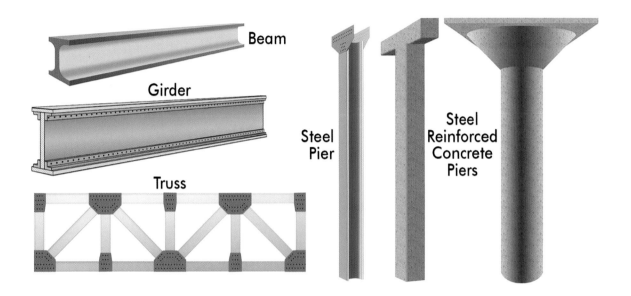

Beam

Girder

Truss

Steel Pier

Steel Reinforced Concrete Piers

THE GREEK AND ROMAN ORDERS

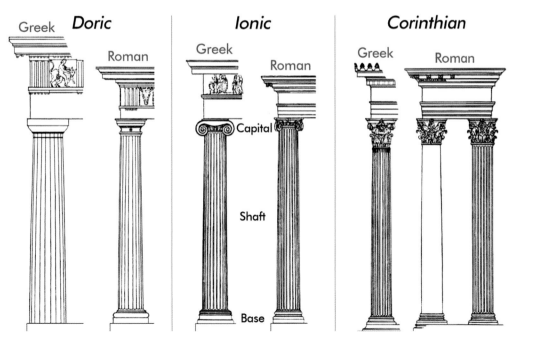

Doric

Greek

Roman

Ionic

Greek

Roman

Capital

Shaft

Base

Corinthian

Greek

Roman

BRICKWORK

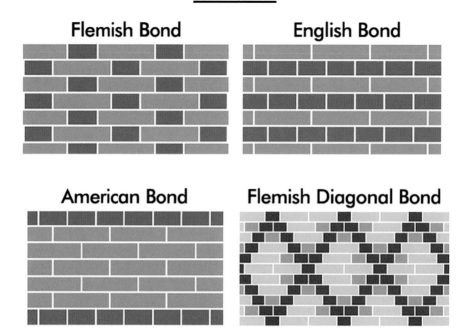

Flemish Bond

English Bond

American Bond

Flemish Diagonal Bond

STRUCTURAL SUPPORT METHODS

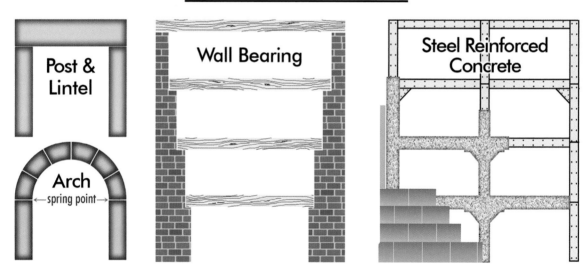

Post & Lintel

Arch
←— spring point —→

Wall Bearing

Steel Reinforced Concrete

ARCH TYPES

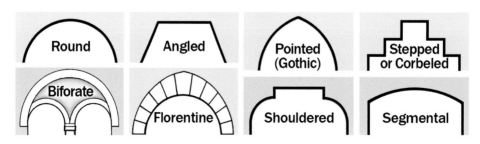

Round

Angled

Pointed (Gothic)

Stepped or Corbeled

Biforate

Florentine

Shouldered

Segmental

ROOF TYPES

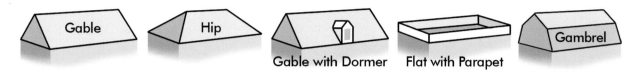

Gable · Hip · Gable with Dormer · Flat with Parapet · Gambrel

MODERN BUILDING PARTS

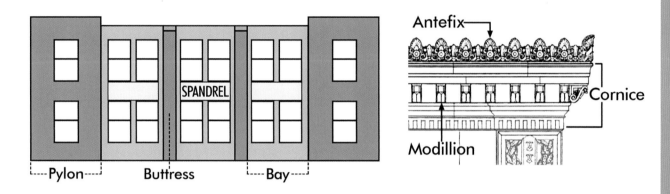

SPANDREL

Pylon · Buttress · Bay

CLASSICAL CORNICE FEATURES

Antefix

Cornice

Modillion

WINDOW AND DECORATIVE DETAILS

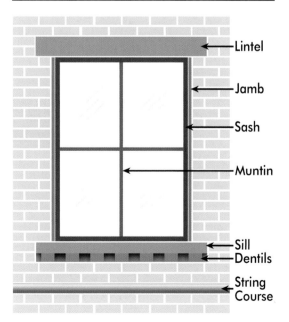

Lintel

Jamb

Sash

Muntin

Sill
Dentils

String
Course

WIRT C. ROWLAND

1878–1946

PREFACE

"They don't build 'em like they used to" was a comment I often heard when photographing Detroit's Guardian or Penobscot Buildings. Implicit in the comment is the view that buildings dating from the 1920s command a certain admiration, and even fascination, in part, owing to the luxurious materials that compose the structures. But something less tangible is at work as well. These buildings were made to be seen, and clearly, a great deal of effort was expended on crafting their outward appearance—a circumstance of which even the most casual observer is aware.

Over the years, a number of the city's buildings—not just these two skyscrapers—became favorites of mine. The Bankers Trust Company Building on the corner of Congress and Shelby Streets; a modern, limestone-faced building on East Jefferson Avenue with bold, stepped arches; an ivy-covered, red brick building further down Jefferson that housed the Ross Roy advertising agency; and looming over the Lodge Freeway, a former Michigan Bell warehouse topped with a commanding tower of brick and terra-cotta were all on my list. Outside of downtown Detroit, the plain but welcoming Hatcher library at the University of Michigan, with its enormous reading room, and the dramatic—and unexpected—Kirk in the Hills church in Bloomfield Hills, were both on my list. I couldn't pass by these structures without admiring their unique designs, well-composed facades, and carefully detailed exteriors.

In 2011, I was asked to conduct a tour of downtown Detroit for a small convention, requiring that I bone up on the city's history and architecture. Shortly after beginning my research, I discovered that all my favorite buildings were designed by one architect: Wirt Rowland. It surprised me that a modern master could leave behind such a visible legacy of achievement and not be well known.

Driven by a desire to learn about Rowland and discover more of his buildings, I delved further into his life and work. What fascinated me most was Rowland's resolute commitment to the view that success in any creative field, be it art, music, poetry, writing, or architecture, is achieved only through deep study, and mastery through repeated use, of the lawful principles underlying the activity.

March Phillipps—an author recommended by Rowland for his insight into the wellsprings of creative thought—once wrote: "Results of two very different kinds may be obtained from the study of art. Either we may obtain an insight into the laws and principles of art itself, or we may obtain an insight into the lives and characters of those by whom the art was evolved" (*The Works of Man*). This book, *Designing Detroit*, strives to illuminate both, examining the architecture community in one of the country's fastest-growing cities during the first half of the twentieth century, and presenting an overview of the methods by which one architect achieved consistent success in designing buildings of great beauty.

Buildings dating from the early decades of the last century are tightly intertwined with the history of the period; one can hardly become enlightened about one without the other. This book considers buildings within their historical context, as integral outgrowths of the economic, social, and technological circumstances existing at the time.

Rowland was systematic in his approach to design, as exemplified by his use of geometric methods for composing facades; even a cursory understanding of these methods affords one a more profound appreciation of his buildings. The approach taken herein is to explain these fascinating methods in such a way as they may be grasped by the nontechnical reader. In fact, the approach taken throughout this book is to assume no technical familiarity with architecture or architectural terms on the part of the reader.

It is hoped that in addition to stoking a greater admiration for Wirt Rowland and the architecture of his time, this book will aid in preserving his architectural legacy. Few of Rowland's buildings—too few, really—are listed on the National Register of Historic Places. His lesser works fall to the wrecking ball on a regular basis. While this is an unavoidable consequence of economic progress—earlier structures were demolished to make way for Rowland's buildings—perhaps more widespread knowledge of the history of a particular building may tip the scale in favor of reusing rather than replacing.

INTRODUCTION

Architecture, being the most broadly human of all the arts,
is the richest in human character.

—Lisle March Phillipps, *The Works of Man*, 1911

"It can't be quite right," wrote Florence Davies, art critic for the *Detroit News*, in a 1928 article quoting a typical reaction to the orange, forty-story building rising at Griswold and Congress Streets in Detroit's financial district. "'Do you like it?' is a question one hears on the street, and in the studios of Detroit artists, often with a good deal of doubt implied in the asking." "The disturbing factor seems to be color," she concluded.[1]

The *Wall Street Journal* noted the new building "is conspicuous for its modern design, employing lavish use of color."[2] The *Christian Science Monitor*, betraying a bit more emotion, described the structure as "astonishing."[3] A Detroit business journal, reporting on the widespread attention received by the half-finished building, commented: "The idea of constructing a skyscraper in which the exterior treatment is in this new orange shade has excited unparalleled enthusiasm and interest in all parts of the country and letters have reached Detroit from all the metropolitan territories."[4]

The building's forty-nine-year-old designer, Wirt Clinton Rowland, found many of his peers in Detroit's architectural community viewed the unusual structure with disdain.[5] Rowland's former employer, renowned architect Albert Kahn, was confident in Rowland's skills but perplexed by his latest design; he confided to a fellow architect: "there must be something to it, Rowland did it."[6]

Even among those directly involved in the building's construction, controversy raged. Mary Chase Perry of Pewabic Pottery, manufacturer of colored tiles for the structure, wrote: "An effort to classify the style of this building was the occasion for many conjectures—as to the period; as to the type of ornament—if any; as to the choice of colors both for the brick and tile; in fine as to the expediency of such a building anyway." On these topics, said Perry, there were "several heated discussions—not to say agitated debates."[7]

It is understandable that nonarchitects were surprised and puzzled at the sight of an unusual building, but that so many in the art and architecture community reacted with scorn—and did so even before half the structure's exterior was in place—reveals a shortcoming in outlook: fresh efforts are often judged in comparison with what is familiar and well established. Innovators, particularly those with uncommon ability and great personal motivation, frequently operate beyond the horizon, engaged in developing new methods. Although these new efforts may be disparaged when first unveiled, once understood, they often become widely adopted.

Wirt Rowland was a pioneer and one of the most consistently innovative building designers of the early twentieth century. The sculptor Corrado Parducci (1900–1981), who worked with architects throughout the country, said of Rowland: "he reached out, rather than looking back . . . a revolutionary in his ideas. He was very progressive, and I held him in high esteem."[8] During his lifetime, Rowland's work was recognized nationally, not only for its artistic merit but also for its innovative use of materials and technology. At one time, the tallest building in each of Michigan's four largest cities was a Rowland-designed structure; his buildings may be found on both coasts of the United States, and include the nation's first air force base and first air-conditioned skyscraper. His innovations influenced iconic buildings throughout the country, from the Chrysler Building in New York City to Art Deco style hotels in Miami Beach.

Of the sixteen major skyscrapers in downtown Detroit designed by local architects prior to 1930, Rowland was responsible for five. The balance were designed—with one exception—by two European-born architects: Louis Kamper (1861–1953), from Bavaria, and John Donaldson (1854–1941) from Scotland.[9] Kamper and Donaldson, in designing their tall buildings, adapted European decorative features to a completely new type of structure— the skyscraper. Rowland, on the other hand, saw European-style ornamentation as unfit for use on a building many times taller than those from which the decorations were copied. He sought to develop a distinctly American architectural style, one that showed respect for its Old World roots but was more closely associated with American culture and the revolutionary construction technologies that gave rise to the skyscraper. The Guardian and Penobscot Buildings stand as testimony to Rowland's achievement of this goal; they are widely recognized as exceptional examples of uniquely American skyscraper design. Alastair Duncan, in his 1986 book, *American Art Deco*, wrote: "The Union Trust [Guardian] Building in Detroit stands unquestionably as America's premier Art Deco bank building."[10]

What of the creative individual responsible for bringing these structures into being? Hundreds of books have been written on architects Frank Lloyd Wright, Albert Kahn, and Louis Sullivan; Rowland, who designed more tall buildings than all three men together, has yet to be the subject of a single volume. This lack of attention may be due in part to Rowland's modest and unassuming nature. He cared little for self-promotion or public recognition— seeing his ideas manifest in a completed structure provided his greatest satisfaction. Another factor: Rowland was employed by Detroit's largest and most capable architecture firms and, as far as the public was concerned, the "architect" of a building was the architecture firm—that just one of the firm's employees, the chief designer, was responsible for crafting the layout and appearance of a building was often glossed over.

Although not so well known to the general public, Rowland was revered by his fellow architects for his superb design skills, encyclopedic knowledge of the field, and selfless collaboration with and mentoring of others. He organized and led local architecture clubs, which focused on developing the design skills of members. The longtime editor of the *Weekly Bulletin*, journal of the Michigan Society of Architects, wrote of Rowland: "there is one designer who has been most intimately connected with [Detroit's architectural] development whose name is not so well known to the public. When the history of Detroit's present architecture is written, the name of Wirt C. Rowland will be near the top."[11] The *Western Architect* noted that in Detroit, design "capability is more evenly distributed than in most cities," a circumstance attributed to "a few leaders in architectural design [who] established the associations that welcomed the unattached practitioner and encouraged his development. . . . The work of the few highest in opportunity and ability unselfishly has aided the many to like standards of work."[12] The legacy of this collaborative effort may be seen in the exceptionally high quality of architecture throughout the Detroit area generally, particularly structures dating from the first half of the twentieth century.[13]

Rowland's success as a building designer was aided immeasurably by impeccable timing and the good fortune to have come of age in Michigan. Two nearly simultaneous developments after 1900 in Detroit provided the fertile environment for Rowland's subsequent accomplishments. First was rapid growth in the manufacture of automobiles: an industry that turned out just over 4,000 passenger cars in 1900 mass produced 5.4 million vehicles in 1929.[14] Spurred by the auto industry's dramatic growth, Detroit's population exploded from roughly 300,000 in 1900 to nearly 1.6 million by 1930—an increase of more than 500 percent. The second development was the perfection of a revolutionary new construction technology—steel reinforced concrete—that transformed building design, upending the field of architecture in the process.

Auto industry growth propelled demand for new factories, warehouses, and dealerships; industries related to auto and those necessary to support Detroit's growing population sustained rapid expansion as well: transportation, telecommunications, advertising, banking, housing, and education. Although marginally involved with the auto industry early on, Rowland was most often concerned with structures serving the needs of a rapidly developing urban center: offices, banks, hotels, telephone exchanges, and schools, nearly all of which were constructed with steel reinforced concrete. Rowland designed more than twenty schools and dozens of telephone exchanges, but his most substantial—and elaborate—type was the bank building, particularly bank headquarters buildings. The remarkable economic expansion that took place in Michigan between 1900 and 1930 greatly strained the state's banking resources but fueled considerable growth among these institutions, providing a windfall of work for Rowland. Of the seven skyscrapers he designed throughout the state, six were bank headquarters buildings.[15] It was the exceptional and peculiar growth of the banking community during the 1920s that largely defined Detroit's skyline, and Rowland's most visible legacy.

With construction booming in Detroit, the city became a nationally recognized hotbed of architectural innovation. The journal *Cement World* noted in 1907: "in Detroit, many large structures of reinforced concrete, monumental in size and design, are being constructed. It was forcibly shown on all sides that Detroit is far ahead of Chicago in reinforced construction."[16] In 1915, a writer for *Architecture* offered his impressions of the city: "I have not seen anywhere such a great proportion of new work, not only interesting, but of permanent value in architectural development as in Detroit, and this applies . . . to the whole range of building activities, banks, hotels, office buildings, factories, churches and residences, and with the tremendously high standard that has been set."[17] The *Western Architect* devoted its October 1916 issue to Detroit architecture, with an introduction stating: "The phenomenal growth of Detroit during the past decade, aside from its exceptional advancement in architectural design, has attracted the attention of the profession to the work of Detroit architects . . . from the lowly bungalow to the apartment buildings which rival in design the best that our cities, East and West, afford."[18]

The new construction technology created enormous opportunities—and challenges—in the design of buildings, particularly for an entirely new type of structure that it made possible, the skyscraper, for which there was no historical design precedent. Arriving in Detroit in 1901 to work as an apprentice architectural draftsman, Rowland was ideally positioned to contribute to this wave of growth. His exceptional potential as a designer was quickly recognized, and over the subsequent three decades he worked for the city's foremost architects: George D. Mason, Albert Kahn, and Smith, Hinchman, and Grylls—Mason and Kahn were two of the country's earliest pioneers in the use of steel reinforced concrete for a wide range of buildings. By 1905, Rowland achieved the position of lead designer, with responsibility for fashioning a building's outward appearance and crafting its shape and layout to best suit its intended purpose. Throughout the years of brisk construction, Rowland designed an astonishingly wide range of structures, and in the process, devised a new approach to building design, based on classical principles but adapted to modern construction methods, materials, and lifestyles.

With the onset of the Great Depression, the heyday of construction came to an end, and, though Rowland had many fewer projects, he continued to innovate, particularly in the use of new materials. He put these years to good use, as well, by churning out a great deal of writing on architectural subjects.

As is sometimes the case with those for whom creative endeavors are all-consuming, Rowland was a workaholic, relentlessly immersed in exploring architecture problems and furthering his knowledge of the field. It was for this reason, most likely, that Rowland never married.

Rowland's interests, however, were far from narrow; he had an intense love for music, poetry, great literature, and, in particular, drawing. From an early age, he made freehand sketches in pencil, thereby refining his perception of the works of both man and nature. Later in life, he would recommend freehand drawing as the best preparation for one contemplating a career in architecture.[19] Rowland's musical skill was evident in his learning to play organ and piano at a young age and in his participation as a vocalist in the church choir.[20] Music, too, he would later recommend as a path by which architectural designers could acquire a well-rounded understanding of the universal principles of art.

Unlike many successful architects, Rowland never designed for himself a lavish home, living instead in a rented room and spending his money on fine food, clothing, and frequent travel. He also owned an automobile, though he never learned to drive, coaxing friends into taking the wheel on his behalf. He often spent weekends at the family home in Clinton, Michigan, luring drivers with free room and board and trips to the Irish Hills. After his mother's death in 1915, Rowland inherited the home, which he used as a weekend retreat, remodeling and expanding it in 1927.

The Village of Clinton, Michigan, was settled in 1829 by New Yorkers who named the town for DeWitt Clinton, governor of their former state. Located fifty miles from Detroit on Michigan Avenue, the road to Chicago, the town thrived as a trading and manufacturing center in the late nineteenth century.[21] Rowland's parents were both born in New York State, Clinton Charles Rowland in 1831 and Ruth Melissa Willis in 1842, but how they came to be married and living in Clinton is unclear. Records show Melissa Willis married James E. Burton in 1861, but nothing more was heard of the ill-fated Mr. Burton other than that he was buried in Clinton's Riverside Cemetery in 1863, suggesting he may have died in the Civil War. In any event, in 1867 Melissa and Clinton Rowland were married.

Clinton Rowland was employed as an engineer running the great Corliss steam engine that powered equipment in the Clinton Woolen Mill, one of the country's largest manufacturers of wool.[22] Melissa Rowland was active in the town's First Congregational

Church where she taught Sunday school for more than fifty years.[23] In 1867, a daughter, Grace Gail, was born to the Rowlands. Soon after, the couple purchased a house at 307 West Franklin in Clinton. On Sunday, December 1, 1878, at 6:00 p.m., Wirt Clinton Rowland was born.

At the age of eight, a quest for reading material brought Rowland to a stack of *Harper's* magazines, one of which featured a seventeen-page article on London's Lambeth Palace. Rowland was fascinated by the building's details and, particularly, its plans.[24] His career choice was sealed when he realized: "an idea became a plan and a plan became a building, the three were inseparable and one with me the rest of my life."[25] "I straightaway began planning my own castles," wrote Rowland of the aftermath, "with all the fireplaces, galleries and secret staircases in great number. But my mother was always critical of the amount of space to be used for clothes closets."[26]

Around the same time, young Rowland received a lesson in the shortcomings of existing construction methods when the Clinton Woolen Mill burned to the ground. Manufacturing buildings such as the Clinton mill were constructed with wooden floors supported by heavy timbers anchored to the masonry outer walls of the structure. Fire was an ever-present danger, due to the building's wood construction, though the large timbers burned slowly, hopefully giving occupants adequate time to escape. At around 6:30 a.m. on December 11, 1886, just after workers had arrived at the mill, an explosion occurred near the elevator shaft of the nine-year-old building, sparking a fire that quickly enveloped the

1. The Rowland home in Clinton. (Sharon Scott)

2. Rowland (*first row, far right*) with his class at the Clinton Union School, April 21, 1886. (Historical Society of Clinton, Michigan)

structure. Clinton Rowland was at work in the engine room adjacent to the main building and happened to be standing near the outlet of a drain pipe that extended from the elevator shaft. When the explosion occurred, flames shot down the pipe, burned the hair from his head and face, and blew away the window and sash behind him. Although Rowland received burns on his face and hands, he considered himself fortunate to have escaped with his life.[27] (The mill was quickly rebuilt after the fire but succumbed once again to flames in 2007.)

Shortly after this narrow brush with death, the family again faced tragedy: Grace Gail became ill and died from unknown causes the same month. Wirt Rowland later penciled an epitaph to his sister in the family Bible.

> W. C. Rowland is the son of C. C. Rowland & R. M. Rowland. He is
>
> now 11 years old
>
> Written by W. C. Rowland in 1890
>
> Grace Gail Rowland died December 1886. She was 18 years old
>
> W. C. Rowland was born on December 1st 1878
>
> G. G. Rowland was born October 1867[28]

Among the Rowland family's relatives in Clinton were Genevieve Lancaster Burroughs (1864–1895)—daughter of Clinton Rowland's sister Mary Elizabeth Rowland Lancaster— and Genevieve's husband, Charles Silvers Burroughs (1857–1937). Wirt developed a particularly close relationship with their son, Frank Burroughs (1884–1973), which the two

maintained throughout their lives, even after Rowland moved
to Detroit and Burroughs to Grand Rapids.

Rowland graduated from Clinton High School in
1896, having filled the flyleaves of his school books with
"sketches of every possible project." "I didn't like mathematics," he said, "but solid geometry—I had them there, and
passed perfect on my final exam in that subject."[29] Rowland
did not attend college, though later in life he wrote of the
importance of doing so: "the literary course in college is the
basis of all life training. It teaches one to think, to discipline
the mind, and its experience compiles and builds up permanent ideas and ideals concerning human affairs. It fits

3. Grace Gail Rowland from
a school photo. (Historical
Society of Clinton, Michigan)

one for a broader place in any profession."[30] Rowland nevertheless acquired the "literary course" through his own efforts, evidence of which appears in his writings, where he
cites, among others, Samuel Coleridge, Joseph Conrad, Thomas Hardy, John Milton, and
Friedrich Nietzsche.

Rowland's first job was at the woolen mill where his father worked, a position that
instilled in him an appreciation for adequate light and ventilation in the work environment
but offered little opportunity to exercise his artistic skills. However, Rowland was able to
advance toward his goal of becoming an architect by means of courses he took through the
International Correspondence School. After a few months at the mill, he was offered a clerk-
ing position at Smith-Richmond and Company, a private bank in Clinton. Rowland joked
that when an acquaintance commented to his mother, "I hear your son is in the bank," his
mother responded, "Yes, he's mopping the floors and tending the furnace."[31] Nevertheless,
this was the first of many occasions when banks and bankers would play a significant role in
Rowland's life.

The First Congregational Church of Clinton was constructed in 1844 as a simple
but attractive structure. In 1899, the congregation constructed a new belfry, the design
and plans for which were provided by Rowland, his qualifications having been acquired
entirely through self-study, including the correspondence courses he had taken.[32] Yet the
belfry was a suitable addition of appropriate design and remains in place atop the church,
essentially unchanged.

Although Rowland was certain of his desire to become an architect, he continued
to labor away, day after day, in the bank, while many of his contemporaries, possessed
of the same career aspirations, sought out apprentice positions with architects in their

4. Michigan Avenue in Clinton. Smith-Richmond and Company was located in the brick building right of center. (Historical Society of Clinton, Michigan)

local communities or in large cities. At the time, the chief route to a career in architecture was through on-the-job training, as architecture schools in the United States were just being established; Harvard's school of architecture was begun in 1893 and the University of Michigan's architecture school was not opened until 1906. Rowland could easily have boarded a train to either Detroit or Chicago and sought work in an architecture firm, but he failed to do so.

The cashier of Smith-Richmond, and youngest of its four founders, Leander W. Kimball (1868–1955), became good friends with Rowland and an admirer of his raw talent. Fearing that this great talent might go to waste, in early 1901 Kimball seized control of Rowland's destiny by securing for him a position with an architecture firm in Detroit.[33]

FIRST CONGREGATIONAL CHURCH
CLINTON, MICH. 1265

5. Rowland designed the belfry for the First Congregational Church of Clinton in 1899, and later provided plans for the Kirker Memorial, the two-story addition to the building completed in 1923. (Historical Society of Clinton, Michigan)

1
WORKING FOR "THE DEAN"

The importance of a study of history is acknowledged by all. To the architect it must be a never-ending source of idea and inspiration. It forms the firm foundation upon which we must build our architectural aspirations.

—Wirt Rowland, "The Making of an Architect," 1920

Rowland arrived in Detroit in March 1901, working first for Rogers and MacFarlane, a consequential architecture firm that later designed the massive United States Tire Company (Uniroyal) plant in Detroit on East Jefferson Avenue at Grand Boulevard.[1] Rowland became fast friends with the firm's sole draftsman, H. Augustus "Gus" O'Dell (1875–1965).[2] In May of the following year, Rowland left the firm, taking advantage of an opportunity to work for George D. Mason (1856–1948), one of the city's foremost architects, often respectfully referred to as the "Dean of Detroit architects." Mason began his career in architecture in 1873, and in 1878[3] formed Mason and Rice, a partnership with Zachariah Rice. Over the next twenty years, the firm produced many notable structures, including Mackinac Island's Grand Hotel (1887) and Detroit's First Presbyterian Church (1889, on Woodward Avenue at Edmund Place).

When the partnership with Rice ended, Mason joined with his former employee, Albert Kahn, in the firm of Mason and Kahn. Although the partnership lasted only from March 1901 to March 1902, it produced a number of notable structures, including the Palms Apartment Building, Belle Isle Aquarium, University of Michigan West Engineering Building, and Temple Beth El (Bonstelle Theater).[4] Although their partnership ended in March 1902,[5] the two men jointly oversaw completion of buildings under construction.[6]

Mason's next business arrangement, beginning in March 1902, was Mason and Reed-Hill, with William Reed-Hill (1870–1945) and associate architect Walter S. Painter (1877–1957). It was during the tenure of this enterprise that Rowland began working for Mason. Painter's major project at the time was the widely admired Quebec Auditorium (Capitole de Québec).[7] The partnership came to an abrupt end on June 9, 1903, when

Reed-Hill filed suit against Mason, claiming Mason had seized control of the business.[8] Mason and Painter subsequently formed a partnership that carried on until around 1904, when Painter left to become chief architectural designer for the Canadian Pacific Railway, for whom he designed the massive Banff Springs Hotel. Mason, having wearied of partnerships, established his own firm.

Rowland benefited greatly from his eight years working for Mason, from whom he received instruction in all facets of architecture. Mason, according to Rowland, "had the patience of a saint and was like a father to me."[9] Equally important was Mason's extensive library of architectural publications.[10] Rowland, a voracious reader, immersed himself in this material and quickly mastered it. So quickly, in fact, that when Mason received commissions in 1905 for two large hotels, he delegated to Rowland responsibility for building design and drawing plans for both.[11] That Mason could entrust responsibility for the two largest private building contracts in the city's history to a twenty-seven-year-old with just four years of career experience is astonishing.[12]

These two projects, Hotel Pontchartrain and Tuller Hotel,[13] exemplified the maturation of a revolutionary building technology: steel reinforced concrete. In the latter part of the nineteenth century, the invention of the elevator made it practical to contemplate tall buildings, but the method by which buildings were constructed at that time was not suitable for tall structures. Buildings were supported by thick walls of masonry—brick or stone—and the taller the structure, the thicker the outer walls had to be in order to support the weight above. Windows reduced the load-bearing capacity of walls, and so were limited in number and made as narrow as practical. Floors were supported by heavy wooden beams strung between the exterior masonry walls, thereby transmitting much of the weight of the building's contents to the walls as well.

In addition to the practical size limitations inherent in load-bearing masonry walls, these structures were particularly susceptible to complete and rapid destruction by fire. Blazes easily spread from one floor to another until the entire structure was engulfed. In fact, the ends of the beams supporting the floors were "fire-cut," set into the masonry with extra space above them, or cut at an angle, so that if they burned and snapped, the beam ends would not pull the supporting wall down and collapse the building.

6. Diagram of a typical masonry construction building, with floors supported by wooden beams and exterior load-bearing walls.

7-1 & 7-2. The Ford Piquette Avenue Plant, completed in 1904, is of masonry construction: wooden floors, beams, and piers, with exterior walls of brick. The beams beneath the floors are supported by interior piers and exterior brick walls; beams are held in place atop the piers by cast iron caps. The long building is broken up into sections by brick firewalls, equipped with a solid wood fire door, which would close automatically in case of fire. Firewalls and fire suppression systems, in the form of overhead sprinklers, were intended to provide the building's occupants with time to escape a fire but rarely prevented fire from consuming the structure.

8. The Vinton Building at 600 Woodward Avenue under construction in April 1917. The building's steel skeleton is exposed on the two upper floors, while the floors below have wooden forms in place into which concrete will be poured, forming the building's frame. (For a technical discussion of the type of steel reinforced concrete construction employed here, see *Cyclopedia of Architecture, Carpentry, and Building*, American Technical Society, volume 4, beginning page 107.) (Construction of the Vinton Building, Detroit, MI—April 9, 1917, Albert Kahn Papers, Albert Kahn Associates, Inc., and the Bentley Historical Library, University of Michigan)

9. The Vinton Building in May and November 1917. On the *left*, the building frame members on the upper floors are wrapped in wooden concrete forms; the lower floors have been poured, the forms removed, and the concrete frame is visible. On the *right*, the building is complete with its skin of bricks and windows covering the concrete frame. (Construction of the Vinton Building, Detroit, MI, April 15 and 21, 1917, and November 1917, Albert Kahn Papers, Albert Kahn Associates, Inc., and the Bentley Historical Library, University of Michigan)

In the 1880s, a successful effort to supersede masonry supporting walls was achieved by employing a rigid internal framework of iron and steel. It was quickly discovered that heat from a fire in the building softened the steel frame, leading to collapse. To fireproof the steel, all frame members had to be completely encased in terra-cotta tiles, an additional and costly process.

Introduction of the rotary cement kiln around 1890 dramatically reduced the cost of Portland cement, spurring greater use of concrete in place of costlier steel. Concrete could support enormous weight, and steel provided great strength—used together, the two appeared to compose the perfect construction technology. By 1900, a number of systems were in use for reinforced concrete construction. Although these systems were generally successful, slight deviations from rigid design requirements or procedures for handling the concrete resulted in dramatic failures. The four-story Otsego Hotel in Jackson collapsed while under construction in 1902,[14] killing one worker and seriously injuring two others, and in 1904, the nearly completed Boos-Basso Building in Battle Creek suffered extensive damage when the fifth floor gave way, taking out the floors beneath as it fell.[15]

Mason and Kahn recognized the enormous potential of the technology and used reinforced concrete for the floors of the Palms Apartments, completed in 1902, and the 1903 Engineering Building at the University of Michigan.[16] Kahn, however, later acknowledged the risk in using a "system then little known"; there were few firms in the country experienced in the architectural use of concrete—the floors of the Palms Apartments were constructed by a firm that built concrete sidewalks.[17]

Unlike a beam of wood or steel, which bends or cracks at the center when loaded beyond its maximum strength, concrete crumbles unpredictably. It could be made stronger by embedding steel reinforcements within, but a systematic method of doing so had yet to be discovered, making it difficult to calculate with any certainty the maximum load-bearing capacity of the material. "In calculating the strength of a beam," explained Albert Kahn's brother Moritz, "we assume that under a uniformly distributed load the maximum bending moment occurs at the center, and this is where the beam will fail. If in actual test to destruction we find it failing at some other point, our original assumption is wrong and all our subsequent calculations count for naught."[18]

The problem was solved in 1903 by another of Albert's brothers, Julius Kahn, Kahn's chief engineer. The "Kahn System," as Julius's system was called, relied on steel reinforcement bars set at a 45-degree angle to the concrete member so that the steel and concrete would function together as a truss, with the steel resisting tension, and concrete, compression. When tested, failure would result from the steel pulling apart, so the strength of the member could be reliably calculated based on the maximum strength of the steel. A structure could now be confidently designed to require the minimum amount of costly building material needed to attain adequate strength for the intended purpose.[19]

The Kahn System was increasingly adopted as the preferred method for constructing reinforced concrete buildings, resulting in concrete rapidly displacing both masonry and fireproofed steel as the means for supporting buildings. Nowhere was that advance more manifest than in Detroit; *Cement Age* noted in 1906: "Reinforced concrete construction . . . has created such a demand for cement in Detroit . . . that the various factories of Michigan are running to their full capacity and then cannot keep up with their orders."[20] In some cities, skepticism over the method's safety delayed wide adoption

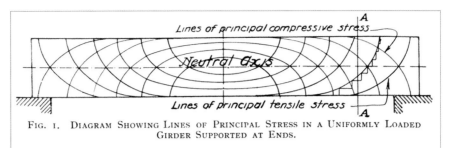

FIG. 1. DIAGRAM SHOWING LINES OF PRINCIPAL STRESS IN A UNIFORMLY LOADED GIRDER SUPPORTED AT ENDS.

FIG. 2. TEST OF UNIFORMLY LOADED SLAB. FAILURE BY SHEAR.

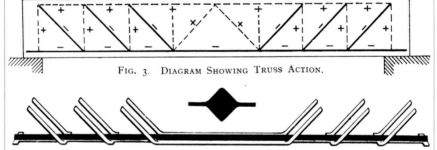

FIG. 3. DIAGRAM SHOWING TRUSS ACTION.

FIG. 4. CROSS SECTION AND VIEW OF KAHN TRUSSED BAR.

FIG. 5. TEST OF UNIFORMLY LOADED BEAM REINFORCED WITH KAHN TRUSSED BARS.
(Compare with Fig. 2.

10. An article by Moritz Kahn in *Concrete and Constructional Engineering* from March 1906 contains photos of concrete slab tested to failure. In the first photo, the concrete failed in shear at its ends, along the lines of stress. In the second photo, a concrete beam reinforced with Kahn System trussed bars failed in the middle, as expected, due to the the steel truss failing under maximum load.

and resulted in limits on the height of concrete structures. New York City's Bureau of Buildings refused to grant permits for reinforced concrete construction (except for private residences) until 1905.[21] In Cleveland, a sixteen-story hotel was derailed in 1907 by the city's building code, which limited concrete structures of any kind to six stories.[22]

Construction of the ten-story Tuller Hotel on Park Avenue at the west end of Grand Circus Park began late in the summer of 1905. Although the building's owner, Lew Whiting Tuller (1869–1957), was an architect, he lacked the qualifications to design a large, reinforced concrete structure. For this, he hired George Mason, who provided the design, structural details, and working drawings.[23] Mason, in turn, delegated the building's design and preparation

11. A typical steel reinforced concrete structure of the early twentieth century, this warehouse has been partially stripped of its outer skin, and its concrete frame is clearly visible. Floors are supported by piers topped with a spread capital and drop panel to spread the floor's weight over a larger area. The outer walls are made of hollow terra-cotta structural tile, which fills the space between frame members. The structure is sheathed with a skin of bricks secured by steel tabs embedded in the concrete. Bricks are supported above the windows by, in this case, a steel bracket attached to the frame.

of working drawings to Rowland while retaining for himself the structural engineering.[24] When the Tuller opened in July 1906, it was the second reinforced concrete hotel in the Midwest and second tallest in the nation.

Tuller operated three large apartment buildings in Detroit. The Tuller Hotel was originally intended as the fourth in his collection of high-class lodgings, which is why the building had the appearance of a large apartment building (such as the Palms on East Jefferson) and why it was located on Grand Circus Park, far from the main business area.[25] The exceptional shortage of hotel rooms in Detroit at the time might have spurred Tuller to market his new venture as a hotel.

Advertisements for the hotel prominently described it as "fire proof," a point not lost on travelers as hotel fires were quite common. Big city hotel fires were the deadliest, but smaller blazes added to the toll. In Michigan, a 1903 fire at the Travelers' Home in

Menominee left one dead and three burned.[26] The following year, the Bryan Hotel in Lansing "burned like tinder," killing at least four and leaving four more burned or injured.[27] One year later, the Pacific Hotel in Big Rapids "burned to the ground," resulting in one fatality.[28] Steel reinforced concrete construction, if not truly "fire proof," is far more fire resistant than masonry structures of brick, wood, and iron. For this reason alone, as construction with reinforced concrete became routine, it was the method of choice for hotels, schools, theaters, factories, and public buildings.[29]

The Tuller Hotel occasioned little fanfare as it rose from the corner of Park and Adams. However, the second of George Mason's hotel projects, a replacement for the 1881 Russell House, received much publicity in the Detroit papers. This was due in part to the building's highly visible location on Woodward Avenue and Cadillac Square, and anticipation that the new hotel's four hundred rooms would help alleviate Detroit's shortage of accommodations. (An August 17, 1905, article on the new hotel in the *Detroit Free Press* began: "It is not an exaggeration to say that the business men of Detroit are crying for better hotel accommodations."[30])

Absolutely Fire Proof.

12. The Tuller Hotel in its original configuration, prior to the addition of four floors in 1909. (Detroit Publishing Company)

The hotel's owner—the Detroit Hotel Company—was composed of interests in Detroit, Cleveland, and New York City. In addition to Mason, two architecture firms in New York submitted proposals to the owners, who decided in early August 1905 to hire Mason but employ the prominent New York firm of McKim, Mead, and White as consulting architects.[31] Another New York–based firm, Westinghouse, Church, Kerr, and Co., was selected to construct the building. Within three weeks, Mason and Rowland had prepared preliminary plans for the building, and on Thursday, September 7, the plans were approved by the Detroit interests at a meeting in Mason's office. Blueprints in hand, at 3:40 that afternoon Mason and Rowland boarded a train for New York City, arriving the next morning

13. Hotel Pontchartrain on Woodward Avenue under construction in 1907. The structure at this stage would have presented a puzzling spectacle to observers accustomed to seeing a building's exterior supporting walls built from the ground up. (Detroit Publishing Company Photograph Collection, Library of Congress Prints and Photographs Division)

at eight. They met first with William Mead of McKim, Mead, and White and then with representatives of the construction firm. Their work done for the day, the two men took in Coney Island Amusement Park that evening.[32]

The Russell House was razed beginning in December 1905, and by the end of the month, complete plans for the new hotel were approved, with the exception of the layout of the hotel room floors. The hotel manager wished the rooms to be made larger, which required redrawing the floor plans. Mason and Rowland spent New Year's Day, 1906, in the office completing these final revisions. Finishing late in the afternoon, Mason caught a train to New York City, delivering the final plans to the consulting architects and construction firm the following day.[33]

By spring, work was under way on the southeast corner of Woodward and Cadillac Square on what was now called "Hotel Pontchartrain." Like the Tuller, Hotel Pontchartrain was to be ten stories high, with a foundation adequate to support a later addition of four floors. The building had three basement stories that extended below the surface to a depth of forty feet. Unfortunately, once the basement had been excavated, testing of the earth beneath revealed numerous pockets of quicksand within the clay.[34]

Development of steel supporting frames made tall buildings practical, but steel frames require a much different foundation than masonry-wall-supported structures. The weight of a steel frame building is concentrated on the frame's piers, much like the weight of a table is supported by its legs. The relatively small face of each pier carries an enormous amount of weight. If the piers are not standing

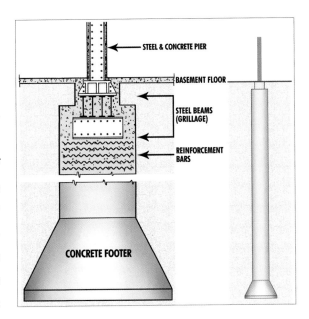

14. Typical method for supporting a large steel frame building. Each pier of the building's frame stands on a web of steel beams set within concrete. Beneath is a reinforced concrete foundation pier extending down into the earth. The bottom of the pier—the footer—is placed at a depth that assures adequate support for the building and is often bell shaped to spread weight over a larger area.

upon bedrock, then, in order to spread weight over a larger surface area, the pier typically rests on a broad platform of steel beams set side by side (called grillage). This arrangement is encased in concrete, and usually sits atop a reinforced concrete pier, which extends as deep into the earth as is necessary for secure footing. For tall buildings, placing piers upon bedrock is ideal. However, bedrock is often located so far beneath the surface that reaching it with the digging equipment available in the early twentieth century was cost prohibitive. Hardpan, a dense, impermeable layer of soil, is satisfactory, with hard clay the next best alternative. Beneath downtown Detroit, to a depth of about eighty or ninety feet, is clay—mostly blue clay—interspersed with occasional layers of wet sand and gravel (essentially "quicksand"). Below the clay is a layer of gravel, hardpan, and finally limestone bedrock at around 100 to 130 feet down.[35]

The piers for the Pontchartrain could not rest upon quicksand, so it was decided by Westinghouse, Church, and Kerr to abandon the original plan of using large concrete piers with footers and instead sink a forest of three thousand tightly spaced steel piles extending forty feet below the basement floor. On top of these piles was constructed an immense concrete foundation, three feet thick and reinforced with twisted steel bars.[36] The piers of the Pontchartrain's steel skeleton rested upon this foundation. Of this weighty structure, Wallace Franklin, Michigan manager of the construction company, said, "If any one ever wants to go any further down, should the new hotel be deemed too small in the coming centuries, the contractors will have a beautiful job getting through that three feet of rock and steel."[37] (Although wrong on the reason and date, Franklin correctly anticipated the great difficulty of cutting through the nearly impenetrable foundation.)

Once problems below the surface were resolved, construction proceeded rapidly, and the Pontchartrain opened with a gala dinner on October 29, 1907. As over four hundred invited guests dined, more than four thousand sightseers crowded outside, awaiting a turn to stroll through the lobby.[38]

15. Sketch prepared by George Mason's office in 1905 showing how the Hotel Pontchartrain would look as a fourteen-story building, once the final four floors were added. (Detroit Publishing Company Photograph Collection, Library of Congress Prints and Photographs Division)

A beneficial feature of the Pontchartrain—and characteristic of Rowland's designs—was provision for generous amounts of natural light and ventilation. In order to maximize the number of rooms, hotel buildings were often designed with some "inside" rooms having windows that opened onto a narrow courtyard affording little in the way of natural light and ventilation. Rowland, however, designed the Pontchartrain so that every one of the guest rooms was an "outside" room. Rooms in the building's rear faced a large, open area above the dining room and a majority had bay windows, allowing even more light and air to enter. The hotel's dining room, located in the rear of the building, had floor-to-ceiling windows facing a courtyard and a huge skylight occupying roughly one-quarter of its ceiling.

Mason came to greatly respect Rowland's skill in design and promoted him to lead designer. In a letter of recommendation written shortly after Rowland's departure from the firm, Mason said, "Rowland is one of the best Designers and Draughtsman that I have ever had in my office. This is saying a good deal, but he seems to have a natural fitness that few Designers possess. We have often made the remark that [Rowland] 'could draw Greek Architecture like a Greek,' his perception of line and form being so thoroughly acute. He has the right conception of architecture, and all his sketches thoroughly illustrate this fact."[39] Mason also found Rowland's ability to communicate with clients to be a valuable asset, particularly when advocating on behalf of good design principles, so Rowland frequently accompanied Mason on client meetings. Eventually, Rowland became an associate (junior partner) of the firm.[40]

Between 1905 and 1910, George Mason landed a number of projects that epitomized Michigan's growing economy, including two auto dealerships, three banks, and a lumber company. The Postal-Doherty Auto Company Building is notable in that it displayed design characteristics common on Rowland's later buildings: carefully composed brickwork patterns, colorful terra-cotta accents, and heavy vertical piers. This handsome dealership for Oakland and Welch automobiles was located on the east side of Woodward Avenue just south of Parsons Street.

One of the extraordinary designs Rowland produced during this period is the administration building of Herman Kiefer Hospital. Planned by the Detroit Board of Health as a contagious diseases hospital, it is located on a large parcel of land at the northwest corner of Hamilton Boulevard and Pingree Street (Hamilton in this area is now the John C. Lodge Service Drive). The Board of Health operated under tightening budget limitations

16. The Postal-Doherty Auto Company Building, completed in 1908, was located on Woodward south of Parsons. Evident here are features that would appear in Rowland's later designs. (George D. Mason and Co., courtesy of the Burton Historical Collection, Detroit Public Library)

imposed by the Detroit city council, necessitating a rather austere design. Some cost savings were achieved by building only the first stories of the buildings and adding the second floor at a later time. Drawings were delivered to the Department of Health in June 1909, and the first two of the three originally planned buildings were completed in 1911.[41]

The complex is comprised of two identical ward buildings facing each other north and south across an open courtyard. At the west end of the courtyard, facing east toward Hamilton Boulevard, is the administration building. Raised walkways extend from the wings of the administration building to the ends of the two ward buildings. The entire arrangement is bilaterally symmetrical about the central axis of the courtyard and reminiscent of the villa designs of Italian Renaissance architect Andrea Palladio (1508–1580), particularly reflecting his drawing for Villa Godi.[42] As a result of Rowland's superb design, the administration building, though small, has a commanding dignity about it. To all appearances, Rowland adapted Palladio's ancient design principles (based on Greek and Roman predecessors) to modern materials and circumstances, resulting in a simple, functional building expressing understated classical beauty. It was a fitting conclusion to this chapter of his career.[43]

It is worth noting that the architecture of the Herman Kiefer Hospital administration building would have been readily appreciated by most Detroiters during the first half of the twentieth century. The Detroit public schools provided students with a comprehensive education in architectural history and construction methods. The curriculum for fourth grade students, for example, covered architecture of the Greek period—"The

17. Herman Kiefer Hospital administration building, constructed in 1911 for the Detroit Board of Health. Walkways extending from the wings connect to two ward buildings.

18. The design sketch made by Andrea Palladio for the Villa Godi, published in his *Four Books of Architecture* in 1570.

architecture is based on the lintel construction with the most perfect proportions of all times"—and Roman period—"The distinguishing characteristics of Roman architecture are the arch and vault plus the Greek column and entablature, which is no longer constructive, but ornamental in its application." The "standards of attainment" for the subject included: "gain a beginning knowledge of the important public buildings in Detroit; the architecture, location and use, and influence shown of historic architecture," and "develop a general understanding of Greek and Roman architecture; the construction features, decoration, use and ideals of the civilization." In grade six, students studied Gothic architecture—"The characteristics of Gothic architecture were an ever increasing height of vaults, enlarged open spaces and windows. Exquisite wood carving and stained glass windows developed." "This architecture developed two principles: (a) concentration of strain on points of support; (b) transmitted thrust—i.e., a thrust resisted by a counter-thrust."[44]

During the years Rowland worked for Mason, his leisure hours were spent studying architecture books and journals and participating in community activities. He had a lifelong interest in music and was a superb vocalist, able to sing both bass and baritone. By fall 1902, he secured one of four vocal positions with the quartet choir of the Forest Avenue Presbyterian Church.[45] He regularly attended educational and social meetings at the YMCA and often performed vocal solos as part of the program.[46] As Rowland's reputation grew, he performed before ever larger audiences, singing before the Newsboys' Association at the Detroit Orchestra's Philharmonic Hall in 1905.[47] At Christmas that year, Rowland assisted with a performance for the children of the Protestant Orphan Asylum—playing the part of Santa Claus.[48]

The following year, Rowland found himself as the first of two vocalists providing entertainment for the graduation ceremonies of the Farrand School for Nurses (Harper Hospital School of Nursing). The audience, according to news reports, "considerably exceeded the seating capacity of the lower floor of Swain Hall," perhaps due to the entertainment, or because diplomas were presented by J. L. Hudson, president of Harper

Hospital's Board of Trustees.[49] The second vocalist was accompanied on keyboard by Ada May, a talented Detroit pianist the same age as Rowland. May studied piano from a young age under Margaret W. Wiley, eventually becoming an assistant piano teacher in Wiley's music studio on Witherell Street.[50] Later, May joined the Ganapol School of Musical Art and, in 1910, opened a branch on Blaine Avenue where she taught piano classes.[51] Rowland and May were both enthusiastic musicians with a passionate devotion to their work, and after meeting at the Farrand School graduation, the two began a relationship that would last until Rowland's death.

19. Accomplished pianist Ada May in a 1911 photo of the staff of Detroit's Ganapol School of Music. (Baker Studio, courtesy of the Burton Historical Collection, Detroit Public Library)

By 1908, Rowland's income was adequate to cover the cost of an extended trip to Europe. Aspiring architects of the period often toured in Europe after graduate school to study firsthand the great architecture of history. A lengthy stay on the Continent afforded the opportunity to sit for hours and sketch buildings, and acquire an intimate familiarity with the structures. As Rowland had yet to see the historic buildings he had studied in books, he took leave from Mason's office and set out on a tour of England, France, Italy, and Algeria. Rowland's improved financial situation also permitted him to move from the house at 1272 Twenty-Fourth Street in southwest Detroit, where he had boarded since 1902, and take a room at the downtown YMCA.

In 1909, Rowland achieved what was likely the pinnacle of his success as a vocalist in *The Mikado*, performed at the Detroit Opera House as a benefit for the East Side Settlement Association. Endorsing the choice of Rowland for the title role of Mikado, the *Detroit Free Press* noted, "in such a presentation as will be given by the conservatory, experienced soloists are required and the cast embraces such well known members as Wirt C. Rowland."[52] One review, "'Mikado' Cast Full of Stars," described the performance as "the most successful affair, artistically, socially and financially of the winter. 'The Mikado' was presented by a company of amateurs, but there was no amateurish note in all the performance."[53]

Later that year, Rowland joined the quartet choir of Temple Beth El, and in November, sang the part of Dick Deadeye in a performance of Gilbert and Sullivan's *H.M.S. Pinafore*. Early in 1910, he became a member of the quartet choir of Central Methodist Episcopal Church.

At the same time, Rowland was active in the Detroit Architectural Club, serving in 1909 on its board of directors, followed by his election as president the following year. The club carried on a variety of social and educational activities and boasted a membership of over one hundred, meeting twice a month. Club activities afforded an opportunity for younger members to hone skills through friendly competitions and learn from older members. Another benefit was the opportunity to enhance one's career potential by developing relationships with the principals of growing architectural firms.

20. A *Detroit Free Press* article from January 31, 1909, described the upcoming benefit performance of *The Mikado*.

2

BACK TO SCHOOLS

The study of architectural history and its value in the training of the practical architect [is]
not for the purpose of being able to copy or follow with more or less accuracy the forms of
this or that style, but for the purpose of really penetrating the underlying meaning
of architectural form.

—H. Langford Warren, "The Study of Architectural History," June 1912

Albert Kahn, after leaving the partnership with Mason in 1902, opened his own firm,
hiring designer Ernest Wilby (1868–1957) the following year.[1] Business grew rapidly, in
large part due to the firm's early mastery of steel reinforced concrete construction methods.
The explosive growth of Detroit's auto industry fueled the expansion of Kahn's firm as
well, reinforced concrete being used for nearly all factory construction after 1906. In the
eight years from 1902 to 1909, Kahn's office took in nearly two hundred jobs, including
forty-one factories, twenty-two office buildings, sixteen stores, ten banks, and fifty-two
residences. Eighteen of the factories were vehicle or vehicle component manufacturing
facilities, four of which were located outside of Michigan.[2]

Kahn's largest client was Henry B. Joy, majority owner of Packard Motor
Company. In 1901, Joy hired Kahn to design an auto dealership building (now known as
the DuMouchelle Building, 409 East Jefferson), a two-story structure to which four floors
were added in 1904.[3] In 1903, when Packard Motor moved to Detroit from Ohio, Joy
had Kahn's firm design a factory complex on the northwest corner of Grand Boulevard
and Concord Avenue. The buildings were constructed using traditional masonry or mill
construction methods.

Then came an almost overnight change. Albert and Julius Kahn realized the Kahn
System of steel reinforced concrete could revolutionize factory construction. During the
first six months of 1906, the firm secured contracts to construct four automobile factories. An addition to the Packard plant (Building Number Ten) was Kahn's first reinforced
concrete automobile factory,[4] followed soon after by factories for E. R. Thomas and Pierce-
Arrow in Buffalo, and Garford in Elyria, Ohio.[5] By the end of 1906, Kahn's office had
completed six reinforced concrete factories; the following year, nearly a dozen more were

begun, including Henry Ford's Highland Park complex, the first of many projects for Ford Motor Company.

In 1909, Kahn's office designed four service and sales buildings for Ford and Packard (located in Kansas City, Missouri; Long Island and Albany, New York; and Boston, Massachusetts), a type of structure that would proliferate in the following decade. Service and sales facilities, unlike factories, required an appealing architectural design. It was, perhaps, the advent of these structures, along with the growing concern of auto companies with the appearance of their administration (headquarters) buildings, that increased the design workload beyond what Wilby, Kahn's head designer, could handle. To bolster the design capability of his firm, Kahn offered Rowland a position, which he accepted, and began work with the firm in January 1910.

Rowland at first found working for the rather intense Kahn to be challenging, particularly when Kahn would, as Rowland put it, "run quickly down the aisle," a practice that rankled Rowland.[6] He soon became accustomed to Kahn's behavior and, despite the rocky start, thirty years later Rowland said of Kahn, "I have never had an unkind word from him."[7]

As it turned out, 1910 was a big year for Kahn's firm: fifteen factories, six office buildings, three service buildings, four stores, and assorted banks, libraries, theaters, and apartments; there was more than enough business to keep both Rowland and Wilby busy. Kahn's office had grown into a large firm, with many specialized employees working in

21. The drafting room of Albert Kahn, Architects and Engineers in the Marquette Building, around 1918. (*Architectural Forum*, November 1918)

ALBERT KAHN

J.R.BOYDE
WM. C.BUNCE
F.A.FAIRBROTHER
H.G.KNAPP
W.C.ROWLAND

ERNEST WILBY   LOUIS KAHN
J. F. HIRSCHMAN   ASSOCIATES
ARCHITECTS & ENGINEERS
MARQUETTE BUILDING
DETROIT, MICHIGAN

J.T.N.HOYT
CHIEF STRUCTURAL ENGINEER
F.K.BOOMHOWER
CHIEF MECHANICAL ENGINEER

22. The letterhead of Albert Kahn, Architects and Engineers, from 1922 lists the firm's key employees, including Rowland.

teams, so it was not uncommon for both Rowland and Wilby to collaborate on major projects. Kahn—almost certainly the most brilliant architectural entrepreneur of the century—had by this time settled into a largely managerial role overseeing business activities for the growing firm. He had little involvement in architectural design, which was left to his highly paid designers, Rowland and Wilby.

Kahn's firm is commonly referred to as "Albert Kahn," resulting in confusion between "Albert Kahn" the architect and "Albert Kahn, Architects and Engineers" the architecture firm. Albert Kahn was to Albert Kahn, Architects and Engineers, what Henry Ford was to Ford Motor Company; Rowland and Wilby were to Kahn's firm what artist Norman Rockwell was to the *Saturday Evening Post*. The headquarters building for the Hudson Motor Car Company, for example, was designed by the firm of Albert Kahn, Architects and Engineers, not by Albert Kahn personally; Kahn's employees Ernest Wilby and Wirt Rowland were the architects responsible for the building's design. By at least 1910, if not well before, buildings designed "by Albert Kahn" were a product of various employees of Kahn's firm.

Albert Kahn, Architects and Engineers, was typical of a large architecture and engineering firm of the day, with division of labor into multiple departments according to specialty. The technical division drafted plans for structures, beginning with the designing department, which initiated a project by developing a series of proposals based on the client's requirements. Frequently these proposals entailed a spreadsheet analysis of every square foot of the prospective building to establish accurate cost information and determine the client's potential return on investment. These data often impacted the ultimate size of the structure and the amount spent on appointments. Once a detailed proposal was approved by the client, the designing department, along with the architectural, structural, and mechanical departments, developed detailed plans for construction of the building and its mechanical systems. Each department had a job captain responsible for overseeing progress and coordinating with other departments. Once construction began, superintendents from the architecture firm oversaw onsite work carried out by the construction contractor.

A complete set of plans for a commercial building included three subsets: architectural (beginning with sheet 1), structural (beginning with sheet S-1), and mechanical (beginning with sheet E-1). More recently, *P* for plumbing, *M* for mechanical, and *E* for electrical plans have become common. Structural plans are primarily concerned with the steel framework of the building; mechanical with electrical (wiring, lighting, outlets, and transformers), ventilation, fire suppression, elevator, plumbing (drinking water, hot and cold running water, and waste), and telephone. Everything else appears in the architectural plans.

Architectural drawings generally present either a plan view—as if seen from above—or an elevation—as if seen head-on. For example, a sheet labeled "Plan of 4th to 16th Floors" shows one of the building's floors as if it were a dollhouse with the roof removed. The sheet labeled "East Elevation" depicts the facade of the building that faces east, as if viewed straight on. Additional sheets show particular sections of the structure, both interior and exterior, in greater detail than can be displayed on a view of the full facade. Every sheet includes a block containing a description of the sheet, job number, sheet number, and date. The name or initials of the individuals who drew, traced, checked, and approved the sheet typically appear as well. Until the 1970s, architectural drawings were

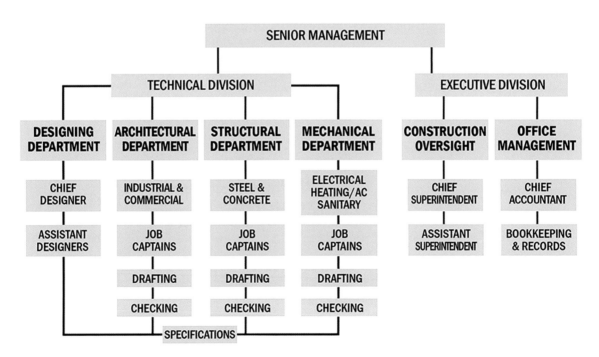

23. A simplified organization chart showing the various departments of a large architecture and engineering firm of the twentieth century such as Albert Kahn, Architects and Engineers.

made on drafting linen, a cloth material coated with a smooth surface that was durable and suitable for sharp ink lines. A designer, architect, or engineer began the process by creating an original drawing, which was then traced by a draftsman onto the drafting linen. This drawing was checked for errors and, occasionally, revisions were made. Only after the sheet was approved—typically by an officer of the firm—was it used for construction.

In addition to the full set of plans, an additional series of detail drawings, often in half or full scale, were produced for individual features, such as handrails, carved stone figures, marble pieces, drinking fountains, flag poles, screens or gates, and teller wickets. In Rowland's day, blueprint copies of these detail drawings were distributed to outside vendors and craftsmen (such as Corrado Parducci) as a means of conveying the exact size, shape, and appearance of the required item.

Early in 1910, Rowland and Wilby collaborated on a reinforced concrete administration building for the Hudson Motor Car Company. The exterior surface of the administration building was constructed entirely of white concrete, an unusual treatment intended to contrast with the darker, brick-trimmed factory buildings behind.[8] The most prominent feature of the facade was the company's name in large bronze letters running nearly the full width of the building.

During the summer, Rowland was given responsibility for designing the Dollar Savings and Trust bank building in Wheeling, West Virginia. Dollar Savings was the foremost bank in the region, and its president desired a well-designed structure, both as to function and appearance. In the early twentieth century, due to the widespread use of cash, the nature of bank buildings was much different than today. Banks handled and kept on hand substantial amounts of currency, sometimes enough to cash payroll checks for an entire shift at a nearby factory. In addition, they typically maintained large safe deposit vaults where customers stored cash, bonds, and other valuables. Bank design, consequently, was a specialized field requiring architects and engineers with knowledge of bank security, procedures, and requirements. Banking

24. Title block from the Dollar Savings and Trust Building plans, job number 464, sheet 8, dated August 1, 1910, drawn by "W. C. R." (Wirt C. Rowland), traced by "C. W. P." (Clarence W. Palmer) and "P. J. S." (Perry J. Smith), and checked by "A. K." (Albert Kahn).

25. The Hudson Motor Car Company administration building, front elevation, drawn by Rowland and dated April 7, 1910. The design bears a similarity to the 1908 Postal-Doherty Auto Company Building and the later Detroit News Building. (Albert Kahn Papers, Albert Kahn Associates, Inc. and the Bentley Historical Library, University of Michigan, Construction Drawings of Office Building for Hudson Motor Car Co. [Job 450-A] by Albert Kahn, Architect, Ernest Wilby, Associate, drawer 24, folder 2)

firms in smaller towns usually had to seek an architecture firm in a major city if they wished the most up-to-date, efficient, and secure bank building. During Rowland's tenure with George Mason (1902–9), for example, the firm designed five buildings in Michigan, outside of Detroit. Of these, four were banks: First National Bank of Ludington, Jackson State Savings Bank, Mt. Pleasant Savings Bank, and First National Bank of Traverse City.

The Dollar Savings and Trust building was typical for banks of the era; a large banking room, nearly thirty-four feet in height from floor to ceiling, filled almost the entire structure from the front entrance to the vault and restrooms in back. The building contained four vaults: a large safety deposit vault and smaller vaults for cash, accounting books, and general storage. A sizable skylight illuminated the interior, which was necessary because the building was not located on a corner and had windows only in the front. Throughout the interior, extensive use was made of marble, an expensive material that required the architect provide exact specifications.

Although Rowland was a "designer," his expertise ranged far beyond; he created nearly all the drawings for the Dollar Savings and Trust Building, including foundation, floor plans, sections, and elevations. That Rowland could produce the plans for such a specialized building gives some sense of the extent and depth of his practical knowledge of the field—supplemented, perhaps, by his previous experience working for the bank in Clinton. Rowland's design of the building's facade was well received. The journal *Architecture*, in its October 15, 1911, issue, ran full-page photos of the building, accompanied by an article

26. Hudson Motor Car Company administration building after its completion in January 1911. The structure's white concrete cladding was unusual, and allowed the building to stand out against the darker brick and concrete factory behind; Pewabic tiles, commonly used as an accent on brick buildings, were used here as well. (Albert Kahn Papers, Albert Kahn Associates, Inc. and the Bentley Historical Library, University of Michigan)

stating: "Albert Kahn has designed an intelligent and satisfactory building for the Dollar Savings and Trust Company. It is the work of a thoroughly trained architect, and . . . a substantial, dignified, worthy piece of architecture, adequate for its purpose and an ornament to its city."[9]

Ironically, the International Correspondence School, which provided the courses from which Rowland acquired his basic knowledge of architectural drafting, used his drawings of the Dollar Savings and Trust Company building to illustrate the course "Reading Architect's Blueprints (Part 1)." The drawing is used as an example of how to indicate individual stones on an elaborate cut-stone facade.[10]

A program established by Harvard University awarded annually three scholarships in architecture to members of the Architectural League of America (of which the Detroit Architectural Club was an affiliate). Two of these scholarships were awarded through an architectural design competition specified and judged by the college's architecture department.[11] In 1910, the competition scholarships were won by Robert Finn, who later designed the Wurlitzer Building in downtown Detroit, and Henry Janssen, both young draftsmen in Albert Kahn's office. According to Kahn, both men "were coached by Mr. Rowland," though "they occupy positions in this office far below him."[12] Rowland was generous with his time, in the office and through his work with the Architectural Club, willing to tutor and mentor young draftsmen wishing to learn the profession.

It was ironic that Rowland, with no college education, facilitated the admission of two younger coworkers to Harvard's architecture school. The irony was not lost on Rowland;

later that year he applied to Harvard for admission to the architecture school as a "special student" (for applicants lacking an undergraduate degree). In his letter to the administrative board, Rowland wrote that he wished to "concentrate my study upon many things in Architectural design in which I feel I need drill—also a better foundation in Architectural History." Rowland requested his application be given special consideration as "an extreme case," noting that individuals typically do not "pause in the midst of work to take studies at college," particularly when the "demands upon him are what mine are." Nevertheless, Rowland assured them, he had the "determination to shelve all these" for much of the year.[13] Both Albert Kahn

27. Dollar Savings and Trust Company, Wheeling, West Virginia. (Albert Kahn, Architects and Engineers as published in *Architecture*, October 1911)

and George Mason wrote glowing letters of recommendation on Rowland's behalf. Primarily on the strength of these letters, Harvard's administrative board was convinced Rowland was "an exceedingly strong applicant" and voted to admit him—the only one of six special student applicants accepted.[14]

True to his word, Rowland signed up for two architecture history courses, Technical and Historical Development of the Ancient Styles and Technical and Historical Development of the Mediaeval Styles of Architecture, both taught by Herbert Langford Warren (1857–1917). Warren, prior to joining the faculty of Harvard as head of the Department of Architecture in 1893, had been a practicing architect: five years under the influential American architect Henry Hobson Richardson, who developed the popular style that bears his name, "Richardson Romanesque," and then in his own firm, beginning in 1885.[15] Warren authored *The Foundations of Classic Architecture* and edited *Vitruvius: The Ten Books on Architecture*, both of which remain important sources to this day.

Warren enriched and decisively influenced Rowland's view of architectural history, which in turn affected Rowland's approach to future design challenges. In Warren's view, great architecture results from the combination of long-proven principles of art and design with current construction technology to solve new problems. He was a functionalist—a well-designed building derives its beauty in great part by expressing structural functions: "beautiful architectural forms are organic expressions of structural functions"; Greek and Roman columns, for example, are "vital and beautiful expressions of structure."[16] Rowland fully embraced this concept as a fundamental principle underlying his subsequent work, and he referenced it often in his later writing.

Warren's view—art is created through the knowledgeable application of well-understood principles—flew in the face of Romanticism, a popular view (then and now) that held that artistic inspiration arose from untutored emanations of the creative psyche. Warren urged designers to "avoid . . . capricious innovation for the sake of novelty."[17] This too resonated strongly with Rowland, who believed the only route to artistic achievement was through dogged study of history combined with mastery acquired through repeated application to real-world

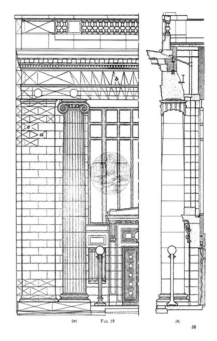

28. The International Correspondence School's course "Reading Architect's Blueprints (Part 1)" includes a reproduction of Rowland's drawings for the Dollar Savings and Trust Company.

problems. Rowland believed in creative insight but understood that minds well prepared by study and practice have more and far better creative insights.

Among the reading assigned by Warren were works by French architect Eugène Emmanuel Viollet-le-Duc (1814–1879), a prolific writer on architecture history. Viollet-le-Duc advanced two key points that influenced Rowland's approach to design. The first was a unified view of the history of architecture, that a body of knowledge, developed by the ancient Egyptians, was passed on to the Greeks and developed by them to a high art. These Greek artisans continued to practice in later centuries under Roman rule, conveying the knowledge from generation to generation through families and guilds. With the collapse of Rome, descendants of these artisans carried on their art under the Eastern Roman Empire and into the early Middle Ages, where in Europe they produced the architecture we now call Romanesque, and then Gothic. With the advent of the Renaissance, this enduring corps of practitioners finally dissipated; their principles of architecture and art faded and were lost.

The second key element was the knowledge exploited by these artisans. The use of geometry, argued Viollet-le-Duc, was the essential component passed from one architect and artist to another over many centuries. These practitioners relied on a limited number of geometric figures, according to Viollet-le-Duc, equilateral and Egyptian triangles in particular. The use of these simple triangles for designing and constructing buildings most likely arose as an expedient in an age lacking not only accurate linear measuring tools but also any type of standard length. In place of linear distances, the ancients likely used triangles, which required only a string or chain, as a method of measuring and building to a specified standard. This simple geometry, based on well-understood characteristics of basic triangles, would have provided the engineering know-how to erect buildings that would remain standing. As structures became more sophisticated, it is likely that the very same geometric methods used to erect stable buildings were increasingly deployed for aesthetic purposes.

Viollet-le-Duc took pains to point out that geometry used in this manner constituted a *generative principle* underlying the proportions of a structure: "the application of these triangles to architectural designs obliges the designer to keep to certain proportions between heights and widths; while he has perfect liberty to assume certain heights or widths according to the practical conditions he has to fulfill, he is constrained by his system of proportions to adopt corresponding widths or heights, which, however much difference there may be between them, must always be in harmonious relations with each other."[18] This highlights Viollet-le-Duc's fundamental concern: beauty in a structure depends upon proportion, a harmonious relationship of the parts to the whole, "these relations being imposed, not by the parts on the whole, but by the whole on the parts."[19] Unlike a system of design that relies on linear measurements, a system based on geometric figures may be scaled to suit the circumstances, and the resulting proportions will always reflect the proportions of the underlying geometry—the "whole" imposes its proportions on each part.

Viollet-le-Duc aptly uses the term "harmonious" to describe proper relationships between the parts of a building; in arguing for geometric principles of proportion, he makes the comparison to music. "If absolute rules and geometrical principles, in application, gratify the eye, it is because sight is a sense, like hearing, which can never suffer a discord without being offended, however little culture the ear may have received in music."[20] If one's eye is pleased by the design of a structure, it is so because the designer has achieved visual harmony through the application of geometric principles of composition. "I do not believe in chance, especially in architecture," explains Viollet-le-Duc. "If a work is good, it is because it is based on a good principle, intelligently and loyally followed."[21]

Rowland absorbed this viewpoint and made it his own. He set about mastering the geometric principles of composition that underlie great architecture from the ancients through the early Renaissance and employed them as fundamental design tools. Rowland's writing makes frequent and specific references to these crucial methods of design. In 1931, he wrote, "The beauty of proportion, articulation, and structure [were discovered by] the Greeks. . . . I believe the most important and significant fact which remains for us to be their . . . control of placing and proportion by the laws of mathematics."[22] And in 1932, "The Greeks were masters of geometric principles which . . . helped them attain mastery of expression."[23]

Rowland was in full agreement with Viollet-le-Duc's view of architecture history as the employment of a set of geometric principles by generations of Greek artisans (or their disciples) to the particular building technology, materials, and purposes of successive cultures. "It is to be noted," Rowland wrote, "that, in what followed from the Periclean age [of Greece] to the decline of the Gothic in France, wherever and whatever the Greek may have touched either in influence or through actual contact through succeeding generations of artisans, he left inevitable marks of his logic. And it is not hard to believe that he was responsible even though it may be indirectly, for the highest order of articulation which we find in the best of French Gothic cathedrals."[24] What we today may view as relatively distinct "styles" of architecture—Greek, Romanesque, Gothic—are, in this context, varied manifestations of fundamental geometric principles applied to different circumstances.

To understand Rowland's view of himself as a "modernist," one must understand his view of architecture history, a view he shared with Viollet-le-Duc and Warren. Rowland did not wish for his building designs to imitate any particular historic style, nor did he seek to break entirely from the past—approaches practiced by many of his peers. His desire was to master the *generative principles* from which Greek architecture, in particular, was derived and apply those same principles to today's problems using today's materials and technology. Writing in 1921 Rowland said, "As far as architecture is concerned, any attempt to revivify it fails when any effort is made to change its outward forms without attention to its inner principles. We must invest our work with those principles, and if buildings . . . have shown progress, it has not been through any desire to create a new type, but through the application, from problem to problem, of those essentials which are incorporated in the great architecture of the past."[25] It is pointless, then, to categorize Rowland as loyal to any particular historic style. He respected and admired characteristics of many styles but was loyal only to the unchanging principles "of placing and proportion" employed over many generations to design and build.

The geometric system Viollet-le-Duc describes, in its simplest form, makes use of the equilateral triangle to define the proportions of a building and to determine the location of major building features. Large triangles employed to proportion the mass of the structure are subdivided into a lattice of smaller triangles. Structural and ornamental elements—points that are visually distinctive—are placed where these lattice lines intersect.

In a more complex example, Viollet-le-Duc demonstrates how proportions for the Arch of Titus in Rome were derived, not from a single equilateral triangle but from a combination of triangles large and small. "The arch of Titus at Rome, small as it is fully satisfies the eye. Let us ascertain on what principle its proportions were obtained. Here again we find that the generative principle by which the lines were disposed was the equilateral triangle. The key of the arch is at the apex of an equilateral triangle, and the axes of

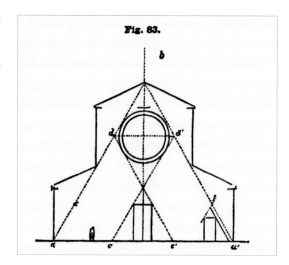

29. From Viollet-le-Duc's *Discourses on Architecture*, his figure 83 shows how a basilica might be designed by means of an equilateral triangle to first establish the ratio of height to width, and then locating the major building features by subdividing into smaller triangles. (Drawing from English version, published 1875)

the piers on either side are perpendiculars elevated from the two extremities of its base *a b.* The opening *c d* of the archway up to the line *e f* of its springing [point] is a perfect square, and the apex of an equilateral triangle, constructed on the line *e f* as a base, fixes the lower line of the main cornice."[26]

Viollet-le-Duc includes in his discussion of proportion the design of a building such that the height suggested by an equilateral triangle would be impractical. As an alternative, "an harmonious relation between the extreme width and height" may be obtained by setting the height "equal to one half the [width] of the entire facade."[27] A building with a height equal to one-half its width will, of course, fit within a rectangle comprised of two squares.

Toward the end of his studies at Harvard, Rowland entered one of his sketches in the Boston Society of Architects competition, and won first prize. His entry was later published in the journal *Architecture and Building* as part of an article describing the educational methods of the School of Architecture at Harvard.[28]

Rowland completed his studies at Harvard in the spring of 1911 and returned to work in Albert Kahn's office. Awaiting him was an important project for the University of Michigan, and an opportunity to apply his newly acquired design skills. Arthur Hill was

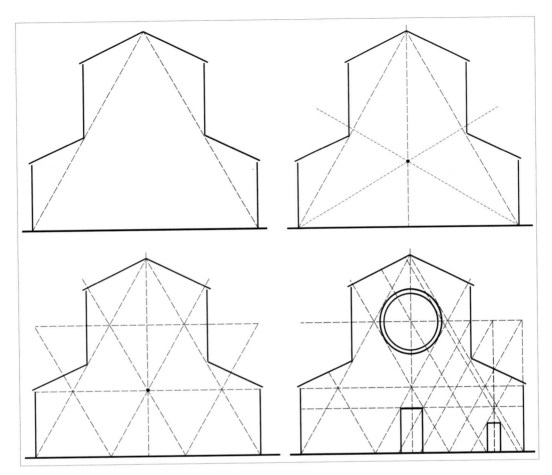

30. A step-by-step elaboration (by Michael G. Smith) of Viollet-le-Duc's simple diagram demonstrates that the triangle-based lattice system results in relationships between the building's features in both proportion and location. An equilateral triangle is drawn and the building's outline is added conforming to the proportions of the triangle (*upper left*). The triangle's sides are bisected (*upper right*) to locate points through which subdividing lines are drawn, forming a lattice (*lower left*). By locating all features according to the intersection of lines within the lattice, harmony of proportion and location is achieved (*lower right*). Note, for example, lines tangent to the large window establish the location and size of both the large center door and smaller door on the right.

a civil engineer educated at the University of Michigan who amassed a fortune in lumber and steamships, and when the Saginaw man died in 1909, he left the university money for the purpose of building a large auditorium. The Arthur Hill Memorial Hall would later be described by noted architecture critic Lewis Mumford as "the best auditorium in the country."[29]

The building's designers faced two challenges, the first being the university's desire for the building's appearance to be innovative, attractive, and appropriate to its midwestern location. The second was the need for a speaker or performer to be heard clearly in every one of the auditorium's five thousand seats—electric amplification systems were not yet in use. As it turned out, both challenges were met with a bit of assistance from Harvard University.

The leading researcher in the field of acoustics, Wallace C. Sabine (1868–1919), a physics professor at Harvard, discovered in 1898 a formula for calculating reverberation and sound absorption. Sabine later became dean of Harvard's graduate school of applied science, and one of his duties was handling "special student" admission requests. It was Sabine to whom Albert Kahn's 1910 letter of recommendation for Rowland was addressed. The following year, Kahn took advantage of this relationship and wrote again to Sabine requesting advice on the feasibility of constructing an

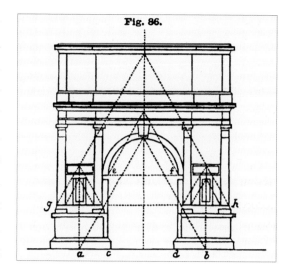

31. Arch of Titus at Rome; figure 86 from Viollet-le-Duc's *Discourses*.

acoustically satisfactory auditorium of the size the university envisioned.[30] Kahn then hired as consulting engineer for the project 1891 Harvard grad Hugh Tallant (1870–1952), an architect who successfully employed Sabine's acoustics research to the construction of large theaters. Tallant published an extensive article, "Hints on Acoustics," in the architecture

journal *Brickbuilder* in May 1910 and was almost certainly the leading expert on architectural acoustics.

Tallant described the auditorium problem as one in which volume is "much too loud near the speaker and correspondingly too faint elsewhere." "If the sound could be equally distributed throughout the entire auditorium," he pointed out, "the result would be ample loudness at all points."[31] Tallant observed that parabolic reflectors were successfully used

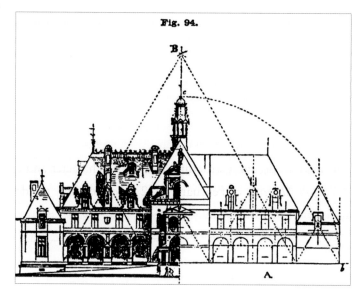

32. Demonstration by Viollet-le-Duc (from *Discourses*) of a method to establish the proportions of a structure when adopting the full height of an equilateral triangle was impractical. The height at *c* (equal to one-half the width of the facade) should be used, which could be determined by drawing the compass line *b c*.

to focus and cast light over great distances; why not use the same method to project sound? Hill Auditorium, then, was designed much like a large parabolic reflector, with appropriate adjustments as required by architectural necessity.

Responsibility for the building's design fell to Rowland and Wilby, and, according to Rowland, was a collaborative effort of both men.[32] Most likely, it was Rowland who gave the building its overall shape, proportion, color, and style, while Wilby attended to the details of windows, doors, roof, awnings, and interior appointments.

The university trustees desired a fireproof building large enough to accommodate the entire student body for occasions such as the annual May Festival and commencement. The funds available for the building were adequate, provided the exterior design was modest. The building would have to be clad mostly in brick,

33. Rowland's prize-winning entry from the 1911 Boston Society of Architects competition to design a "Ceremonial Loggia on a State Capitol building, in which the Governor might stand on occasions of public functions." (Architecture and Building, May 1912)

with stone accents; a marble-clad, classical design, as was typical among well-funded eastern schools, was out of the question. Nevertheless, this constraint was turned into an opportunity to design a structure true to the character and sympathies of the Midwest. The *Michigan Alumnus* of February 1912 described how the design produced by Rowland and Wilby achieved that goal: "Architecture in America is often divided into two schools—the Eastern and the Western. The Eastern school is known by its adherence to classic tradition; the Western school by its freedom from traditional form. Considering this fact, some may discern in this building a character which is appropriate to the ideals of a middle-Western University, because it fuses the spirit of the classic and conservatism of the East with the freedom of idea which becomes the new West."[33] This brief passage captures the architectural currents of the time and the character of the building quite well and was likely copied or paraphrased from a description of the building provided to the university by Rowland.

34. Hill Auditorium at the University of Michigan, Ann Arbor, completed in 1913.

In appearance, Hill Auditorium combines elements of Prairie School style with classical features in a very original design. In the years preceding, the highly original school buildings of Dwight Perkins (1867–1941), architect of the Chicago Board of Education, were lauded in the architectural journals. Perkins designed simple (by the standards of the day) school buildings that were attractive in form, with minimal ornament, reflecting the Prairie School style popular in the Midwest. The *Architectural Record* described his Rogers School as an example of "what can be done on a building of supreme simplicity in design and carefully studied proportions in its various parts."[34] Rowland may have been influenced to some degree by Perkins, but it's more likely both men were operating in parallel, seeking to produce modern designs reflecting contemporary, regional tastes within a modest budget. Perkins had been associated with Frank Lloyd Wright and other Prairie School architects, and his work more strongly reflects that style. Rowland, on the other hand, employed modest Prairie School cues to give Hill Auditorium a midwestern regional character. The building also features Greek antefixes (ornaments projecting vertically along the edge of the cornice), tying the building to the Old World as well.

The building is a superb example of Rowland's newly acquired skills in geometric design methods. Beginning with a shape one-half as tall as it was wide (exactly as Viollet-le-Duc recommended), Rowland quite likely divided this shape into thirds, each third composing the base of an equilateral triangle. A horizontal line along the apex of the triangles and vertical lines from the apex of the first and third triangles to the base of the figure defined the location of the prominent decorative band on the building's facade. In a similar manner, the size and location of all features of the building's facade—including the angle of the roof—were determined, as explained in detail by the accompanying figures.[35]

It should be clear from the foregoing figures that the building's shape and proportion, as well as the location of all its decorative elements, were determined by Rowland in an exacting and methodical manner. Nothing was "left to chance"; some principle was employed by Rowland to place each and every feature that catches the eye. As a consequence, prominent features of the building bear a geometric relationship with each other reflecting the lines and angles of the grid—features line up, not just vertically and horizontally, as one would expect, but also along the parallel angular lines. We easily perceive vertical and horizontal patterns in man-made objects, particularly buildings. We are less accustomed to angular align-

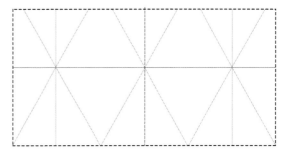

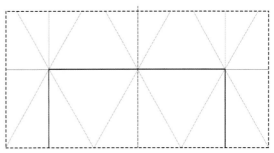

35. For Hill Auditorium's facade, Rowland likely began with a shape having a height equal to one-half the width (a rectangle comprised of two squares). This shape is divided into three sections of equal width, each of which serves as the base of an equilateral triangle. A horizontal line passing through the apex of each triangle is combined with vertical lines bisecting the left and right triangles to determine the centerline location of the prominent decorative band on the building's facade. (These overlay drawings are by Michael G. Smith.) The drawing used as the basis for these overlays is "Front Elevation," sheet 8, drawn by Wirt Rowland and Ernest Wilby, job 494, October 5, 1911, scanned at the Bentley Historical Library, Ann Arbor, Michigan.

ments and less likely to notice when they occur, yet such patterns are perceived to some degree on a subconscious level and contribute to our sense that a design is well thought out, balanced, harmonious, and symmetrical. (This applies to the building as it was planned. Changes made during construction may not conform to the architect's intent, such as the round designs added to the upper horizontal band, which do not appear in the plans.)

Rowland's system may appear at first glance to be tedious and complex; the truth, however, is just the opposite. Rowland knew the system was sound and would produce an attractively proportioned, balanced, and harmonious composition. With a specific vision of

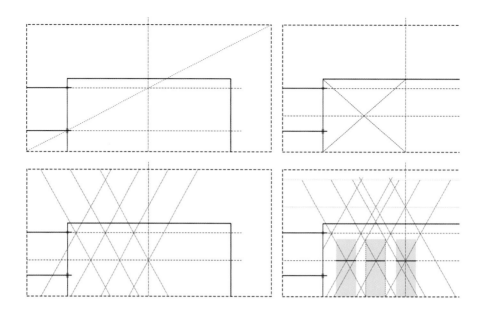

36. A diagonal line bisects the figure and determines the location of a horizontal line dividing the figure in half vertically. A second horizontal line is drawn where the diagonal intersects the decorative band (*upper left*). Two diagonals are used to locate the vertical center of the facade subsection (*upper right*). Equilateral triangles are drawn with bases on the horizontal centerline of the facade subsection and apexes on the building's horizontal centerline, forming a lattice of triangles. Round designs in relief are placed at these apexes (*lower left*). The bays for the windows and doors are centered within triangles and extend to where the lattice lines intersect the base of the figure. The windows sit upon the horizontal line bisecting the facade subsection vertically. Where the lattice extends above the facade section, two more horizontal lines are drawn at intersection points, the uppermost being the top of the roof, the second being the location of the cornice (*lower right*). (Overlay drawings are by Michael G. Smith.)

the building's layout and features in mind, he could use this geometric method to quickly and easily finalize the exact size, shape, and location of every element composing the final design. The alternative was trial and error: sketching a proposal, tweaking by eye, and then sketching again, over and over until further improvement seemed unlikely—a far more tedious, inexact, and time-consuming approach.

Rowland's use of geometric lattices may be inferred, as has been done here, from the original architectural drawings, based on measurable geometric relationships. These drawings, being traced copies of the designer's original measured sketch, do not bear any direct evidence of the designer's work methods. However, there is verification that Rowland used geometric lattices. Interviewed for a 1925 article on design that appeared in the architecture journal *Pencil Points*, Rowland made a quick sketch for author John C. Breiby. In the margin of the sketch appears an elaboration of the geometric lattice system.[36]

Around this time Rowland aided his hometown neighbors by providing, for the Culture Club of Clinton, the design for a chapel to be built in the village's Riverside Cemetery.

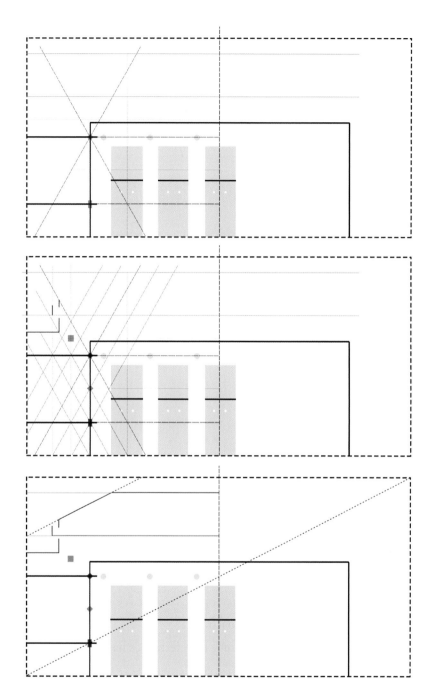

37. An equilateral triangle is drawn with its apex at the intersection of the centerline of the figure and the left vertical of the decorative band (*top*). The equilateral triangle is expanded to a lattice. A brick-work design is located in the center of two opposing triangles (this design is difficult to discern on the building but is prominent on the elevation plan sheet). The lattice line to the left of this design extends from the center of the far left door/window bay and locates the point at which the side wing extends from the building. The line to the right locates the point where the building's roof terminates (*middle*). The angle of the roof (30 degrees) is equal to the figure's bisecting diagonal (*bottom*). (Drawings are by Michael G. Smith.)

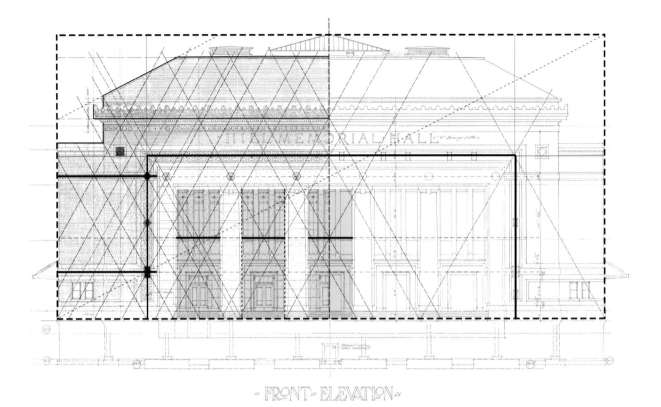

~ FRONT ELEVATION ~

38. The front elevation of Hill Auditorium as drawn by Rowland and Wilby with the design lattices of triangles overlaid. (Overlay drawings are by Michael G. Smith; base drawing: Albert Kahn, Architects and Engineers, job number 494, sheet 8, October 5, 1911)

A cornerstone-laying ceremony was held in September 1912, and, although the weather was foul the day of the event, a large number of people gathered, including many from the surrounding towns. Following an impressive ceremony by representatives of the Grand Lodge of Freemasons, the audience sang "Praise God from Whom All Blessings Flow," and Rowland offered a solo, later described in the local paper as "especially fine."[37]

Building the chapel was truly a community effort, made possible by donations of labor, stones, sand, money, and even the cornerstone; more than any of Rowland's projects, the chapel came into being in a manner similar to that of the cathedrals of the Middle Ages. The colorful stones used for the walls were donated by local farmers and carefully selected by livestock dealer Solomon Tate. Masonry work was provided by William Sr. and William Jr. of William Uhr, Sr. and Sons Masons of nearby Manchester; superbly executed, the stonework adds greatly to the attractiveness of the building. Dedicated in August 1913 at a well-attended ceremony,[38] the chapel is simple in design, but elegant; its picturesque appearance and the sophisticated treatment of its windows and door are unexpected in such a diminutive structure.

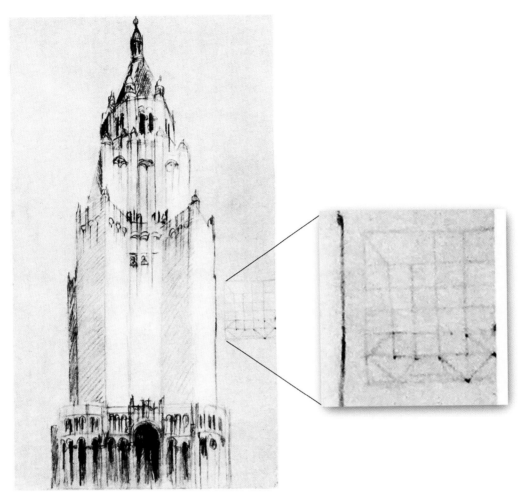

Figure 6. Suggestive Sketch Study for an Office Building.

39. A sketch made by Rowland for author and architect John C. Breiby for a 1925 article in *Pencil Points*. To the right is an enlarged version of the geometric lattice Rowland drew in the margin of the sketch.

     Rowland's closest friend was Herbert G. Wenzell (1883–1939), an architectural designer who began working for George Mason during Rowland's earliest years with the firm. The two men shared a deep interest in architectural history, and late in 1911, they jointly prepared an entry for a design competition held by the *Brickbuilder*, an architecture journal. Rowland and Wenzell's *Brickbuilder* entry received a "Fifth Mention," awarded by the judges "on account of the broadness given to the bays and the simple and utilitarian spirit sought by its author[s]." The judges commented, however: "The two entrances appear to have been put in after the building was designed, and one wonders why the piers were terminated like chimneys."[39] An unusual aspect of Rowland and Wenzell's entry was its vibrant color scheme: the building was Indian red; the ornament, green and golden brown with olive green background, and the lower ornament in yellows—other entries in the competition were preponderantly cream, ivory, and buff.

Rowland upgraded his living circumstances again in 1912, moving from the YMCA to a boarding house at 1536 Pennsylvania Street run by Grace Ritchie. "Mrs. Ritchie," as she was known to all but relatives, was widowed at an early age when her husband, attempting to board a boat, fell and drowned. She turned her six-bedroom home into an upscale boarding house catering to unmarried men and women, who received, in addition to a room, dinner served in grand style.[40] The home's location, one block from Jefferson Avenue, made for an easy commute by streetcar or jitney to downtown, and for Rowland, an easy walk to Pewabic Pottery, just over one block away.

Ritchie's nephew, Dr. Kenneth Olson, fondly recalled that Rowland, though a famous architect, nevertheless took time to get to know him. Rowland was a sharp dresser and often passed along his expensive ties to Olson, a much-appreciated gift as Olson was required to wear a necktie to high school.[41]

In the early twentieth century, jobs in Detroit's booming auto manufacturing business attracted to the city so

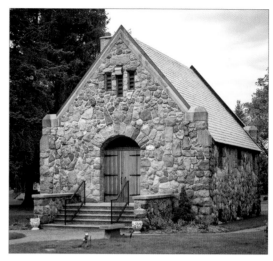

40. The Village of Clinton's Mortuary Chapel in Riverside Cemetery, completed in 1913.

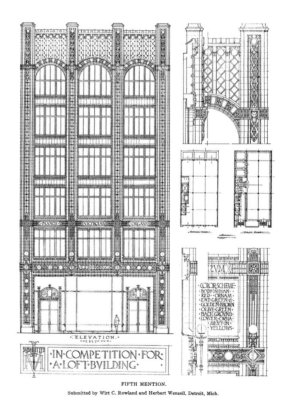

41. Entry for the design of a loft building by Rowland and Herbert Wenzell from the February 1912 issue of the *Brickbuilder*. The unusual color scheme is listed in the lower right corner.

42. The boarding house at 1536 Pennsylvania Street, where Rowland lived for thirty-four years, and Mrs. Grace Ritchie, proprietor. (Dr. Kenneth Olson in the collection of the Historical Society of Clinton, Michigan)

many workers and families that housing and city services were stretched beyond capacity. Between 1904 and 1915, the city's population more than doubled, the number of jobs tripled, and total wages paid increased by 400 percent.[42] Public school enrollment, 44,000 in 1905, more than doubled to 92,000 by 1915.[43] The Board of Education President's Report in 1913 stated: "the terrific growth of the city has continued to the end that many pupils have to be satisfied with half day sessions on account of the present school buildings being badly overcrowded."[44] Indeed, in 1913, over seven thousand students were attending only one-half day of classes to permit school buildings to accommodate twice the number of students. Classes met in portable rooms and in the basements of many schools; principals vacated their offices so recitation classes could be held.[45] Class sizes in primary grades averaged well over fifty students (though, based on average attendance rather than enrollment, the number was closer to forty). Just keeping pace with the annual increase in students required the construction of six elementary schools each year.

Increasing enrollment wasn't the school board's only construction challenge. Existing schools built of masonry and wood were far more dangerous in the event of fire than modern "fireproof" reinforced concrete structures. This was not a theoretical concern by any means as Detroit's only high school had been destroyed by fire in 1893, and in 1909, a conflagration gutted the city's Cass High School. Outside Detroit, flames consumed two other southeast Michigan high schools during the same time period: Owosso in 1900 and Port Huron in 1906.

The school board had, since 1894, employed the firm of Malcomson and Higginbotham as the primary provider of architectural services for the school district. However, in late April 1912, that relationship nearly came to an end over the school board's concern that the firm lacked sufficient experience in fireproof (reinforced concrete) construction. School board member Clarence M. Burton opposed renewing the firm's annual contract, stating: "the proposition of fireproof construction is a new one so far as the board's investigation is concerned. We do not know what this

43. Detroit's Capitol High School was destroyed by fire on January 27, 1893. Erected in 1828 as a courthouse, the building later served as Michigan's capitol and then the city's first high school. The building stood on State Street at Griswold in what is now Capitol Park. (Courtesy of the Burton Historical Collection, Detroit Public Library)

firm can do along that line and we ought to investigate." Burton had concerns with Malcomson and Higginbotham's previous work as well, claiming architectural mistakes had been made on one school and that another, recently constructed, was a "monstrosity."[46] Burton was not alone in his apprehensions, as the school board voted to table the architecture firm's contract offer until the matter could be reviewed by the board's real estate and buildings committee. The committee met the following week and interviewed a number of architecture firms, apparently ready to make a change, but concluded that the contract terms Malcomson and Higginbotham offered were too advantageous to forego at that time, given the tight budgets allowed for construction.[47]

This was a narrow escape for Malcomson and Higginbotham and, considering that school board commissions composed most of the firm's business, losing the contract would have been devastating. The firm's principals, William G. Malcomson (1853–1937) and William E. Higginbotham (1858–1923), knew they had to bolster the firm's expertise in concrete construction and design or face the possibility their school board contract would not be renewed the following year. The two men were fortunate to find in thirty-four-year-old Wirt Rowland more than adequate skills in both areas. Rowland's extensive experience with reinforced concrete construction, gained in Mason's and Kahn's offices, and his established contacts with appropriate vendors of steel reinforcement and concrete, brought expertise and credibility to Malcomson and Higginbotham. His design skills were, of course, well known throughout the architecture community. Kahn's firm was larger, with a more diverse range of clients than that of Malcomson and Higginbotham, but 1911 and 1912 were relatively slow years for Kahn's office, offering few opportunities for Rowland to exercise his creative skills. Malcomson and Higginbotham, on the other hand, had the prospect of at least one high school building, and probably two more in the near future, as well as six or eight elementary and middle schools each year. As part of the arrangement to bring Rowland into the firm, Higginbotham and Malcomson made him a junior partner and the firm's name became Malcomson and Higginbotham, Wirt C. Rowland Associate, effective in October 1912.[48]

At the time Rowland started with Malcomson and Higginbotham, the firm was overseeing construction of Northwestern High School (opened January 26, 1914) and Bennett Elementary (February 1913), and completing plans for several sixteen-room elementary school buildings of a design similar to Bennett, including Burton (January 1914) and Hillger (January 1914).[49] Although plans for Burton and Hillger were essentially complete, Rowland made cosmetic revisions that improved the appearance of both.

As anticipated, the school board proceeded with two new high school buildings in 1913, purchasing property for Northeastern and Northern High Schools and requesting that Malcomson and Higginbotham prepare plans for both. Plans for Northeastern (4830 Grandy Street, demolished) were completed early in 1915, and the school opened on January 31, 1916. Although plans for Northern High School (9026 Woodward Avenue) were completed shortly after those for Northeastern, Northern did not open until January 29, 1917, due in part to a lack of funds.[50]

Northeastern High was a handsome and straightforward building, clearly different in appearance than Northwestern High, completed the previous year. Northwestern had wings that extended from the building's central section, the front facades of which had large areas lacking windows, giving the structure somewhat the look of a mausoleum. Rowland's design for Northeastern corrected this flaw. He gave the building a more dignified appearance—akin to an important university structure and less like a grade school—by employing features from buildings he had recently designed in Kahn's office: bold corner pylons, prominent vertical piers with buttress-like decorations, a broad band of bricks set in diamond patterns, and a hip (instead of flat) roof. Bold horizontal bands of light-colored stone provided contrast with the brick.

Northern High, though having the same basic shape as Northeastern, departed significantly in appearance. In designing Northern, Rowland clearly reused many ideas that

44. Detroit Northwestern High School (demolished) was designed by Malcomson and Higginbotham in 1911, prior to Rowland joining the firm. (Detroit Publishing Company Photograph Collection, Library of Congress Prints and Photographs Division)

first appeared on Hill Auditorium: the large area of windows in front, separated by light-toned piers and framed by brickwork. On Hill Auditorium, this treatment seems natural because we know that behind the windows is a single, large auditorium. On Northern High, this treatment unifies the facade, eliminating the otherwise typical perception that the building is merely a box containing identical classrooms. Surrounding this windowed area are decorations in terra-cotta, most in a buff color, which complements the brick, though one band has a background of pale blue. Terra-cotta sections beneath the eave bear unusual overlapping zigzag shapes—interesting because the same design reappeared more than a decade later on many Art Deco style buildings. Zigzag designs did not originate with Rowland; they were employed as decorations going back at least as far at the eleventh century.

The brickwork on the building is worthy of attention as Rowland somehow convinced the school board to provide an additional $2,500 (the total cost of the school was $650,000) for "Flemish bond" brickwork (every other brick is laid narrow end out). The bricks, which were of a less expensive type, range in color from deep red to pink and are set with unusually thick mortar joints.

Northern High School was well received by the architectural community. The *Western Architect* published a photo of the nearly completed school in its October 1916 issue,[51] and the *American Architect* ran four photos of it in the January 18, 1922, issue.[52]

45. Detroit Northeastern High School, designed by Rowland, opened in January 1916 (demolished). (Courtesy of the Burton Historical Collection, Detroit Public Library)

Early in 1915, the school board resolved to build a high school in the southeastern section of the city, and a site at the corner of Fairview and Goethe was selected. At the school board meeting of August 13, 1914, the Kercheval Avenue Citizens' Improvement Association objected to the location as it was not on a streetcar line, the nearest being the Mack Avenue line about one-quarter mile north. School board member Samuel Mumford dismissed the objection, suggesting that "walking [is] a healthy exercise for school boys and girls."[53] Plans were approved in early 1915 and Southeastern High School, though not complete, was opened for students on January 3, 1917.

In appearance, Rowland's design for Southeastern was a striking fusion of Northern and Northeastern, combining the stone piers of Northern with Northeastern's repeating vertical bays of windows topped by arches. All three schools had hip roofs, but Southeastern's overhang the walls, making the roof a more prominent visual feature. Banding in the arches and diamond shapes within the spandrels (between the second and third floors) are eye-catching at a distance; closer inspection of the building reveals myriad subtle designs in red terra-cotta. The most unusual treatment is the area above the window arches: a field of complex terra-cotta designs in red, blue, and tan. When examined close up, these designs appear somewhat strange, but viewed as they were intended—from a distance of at least thirty feet—they look like a fine quilt and give the building an unusual and colorful texture. The bricks used on Southeastern were, like those of Northern, inexpensive but set in Flemish bond with thick mortar joints.

46. Detroit Northern High School at 9026 Woodward Avenue opened in January 1917.

Due to extremely tight spending limits imposed on the school board by city government, school construction budgets were austere in the extreme, particularly for elementary schools. In the original contract for the Majeske Elementary School, for example, drinking fountains were cut from the plans "on account of lack of funds."[54] The fountains were restored during construction the following year under a new budget. Naturally, with such tight financial restrictions, little money was available for purely aesthetic purposes, and the appearance of school buildings suffered. This problem was brought to the public's attention in January 1914 when several members of the city's board of estimators—responsible, in part, for city budgets—toured recently completed elementary schools (designed by Malcomson and Higginbotham prior to Rowland's employment). One estimator stated, "The Barstow and Marcy schools looked like factories,"[55] while another commented, "No public building should look like a warehouse."[56] As a consequence of these criticisms an additional $5,000 was added to the 1914 construction budget for each new school to cover the cost of "exterior adornment."[57]

It fell to Rowland to plan the next generation of elementary school buildings, and the result was a design with twenty classrooms suitable for grades kindergarten through eight, though this "standard intermediate school," as it was called, sometimes served high school grades until additional buildings were constructed. Even with additional funds allowed for appearance sake, designing attractive grade school buildings required ingenious

47. Detroit Southeastern High School at the corner of Fairview and Goethe streets opened in January 1917.

exploitation of inexpensive materials. Rowland used lighter-toned or brightly colored bricks and employed brickwork designs, often set within contrasting stucco. The "warehouse" look of the older schools (Bennett and Northwestern) derived in part from having flat roofs and two massive blank walls on the front facade. Rowland's twenty-room schools, by contrast, had a cleverly designed hip roof on three sides—the central portion and rear of the building were covered by a gently sloping roof, which aided water runoff. By adding gables or other adornments to the basic hip roof, Rowland was able to give each building a distinct appearance. Windowless walls were eliminated, and some variety in the shape of windows was introduced, often in the form of an arch. Even though these twenty-room schools incorporated additional aesthetic features, they were, on a per room basis, less expensive to build and operate than the sixteen-room design.[58] The first school of this type, Thirkell Elementary, opened in September 1915, followed by Joyce (January 3, 1916), Ellis (January 31, 1916, demolished), Marxhausen (January 31, 1916, demolished), Nordstrum (September 11, 1916), Breitmeyer (February 1917, demolished), and Harms (March 29, 1917).

Malcomson and Higginbotham was actively engaged outside of Detroit during Rowland's time with the firm, designing three schools and the Elks Temple in Flint, Michigan. Voters in that city passed a bond issue in November 1912, and within thirty days Malcomson and Higginbotham had been selected as architects for two twelve-room schools of similar design.[59] Homedale (1501 Davison Road, demolished) and Parkland (North

Street at East Pasadena, demolished [at the time Parkland School was built, Pasadena was known as Durant Street]) opened at the beginning of the school year in 1914. Although small, these two Rowland-designed schools incorporated unusual features, such as high arched windows in the building's central section and vibrant colors. Homedale had a flat roof, but on the building's center section, running from the roofline down to the springing point of the window arches, ran a bold band of tan artificial stone accented by buff-colored insets. This center section was flanked by two large pylons topped with ornate Prairie School–type designs. A medium red brick gave the building a bright look and coordinated well with the buff and tan accents.

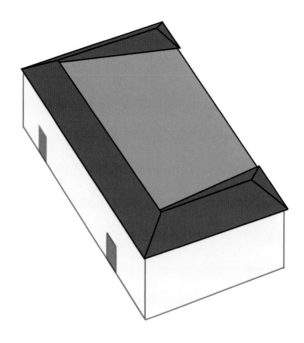

48. Rowland's design for twenty-room schools had a hip roof on three sides and a large sloped roof covering the midsection and rear.

Parkland Elementary was essentially identical to Homedale, but Rowland gave it a distinctly different look with a gabled roof (and matching roofs over the two entrances), prominent arched window muntins, and ornate gutters.

In early 1915, Malcomson and Higginbotham was selected to build the Flint Fairview School (1243 Central Avenue, demolished [Central Avenue is gone, replaced by a Buick plant (also gone); it was the next street south of Leith Street and the school was located about where James P. Cole Boulevard runs]), completed the following year. Fairview shared the same basic design with its two predecessors, but once again, Rowland introduced enough variation to make the school distinct—a full hip roof with an overhang (with matching roofs covering the entrances) and segmental arches above the second-floor windows.

The city of Hamtramck chose Malcomson and Higginbotham to design the tiny John Lynch School (Palmetto Street, just west of Van Dyke) in 1914. This simple, eight-room school is topped with Rowland's characteristic hip roof (with dormers in this case) and a nicely styled entrance having an orange brick and light stone surround.[60]

Rowland's school buildings were fresh designs (Rowland would have referred to them as "modern"), and they remain fresh a century later. He used no classical columns or Gothic pointed arches, features that adorned many other school buildings of the period.

49. Isabel F. Thirkell Elementary School at 7724 Twenty-Fourth Street as it looked upon completion in 1915. One interesting aspect of the school is its similar appearance to the Hudson Motor Company administration building designed by Rowland and Wilby in 1910. (Courtesy of the Burton Historical Collection, Detroit Public Library)

50. Thirkell School in 2013. Although some of the ornamental features have been removed, the building looks much like it did nearly one hundred years ago.

Instead, he incorporated visually satisfying embellishments of his own design. Rowland employed color to add interest and variety, sometimes in broad areas through brightly colored bricks and occasionally as a subtle accent or background. By adding more and larger windows and a hip or gabled roof, his grade school buildings looked less stark and warehouse-like than earlier Detroit schools. His high school buildings were particularly unique and innovative, their designs expressing a grandeur and dignity more typical of important buildings on a university campus.

Another project that occupied Rowland's time during his employment with Malcomson and Higginbotham was a design for the Detroit Public Library. The city of Detroit held a design competition to select an architect for the new main library building to be constructed on Woodward Avenue south of Kirby Street. Entries were judged on the practicality of the interior layout and attractiveness of the exterior design. The library commission invited four prominent New York architectural

51. Nordstrum School on Fort Street in southwest Detroit, completed in 1916, served initially as a high school until the adjacent Southwestern High was constructed.

firms to provide entries: McKim, Mead, and White (architects of Detroit's State Savings Bank); Cass Gilbert (Belle Isle's Scott Memorial Fountain); Carrere and Hastings (Merrill Fountain in Palmer Park); and H. Van Buren Magonigle (Stevens T. Mason Monument in Capitol Park). In order to encourage participation by Detroit architecture firms, the competition was divided into two phases; the first was open only to Detroit-based architects. From among these local entries, two winners were selected to compete in the second phase with the four New York firms.[61]

The competition was announced in early February 1913 and the deadline for entries in the first phase was March 15. Sixteen firms entered the competition, including Albert Kahn, George Mason, John Scott and Co., and Van Leyen and Schilling. After two weeks of deliberation, the library commission announced that the two winners of the first phase were Malcomson and Higginbotham and William B. Stratton.[62] The competition's second phase was judged by Herbert Putnam, Librarian of Congress, and architects Paul Philippe Cret (who later designed the Detroit Institute of Arts) and John L. Mauran. In early June it was announced that Cass Gilbert had been selected as architect for Detroit's new library.

One of the country's foremost library designers, Edward L. Tilton (1861–1933), was not represented in the competition, though Tilton had more than twenty library buildings to his credit (he subsequently designed Highland Park's McGregor Public Library on Woodward Avenue). Malcomson and Higginbotham's entry, presumably designed by Rowland, took advantage of Tilton's absence with a design similar in many respects to Tilton's Springfield, Massachusetts, Central Library, designed in 1907.[63] Rowland's design, though, was less influenced by the prevailing classicism of the period and exhibited superbly balanced proportions, likely achieved through careful application of his geometric design method.

At some point in 1915 Rowland decided to leave Malcomson and Higginbotham, though it is not definite why or exactly when. One factor may have been the incessant attacks on Malcomson and Higginbotham by certain school board members—covered in the local papers as high drama—causing Rowland to question the firm's future prospects. On March 24, Rowland's seventy-two-year-old mother, Melissa Rowland, suffered an incapacitating stroke. Her condition slowly deteriorated over the next two months until, on May 25, she passed away.[64] As the only relative available to attend to his mother's needs, Rowland likely took a leave of absence from Malcomson and Higginbotham to remain with his mother in Clinton during her illness, returning to Detroit after attending to her affairs.

When Rowland left Albert Kahn's office to join Malcomson and Higginbotham in 1912, Kahn hired as a replacement Amedeo Leone (1892–1984), a promising New York City architectural designer. Two years later, however, Leone quit and joined the staff of Smith, Hinchman, and Grylls, once again leaving Kahn short one designer.

52. Harms School on Central Avenue in Southwest Detroit was completed in 1917 and features an unusual decorative treatment of the entrance.

53. Breitmeyer School (demolished). (Timothy Boscarino, Historic Designation Advisory Board, City of Detroit)

54. Carstens School (derelict). (Timothy Boscarino, Historic Designation Advisory Board, City of Detroit)

Kahn courted Rowland, and by summer's end, 1915, Rowland was back working in Kahn's office.[65]

Between June and November 1915, an unusual building rose in downtown Detroit on Woodward Avenue at Grand River: the T. B. Rayl Hardware Company Building. In describing the new structure, the *Michigan Manufacturer and Financial Record* said, "The building has a striking architectural design. The walls are of special reddish terra cotta, which makes the building stand out strongly in contrast with the white glazed terra cotta so commonly used at present."[66] In 1968, Hawkins Ferry wrote approvingly of the building, "The red terra-cotta exterior with its rich surface ornament, the slender piers terminating in arcades, and the cavetto cornice harked back to [Louis] Sullivan's Guaranty Building (1895) in Buffalo."[67] The 1998 historic district report for the neighborhood states, "This building is one of downtown Detroit's unrecognized gems."[68] The *American Institute of Architects Guide to Detroit Architecture* (2003) says, "This splendid corner building exhibits a sophisticated composition of form following structural function. The red terra cotta surfaces crisply distinguish supporting elements from nonsupporting surface ornament. Slender piers terminate in a visually relieving arcade. Among the finest Sullivanesque

55. Flint Homedale School (demolished). (Courtesy of Kettering University Archives)

56. Flint Parkland School (demolished). (Courtesy of Kettering University Archives)

57. Flint Fairview School (demolished). (Courtesy of Kettering University Archives)

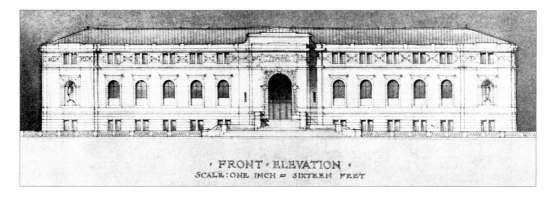

· FRONT · ELEVATION ·
SCALE: ONE INCH = SIXTEEN FEET

58. Rowland's entry for the Detroit Public Library design competition of 1913.

designs in Detroit."[69] The architects of the Rayl building were Frank Baxter, Dewey Halpin, and Augustus O'Dell of the firm Baxter, O'Dell, and Halpin, a competent firm, but one whose previous (and subsequent) designs were unremarkable—certainly not "striking" architectural designs.

The Rayl Building is a fascinating case of great architecture appreciated for its own sake, in spite of the building's attribution to the undistinguished firm of Baxter, O'Dell, and Halpin. Nevertheless, great art and architecture are seldom produced by individuals who have not invested thousands of hours in study and practice to attain the highest levels of skill in their profession. Such is the case with the Rayl Building, which was designed during the spring of 1915, not by Baxter, Halpin, or O'Dell but by Wirt Rowland. Augustus "Gus" O'Dell, it will be recalled, worked with Rowland at Rogers and MacFarlane, and the two remained good friends. Prior to 1915, most of the projects designed by Baxter, O'Dell, and Halpin had been factories, stores, and residences. The firm likely had the expertise to design a seven-story building, but not one that so successfully overcame the particular challenges posed by the Rayl Company. The building might have turned out differently were it not for the close relationship between O'Dell and Rowland; O'Dell was confident Rowland's design skill and depth of experience with reinforced concrete construction would result in an outstanding building, attractive and well-suited to its purpose. O'Dell could also count on Rowland's extraordinary modesty to make it unnecessary that Rowland be recognized for the building's design, thereby assisting O'Dell to secure future work based on the building's success. Quite possibly, Rowland worked on the building while attending to his ailing mother in Clinton—Rowland added a large studio to the home in 1927, suggesting that he was in the habit of working while staying there. In the 1930s, Rowland hired himself out to other architects for what he called "freelance" work, indicating his familiarity with and acceptance of the practice.[70]

It appears that at least a small number of fellow architects were aware of Rowland's authorship of the Rayl Building's design. The draft of Rowland's obituary, written for the *Weekly Bulletin of the Michigan Society of Architects*, included the line: "The Rayl Bldg., at Woodward and Grand River Avenues, was one of the first to make use of terra cotta and other modern materials. It was designed by Rowland for Baxter and O'Dell."[71] The obituary was likely written by Talmage C. Hughes, longtime editor of the *Weekly Bulletin* and a good friend of Rowland—the two had worked together in Albert Kahn's office.[72] Hughes had an encyclopedic knowledge of Detroit architecture and architects and was the primary source on those topics for the *Biographical Dictionary of American Architects*, 1956, by Henry and Elise Withey. The published obituary, however, omitted these lines, perhaps as a face-saving measure for O'Dell, a former president of the Michigan Society of Architects and a practicing architect at the time of Rowland's death.[73]

59. T. B. Rayl Building at 1400 Woodward Avenue as it appeared on May 8, 1925. The small building on the left is being demolished to make room for an addition to the Rayl Building. (This is a black-and-white photograph that has been colorized.) (Courtesy of the Burton Historical Collection, Detroit Public Library)

The interior of the building was a cornucopia of clever applications of new technology and materials. Rowland took maximum advantage of the Kahn System of concrete reinforcement (manufactured by Julius Kahn's Trussed Concrete Steel Company) to produce a building ideally suited for its role as a retail store. Floretyle, manufactured by Trussed Concrete, was a hollow steel spacer set within the building's concrete floors, lessening the amount of concrete required and reducing the overall weight and cost of the building. Floretyle permitted the floor's support beams to be the same depth as the floor, resulting in flat ceilings, unobstructed by beams. The combination of the Rayl Building's flat ceilings and very tall windows allowed the maximum amount of daylight to enter and penetrate to all areas of the floor.

Floretyle arrived on the construction site nested in compact stacks, a consequential advantage over the bulky terra-cotta spacers they replaced. Downtown construction locations often lacked adequate space in which to store the tile sections, resulting in delays if scheduled deliveries did not arrive on time. Incredibly, Rowland's selection of materials and construction methods allowed the seven-story (plus basement) building to be erected in a mere five months.[74]

The large windows on the first and second floors of the Rayl Building were designed to serve as displays for merchandise. In order for these windows to remain unobstructed, the supporting piers of the structure's frame were inset from the building line, and the sections containing the windows were supported by cantilevers.[75]

The building was so successful that the Rayl Company acquired the adjacent property and in 1925 added a nearly identical section to the north end of the structure. Sometime later, an additional floor was added. Unfortunately, the unusual cornice was removed in the 1990s.

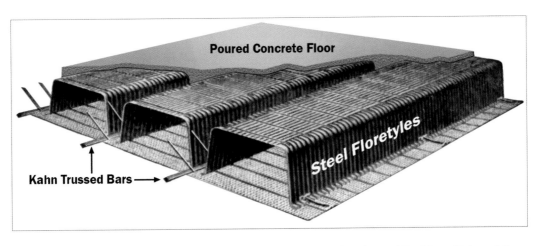

60. Kahn System of construction with Truscon Floretyle, as used in the Rayl Building. (Adapted from *Truscon Floretyle Construction*, 1923)

3

THE CITY'S TOP DESIGNER

If buildings for commerce and industry have shown progress, it has not been through any desire to create a new type, but through the application of those essentials which are incorporated in the great architecture of the past.

—Wirt Rowland, "Architecture and the Auto Industry," 1921

World War I began in July 1914, and, as fighting continued unabated, many believed the United States would eventually be drawn into the conflict. The nation was woefully unprepared to intervene in Europe, or even defend itself against aggression; the US Army, with 100,000 in uniform, compared poorly with the German army's more than 1.5 million. On May 7, 1915, the British ocean liner RMS *Lusitania*, en route from New York to Liverpool, was sunk by a German U-boat, killing nearly 1,200, including 128 Americans. Overnight, concerns over preparedness became front-page news. At a meeting of the Harvard Club, General Leonard Wood, former army chief of staff and a Harvard graduate, proposed a military training camp for business and professional men who might be called upon to serve as officers in the event of war. The project quickly gained momentum through the involvement of other university alumni organizations. The organizers arranged with the War Department to conduct a four-week military training camp from August 10 through September 6 in Plattsburg, New York; in June 1915, invitations to attend were sent to 15,000 alumni.[1] The War Department provided training, yet each attendee was required to pay for their food and uniform.[2]

Most of the camp's attendees were businessmen and professionals in their thirties and forties; they received instruction in basic military discipline, close order drill, tactics, trench digging, and riflery. Among the trainees were John P. Mitchel, mayor of New York City; former assistant secretary of state Robert Bacon; *New York Times* general manager, Julius Ochs Adler; and thirty-six-year-old Detroit architect Wirt Rowland. As a former Harvard student, Rowland likely received one of the invitations and, by August, having completed design work on the Rayl Building, volunteered to serve his country. Rowland apparently was less than satisfied with his uniform, commenting, "I came back with the seat of my trousers even with the backs of my knees." Upon his return to Detroit, he was hailed: "Here comes the man who won the war!" or so he claimed.[3] Rowland's military career having concluded, he returned to work at Albert Kahn's office.

The first major project to receive Rowland's attention was a building that would be widely regarded as a significant architectural achievement and more than twenty years later described by Albert Kahn as "the best industrial building we have designed to date."[4] The *Detroit News*, a local newspaper established in 1873, had grown dramatically under the leadership of its president, George Booth; circulation in 1913 was 140,000 and by 1916, topped 190,000.[5] Booth engaged Kahn's firm to design for the company a building highly customized to the particular requirements of producing a daily paper—a novel request at the time as even large dailies leased or built standard space that could be reused for other purposes. Every aspect of the News Building's plan was intended to maximize the efficient production of the newspaper. The appearance of the building was also important to Booth, who sought "a structure of superior design," unusually attractive, yet dignified and reflective of the firm's civic mission.[6]

Rowland, collaborating with Ernest Wilby, succeeded in meeting both requirements beyond Booth's expectations. A 1918 article in *Architectural Forum*, headlined "An Imposing Example of Commercial Architecture and an Efficient Newspaper Plant," described the building as "one which presents an ideal solution of the newspaper plant, both from its architectural expression and its perfectly co-ordinated plan."[7] In his 1928 book, *The American Architecture of To-Day*, George Edgell wrote of the building: "The proportions of arcades, windows, and attic are exceptionally fine. The ornament, classic in feeling, but modern in design, is sparing and appropriate." "One senses immediately the lightness and functional practicality of the work, while one delights in its proportions and refinement."[8] The *Michigan Alumnus* in 1919 said: "the largest plant ever assembled for exclusively newspaper purposes" embodies "a unique architectural idea, being perhaps the only structure of its kind in which the artistic plan and the utilitarian purpose have from the beginning received equal attention. So completely have these disparate aims been reconciled."[9]

Is it true that "utilitarian purpose" and "artistic plan" are "disparate aims"? Rowland, Langford Warren, and Viollet-le-Duc would disagree. These men believed the beauty of an object arose from the fitness of its design to perform the task for which it was intended. Viollet-le-Duc describes how a primitive copper pot, being well adapted to its use, has "style" or beauty: the bottom of the vessel is broad and flat, to prevent spillage; the top edge has a lip to facilitate pouring; handles provide a means to lift the pot, but they do not extend

61. The Detroit News Building, Fort Street (rear) entrance.

above the lip in order that the pot may lie flat when turned upside down.[10] In a misguided attempt to make the pot more stylish, a subsequent coppersmith rounds off the bottom and extends the handles above the lip, thereby making the utensil less well suited to its purpose and, according to Viollet-le-Duc, less stylish. "A thing has style when it has the expression appropriate to its uses."[11] Rowland spoke of "the satisfaction we should find in a machine which is economically proportioned to its parts and those parts formed to properly carry out their duty. If this be called beautiful, the underlying idea of functional proportioning is that which makes it beautiful, the conformance with nature's laws of motion and mechanics, and not the free and unrestrained ideas of form which man may apply out of the figments of his imagination to create what he may call art."[12]

The artistic treatment of the Detroit News Building was not a disparate aim needing to be reconciled with functional design requirements, but a consequence of the functional design of the structure. The structure, by the standards of Viollet-le-Duc and Rowland, was well designed for its purpose and, therefore, beautiful. Rowland and Wilby, as artists, amplified and further developed the building's inherent beauty by structuring its outward appearance according to principles of design. Adding subtle embellishment and decoration, they made it a work of art.

The basic layout of the structure was determined by three primary physical considerations. First, the printing presses, two hundred feet in length, had to reside within a large, open area on the ground level. Second, the various departments had to be located relative to each other so as to achieve maximum productive efficiency. Third, given the inadequacy of artificial lighting at the time, expansive windowed areas were required to facilitate the entry of daylight.[13] From these requirements emerged a building one full block in length (280 feet) and three stories high (plus basement and mezzanine). The building's first floor was almost entirely consumed by the press room and adjacent shipping department, where newspapers were loaded on trucks for distribution. Above the first floor, the building took on a U shape, enhancing daylight illumination of offices on the west side of the upper floors and making room for skylights over the shipping department. On the second floor were the editorial, circulation, advertising, and business offices, one flight away from both the composing room above and press department below (should anyone need to run down and yell "Stop the presses!"). The original preference of *Detroit News* man-

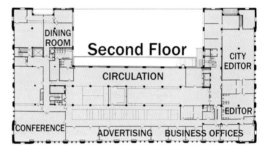

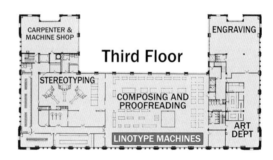

62. Floor plans for the Detroit News Building.

agement was to locate business offices on the first floor, easily accessible to the public. Placement of the press room and shipping department on the first floor, however, made this impossible. Once the idea of locating offices on the second floor was accepted, the advantages of doing so became clear: all offices were located in close proximity—business, circulation, advertising, and editorial. The third floor housed the engraving, art, composing, and proofreading departments, all of which required above-average lighting for efficient and accurate performance. The engraving and art departments were located on the building's corners, well lit by windows. Illumination for the composing and proofreading departments was augmented by a large monitor (a raised portion of roof with windows, often used on industrial buildings of the time).

The structure's specific form having been determined by practical considerations, structural engineers set about determining the most efficient method of construction. The

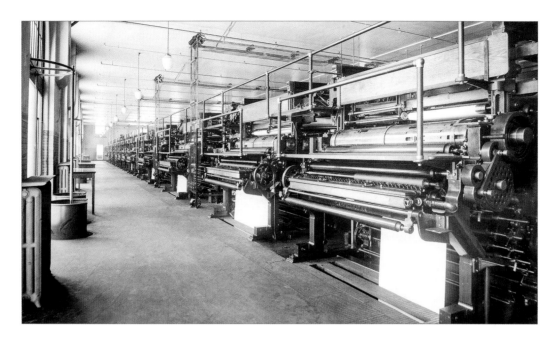

63. The printing press on the first floor of the Detroit News Building was actually comprised of multiple units feeding into a central stream of paper, or "web," which was folded and cut into individual newspapers at the end of the press. Rolls of paper were located in the basement and fed, uncut, into individual press units through slots in the floor seen here. On the far left is one of the fireman's poles used by pressmen to quickly access the paper roll in case of a problem. (Albert Kahn Papers, Albert Kahn Associates, Inc. and the Bentley Historical Library, University of Michigan: Evening News Association [Detroit News] Building, Detroit, Michigan [1916], Job No. 641, photographs of exterior and interior, photos by Hance, Volume 29)

entire building is of steel reinforced concrete (except for a portion of the third floor roof), but a variety of methods were utilized, depending on the use of a particular area. The ceiling of the press area, for example, contained deep beams in order to eliminate a forest of supporting piers, while other areas employed Floretyle for light weight and a smooth, light-reflecting ceiling.

One of the unusual features of the building was air-conditioning, an emerging technology that improved the efficiency of the printing process.[14] Paper and ink react to changes in humidity, causing problems during printing. Air-conditioning permitted a constant level of humidity and temperature to be maintained and, as a side benefit, allowed the building's windows to remain closed, eliminating sudden breezes that sent paperwork flying.

The exterior surface of the building is really nothing more than a limestone skin over the concrete frame, a fact noted by the journal *Architectural Forum*: "The Detroit News Building is characterized chiefly by an expression of structure. Its frame is of reinforced concrete, and this fact is easily apparent from the series of strongly accentuated piers and

64. The third floor of the Detroit News Building housed the composing and proofreading departments. The square arrangement of desks in the foreground is the proofreading area. On the far left in the foreground are full pages set in metal type sitting atop wheeled trucks. Behind the column, galley proofs are being pulled from typeset forms. In the background along the windows are two rows of Linotype "hot lead" typesetting machines. The monitor skylight above the room is visible in the upper right corner. The steel truss roof was necessitated by the monitor and is the only part of the building not of reinforced concrete. (Albert Kahn Papers, Albert Kahn Associates, Inc. and the Bentley Historical Library, University of Michigan: Evening News Association [Detroit News] Building, Detroit, Michigan [1916], Job No. 641, photographs of exterior and interior, photos by Hance, Volume 29)

spandrels."[15] (It was—and still is—common for architects to clad a steel and concrete frame building to appear as a masonry wall supported structure, a practice Rowland viewed with disdain.[16]) Both Rowland and Wilby believed a structure's beauty arose in part from its freely expressing the means by which it opposed gravity, an effect encouraged by the external expression of the internal supporting structure. Wilby saw in beautiful architecture "the story of gravity, strain and stress, in pier, column, lintel and arch."[17] Rowland had learned from Langford Warren that "beautiful architectural forms are organic expressions of structural functions,"[18] and Rowland similarly asserted, for a building to be attractive, "there must be some visual evidence in it of performing its work as a structure."[19] Even the plain wall was found wanting by Rowland for having "no visual articulation of natural forces."[20]

The vertical elements of the News Building's structural frame are emphasized by piers that extend from street level to slightly above the parapet. Massive pylons anchor the building's corners, each topped with a stepped pyramid roof. The piers project somewhat from the adjacent surface of the flanking bays, while the four corner pylons project further, giving them greater prominence, like the sturdy legs of a heavy table, an effect enhanced by their having only a single column of windows. Spandrels above and below the third-floor windows emphasize the horizontal aspect of the structure's frame. First-floor windows are taller than those above in order to admit maximum light into the high-ceilinged pressroom and offices located on a small mezzanine in the front of the building. The arches provide a contrast to the vertical and horizontal lines of the building and are plain, save for a single band of ornate carved design.

65. Front entrance of the Detroit News Building on Lafayette Boulevard as it originally appeared. (Albert Kahn Papers, Albert Kahn Associates, Inc. and the Bentley Historical Library, University of Michigan: Evening News Association [Detroit News] Building, Detroit, Michigan [1916], Job No. 641, photographs of exterior and interior, photos by Hance, Volume 29)

An extraordinary feature of the building is the sculpture adorning the exterior. On the building's front, larger-than-life statues of history's most renowned printers and publishers stand watch along the parapet: Johannes Gutenberg, Christophe Plantin, William Caxton, and Benjamin Franklin. Also on the parapet are raised inscriptions describing the newspaper's mission, authored by University of Michigan professor Fred N. Scott.[21] Carved in the spandrels between the second- and third-floor windows on three sides of the building are the printers' marks of distinguished publishers of the past.[22]

Architectural sculpture was a long established form of expression, but its use on a commercial, rather than public or religious, building was innovative. On one level,

Rowland's belief that "carved ornament of an appropriate character may add a human touch, a need often felt in buildings where the lines are otherwise rigid and geometrical," justifies its use here.[23] On a deeper level, the sculpture on the News Building was the manifestation of a concept unifying the building's design. Lee White of the *Detroit News* wrote: "Escape was sought from the classic and Renaissance traditions which have too often been indifferently appropriate to modern needs, and by daring adaptation of medieval precedents a building that acknowledges its European prototype, and yet is essentially American, was realized."[24] "Medieval precedents" was a reference to "Romanesque" architecture, which Rowland described as "characterized by round arches and bold, simple surface decorations."[25] The most commendable feature of Romanesque architecture, according to Rowland, was "the craft of its structural ornament,"[26] though not as independent works of art, but as part of the building. To the Romanesque craftsman, said Rowland, "building and art were one and the same thing and could not be separated into a steel frame and an art which is *pasted* on it—as in our time." "Structure and art go arm in arm, in fact annealed into one and the same expression."[27] The Detroit News Building, then, epitomized the Romanesque concept of architecture: art and structure formed a unified entity.[28]

Why was Romanesque style well suited for modern buildings? White's comment on the inappropriateness of classic and Renaissance traditions closely reflected Rowland's views. In fact, White was most likely quoting from or paraphrasing a description of the building prepared by Rowland; such descriptions were typically prepared by the designer so those lacking expertise in architecture could confidently write and speak about a building without risking embarrassing misstatements. Architecture, as a fine art, had been in decline, according to Rowland, since the early Renaissance: "with the inception of the Renaissance, architectural expression lost any vitality with which it began in the Periclean age."[29] (This was the outlook of Viollet-le-Duc as well.) The Renaissance, it should be recalled, was characterized by imitation of earlier periods of architecture. Absent an understanding of the fundamental principles employed to generate the original examples, imitation produces lifeless results: architecture lacking *vitality*.

As for classic traditions, Roman architecture suffered from being either imitative of earlier Greek buildings or, as Viollet-le-Duc argued, designed by skilled Greek artisans compelled against their better judgment to produce the flamboyant structures desired by their less cultured Roman masters. On the other hand, ancient Greece witnessed, in Rowland's view, "the greatest and most complete development of architecture."[30] "I believe," said Rowland, "the most important attainment in building which the world has ever seen was the Greek temple of the Periclean age."[31] Given his clear admiration for Greek architecture, why not employ it as he did Romanesque? Greek architects applied the most advanced principles and materials known at the time to their construction problems. Their building technology was simple post and lintel: vertical columns supporting horizontal lintels or beams. Columns were the supporting structure of Greek buildings and their appearance clearly conveyed that role. Believing as Rowland did that a building should honestly reflect its supporting structure, making apparent the means by which it counters the force of gravity, there was little Rowland could honestly borrow from the Greeks that wouldn't convey the false impression that the building was supported by stone columns. Although it was popular at the time to place sham classical columns on the facade of a building, Rowland

66. Wood paneling and hand-carved details in what was once the office of *Detroit News* vice president William E. Scripps. The door opens into the office once belonging to president of the *News*, George G. Booth.

believed pasting imitation Greek supporting columns on a steel and concrete frame building was a farce. "If we adopt a style," said Rowland, "without applying its principles to our own conditions, we are charlatans."

Viollet-le-Duc explained the concept using examples in which the technological component was more apparent than with architecture: a sailing ship's appearance is a consequence of its design to meet a particular purpose, giving it a certain beauty. For the same reason, a steamship expresses a different appearance. A steamship, however, "which conceals its motive power to assume the appearance of a sailing-vessel" is completely lacking in beauty. A rifle has beauty, "but a rifle made to resemble a cross-bow does not."[32]

Unlike classical columns, Romanesque architectural sculpture was not structural in nature nor was it necessarily tied to a particular construction technology. Moreover, Rowland's design for the Detroit News Building employed these decorations in a manner consistent with their original use as architectural sculpture.

For those areas of the building's interior where decoration was employed, Rowland continued the Romanesque theme, thereby unifying the structure's exterior and interior. The library, lobby, and many of the interior offices feature exceptional, carved wood doors, panels, and bookcases with designs devised by Rowland. Much of the furniture, both case goods and upholstered, was custom made to complement the Romanesque decor. The library overlooks Lafayette Boulevard and has an interior wall of leaded glass windows providing additional insulation from street noise. The oak framed casement windows are composed of small panes held in place by medieval style muntins, all executed with superb materials and craftsmanship. Some individual panes contain small, hand-painted inscriptions or figures. The inscriptions, set at eye level, add a cozy intimacy to the massive building.

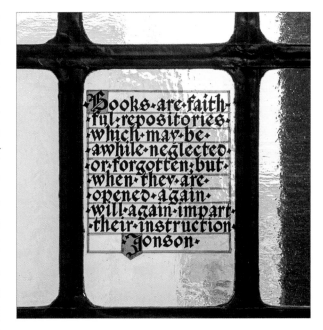

67. One of a number of small inscriptions on the inner windows of the Detroit News Building's third-floor library. The quote is from English poet Ben Jonson (1572–1637).

There are four pairs of larger, hand-tinted glass windows celebrating Art, Music, Literature, and Science, with images of practitioners and technology of the Middle Ages. The lobby and public areas of the building contained many decorations in wrought iron, executed by renowned blacksmith Samuel Yellin of Philadelphia (who also produced a number of wrought iron gates for the home of *News* president George Booth).[33]

In the lobby was a large hanging fixture in the shape of a globe, constructed of iridescent glass. The globe's land masses were represented according to the medieval view of the world. This was a particularly apt bit of artwork as it brought to mind the dramatic increase in knowledge since the Middle Ages, in part as a consequence of the printing press. The medieval style globe was illuminated by one of the modern era's most revolutionary inventions—the electric light—neatly paraphrasing one inscription on the building's exterior: "Dispeller of ignorance and prejudice. . . . A light shining into all dark places."

The building's main stairway began at the elevator lobby, rose to the mezzanine, and then to the second and third floors, each of which was different in height. Complicating matters, doors, windows, and arches opened from the stairway into other areas. Each of the three landings between floors was different; the first had a large doorway open to the press department, the second, a large exterior window, and the third, a window and intermediate flight of stairs. The climb from the second to third floors involved four flights,

68. The Detroit News Building main lobby with lighted globe as it appeared shortly after the building's completion. The furniture was custom made to complement the building. (Albert Kahn Papers, Albert Kahn Associates, Inc. and the Bentley Historical Library, University of Michigan: Evening News Association [Detroit News] Building, Detroit, Michigan [1916], Job No. 641, photographs of exterior and interior, photos by Hance, Volume 29)

three landings, and a 270-degree change in direction. Yet the stairway occupied a minimum amount of space, was well lit with natural light, and each floor presented a unique appearance. Drafting stairway plans was typically a mundane task, but this stairway presented such a three-dimensional conceptual challenge that Rowland personally produced the drawings (one of three sheets for the building which bear his initials).[34] His drawings for the stairway are reminiscent of several well-known etchings by Dutch artist M. C. Escher.

The *Detroit News* remained in its building for ninety-seven years, from 1917 until 2014. During that time, the newspaper firm grew and added to the building, at one point filling in the open area above the shipping department—the fluorescent lamp having eliminated the need for natural light. In 1967, the *News* moved print production to a suburban plant, and in 1998, reflecting the declining fortunes of big city daily papers, the rival *Detroit Free Press* abandoned its own building and moved to the News Building (the two papers signed a joint operating agreement in 1989). Overtaken by changing news consumption habits, the *Detroit News* no longer required the vast amount of space and overhead costs of their building; in October 2014, they moved to new office space. Some employees were disheartened by the move; unlike the Detroit News Building, "The new offices lack character," they said.

In the latter part of 1915, Rowland designed the Detroit Savings Bank branch located on Woodward Avenue at the corner of Milwaukee Avenue in the New Center area. This was the first of at least four identical branches constructed for the bank; the others were Fort Street at Campbell (begun 1919), Warren Avenue at Junction Street (1920), and Hamilton Avenue at Collingwood (1920). Rowland's design is notable for its departure from traditional bank designs of the period and for its imposing, almost haunting appearance. The *Detroit Free Press* described the building as "a fine example of pure Greek architecture, its severe plainness being relieved only by the Greek key border design carved on the front facade."[35] Whatever the origin of the quote, it conveys a partial truth while overlooking an important point: the building is an extraordinary blend of classical and modern elements.

Given the strong traditions of the time regarding the appearance of bank buildings, Rowland was likely not at liberty to dispense with enormous classical columns bestriding the entrance, so he selected Greek Doric columns, the least ornate of the various orders. Around these he wrapped an upside-down U-shaped field of stone inscribed with simple designs. The layout of the incised design on the building's face is nearly identical to those on Hill Auditorium and Northern High School, where a three-sided frame encloses the central

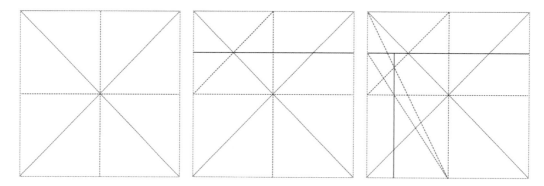

69. Rowland likely started with a square shape for the Detroit Savings Bank. The square is bisected from corner to corner to find the middle, from which it is split vertically and horizontally (*left*). A diagonal line is drawn in the upper left square to locate its center, and a horizontal line is extended through that point (*middle*). A line is placed from the upper left corner to the midpoint of the square, and where this line intersects the shorter diagonal, a vertical line is drawn. (Alternatively, a line bisecting the rectangle formed by the previously drawn horizontal line intersects the midline of the square on the same vertical line.) The horizontal and vertical lines thereby established the location of the decorative band around the facade (*right*). (Overlay drawings are by Michael G. Smith.)

windowed area and entry, with decorative bands extending from the top side of the frame to the corners of the building. The doorway is, like the entrances on both Hill and Northern High, surrounded by a plain, flat stone frame.

Detroit Savings Bank and the earlier Dollar Savings and Trust (1910) share the same basic facade arrangement, but the differences are instructive. Balustrades, various sizes

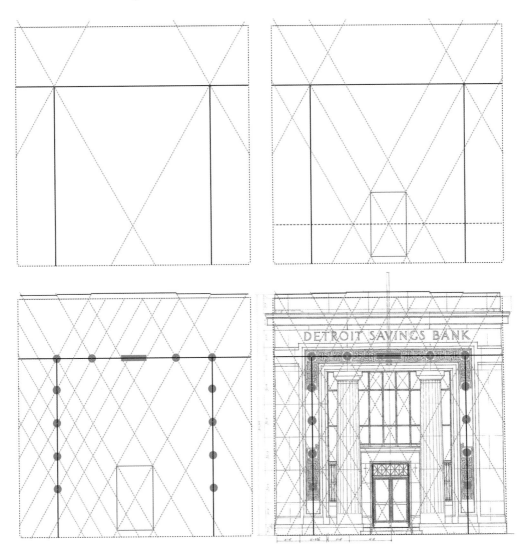

70. Equilateral triangles are drawn from the intersection of the horizontal and vertical lines (*top left*). A horizontal line is drawn through the point at which the sides of the triangles intersect. From this line are added parallel lines forming a lattice of equilateral triangles. The doorway location is established within the triangles centered on this point (*top right*). Additional lines forming a smaller lattice of equilateral triangles provide for the exact location of the decorative roundels and rectangle as well as the location of the steps (notches) in the roof parapet (*bottom left*). The points where lines intersect (the corners of the triangles) determine the midline of the columns and joint locations between individual facing stones (*bottom right*). (Overlay drawings are by Michael G. Smith.)

of dentils, ornate capitals, and bases for columns, and a highly stylized surround for the entrance characterized Dollar Savings (figure 27, p. 36), but are entirely absent from Detroit Savings. Less obvious, but more significant, is the apparent structure of Dollar Savings: the horizontal "lintel" section of the building appears to be supported by massive columns and walls, mimicking traditional Greek post and lintel construction. In contrast, the facade of Detroit Savings is a unified and unbroken expanse of flat stone, relying for its attractiveness primarily on the composition of

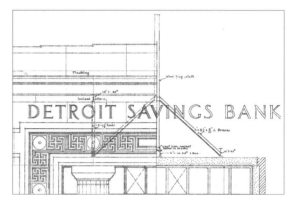

71. Drawing for the Detroit Savings Bank showing the location of incised letters. Note that the left side of the letter *D* aligns with the carved detail on the facade and the letter *V* exactly bisects the building centerline. (Albert Kahn, Architects and Engineers, job 689A, sheet 6, December 20, 1915, drawn by Hugh T. Keyes)

major elements (rather than ornamentation) and consistent with the modern view that the exterior of a building should honestly reflect its actual internal structure.

Once Rowland had a clear idea of how the facade would be arranged, he likely employed his geometric method to determine the exact placement of each feature. The method was entirely consistent with the procedure he used for Hill Auditorium, but the application was slightly different owing to the smaller size of the structure and its square, rather than rectangular, shape. The accompanying illustrations show a step-by-step process.

One interesting—and unusual—feature of the facade demonstrates the meticulous care Rowland lavished upon his designs: the placement of letters in the building's carved inscription. The three words "Detroit Savings Bank" are centered on the building and contain eighteen letters and two spaces, so one would expect the centerline of the building to fall between the tenth and eleventh letters—between the *A* and *V* in "Savings." This, however, is not what is shown in the plans; the letter *V* in "Savings" is exactly aligned with the building's centerline, accomplished through subtle manipulation of letter spacing, a common practice employed by graphic artists when setting headline type for printed material. Placed exactly on center, the letter *V* reinforces the bilaterally symmetrical appearance of the facade and also reflects, almost exactly, the equilateral triangles used in its composition. Unfortunately, the stonecutters failed to heed the carefully drawn plans and the *V* ended up off center.[36]

In 1915, the University of Michigan managed to secure from the state legislature partial funding for a new undergraduate library, in spite of "strenuous opposition in the

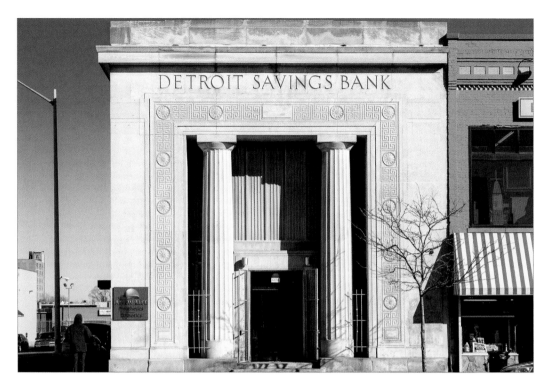

72. Detroit Savings Bank on Woodward Avenue at Milwaukee Avenue. The facade of the building is largely unchanged, though the windows have been covered by steel panels. Note that the *V* in *SAVINGS* was not aligned with the centerline of the building as indicated in the plans.

legislature from those who urged strict tightening of the purse strings and from the element in the legislature none too friendly to the great college."[37] In building a new library, the university sought to satisfy both its present and long-term book storage requirements, and do so in a fireproof structure. Secondarily, the school sought a generous amount of space for reading, studying, and research, all with ample illumination.[38] With a desire for the largest possible building ultimately clashing with the stingy allocation of funds, there was little likelihood that much of the available budget would be expended strictly for appearance sake.

Although plans for the building were complete by September 1916, construction was delayed by World War I. The state legislature did not allocate the balance of funding for the project until 1919, at which point construction progressed quickly, and the building was opened in October 1919. At the dedication ceremony, Albert Kahn noted that the building contained 2.1 million cubic feet (including stacks), acquired at a cost "lower [per cubic foot] than the plainest sort of factory work to-day."[39] The enormous amount of space under roof met the university's book storage needs for more than fifty years, even though the student population tripled during that period.

73. The Reading Room of the Hatcher Graduate Library at the University of Michigan. Each end of the room features a canvas painted by Detroit-born artist Gari Melchers (1860–1932). Melchers produced the two paintings, *The Arts of Peace* and *The Arts of War*, for the 1893 Chicago World's Fair. They were later given to the university.

According to Rowland, the library was designed by himself in collaboration with Ernest Wilby, though Wilby makes no mention of the project in his own list of works, and his initials do not appear on any of the drawings.[40] Rowland's involvement was extensive, as his initials appear on ten of the twelve elevation and detail drawings and on all drawings for the main reading room and delivery corridor on the second floor.

The main reading room is the building's sole aesthetic extravagance. Located on the second floor behind the front facade and running the width of the building, it is 170 feet end to end, fifty feet wide, and fifty feet high. The ceiling is barrel vaulted and, because the width of the room is equal to its height, the room is square in section. The space occupied by the ceiling vault

74. Library of the University of Michigan, now known as the Harlan Hatcher Graduate Library, designed in 1916 and opened in 1919.

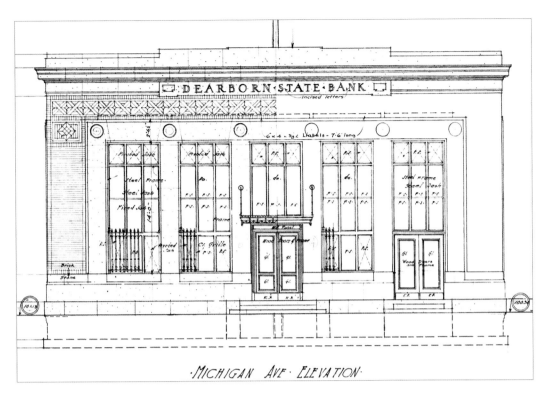

·MICHIGAN· AVE· ELEVATION·

75. A proposal drawn by Rowland for the Dearborn State Bank dates from August 1915 and bears a strong resemblance, both in design and finish materials, to Hill Auditorium and Northern High School. This structure would have been located on the southwest corner of Michigan Avenue and Mason Street in Dearborn. After considering a smaller version of this design, the bank ultimately decided on a smaller building clad in limestone and fronting on Mason Street, roughly 120 feet from the corner. Although the brick was replaced by stone, the basic design and decorative features of the structure were retained. (Albert Kahn, Architects and Engineers, job 502, sheet 4, August 26, 1915)

is accommodated within the building's hip roof. The nineteen-foot-high windows along the front and ends of the room admit an abundance of light during the day. At night, light was originally provided by fixtures atop the bookcases and diffused task lighting built into frames on the study tables.

The plans for the building show that stone, or a stone-like material, was to be placed around and between windows of the front facade in nearly the same manner as on Northern High School. This apparently was sacrificed at a later date as a budget concession and was replaced with brick and a horizontal polychrome band of square- and diamond-shaped designs. This was unfortunate, particularly as the north-facing facade is typically in shadow, an effect accentuated by adjacent tall trees. Nevertheless, the building was well designed for its intended purpose, which it continues to serve with minimal alteration. Testimony to that effect comes from the building's users. In an *Ann Arbor News* article, "Eight Great Places to

Study on University of Michigan Campus," Kellie Woodhouse writes of the reading room: "This room is usually pretty busy, but it's also very quiet. Graduate student Leigh Stutler says students flock to it because it's 'pretty' and 'dead quiet' at the same time. Students who use the room are 'really focused and intent on actually studying,' Stutler says."[41] Blogger "So Midwestern," a former Michigan student, writes: "the reference room is gorgeous and I have always been amazed at how it is always packed with students but still manages to be nearly silent."[42]

During the course of 1916, ill health forced Ernest Wilby to give up the active practice of architecture, though his name remained associated with the firm until 1918 when it became obvious he would not return.[43] It is unclear what illness or incapacity Wilby suffered, though in a 1938 letter he states "I went through a quite serious operation lately and have lost the complete use of one eye. The other is very weak and deficient."[44] In a 1941 letter he stated he was "badly handicapped by impaired eyesight which is sufficiently severe to require that I be accompanied by someone whenever I venture away from my home."[45] Years after Wilby's retirement from the firm, Albert Kahn said, "One of the best investments I made early in my professional career was the engagement of Ernest Wilby. I flatter myself at having had the courage to engage him at a salary considerably higher than what I expected to earn for myself—but it proved a wise move."[46] Wilby was an important presence in Kahn's office, not merely as a designer but also as a guide and mentor to those who strove to understand the art of architecture. Rowland said of Wilby: "Probably no other man who worked in this city has had such a fine influence, both architecturally and personally, on the younger element in the profession."[47] Next to Langford Warren, Wilby was likely the most influential figure in Rowland's professional life. Wilby's philosophy of architectural beauty was both logical and spiritual, and, like Warren, Wilby understood that the ability to create great art rested upon mastery of principles. Explaining his philosophy, Wilby said, "artistic instinct is a very poor crutch on which to lean. . . . If a thing is good there is almost always a reason for it, a reason which can be set forth in words, or proved by a diagram."[48] (Wilby's comment closely echoed the views of Langford Warren and Eugene Viollet-le-Duc: "If a work is good, it is because it is based on a good principle, intelligently and loyally followed.")

Wilby had a knack for putting into plain language his view of the artist: "a man given the power to see concealed beauty in all things material and practical and able to bring this beauty out into the open, so that we who do not have this gift and vision can see and enjoy it also." To be successful as an architectural artist, according to Wilby, "It is far more important to know the principles of good art and beauty not confined to architecture or any school but as a force in all things made by God or by man . . . you cannot be an artist in one thing without being an artist in all things."[49] These principles, said Wilby, derive from "the natural laws the great Master uses to give beauty to this world we live in."[50] This hallowed view of artistry made an impression on Rowland, who referred to Wilby as his "spiritual father" and called him "Pop," though the difference in age between the men was only ten years.[51]

Wilby's most significant accomplishment in architecture revolutionized manufacturing buildings and is evident on an inestimable number of such structures. When designing the Highland Park plant for Henry Ford, Wilby had the idea of dispensing with traditional windows held in place within a brick wall, and instead, filling the space between each concrete column with glass.[52] The individual window panes were held in place by steel sash of a new design; the only relic of the brick wall was a small section beneath the windowsill. The vast increase in window area dramatically improved interior illumination and reduced construction costs. Of this innovation, architectural historian Fiske Kimball wrote in 1928: "Almost overnight the scheme was adopted in thousands of American plants, and foreign imitation soon followed. . . . The whole physiognomy of industrial buildings was quite changed."[53]

Although he did not return to architectural work, Wilby began teaching architecture at the University of Michigan in February 1922, continuing until retirement in 1929.[54] In spite of his career-altering illness, Wilby lived to eighty-nine, passing away in December 1957 after spending his final years happily puttering around the garden of his home in Windsor, Ontario.[55]

With Wilby's departure from Kahn's office, a greater burden of work fell upon Rowland, including responsibility for industrial buildings. Fortunately for Rowland, and due largely to his efforts, Kahn's office was a powerhouse of talented, up-and-coming designers, including Clair Ditchy, future suburban home designer and national president of the American Institute of Architects; Austin A. Howe, who would later design Detroit's Anthony Wayne, Jared Finney, and Von Steuben schools; Gerard Pitt, who became one of Miami's most prolific art deco architects; brothers John and Coulton Skinner, who designed many of southern Florida's most significant buildings; and Wayne Yates, architect in charge of the Fisher Building.[56]

Projects handled by Kahn's office during 1916 and 1917 were primarily commercial and industrial in nature, dominated by automobile service buildings in the east and Midwest. Nearly twenty factories were designed, mostly in Detroit, and roughly a dozen store buildings—primarily two-story retail and rental structures. Hospital buildings constituted a significant specialty, and during this period Kahn's office designed buildings for Harper, Henry Ford, and Grace Hospitals. The most significant office building was the twelve-story Vinton Building (located in Detroit's financial district on Woodward at Congress Street), one of Wilby's last projects for Kahn. He was assisted by Henry Janssen, the young man who, under Rowland's tutelage, won a scholarship to Harvard.[57]

The war in Europe was an increasing concern, particularly for those who appreciated how woefully unprepared the United States was to enter the fight. American factories were kept busy supplying Great Britain with ships, munitions, and other long-standing implements of warfare. War, however, tends to accelerate the advancement of technologies that provide an advantage on the battlefield, and during the early years of World War I, aviation rapidly advanced from novelty to a decisive factor for both offensive and defensive operations. Aircraft were first used for observation behind enemy lines, providing insight into the enemy's strength, fortifications, and intentions. When machine guns and bomb-carrying capacity were added to these aircraft, they acquired the offensive capability to cause damage and casualties, forcing the enemy to defend from attacks in three dimensions. To repel these attackers, pursuit aircraft were developed to chase and shoot down enemy planes. By 1917, Great Britain, France, Italy, and Germany had well-trained crews operating highly sophisticated aircraft.

Taking heed of the looming potential for armed conflict, the federal government established a number of advisory committees comprised of highly qualified leaders from various industries. The Council of National Defense, established in 1916, was headed by Howard E. Coffin, vice president of Detroit-based Hudson Motor Company and the chief force behind standardization of automotive parts. However, with no authority or budget, these committees could do little more than gather data on the productive capacity of American industry.

The country faced many challenges in gearing up to fight, but none more daunting than the need to build an air force nearly from scratch. The US Army's air service was essentially nonexistent, having only fifty-five training planes and thirty-five flying officers, mostly recent graduates, none of whom had ever flown a modern warplane.[58] The traditional forces of the army and navy, though small, needed only to be scaled up, a straightforward goal accomplished by the existing core of professional soldiers and sailors. The air service, however, lacked the core cadre of pilots, gunners, observers, and mechanics that were needed to train others. For more than a decade prior to 1917, leaders within the military—and interested outside groups as well—badgered Congress to appropriate funds for aeronautical research and military aviation, to no avail. Even after the *Lusitania* was sunk, Congress was unwilling to adequately fund military aviation, though the significance of aircraft in waging war had become obvious. As late as 1916, the US Army air corps had less construction under way than the Salvation Army.

Henry B. Joy, president of Detroit's Packard Motor Car Company, was an early advocate for aviation. Prior to 1910, he acquired a large tract of land near Mount Clemens, which he put to use as an airfield called Joy Field. After war began in Europe, Joy became alarmed at the lack of progress made by the United States in developing military air capability. From late in 1915 on, Joy offered to sell at cost or lease his flying field to the US government for the purpose of training pilots and testing aircraft.[59] In a letter to the editor in the *Detroit Free Press*, Joy pointed out that "America does not own a single flying field. Those used are rented and equipped scantily and ridiculously by reason of no appropriations by Congress."[60] Joy's description of the equipment was no exaggeration. Air force general Hugh Knerr described the condition of the army's top flying school upon his arrival there as a cadet: "a few wooden hangars alongside the dusty field and some small airplanes lined up in front of a crude operations office, where men in flying gear were lounging on benches in the shade."[61]

On August 6, 1917, the United States declared war against Germany, and the army finally began its effort to establish a credible air service—an effort led almost entirely by individuals hailing from Michigan. The commander of the Army Signal Corps, which included the Army Air Service, was General George Owen Squier.[62] Squier was born in Dryden, Michigan, in 1865, graduated from West Point in 1887, and later secured a doctorate from Johns Hopkins, where he studied mathematics, physics, and ballistics. By the time of America's entry into World War I, Squier had nearly sixty patents to his name, many of them related to radio telegraphy. An early advocate of military aviation, in 1908, Squier became the first military airplane passenger when he was taken for a flight by Orville Wright.[63]

Howard Coffin, now chairman of the Aircraft Production Board, recommended to Squier that Detroiter Clinton Goodloe Edgar (1873–1932) be appointed to head the Signal Corps construction division, responsible for building aviation training fields. Edgar was the managing partner of the W. H. Edgar and Son sugar company, president of Continental Sugar, and a director of the First National Bank of Detroit. In 1916, Edgar had attended the Plattsburg military training program and was made a captain in the Reserve Corps. With the declaration of war, Edgar reported for active duty and, almost immediately, was tapped by Squier to head the construction division, starting work the first week in May.[64]

Lacking any plans or examples of operating aviation training camps in the United States, Edgar traveled to Canada's Camp Borden to observe their pilot training operation, returning with a set of plans and specifications for the flying field. Squier's expectation was for Edgar to set up and manage an army architecture office to design and oversee construction of the new fields. Given the urgent need to get construction under way, Edgar told Squier there was no time to establish an architecture department and recommended instead an outside firm be hired. Although it was unusual to employ nonmilitary architects, Squier agreed. Edgar returned to Detroit and hired Albert Kahn, Architects and Engineers, to draw up the plans and specifications for the army's training fields.[65] Edgar was well acquainted with Kahn's firm, having employed it in 1915 to design both a store and his Grosse Pointe residence.[66] Also, as chairman of the loan committee of First National Bank, Edgar inspected and approved loan requests, including those for Packard, Hudson, and other automobile companies seeking to construct new plants, many of which were Kahn projects. Describing his arrival at Kahn's office, Edgar said: "I cleared out every bit of work he had in it, took his entire force, and we got out the plans for 54 buildings in about 10 days."[67]

The pace of activity was now quite rapid. Congress appropriated the inconceivable sum (for the time) of $500 million for aviation training field construction and outfitting. With cash available, the army quickly arranged in mid-May 1916 to acquire Joy Field, renaming it Selfridge Field[68] for military aviation pioneer First Lieutenant Thomas Selfridge, killed in the 1908 crash of a plane piloted by Orville Wright. Selfridge is considered the first person to die in the crash of a powered aircraft. By May 19, Kahn's firm had plans drawn and, before the month ended, contracts were let for construction of Selfridge Field, the first of the new aviation training fields.[69] By the beginning of June, construction was under way at Selfridge and, incredibly, the field opened by the middle of July, in spite of construction interruptions due to heavy rains.[70] In less than two months, 180 acres of land had been cleared; swamps drained; roads built; water, sewer, and electrical systems installed; and more than fifty buildings and hangars erected.[71]

Three other fields were also placed under construction: Champaign, Illinois (Chanute Field); Dayton, Ohio (Wilbur Wright Field); and Mineola, Long Island, New York (Hazelhurst Field). These four fields, along with more than twenty-five others that followed soon after, were constructed according to the standardized plans hammered out in Kahn's office during Edgar's ten-day marathon session. The plan for an entire training base of fifty-four buildings was contained on forty-seven sheets of drawings, accompanied by a specification booklet: *Specification No. 809, for a Group of Buildings for an Aviation Training Camp for the United States Signal Corps.* (The number 809 was Albert Kahn, Architects and Engineers, internal job number for Selfridge Field.) Each camp was planned to house 972 individuals, but in practice, the number sometimes exceeded 2,000, with many living in tents.[72] These camps were intended to be temporary, the chief design consideration being speedy completion so training could begin at the earliest possible moment. Buildings were constructed of white pine on concrete foundations with common hardware and structural sections built up from standard lumber, all of which could "be assembled and erected by the ordinary house carpenter."[73]

76. Hanger 9 at the former Brooks Air Force Base, San Antonio, Texas. Built in 1918, it is the only remaining Kahn-designed World War I temporary hanger and is the oldest former US Air Force hanger in the country. (Adam Smith)

The airplane hangars were the most numerous of the structures composing the standard flying field. They were large—66 feet wide by 120 feet long on the inside—with extensive window area to allow adequate illumination. To accommodate the maximum number of aircraft, the hangar had to be free of interior piers and other structural bracing. Yet they had to be quite strong: being large, hollow structures located in open areas, they were particularly susceptible to wind damage. To eliminate internal structural components typically used to brace walls, Kahn's designers placed angled structural supports on the *outside* of the building. The sidewalls supported ceiling trusses that spanned the sixty-six-foot distance between them. Planks that composed the trusses were spaced in such a manner as to fit together with those of the wall supports like finger joints. The structure was strong enough to permit aircraft to be suspended from the truss. Another innovative feature was the full-width hangar door. The telescoping wooden door panels hung from a guide that extended beyond the hangar's outer walls, allowing the full width of the hangar to be open. At least one of these "temporary" hangars still stands: Hangar 9 at the former Brooks Air Force Base, the oldest military hangar in the country.

As for the other structures, they were so well designed that only one notable alteration was made subsequent to completion. Barracks buildings provided four hundred cubic feet of space per person; in 1918, the Army Medical Department decreed that each inhabitant must instead have five hundred cubic feet. To meet this requirement, the front wall of already completed buildings had to be moved forward, eliminating the front porch and absorbing its area within the building's interior.[74]

In addition to the temporary airfields, Kahn's office was hired to design buildings on two permanent bases: Langley Field, near Hampton, Virginia, and Rockwell Field, on North Island, San Diego, California. Rockwell was already operating (in theory at least) as a Signal

Corps training field in early 1917, but facilities were primitive. At Langley, the newly established National Advisory Committee for Aeronautics (NACA) (which was replaced in 1958 by the National Aeronautics and Space Administration [NASA]) under the direction of General Squier sought in late 1916 to establish "the world's finest aviation research and development station."[75] Congress appropriated funds to acquire the property and construct a laboratory, plans for which were completed by the architectural firm of Donn and Demming.[76] Early in 1917, NACA engaged Albert Kahn's company to design the balance of the buildings. This commission probably came to Kahn through a recommendation from Howard Coffin, whose work on the civilian advisory committees intersected with NACA. Some of Langley's important structures—such as the wind tunnel—entailed unusual structural and electrical requirements, and, in the view of Coffin and NACA, the extensive manufacturing plant experience of Kahn's firm likely made them the best qualified to take on the project.[77]

77. A 1920 photo showing the Langley Field laboratory (administration building) with three of the civilian housing duplexes. (US Air Force)

When the United States declared war, construction of Langley and Rockwell Fields became high priority. Although completion of the base was to be rushed, "each building necessarily must have a certain amount of careful study."[78] The original contract with Kahn foresaw Langley becoming a significant pilot training field, "the West Point of aviation,"[79] and called for the design of roughly seventy-five buildings.[80] Construction began

78. The laboratory (administration building) now serves as the US Air Force Air Combat Command Headquarters. (US Air Force)

in July 1917 on the most urgently needed structures, but rapid progress was hampered by a shortage of labor. The Signal Corps, desperate to begin development work, moved much of the testing program to McCook Field in Dayton. As the war neared its end in 1918, many of the structures not yet begun were canceled. When construction ended, thirty-two buildings designed by Kahn's office were complete: laboratory, machine shop, wind tunnel, storehouse, truck shed, two hangars, and various housing fa-

79. Main entrance to Langley Field's laboratory (administration building) showing brick and stonework. (US Air Force photo by Senior Airman Kayla Newman)

cilities, all of which continue in use to this day, virtually unchanged. The two hangars are the oldest in the active American military inventory, and the thirty-two buildings constitute the "oldest and largest group of buildings historically associated with the Army air arm" and US Air Force.[81]

As originally envisioned, Langley was to be the country's center for aeronautical research; the appearance of the buildings needed to reflect this significant role. Given the large number of structures, it was an enormous design undertaking, yet was well suited to Rowland's skills. He avoided the often monotonous look of a military installation by introducing a great deal of variety in the appearance of the buildings, yet maintained an

understated theme respectful of the military and scientific purpose of the base. All of the buildings, including those for housing, were of reinforced concrete construction.

The most substantial of the buildings was the laboratory, a two-story brick structure with red tile hip roof, large windows, and expansive interior spaces. Many of its design attributes were similar to those of Rowland's grade schools. The most

80. End wall of one of two permanent hangars designed by Rowland at Langley Field. (Black and white, US Air Force; color, US Air Force photo by Senior Airman Kayla Newman)

81. This duplex on Eagan Avenue has a ceramic tile roof. Originally, the porch was screened; the windows and door were added later. (US Air Force photo by Senior Airman Kayla Newman)

exceptional feature of the laboratory is its ornate brickwork, beginning with the durable and attractive English bond used for the walls. Beneath the eaves, contrasting brick and light stone were used in a diaper pattern, and the spandrels were filled with patterns composed of smaller pieces of brick. Entrances are surrounded by dramatic brickwork, contrasting stone, and carved emblems cast in concrete. The laboratory, due to the shifting mission of Langley, was used from the beginning as an administration building, and serves today as the US Air Force Air Combat Command Headquarters.

Like the laboratory, the machine shop, storehouse, truck shed, and, particularly, the hangars featured fine brickwork with complementary accents and light stucco highlights. Most interesting, perhaps, are the cast emblems used on all the buildings—each one different and carrying a specific meaning related to the mission of the base. Contained within the emblem on the former storehouse (corner of Thornell and Douglas) is a gyroscope, the device that makes instrument flight possible. The machine shop (219 Dodd) emblem has metalworking tools and a bevel gear. Other emblems show propellers, wings, shields, and other insignia of the air service.

Adjacent to the laboratory are duplexes intended to house the base's civilian and military employees. Laid out eight to a block in a nearly symmetrical arrangement, they

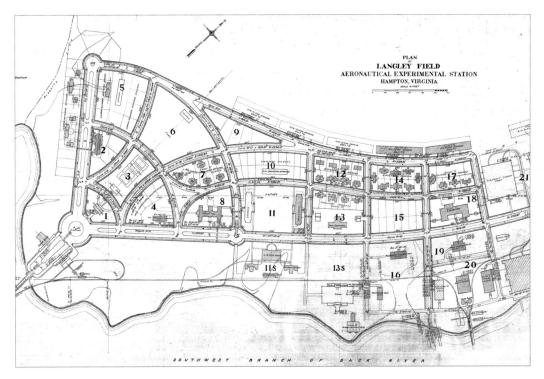

82. Site plan produced in August 1917 by Albert Kahn's office showing street layout and location of buildings: commissioned officers' quarters (2), bachelor noncommissioned officers' quarters (4), noncommissioned officers' houses (7), civilian homes (south side of 12, north side of 13, 14, and 17), laboratory/administration building (18), hangars (north of 14 and 17), truck shed (left side of 20), storehouse (right side of 20), wind tunnel (lower left of 16), and machine shop (out of view to the right of 18). (Albert Kahn Papers, Albert Kahn Associates, Inc. and the Bentley Historical Library, University of Michigan, Langley Field Aeronautical Experimental Station, Hampton, Virginia [1917–18], job nos. 796 and 76, Plan of Langley Field (4), August, 2, 1917, [30 1/4 x 68 1/2 inches], tube 57)

vary from each other in floor plan and exterior appearance, though all look much like English cottages. That some of these buildings still retain their original tile and slate roofs speaks to the care with which they were designed and built. (The original Rowland-designed buildings are on both sides of Eagan Avenue between Bowen and Thompson; the block bounded by Eagan, Sweeney, Plum, and Thompson; and on the north side of Eagan between Plum and Douglas.)

To the east, in the block bounded by Eagan, Glover, and Bryant Avenues, are the six original noncommissioned officers' houses. These are duplexes, symmetrically arranged, but smaller than the civilian homes, with less elaborately fashioned exteriors. On the northwest corner of Dodd and Wright is the bachelor noncommissioned officers' quarters (now known as Dodd Hall), a two-story stucco building with a hip roof. Finally, at the corner of Hammond and Wright avenues, is the commissioned officers' quarters. More formal in appearance, its large first-floor windows are surrounded by light stone frames that contrast with the brick veneer.

All of these buildings are sited within a street layout reminiscent of traditional rectangular blocks, but exact right angles at street intersections were avoided. Streets that parallel the coastline reflect its gentle curve and come together at the southwestern end of the base in a cleverly designed and nearly symmetrical radial. The gently curving streets and English cottage–style housing give the impression more of a quaint village than a military installation.

Rockwell Field, located on North Island in San Diego Bay, was intended as a West Coast version of Langley, offering pilot training and experimental facilities, but without the NACA presence. Planning for the joint army and navy aeronautical station on North Island began in mid-August 1917 with a meeting between the commanding officer of Rockwell Field, the senior navy commander, and Albert Kahn. They devised a plan for dividing the island between the army and navy and establishing more direct rail and roadway connections to the mainland. One week later, Kahn's office submitted to the army a plan for construction of Rockwell Field.[82] General Henry "Hap" Arnold described the plan as "ideal in that it grouped all buildings for noncommissioned officers and the hospital together where a splendid view of the bay was to be obtained and located the officers' quarters at the extreme end of the island facing the ocean."[83] Arnold described the plan's transportation infrastructure: "The system of roads contemplated a main avenue leading from the dock all the way to the south end of the island. A new dock was to be constructed which would provide better unloading facilities."[84]

The structures at Rockwell are of significant interest. In the words of archaeologist Andy Yatsko, the buildings "represent the work of a master, being unique examples of his use of the Mission/Spanish Colonial Revival style in an architectural genre outside his recognized area of mastery. In this, they possess high artistic values."[85] The style today referred to as "Spanish Colonial Revival" was at the time of Rockwell's construction known as "California Mission." California Mission, along with Santa Fe style and Pueblo Revival, were variants arising from the same source: the architecture, construction methods, and building materials employed by Native Americans of the Southwest and, later, their Spanish conquerors. The indigenous people of the Southwest lived in large communities of interconnected buildings—either cliff dwellings, built within sheltered areas beneath a rock overhang, or pueblos, usually sited in the open upon high ground. These dwellings were constructed primarily of mud and were often several stories high. The thick mud walls were well suited to the climate of the region, providing some respite from the sun and heat. Pueblo communities often encircled a central courtyard; the structure's windowless outer walls provided protection against attack. Spanish missionaries arrived in the sixteenth century and adapted native construction practices and material to their own needs, evolving over time to a more ornate style. The most notable Spanish buildings were the many missions constructed throughout the American Southwest and in California.

83. The Guard House, completed in 1918, at the entrance to the former Rockwell Field, is a fine example of California Mission (or Spanish Colonial Revival style); a simple, but elegant structure. (US Navy photo by Andy Yatsko)

In the late nineteenth century, architectural designers began to incorporate elements of these centuries-old structures into new buildings as an alternative to traditional European architectural styles. In California, designs were inspired by the look of California missions, and often featured exterior walls of stucco, arched openings, and gabled roofs covered in red clay tile. In New Mexico, Santa Fe style was patterned after more primitive Spanish structures, such as San Estevan del Rey Mission Church at Acoma Pueblo. Distinct features of the style include flat roofs, square openings (rather than arched), lack of curved shapes, and natural adobe colors. This style was heavily promoted, beginning around 1910, by the Santa Fe Railroad and Fred Harvey Company. Pueblo style (now called Pueblo Revival) was similar to Santa Fe, but more austere, and was the last of the three to emerge.[86]

These styles, though widely employed only in the American Southwest, were of particular importance to American architects for the reason that the architecture of the pueblos and cliff dwellings represented the sole truly *American* architectural modes. All other significant styles employed by American architectural designers originated in the Old World; even Richardson Romanesque Revival, developed by American architect Henry Hobson Richardson (1838–1886) was, as the name implies, a modern variation on European Romanesque architecture of the Middle Ages. Rowland, a passionate student of architecture history with a penchant for devouring journals covering the field, was well versed in California Mission style and likely admired the superb adaptation of the methods, materials, and structures to the resources and conditions of the region.

Rockwell Field presented Rowland with an opportunity to practice "Western school" architecture on its home turf. A total of twenty-two buildings were designed by

Kahn's office, and construction began on February 4, 1918.[87] When the armistice was signed on November 11, all building programs were suspended.[88] The structures completed were the hospital, medical research laboratory, three hangars, a guard house/meter room, and four commissioned officers' homes (two duplex buildings). All the Rockwell structures have modern steel reinforced concrete frames, with walls between frame members built up with hollow terra-cotta tile. The exterior finish is buff color stucco. The buildings, including the three hangars, have gabled roofs covered with red clay tiles. The hangars, guard house, and commissioned officers' homes remain in service.[89] The hospital and adjacent research laboratory were demolished at the time runway 29/11 was constructed.

84. Officers' homes at Naval Air Station North Island (formerly Rockwell Field) built in 1918. (Navy Public Affairs Support Element West)

4

COLUMNS OF STONE, COLUMNS OF WORDS

What we need is to understand more fully those fundamental principles of our art which
underlie the best work of all times and all styles: to understand and know thoroughly
the architectural forms of the past and appreciate how in them these principles were
expressed: to use these forms in our own work freely, varying from them not capriciously,
but according to principle, as changed conditions, changed modes of construction,
changed ideals seem to require.

—H. Langford Warren, "The Influence of France upon
American Architecture," November 1899

With the war's end, government work in Kahn's office was quickly wrapped up. Almost immediately, two enormous projects were begun: a headquarters for the General Motors Corporation and an office building with bank for First National Bank of Detroit. When completed in 1923, the General Motors headquarters was the second-largest building in the country, and the First National Bank Building, completed in 1922, was the tallest in the state of Michigan.

The announcement by General Motors of their commitment to proceed with the headquarters building was hailed in Detroit's financial press as "the pistol shot signaling the resumption of the race" by those "trying to see through the cloud of uncertainty enshrouding them after the sudden termination of the war."[1] Quite a pistol shot it was, too: the building covers an entire city block, has a floor area of thirty acres, and cost $20 million to build (ten times the cost of the Detroit News Building).

When planning for the building began in 1919, General Motors was headquartered in New York City, but key managers desired a move to Michigan where a majority of the firm's operations were based. Unable to locate a large parcel of land available at a reasonable price within downtown Detroit, the company acquired land three miles north of the city center on West Grand Boulevard in what became known as the New Center. Grand Boulevard in the block acquired by GM was, at that time, primarily residential, with the sole exception of the Hyatt Roller Bearing Building. Given the relatively low value of the land, GM was able to acquire it at a highly favorable price. Although the war had driven steel prices to record highs, the war's end resulted in plentiful labor (of the total cost of a structure, 70 percent was thought to be labor).[2] General Motors anticipated renewed business activity would reverse this situation, and so rushed to get construction of their building under way.

Even before building plans were complete, excavation of the entire block to a depth of sixteen feet was begun. Starting June 2, 1919, three steam shovels and thirty-five trucks worked twenty hours a day for nearly three months hauling away blue clay. Ramps dug into the excavation permitted trucks to drive down to the work area, but when fully loaded, they required the aid of a hoist to pull them up the grade from the giant hole. The apartment buildings on the property were to be razed, but, as Detroit was in the midst of a long-term housing shortage, many renters refused to leave before the end of their lease, forcing excavation to proceed haphazardly.[3]

The most extraordinary aspect of the excavation was the treatment accorded the Hyatt Roller Bearing Building. Hyatt, at this point a General Motors subsidiary, had only just occupied their three-story, steel reinforced concrete building in 1916. Being located on the southwest corner of West Grand and Cass Avenue, it was directly within the footprint of the big GM building. It turned out that moving the 95 by 60 foot, 3,600 ton structure made the most economic sense, so the building was relocated 418 feet to its new foundation between June 20 and August 4, 1919. In spite of the various curbs and streetcar tracks that had to be crossed, headway was made at an average rate of sixty feet per day. This all sounds fairly unspectacular until it's learned that Hyatt's employees continued their normal work activities within the building, even as it was moved![4]

For the General Motors Building, Rowland was responsible for establishing the overall layout of the structure and its exterior design. At the time, the most significant challenge facing designers of office buildings was providing tenants with adequate window exposure—the primary source of both light and ventilation. It was found that a work space should be no more than twenty-six feet from a window, or light and air were considered inadequate.[5] Consequently, window exposure constrained the maximum width of a building to about sixty feet: an eight-foot corridor, with offices no more than twenty-six feet deep on either side. The prevailing habit of designers was to begin at the street—the front of the lot—and design the structure from front to back (a habit carried over from the days of masonry "storefront" buildings). For offices overlooking the street, window exposure was more than adequate; for others, however, passageways admitting light and air had to be provided, usually in the form of narrow courtyards or "light courts." As a result, buildings were often

U shaped; the bottom of the U abutted the street with two wings extending to the rear and a narrow light court between them. The Ford Building, on the northwest corner of Congress and Griswold Streets in Detroit's financial district, is an example of the U-shaped layout. The Dime Building (now Chrysler House), on the northwest corner of Fort and Griswold Streets, is as well, but the light court faces the front instead of the rear

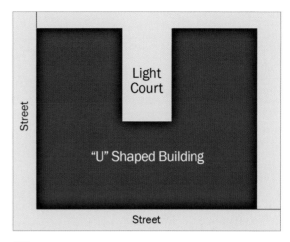

85.

of the building. Depending on the size and form of the lot, other shapes were common. Enclosing the light court entirely by closing the open end of the U resulted in an O-shaped building; one with light courts at both ends resulted in an H shape.

Offices located on a light court typically suffered less adequate light and air, making them less desirable than offices on the building's outside. As a consequence, space near the front of a light court was discounted 20 to 30 percent, while space deep within a light court—known as secondary space—was discounted 50 to 65 percent. (There was also "dark space," located on a wall abutting an adjacent building and generally usable only for elevator and service shafts.[6])

Rowland disliked light courts and viewed them as a design failure; a primary requirement of any building is to optimally meet the needs of the humans within, particularly as to adequate light and air. Rowland began his design effort by determining how to best satisfy the purpose for which the building was to be constructed—including the provision of

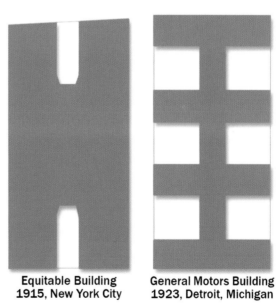

Equitable Building 1915, New York City   **General Motors Building 1923, Detroit, Michigan**

86. New York City's Equitable Building, completed in 1915 (*left*), was the world's largest building at the time the General Motors Building, the second largest, was completed (*right*). The Equitable Building incorporated two narrow light courts as a means of providing light and air to interior offices. The GM Building's offices were all on the outside.

87. The General Motors Building on Grand Boulevard in Detroit.

optimal working conditions for its inhabitants—and then allowing the building design to emerge as a consequence.

By prioritizing the requirement that all offices be outside, with full access to light and air, and dispensing with the convention that an office building be massed along the street, Rowland devised a strikingly effective arrangement for the General Motors Building. By moving the central section of the building—the section typically located "in front" on the street—to the center of the lot, with wings radiating out from this section in a symmetrical layout, all offices had outside exposure. There were other important advantages to this arrangement: elevators, stairwells, and conduits could be located in the windowless areas where the wings joined the central section. As a consequence, and due to the symmetrical form, the building had no unsightly back side and looked attractive from any direction. Having elevators, restrooms, and stairways centrally located also maximized tenant convenience. Yet this arrangement for the office floors did not detract from the quantity of rentable retail space on the ground floor as the office section sat upon a base that extended over the entire lot.[7]

From early in 1919, when the building was first announced to the public, it was reported that the unusual layout was devised so that: "Every office has an abundance of natural light and fresh air. Artificial light is hardly ever necessary, all offices being on the outside."[8]

This feature was also trumpeted by the company in ads aimed at prospective tenants. Non–General Motors tenants, in fact, occupied the second through the seventh floors of the fifteen-story building, providing rental income and additional space into which the company could expand as needed.[9]

The massive building was exceedingly well equipped. In addition to eight automobile showrooms and a 1,500 seat auditorium on the first floor, the basement held two swimming pools (men's and women's), a gymnasium, twelve bowling lanes, thirty-one billiard tables, and a barber shop. On the fourteenth floor were the executive offices, with private dining rooms, barber shop, and living suites for executives visiting from out of town. The fifteenth floor held two dining rooms capable of feeding the entire building's population of six thousand in less than an hour and a half.[10]

The structure is supported by a steel skeleton; steel reinforced concrete was used only for the floors. The steel beams and piers in the building were enclosed in terra-cotta tile, effectively fireproofing them. In order that large areas of the first floor remain unobstructed by piers, the weight of the upper stories is carried by enormous girders, the largest of which is nearly one hundred feet long and weighs over one hundred tons.[11]

The General Motors Building was the first significant office structure taken up by Albert Kahn's firm since before the war, and its appearance deviates considerably from earlier designs, particularly the Detroit News Building, which pushed modern design into new territory. With the News Building, "Escape was sought from the classic and Renaissance traditions which have too often been indifferently appropriate to modern needs"; cornices, classical columns, and other stock features of neoclassical designs were abandoned. The GM Building's exterior, however, was uncharacteristically retrograde, incorporating classical columns, entablatures, and an ornate cornice. The building received attention in the architectural journals for its size, layout, and construction, but little was said regarding its style.[12] Architectural historian George Edgell, who lavished praise on the News Building, wrote of the General Motors Building: "Though the detail of the entrance and lower colonnade is architectural and fine, the overpowering effect of the building is produced by the simplest and most logical arrangement of enormous masses." He then proceeded to discuss New York's Cunard Building: "A building of a more elaborate architectural treatment [than the GM Building]."[13] Had this shift to classical style been limited to the GM Building, it might be attributable to customer preference, but similar features characterized other significant buildings of the period produced by Kahn's office.

What role did Rowland play, if any, in this reversion to classical forms? In an extensive article for the June 1921 issue of the *Architectural Forum*, Rowland discusses the use

88. Rear view of the General Motors Building and attached laboratories building, fronting on Milwaukee Avenue.

of historical styles for modern buildings. "History furnishes us a rich store of precedent . . . among the examples of the Lombard Romanesque" and "from the Gothic—of the relation of tall openings to buttress piers. In these two styles there is much material for study, not to say inspiration."[14] "Classic form," Rowland wrote, "is too impersonal and too universal." Designers with deep knowledge of classic forms had employed them on modern buildings with only limited success, because, as Rowland caustically pointed out, "their interest was not in the actual solution of commercial problems, however masterly their knowledge and use of classic forms."[15] Using classic forms to solve "problems which are distinctly modern is modified not only by practical and economic restrictions, but also by its own very principles. It is not the clever adaptation of its parts to a modern frame work, but an actual dismember- ment and a building up again according to those principles, which will create and endure."[16] In this last statement, Rowland reveals the core of his outlook: successful building designs won't come from ingeniously grafting historic features onto modern structures; instead, we must return to the fundamental design *principles* employed by the Greeks, from which we can create a modern architecture consistent with our own era's technology, materials, and requirements. Simply put, copying Greek features is a fundamentally flawed approach to design; instead, the principles of design employed by the Greeks must be adopted.

Considering Rowland's clearly stated views on the use of classic forms, and within the context of his earlier building designs and those he designed after leaving Kahn's office, the most probable explanation for this change to classical forms is that it was imposed by Albert Kahn. There is direct evidence to support this view: renowned Detroit sculptor Corrado Parducci in a 1975 interview stated Rowland quit his position with Kahn "in order to free himself from the restrictions that Kahn imposed on his designers."[17] Although the reason for Kahn imposing certain requirements on his designers at that time is unclear, his motivation may have been a lack of confidence in the permanence of modern design. In 1929, Kahn wrote: "The First National Bank Building is of a conservative type. Though less radical than some of our modern structures, it serves its purpose as well and will stand as an exemplar of well tried work. . . . When much of the present day modernism has passed its vogue, this building will continue to carry on the better traditions of the architecture of the past."[18]

Nevertheless, if classic it must be, Rowland was certainly the right person to execute the design. The ornamental details of the General Motors Building are generally restrained, the most prominent being the cornice with its cast metal antefixes and terra-cotta modillions. Beneath the cornice are columns topped with ornate Corinthian capitals, but the columns themselves are smooth (rather than fluted), making them less noticeable and less obviously classical.[19]

The front entrance of the building is surrounded by a portico, of nominally classical design, and exceptionally well scaled—large enough to complement the enormous building, but not out of scale with humans. Inside and out, the portico is clad in gray stone, set off by brass doors; highly polished, rose-colored marble columns; and light fixtures of

89. Front portico of the main entrance to the General Motors Building.

green metal. The ceiling of the portico is groin vaulted and coffered. Taken as a whole, the portico is quietly restrained, impressing with subtlety rather than opulence.

In spite of any duress Rowland may have been under to use a classical motif, this entrance exemplifies good architecture. It serves its utilitarian functions admirably well: protecting pedestrians from the elements as they prepare to enter the building or wait to leave; and by its appearance—including the flag, sculptured figures, and clock above it—the portico clearly identifies the building's entrance for first-time visitors. The uncomplicated beauty of the portico may be appreciated by those with little knowledge of architecture—it was designed by an architect, not for the approval of fellow professionals, but for the masses. Unsurprisingly, the plans for the portico and its details were drawn by Rowland.

Meanwhile, three miles south at the corner of Woodward Avenue and Cadillac Square, the Hotel Pontchartrain was struggling to remain open. The decision of the hotel manager to enlarge the guest rooms, made late in the planning of the building—requiring Rowland and George Mason to spend New Year's Day 1906 reworking the plans—was ill-conceived. Enlarging the rooms reduced the number of rooms available to rent, diminishing the hotel's potential revenue.[20] In January 1919, it became clear that Prohibition would soon become law and Pontchartrain's liquor sales revenue would be lost. The end came in March 1919 when the hotel was sold to the First National Bank of Detroit for a new headquarters and office building.[21]

The original conception of the bank was to strip the hotel building to its frame and build it out again as a modern office building with public banking facilities on the second floor. This approach would have eliminated the cost of excavation and significantly reduced the amount of high-priced structural steel required.[22] Subsequently, however, it was decided that increasing the height from fifteen to twenty-four stories would be advantageous, and more rentable space could be had at little cost by adding a small wing to the rear of the building. Then, instead of terra-cotta cladding it was decided to use limestone, a heavier material, and to eliminate some of the supporting piers obstructing the banking lobby. Taken together, these changes meant that the Pontchartrain's skeleton and its foundation could not be reused. An entirely new structure would need to be built within the existing excavation on a foundation capable of supporting the greater weight of the new building. At this point, the remark made in 1906 by Wallace Franklin concerning the Pontchartrain's foundation—"If any one ever wants to go any further down, the contractors will have a beautiful job getting through that three feet of rock and steel"—highlighted a daunting challenge to be overcome. It was decided the new building should be supported by concrete piers, five to nine feet in diameter, extending eighty-five feet below street level, with three bell-shaped footers at various depths. Excavating caissons (within which the piers would be constructed) required cutting holes in the existing three-foot-deep reinforced concrete foundation and then removing or cutting off the forest of piles that had been sunk beneath, all of which was accomplished with great difficulty.[23] Once completed, some of the original sub-basement walls of the Hotel Pontchartrain were retained and incorporated within the basement of the new building.

Overseeing construction of the new building was the same team of individuals who, two years earlier, constructed Rockwell Field in San Diego. After leaving the army, Colonel Clinton Edgar returned to his business pursuits in Detroit, including serving as a director of the First National Bank of Detroit. Due in part to his construction experience in the army, Edgar was appointed chairman of the bank's building committee. Edgar in turn hired thirty-three-year-old Captain William H. Carruthers as secretary of the committee, with responsibility for auditing construction transactions and mediating between the committee, architect, and general contractor. Carruthers had worked under Edgar in a similar position overseeing construction at Rockwell Field until his discharge in June 1919.[24] Naturally,

90. Within the basement of the First National Bank Building is the earlier basement of the Hotel Pontchartrain. The smooth, painted section of wall here is from the Pontchartrain; above it, the rougher concrete poured for the bank building's basement.

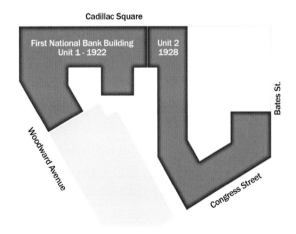

91. The First National Bank Building was constructed as two units. The Rowland-designed unit 1 wraps around the corner of Woodward and Cadillac Square. The unit 2 addition attached to the end of the original building and continued on a snake-like path to Congress Street. With the exception of the minor wing projecting south from the building, unit 1 occupies the same footprint as the original Hotel Pontchartrain.

Edgar secured Kahn's services as architect for the building.

Rowland was responsible for the preliminary and exterior design work on the bank building.[25] Having also designed the Hotel Pontchartrain for the same lot, Rowland was likely the first ever architect to design and build two reinforced concrete skyscrapers on the same location. The First National Bank Building fit the same footprint as the Pontchartrain, with the exception of a minor wing protruding from the rear of the building. Although the bank promoted its rental offices as having "an abundance of natural daylight and healthy fresh air," a light court of sorts resulted from the addition of this wing, invalidating any claim that every office was outside.

Located on the second floor was the building's most dramatic feature: a bank lobby,

92. The First National Bank Building receives finishing touches on its cornice (since removed) in 1921. (Detroit Publishing Company Photograph Collection, Library of Congress Prints and Photographs Division)

one of the five largest in the country, thirty-six feet high with sixty-nine teller windows. The room was illuminated by windows, three stories in height. Like the General Motors Building, the bank building is decorated with classical details, fluted Corinthian columns flanking the bank lobby windows being the most noticeable. A description of these details, almost certainly paraphrased from Rowland, appeared in the *Detroit Free Press*: "The decoration is an application of classic architecture to modern conditions." Exactly reflecting Viollet-le-Duc's view of architecture history, the article continued: "The building is treated rather more in a Greek spirit of refinement, which recalls that the best Roman work was executed by Greek workmen." As to the columns, "it may be noted by those who have trekked down the Mediterranean," as Rowland had in 1908, "the Corinthian pillars are patterned as nearly as possible after the columns of the Temple of Castor and Polux in the Roman forum."[26] Along the building's top was a cornice (since removed), similar in style to that of the GM Building. Although Rowland may not have had complete freedom in his design of the building's exterior, it is an impressive and dignified structure, well adapted to its location and purpose.

The interior of the building made extensive use of marble, particularly in the public lobbies and banking areas. Offices throughout the building were trimmed in walnut, much of which was harvested during the war by the Boy Scouts for use as rifle stocks and that remained unused after the armistice.[27]

From 1911 until 1919, Rowland appears not to have had much involvement in the organized leisure activities that characterized his earlier life. This was likely due to some combination of a smothering workload and his passionate pursuit of architectural knowledge. Quite suddenly, however, in the fall of 1919 Rowland became involved in numerous outside ventures. It was at this time his designs for the General Motors and First National Bank Buildings were formulated. If, as Parducci claimed, Rowland's design freedom was restricted and he was precluded from developing new styles, his work may have become tedious and unsatisfying and, perhaps, Rowland's new spare time activities provided an alternate outlet for his frustrated creativity.

Rowland surfaced first in August 1919 as chairman of the Committee on Publication of the monthly journal *Michigan Architect and Engineer*, recently established as the official publication of the Michigan Society of Architects and Michigan chapter of the American Institute of Architects. Then in the early fall, a new architecture club appeared (the Detroit Architectural Club having disbanded some time previously), founded by Rowland, Amedeo Leone, William Kapp, Lancelot Sukert, and Joseph French. Amedeo Leone was employed by Smith, Hinchman, and Grylls; William Kapp was at Wills-Lee Automobile Company; and Lancelot Sukert and Joseph French were with Albert Kahn, Architects and Engineers. Meetings were held at the chamber of commerce, and in November, with ninety members in attendance, Rowland was elected president.[28] The "Thumb Tack Club," as the organization was called, was modeled after the Boston Architectural Club and T-Square Club of Philadelphia; its primary mission was to provide an opportunity for architects and draftsmen with an interest in design to develop their skills under the tutelage of the city's more experienced designers. The club also strove to advance the public's appreciation of architecture through lectures and an annual exhibition.[29] In a bit of pique, the club announced it would "campaign against all intrusions of the city and parks with hideous examples of building and monuments."[30]

The club rented an old house at 83 Fort Street,[31] using the second floor for club rooms and the attic for classrooms. A contest was held to select an emblem for the club. The winning entry was chosen by Maxwell Grylls of Smith, Hinchman, and Grylls and was submitted by Wayne Yates, a designer in Albert Kahn's office.[32] (Of the six finalist entries selected, four of them were by Yates, who would later play a key role in the design of the Fisher Building as "architect in charge.")

On January 13, 1920, the club dedicated its club rooms with an Egyptian-themed gala that included two dramatic presentations by members. The cast was as follows:

"A Night on the Nile"—Time: Right Now

Ah-Koostik, Trumpeter, Aloys F. Herman

Doh-Rik, Arc-o-light of the Short-Order, John Strain

Ioh-Nik, Arc-o-light of the Dis-Order, William Bunce

Uppah-Sahsh & *Loah-Sahsh*, Double Hung Guards of the Sacred Astral Urn, L. C. Bauman and Paul Garlick

Khan-Sole, Standard Bearer, Harry Meyer

Pah-Rha-Pett, High Priest of Osiris, Wirt C. Rowland

Tyhm-Kahd & *Tyme-Klok*, Guards of the Prisoner, Gus Muth and Frank Barcus

Hate-th Hour, Prisoner to be sacrificed, Harry Hoffman

Mob of Egyptian Rabble, Draughtsmen [draftsmen]

Scenario, Dialogue and Lyrics by Yates and Sukert

Music (selected by Rowland), Verdi & Mozart (Used by special permission of the composers)

Costumes designed and executed by Chas. Crombey; sandals and corset worn by Rowland executed by Thompson Starret Construction

"Jipping the Egyptians"—In five reals and one imitation; Time: Morning, Second Dynasty

Pinky Peer A'mid, The Office Rapscallion, Ed Shepherd

Menuch and *Eunuch*, Office Slaves, F. C. O'Dell and J. Ivan Dise

Khan Q Byne, A low relief (very low) Mistress of the Mayor's Chamber recently escaped, Wallace Frost

Ahl Birt Karnak, A Nile-ist, E. E. Eicherbaum

Bull-Fee-Sees, Mayor of Phlyverus-on-the-Nile, Aloys F. Herman

Doughnuts by French and Cider by God!![33]

93. "A Night on the Nile" presented by the Thumb Tack Club, January 13, 1920. *Left to right*: George Lannoth, William Bunce, Harry Meyer, L. C. Bauman, Wirt C. Rowland (*center, standing*), Paul Garlick, John Strain, Gus Muth, Harry Hoffman, and Frank Barcus. (*Weekly Bulletin of the Michigan Society of Architects*)

The gala was a huge success, so another, even more ambitious event was planned for the following month: a costume dance party, promoted as "A dashing, daring display of dangerous deeds, delightful designs, dexterous dancing, dapper draughtsmen and delectable damsels." Coulton Skinner, a young designer in Kahn's office, was selected to act as "Ringmaster" of the "Circus Day Party."[34] This event too was a stunning success; partiers carried on until 3:00 a.m. and a photo appeared in the *Free Press* rotogravure section.

The educational efforts of the Thumb Tack Club, however, met with challenges. A May 1920 article stated, "it is a fact that both the 'Atelier' (as the design class is called) and the 'Life Class' have not been and are not at present an outstanding success, in so far as popularity and attendance go."[35]

The Thumb Tack Club served as an informal social venue during the workday, with a small group gathering regularly for lunch. The *Michigan Architect and Engineer* reported that during lunch, "Wirt C. Rowland presides over a Russian 'Olga Samovar' from which tea, coffee or bouillon is created."[36]

The club's success enabled a move in January 1921 to larger quarters at the rear of 150 East Larned, which was equipped with a fireplace and kitchen. One member provided

94. "Circus Day" costume party held at the Thumb Tack Club, February 17, 1920. Rowland is wearing a matador costume with tie tucked in his shirt, standing about one-quarter of the way in from the right side. This photo appeared in the *Detroit Free Press* Sunday, March 14, 1920. (Private collection)

directions for accessing the club rooms: "I ascended some steps and through a stair hall to a door which opens on an inner court, up another short flight and thence across an old bridge and through another pair of doors." To initiate the new club, a dinner party was held, followed by a "smoker." A report on the event noted, "The smoker started before the dinner and extended through all of the evening's activities, also the club rooms and the hall." Apparently, the club's new amenities had not been fully tested, as the report further stated, "It will long be remembered as the thickest smoker held by the Thumb Tack Club, and never again can it be equaled, for the temporary ailments of the fireplace will be remedied."[37]

The club's most successful enterprise was the annual architectural exhibition, first held October 17 through 31, 1921, at the Detroit Institute of Arts. Photographs and sketches were displayed of buildings and monuments, both recently constructed and planned. The works of many of the country's leading architects were represented at the show. Speakers included eminent New York architect Cass Gilbert, designer of the Detroit Public Library and, at the time, engaged on the Scott Fountain at Bell Isle, and Boston architect

R. Clipston Sturgis, president of the American Institute of Architects. To help raise money, the club published a hardbound yearbook with photographs of many of the exhibits. Once expenses were paid, the club netted a $1,700 profit on the exhibition[38] (a Ford Model T Runabout sold for $325 at the time). Shortly after, Rowland was again elected president of the club, taking over from Lancelot Sukert, who had served during the club's second year.

In October 1919, while organizing the Thumb Tack Club, Rowland spent three weeks in Cambridge, Massachusetts. The purpose of his trip was to visit Harvard music professor Archibald T. Davison (1883–1961) and attend "many of the classes in theory of music . . . in preparation for his contemplated work in community music for the Chamber Music Society of Detroit."[39] Thus began another experience that would dramatically affect Rowland's future building designs. Detroit's Chamber Music Society was founded in 1907 by Clara E. Dyar and Lillian E. Baldwin.[40] Dyar was active in many benevolent and arts organizations, and Baldwin, along with her husband, architect Frank Baldwin, was heavily involved in the city's Arts and Crafts movement. By 1919, the Chamber Music Society was arranging well-attended public performances and lectures, often at the Detroit Institute of Arts. During January and February 1919, the society presented a series of three lectures by "the leading musical educator in this country,"[41] Thomas Whitney Surette (1861–1941) of Boston. Surette was a professor of music at Harvard University, a "composer of note," and, in collaboration with Professor Davison, author of many songbooks and books on music theory.[42]

Surette's view of music was much the same as Wilby's view of architecture: the two fields merely represented different means of expressing the same universal artistic skills. Surette described an artist as one who has a "greater power of seeing the significance of things." A painting "is not so much a simulation of the thing seen, as a record of [the artist's] reaction to it. The thing in which he is interested is the work of art itself and obviously this should be the purpose of the observer as well." The object of the writer is "to present the world he deals with in terms of his own imagination. The more closely he presents actual things, by themselves, the less likely he is to arrive at the truth." Music functions in the same manner, differing only in that it is not representative, but is a "pure and unadulterated record of [the artist's] reaction."[43]

Surette recognized, of course, that music is appreciated most simply in an emotional response, "but that appreciation may be greatly enhanced by a vivid response on our part to *all* its elements, i.e., the meter, rhythm, play of the counterpoints, and arrangement of the themes into a coherent form."[44] As most people lacked the time and motivation to acquire a musical education, Surette devised an effective alternative: public singing. Surette found that musical themes and counterpoint could be comprehended when small groups of individuals sang easily learned sections of musical pieces. Even sophisticated musical works became readily accessible through this method, even for those with no musical education.

The first musician in Detroit to promote the broad potential of Surette's approach was Rowland's friend Ada May, who taught piano at the Ganapol School of Music.[45] The school and its instructors were active in Detroit's rapidly growing music community and, beginning in 1912, gave many faculty concerts to encourage music appreciation. May realized Surette's method would be more effective at bringing appreciation of classical music to a much larger audience. In 1917, at a meeting of the Musical Art Club, held at the Ganapol School, May gave a presentation on "Points in the Teaching of Mr. Thomas Whitney Surette."[46] Her proselytizing paid off, resulting in the Chamber Music Society sponsoring Surette's three lectures in early 1919.

May was also successful in arousing Rowland's interest in Surette's approach. Rowland was a trained musician, but Surette presented a view of music that was wholly new to Rowland, and one directly applicable to his design work. Surette explained that music first developed from folk songs that, in their simplest form, contain some thematic "element that binds the whole tune together."[47] Using Shelley's "Ode to the West Wind" as an example, Surette notes how "the words 'Hear, oh! Hear' bind the whole together. The principle is found in design everywhere."[48] As music evolved beyond the simple folk song, a second voice was added, resulting in "polyphony." The second voice was termed "counterpoint" and, as Surette explained, "counterpoints were derived from the original melody. This principle is one recognized in all art, namely, that the detail should grow out of the structure. It applies especially to architecture, but also to painting, literature, and sculpture."[49] Bach's Fugue no. 5 in D Major from the second volume of the *Well-Tempered Clavier* "is a composition in four 'voices,' each one entering in turn, while the other (or others) continues with phrases drawn from the theme itself." "This is an interesting example of that kind of economy in the use of material which is characteristic of great art. Practically the whole piece is made from the first phrase which contains but eleven notes."[50]

Music is an art form that exists in time rather than space. It is characterized by "development," "a process through which the small rhythmic units, characteristic groups of notes, take to themselves for the time being an independent existence; they may be lengthened or shortened in time (i.e., played faster or slower); they may be turned upside down or they may form a little tune of their own; they may be given entirely different chords than were formerly used; they may be intensified by the tone color of another instrument. In this process is comprised the very essence of the art of music."[51] These principles of music could not, obviously, be directly adapted to architectural design, but in a larger sense as *principles* of art, Rowland believed they could.

Rowland was so enthusiastic about Surette's methods and views that he wished to assist Surette and Ada May conduct the next round of lectures and community singing classes. The three Surette lectures in early 1919 had been so successful, the Chamber Music Society, now with support from the Detroit Institute of Arts, scheduled classes over twenty-three weekends between October 1919 and May 1920. Two classes were held on Saturday—a morning class for children and afternoon class for schoolteachers—and one on Sunday open to all. Surette traveled to Detroit to conduct classes one weekend each month. Classes on other weekends were taught by May and Rowland.[52]

To this busy schedule, Rowland added yet another creative task: authoring articles for *All the Arts*, the monthly magazine of the Detroit Orchestral Association. Through Rowland's work with the Chamber Music Society he made the acquaintance of Newton J. Corey, manager of the Detroit Orchestral Association and editor and publisher of *All the Arts*. Rowland's first article, promoting the Thumb Tack Club, appeared in January 1920.[53] The following month, Rowland's "The Making of an Architect" was published. More philosophical than the first, it touched on views of architecture history traceable to Langford Warren and Viollet-le-Duc.

Rowland's next effort appeared in the March issue, an astonishing article titled "An Architect's Attitude towards Music." In a mere one thousand words, he quite capably recapitulated Surette's views and explained the close relationship between music and architecture through "elements common to all great art." Rowland urged his fellow architects to consider music, like architecture, "may have ordered beauties, regulated by principles both as fixed and as fluid as those of any art." The laws of structure in architecture may seem different from the structural principles of music, "nevertheless the two fundamentals of unity and contrast obtain in music as they do in any true phase of art."[54] Many architects are well versed in allied crafts such as sculpture and painting, but outside the realm of the eye, they "sit perplexed when asked to consider seriously a symphony of Brahms, a string quartet by Beethoven, or a Bach Fugue, little knowing that he is being led blindfolded along the Acropolis, or through the aisles of Rheims." Rowland refers here to musical selections characterized in particular by theme development through counterpoint or fugue (for example, Brahms, Symphony no. 4, op. 98; Beethoven, Great Fugue string quartet, op. 133; and Bach, Fugue in E Flat Major, BWV 552). Rowland satirized a popular canard of the time, that "architecture is frozen music," commenting, "The present day may admit of the thawing of many things frozen, and the efficacy of zero weather for others." He derided as

95. The United Savings Bank Building on Griswold as it appeared in a photo from the *Architectural Forum*, June 1923.

well the interpretation "fate knocks at the door" as applied to Beethoven's Fifth Symphony: "Fate shall knock at the door of such nonsense, for the time will come when those opening measures of that wonderful symphony will be recognized as the cornerstone of that which is built up in terms of tone and rhythm into as sure and substantial a structure of music as any temple or cathedral has been built of stone."[55]

Late in 1920, Rowland designed the United Savings Bank of Detroit, a six-story bank and office building located at 1133 Griswold (between Michigan Avenue and State Street). Construction began in May 1921 and was completed in November. The building featured both classical details and restrained modern styling. Working under Rowland's supervision, plans for the structure were drawn by up-and-coming designers Joseph French (1888–1975), Robert Hubel (1891–1944), and Wayne Yates (1886–1928)—three individuals whose efforts were key to launching the Thumb Tack Club.

Both Hubel and Yates were designers whose entries had won or been mentioned in a number of Thumb Tack Club and other contests. Nevertheless, though the younger men possessed talent, they lacked experience and required Rowland's guidance, a point illustrated by a competition to design a small city bank, sponsored by the Michigan chapter of the American Institute of Architects. The contest was judged by George D. Mason, William B. Stratton, Louis H. Boynton (professor of architecture at the University of Michigan from 1910, and prior to that, a practicing architect who had worked for McKim, Mead, and White, and Cass Gilbert), and Edmund D. Fisher, vice president of the Bank of Detroit. Robert Hubel was awarded second prize, but the judges' comments on his entry reveal much about the limits of his practical experience: "an admirable floor plan and an artistic interior. Too much space, however, is devoted to offices and too little for clerical purposes. While nine cages are provided, they are a trifle too small, and also encroach upon the work space. The clerical department has only one window on each side, and probably would require an abnormal amount of artificial light. Mezzanine is lighted only from the front of the bank."[56]

The United Savings Bank Building was unusual in that it was not festooned with large classical columns, as were most banks of the era.[57] The bank lobby was located at street level, behind arched windows, and the entrance was within the center arch. To the right was a second entrance providing access to elevators servicing floors above the bank. This entry was marked by a plain rectangular surround protruding slightly from the building's surface. Above it, a round window within a square frame balanced out the large arched openings to the left. The lower section of the building (first and second floors) was characterized by clean lines, plain surfaces, and large arches. The only decorative features were two bas-relief carvings flanking the bank doorway, a smaller carving over the second entry, a modest amount of cast iron decoration surrounding both doors, and dentil molding beneath the second-floor windows. As with the Detroit News Building, the frame of the structure was expressed vertically by prominent, undecorated piers. The attractiveness of the lower section resulted in large part from the contrast of the simple arches with the rectangular elements surrounding them. Features were brought to attention by the careful control of shadow and light. The arches were deep and framed by a circular lip or torus that protruded from the building surface, functioning much like a torus on the base of a classical column—casting a shadow and reflecting a highlight. A similar effect was achieved by the dentil molding—both trapping and reflecting light in order to create a visually interesting, horizontal division between the bank lobby and office section of the building. This design approach was exemplary of Rowland's employment of the *principles* of Greek architecture, rather than merely attaching copies of Greek architectural elements.

At the top of the building, however, classical features were applied without regard to the successful modern design five stories below. Considering the prominence given the piers, it seems reasonable they would have extended to, or above, a parapet, as with the News Building, and many earlier commercial structures from Kahn's office. Instead, a large cornice terminates the otherwise unbroken piers. Above the cornice is a large band of ornate metal cresting, and below it, a heavy belt of carved ornamentation, too finely detailed to be seen distinctly from the street. The building is located on an angled lot and the acute angle of the corner would have been unnoticeable but for the cornice, which projects out absurdly like the prow of a ship, calling attention to the odd shape of the building.

The contrast in appearance between the building's neoclassical upper and modern lower sections suggests Rowland was allowed more design freedom in some areas than in others. The First National Bank and General Motors Buildings had similar cornices—perhaps Kahn was uneasy with omitting the cornice from a formal building, particularly one where classical columns—the standard decorative prop for banks—had been rejected.

Kahn's office handled fewer projects in 1921 than the previous year, likely due to the Depression of 1920–21. Rowland took advantage of this lull in business to travel in Europe, arriving there in July 1921 and touring France, Italy, Switzerland, and Germany. This was his second trip to France, a country he would visit on each of his four journeys to Europe between 1908 and 1930.

5

NEW WORK, NEW FREEDOMS

The painter's expression is his painting, the figure, that of the sculptor, and performed symphony, that of the composer. In like manner, the most effective thing the architect may have to say is in his completed building.

—Wirt Rowland, "Human—All Too Human," April 1939

1922 was a pivotal year in Wirt Rowland's career. His designs for numerous significant buildings, including the massive General Motors headquarters, placed him among the most experienced and accomplished architects in the world. Yet as other gifted architects were developing new and less traditional building designs, the restrictions imposed in Kahn's office hampered Rowland from doing so.[1] At age forty-two, he was impatient to leave behind classical motifs and focus his efforts on modern buildings of his own design.

Detroit's oldest architectural firm, and one of its largest, Smith, Hinchman, and Grylls, Architects and Engineers,[2] was, along with Albert Kahn, Architects and Engineers, one of the few firms in the city to offer both architectural and engineering services.[3] By 1920 Smith, Hinchman, and Grylls counted among its clients Detroit Edison, Detroit Public Lighting Commission, Michigan State Telephone Company (predecessor to Michigan Bell), and Detroit Board of Water Commissioners. Much of Smith, Hinchman, and Grylls's business was industrial in nature—manufacturing plants in auto or auto-related fields.[4] Retail store buildings were a sub-specialty; the firm designed the structures housing the city's three major department stores: J. L. Hudson, Crowley-Milner, and Ernst Kern.[5]

In 1921, Smith, Hinchman, and Grylls was approached by Arthur H. Buhl (1878–1935), of the Buhl Land Company, concerning construction of a large office building on the southwest corner of Griswold and Congress Streets in Detroit's financial district. The structure Buhl had in mind would be taller than any previously designed by Smith, Hinchman, and Grylls, taller, even, than any building in the state of Michigan. This skyscraper would replace the Buhl Land Company's existing building, known as the "Buhl Block," composed of three buildings constructed between 1869 and 1884 and home to many of the city's attorneys. Inefficiently heated by drafty stoves, and having no running water on four of the oldest building's five floors, the structure was obsolete.[6]

Looking ahead toward replacing the aging Buhl Block, the Buhl Land Company had, prior to World War I, commissioned a study of financial districts worldwide. Their concern was that Detroit's financial district might migrate as the city grew. It was found, though, that established financial districts were stable and unlikely to change location over time.[7] Further progress on a new building was delayed, however, by America's mobilization for and entry into the war, during which structural steel prices and other building costs soared—steel tripled in price between 1914 and 1917.[8]

By the end of 1921, prices finally declined to near prewar levels, and in May 1922 Arthur Buhl informed Smith, Hinchman, and Grylls the Buhl Land Company was ready to proceed with the project.[9] But, was Smith, Hinchman, and Grylls ready? The firm had designed large, steel reinforced concrete structures that were single-purpose, owner-occupied industrial and retail buildings. Unlike these structures, which house a single business, an office building *is* the business, and one that competes directly with its neighbors on rental rates, attractiveness, amenities, appointments, flexibility of office layout, view, location, and other factors. To assure profitability, the Buhl Building had to be designed in accordance with criteria different from those of Smith, Hinchman, and Grylls's previous projects.

In addition to the requirement of providing tenants with adequate window exposure—the primary source of both light and ventilation—office building designers faced vertical challenges as well: taller buildings required more elevators, but additional space for elevator shafts typically came at the expense of rentable floor space. Moreover, elevators had to be centrally located, or placed in more than one location, to preclude lengthy walks from office to elevator. Finally, there was the exterior appearance of a building, which reflected on the firms located within. Albert Kahn once said, "people prefer to do business with concerns housed in handsome structures just as they prefer to do business with well-dressed individuals."[10] Over time, a building will face increasing competition from newer

96. A photograph of Rowland taken while he was with Smith, Hinchman, and Grylls. (Unknown source)

and perhaps taller competitors. A structure with an attractive exterior that ages well, and is viewed by the community as an asset to the city skyline, will more likely attract and retain tenants, and continue to command high rental rates.

The principals of Smith, Hinchman, and Grylls appreciated that the Buhl project—and future opportunities—required a superb building designer, experienced with large office structures, and familiar with the architectural tastes of Detroit. Smith, Hinchman, and Grylls had previously hired outstanding professionals as a means to fuel their growth; designer Amedeo Leone was lured from Albert Kahn's office in 1914,[11] and in 1918, the firm brought on William Sidney Wolfe (1889–1944), an exceptionally gifted architectural engineer. The ideal candidate to shore up Smith, Hinchman, and Grylls's weakness in office building design was Wirt Rowland, and the firm wasted no time, approaching him shortly after Arthur Buhl indicated his desire to proceed with the new building.

Already the highest-paid designer in the city,[12] Rowland was offered even more money,[13] and the opportunity to design the city's tallest and most important new building. The greatest inducement would have been Smith, Hinchman, and Grylls's willingness to cede to Rowland complete independence as a designer. By the end of June, Rowland left Kahn and joined Smith, Hinchman, and Grylls as chief designer.[14]

In this new role, Rowland oversaw all design work for Smith, Hinchman, and Grylls. In practice, Rowland was responsible for most of the designs, though not all, depending on the client and type of building desired. The design department of Smith, Hinchman, and Grylls had a number of talented designers, foremost among them, Rowland's fellow cofounders of the Thumb Tack Club, Amedeo Leone and William Kapp (1891–1969). Leone, born in Italy, studied architecture in New York City and was brought to Detroit by Albert Kahn in 1913 to assist in designing the Detroit Athletic Club.[15] Leone was hired by Smith, Hinchman, and Grylls in 1914, and in 1918, he designed the Fyfe Shoe Store building.[16] William Kapp was born in Toledo, Ohio, began practicing in 1909, joined Smith, Hinchman, and Grylls in 1914, and became a partner in the firm in 1924. Clients seeking a modern-style building would work with Rowland, while those seeking a classic look would typically work with Leone.[17] Due to the large volume of work the firm was handling, Kapp's time was primarily occupied with overseeing architectural teams on large projects and meeting with clients during planning and construction.

As Rowland and his team began work on the new Buhl Building, their first concern was how to most effectively utilize the lot. Building owners, not surprisingly—given the high cost of prime city real estate—favored designs that extracted the greatest amount of rentable square footage from each floor of the building. The Buhl property was a corner lot, 188 feet along Congress Street and 120 feet along Griswold and, given the proportions of the lot, a U-shaped building would have leaped to mind for most architects of the time. Rowland's practice, however, was to prioritize adequate light and ventilation for the building's inhabitants by placing all offices on the outside. This was easily accomplished by the same means as with the General Motors Building: placing the building in the center of the lot with wings extending outward, resulting in a cross-shaped building.

Rowland and his team subjected ten layouts to a detailed spreadsheet analysis of potential return on investment.[18] The analysis suggested that the U-shaped layout, with a large light court facing the alley behind, offered a total return on investment of 21.3 percent, which was slightly more than the cross shape's return of 20 percent.[19] However, by forgoing a small amount of rentable space, the cross shape offered significant practical and aesthetic advantages. As every office was an "outside" office, the leasing manager would not need to juggle multiple types of space—prime, light court, secondary, and dark. The elevators, toilets, stairways, and building mechanicals could be located in the central, windowless area

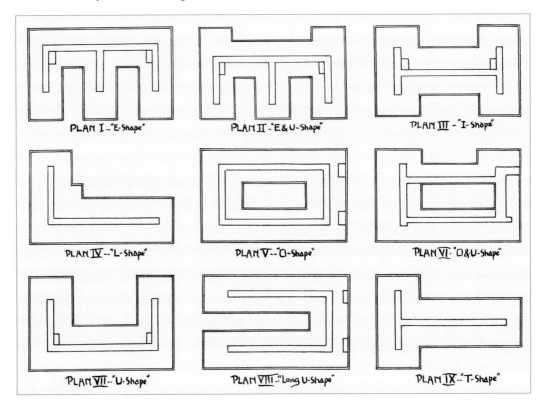

97. In addition to the cross shape, nine possible building layouts were considered for the Buhl Building. Inner outlines show corridor locations and small rectangles represent elevators (if more than one set). This diagram appeared in *Buildings and Building Management*, September 17, 1923. (*BUILDINGS* magazine, Stamats Communications; drawing: Smith, Hinchman, and Grylls and SmithGroupJJR)

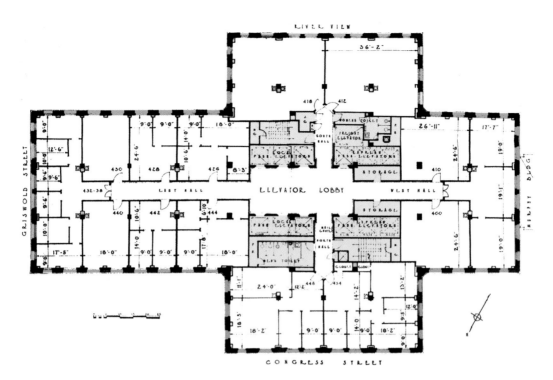

98. The sample floor plan distributed by the Buhl Land Company showing the wide range of possible office layouts and sizes. (Smith, Hinchman, and Grylls)

where the two arms of the building cross, readily accessible to tenants. As the building had no obvious back side, a dignified facade was presented in every direction.

Due to its clear superiority, the cross shape was not only accepted by the Buhl Land Company, it became the chief feature of its marketing effort. In promoting the building, the Land Company went so far as to say its design permitted smaller, less costly offices: "layouts are so efficient, so compact, that ample room may be obtained in smaller space than would be required in a building of lesser efficiency."[20]

The exterior appearance of the proposed building evolved over time; an early rendering of Rowland's concept clearly displays characteristic features of the completed building: a large base supporting a cross-shaped office tower, each wing of which is topped by a peaked parapet, with prominent piers rising from base to roof.[21] Capping the building was a penthouse with pyramid roof (essentially a square hip roof). On the longer, east/west wing were setbacks giving the building a "stepped" appearance. They were later eliminated, not for aesthetic reasons, but as a practical, financial consideration: setbacks reduce the amount of rentable space.[22]

Another change from this early concept was a shift from a symmetrical cross shape to a Latin cross, achieved by moving the shorter arm of the structure closer to the west end of the building. There were likely two reasons for this, the first being the slight flexibility in accommodating tenants gained through having one of the four wings of each floor be relatively larger than the other three. The square footage of the area east of the elevator lobby (toward Griswold Street) is roughly twice the size of the area west of the elevators.[23]

The second reason addressed a concern the Buhl Land Company must have had for the future. The site for the building was adjoined on three sides by streets and an alley, precluding future construction of a window-obstructing adjacent structure. On the fourth side, however, was the six-story Murphy Building; completed in 1903, it was of modern steel frame construction and far from obsolete. There was no way of knowing, though, if or when the Simon Murphy Company, owners of both the Murphy and its neighboring Telegraph Building, might decide to replace them with a large skyscraper abutting the Buhl Building's westernmost facade. Shifting the shorter cross arm of the Buhl Building to the west reduced by 1,200 square feet on each floor the amount of space at risk in the event of such a development.

99. An early proposal for the Buhl Building by Smith, Hinchman, and Grylls showing the parapet and prominent vertical lines, which appear on the completed building, as well as the setbacks and roof later eliminated. (Smith, Hinchman, and Grylls and SmithGroupJJR)

The advent of skyscrapers late in the nineteenth century presented architects with a design quandary: how should a tall building look? Existing design principles were upended as buildings were turned on end, becoming tall and narrow, instead of wide. Early design efforts often had the appearance of multiple buildings piled one atop the other.[24] Then in the 1890s, Chicago architects Dankmar Adler and Louis Sullivan designed two skyscrapers exhibiting a much different appearance, the Wainright Building in Saint Louis and Guaranty Building in Buffalo. Sullivan maintained that a revolutionary shift in building construction—from masonry supporting walls to steel frame—required a corresponding shift in the outward appearance of the structure. Rather than cloaking a building in a skin made to look like the heavy masonry of wall-supported structures, Sullivan suggested the covering should honestly reflect the framework within. In contrast to the "piling up" approach, Sullivan's skyscrapers had a base, shaft, and attic (or capital), much like a classical column. Sullivan and his Chicago School followers enjoyed a period of success, and Detroit has a number of good examples of the style: the T. B. Rayl Hardware Building and the L. B. King and Company Building at 1274 Library Street, designed by Rogers and MacFarlane and completed in 1911.

The untimely demise of the Chicago School style is generally attributed to the 1893 World's Columbian Exposition held, ironically, in Chicago. With the sole exception of Sullivan's Transportation Building, the exposition's structures were classical in style, boosting the popularity of that approach. In the aftermath, classically inspired designs increasingly prevailed as the Chicago School's influence waned.

100. The Rookery Building in Chicago was designed by the firm of Burnham and Root and completed in 1888. It has both exterior load-bearing walls and an internal steel frame. The building's facade is comprised of multiple horizontal layers, as if several buildings were piled one atop the other.

For the Buhl Building, Rowland sought a new approach to the design of tall buildings, one that did not employ classical forms and moved beyond the Chicago School. To achieve this, Rowland addressed two design challenges: a unified exterior treatment, and a complementary and versatile ornamental scheme. The Detroit News Building contained the basic elements from which his design for a taller structure could be derived, and its Romanesque decorative theme could be further evolved as a workable ornamental scheme. Rowland built upon the News Building's expression of the structural frame through prominent piers and pylons. The Buhl Building's piers rise from street level to the very top of the building, unifying the structure vertically and serving as its primary design element. On each corner of the building's base are massive pylons that project above the roof line of the base and contain a single column of windows, which, being narrower and more deeply inset than the structure's other windows, emphasize the pylon's bulk. The wings of the upper office section of the building appear to pass through the base section, each corner supported by a pylon identical to those on the corners of the base, except that these pylons extend to the building's roof.

Piers were commonly employed to emphasize the soaring verticality of skyscrapers; however, piers were often broken by prominent string courses of stone, visually separating the building into sections. In other cases, piers from the shaft are terminated above or within the base, with the same visual result. This was the case even with two of the most innovative designs of the period, the American Radiator Building in New York (1924) and Eliel Saarinen's (unbuilt) design for the Chicago Tribune Building (1922). Another feature reinforcing visual segmentation was the common practice of cladding the base in stone while using less costly brick above. The Pontiac Commercial and Savings Bank (northeast corner of Saginaw

101. Chicago's Brooks Building, designed by Holabird and Root and completed in 1910, is typical of the Chicago School style. (Ken Lund)

and Lawrence Streets), designed in 1922 by Smith, Hinchman, and Grylls, is characteristic of this approach: limestone on the lower floors and brick with terra-cotta accents above. That option was rejected for the Buhl Building in favor of terra-cotta cladding overall, further unifying the structure from top to bottom.[25] The terra-cotta cladding was colored to resemble granite and cast in seemingly random-sized blocks, providing an attractive finish at moderate cost. This clever treatment was used previously on the Fyfe Shoe Store Building (10 West Adams, Detroit), designed in 1918 by Smith, Hinchman, and Grylls, so, presumably, the idea did not originate with Rowland. With the Buhl Building, use of the finish was noteworthy enough to result in its being featured in a promotional ad by the National Terra Cotta Society: "A cherished speculative formula went to the winds in the designing of the Buhl Building. Costly lower-story finish at the expense of finishing the shaft above formed no part of the conception in this fine office building. It is faced throughout with Terra Cotta in a beautiful mottled grey glaze."[26]

Rowland further harmonized the building's base with its top by essentially repeating on the top floors of the building the design appearing on the facade of floors two through four. Rowland was keenly aware of the effect distance has on perception and, as the

102. The wings of the Buhl Building appear to pass through the base; corners are emphasized by stout pylons.

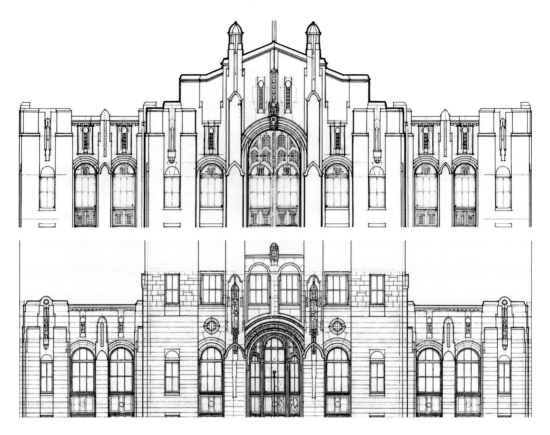

103. Comparison of the Buhl Building's base and top showing similarities in design. (Adapted from the original Smith, Hinchman, and Grylls Buhl Building plans)

top of the building was viewed from a greater distance than the lower floors, the decorative elements on the upper floors were exaggerated in size, bolder, and less detailed than those far below.

The row of arches above the building's fifteenth-floor windows were probably not added for decorative reasons. A pipe gallery, about five feet high, was required below the sixteenth floor, leaving extra vertical space between the windows of the fifteenth and sixteenth floors. The addition of arches over the fifteenth-floor windows was the least distracting manner in which to treat the incongruous spacing between floors.

For Rowland's purposes, Romanesque figures, ornaments, and moldings added eye-pleasing character to parts of a building viewed at close range. In a particular irony of the machine age, Romanesque features, which in the Middle Ages required great skill and time to produce, could be manufactured in quantity from a single hand-carved model and fit together to cover large areas.

The Griswold Street facade is a showplace for Rowland's Romanesque designs and the superb carved figures of Corrado Parducci. As with the General Motors Building,

In devising an exterior design for the building, Rowland drew on his extraordinary breadth of knowledge of past architectural styles, but realized he could also draw from the unique culture and art of the American Indian. Rowland shared with many American architects a deep desire to lessen the Old World's influence and develop a uniquely American style for buildings; incorporating native influences was seized upon by Rowland as an exceptionally promising route to that end. The most prominent and identifiable decorative feature adorning the Buhl Building is not European in origin, but *American*: sculptural representations of Native Americans. Formerly consigned to the role of tobacco store icons, these figures were elevated by Rowland to the role of humanizing and dignifying the entrance to the home of important law firms and businesses. At the time the Buhl Building opened, observers would have viewed the American Indian figures as a clear reference to America and her frontier—Arizona and New Mexico had only joined the union thirteen years earlier. Although the decorative treatment of the Buhl Building's exterior honors its European heritage with Romanesque features, the prominent Native American

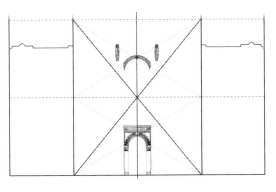

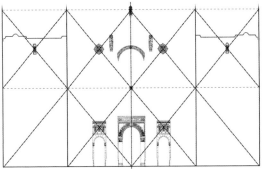

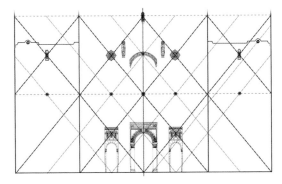

107. Two lines bisecting the rectangle formed by the equilateral triangles (*top*) form the basis for a lattice of triangles. The points where these triangles intersect provide the locations for other prominent features of the facade, including a large eagle at the apex (*middle*). By adding intermediate lines to the lattice, additional details were located at intersection points (*bottom*).

figures identify the building as a product of modern American culture.

The Buhl Building owes its balanced and harmonious appearance to the triangle-based geometric scheme Rowland employed in determining the placement of each design feature. Unlike Hill Auditorium, where Rowland began with a large, nearly blank

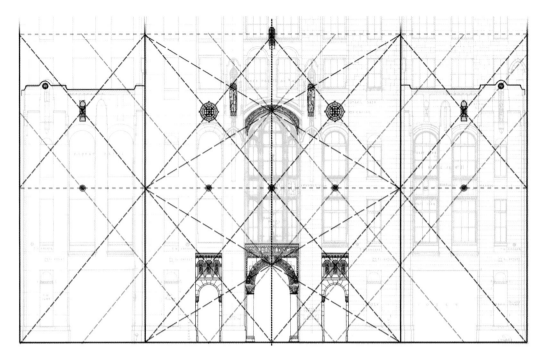

108. The scheme Rowland likely used to arrange the decorative elements of the facade super-imposed over the original elevation for the Griswold Street side of the Buhl Building. (Overlay drawings are by Michael G. Smith; Smith, Hinchman, and Grylls Buhl Building plan sheet 32, November 1, 1923)

canvas, the Buhl Building's Griswold Street facade was largely predetermined by practical and economic considerations—piers and pylons conformed to the width of the building's wings, and floor heights were determined by rental requirements and ventilation conduits—so Rowland cleverly adapted the method to the available space within which he could work.

By early February 1923, Rowland and his team had established the basic design and exterior appearance of the structure, and the Buhl Land Company publicly announced their intention to construct the building. Sketches and a detailed description of the advantages of the Latin cross layout appeared in the press and, though the building existed only on paper, its design had an impact on other buildings being planned. The David Stott Building, in the planning stages since 1920, might have begun construction in 1924, but the announcement that the Buhl Building's offices would all have outside light and no light courts sent Stott Building architects John M. Donaldson (1854–1941) and Walter R. Meier (1887–1931) back to the drawing board. Their building layout in early 1923 was a standard U shape with a light court. To better compete with the Buhl Building, it was revised to an L shape, eliminating the interior light court. The elevators were also moved from the eastern wall of the building to the center of the floor, a change architect Walter Meier stated made them more "conveniently located."[31]

109. Building Planning Service Committee meeting, August 25, 1923. Architect Fred Smith is at the far left, seated, facing the camera. Architect Theodore Hinchman is the first person seated on the opposite side of the table, far left. Directly behind Hinchman, fourth from the left in the group standing, is architect William Kapp. To the right of Hinchman is Donald Kiskadden of the Buhl Land Company. A sketch of the proposed building hangs on the wall behind Kiskadden. (*BUILDINGS* magazine, Stamats Communications)

At the behest of the Buhl Land Company, the building's plans and spreadsheet analysis were studied in August 1923 by the Building Planning Service Committee of the National Association of Building Owners and Managers (now known as Building Owners and Managers Association, or BOMA) at a special meeting in Detroit. The association had established the committee one year earlier to help reduce the financial risk entailed in putting up a new office building; plans were subjected to a critical review by ten or twelve of the country's most experienced building managers. Smith, Hinchman,

110. A sketch by Wirt Rowland of the Detroit riverfront as it would look once the Buhl Building was completed. (Published in "Design in the Drafting Room" by John C. Breiby, *Pencil Points*, June 1923)

and Grylls was represented at the two-day meeting by Fred L. Smith (1862–1941), Theodore H. Hinchman (1869–1936), and William Kapp, and the Buhl Land Company by Donald Kiskadden. As these meetings focused on operational concerns of the completed building, Rowland's presence was not required. William Kapp, team captain overseeing the Buhl Building project, was well qualified to explain to the committee any aspect of the plan. Both Smith and Kiskadden later said the meeting provided value beyond their expectations (more so as to operational, marketing, and management, than architectural or structural concerns).[32]

Having received the endorsement of the Planning Service Committee, Smith, Hinchman, and Grylls proceeded to finalize plans for the building. The full set of plans, dated November 1, 1923, comprised 112 sheets—fifty-five architectural; twenty-three structural; and thirty-four electrical, mechanical, and plumbing. Of the nine sheets that illustrated the exterior details of the building, all were drawn by Rowland—each spandrel, panel, figure, and feature meticulously rendered with dimensions noted. Even the height of each individual course of terra-cotta cladding was specified.[33] Rowland's involvement did not end with completion of the plans as he closely supervised all matters relating to the building's exterior appearance.

For the decorative work on the building's exterior, Rowland created freehand detail drawings. From these, sculptor Corrado Parducci produced models, which other craftsmen copied in stone, or as molds for terra-cotta or cast iron.[34] Parducci's models for the decorative terra-cotta tiles were copied by the Northwestern Terra Cotta Company in Chicago, and Rowland carefully inspected their work at the factory to assure the finished product was satisfactory.[35]

On January 8, 1924, two contractors, Davis and McGonigle and W. E. Wood, presented bids to construct the building. Wood promised a complete building by May 1, 1925, while Davis and McGonigle would commit to only 90 percent by that date and completion by June 1.[36] The contract was awarded to Davis and McGonigle, as their bid of just over $3.5 million was $100,000 lower than Wood's.

Work began immediately; existing buildings on the lot were razed beginning January 17.[37] Work on the caissons began March 1, erection of structural steel was started May 26, and by August 16, the steel framework was complete.[38] Although planning of the building had taken a leisurely and cautious course, by early 1924, speed had become an important consideration. One reason was the commitment the Buhl Land Company had made to prospective tenants of the building, including displaced tenants from the old Buhl Block, that their new offices would be ready by May 1, 1925. Less obvious was competition the Buhl Building would soon face from other new office structures whose planning was already well advanced.

Tenants began moving into the Buhl Building on April 21, 1925, and the building opened as promised on May 1.[39] On that day, Kiskadden announced that half of the building's 320,000 square feet had been leased,[40] well ahead of the 30 to 35 percent typical of similar buildings of the time.[41] In July 1925, the newly formed Guardian Trust Company opened its office on the ground floor of the building, its entrance graced by two bronze doors featuring the sculpted figures of a man holding a key and a woman with a horn of plenty—both modeled by Corrado Parducci.[42] In 1928, the Savoyard Luncheon Club was constructed on the roof of the building.

In the four years following the Buhl Building's opening, eight more large office buildings were completed in downtown Detroit (Michigan Building, Book Tower, Cadillac Tower, Industrial Bank Building, United Artists Theater Building, David Broderick Tower, Greater Penobscot Building, and Guardian Building). Despite this, the Buhl Building reported in May 1929 an occupancy rate of over 92 percent, a tribute to the structure's superb design.[43] Later that year, the Detroit chapter of the American Institute of Architects awarded a medal recognizing the Buhl Building as among the city's finest architectural work.[44]

The Buhl Building's success as a business venture for the Buhl Land Company, and as an admired addition to Detroit's skyline, yielded immediate benefits for Smith, Hinchman, and Grylls in the form of new commissions. In the three years 1924 through 1926, the firm was selected to design four office towers, three of which would be the tallest buildings in the state's three largest cities. The stream of work for Rowland was so considerable that his outside activities, quite extensive prior to joining Smith, Hinchman, and Grylls, were largely displaced by work.

In 1920, the citizens of Detroit voted to construct a street railway system and operate it as the Department of Street Railways. The city subsequently acquired the assets of the privately owned Detroit United Railway. One factor favoring public ownership of the system was the city's ability to readily supply power to the electrically operated railway through the existing public lighting system. At the time, Detroit had the largest arc lamp street lighting system in the country; however, there was insufficient excess capacity to operate the streetcar system. As a consequence, in 1922 the Detroit Public Lighting Commission (DPLC) embarked on a major expansion of its power producing and distributing capacity, the key element of which was construction of the Mistersky Power Station (designed by Amedeo Leone and named for Frank R. Mistersky, general superintendent of the DPLC) at the foot of Morrell Street in southwest Detroit. Smith, Hinchman, and Grylls was DPLC's preferred

111. The Detroit Public Lighting Commission Palmer Park substation on Woodward Avenue, completed in 1923.

vendor for engineering services and was contracted to design Mistersky and the substations (Smith, Hinchman, and Grylls partner, engineer Theodore Hinchman, was a commissioner of the DPLC from 1905 to 1910).[45]

In 1922, DPLC had Smith, Hinchman, and Grylls design the Palmer Park substation—located on Woodward Avenue at Merrill Plaisance Street—the first new installation intended to meet the needs of the street railway.[46] Located on the city's main thoroughfare, within a city park, and in a growing area characterized by expensive homes and upscale apartment buildings, the substation required an attractive exterior design to avoid inciting the ire of nearby residents. Palmer Park was given to the city in 1893 by Thomas Palmer, and it contained a home—designed in 1885 by George D. Mason and Zachariah Rice—presenting the appearance of a rustic log cabin. Rowland's design for the substation blends in with the park's natural forest and log home—the rough-hewn stone walls of the substation look almost ancient.[47] In stark contrast to the roughly cut stone, the building sports sophisticated French Renaissance accents—ornate pediments, smooth cut stone, and escutcheons—evoking a cosmopolitan feeling. The building effectively complements both the park and the nearby high-density apartment buildings.[48]

During the 1920s, motor vehicle manufacturing powered Michigan's unprecedented economic expansion, and vehicle production, in turn, spurred growth in other industries, telecommunications and banking in particular. Michigan Bell, the state's dominant telephone service provider, sustained extraordinary growth over the decade, both through organic expansion and acquisition of seventeen competing firms.[49] In 1920, the company had 275,000 phones in the state and 850,000 miles of wire. By 1930, the number of phones more than doubled to 675,000, and miles of wire increased over 400 percent to 3,811,000.[50] Michigan Bell reported in June 1925 that, in the prior year, its subscriber base in Detroit had grown from 104,000 phones to 223,000, leading the *Wall Street Journal* to say that the city's growth was so rapid, "utility companies are confronted with problems of expansion comparable with difficulties met during the war."[51]

Although less visible than phones and wire, Michigan Bell switching equipment was an essential component of the system. Every phone was connected to a local central office that housed equipment for routing calls to the network's trunk lines.[52] To accommodate an increase in telephones, Bell had to construct new and larger central offices. At the same time, the company was replacing manual service (operator connected) offices with new central offices equipped with automatic (direct dial) capability. The city of Detroit had fourteen central offices handling 115,250 phones in 1917.[53] By 1930, there were thirty central offices handling 352,000 phones,[54] 100,000 more phones than in all of Italy.[55] Statewide, as of the end of 1929, Michigan Bell had completed twenty-five new central offices in the previous three years, with eleven more under construction.

The size and weight of equipment housed in a central office building necessitated an industrial type structure with ceilings of eleven to fourteen feet and floor loadings of 150 pounds per square foot (a typical office building had ten- or eleven-foot ceilings and floor loadings of sixty to seventy-five pounds). Yet as most central offices were located in, or adjacent to, residential areas, these buildings had to be attractive and in harmony with surrounding architecture, or the phone company might face local resistance to construction plans.

Michigan Bell established a strong relationship with Smith, Hinchman, and Grylls prior to World War I, in part because of Smith, Hinchman, and Grylls's strengths in both engineering and design. The phone company's enormous growth during the 1920s made them the architecture firm's largest customer; between 1923 and 1929 Smith, Hinchman, and Grylls turned out an average of seven buildings per year for Bell, including an eight-story Saginaw office, eleven-story Oakwood Boulevard warehouse, five-story Grand Rapids building, and twelve-story addition to the Cass Avenue headquarters. The importance of Bell as a client, particularly in light of the genuine design challenges posed by their buildings, dictated that Rowland handle their design work. The considerable number of Michigan Bell buildings produced by Rowland during these years—nearly all of which still stand—provides an extraordinary record of his rapidly evolving vision of modern design as well as his facility in adapting a wide range of historical styles to modern use.

112. Smith, Hinchman, and Grylls sketch from 1923 of the proposed Michigan Bell Ann Arbor central office. (Drawing: Smith, Hinchman, and Grylls and SmithGroupJJR)

Having Michigan Bell as a client entailed certain advantages of particular interest to Rowland. Their structures were, for the most part, industrial buildings, reducing some of the often confounding challenges entailed by office buildings, banks, and schools. Michigan Bell, a near monopoly and exempt from antitrust regulation, had somewhat less concern for the cost of buildings than most Smith, Hinchman, and Grylls clients; at the very least, the volume of structures made construction budgeting a routine matter, and Rowland could design to an adequate—perhaps even generous—budget, confident that the client wouldn't get cold feet and insist on stripping away design features to reduce the cost. Moreover, given the number of phone company projects, and the nature of the large company's manage-

ment structure, there was little tinkering by the client with the architect's design, as was often the case when more modest firms built large buildings.

Rowland's first two projects for Michigan Bell commenced in 1923, an automatic dial central office in Ann Arbor and the western Michigan headquarters building in Grand Rapids. The location of the Ann Arbor building, on East Washington between Division and Fifth Streets, was in the city's business district, not far from the University of Michigan campus. The nearby masonry buildings, dating mostly from the late 1800s, featured

113. Smith, Hinchman, and Grylls rendering of the Michigan Bell Ann Arbor central office with the planned third-floor addition. The clay tile hip roof, shown here, was not built. (Drawing: Smith, Hinchman, and Grylls and SmithGroupJJR)

114. The Michigan Bell Ann Arbor central office in 2015. The pedestrian gives a sense of the true size of the structure. The original door was larger and more in keeping with the building's scale.

round-headed windows and large cornices. Rowland's Ann Arbor central office complemented those features; the building's midsection windows were grouped within a simple Romanesque style arcade topped with terra-cotta arches echoing several of the more ornate buildings on nearby Main Street. The building is faced in red brick of varying shades, complementing many similar red brick structures on the University of Michigan campus.

Constructed in 1925 of steel reinforced concrete, each of the building's two floors and basement had high ceilings typical of central offices and, as a consequence, the building was taller than nearby structures having the same number of floors. By scaling up in size the building's features, Rowland made it appear similar in scale to the smaller buildings nearby. The true size of the building is difficult to judge without benefit of a passerby.

To accommodate future growth, Michigan Bell central offices were designed to permit the addition of more floors. When possible, Bell would acquire adjacent property so the building could expand horizontally as well. Ann Arbor's growth was such that in 1927, the building's cornice was removed and a third floor was added, and later, a three-story wing to the building's west side. The third-floor addition, most likely designed by Rowland as part of the original two-story plan, was completed without the planned decorative clay tile roof visible in the design sketches.

115. The Grand Rapids Michigan Bell office building has a stone base that almost imperceptibly shifts to brick within the second floor. The corner pylons of the building appear wider due to the illusion they are overlapped by the central facade. The illusion is enhanced by the parapet atop the pylons and the uncentered column of windows on the pylons. Colorful accents highlight the Romanesque style upper windows. This photograph depicts the original building without the upper stories added later.

By the 1920s, Grand Rapids was the headquarters for Michigan Bell's operations in the western half of the state, and in 1923, Bell acquired Citizens' Telephone Company and its 23,000 Grand Rapids area subscribers. Consolidating the two companies required construction of a five-story building on the northeast corner of Fountain Street and Division Avenue to house new, automated central office equipment and larger divisional business offices.

When considering a design, Rowland weighed the local context within which the building was to be constructed, paying particular attention to major buildings nearby and any characteristic cultural features of the area. Some architects, Rowland observed, were guilty of seeking personal recognition for their designs at the expense of harmony among neighboring structures. He wrote in 1931: "the architect is still absorbed in the petty embellishment of this creature that it may be distinct from its neighbors; for to bring it into the general order and character of massing of a street would be to forfeit a prized individualism."[56] Across the street from the proposed Bell building was the new Fountain Street Baptist Church (now known as Fountain Street Church), a substantial structure, beautifully designed in an authentic Romanesque style. Rowland elected to continue the existing Romanesque theme with the new Michigan Bell building.

The design Rowland devised for Michigan Bell's Grand Rapids building is understated, with subtle decorative embellishment. A limestone base gives way almost imperceptibly to buff-colored brick, doing so in the middle of a floor in order to minimize the visual segmentation of the building into sections. Interesting textures within the spandrels, created through the use of patterned brick, are bordered by light-toned terra-cotta. The large expanse of gray and buff is punctuated by pale blue, green, and yellow accents on shields set within the spandrels and, above the fifth-floor windows, bolder blues and yellows. The (original) cornice above the fifth floor unifies the structure horizontally, while massive pylons on all four corners do so vertically—much like the Buhl and Detroit News Buildings. Lacking sufficient width to allow for pylons of a size Rowland felt appropriate, he employed an illusion to make them appear wider. The central facades of the building, which are capped by a cornice, seem to overlap the pylons, which are slightly recessed—an effect that is quite evident when one looks at the portion of the pylons extending above the cornice. (Unfortunately, much of this effect was lost when additional stories were added on top of the original building. The effect is best appreciated in photos taken prior to the addition.)

Rowland's design echoes the Romanesque features of the neighboring church, particularly the biforate arches above the fifth-floor windows.[57] This distinct arrangement of paired, arched windows set beneath a larger arch had been popular in the United States (see Wayne State University's "Old Main," 1895), but by the 1920s had, except for churches, largely fallen from favor.

Like the Buhl Land Company, the directors of the Second National Bank of Saginaw had been awaiting a drop in steel and construction prices before proceeding with a prestigious new headquarters building. In September 1923, the directors appointed a building committee to plan the structure, recommend an architect, and secure contracts for construction. The committee visited two recently completed bank buildings that contained, in addition to the bank's offices, a number of floors with rentable office space: the Industrial Savings Bank Building (432 North Saginaw Street) in Flint and the Pontiac Commercial and Savings Bank Building (30 North Saginaw Street) in Pontiac.

Initially, the bank contracted with the Chicago architectural firm of Weary and Alford,[58] but their relationship became contentious and the Chicago firm of D. H. Burnham and Company[59] was invited to submit a proposal.[60] The committee also arranged a meeting with Fred Smith of Smith, Hinchman, and Grylls, architects of the Pontiac bank they had visited and the only Michigan-based firm considered. The committee was particularly impressed when they learned the firm had designed the proposed Buhl Building in Detroit.

Through November and December 1923, D. H. Burnham and Smith, Hinchman, and Grylls offered various plans to the committee, and on December 7 the committee members informally voted to ascertain which architecture firm had garnered more support. Smith, Hinchman, and Grylls was the first choice of four of the six committee members.[61] Four days later, Daniel Burnham

116. The sketch presented by Smith, Hinchman, and Grylls partner Fred Smith to the Second National Bank of Saginaw building committee on February 1, 1924. The design at this point included a hip roof and modest cornice. (Drawing: Smith, Hinchman, and Grylls and SmithGroupJJR, from the collection of the Castle Museum, Saginaw)

Jr. (of D. H. Burnham, son of noted architect Daniel Burnham) made an "unexpected" visit to Saginaw, and the building committee was hastily called into session to view a model of Burnham's proposed banking room. Burnham's pitch was for naught, though, as the committee voted the following week in favor of hiring Smith, Hinchman, and Grylls.

One of the reasons for the break with Weary and Alford was the building committee's stubborn preference for a square office tower. On February 1, 1924, Fred Smith presented the committee with drawings of the square tower structure they had requested, but also showed them a sketch, prepared by Rowland, of an L-shape building as it would appear from the rear. The sketch illustrated that, by applying the same design features and exterior finish to all sides, the back side of the tower would not appear unsightly, as the committee feared. Smith pointed out the important advantages of the L shape: it allowed for all offices

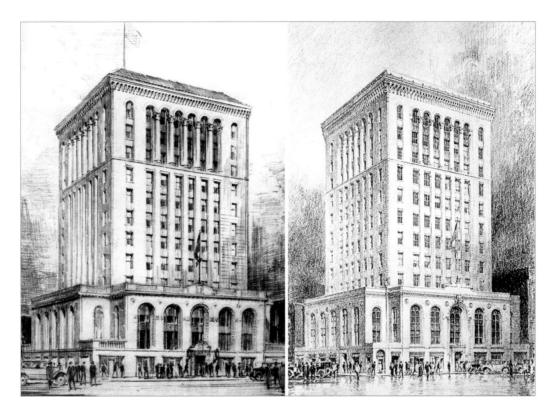

117. *Left*: Second Smith, Hinchman, and Grylls sketch for the proposed Second National Bank of Saginaw showing a larger hip roof and slightly enlarged cornice. A projecting string course separating the top and middle sections of the building was added, and the flat piers between the windows in the top section have been changed to columns. (Drawing: Smith, Hinchman, and Grylls and SmithGroupJJR, from the collection of the Castle Museum, Saginaw) *Right*: The final design rendering for the building shows the hip roof replaced by a larger, more ornate cornice and the windows of the three-story base changed to a Romanesque style. (Drawing: Smith, Hinchman, and Grylls and SmithGroupJJR)

to have outside exposure with excellent light, and the space could be more easily divided into typical office sizes. Although the L-shape plan had, compared with the square tower, less rentable space on each floor, adding one more floor to the building would make up for the lost space—the cost of a square tower being about the same as an L-shape tower with one additional floor.[62] The committee was sold and voted unanimously to adopt the L-shape plan.

The February 1 sketch expressed Rowland's early vision for the building: Romanesque decorative elements, a hip roof, arched top-floor windows, and a modest, arcaded cornice.[63] The building committee members, likely influenced by the more traditional appearance of the two banks they had toured, pushed back, insisting on a more classic look they believed appropriate for a large bank. A later sketch shows a prominent horizontal string course was added between the ninth and tenth floors, sacrificing vertical unity and visually separating the building into three sections—a more traditional style. Between the windows on the top three floors, the square piers were replaced with more traditional half-round columns.[64]

Ultimately, the hip roof was eliminated and replaced with a larger and more ornate cornice, and the large window panes on the second and third floors (visible in the second sketch) were replaced with traditional Romanesque biforate arch windows similar to those on the Grand Rapids Michigan Bell building. The end result was a compromise between Rowland's Romanesque

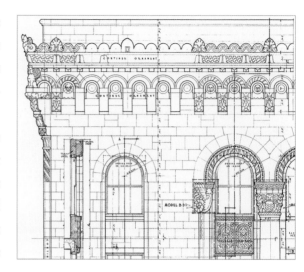

118. Second National Bank of Saginaw arcaded cornice, arched windows, and other upper-story details drawn by Wirt Rowland. (Smith, Hinchman, and Grylls plans, sheet 26, June 2, 1924)

accented modern structure and the building committee's desire for a more traditional appearance. Nevertheless, Rowland's familiarity with Romanesque enabled him to adapt and extend the style in a manner appropriate to the structure and its purpose.

The highlight of the Second National Bank Building is the beautiful, Romanesque style terra-cotta work, a product of Rowland's close collaboration with sculptor Corrado Parducci.[65] The entrance on Washington Avenue is extraordinary, with its contrasting white marble door frame set against a three-story tour de force of Romanesque patterns and grotesques. The arched entrance is topped—as many of Rowland's buildings were—by an eagle, and above the door frame the Great Seal of the State of Michigan is carved in marble.

During construction, Rowland spent several days at Atlantic Terra Cotta's Princeton, New Jersey, plant approving the firm's conversion of Parducci's models into molds for individual terra-cotta pieces. Subsequent work was approved by Rowland from photographs sent from the factory.[66] Atlantic Terra Cotta's journal later carried an extensive article on the bank, describing it as "the highest type of modern construction, well conceived and well executed."[67] The journal *Architectural Forum* ran an article on the building as well, including photos and a plan of the first-floor shops and bank lobby.[68]

As with the Buhl Building, Rowland did not design the interior, with the exception of the ornate wrought iron work for the bank's lobby entrance, screens, and grilles of the vault and safe deposit lobbies, balcony rails, and the ornate teller screens—all in beautiful patterns consistent with the exterior.

Plans for the building were completed and presented to the bank committee July 9, 1924. By the end of July, bids were requested from contractors, and W. E. Wood Company, still smarting from its loss to Davis and McGonigle on the Buhl Building, fared better this time; they were selected as general contractors based on their bid of roughly $850,000. The total cost of the building had, by this point, risen somewhat beyond the bank's budget limit of $1 million, and some expense was saved by an ingenious substitution of bronze-colored terra-cotta for the decorative cast iron on the building's exterior.[69]

Construction began in September 1924. The elevators were ready for use on September 1, 1925, and tenants began moving in. The bank, however, was not operational until early in December, at which time the Second National Bank Building, Saginaw's tallest building, was formally opened to the public.

Rowland's use of Romanesque-inspired features enabled him to solve a number of problems related to exterior adornment. On the Buhl Building they create interest and character at street level, and on the Saginaw bank building, more extensive Romanesque adornment is a unifying factor. In spite of Rowland's strong admiration for the style, he did not believe it to be an ideal standard for modern, tall buildings. The carved designs, for example, were visible only at short range, so using them on the upper floors of a tall building was pointless.

119. The Bankers Trust Company Building at Congress and Shelby Streets, Detroit.

On a small building, however, the style could be exploited to its best advantage, and in 1924, just such an opportunity arose, as Smith, Hinchman, and Grylls was selected to design a bank and headquarters building for the Bankers Trust Company of Detroit.

In the early 1900s, banks seeking to build in downtown Detroit were locating along Fort Street, west of Griswold. Among the bank buildings constructed between 1900 and 1924 on Fort Street were the Peoples State Bank, Peninsular State Bank, National Bank of Commerce, Detroit Trust Company, and Bank of Detroit.[70] All were three to five stories in height, clad in limestone or even marble, and featured very

120. The Bankers Trust Company Building is decorated with traditional Romanesque as well as modern designs. Here may be seen stylized eagles with stars, much like a United States dollar coin, and the "whirling wind" (swastika) symbol in the form of four leaves rotating within a sunburst.

formal, classical facades with enormous columns. Bankers considered the appearance of their building to be a critical factor in attracting and keeping customers. In 1921, Bank of Detroit vice president Edmund Fisher stated that the most important consideration in the plan for a new building was "advertising value, growing out of its exterior and interior appearance, and, the probable psychological effect upon the mind of the average depositor because of the impression it gives of solidity and strength."[71] According to a report authored by the Peoples State Bank of Detroit, the principal consideration when designing a bank "is to make the structure as attractive as possible to the public and employees . . . and in this way to impress the public through [the bank's] architecture."[72]

Although land was available on Fort Street, the Bankers Trust Company opted to acquire a less costly lot on the southwest corner of Congress and Shelby. Surrounding the lot were garages, warehouses, a manufacturing building, and the rear of the block-long Peoples State Bank.[73] Bankers Trust officers may have been put off by the cost of constructing a building on Fort Street similar in style to existing structures, and reacted favorably when Smith, Hinchman, and Grylls suggested an alternative that was modern, distinctive, yet less costly. Rowland's design for the bank was attention grabbing, yet conveyed the qualities of strength, stability, and security, so important to bankers and their customers. The bank's board of directors, which included Leo Butzel, an original partner of Detroit's Butzel Long law firm, Edwin Denby, former secretary of the navy, and William Kales of the Whitehead and Kales engineering firm, made a bold decision to accept Rowland's plan for the building.

Rowland created a fascinating blend of carefully emulated Romanesque features set side by side with modern imagery. A close look at the building reveals scallops, chevrons, zigzags, vine leaves, and other moldings nearly identical to those used on Lombard or Norman Romanesque buildings. However, one also sees an eagle with stars, symbolic of the United States, and the Native American revolving sky symbol, rendered as four spinning leaves. Although the building's arches recall the open arcades of Romanesque structures, the lines of the building are entirely modern, and, unlike Romanesque buildings, the arches contain broad expanses of window.

One significant feature of the Bankers Trust Company Building is its corner entrance. It was common at the time for branch banks located on corner lots to have a corner entrance, but for a bank headquarters—or any other major building—within the downtown business district, it was unheard of. Rowland rejected the dictum that a building's entrance be centered within the side of the building facing the more important street, and instead chose to place the entrance on the corner. This additional facet makes the building appear larger, with a more commanding presence, and permits the entrance to be seen from either Congress or Shelby Street.

Facing northeast and surrounded by much taller structures, the building is rarely in direct sunlight. Rowland was keenly aware of how direct light brings out color and emphasizes details through changing patterns of highlight and shadow. To counteract the effect of its shadowy location, Rowland deeply recessed the first-floor windows within large, layered arches. The second floor, too, has deep arches over free-standing columns ornamented in varied patterns. The designs in the terra-cotta molding used on the arches and horizontally across the facade capture light and create dark shadows that set off the building's features. Even on a sunless day, the building produces enough shadow and detail to please the eye.

Green marble columns and green window frames accent the light colored terra-cotta. Two marble columns flanking the entrance actually project out from the front of the building, but due to the angled corner, the columns remain within the building line. The green marble inserts in the last of the Shelby Street windows and two of the Congress Street windows add to the effect; their primary purpose, however, is hiding from view the floor of the mezzanine above the private bank offices (the building actually has three stories).

The flat roof of the building is hardly noticeable, given the extraordinary treatment of the building's facade, but it is entirely possible that Rowland intended there to

121. The George Harrison Phelps Building on Jefferson Avenue at Joseph Campau. The unusual brickwork on the building includes Flemish diagonal bond patterns on the turret and within the gable above the two large arched windows.

be a decorative clay tile hip roof. If so, then, as with the Michigan Bell Ann Arbor central office and the Second National Bank of Saginaw, the roof was removed from the plans or not completed.

Just over a mile east of downtown, Rowland again employed Romanesque features on the George Harrison Phelps Advertising Agency Building, constructed in 1926 on the corner of East Jefferson Avenue and Joseph Campau (Campau has since become part of the building's parking lot). As with the Bankers Trust Building, the Phelps Building demonstrates Rowland's extraordinary ability to apply a historical style to a modern reinforced concrete structure, and to wring from the same Romanesque style two entirely different effects.[74] The Bankers Trust Building is symmetrical and formal, with broad arches and large expanses of glass, while the Phelps Building is unsymmetrical, rustic, and whimsical.

The primary challenge faced by Rowland in designing the exterior of the Phelps Building was accommodating the unusual arrangement of windows required for the interior floor plan. The southeast corner of the building contained a large, two-story studio for George Phelps, the lighting for which came primarily from two enormous windows on the Jefferson side of the building. On the east (Joseph Campau) side, to avoid excessive direct sunlight in the morning and provide a large, unobstructed interior area for large wall hangings, the studio had only three small windows.

122. One of the George Phelps Building's unusual features is often obscured by ivy: a stone carving of the town crier perched on a ledge midway up the structure's southeast corner. On the left, the figure as it appeared on sheet 13 of the original Smith, Hinchman, and Grylls building plans, dated July 15, 1925. On the right, a photograph of the building.

The varied sizes and purposes of the rooms—particularly the two-story studio—resulted in a structure with unavoidably inconsistent window sizes and placement. Instead of obscuring the problem, Rowland embraced it, resulting in an unusual and appealing building. In spite of the asymmetry, the building is well balanced. On the Jefferson Avenue facade, the large studio windows on the right are balanced by a projecting turret on the lower left and the left-of-center front entrance. On the Joseph Campau facade, the large biforate arch windows unify the structure horizontally at street level; above them, the largely windowless area toward the front is separated from the windowed rear section by a massive chimney and shifting roof-line. The lack of windows toward the front is partially offset by an unusual projecting balcony.

The structure's atypical window arrangement wasn't the only challenge. Rowland also sought to blend the design with the surrounding neighborhood. At the time, East Jefferson was primarily residential in nature, with two- and three-story mansions dating from the late 1800s—two of which still stand on the east side of the building's parking lot. While Rowland's inclusion of the turret on the building's front was consistent with its Romanesque style, his choice was almost certainly motivated by a desire to integrate the building with the surrounding homes, many of which were turreted.

123. This building at 1900 East Jefferson Avenue was designed by Smith, Hinchman, and Grylls for the Kales Realty Company. Completed in 1926, it was originally known as the Jefferson Terminal Warehouse. The building's limestone cladding is unusual for a warehouse, as is its well-designed facade, the broad arches of which recall both the Detroit News and Bankers Trust Company Buildings. The structure could support an additional six stories, but none were added.

Less obvious to the casual observer is the sophisticated (and expensive) detail work on the building. The brickwork is a modified Flemish Bond, with lengthwise bricks set in pairs—without mortar between their ends—to present the appearance of longer Roman bricks. The mortar joints are thick, providing more contrast with the brick. The original roof was of handmade tile with natural variations in color. Like the Detroit News Building's offices, many of the windows were of leaded glass with painted illustrations. Among the deluxe features of the building were a squash court, laundry, a two-bedroom apartment in the basement for the caretaker, and even a volleyball court outside.

As Rowland's workload grew, the task of drawing final building plans was increasingly delegated to other designers. Plans for the Phelps Building were drawn by Rowland's team members Lester "Andy" Anderson and Edgar D. Giberson.[75]

Having designed the tallest buildings in Detroit and Saginaw, Rowland turned his attention to Grand Rapids. In early 1925, the Grand Rapids Trust Company contacted Smith, Hinchman, and Grylls seeking plans for a combination bank and rental office tower, much like the Second National Bank of Saginaw. With this building, Rowland made significant progress in further developing the modern American style he had fashioned for the Buhl Building.

The lot for the Grand Rapids building, on the northwest corner of Monroe and Ionia, was a square, 88 feet on each side, making it impractical and unnecessary for the base

124. The Grand Rapids Trust Building, completed in 1926.

of the building to be larger than the office tower, as with the Buhl and Saginaw buildings. However, like the Saginaw bank building, optimal office layouts and outside exposure for all offices were achieved with an L-shaped structure.

The Buhl and Grand Rapids Trust Buildings share the same terra-cotta cladding, and expression of the building's supporting frame through exterior piers and pylons. However, the piers and pylons of the Buhl Building—some projecting, others recessed—are the dominant feature of the structure's outer surface. On the Trust Building, the plane of the wall surface has a smooth appearance, nearly unbroken by projecting features. Rowland created texture and depth on the base of the Trust Building with large and deeply recessed arches, each having several layers of understated ornament that wraps, unbroken, around the entire opening. Whereas the large, corner pylons of the Buhl Building are prominent, those on the Trust Building are recessed, giving greater emphasis to the central facade—Rowland made "the core of the building appear its strongest part. He set about to weaken the appearance of the corners instead of making them look like pylons upholding the mass."[76] This was an important step in Rowland's development of a modern style: the expansive face of the building was made a point of interest. Rather than viewing the face of the building as a surface upon which interesting features were to be placed, the vast surface is itself a feature. By recessing

125. An American Indian on the corner of the Grand Rapids Trust Building wears a necklace of the type made by Navajo, Hopi, and Zuni craftsmen. The two cast iron pieces above the figure are decorative rosettes, modeled by Corrado Parducci, in the center of which is a trolley wire hanger.

everything behind the central facade, the facade is perceived as a massive, vertical solid, as if it were an enormous single piece. This effect is accentuated by extending the central facade two stories above the corner pylons.

With these key advances—the broad mass of building as a design feature, and less prominent ornamentation—Rowland moved much closer to the strikingly modern designs he would soon produce. Still lacking—and Rowland was well aware of this problem—was some form of ornamentation or adornment to replace the Romanesque features on which he had been relying.[77] The Romanesque decorations used on the lower portion of the

Grand Rapids Trust Building are notably more subdued than those on the Saginaw bank building; they are less important to the overall design, their role superseded by the defining shapes of the structure: the arches, windows, and surface.

Rowland's evolving approach to finishing off a building's top is evident here as well. His previous structures had a decorative tile roof or peaked (gable wall) parapet, or in some cases, a traditional cornice (or cornice-like band of ornament). The Grand Rapids Trust Building's flat roof, however, is plainly evident, the roof line broken only by piers, between which are spandrels with deeply inset arch designs and other Romanesque-inspired ornament.

The uppermost corners of the structure are adorned with carvings of Native Americans. Prominently featured on the second floor, facing into the intersection of Monroe and Ionia, stands a full-size American Indian figure, wearing a necklace of a type common among Native Americans of the Southwest.

The front entrance of the building was originally flanked by a pair of red marble columns—much like the Bankers Trust Company Building entrance. Atop the columns were the carved figures of

126. A freehand detail drawing by Rowland showing how the figures atop the columns flanking the entrance to the safe deposit lobby should appear. Smith, Hinchman, and Grylls distributed these detail drawings to the craftsmen who would execute the carving, in this case, Corrado Parducci. (Drawing: Smith, Hinchman, and Grylls and SmithGroupJJR, Hinman Co. Collection)

127. The two completed figures as they appear in the Grand Rapids Trust Building today. When the bank was closed, the columns were moved from the safe deposit lobby to the women's restroom off the second-floor banking lobby, which now serves as a ballroom.

two wolverines holding shields upon which were representations of river rapids and men in canoes.[78] On the front entrance door jamb is carved an image of river rapids, the city's namesake, while a second carving shows a tree—raw material for the city's dominant industry of furniture manufacturing.

The Trust Building is a particularly good example of Rowland's commitment to blending new structures with those nearby. Each face of the Trust Building has three arched bays of windows, two stories in height, and above each, a pair of smaller arched windows. This arrangement is flanked by six windows—three on either side—within recessed pylons. Across the intersection, the former Grand Rapids Savings Bank Building at 60 Monroe Center, built in 1916, has the same arrangement (except columns and lintels instead of arches). The lowest of the three corner windows on the Savings Bank Building are set within a projecting rectangular frame, topped by an entablature that resembles that above the three large bays of windows. Rowland echoes this feature on the Trust Building: a projecting rectangular frame surrounds the lowest of the three corner windows and contains a decorated arch reflecting the adjacent large arches.

The Grand Rapids Trust Building now goes by the name 77 Monroe Center. The building's owner, Roger E. Hinman of the Hinman Company, has spared no expense in maintaining and preserving the structure, an investment that results in high office occupancy rates and heavy bookings for the ballroom located in the former banking lobby on the second floor.

In 1925, Michigan Bell inaugurated an enormous expansion of plant and equipment it anticipated would be required to keep pace with growth in the state's telephone use. That year Smith, Hinchman, and Grylls began fourteen projects for Bell, including four major central office buildings in Detroit and a twelve-story addition to the Cass Avenue headquarters building.[79]

128. The Michigan Bell Longfellow central office in Highland Park, designed in 1925 and placed in service in August 1927. Notice the Florentine arches on the first floor and shouldered arches above the second-floor windows.

Among the projects begun that year by Rowland were the Longfellow exchange in Highland Park and Royal Oak's central office, both of which were two-story structures of similar design (though the later addition of two floors and a rear extension to the Royal Oak building altered its appearance). As with the Buhl, Saginaw bank, Bankers Trust Company, and Grand Rapids Trust buildings, both of these central offices were clad in buff terra-cotta—the last of Rowland's designs to be finished in this manner.

129. Michigan Bell's Royal Oak central office was designed in 1925 and placed in service in November 1927. When completed, the structure looked much like the Highland Park building. Later, two floors were added and the rear of the building was extended.

Rowland broadened his source of historic inspiration for these two buildings: the entrance and large first-story windows are topped by Florentine arches, a common feature of early Renaissance buildings. The second-floor windows have shouldered arches, a departure from the round or square window openings Rowland used in the past. With its Renaissance-style arches, clean lines, and minimal ornamentation, these buildings look very much like modern versions of an Italian Renaissance palazzo.

To house a Michigan Bell central office for Redford, in 1925 Rowland designed a handsome structure for the northwest corner of Grand River and McNichols Road (6 Mile). The building exhibits a rigorously developed symmetrical design and Romanesque features. Rowland imparted depth and interest to the otherwise two-dimensional facade by adding layers of arches and bevels, all formed using just the bricks of the building's outer skin. The piers that flank the four arched window bays of the first floor are beveled (chamfered), while the segmental arches are composed of three layers of bricks. Just below the roofline, an arcaded cornice was created using bricks and stone corbels. Capping off

130. Former Michigan Bell Redford Central Office on Grand River at McNichols in Detroit.

the building is an ornamental red clay tile roof, probably similar in style to those envisioned for the Ann Arbor central office, National Bank of Saginaw, and, possibly, the Bankers Trust Company Building.

The headquarters for Michigan Bell was the Bell Telephone Building at 1365 Cass Avenue in Detroit; the seven-story structure housed business offices as well as extensive switching equipment. Designed by Smith, Hinchman, and Grylls and built between April 1917 and August 1919,[80] the building was designed to accommodate twelve additional floors as needed. By 1925, the company had grown beyond the building's capacity and was leasing additional office space nearby. In the eight years since the building had been designed, architectural styles had changed so dramatically that the previously conceived plan for the building's addition was outdated. Rowland was charged with reworking plans for the addition to achieve a more modern appearance for the entire building—a challenging task, given that the existing, classically styled structure was "set in stone."

Rowland used the building's height (only six feet less than the Buhl Building) to advantage in altering its style; the nominally Romanesque features he employed on the upper floors are seen from a distance, while the columns and other classical features of the original structure are viewed only by a near observer.

131. Michigan Bell Telephone Building on Cass Avenue as it looked between 1919 and 1927. (*Mouthpiece*, April 1927)

132. The Michigan Bell Building in September 1927. Wooden forms are being constructed around the steel skeleton in preparation for pouring concrete. (Bentley Michigan Bell collection, Michigan Bell photo, appeared in the *Mouthpiece*, October 1927, 6)

The building's top is a scaled-up version of the Grand Rapids Trust Building, rendered primarily in brick and terra-cotta. Three-story, deeply recessed arches and inset building corners create depth and attract the eye to the upper section. Piers along the roofline are adorned with pedestals, from which hangs a bell. Upon the pedestal stands the figure of a woman. ("Ma Bell"? It's possible; the telephone company's nickname of "Ma Bell" was in use within Michigan prior to the building's design.[81]) Between the buttress tops are sections of small, recessed arches separated by projecting colonettes. Rowland avoided placing detailed elements at such a great distance from the street as an observer would be hard-pressed to make them out. The details, therefore, of these elements are not finely wrought, but simple shapes intended to

133. The Bell Telephone Building on Cass Avenue at Times Square in Detroit was built in two phases. The lower seven stories were completed in 1919 and the twelve-story addition, designed by Rowland, was constructed from 1927 to 1928.

provide interesting surface texture by trapping light and creating shadows. From the projecting figure of the woman, to the window panes deep within the arches, there are at least seven planes of detail.

The top of the building is finished off with an ornamental hip roof of copper. Due to the large size of the building and the roof's distance from the ground, Rowland likely anticipated that a red clay tile roof, as he had employed (or planned) on other buildings, would look out of place. Buildings capped with a full copper roof were common at the time; Rowland's innovation was the partial roof, rather than a full roof rising to a peak. The green patina of the aged copper adds color and complements the bricks and spandrels of the building.

Late in 1925 Rowland began work on the Michigan Bell Hogarth central office, a three-story structure on the corner of Plymouth Road and Northlawn Street. The building is clad in bright red brick accented with narrow bands of light trim.

134. The Bell Telephone headquarters building in Detroit features a copper hip roof. The ornamental details below the roof are set at a multitude of depths, giving the upper part of the structure texture and dimensionality.

Like the Detroit News Building, which in key aspects it resembles, the vertical lines of Hogarth's facade are emphasized with simple piers. The building has no cornice, parapet, or visible roof to mark its top. Rather—as with the Grand Rapids Trust Building—the piers project above the roof, breaking its long horizontal line at regular intervals. As originally constructed, Hogarth had a band of light-toned ornamentation between the buttresses, very similar to the Grand Rapids Trust and Michigan Bell headquarters buildings. On the northeast corner of the building was a carved figure of a woman standing upon a bell—similar to the Bell headquarters building. When a fourth floor was added, the decorative panels, ornamented pier caps, and carved figure were removed.

As the building faces north and east, the two main facades are in shade from noon on. The design on the spandrels between the second and third (and subsequently, third and fourth) floors are deeply carved and, along with the inset windows adjacent to the

135. Michigan Bell Hogarth central office in its original configuration as a three-story building. The carved figure of a woman on the corner, decorative spandrels, and ornamentation on top of the buttresses—all of which have since been removed—are visible in this photo. (Indiana Limestone Photograph Collection, Indiana Geological Society)

projecting piers, aid in creating shadows that give texture to the surface of the building.

Rowland took a particularly novel approach with the entrance, located on the building's southeast corner. (This entrance, on Northlawn, has now been mostly bricked up and employees enter through a door off the parking lot on the south side of the building.) The entrance is located within a slightly recessed section of the building and, but for this section, the facade of the building would be symmetrical. The entrance itself is asymmetrical, flanked by two buttresses that are identical except for the section above the second-floor windowsill, where the right buttress reaches higher and wraps around the slight corner of the building. The entryway opening is topped by a round arch, within which are three round-headed windows, and just left of the entry is another arch-topped window. These round windows contrast with the building's other windows, all of which are rectangular in shape. The appearance of the entrance is unexpected, a clever bit of intentional asymmetry and contrast, included by Rowland to add interest to an otherwise staid building.

When Rowland commenced employment at Smith, Hinchman, and Grylls, in addition to the Buhl Building, another project received his immediate attention: the Jefferson Avenue Presbyterian Church. Construction of the church was prompted by the merger of two congregations, Bethany Presbyterian and Jefferson Avenue Presbyterian. Downtown-based

136. Michigan Bell Hogarth central office at the corner of Plymouth Road and Northlawn Street after the addition of the fourth floor.

Jefferson Avenue, with fewer than three hundred congregants, was shrinking, while Bethany, three miles east and with over one thousand members, was growing beyond the capacity of its existing building—both effects due to the relocation of increasingly mobile residents away from the city center.[82] An article in the *Detroit Free Press* explained: "In recent years, the Newberrys, Joys and others, who were as much a part of [the Jefferson Avenue Church] as its bricks, gave up their homes on Jefferson Avenue and, moving to Grosse Pointe, gradually withdrew from any personal activity in the affairs of the church."[83]

Smith, Hinchman, and Grylls partners Theodore H. Hinchman and Fred L. Smith were both members of Jefferson Avenue, making Smith, Hinchman, and Grylls the obvious choice as architects. (Both men made generous pledges to the building fund.[84]) In 1918, the church acquired a site on East Jefferson between McClellan and Parkview Streets,[85] and in 1920, a design prepared by Smith, Hinchman, and Grylls for an expansive church, parish house, and manse was published.[86] It became evident, however, that the proposal was beyond the budget of the combined congregations, so the site was sold and a smaller lot at the corner of Jefferson Avenue and Burns was purchased.[87]

Plans for a more modest structure at Jefferson and Burns were drawn by Smith, Hinchman, and Grylls designer William Kapp in 1921.[88] When Rowland arrived at the firm the following year, he was asked to quickly develop a new design for the exterior of

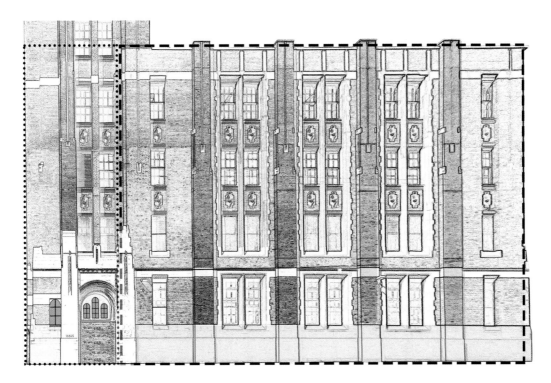

137. The Northlawn Street facade of Hogarth. The section containing the entrance (enclosed in dotted outline) extends to the left from an otherwise symmetrical five-bay section (dashed area).

the building. William Kapp's design for the interior was retained, but modified as required to accommodate Rowland's revised exterior. That Rowland, an architect experienced in modern commercial, industrial, and school architecture, could turn out, in three months, a successful design for such a beautiful, English Gothic style church is a tribute to his vast and detailed knowledge of architectural history.

By November 1922, church officials had approved the new plans and contracted with Bryant and Detwiler for construction of the foundation and basement, completed in early 1923. However, before contracts were signed for the balance of the building, rising construction prices, driven in part by Detroit's construction boom, increased the building's cost by over $105,000 to $656,000. The church building committee sought cost-cutting suggestions from Smith, Hinchman, and Grylls, a number of which were implemented, including reduced use of the most expensive type of granite on the exterior and elimination of the porte cochere (covered entrance extending from the west side of the chapel). Nevertheless, the higher price tag halted further progress on construction.

Finally, on January 31, 1924, representatives of Bethany and Jefferson Avenue congregations met to formally merge the two, becoming the Jefferson Avenue Presbyterian

Church (JAPC). They elected twelve trustees, including architects Theodore Hinchman and Louis Kamper, and voted to accept a proposal from W. E. Wood Company to complete the building. Yet even after the cornerstone was laid in June 1924, church trustees continued to revise the plans to further reduce costs.[89]

By the spring of 1926, the building neared completion. Among the last items added to the exterior was the stone carving work of Detroit artisan Peter Bernasconi. One of the country's leading stone carvers, Bernasconi learned his trade in Italy and Germany prior to immigrating in 1913 to the

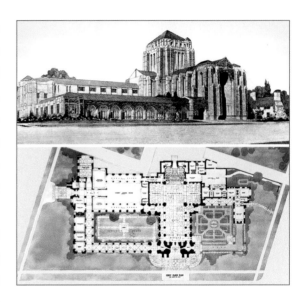

138. Sketch and plan of the proposed Jefferson Avenue Presbyterian Church prepared by Smith, Hinchman, and Grylls for the lot located on Jefferson between McClellan and Parkview Streets. (*Michigan Architect and Engineer*, November 1920)

United States. He often worked, as in this case, turning models created by Corrado Parducci into the carved stone features on buildings. His many commissions in Detroit include the carved stone on the Guardian Building, Livingstone Memorial, Ford Motor Engineering Lab, and Saint Aloysius Church.[90] Bernasconi's work adorns the exterior of the church, most prominently, over the front entrance to the chapel where the burning bush and figure of Saint Michael may be seen.[91]

Another well-known and highly regarded local craftsman who left his mark on the building was Thomas DiLorenzo. Among his many projects are the ceiling of the Guardian Building's banking lobby,[92] and the painted decoration in Detroit's Music Hall (Wilson Theater).[93] Within the church, DiLorenzo was responsible for the painted decorations on the ceilings throughout, including the special treatment of the wood and plaster

139. A 1922 sketch of the church showing the porte cochere (between the front entrance and tower entrance) but otherwise indistinguishable from the completed building. (Drawing: Smith, Hinchman, and Grylls and SmithGroupJJR)

140. Laying the cornerstone of the Jefferson Avenue Presbyterian Church, June 1, 1924. In the center, the front wall of the parish house is under construction, to its right is the steel framework of the second floor, and to the left, a pile of hollow terra-cotta structural tiles that back up the stone and constitute the walls. The homes behind are on the west side of Burns Avenue. (Collection of the Jefferson Avenue Presbyterian Church)

ceiling of the chapel. The chapel ceiling, according to JAPC pastor Peter Smith, has never been repainted.

In a 1924 memo to the church trustees, William Kapp characterized the architectural style as "a modified English Gothic." (Gothic churches built in England typically did not require flying buttresses as they were built, as explained elsewhere by Rowland, "over the foundations of monastic ruins, Norman or Romanesque, and they [the builders] did not bother to change the original structural system."[94]) He asserted that the church "ranks with the finest in this part of the country."[95] While self-serving, the claim is not without merit as the church subsequently received significant attention in national publications; photos of the completed building were featured in four of the leading architectural journals.[96] The weekly *Detroit Saturday Night* described the church as "one of the most beautiful buildings in the city."[97] *Worship in Wood* by Thomas M. Boyd (1927) featured a photo of JAPC's organ and pulpit as the book's frontispiece. Renowned Gothic architect Ralph Adams Cram included photos of the church in his 1929 book, *American Church Building of Today*.[98]

The church does not differ markedly in general appearance from others built around the same time (see the Westminster Presbyterian Church in Saint Louis by Albert Groves, completed in 1925). Rowland's design, however, exhibits superb balance, proportion, and composition of elements. His careful selection of materials, according to color and texture, gives the structure a substantial, yet warm and welcoming appearance. As with his other buildings, Rowland emphasizes the vertical, but horizontal elements play a key supporting role. The horizontal lines of the smooth limestone coping (where walls meet roof) and buttress steps contrast with the darker and rougher granite. Important focal points—the large tower windows, front window, and doorways—are bounded by prominent horizontal features. The building's design is harmonized through repetition of certain elements; the paired windows of the tower, for example, are reprised in small scale above the main Jefferson Avenue window, above the door at the base of the tower, and then again as rectangular windows flanking the entrance to the chapel.

One unusual aspect of the design is found on the southwest corner of the belfry, a highly detailed, small tower with a copper-sheathed roof. Rowland's knowledge of Gothic architecture, as practiced during the twelfth through the fourteenth centuries, was extensive and was acquired through academic study as well as trips abroad to view many Gothic structures firsthand. In a 1938 article by Florence Davies in the *Detroit News*, Rowland is quoted: "Gothic is something that grows as a vine or a tree—from roots. As symbolized by any vertical member or molding which may start from a base, it never stops until it vanishes into mid-air by means of points and pinnacles, disappointed, as it were, because it cannot ascend farther."[99] In JAPC's small tower, Rowland has given life to a "vertical member" that "vanishes into mid-air by means of points and pinnacles." Looking at this highest point on the church, one can almost sense the little tower's pride in being that part which is closest to God. When viewed from Jefferson Avenue, the small tower may evoke images of the Statue of Liberty's torch, conveying a welcoming message to all.

The use of fine materials, both inside and out, contributes to the building's appearance. The largest single construction expense was for the square-cut stone (ashlar) exterior, purchased from Plymouth Quarries, Boston, Massachusetts. The gutters, downspouts, and hardware are of copper and decorated with a multitude of religious symbols. The roof of the building is graduated slate. Hardware throughout the interior is hand-wrought iron, and the wood furnishings feature many hand-carved details.

The foundation (and basement) upon which the building rests is steel reinforced concrete, while the superstructure is masonry and steel frame. Although the granite facing is four inches deep, it does not support the structure.[100] The walls are made of fireproof, load-bearing blocks that support the building's weight and secure the facing in place.[101] One of the builders is reported to have said: "This is the most substantial building of any kind that I have ever erected."[102]

The first service in the new church was private, held for the workmen and their families Sunday, March 21, 1926. One week later, on Palm Sunday, March 28, 1926, the first public service for the congregation was held. Wirt Rowland once wrote that "no architect who had not the spirit of God in his heart could design

141. A 1927 letter from Rowland to the children of Frank and Opal Burroughs: Frank Jr., Nancy, Genevieve, and Mary. (Collection of Genevieve Burroughs Baker)

a beautiful church."[103] The Jefferson Avenue Presbyterian Church was, according to Corrado Parducci, "one of Rowland's favorite projects,"[104] perhaps because it allowed Rowland to express his spiritual side.

Despite Rowland's busy schedule, he kept in touch regularly with his cousin Frank Burroughs, now living in Grand Rapids. Frank had married in 1916 and he and his wife, Opal, now had four children, Frank Jr., Nancy, Genevieve, and Mary. Rowland doted on the children much as a devoted grandparent, and often visited the family, staying with them for holidays and in the summer to gain a respite from the heat of the city.

6

A BREAKTHROUGH

Architecture, like music, is difficult to discuss. It stands as it is, for people to see, to understand or misunderstand, to condemn or admire. A certain design may be explained, but must be understood by one whose comprehension is the same as the person who tried to explain it.

—Wirt Rowland, "New Note in Architecture Struck," 1929

Between 1923 and 1925, Rowland made significant headway in his effort to develop a uniquely American design for the skyscraper. His ideas evolved from the Buhl Building, the design for which was completed in November 1923, to the Grand Rapids Trust Building, designed during the summer of 1925. Instead of the prominent piers and corner pylons of the Buhl, the Grand Rapids Trust Building emphasized the slab-like mass of its central facade. The gabled roofline of the Buhl gave way on the Grand Rapids building to a flat roof. The advances represented for Rowland the fully developed exterior treatment he sought for tall buildings. Rowland's second challenge, to develop a complementary and versatile ornamental scheme, remained problematic. Romanesque carving was beautiful and versatile, but as buildings grew ever taller, the use of carved designs many hundreds of feet in the air—too distant to be clearly perceived by the human eye—was impractical.

Rowland's approach to these two concerns was altered as a consequence of his work with Thomas Whitney Surette. As Rowland came to understand how a significant musical work was built up from, and unified by, a series of notes constituting a theme, he realized the same concept ought to apply to architectural design as well. This insight particularly affected his view of architectural ornament and the decoration of tall buildings. A skyscraper cannot be taken in with a single view. The building may be seen from a distance, and up close; from many locations and angles; and from outside and inside. In short, an observer's perception of the structure develops over time as more of the building is viewed—a process similar to the manner in which a musical work becomes known to the listener. Rowland realized he could take advantage of this temporal dimension to allow for theme development within the design of a building. As with music, theme development is a subtle feature, but one that permitted Rowland to add an important new level of artistic expression, one that could be appreciated by an interested and motivated observer.

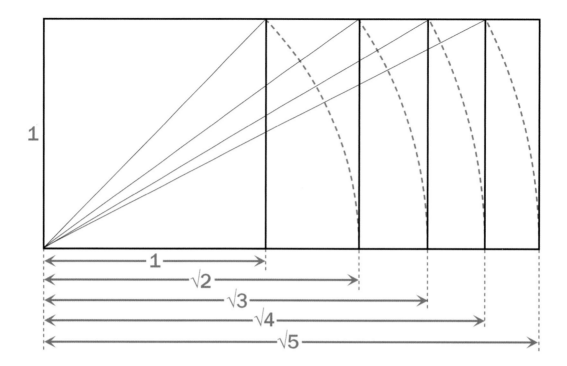

142. Root rectangles are formed one from the other, beginning with a square. A square with sides equal to one has a diagonal equal to the square root of two (√2). If the diagonal of the square is rotated to form the long side of a rectangle, its sides will be equal to one and √2: a "root two" rectangle. Each new root rectangle is formed from the diagonal of the preceding rectangle.

As Rowland mulled over the import of Surette's work, there were major developments in art and architecture that also influenced his thinking. The key to the Greeks' unmatched talent in designing beautiful architecture and sculpture had long been sought. Of this lost talent, Viollet-le-Duc wrote: "We have very little information" on the methods of establishing proportion in architecture used by the Greeks; we have lost "the thread which guided the architects of old through that labyrinth of mysterious knowledge."[1]

Around 1900, an American artist by the name of Jay Hambidge (1867–1924), conducting research for an architectural mural, discovered a surprising fact about Greek architecture: the Greeks did not use linear measure as we do today; they measured areas and volumes using geometry. Specifically, the Greeks employed "root rectangles" (and variations)—figures having sides that, in ratio, are incommensurable (have no common standard of measurement). The length of at least one side of a root rectangle is an irrational number—a number that, as a decimal, continues indefinitely. By dividing root rectangles or combining them according to known rules of geometry, the Greeks could measure and proportion as needed, the only tool required was a compass, or even just a string.

Hambidge demonstrated numerous ways in which root rectangles may be divided, the most important being the reciprocal of the rectangle. A line drawn from a corner at right angles to the diagonal of a rectangle defines an area proportionally identical to the parent rectangle, only smaller. This smaller reciprocal rectangle may be further divided in the same manner, and so on to infinity. Root rectangles may also be subdivided by adding, or "applying," squares.

One rectangle Hambidge referred to as the "rectangle of the whirling squares," so named because each reciprocal cuts the parent rectangle into a smaller rectangle plus a square. The whirling square rectangle is constructed from the root five rectangle, which has one side equal to 1 and a second side equal to the square root of five, or approximately 2.236. The whirling square rectangle has one side equal to 1 and a second side equal to $(1 + \sqrt{5})/2$, or 1.618 . . . ; its reciprocal is equal to 0.618 . . . A whirling square rectangle (1.618 . . .) added to its reciprocal (0.618 . . .) is a root five rectangle (2.236 . . .). Those familiar with design theory will recognize the ratio 1:1.618 as the "golden rectangle" or "golden ratio," which is found throughout nature. This ratio defines, for example, the arrangement of scales around a pine cone, rows of seeds around a sunflower disc, and proportions of the human face.

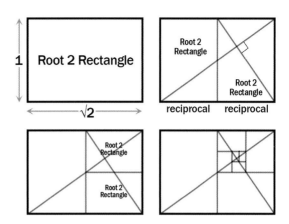

143. Drawing a diagonal to a root rectangle and then a line from one corner cutting the diagonal at right angles divides the rectangle into its reciprocals, each having the same proportions as the parent. A root two rectangle divides into two reciprocals, a root three into three, a root four into four, and so on. The subdividing process can be continued indefinitely.

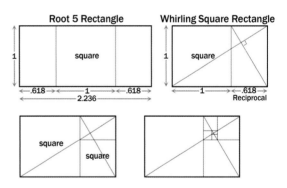

144. From the root five rectangle (*upper left*), the "whirling square" rectangle is derived. The reciprocal of the whirling square rectangle is equal to 0.618 . . . , leaving a remainder equal to 1, or a square (*upper right*). Each reciprocal can be further divided into a smaller rectangle—of identical proportions to the parent—and a square (*lower left*). These squares appear to "whirl around" the eye of the figure to infinity (*lower right*). The ratio of the sides of a whirling square rectangle is 1:1.618. . . . If a square (ratio of 1:1) is subtracted, it results in a reciprocal figure with a ratio of 1:0.618.

It was this relationship of root rectangles to nature that led Hambidge to refer to proportional relationships based on root rectangles as "dynamic symmetry," "dynamic" because they are based on the same proportional arrangements exhibited by growing organisms in the natural world. "The essential point," said Hambidge, "is that this simple construction enables the designer to introduce the law of proportion into any type of composition, and that, too, in much the same way as it appears in the plant and the shell."[2] Proportional relationships not based on root rectangles were labeled by Hambidge as "static."

Hambidge made the significant point that static symmetry may be achieved unintentionally or instinctively, while dynamic symmetry cannot.[3] Hambidge demonstrated that dynamic symmetry was found in the design of pottery and architecture dating from the Periclean age of Greece and, to a lesser extent, the early Egyptians. Although Hambidge's methods had much in common with Viollet-le-Duc's lattice of triangles, dynamic symmetry offered designers and artists a more refined system.

In 1902, Hambidge presented his theories to the British Society for the Promotion of Hellenic Studies and was immediately invited to address the organization again once his research was more fully developed. His second presentation was planned for 1914, but did not occur until 1919 due to the outbreak of war. The address was published as a nine-page article in the November 12, 1919, issue of the *American Architect*: "Symmetry and Proportion in Greek Art."[4]

Hambidge's ideas were polarizing; in the arts community, partisans and doubters were said to be evenly divided.[5] When *Architect's Journal* of London wrote that Hambidge's visit there "did not make many converts to his theories," it provoked an incensed response from the *American Architect* (April 21, 1920): "[Hambidge's] facts are indisputable." A negative review by the *Nation* of Hambidge's *Dynamic Symmetry—the Greek Vase* prompted a storm of outrage on the pages of the *American Architect*; the first salvo was fired by architectural historian William H. Goodyear (1846–1923), fine arts curator of the Brooklyn Museum (November 24, 1920), followed by a letter endorsing Hambidge from Gustave Eisen of the California Academy of Sciences (December 1, 1920).

Later that same month, the *American Architect* published an interview with American painter George Bellows (1882–1925). Bellows was critical of the state of American architecture: "I am sick of American buildings like Greek temples . . . it is tiresome and shows a lack of invention. . . . All living art is of its own time. . . . Few architects seem to grasp this."[6] On the topic of dynamic symmetry, Bellows commented, "Hambidge has shown me a great many things that are profoundly true, and I believe any serious architect who will take the time to study this theory will be greatly helped. . . . Not only do I regard [dynamic symmetry] as of vast importance and as expressing a fundamental natural truth, but even if it were not absolutely correct, it is anyhow useful to me."[7] Bellows, like Rowland, was an innovator and in the forefront of his profession. "There is no new thing proposed that I [as a painter] will not consider," said Bellows. "The fact that a thing is old and has stood the test of time has become too much a god."[8] Yet in his utilization of dynamic symmetry—a method dating back thousands of years—Bellows demonstrated that great art is produced when innovation is guided by well-established and deeply understood principles.

In November 1921, the journal *Architecture* published "Dynamic Symmetry and Modern Architecture" by Hambidge.[9] Mincing no words, Hambidge began the article, "The great weakness of architecture today lies in the fact that it does not disclose concrete proportion of the right type. We might say that architecture today is almost without proportion. The prevailing practice of putting together unrelated design elements as they are lifted or adapted from the sources of the past has resulted in a hodgepodge." He stated that with the Greeks, the "most characteristic element of the design is the bonding or knitting together of composing units. This is due to proportion. A better word would be symmetry." "The design conception as a whole," Hambidge explained, is the "dominating symmetry factor. When this is fixed everything else depends on it." Hambidge compared the methods of Viollet-le-Duc with those based on dynamic symmetry: "The design history of the past shows us that artists have fixed this dominating symmetry in at least two ways: one by the use of the regular figures of geometry such as the square and the equilateral triangle or by lengths of line determined by some measuring unit, the other by employing areas possessing peculiar properties of measurableness." Hambidge was clearly speaking to designers, such as Rowland, who employed some form of geometric design method in their work.

Beginning in 1920, discussion of dynamic symmetry spilled over into popular culture as articles on Hambidge's theories appeared in leading newspapers and periodicals. The July 4 issue of the *New York Times* ran "Art: Re-Discovered Principles of Greek Design."[10] The *Chicago Daily Tribune* followed with two articles in April 1921.[11] Then *Scientific American* in its July 1921 issue published an extensive and detailed article, "Dynamic Symmetry: The Rediscovery of the Basic Principles of Greek Art."[12] Interest in dynamic symmetry resulted in a series of lectures on the topic by Professor Rose Netzorg of Kalamazoo Normal College, hosted by the University of Michigan's architecture school.[13] A 1923 book, *Teaching of Industrial Arts in the Elementary School*, included instruction on the use of dynamic symmetry, stating, "Dynamic symmetry is in wide use in the industrial world at the present time."[14] The concept found its way into consumer marketing efforts; an advertising campaign, beginning in 1926 for Chrysler automobiles,[15] stated, "Just to sit in the car and look about reveals first a quality all Americans love—compactness, conservation of space, dynamic symmetry, artistry and a complete elimination of unnecessary elements."[16] At least one brand of women's hose was, according to the *New York Times*, designed according to the principles of dynamic symmetry.[17]

Dynamic symmetry was added to the subjects taught in Detroit's schools and colleges. The bibliography of the Detroit Public Schools, *Course of Study, Art Education, Elementary Schools,* from 1925 lists under "Fine Arts" four books on design, one of which was Hambidge's *Dynamic Symmetry*.[18] The University of Michigan's *General Announcement* for the Colleges of Engineering and Architecture, 1926–27, under "Decorative Design" lists the course "Geometric Relations (Dynamic Symmetry)."[19] The Detroit Public Library added Hambidge's *Parthenon and Other Greek Temples: Their Dynamic Symmetry* (1924) to their architecture section.

An insightful article in the February 3, 1924, *New York Times*[20] presaged the significance dynamic symmetry would have for Rowland's work. The article was written by Wilford S. Conrow (1880–1957), an artist and collaborator with the aforementioned William H. Goodyear. Conrow stated that Hambidge's "rediscovery of the principles of Egyptian and Greek design, called 'Dynamic Symmetry,' makes it possible to have interrelated proportion of area in the design of grounds, buildings, interior decorations and furnishings." To successfully bring about such interrelations in a single project would require "a great body of highly trained men and women working together under a single head," with "complete understanding and cooperation, inspired by intense enthusiasm among all employed."

As these discussions in the world of design and architecture unfolded, important developments in Detroit's banking community were quickly bringing about the circumstances that led to the construction of Rowland's two most significant buildings: the forty-story Guardian Building (originally known as the Union Trust Building, the name by which it will be referred to here) and forty-seven-story Greater Penobscot Building.

In Michigan, state banks were permitted to operate branches—a practice prohibited in most other states at the time. As a consequence, Detroit had larger banks, but fewer of them than cities of a similar size. By 1922, most transactions in Detroit were handled by thirteen state banks (with 184 branches) and three national banks.[21]

Automobile manufacturing, which by the 1920s had become the country's largest industry, required increasing amounts of capital to finance domestic and international expansion, dealer inventories, and customer credit.[22] Much of this capital was supplied through the financial markets in New York City, an arrangement that sometimes tested the patience of Detroiters. Friction between Ford Motor Company and the New York financiers turned to outright hostility in 1920 when bankers demanded representation on Ford's board of directors as a condition for a large loan. Five years later, on May 19, 1925, a front-page story in the *Los Angeles Times* carried the headline: "Ford Banks in Gotham; Millions Invade Wall Street; Believed Beginning of Huge Financial Enterprise of Auto Magnate." "Henry Ford," said the article, "entered New York's financial district with what appeared to be a banking house of his own." "The announcement came in the form of an advertisement that went entirely over the highest Wall Street heads until some genius saw its potential possibilities. In the advertisement, Kean, Higbie Company announced the discontinuance of their New York office and said that the business would be transferred to the Guardian Detroit Company, 120 Broadway, New York, and Buhl Building, Detroit."[23] The *New York Times*, in its own front-page story on the "Ford invasion," pointed out Guardian Trust (a subsidiary of Guardian Detroit Company) would offer Ford many advantages, including the ability to sell public shares in Ford Motor "without the usual negotiations with bankers or underwriters."[24] In July 1925, Guardian Trust Company opened its offices in Detroit on the first floor of the new Buhl Building.

Henry Ford had led the charge, but when Guardian opened its doors, it was backed by "Detroit's best known financial, industrial, legal and general business figures, including leaders in practically every field of large activity in the city."[25] Founders, officers, and directors of the firm included:

William Robert Wilson, *president*, former president of Maxwell Motor Corp.

Lawrence D. Buhl, *director*, vice president of Buhl Land Co.

Roy Chapin, *chairman of the board*, chairman of the board of Hudson Motor Car Co.

Howard E. Coffin, *director*, vice president of Hudson Motor Car and president of Transcontinental Air Transport (subsequently TWA); chairman of National Air Transport (United Airlines)

Fred J. Fisher, *director*, president of Fisher Body Corp. and vice president of General Motors

Edsel Ford, *director*, president of Ford Motor Co.

Carlton M. Higbie, *director*, director of Reo Motor Car Co.

Sherwin A. Hill, *director*, director of Graham-Paige Motors

Ernest Kanzler, *director*, vice president of Ford Motor Co. and brother-in-law of Edsel Ford (Kanzler later left Ford Motor to become executive vice president of Guardian Detroit Bank)

Alvin Macauley, *director*, president of Packard Motor Car Co.

Charles S. Mott, *director*, vice president of General Motors; president of Industrial Savings Bank (Flint)

Fred T. Murphy, *director* (later succeeded Chapin as chairman of the board), Simon J. Murphy Co. (owner of the Penobscot Building)

Charles Van Dusen, *director*, president of S. S. Kresge Co.[26]

Hiram H. Walker, *director*, Hiram Walker and Sons, Ltd.

The list of stockholders in the company was even more diverse: former US senator and secretary of the navy Truman Newberry; Walter Briggs, president of Briggs Mfg. Co. (and later, owner of Briggs Field/Tiger Stadium); Senator James Couzens; Standish Backus, president of Burroughs Adding Machine; John C. Lodge, president of Detroit Common Council; and Earl and George M. Holley of Holley Carburetor.[27] Clearly, Guardian represented a mass movement of Detroit business interests seeking independence from out-of-state financial institutions.

One block north of Guardian's office in the Buhl Building sat the aging, six-story Moffat Building, constructed in 1871 on the southwest corner of Fort Street and Griswold. In December 1922, it was announced that the Simon J. Murphy Company had acquired the Moffat Building and planned to construct on the site a large office structure. Murphy Company founder, Simon J. Murphy (1815–1905), was born in Maine, found work in a sawmill at the age of eighteen, and later, established a prosperous lumbering partnership. In 1866, Murphy moved his family to Michigan, eventually growing his lumber firm into one of the state's largest. He built the first Penobscot Building (141 West Fort Street) in 1905 and named it for the Penobscot River in Maine, along the banks of which he played as a child. (The river took its name from the Penawapskewi, a tribe of Native Americans who lived in Maine and Canada.) Upon Murphy's death, one of his twelve children, William H. Murphy (1855–1929), became president of the Murphy Company and subsequently built the twenty-three-story Penobscot Building Annex (144 West Congress), completed in 1913. Both Penobscot buildings were independent structures abutting each other at the rear, with continuous corridors between them on each floor.

The architecture firm of Donaldson and Meier designed the first two Penobscot buildings and the Murphy Company selected them once again for the third iteration.

Interestingly, the Murphy Company sought input from the Building Planning Service Committee of the National Association of Building Owners and Managers before proceeding with any serious plans. These meetings took place December 13 and 14, 1924 (less than four months after the same committee had reviewed final plans for the Buhl Building). The consensus of the committee was that the excellent location of the site suggested a building of at least thirty stories with a commercial bank on the second floor, a trust office on the first floor, and the third floor left unfinished to provide for future bank expansion.[28]

In June 1926, the Murphy Company publicly announced plans for its new, forty-five-story Penobscot Building and indicated construction would begin in the fall. By November, demolition of the Moffat Building was under way and the Murphy Company was running ads promoting the new structure.

145. A promotional advertisement for the Greater Penobscot Building appeared in *Detroit Saturday Night* on October 16, 1926, one of many to appear prior to the start of construction. In this sketch by the architecture firm of Donaldson and Meier, the main building entrance is on Fort Street.

Across Griswold Street from the doomed Moffat Building was the Union Trust Company, with headquarters on the northeast corner of Griswold and Congress. The Union Trust Company (of Detroit) was established in 1891 with two employees; its first president was Detroit seed tycoon Dexter M. Ferry. In 1896, the company constructed a headquarters building at Griswold and Congress, the ten-story Union Trust Building, designed by Donaldson and Meier. In 1907, a number of the trust company's investments went bad, and the formerly prosperous firm suddenly faced a crisis so grim, the company's directors were prepared to place the firm in receivership.[29] It was agreed, however, to allow time for several of the directors, including Henry Russel, to try and save the company. Although Russel was able to raise desperately needed capital, his effort to secure a new president to lead the firm was proving exasperatingly difficult; the position was turned down by nearly twenty individuals.[30]

Finally, the position was accepted by thirty-eight-year-old Frank W. Blair (1870–1950), auditor of Peoples State Bank.[31] Blair was born in Troy Township, where his parents were farmers; his grade school was a log cabin, and he attended Birmingham High School, to which he walked nearly five miles.[32] In 1890, Blair found work at the Birmingham General Store, spending his nights studying to become a registered pharmacist.[33] The store's owners ran a private bank out of the same location and Blair educated himself so thoroughly in banking and accounting that in 1901 he secured a position with the state's auditor-general's office in Lansing. In 1905, Blair was promoted to the state bank examiner's department. In this position, Blair came to the attention of Henry B. Ledyard, a director of Peoples State Bank, who arranged for Blair to be hired as the bank's auditor. Two years later, Ledyard, also a director of Union Trust, suggested Blair for the position of president.

Blair's performance as head of the trust company was phenomenal; he grew the company from around seventy employees in 1908 to over one thousand by 1926.[34] To house these additional employees, the company absorbed all the rental space in its existing building and leased additional space in nearby structures.[35]

Under Michigan law, trust companies were prohibited from engaging in banking; the state legislature, however, had recently relaxed restrictions on banks, permitting them to offer trust services, thereby placing the trust companies at a serious competitive disadvantage. To continue growing, Union Trust viewed expansion into the banking business as essential, so in 1925 they endeavored to convince the state legislature to permit trust companies to offer banking services. When this effort failed, the firm embarked on a strategy to enter the banking business by acquiring or merging with an independent bank.[36]

Given the trust's rapidly growing need for office space and its anticipated expansion into banking, it was clear the existing headquarters building was inadequate, yet the prospect of acquiring a parcel of land in the financial district suitable for a large building was not promising. Persistence and ingenuity, however, paid off; in February 1925 Union Trust acquired four of the five buildings (Huron, Lewis, Burns, and Butler) on the east side of Griswold between Congress and Larned Streets. The fifth building, on the northeast corner of Griswold and Larned, was owned by the Standard Savings and Loan Association (later known as Standard Federal Bank until 2008 when it was acquired by Bank of America), of which Frank Blair was a director.[37] To secure this final property, Union Trust acquired a parcel on the northwest corner of Griswold and Jefferson and swapped it for Standard Savings and Loan's existing building.[38] Union Trust now had the entire block of land it required, and Standard Savings had a desirable property on which to build a new headquarters. The arrangement permitted Standard Savings to remain in its building until the fall of 1927, when their new, eight-story headquarters building—designed by Rowland's good friend Herbert Wenzell of George Mason and Company—was to be completed. Until that time, therefore, Union Trust was precluded from beginning construction, allowing them a lengthy period in which to plan their new building and court banking firms with which to merge.

To oversee construction of the new structure, Union Trust established a building committee comprised of Frank Blair and five company directors. Chairman of the committee was civil engineer Francis C. McMath (1867–1938), founder and president of the highly successful Canadian Bridge Company of Walkerville, Canada. McMath, a member of the Jefferson Avenue Presbyterian Church, had served as chairman of the church building committee and as a church trustee simultaneously with Smith, Hinchman, and Grylls partner Theodore Hinchman.[39] Union Trust might have independently settled on Smith, Hinchman, and Grylls to design their building, but surely the connection between McMath and Hinchman through Jefferson Avenue Presbyterian, and McMath's familiarity with the superb design and construction of the new church, must have influenced the decision.

Early in 1926, Union Trust's building committee approached Smith, Hinchman, and Grylls with their headquarters building project. It was of great importance, they emphasized, that the appearance of the new building convey two qualities with which the

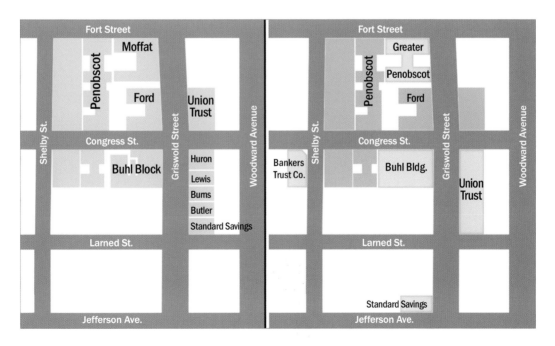

146. Detroit's financial district in 1920 (*left*) and 1930 (*right*) showing locations of the Greater Penobscot, Buhl, Union Trust and Standard Savings Buildings.

company wished to be identified: *strength* and *progress*.[40] To achieve this goal, Union Trust was willing to grant Rowland a great deal of liberty in conceptualizing the design.

Fortunately for Rowland, office building construction in Detroit in 1926 had slowed somewhat from the feverish pace of the previous two years,[41] a trend reflected in the volume of work handled by Smith, Hinchman, and Grylls. This allowed Rowland time to take a much-needed vacation and conduct an unhurried study of the challenges posed by the Union Trust's complex project. He spent most of the summer and early fall traveling through Europe, beginning in England, then Belgium, France, and finally, Spain, where he spent nearly two months.[42]

Before embarking on his trip, Rowland had begun to formulate a remarkable approach to conveying—through architecture—the qualities of strength and progress. In his quest to devise a method of design better suited for tall buildings than the Romanesque features he had used previously, Rowland wondered: What would be the result if *ornament is eliminated*? "Color," Rowland thought, "is an answer to a lack of ornament, but it must be regulated by scientific knowledge and not on past aesthetic and academic values."[43] Previously, Rowland had used geometric systems when placing ornament and decoration

147. The Union Trust (Guardian) Building and Greater Penobscot Building dominate Detroit's financial district.

on the facade of his buildings; why not, Rowland thought, eliminate the ornament and represent the underlying geometric pattern directly, through the use of colored material?

This was an enormous breakthrough, and just the one Rowland needed. He was now ready to leave the past behind and leap into the future.

The use of colorful geometric patterns as an architectural treatment had precedent in the Moorish architecture of Spain, dating from the tenth through fourteenth centuries. Rowland was certainly aware of these structures from his studies, but the idea of traveling to Spain in 1926 to investigate the use of colored tile as an architectural treatment may actually have been suggested by Mary Chase Perry (1867–1961), founder of Pewabic Pottery. In the early 1920s, Perry was

148. Ceiling of a room in the Alhambra Palace of Granada, Spain. (Daniel A. Smith)

hired to produce decorative tile designs for the ceiling in the crypt of the Shrine of the Immaculate Conception being built in Washington, DC. To better understand the style sought by the Shrine, Perry traveled with her architect husband, William Stratton, to study "ceramics applied architecturally"[44] in Spain and Italy. In Spain, Perry and Stratton spent weeks studying in detail the geometric patterns of tile adorning the Alhambra, a palace built by the Moors in Granada.[45] Rowland worked often with Perry as Pewabic tile was frequently employed as an accessory on his buildings. Perry's description of the Alhambra may have aroused Rowland's interest in Moorish geometric tile, or, she may have specifically suggested he consider using Pewabic tile in a similar manner to create an unusual effect.

Rowland might also have reviewed Viollet-le-Duc's description of Moorish architecture: "an offshoot from that Persian architecture which had been modified by the Nestorian Greeks. This last reflection of Greek genius has hardly yet ceased to be brilliant."[46] Viollet-le-Duc noted that both western European and Moorish architects used geometry, but for completely different purposes. The former employed it to design the structure and "geometry had ceased its work when the building began to be ornamented." The Moors, however, constructed simple buildings of bricks and mortar; "geometry had little part except in the decoration." With only a "square and compass" at their disposal, Viollet-le-Duc noted, the Moors "succeeded in creating marvels of architectural beauty . . . presenting to the astonished eye intricate geometrical decorative combinations."[47] In the decoration of their architecture, "proportion was everything"; geometry *was* the ornamentation.[48] This was an important distinction for Rowland, as ancient temples, Romanesque and Gothic cathedrals, and public buildings were designed in compliance with harmonious geometric schemes, but the design of an office building was almost entirely determined by functional and economic considerations, often making a geometric approach unfeasible. If Rowland wished to employ geometric systems of design, then he, like the Moors before him, could bring them to bear on surfaces of the structure, rather than the structure as a whole.

During Rowland's 1926 trip to Spain, of particular interest was the Alcázar of Seville, a Moorish palace similar to the Alhambra in its extensive use of colorful ceramic tiles set in geometric patterns over large expanses of interior walls. Rowland also visited Parque Güell in Barcelona, where he admired the colorful mosaic tile benches, and the unusual Sagrada Família Cathedral, designed by architect Antoni Gaudí (1852–1926).[49] By the time he returned home, Rowland had a firm concept of how he could replace traditional ornamentation with colored material, arranged in geometric patterns, to decorate the Union Trust Building.

But Rowland had in mind an effect that would go beyond Moorish style decoration of surfaces. A 1915 book, *Form and Colour*, by Lisle March Phillipps, deeply influenced Rowland's view of color used architecturally and provided him with the "scientific knowledge" he sought.[50] Phillipps analyzed color—as a feature of art and architecture—from a historical and perceptual context. Classical Greek structures were studies in form; color was used only decoratively, applied to the surface, conforming to and emphasizing architectural forms. Form remains the dominant characteristic of Western architecture

149. Tile pattern on a wall of the Alcázar Palace in Seville, Spain. (Daniel A. Smith)

to the present day, with the important exception of Byzantine architecture, described by Phillipps as "an adaptation by the Greeks of Oriental ideas of color."[51] In certain examples of Byzantine architecture, color, as mosaic tile, is the *primary* architectural feature—"never used decoratively but structurally throughout."[52] Although the Moors employed both color and geometry in a manner that held great promise, it was Phillipps who provided Rowland with the theoretical guidance required to use color as more than surface decoration.

Rowland was confident his plan to use color instead of traditional ornamentation would adequately convey the idea of progress. In order to convey the quality of strength, Rowland faced a significant challenge. The lot for the Union Trust's building measured 80 by 270 feet—particularly long and narrow. "It is no small task to give such high and narrow masses an appearance of stability," said Rowland, "particularly when the upper part of the building, the rental floors, must be well nigh half in window openings."[53] To insure adequate light and air, the maximum office depth limited the width of the building (above the base) to around sixty feet. While there was no risk the forty-story building would topple, when viewed from the end, the structure might appear precarious—quite opposite the effect sought.

Rowland addressed this concern in part by arranging the building in the shape of a dog bone, achieved by placing the elevators—typically located near the center of a building—at each end (the smaller set of elevators near Larned Street were for private use by the trust company). This allowed the ends of the building to be as wide as possible, while the main bulk of office space was located in a narrower, middle section of the building, set back twelve feet from the property line. The setback prevented the offices in this section from being overly deep, with poor light and ventilation. This arrangement also suited the trust company's desire to reserve most of the ground-level floor for an enormous banking lobby, 43 feet wide and 154 feet in length, unencumbered by support piers. Banking lobbies were often located on a building's second floor so the ground floor could be occupied by retail stores paying premium rental rates. The trust company elected to forego retail shops, perhaps believing the presence of retail stores in their headquarters would detract from the dignity of the building or compromise their carefully cultivated public image.

In spite of occupying the full width of its lot, Rowland was concerned that a forty-story building only eighty feet wide would fall short of presenting the rock-solid appearance the trust company sought. Perhaps the way to make the building look rock solid was to give it the appearance of rock. Fascination with the American West during the early twentieth century was fueled in part by admiration for the extraordinary rock formations of Colorado, Arizona, and Utah. Those who had yet to see these immense fortresses and castles of stone were familiar with them through publications, promotional material, and postcards. The Fred Harvey Company, Santa Fe Railroad, and Union Pacific Railroad heavily promoted western travel, often with colorful photos showing dramatic geologic features. The high-quality Photochrom/Phostint

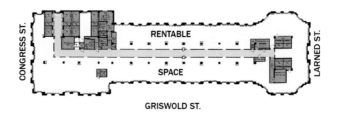

150. In order for the Union Trust Building to expand to the full width of the lot on both ends, the building was given a "dog bone" shape. This allowed for the main section of offices in the narrower middle section to avoid being unduly deep and poorly lit. (Adapted from the original plans)

color postcards distributed by the Harvey Company were printed in Detroit by Detroit Publishing Company, which also sold the postcards through retail stores in Detroit and other major cities.

Among the many postcards from Detroit Publishing (they printed seven million annually) depicting glowing orange rock formations was one in particular that may have caught Rowland's eye: Canyon de Chelly, Arizona. This card carries a colorized photograph of Spider Rock, a tall, slender formation that rises over 750 feet from the canyon floor. Intuitively, adopting the well-known color of these sturdy rock formations made sense, but Rowland would have sought scientific justification. The psychology of color was then (and remains) a field with little scientific certainty, but a number of writers had settled on at least one area of agreement: light blue, the color of the sky, is generally associated with a lack of solidity.[54] By the same logic, orange, the color opposite light blue on the color wheel, is perceived as the most solid. "Orange," said Rowland, "is recognized as a color which gives greatest solidity to wall surfaces at the greatest distance."[55] The brick selected by Rowland to clad most of the building is close in color to the illustrations of rock formations on these postcards. Moreover, the building's side profile is strikingly similar to that of Spider Rock.[56]

Rowland's rough ideas for the building were presented to Blair and the building committee, and they responded: "Go ahead, and let's see how the idea works out."[57] Rowland and his team then prepared detailed sketches using crayon and colored pencil to convey the appearance of the proposed building as clearly as possible. Once again, Blair and his committee expressed confidence in Rowland's judgment: "If you think that that is what we should have and you recommend it, we'll go along with you."[58]

As planning for the Union Trust Building proceeded, an extraordinary situation arose in the offices of Smith, Hinchman, and Grylls, brought about by the actions of Guardian Trust. In November 1926, the Moffat Building was being demolished to make way for the Greater Penobscot Building, and the architecture firm of Donaldson and Meier was taking bids on the new building's construction. The Guardian Trust Company concluded—as had Union Trust—that future growth depended on entering the banking field, and due to Guardian's broad support within Detroit's business community, it was decided to establish a new commercial and savings bank. Confident the

151. Postcard produced in the early 1920s for the Fred Harvey Company by the Detroit Publishing Company shows a colorized photograph of Spider Rock in Arizona's Canyon de Chelly.

new Guardian Bank would be a large enterprise from the beginning (as, in fact, it turned out to be), Guardian Trust set out to locate larger quarters.

The obvious choice was to reserve space in the soon-to-be-built Penobscot Building, plans for which included a modest banking lobby on the second floor, with additional bank offices available on the first and third floors. The amount and quality of space, however, were less than what Guardian sought. The Murphy Company inquired of Donaldson and Meier if the banking lobby could be enlarged to the impressive size—unimpeded by piers—sought by Guardian. Either Donaldson and Meier responded that the banking lobby envisioned was beyond their firm's engineering capabilities, or the cost figure they provided to Murphy was off-putting. Consequently, late in 1926, the Murphy Company approached Smith, Hinchman, and Grylls seeking a second option on the matter.

Providing, within a tall building, an expansive open area, unimpeded by support piers, presented two challenges. First, the floors above the open area had to be supported by large girders or trusses, but not so large that constructing and installing them was impractical. Second, the support piers at each end of the girders or trusses carried a great deal of weight that had to be distributed to nearby frame members and to the foundation. The engineering department at Smith, Hinchman, and Grylls, under the leadership of William Wolfe, was well qualified to meet this exceptional challenge, in part due to having already overcome similar difficulties in designing the banking lobby within the Union Trust Building. They quickly devised a solution that met Guardian's requirements for a banking lobby at a cost acceptable to the Murphy Company, resulting in Donaldson and Meier losing the job to Smith, Hinchman, and Grylls. (Donaldson and Meier were apparently displeased enough by the loss of this job that they relocated their offices in 1928 from the 1905 Penobscot Building, in which they had resided for more than twenty years, to the nearby First National Bank Building.) The designers and engineers of Smith, Hinchman, and Grylls unexpectedly found themselves working up a new plan for the Greater Penobscot Building on a rush basis, and as the calendar turned from 1926 to 1927, the firm was simultaneously planning the state's two tallest buildings.

On February 9, 1927, Guardian Trust went public with their plan to establish the Guardian Detroit Bank. In order to skirt the state's prohibition against trust companies directly engaging in banking, the Guardian Trust Company and Guardian Detroit Bank were subsidiaries of a parent firm, the Guardian Detroit Group. A page one article reporting the announcement in the *Michigan Manufacturer and Financial Record* began with the jubilantly frank comment: "Financial Detroit's long-sought independence of outside banking interests in the financing of the city and state's business and industrial growth was measurably advanced by the announcement of plans . . . which will add greatly to the city's prestige as a financial center."[59] The bank was to operate temporarily from enlarged quarters in the Buhl Building until their permanent home "in the first five floors of the Greater Penobscot Building" was completed.[60] Shortly after, Guardian Group hired forty-one-year-old Robert O. Lord, vice president of Harris Trust and Savings Bank in Chicago, to head up the Guardian Group as its president.[61]

Incredibly, by March 1927, Rowland, Wolfe, and other team members working on the Penobscot Building had completed the design. By mid-May, nearly all plan drawings were complete: more than sixty sheets of architectural drawings, forty structural sheets, and thirty for mechanicals (plus four from Detroit Edison and twenty-one from Michigan Bell). To expedite the planning process, and avoid unduly delaying Smith, Hinchman, and Grylls's work on the Union Trust Building, the Penobscot project was split into two jobs, the first being the Greater Penobscot Building, on which work was commenced immediately (excavation of the foundation proceeded even as plans for the building above were still being drawn). The space within the building to be occupied by Guardian Group was the second job, which was set aside until design work on the Union Trust's building was completed in August. Guardian's offices consumed most of the space on five floors of the building—the second, second mezzanine, and third floors and first and second basements—all of which required more than thirty sheets of architectural drawings, completed by March of the following year.[62]

With the new design for their Penobscot Building in hand, the Murphy Company restarted its marketing campaign in March 1927, running ads showing a rough sketch of the Smith, Hinchman, and Grylls design for the structure in place of the Donaldson and Meier version. Then on April 2, the company released to the press a detailed sketch of the proposed building and explained the redesign had been carried out to accommodate the Guardian Detroit Bank.

Having remained silent while developments with Guardian unfolded, on April 9, 1927, Union Trust announced, to great fanfare, plans for its new, forty-story headquarters building. A rough sketch of the proposed structure accompanied numerous articles in national journals and local papers, including the *Detroit News*, which referred to it as "a cathedral devoted to finance"—later shortened to "cathedral of finance," a moniker that stuck.[63] Although the description of the building mentioned a bank lobby, Union Trust provided no explanation as to why. The following week, however, Frank Blair revealed publicly Union Trust's intention to enter the banking field, "either by the organization or the acquisition of a bank."[64]

Later the same month, Blair created a stir nationally when he and others from Union Trust traveled by airplane to the American Bankers' Association convention in Hot Springs, Arkansas. "We made the trip from Detroit to Hot Springs, 850 miles," Blair pointed out, "in seven hours and five minutes. The fastest train service is twenty-seven hours and fifty minutes."[65] Having foreseen that aviation would shrink the globe and become

152. An early design sketch for the Greater Penobscot Building that appeared in an advertisement by the Murphy Company in the March 12, 1927, issue of *Michigan Manufacturer and Financial Record*.

a huge industry in the process, Blair became actively involved in promoting the industry; he headed a number of aviation organizations and served on the boards of Detroit-based aircraft manufacturing firms.[66] Just over a month after the Hot Springs trip, Blair's views on the future of aviation were boosted by the successful nonstop transatlantic flight of another native Detroiter, Charles Lindbergh. Later that year, Union Trust became the first financial institution in the nation to establish an aviation department and acquire aircraft used in conducting business.[67]

That summer, Blair vacationed in Europe with Henry H. Sanger, vice president of the National Bank of Commerce, and Henry Russel, a director for both Union Trust and National Bank of Commerce.[68] The three fell into a discussion of merging their two companies and, based on the clear advantages of doing so, committed to promoting the idea of a merger within their organizations.[69] Within a year, the two firms were joined through a holding company (Union Commerce Corporation), which acquired the stock of both firms.[70] Union Trust was now in the banking business.[71]

Construction work on the Greater Penobscot Building's foundation began in the spring of 1927. Due to the great weight carried by the piers supporting girders above Guardian Group's banking lobby, the building's foundation was planned to rest upon hardpan at about 120 feet below the surface and consist of concrete piers, six to nine feet in diameter.[72] Excavation for the first pier proceeded to hardpan without incident and the base of the shaft was being widened to make room for the bell-shaped footer when, suddenly, water rushed into the shaft, filling it to a depth of one hundred feet within twelve hours. Smith, Hinchman, and Grylls chief engineer William Wolfe surmised that cracks in the hardpan had allowed the water to enter and realized the hardpan layer was too unstable to support the foundation; the piers would have to be sunk to bedrock, fifteen feet farther down. As for the inrushing water, continually pumping it from the excavation might cause the ground to settle beneath nearby buildings, so it was not possible to excavate open wells as planned. Instead, caissons would be built, sealed airtight, and pumps used to increase the air pressure within sufficiently to hold back the water. Workers would have to enter the caisson through an airlock bolted to its top.

Even with high air pressure, water still seeped into the excavation, raising concern that the high sulfur content of the water might in time deteriorate the concrete. The problem was finally solved by adapting a technique used in constructing dams. Small holes were bored down into the bedrock layer until water was encountered; concrete was then pumped in under pressure, displacing the water and filling crevices within the bedrock. Repeating this procedure throughout the site eliminated much of the water seepage and permitted lower air pressure to be employed within the caissons.[73]

Working below ground was, in fact, more dangerous than working in the steel high above. On May 3, George Brill was repairing one of the air pumps inside the caisson when he smelled hydrogen sulfide gas. He yelled for help and then passed out, falling from his perch into water that had begun to rise in the caisson's bottom. Brill's coworker, Victor Jorgensen, heard the cry for help and immediately descended the caisson to offer assistance. Jorgensen, however, was himself overcome by gas and ended up in the water with Brill. Due to the gas and depth of water, efforts by other workers, police, and fire squads to rescue the two men were unsuccessful.[74]

The air pressure used in the caissons made workers susceptible to decompression sickness, or "the bends" as it is commonly called. As a precaution, a treatment facility was maintained on site by the contractor, and those who went through decompression were released wearing badges bearing instructions to return the worker to the job site should they become incapacitated.[75]

The lessons learned on Penobscot's foundation were leveraged to good advantage on the Union Trust Building. One by one, during the spring of 1927, four of the five buildings on the trust company's site fell to the wrecker's ball and, even though the Standard Savings Building remained on the south end of the site, construction work began. (The Standard Savings Building remained occupied; its shallow foundation was shored up and work on the new Union Trust Building was carried out beneath it.) First, borings were made to bedrock and the process employed on Penobscot's foundation of displacing water with concrete was repeated throughout the site.

What followed was an unusual sequence devised by Wolfe to reduce cost and more quickly complete the building. Rather than first excavating the entire site to the level of the lowest basement, shoring up the earthen walls surrounding the hole, and then digging the caissons to bedrock, Wolfe directed instead that the caissons be excavated first. With the foundation in place, the building's structural steel frame was begun and continued upward. Simultaneously, the basement walls were constructed by digging a trench around the site, placing forms, and pouring concrete. Once these walls were in place, the remainder of the basement was excavated, and the basement's structural steel and concrete floor installed. The second and third basements were completed in like manner. By the time the third basement was excavated, the steel work above had been completed to the thirty-fourth floor—Wolfe's method saved considerable expense and compressed the amount of time required to complete the building.[76]

The directors of both Union Trust and Guardian Group well understood the potential advertising value inherent in the appearance of their respective banking lobbies, and the probable "effect upon the mind of the average depositor because of the impression it gives of solidity and strength."[77] Responsibility for maximizing that effect fell to Rowland and Wolfe; together, the two men faced the formidable challenge of designing the great banking lobbies. It might appear that Wolfe's role was to engineer a large space within which Rowland applied decoration, but the reality was much different. Rowland and Wolfe worked closely together from the beginning, evaluating the feasibility and cost of many

153. The Union Trust (Guardian) Building on the southeast corner of Griswold and Congress Streets.

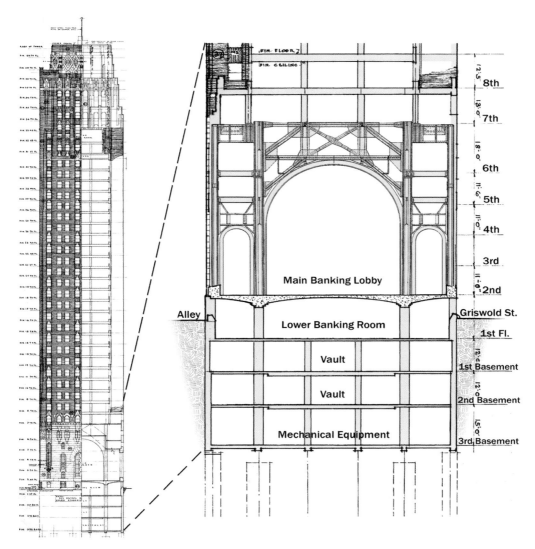

154. Elevation and cross section of the Union Trust Building. The illustration at right shows the unusual truss work required to support the floors above the main banking lobby and how the slab floor of the banking lobby forms the arched ceiling of the lower banking room. (Adapted from the original Smith, Hinchman, and Grylls building plans, August 15, 1927)

options, eventually settling upon a design achievable through existing or foreseeable engineering at a cost acceptable to the customer.

In some cases, Wolfe devised a cost-effective means to achieve a certain effect sought by Rowland. For example, the main banking lobby in the Union Trust's building is forty-three feet wide, and directly below is a slightly wider lower banking room (which contained the savings and bond departments). Wolfe devised a floor for the main banking lobby, "of rather unusual construction," which also served as the arched ceiling of the lower banking room.[78] The floor is comprised of a concrete slab, fifty-six inches thick at the outer end and only nine inches in the center. The slab covers the full forty-seven-foot width of the lower banking room, eliminating the need for supporting piers; aside from the steel reinforcement embedded within the slab, it required no beams. Rowland, having obtained the enormous arched ceiling he sought, had it painted silver. Concealed lighting fixtures reflected light across the ceiling into the room, making the space appear larger and more open.[79]

The stepped tile designs of the lobbies also required close collaboration between Rowland and Wolfe. The colored ceramic tiles are not merely decoration applied to an interior finished surface as would be the case with paneling or plaster, but rather are mounted directly on the concrete structural frame of the building. This approach assured the most stable and permanent tile installation, but required great precision in erecting the concrete forms. The complex step shapes formed by the tiles had to be accurately constructed—in reverse—in wooden forms that held the concrete in place while it set around the steel frame of the building.

In order to eliminate supporting piers within the Union Trust Building's forty-three-foot-wide bank lobby, the twenty-six floors above are supported by large trusses. According to the building's steel contractor, "this presented many difficult engineering

155. The lower banking room with its arched silver ceiling composed of structural concrete; the ceiling is actually the floor of the main banking lobby above. (Smith, Hinchman, and Grylls and SmithGroupJJR)

problems to the architects."[80] The eight trusses above the banking lobby are fourteen feet high in the center, twenty-seven feet at each end, and span just over forty-seven feet between supporting piers. The weight of each ranged from fifty-five to seventy tons—at the time, the heaviest of that type erected in Detroit.[81] Due to the enormous weight supported, Wolfe was concerned about the stress on rivets binding together the individual sections of steel that composed the trusses. His solution was to drive the rivets in three stages as the building went up, using only as many as required to support the weight of the incomplete building. The last group of rivets was driven in only after the steel work was complete and most of the concrete poured. With much of the weight of the building already in place, any deformation of the steel frame had already occurred, eliminating stress on rivets placed in the last group.[82]

By January 1928, the steel skeletons of both the Greater Penobscot Building and Union Trust Building were rising rapidly into Detroit's frigid winter sky. A team of roughly two hundred well-paid and highly skilled steel workers labored on Penobscot's steel frame. More than seventy-five of these men were Mohawk Indians from around Quebec City who had learned the trade building the Quebec Bridge.[83] Despite increased building heights, the safety of steel work had improved over the early days of steel frame buildings. The law

156. Entrance to the lower banking lobby of the Union Trust Building (facing out toward the main lobby).

157. The Union Trust Building under construction, looking south from the main lobby into the banking lobby. Over the banking room the sixth floor is visible, through which pass the large girders supporting the upper floors. At the top of the photo are two temporary wooden frames spanning the width of the room (a third rests upright, leaning on the edge of the banking room floor). Around these frames was constructed a wooden falsework, or form, which would support the concrete ceiling of the main lobby until it hardened. To the left is the elevator alcove, and it can be seen that the stepped shapes of its ceiling were cast in the concrete frame of the building; the colored tile was subsequently applied directly to the frame. (Smith, Hinchman, and Grylls and SmithGroupJJR)

required wooden plank floors beneath the area in which work was conducted, making most falls survivable.

A greater peril, perhaps, than falling workers was falling steel. During construction of Penobscot, a two-ton steel bracket fell from the twenty-first floor and plummeted toward foreman Sam Pentecost working below. It passed within a foot of Pentecost—who "could feel the wind it made as it went by"[84]—before slicing through three wood plank decks and a steel concrete form, coming to rest on the twelfth floor.

In February 1928, consolidation fever within Detroit's banking community spread further with the merger of the city's first and third largest banks. (The two merged banks were the Peoples Savings Bank, headquartered in the State Savings Bank building at Fort and Shelby streets [1900, by McKim, Mead, and White], and the Wayne County and Home Savings Bank, with headquarters at Michigan Avenue and Griswold [1915, Donaldson

158. The ceiling of the main lobby as it appears from within the fourth floor. The ceiling is comprised of a concrete shell—seen here—to which the multicolored ceramic tiles were directly attached.

and Meier, demolished].) The $290 million in financial resources of the new institution, Peoples Wayne County Bank, dwarfed Guardian Detroit Bank's $39 million, and even the $54 million in resources of Union Trust's National Bank of Commerce. The merger gave Peoples a whopping ninety-six branches, the most of any bank in any city of the country.

On March 27, 1928, Greater Penobscot received its final load of steel and, during a dedication ceremony on April 2, the final rivet was driven by William Murphy. Champagne was illegal due to Prohibition, so the structure was christened with a bottle of ginger ale swung from a rope and smashed on the building's frame.[85] Reporter Loren Baker, covering the event for the *Detroiter*, rather astutely noted that the Greater Penobscot Building was "the tallest non-tower office building in the world"[86]—the three tallest buildings achieved their height by means of a slender tower set upon a larger main structure: Woolworth Building (1913), Metropolitan Tower (1909), and Singer Building (1908), all in New York City.

Florence Davies, art critic for the *Detroit News*, began her Sunday, July 8, 1928, column writing: "Wait and see, which is a shorter way of reminding us that children and fools should not see unfinished business. The unfinished business in Detroit which is arousing a good deal of interest just now is the new building of the Union Trust Company."[87] The lengthy column admonished those—particularly in Detroit's art community—who were disparaging the half-finished Union Trust Building. Davies had a sound understanding of architecture and anticipated the Union Trust Building, with its "vigorous and daring use of color," was destined to make "a definite contribution to modern American architecture."[88]

Davies's unusual article was not intended as a defense of Rowland—he hadn't the slightest concern for naysayers—but as a defense of progress in the arts. "Wise ones shake their heads. This is the verdict of the timid. It is always the rule for people to turn thumbs down on things which are new and unaccustomed." Davies, aware that an unfavorable opinion of the building might discourage bold experimentation in the future, wrote: "Wait till this pile of tangerine brick and many-hued terra cotta has taken its place in the vista of the street; wait till the composition is completed and the pattern may be seen as a whole, and then wait for that soft envelopment of light which Detroit's changing atmosphere gives and then let's hear your verdict."

The Greater Penobscot Building opened on October 22, 1928, though the interior work on

159. This photo of the Union Trust Building appeared in the *Detroit News* on July 8, 1928, the same day as Florence Davies's column "Wait and See"—the exterior was less than half complete. Ringing the structure about halfway up is a somewhat rickety-looking catwalk on which bricklayers labor to add the building's skin. The unfinished Penobscot Building is visible along the right. (*Detroit News* collection, Walter P. Reuther Library, Archives of Labor and Urban Affairs, Wayne State University)

the upper floors and banking area was still incomplete; more than half the space in the building was leased.[89] On January 14, 1929, the Guardian Group opened their offices in the new building and garnered greater publicity than that of the building's opening, perhaps due to Guardian Group's importance to the business and financial community of Detroit.

In contrast to the modest publicity that greeted Penobscot's opening, the Union Trust Building's opening on April 2, 1928, was heralded by a monsoon of coverage. The *Detroit News* of Sunday, March 31, ran a special sixteen-page section devoted to the new building, which included a two-thousand-word, page-three article, "New Note in Architecture

Struck," by Wirt Rowland. The Sunday *Detroit Free Press* had an eight-page "Union Trust Building Supplement," almost entirely comprised of photos. The *Michigan Manufacturer and Financial Record* published a supplement with numerous color plates and nearly eighty pages devoted to the structure. A page-four article in the April 1 *Wall Street Journal* described the "magnificent 40-story building" to be occupied by Union Trust. The Clinton, Michigan, paper ran an article headlined "Clinton Man Designed Union Trust Building; Recognized in Detroit as Most Competent Designer and Among Foremost in Country."

There were several references in the *Detroit News* and *Michigan Manufacturer and Financial Record*

160.

to the building as a "cathedral of finance" and even Rowland in his *Detroit News* article, in describing the building's shape, wrote that the "arrangement of mass is disposed to resemble almost the form of a huge cathedral, with the high tower at the north end, the nave, with its clerestory and aisles stretching toward the south and terminated by the apse, or small octagonal tower." Others have suggested the interior lobbies of the building present the appearance of a cathedral. However much or little the building may resemble a cathedral, Rowland would not have intended for there to be a meaningful resemblance, as commerce and worship are entirely distinct functions. Rowland took seriously the idea of religious worship and believed it improper that a building intended for such purposes employ, for example, attention-grabbing signs or commercial-type lighting. Likewise, it was disingenuous to invoke religious themes on a commercial building, not to mention, a lazy approach to design.

For its opening on Tuesday, April 2, Union Trust invited the public to visit and explore the building. Long-term employees of the company were given special training and posted on each floor as guides for visitors.[90] *Forty Stories from Bedrock*, a forty-four-page souvenir booklet containing a wealth of information on the new structure, was presented to each visitor. The open house began at 10:00 a.m. and by 1:00 p.m., so many were gathered outside that the revolving doors were folded, allowing visitors to stream unimpeded into the lobby. The event was planned to conclude at 3:00 p.m., but the crush of visitors was so great, the doors remained open until well into the evening. By day's end, more than thirty thousand had passed through the building.[91]

Union Trust's invited guests, including many from out of town, attended a luncheon at the Detroit Club and dinner banquet at the Book-Cadillac Hotel. At seven thirty in the evening, radio station WJR hosted a talk by Wirt Rowland on "Color in Architecture" and a general discussion of the ideas exemplified by the new building.

In the months following, an unusually large number of in-depth articles on the building appeared in industry journals. Most of the architectural journals were based in New York City and tended to lavish attention on new buildings within their city. The widespread positive coverage accorded the Union Trust Building was unusual for a building outside of New York. The November 1929 issue of *American Architect* included an eight-page photo spread, "Color Dominant in Design of the Union Trust Building." *Buildings and Building Management* filled eleven pages, describing the new structure as "a notable example of the latest architectural style and mode. It represents, very consistently and pleasingly, the modernistic trend." "The first impression made upon the critical observer seems to be due to the novelty and originality of the decorative scheme adopted."[92] The *Metal Arts* devoted two articles to the building in its series, "Drafting for Metal Work," and explained in detail how the architects devised a new method of decoration. "These are especially good examples of modern design because the designs are developed in accordance with the chosen method of working the material." "Building up metal work in sheets welded together in layers adds a whole new range of possibilities to the architect's means of expression."[93] *Through the Ages*, the publication of the National Association of Marble Dealers, carried an eleven-page feature article and wrote of the building: "it *is* different, but also it is refreshingly original—a building that belongs to today."[94]

Periodicals outside the architecture and construction field were even more effusive in their praise of the building. In an article headlined "financial institutions begin to recognize the business value of a friendly, attractive atmosphere," *Bankers' Magazine* wrote: "Many examples might be given of the liberty which the modern school has taken. . . . Outstanding among such, of course, is the Union Trust Building in Detroit, upon which widespread attention has been focused since its completion several months ago."[95]

An enthusiastic and exceptionally informative article on the building was penned for the June 20, 1929, issue of the *Christian Science Monitor* by Dorothea Kahn. "American banks," the article began, "seemed for a long time the appointed guardians of Greek architecture no less than of their depositors' cash show signs of seeking modern expression. Three old established banking firms in Detroit have recently expanded into new quarters; and in accordance with the new trend not one hint of the Corinthian or the Ionic can be found in any nook or corner of any of them. The most astonishing of the three is the Union Trust Company's skyscraper,

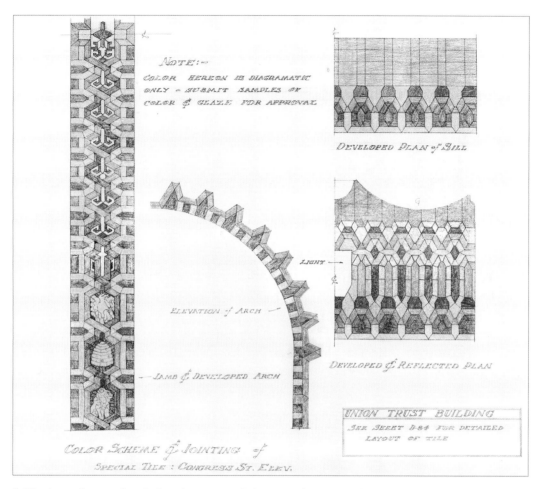

NOTE:—
COLOR HEREON IS DIAGRAMATIC
ONLY — SUBMIT SAMPLES OF
COLOR & GLAZE FOR APPROVAL

DEVELOPED PLAN of SILL

ELEVATION of ARCH

LIGHT

JAMB & DEVELOPED ARCH

DEVELOPED & REFLECTED PLAN

COLOR SCHEME & JOINTING of

SPECIAL TILE : CONGRESS ST. ELEV.

UNION TRUST BUILDING
SEE SHEET D-84 FOR DETAILED
LAYOUT OF TILE

161. One of many detail plan sheets provided to Pewabic Pottery by Rowland's team. These sheets were produced by making blueprint copies of original architectural drawings and then filling in sections with crayon or colored pencil. (Drawing: Smith, Hinchman, and Grylls and SmithGroupJJR, from the collection of Pewabic Pottery)

now receiving finishing touches. It is as gay as a May morning, yet with a basis of reasonableness and strength. Inside and out it has no inhibitions save the dictates of material and time."[96] (In addition to the Union Trust Building housing the National Bank of Commerce, Kahn was referring to the Guardian Bank of Detroit in the Greater Penobscot Building and the First National Bank in the Fisher Building.) In the lobby of the Union Trust Company's skyscraper, "there gleams a glass mosaic design," Kahn continued, "with the motto of the institution glittering in the brave colors of the ceramic entrance. Below it play tiny red, blue and white lights, a device intended to show the progress of the elevators in their up and down course, but actually furnishing a new element of decoration, namely, color in motion." (Elevator position indicator boards had been in use prior to 1929; Kahn seems here to be making a point about its function and appearance within the specific context of this building.)

Rowland, wrote Kahn, "had decidedly interesting reasons for his departure from traditions in this edifice. He feels it is entirely an outgrowth of the conditions he was given. The commission came from a man [Frank Blair] who himself departed from the idea of conservatism in banking and stood for the new trend of making the bank imply service for all, a banker who uses an airplane to go about his business in other cities." "Mr. Rowland has the faculty of looking at the edifice with detachment. 'It shrieks color,' he says. He feels that was necessary to make 'a bite on the public consciousness.' There has been too much fear of criticism about such things. If to some the building seems ultra modern, to its designer it is 'about 20 years behind the times.'"[97]

One of the noteworthy stories to come to light from Kahn's article concerned the mind set of those involved in the building's design. "Once the plans began to evolve, [Rowland] said, the men who worked with him to carry them out caught the enthusiasm engendered by the idea. Some of the vivacity of the building may be explained by this zest that went into its making."[98] Mary Chase Perry—who worked with many of Detroit's architects—wrote of the team: "The local architects, with Wirt Rowland as chief, had formulated every detail with such meticulous care."[99] These comments bring to mind Wilford Conrow's 1924 *New York Times* article on dynamic symmetry's potential application to art and architecture. Conrow suggested the conditions under which a groundbreaking architectural project could succeed: "it is necessary that there be throughout complete and understanding co-operation, inspired by intense enthusiasm among all employed and working under the direction of the master mind in carrying out some given project to completion."

This enthusiasm, pride, and attention to detail were subsequently conveyed to those working on the building, in part through a cash incentive program, but primarily by communicating that superb workmanship was vital to the successful completion of the building. Union Trust offered an award of $100 to one outstanding workman in each of the major trades. The workman's group foreman also received a $100 award. Every worker employed on the building for at least one week received a bronze button inscribed with an image of the building and the words, "Workman Union Trust Company Building, 1927–1928." There were concerns the buttons might be mocked, but they were, in fact, highly prized.

162. Every worker employed on the Union Trust Building for at least one week received a bronze lapel button.

Of the program, the *American Architect* wrote: "The $100 award and the honors which are attached to it have so stimulated the interest of the workmen on this job that several sub-contractors report that assignment of a workman to this building is considered as something of an award of merit."[100] It was common for a plaque naming the architect and officials of the company owning the building to be mounted in the lobby of a structure. The Union Trust Building, however, has a bronze plaque (adjacent to the Griswold entrance) that bears the names of the outstanding workers who received awards.

163. The plaster mold crafted by Pewabic Pottery to fit tiles for the half dome of the Union Trust Building's Griswold Street entrance is seen here being constructed. The object hanging in the center is a scribe used to etch lines in the surface and insure the mold is perfectly round. (From the collection of Pewabic Pottery)

A similarly enthusiastic and inventive approach was taken by vendors who faced challenges in manufacturing the unusual decorative elements for the building. Detroit's Pewabic Pottery under the direction of its founder, Mary Chase Perry, manufactured ceramic tiles for the building, including the half dome over the Griswold Street entrance, containing the figure of an aviator atop the globe. To produce this work of art, a huge plaster mold was built; clay was pressed onto its surface and cut into sizes small enough to fire. As the completed plaster mold was too large to fit within Pewabic's building, it was erected on their front yard.[101] (Pewabic continues to produce tiles for the building, providing replacements for the occasional damaged tile.)

164. The ceramic tile installation produced by Pewabic Pottery for the Union Trust Building's Griswold Street entrance is 21 feet in width. The central figure is an aviator with arms outstretched above the earth. Along the lower section are three emblems illustrating the commercial activities of industry, agriculture, and transportation.

One problem overcome by Pewabic was development of an orange glaze for the accent tiles used on the upper floors of the building. Certain colors had a tendency to fade when fired at the extremely high temperatures required to manufacture tiles that could withstand Detroit's freeze and thaw cycles. Six months of experimentation produced a solution—and a new glaze of interest to artists. "This is exactly the way in which commerce and art should serve each other," said Perry. "The orange glaze which was needed for this commercial use turns out to be a very definite contribution to art."[102]

The widespread use of Monel metal throughout the building for gates, elevator doors, teller wickets, stair rails, furniture, and even inkwells was a radical departure from the standard decorative materials of the day: brass and bronze. A. E. Hanson wrote in *Michigan Manufacturer and Financial Record*: "The Union Trust Company building represents a determined effort to break away from traditional practice not only in the outer aspect of the building but also in the design of the ornamental metal work."[103]

The original plans called for stainless steel, its "white" color better suited to the building's polychromatic interior than that of brass. In addition to providing prices for stainless steel, metalwork suppliers were asked to quote the cost of Monel metal, Benedict-Nickel, and aluminum 17-s. While bids were prepared, Rowland experimented with the four materials to determine maintenance requirements and workability. Benedict-Nickel was found to require nearly continuous attention to retain its color; aluminum was determined to have an unsatisfactory surface, though the metal was easily worked. Vendor quotes subsequently revealed stainless steel was much higher in cost than Monel metal, so Monel was selected.[104]

Metals used for ornamental architectural applications at the time were cast, twisted, cut on a lathe or hammered into the proper shape. It was soon discovered that Monel metal was brittle and could not be worked using these traditional methods. As a consequence, the metalwork had to be built up by welding together multiple layers—sheets or bars—a process that, fortuitously, could be accomplished without leaving visible joints.[105] The decorative aspect of the metalwork, aside from its shape, consisted of lines inscribed into the surface with a router. To add contrast to the Monel surfaces, some were finished in satin, others in a polished luster.[106] Rowland had intended to further enhance the metalwork by enameling sections of it in the colors used within the lobby, but the cost proved prohibitive.[107]

Another notable feature requiring close coordination between Rowland and vendors was the design of the elevator doors. The outer doors of the public elevators in the building's lobby are constructed of highly polished Monel metal; inset within the metal are sections of orange, blue, and black Favrile (Tiffany) glass. In conceiving this scheme, Rowland's intention was not merely to add color to the broad expanse of metallic elevator doors, but to create a colorful light show within the glass shapes. The *Metal Arts* article describes the effect well: "glowing in deep tones in some places and flashing jewel-like elsewhere as the angle of the light changes." "The glass is of the kind used in leaded glass windows, and its changing appearance under the play of light is due to the fact that the door is hollow and the polished inner surface of the sheet of Monel metal that forms the side next to the elevator car reflects the light through the glass in places."[108]

Importantly, the effect was made possible by Rowland having developed the design based on the capabilities of the machining equipment used to manufacture the doors. It was "one of the first practical applications of the principle of designing in accordance with modern machine methods instead of either adhering to old-time methods of craftsmanship or of forcing machines to serve in the execution of designs of hand-work character, which is a thing machines cannot do well."[109] To create openings in the door for the glass inserts, a die was used to punch through the metal—a process much closer to methods of automobile manufacturing than tradi-

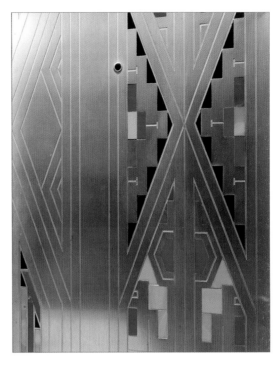

165. The elevator doors of the Union Trust Building are of Monel metal, inscribed with designs routed by machine. Colored glass inserts are mounted within die-cut holes. Originally the glass was clear, resulting in a three-dimensional effect (much like the clear glass tiles currently popular for kitchen backsplashes), but over the years, the surface lost its sheen and became opaque.

tional architectural metalwork. (The surface of the glass shapes embedded in the elevator doors has, over time, become opaque and the effect described has been lost. Polishing the surface of the glass would likely restore the feature to its original condition.)

The Union Trust Building was groundbreaking, not just in appearance and engineering, but in the application of technology to operating systems. The first sixteen floors and two basements were air-conditioned, making it the first air-conditioned skyscraper in the world.[110] A 1929 article in the *Chicago Daily Tribune*, headlined "Detroit Grows Air Minded in Its Building," notified its readers of Detroit's leadership in the application of this coveted technology.[111] The reporter, perhaps probing for a downside to the system, asked building manager Edward Dow whether a tenant dissatisfied with the mandated temperature of 70 degrees might quit his office for quarters in another building. Dow responded, "Here's where Old Man Humidity figures in the situation. When Old Man Humidity steps on the stage, no matter what the temperature is, the audience begins to wilt.

Air conditioning knocks Old Man Humidity out of the picture. And with the old gentleman gone the office which has an even temperature, is going to be a comfortable place to work in."[112]

The circulation system for the air-conditioned floors is entirely contained within the building and out of sight. (The equipment now installed on the roof of the building was a later addition to provide air-conditioning for floors not originally so equipped.) Refrigeration units are located in the third sub-basement and the blowers are on the sixth floor, occupying the otherwise unusable space between the large girders above the banking lobby. Fresh air is brought into the system through large intakes on the building's Griswold Street side; these openings are hidden behind decorative screens.

Elevator systems in the building received a large dose of new technology. Although each car was manually controlled by an employee operator (as was standard at the time), electronics were used to automatically stop the elevator level with the floor. A new device, its first installation being the Union Trust Building, automatically opened the elevator and building doors when the car stopped, a task previously handled by the operator. One of the nonpublic elevators used by banking staff was equipped with a "special dual control," which permitted push-button operation at reduced speed by any staff member, or at full speed when an operator was aboard—essentially (save for the speed restriction) the automatic elevator system in use today.[113]

Not all elevator technology was deployed as planned. Elevator functions were automated with an eye toward eventually eliminating employee elevator operators. It was intended that operators would be replaced by a voice control system whereby "passengers may call their floor stops clearly and loudly." The system was to use a microphone, with the elevator functioning as "a robot."[114] Presumably, the push-button system was found to be more practical.

Another building feature not implemented as planned was a system for opening and closing the gate separating the main banking lobby from the public lobby. As originally envisioned by Rowland, the large Monel metal screen between the two lobbies was to be movable, allowing it to be raised and lowered. (Rowland described it as a "portcullis.") Problems arose in adapting the safety equipment to the construction of the screen, and the plan had to be abandoned. Closing off of the bank was accomplished instead by means of a collapsible horizontal screen.[115]

7

TWO KINGS OF GRISWOLD STREET

All great music is based . . . [on] some basic figure binding the song together. . . .
The principle is found in design everywhere.

—Thomas Whitney Surette, "Music," 1923

"The building shrieks color," and the color of the Union Trust was achieved by the use of colored materials rather than by applying the color to the building's surface (as with paint). In the lobby, for example, Rowland wished to have a band of black along the base of the wall with a deep blood red above, which he accomplished by using Belgian black stone and red Numidian marble (contrary to legend, Rowland did not travel to Africa to secure the marble from a closed mine).[1] Bands of color on the lower stories of the building's exterior are achieved by means of materials possessing the colors desired: Somes Sound granite (light gray), Montrose granite (rose), Mankato stone (cream), terra-cotta (green, white, and gold), and brick (orange and red). "The effect of light, texture of material and the element of form," wrote Rowland, "make up the vehicle through which color carries its impression. Every material has inherent

166. The colors of the Union Trust (Guardian) Building come from the natural gray, rose, and cream tones of different types of granite, and the man-made colors of brick and terra-cotta.

201

beauty of color."[2] Most significantly, the orange color sought for most of the building's exterior comes from brick, which offered other advantages as well. It was low in cost; the savings could be expended elsewhere on the building's design, and it is easily formed into sharp corners, giving Rowland a great deal of freedom in shaping the brick-clad surfaces of the building.

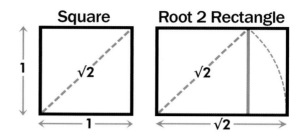

167. The diagonal of a square (which is equal to $\sqrt{2}$) is used to create a "root two rectangle" by rotating it down to form the base of the new figure. A root two rectangle exhibits dynamic symmetry.

Aside from color, the most important design feature Rowland employed was a thematic element to, as Thomas Surette said, "bind the whole together."[3] Of the relationship between musical compositions and architecture, Rowland wrote: "those great compositions, the symphonies, are built up from and around themes which may not be as complete as the ordinary tune. They are themes, in themselves, incomplete, but capable of variation and development into a completely rounded composition with all its decoration by other less important parts. Just so is the design of a building which may become a complete entity by a consistency of its parts with a main motive and its stylistic direction."[4]

Rowland's primary theme for the Union Trust Building is derived from two geometric figures, unified through the principles of dynamic symmetry. It will be recalled that dynamically symmetrical rectangles are derived from the square. A square with sides equal to one has a diagonal equal to the square root of two. The diagonal may be rotated to form the long side of a new rectangle having one side equal to one and a second side equal to the $\sqrt{2}$: a "root two rectangle."

Jay Hambidge illustrates the use of root two rectangles and squares in the design of a Greek fifth century BC bronze oinochoe. The entire jug is contained within a root two rectangle. A square extends from the top of the rectangle to the midpoint (established by diagonals drawn from the corners of the rectangle). The remainder of the space is divided up into squares and smaller root two rectangles. Hambidge wrote: "this design may be understood as a theme in root-two and square."[5]

One method of dividing space using the principles of dynamic symmetry is to join root rectangles and squares in a manner similar to that employed in designing the bronze oinochoe. Any figure formed by joining dynamically symmetrical figures will be dynamically symmetrical. This is the method Rowland used to form one of the two geometrical figures that compose the Union Trust Building's unifying theme.

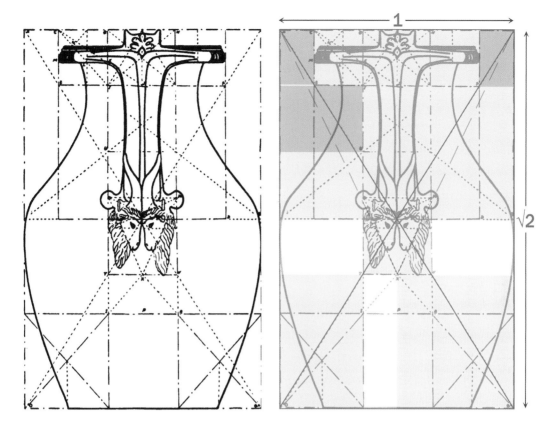

168. An illustration of a Greek fifth century BC bronze oinochoe from *Dynamic Symmetry and the Greek Vase*, by Jay Hambidge, page 52 (*left*). Hambidge described the jug as "a theme in root-two and square." A number of root two rectangles are shaded in green and squares in blue (*right*). It may be seen that the proportion of height to width of the jug is equal to that of a root two rectangle; the space within is divisible by combinations of root two rectangles and squares. The size and location of each feature of the jug are determined by these two shapes. (Shading by Michael G. Smith)

Rowland's geometrical design is formed by first joining a root two rectangle and square. A copy of this figure is superimposed on the original and rotated 45 degrees. This establishes the basic geometric form—45-degree isosceles triangles—from which Rowland develops more complex designs. The geometry may be developed further by

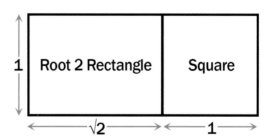

169. A root two rectangle and square joined together form a dynamically symmetrical figure.

adding two additional copies of the original figure to form an eight-sided shape.

It so happens that the eight-sided shape can be represented by a figure less cumbersome to draw: two squares, equal in size, one of which is rotated corner up. Triangles drawn from the base of one square to the corner of the second complete the figure, making it effectively identical to the original eight-sided shape.

Rowland's second geometrical shape is based on the root three rectangle. This rectangle is formed from a root two rectangle in the same manner as the root two rectangle is formed from the square, by taking the diagonal of a root two rectangle (which is equal to the square root of three) and rotating it to become the long side of a new rectangle.

Two root three rectangles super-imposed, with one offset from the other by 60 degrees, form a figure that contains two equilateral triangles with opposed bases. (Adding a third root three rectangle offset by 60 degrees results in a six-sided figure.) Bisecting an equilateral triangle creates two right triangles.

The application of both the 45-degree and 60-degree geometric figures may

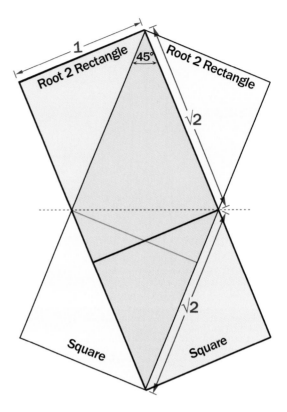

170. Superimposing a figure comprised of a root two rectangle and square over a second, rotating the second by 45° so the two meet at their corners, forms a pair of opposed 45° isosceles triangles (in the area where the two figures overlap).

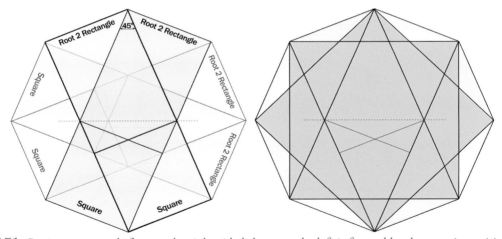

171. Root two rectangle figures: the eight-sided shape on the left is formed by the superimposition of four figures (individually comprised of a root two rectangle plus square), each rotated 45° from the previous. The figure on the right (in orange) is comprised of two squares, one rotated corner up. It is more easily drawn and can be employed in place of the left-hand figure. Many of Rowland's designs are based on this figure.

be seen in Rowland's complex design for the east wall of the Union Trust Building's main lobby. The main entrance to the building is on Griswold Street and opens to the public lobby. Facing the main entrance on the east wall of the lobby is a large and brightly colored mural, flanked on each side by an elevator alcove. Aside from a second entrance on the far left and stairway on the far right, the lobby is bilaterally symmetrical as viewed from the main entrance.

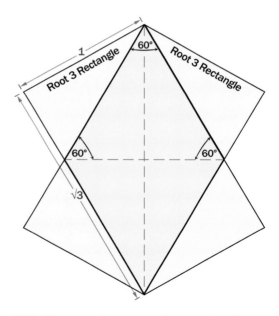

172. A root three rectangle is formed from a root two rectangle in the same manner as the root two rectangle is formed from the square, by taking the diagonal of a root two rectangle (which is equal to the √3) and rotating it to become the long side of a new rectangle.

The design for the east wall of the lobby is almost certainly the most significant feature of the building's interior; first-time visitors see it immediately upon entering, and most of those who work within the structure see it repeatedly. For this reason, the Union Trust building committee elected to place here the colorful mural bearing the firm's foundational statement. The mural is constructed of glass and precious metals and was designed by artist Ezra Winter under Rowland's direction. The mosaic is in the shape of a tree, beneath which is the inscription: "Founded on principles of faith and understanding, this building is erected for the purpose of maintaining and continuing the ideals of financial service which prompted the organization of this institution."

The visual elements of the east wall include the elevator alcoves, their stepped terra-cotta ceilings, stained glass windows, mosaic wall mural, and carved stone ornaments. The locations of the elevator alcoves were determined by structural considerations; the location, shape, and size of the other elements by a root two rectangle-based geometry that harmonizes their proportions to the entire space—including the alcoves.

173. Two root three rectangles joined at the corners form two equilateral triangles in the area of overlap.

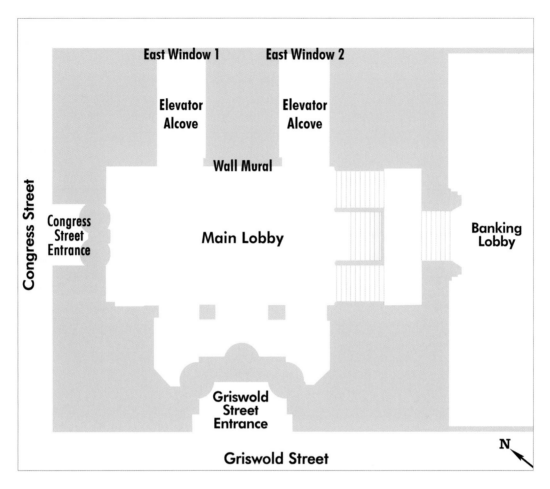

174. Floor plan of the Union Trust Building main lobby.

The following illustrations demonstrate one method to achieve the design, which may or may not be the exact method employed by Rowland; a particular geometric result can often be achieved through more than one series of steps. However, the significant point is not the specific steps, but that all elements of the design are tied together by an underlying principle or theme that harmonizes elements with each other and the structure as a whole.

Moreover, Rowland's use of dynamic symmetry, the system employed by the ancient Greeks, adds further to the interest and subtlety of the overall design.[6]

The complex design of the lobby east wall was worked out by Rowland on a flat sheet of paper, but the components of the design are arranged in multiple planes with a depth of more than twenty-five feet. In addition to these planes, the terra-cotta tiles are stepped and layered. As the design wraps from the surface of the wall to the ceiling of the elevator alcove, tiles are set in numerous layers in three dimensions. It's a wonder the design for the alcove could be drawn, much less constructed. It is likely that the complex design was drawn in full

175. The east wall of the Union Trust Building's main lobby as it appears from inside the Griswold Street entrance. Two elevator alcoves flank a large mosaic mural; at the rear of each alcove is a stained glass window. (The large marble desk was not part of the original building.)

scale on paper and then transferred to a three-dimensional cardboard or wood mockup, from which the forms for the concrete were constructed. The terra-cotta tiles are applied directly to the steel reinforced concrete frame of the building—a masterful example of the advantageous use of concrete to achieve an artistic purpose.

The ceiling of the lobby is one of the most spectacularly colorful surfaces of any building in the world. The colors employed include those of the tile in the elevator alcoves and the mosaic centerpiece of the east lobby wall. The characteristic geometric theme of the ceiling is the root three rectangle.

The tiles that compose the ceiling design are predominantly equilateral triangles and root three rectangles. Rowland could have, of course, constructed the design solely with equilateral triangle shaped tiles, but it would have lacked the intricate and mesmerizing appearance

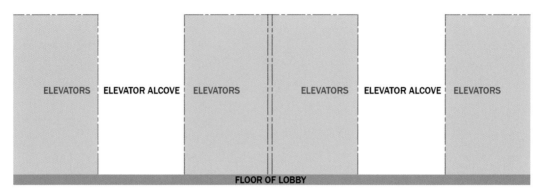

176. The physical layout of the east wall of the Union Trust Building's lobby was determined by the location of the elevator shafts. Twelve elevators in four banks face into two alcoves open to the main lobby.

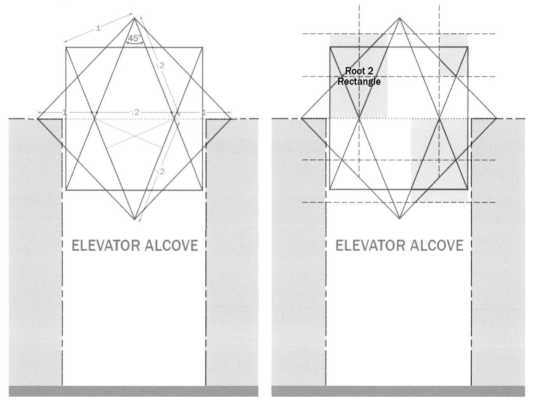

177. The entire design for the lobby wall can be worked out beginning with a root two rectangle figure set atop the elevator alcove (*left*). Lines drawn through intersection points within the figure divide it horizontally and vertically. Additional horizontal lines at equal distance from the center are added (the location is calculated geometrically) (*right*). (Drawing by Michael G. Smith based on analysis and drawings by Rachel Fletcher. [Smith, "Proportioning Systems in Wirt C. Rowland's Union Trust Guardian Building"])

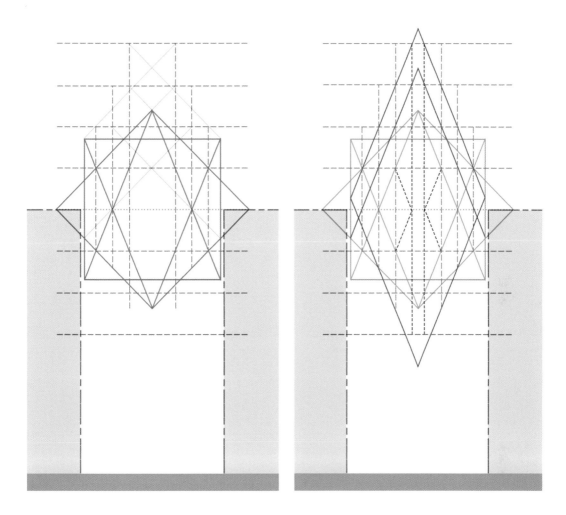

178. Additional horizontal and vertical guidelines that pass through intersection points of the figure are added (*left*). Diagonals drawn through the rectangles within the figure create isosceles triangles parallel to the angles within the original root two figure. Two vertical parallel lines (dotted) are added from points where angled lines cross horizontal lines (*right*).

of the actual installation. To achieve the complexity he sought, Rowland interrupted the field of triangles by adding columns of root three rectangle shaped tiles. Vertically, root three rectangle shaped tiles were inserted every fifth row.

The entire north wall of the lobby is consumed by a unified arrangement of colored tile, glass, and marble nearly five stories high. The doors of the Congress Street entrance occupy the lowest level, above which is a balcony, which bows slightly outward into the room. A window, more than twenty-six feet high and surrounded by bands of reddish tile, dominates the space above and behind the balcony. The window and surrounding tile are inset within a wall enclosing them on three sides and angled at 45 degrees to the plane of the

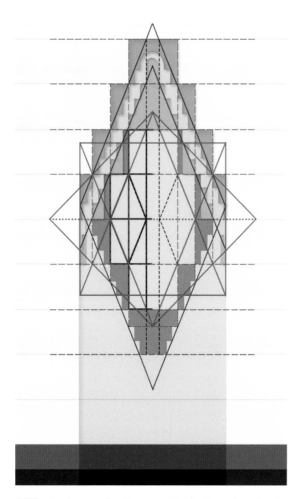 

179. As drawn, the figure perfectly describes the design of the elevator alcoves, from the surface of the east lobby wall (including the seams between rows of marble facing), through the multicolored terra-cotta ceiling, to the muntins separating the panes within the stained glass window on both the interior and exterior of the building.

window. This wall is tiled in the same colors as the ceiling and, in fact, merges into it seamlessly through a series of steps.

Around the top half of the window is a light-colored band, located between the reddish tile and surrounding expanse of blue, green, and orange tile. Just below the midpoint of the window, this band angles outward. Viewed from a distance, this feature gives the appearance of protruding tabs or "ears" on either side of the window. Rowland, being a kind and generous man, presumably added this quirk as a clue to aid in puzzling out the means by which he arrived at his design. As it happens, this odd design feature is located at the midpoint of the root two rectangle overlay figure and aligns with the sides of the two 45-degree triangles.

Generally speaking, Rowland used geometric methods to compose and proportion the design of individual walls or portions of walls. In this respect, he employed these methods

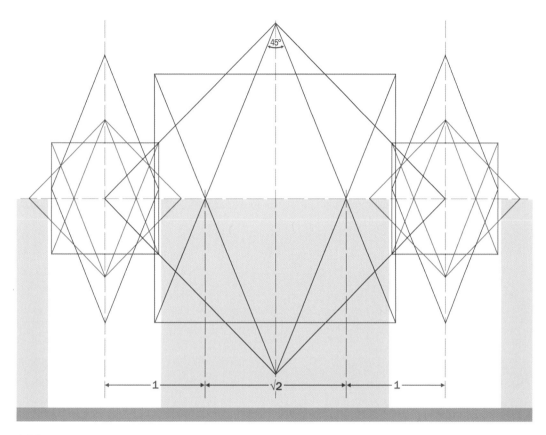

180. The location and size of the mural between the alcoves are established by a root two rectangle figure, the extreme width of which is equal to the distance between the centerlines of the root two alcove figures. (Drawing by Michael G. Smith based on analysis and drawings by Rachel Fletcher. [Smith, "Proportioning Systems in Wirt C. Rowland's Union Trust Guardian Building"])

more broadly than the Moors, whose use of geometry was limited to devising repeating patterns executed in tile. Relative to architects of ancient Greece and the Middle Ages, who used geometric methods to compose entire buildings and establish proportional relationships between various parts of the structure, Rowland fell short. This would not have concerned Rowland, though, for a number of reasons, one of which was the size of the Union Trust Building. While an observer could easily stand before an entire wall of the lobby and study it in great detail, as a practical matter, a forty-story building, particularly one as long and narrow as the Union Trust, situated among other tall structures, could not be viewed in its entirety. For this reason, Rowland focused his creative efforts (and the customer's money) on areas most easily and often observed: lobbies, entrances, elevator alcoves, the exterior at or near street level, and the dramatic tower crowning the top of the building.

With the Union Trust Building, the crowning feature was of particular importance, as without this interesting highlight, the building's profile might have appeared as

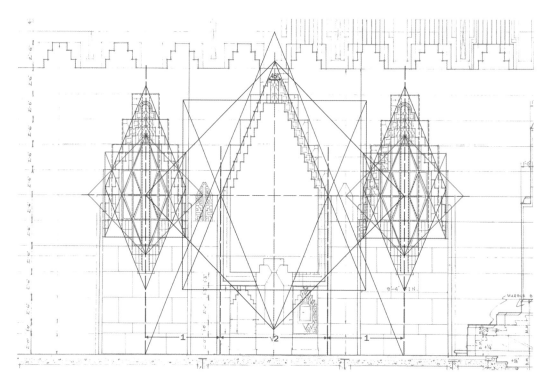

181. The validity of the figure may be confirmed by superimposing it over the original building plans. (Overlay in blue and red by Michael G. Smith; Smith, Hinchman, and Grylls plan sheet 56 for the Union Trust Building)

a rectangular slab (as do many skyscrapers constructed in the latter half of the twentieth century). Traditionally, the uppermost feature of a building was the cornice, but Rowland had long since dispensed with the cornice. On the Grand Rapids Trust Building, Rowland surrounded the flat roof with carved decoration and interrupted the roofline with protruding piers; atop the roof, mostly hidden from view, is a three-story penthouse containing elevator equipment, water tanks, and other mechanicals that needed to be located above the highest occupied floor. The Union Trust Building required two penthouses (one for the bank of elevators at each end of the building), and hiding them would have been difficult on such a narrow structure. Rowland, instead of viewing this as a problem, embraced it as a solution, and turned the two structures into prominent decorative features.

On these penthouses, Rowland unleashed his geometric design technique, employing it to guide both the appearance and shape of the structures. Through the addition on the north side of the building of three small, rentable floors above the main roof (floors thirty-four, thirty-five, and thirty-six), the northern penthouse was raised higher and given greater prominence. To set it off from the rectangular building below, Rowland gave the north tower penthouse an unusual shape. The shape is, of course, derived from one of the

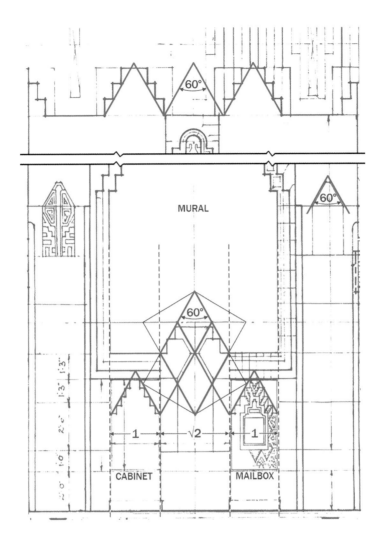

182. The root two composition of the east lobby wall is complemented by smaller features based on the root three rectangle. A stepped design intersects the bottom frame of the mural and is flanked by a cabinet and mailbox topped with similar stepped designs. The shape and location of these features are derived from a root three figure, and the relative widths of the three reflect the root two ratio of the larger composition: $1:\sqrt{2}$. (The plans—shown here—vary somewhat from the completed building.) The stepped design is repeated in the layers of colored terra-cotta above the mural. (Overlay by Michael G. Smith; Smith, Hinchman, and Grylls plan sheet 56 for the Union Trust Building)

geometric figures that gave rise to the complex designs within the lobby—the root two rectangle. The smaller south tower penthouse is also derived from the root two rectangle, but in a subtler manner.

The gold diamond designs encircling the north tower are the building's most prominent decorative feature (with the possible exception of the orange brick). The

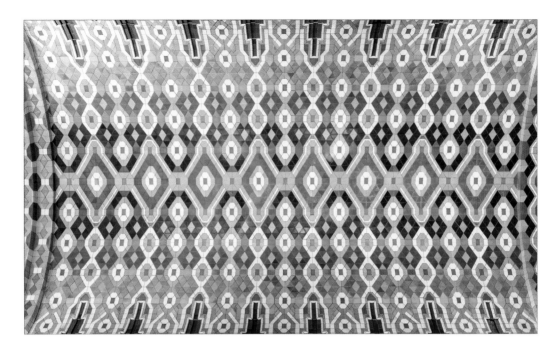

183. The ceiling of the Union Trust Building's lobby. These ceramic tiles were manufactured by Rookwood Pottery in Cincinnati, Ohio. (The ceiling has been restored to its original condition photographically: the floodlights were removed.)

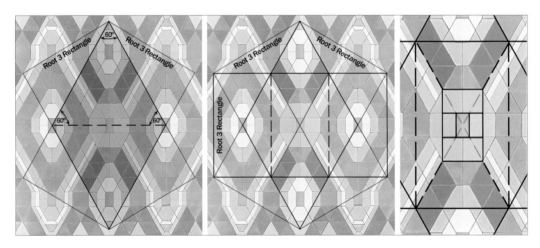

184. The tile pattern in the lobby ceiling of the Union Trust Building is based on 60° equilateral triangles derived from root three rectangles. It is a characteristic of root rectangles that they can be divided into reciprocals having the same proportions as the parent (a root two rectangle divides into two root two rectangles, and a root three rectangle divides into three root three rectangles). The center illustration shows the root three rectangle at the center of the pattern subdivided into three root three rectangles. The further subdivision of root rectangles may be continued to infinity. The illustration on the right shows how one portion of the design divides in this way, and the rectangle shaped tile at its center is a vertical root three rectangle.

diamond figures are seventeen feet high (the black bands above and below add another seven feet) and are comprised of gold, black, and white terra-cotta. Gold over a background of black was believed at the time to exhibit maximum contrast. For this reason, it was the color combination used for painting small signs, as when a company's name was hand lettered on the door to the firm's office. Rowland sought maximum visibility as this feature would be viewed from a greater distance than any other. The diamond pattern is less complex than it appears and is derived from the root three rectangle. (In later years, the floors above the thirty-sixth were converted from storage to rentable space. In the process of converting the thirty-ninth floor, rectangular windows were cut into the building's surface, disfiguring the diamond-shaped designs surrounding the penthouse.)

To further encourage the perception that the north tower designates the building's front, Rowland placed on top of the penthouse an enormous flagpole, eleven stories tall (123½ feet). The pole is hollow, but it weighs more than seven tons and carries a flag forty by twenty feet in size.

Although exceedingly large, the flagpole was by no means an unusual accessory for an important building. It was joined on the penthouse roof by a far more unconventional feature: the Ryan

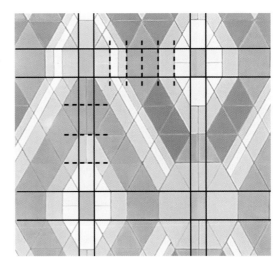

185. A row of vertical root three rectangles was inserted into the pattern every seven rows horizontally and every five rows vertically.

186. The Union Trust Building's main lobby north (Congress Street) wall.

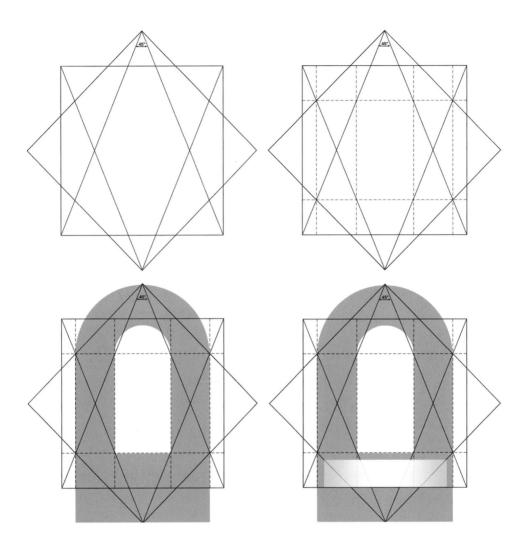

187. The composition of the Union Trust Building's main lobby Congress Street wall can be developed from a root two rectangle figure and its two opposed 45° isosceles triangles (*top left*). Horizontal and vertical lines are drawn through the intersection of the corner up square and the side up square. A second pair of vertical lines is drawn through the intersection of the horizontal lines and the 45° triangles (*top right*). The outer vertical lines align with the full width of the lobby. The inner verticals along with the horizontal lines define the location and size of the rectangular portion of the lobby window (*bottom left*). Below the window is a balcony that aligns with the lower side of the square (*bottom right*).

Automatic Electric Scintillator. Skyscrapers were often brightly illuminated at night so the tall building's promotional advantage was not lost when the sun went down. To simply light up the Union Trust Building seemed unimaginative and incompatible with the structure's colorful theme, so assistance was sought from General Electric Company lighting engineer Walter D'Arcy Ryan, developer of the colored lighting for Niagara Falls in 1907 and the

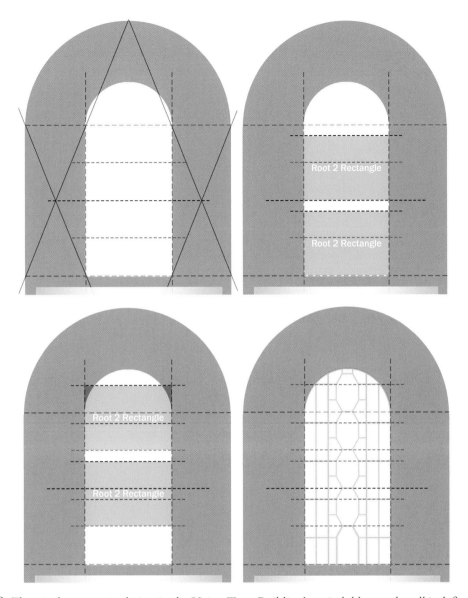

188. The window muntin design in the Union Trust Building's main lobby north wall is defined by the same root two geometric system as the overall wall layout. The rectangular area of the window is bisected by the centerline of the root two geometric figure, forming two equal rectangles. These are each bisected horizontally creating two equal areas (*top left*). Root two rectangles equal to the width of the window are placed, one in each half of the rectangles, to establish two more horizontal lines (*top right*). The root two rectangles are moved up to the second pair of horizontal lines drawn in the first step, establishing another pair of horizontal lines (*lower left*). These horizontal lines define the vertical locations of the muntins within the window (*lower right*).

Panama Pacific Exposition in 1915.[7] The Ryan-designed Scintillator installed on the Union Trust Building was comprised of eight, thirty-six-inch searchlights mounted on reinforced pads atop each of the penthouse roof's eight corners (the searchlights were removed but the pads remain). When in operation, each searchlight rotated horizontally while oscillating vertically; color was added to the light beams by means of filters.[8]

The building's main banking lobby was a workplace, and as such, adequate light and ventilation were essential. With respect to lighting, the narrow width of the building worked to Rowland's advantage as the enormous arched windows on the east and west sides of the building provided an abundance of natural light to the area. The building's air-conditioning system handled ventilation, making operable windows unnecessary. Conditioned air is circulated through large vent openings cut into the marble walls in patterns consistent with the geometric theme.

Due to the great size of the banking lobby, and large number of employees and customers conducting business, Rowland viewed noise reduction as an important objective. To achieve it, he had the ceiling constructed with a thick layer of sound-absorbing material, with canvas applied over the material as the finished surface. The

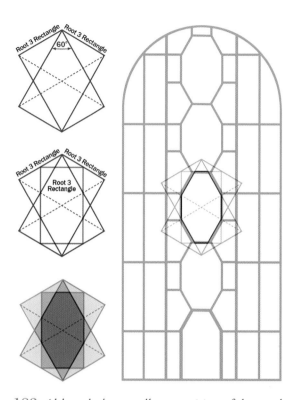

189. Although the overall composition of the north wall of the lobby is based on root two rectangles (45°), the characteristic eight-sided shape of the exterior muntins, however, is developed from root three rectangles (60°). Rowland used this distinctive "octowindow" shape throughout the building. Two root three rectangles overlaid at a 60° angle to each other form a dynamically symmetrical figure (*top left*). Diagonals to each of these rectangles establish four intersection points through which a third, smaller root three rectangle, circumscribed by the larger figure, is drawn (*middle left*). The eight-sided figure takes its shape from the area in which all three root three rectangles intersect (*lower left*). The design is repeated four times along the centerline of the window (*right*).

structure supporting this acoustic mat is somewhat unusual in that it is fairly light in weight and suspended from the frame of the building. Its skeleton is comprised of small-gauge steel ribs arching across the room from one side to the other, and supported by steel hangers attached to the building's frame. The ribs support a lightweight steel framework and a steel mesh screen; everything is held together with wire ties. Plaster applied to the steel mesh screen holds the sound-absorbing material in place.

This installation entailed both problems and opportunities. Canvas, being a soft material, as compared to plaster or marble, necessitated treating the ceiling as a structure suspended from above, rather than an arched vault supported by piers on either side. Throughout the structure Rowland employed material whose inherent color supplied the effect he sought, avoiding the use of paint and other techniques applied only to the surface. Integrating the painted canvas into the overall design of the building was—in theory—problematic. Here again, Rowland turned a problem into a feature. Rather than attempt to disguise the canvas and its painted finish, he seized an opportunity to develop a softer theme,

190. A quirk in the tile design surrounding the Congress Street window aligns with the intersecting 45° triangles in the root two rectangle overlay.

divergent from the hard surfaces of granite, marble, tile, glass, and metal. The edge of the acoustic ceiling liner could have been disguised by placing it flush with the marble-clad piers, but instead, it was constructed as a layer placed over the top of the marble, leaving the rounded corners of the canvas plainly visible. Rowland's choice here was for the ceiling to appear as a soft material suspended from above—almost like a tent—over the hard-surfaced walls and floor below.

As a consequence of this approach, the ceiling presents a different appearance than if it were a hard-surfaced, barrel vault structure. Barrel vaulted ceilings, commonly seen in the lobby of large buildings (Detroit's Fisher Building, for example), were often coffered and painted, and are perceived as a large, structural element. The ceiling of the Union Trust banking lobby, however, with its soft surface and rounded edges, is perceived more as a backdrop on which the colors and geometric patterns take prominence. This is a subtle, but significant, distinction; it is the realization of Rowland's effort to employ color as the primary structural element, in a manner consistent with the Byzantine examples cited by March Phillipps, yet completely modern.

"Hitherto hard building material, such as marble or stone, had dictated architectures of form, which had involved a purely decorative use of colour," wrote Phillipps. "The

191. The north tower penthouse of the Union Trust Building is encircled with gold diamond-shaped designs and contains elevator and other mechanical equipment. The penthouse was given greater prominence by placing it atop three small floors added above the building's main roof; the penthouse at the south end of the building occupies a more typical position immediately above the roof level.

introduction of a soft substance as at once a building material and a colour material placed colour on a new footing. It enabled it to escape from the thraldom of form and to develop its own sensuous character."[9] Phillipps described a room with walls of gold mosaic that exemplified the principle: "The recesses of the chapel are rounded in the mosaic itself, and completely carried out in that material . . . the rounding of the blunt angles in the gold produces on the spectator the impression that the whole wall is formed entirely of this substance."[10] Exactly so is the ceiling of Union Trust's banking room: a soft canvas mat, completely independent of the surrounding stone structure of the walls and floor. Phillipps's description of the mosaics of Saint Mark's in Venice applies just as well to the ceiling of the Union Trust banking room: "The whole of the upper portion of the building is composed of curves.

The edges are blunt, the angles filled in and rounded, the surfaces uneven and slightly undulating. Vaults and cavernous recesses melt into each other. Nowhere is the material broken."[11] The canvas surface of the banking room unashamedly displays the imperfections of its soft composition; where it wraps over edges joining the minor side arches to the central arch, it does so with an almost imperceptible round, rather than sharp, edge. The vibrant geometric designs carry across these edges, further emphasizing the importance of the colored design over the form of the structure.[12]

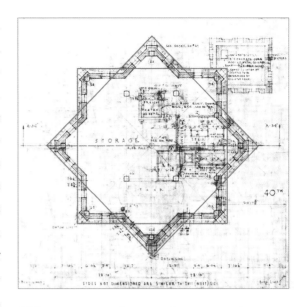

192. The shape of the penthouse atop the Union Trust Building's north tower conforms exactly to the root two figure. The base drawing is from the original Smith, Hinchman, and Grylls building plans, sheet 30, showing the fortieth floor.

The same effect is observed on the apse-like half dome outside above the main (Griswold) entrance of the building: the colored tiles wrap softly over the rounded edges that join the structure to the surrounding stonework. A half dome bearing a mural or mosaic is not an uncommon feature, but is typically executed in a space well defined by surrounding architectural forms, such as ribs, molding, string course, or, at the very least, a sharp angle resulting from the intersection of two surfaces. With the Union Trust half dome, as with Byzantine examples cited by Phillipps, no delineating architectural forms are used; the artwork defines its own extent, rather than being defined by the shape of the structure—the colored tile is viewed as the structural feature rather than the dome-shaped form.

Colors employed on the banking room ceiling complement colors used elsewhere, but are predominantly reds, oranges, browns, black, and white, with accents of blue-green, and silver and gold leaf. This color palette, and the geometric shapes in which they are used, is strongly reminiscent of, in particular, Navajo rugs and blankets from the late nineteenth and early twentieth centuries, and, considering Rowland's fascination with the American West and its inhabitants, it is difficult to imagine his ceiling design was not inspired by Native American art. Navajo rugs and blankets were, at the time, highly prized. A 1919 publication on tapestries by the Detroit Institute of Arts referred to "Navajo rugs so familiar to most of us."[13] In fact, Rowland had American Indian blankets covering twin beds in his

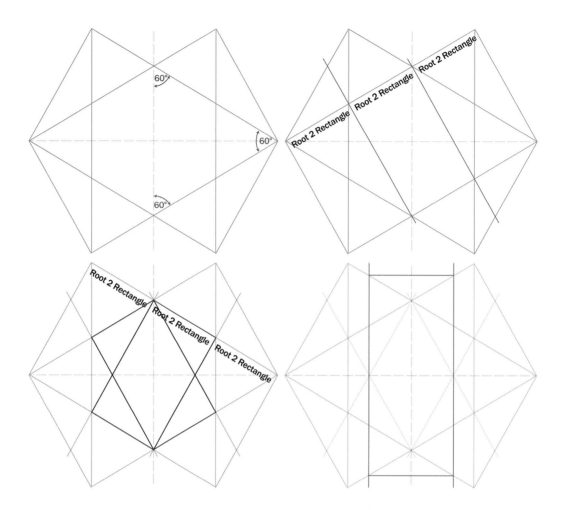

193. The diamond pattern on the penthouse of the Union Trust Building is derived from the root three rectangle figure and is similar to the design on the lobby ceiling. One way to develop the design is to begin with a root three figure rotated 90° *(upper left)*. The two root three rectangles composing the figure are divided into their constituent reciprocals of three root three rectangles, resulting in a second root three figure circumscribed by the first *(upper right and lower left)*. Two vertical guidelines are drawn where the lines of the inner root three figure intersect the horizontal centerline; horizontal lines are drawn between these vertical lines where they intersect the outer root three figure *(lower right)*.

studio in the Clinton home he inherited from his mother.[14] Although designs on Navajo rugs varied a great deal, certain motifs were common, such as the lozenge and stepped terrace seen on the ceiling of the banking lobby. Similar patterns also appear as decorations on Zuni baskets.

This is not to say that Rowland copied Native American designs onto the ceiling or intended the installation to represent a Navajo blanket. He likely saw in the Navajo blankets

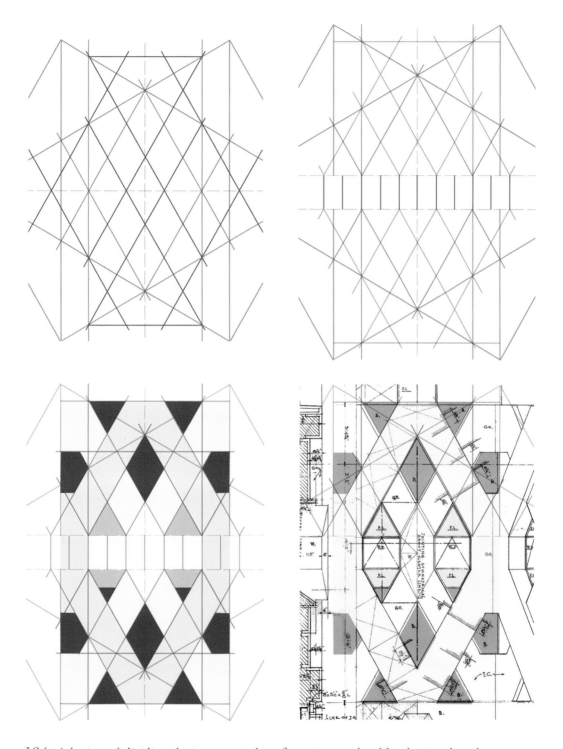

194. A lattice subdividing the inner root three figure is completed by drawing lines between intersection points (*upper left*). The entire figure is split in half horizontally and a row of root three rectangles is inserted to provide space for a row of windows (*upper right*). The design is created by combining shapes and adding color. On the building, color is provided by panels of terra-cotta in gold, black, and white (*lower left*). The final illustration shows the colored geometric figure superimposed over the original Smith, Hinchman, and Grylls plan sheet 42 (*lower right*).

195-1 & 195-2. The space above the ceiling of the Union Trust (Guardian) Building's main banking lobby. A lightweight framework gives shape to the plaster ceiling, supported by hangers anchored to the building's structural members. Plaster was applied to a steel mesh, which is fastened to the frame with wire ties. Only the lower portion of the enormous trusses supporting the upper floors of the building is visible here on the fifth floor. The few structural steel members not buried in the concrete building frame were coated with a fireproof material. The lighting fixtures in white "cans" are not original to the building.

196. Between the main banking lobby ceiling (visible on the far left) and the Griswold Street exterior wall (far right) is a large void space extending from the fourth to fifth floor. On the left is one of the massive girders that support the upper floors of the building over the banking lobby.

197. Main banking lobby of the Union Trust Building (the two rows of recessed ceiling lights are not original).

198. Sound-absorbing canvas on the ceiling of the Union Trust Building's banking lobby was applied in such a way as to accentuate, rather than disguise, its soft and pliable nature.

and rugs a design well suited to a woven material (which canvas is), compatible with the geometric theme of the building and, importantly, uniquely American. Native American art provided the germ of an idea for a theme that he developed fully, employing the same principles of design upon which the entire structure is based. The result was something entirely new, modern, and different. In a similar manner, many lengthy musical compositions are based on simple folk tunes developed into complex symphonies. Describing his Symphony no. 9, "From the New World," Antonin Dvořák said in 1893: "I have not actually used any of the [American Indian] melodies. I have simply written original themes embodying the peculiarities of the Indian music, and using these themes as subjects have developed them with all the resources of modern rhythms, harmony, counterpoint, and orchestral color."[15]

The painted designs on the ceiling echo the stepped figures in colored tile elsewhere on the building, though the ceiling has a decidedly different and simpler feel. Not surprisingly, Rowland derived the design for the ceiling from the root two rectangle, but in a different manner from those of the tile patterns, which derive from multiple rectangles offset from each other. Thomas DiLorenzo has at times been credited with the design of the

199. The interior of Saint Mark's Basilica in Venice. The entire upper portion of the interior is covered in mosaic tile. (Steven Zucker)

ceiling, but as the accompanying drawing from the original Smith, Hinchman, and Grylls plans show, the design was described in detail by Rowland's team (though some of the painted detail specified on the plan was not completed). DiLorenzo's firm was responsible for painting and installing the canvas ceiling.

Flanking the banking lobby on both the east and west sides of the building are enormous windows that serve to admit natural light. As Rowland placed a high value on providing excellent lighting for those employed within, natural illumination was supplemented by general room lighting and task lighting for individual work spaces (teller cages and writing desks in the bank) in the form of lights concealed in a trough above the teller screens. These fixtures were bidirectional, casting light up to illuminate the ceiling and down on the work area. Within the ceiling of the bank lobby are diamond-shaped openings that contain amber-colored glass, above which are light fixtures, their output being filtered through the amber glass, which gives a warm glow to the room on gloomy days.

The illumination was so painstakingly planned and well integrated to the design of individual spaces that *The Lighting Book*, a 1930 work on the science of vision and

200. One section of the ceiling within the main banking lobby of the Union Trust Building. The diamond-shaped panels of amber glass with light behind are original; the recessed lights (only two of which are on here) were added much later.

illumination, made numerous references to the Union Trust Building.[16] For large banking rooms in particular it stated, "The trend is toward the use of concealed lighting," referencing as an example the main banking room of the Union Trust Company, where "principal illumination comes from [the] tops of the banking screen supplemented by luminous panels of glass in the ceiling."[17]

In later years, perhaps when the building was taken over by the United States Army Tank-Automotive Center during World War II, the teller screens were removed from the room, and with them went the concealed lighting fixtures. At some point in time, the arched windows were inexplicably closed off with blue-tinted glass blocks, altering and reducing the natural illumination of the room. Then, to compensate for the lack of light, spotlights were installed in the ceiling—sixty of them in the central arched area alone. The spotlights form two bright rows, emphasizing the length of the room rather than its width and height.

At the south end of the banking lobby is a large mural by Ezra Winter depicting a map of the state of Michigan with its various industries. In the center is a woman holding cornucopias and wearing a gown, down the center of which are stepped designs similar to those in the ceiling. There were at least two mural designs under consideration for this location; the second was by artist Frederick Dana Marsh.[18] Comparing the two works—Winter's completed mural and Marsh's submission—it may be seen to what extent the layout and subject matter were established by Rowland as opposed to being at the discretion of the artist.

In the lower left corner of the work by Marsh, there is a representation of the Ford Rouge plant that is very similar (though not identical) to the well-known 1927 photograph by Charles Sheeler. On the right is the Detroit riverfront with the Union Trust, Penobscot, and Buhl Buildings rising prominently in the background.

The woman depicted in Winter's mural is roughly similar to the figure within the colored glass windows of the elevator alcoves—both wear a similar flowing gown covering all but their feet, with geometric shapes along the center. The two figures carved in stone on either side of the Griswold Street entrance are similarly reposed, but more stylized than the mural or colored glass figures. The upper body features of the figures are well defined, but below the hands, they transform into a series of rectangular shapes where one would expect to see the lower extremities. There is symbolic content—one figure holds a key, the other, a sword; an eagle is perched on the head of both. Considering there are two American

201. A typical Navajo "eye dazzler" rug dating from around 1890 displays similar design patterns and colors as in the ceiling of the Union Trust banking lobby. (Steve and Gail Getzwiller's Nizhoni Ranch Gallery at http://navajorug.com/)

202. Photographs of Navajo rugs and blankets were widely published in the early twentieth century, often in color. From *The Navajo and His Blanket* by Uriah Hollister, published 1903 (*left*). From *American Indians: First Families of the Southwest* by Fred Harvey, published 1920 (*top right*). From *Indian Blankets and Their Makers* by George W. James, published 1914 (*bottom right*).

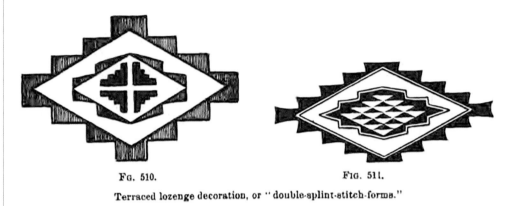

488   PUEBLO POTTERY AND ZUÑI CULTURE-GROWTH.

be enhanced by a consideration of the etymology of a few Zuñi decorative terms, more of which might be given did space admit. A terraced lozenge (see Figs. 510, 511), instead of being named after the abstract

FIG. 510.   FIG. 511.

Terraced lozenge decoration, or "double-splint-stitch-forms."

203. A selection from *A Study of Pueblo Pottery* by Frank H. Cushing showing common Zuni "terraced lozenge decoration," similar to that employed on the Union Trust Building's banking lobby ceiling. Published in 1886 by the Government Printing Office, the book was available at the Detroit Public Library.

Indian figures immediately across the street on the Buhl Building, and another over the entry to Penobscot, it seems the Indian theme might have been carried over to the Union Trust, but there is nothing in the appearance of either figure that indicates a particular identity. These figures were designed by Rowland and Corrado Parducci and carved into stone by Peter Bernasconi.

The large, arched windows—four each on the east and west sides of the banking lobby—contribute to the decorative theme of the building by virtue of the eight-sided shapes formed by the exterior window muntins. These are the same "octowindow" shapes that appear in a vertical band in the center of the Congress Street window; on the bank lobby windows, however, three bands of the design fill each window. When the building is viewed from Griswold Street, these shapes are among the most prominent features of the lower stories. As demonstrated previously, the "octowindow" shape is derived from the root three rectangle (60 degrees). At a glance, it may appear the shape is merely an elongated octagon (stop sign shape), but this is not the case, as a regular octagon is derived from a root two rectangle and has 45-degree angled sides.

In the main building lobby, at the far end of the elevator alcoves, are stained glass windows executed by George Green. Both windows portray a winged figure holding aloft a shield with the word "fidelity" appearing on one and "security" on the other. The shields are eight-sided figures in the same octowindow shape.

In many locations on the exterior and interior of the building, the octowindow shape may be seen, sometimes in a modified form where only the top half of the figure is used. Some of the lesser examples have been lost: the same design appeared on the ceiling of the executive conference room, custom designed carpeting and curtains, and many elevator doors. The backs of office chairs were shaped in this way. Mirrors in the barber shop and beauty salon on the twenty-second floor were octowindows, and the supply cabinet at each barber station was finished in this shape. This form was mistakenly thought by some to have been inspired by Mesoamerican architecture, but Rowland specifically denied this was the case: his March 31, 1929, *Detroit News* article stated that the angled arches "were not derived from any style or from Mayan architecture as often suggested."[19] Nevertheless, the cafeteria on the thirty-second floor of the building was given the name "Aztec Tower." This cafeteria could seat 256 people at sixty-four tables and was often rented to outside groups for special events.

The main lobby of the Union Trust Building, its most celebrated feature, is a magnificent tour de force of color employed structurally. Color, in the form of tiles (rather than the mosaics characteristic of the Byzantine examples cited by Phillipps), defines the room

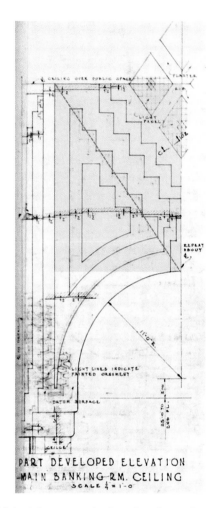

PART DEVELOPED ELEVATION
MAIN BANKING RM. CEILING
SCALE ¾ = 1′-0″

204. The original plan for the ceiling of the main banking lobby of the Union Trust Building, sheet 102. This is a "developed" elevation—it shows the pattern as it appears flat, not as it appears when viewed on a curved surface. It shows only one-quarter of the ceiling; the other quadrants are mirror images of this section. The blue shape is a root two rectangle overlaid on the drawing to demonstrate how the design was derived. The red line is a diagonal to the root two rectangle; the angled features of the design are parallel to this line, including the light fixtures—the diamond shapes in the upper right corner. The lighter markings on the drawing (particularly in the lower left) detail the designs to be painted. (Base drawing from a copy of the Smith, Hinchman, and Grylls plans, sheet 102)

205. The main banking lobby of the Union Trust Building as it appeared upon completion in 1929. The top section of the teller screens concealed fixtures that cast light up at the ceiling and down on the workspace. Check desks in the center of the room had individual lamps. Behind the large screen at the room's end may be seen the illuminated wall fixtures in the main lobby. (Smith, Hinchman, and Grylls and SmithGroupJJR)

and "obliterates the structural features of the old formal styles."[20] Walls, ceiling, corners— end, side, and top—all disappear into a whirl of color.

Of great importance is the *effect* Rowland achieved, an effect he would have described as "emotional" as opposed to "intellectual." Form, according to March Phillipps, is always an intellectual endeavor, while color has the power to affect us emotionally as well. Color, when employed in certain ways, can create a *mood*, something that form cannot achieve. Writing on the architecture of the Middle Ages, Rowland described how craftsmen harnessed light and color to create stirring effects. Visiting Chartres Cathedral, Rowland felt emotion, "powerful and moving," as light, passing through windows of colored glass, "transforms the very atmosphere of the interior, wrapping the worshippers in a glowing and mystical nimbus."[21] Even within the less elaborate buildings constructed by the Moors,

206. The Ezra Winter mural in the main banking lobby of the Union Trust Building (*left*) and a design for the mural submitted by Frederick Dana Marsh in March 1928 (*right*). In some respects, the two are identical, indicating that certain aspects of the design were specified by Rowland. (Marsh Wolfsonian-Florida International University)

Rowland noted, their wall surfaces were covered by "mosaics which provided the color with but very little light from the windows. This created the mystery of the interior."[22]

The successful use of color as a structural feature, according to Phillipps, required that "bright light, suitable for the display of form, was toned down to a solemn twilight in keeping with the effects of rich color."[23] Criticizing the otherwise effective use of color in Santa Sophia (Constantinople; now known as Hagia Sophia, Istanbul, Turkey), Phillipps wrote: "In Santa Sophia the light is brilliant throughout the church, and the consequence is that the mosaics pale their ineffectual fire and fade away into a feeble, ashen grey. It is only in the deep twilight of the later and more typical examples that that deep glow wakes which is the note of the [Byzantine] style."[24]

Having studied this analysis by Phillipps, Rowland understood the importance of proper lighting when color was to serve as the primary design feature. His selection of colors and materials was based on extensive planning and experimentation to assure the desired effect was achieved under the contemplated lighting conditions. How did the colored tiles appear on a sunny day? An overcast day? At night? In the morning with no direct sun, or in the afternoon with sun streaming through the windows? The sun, arcing across the sky over the course of a day, created a wide range of effects as shadows came and went and colors shifted in hue, intensity, and brightness. As the sun shifts its path through the sky from summer to winter, its effect on the building's interior varies ever so slightly as well. All of this was accounted for by Rowland and carefully factored into the type, location, color, and power of the lighting fixtures installed.

Artificial light was originally supplied in the lobby by ten fixtures (five on each side) located roughly thirty feet from the floor and having four lights each. *Forty Stories from Bedrock* offered this description: "Fixtures set high upon the side walls throw an almost horizontal light across the lobby, so that the ceiling is flooded with a softly diffused light."[25]

At some point in the building's history, these fixtures were removed and replaced by a large soffit (containing floodlights aimed upward) running the length of the wall, and recessed floodlights were installed in the tile ceiling. Instead of "softly diffused light" or "solemn twilight," the room suffered a deluge of glaring light, much of it aimed directly into the eyes of those in the lobby attempting to admire the ceiling. Moreover, the soffit along the wall hides the lowest portion of the ceiling's tile pattern and adds a stark, horizontal line dividing wall from ceiling, in place of Rowland's gradual transition. The building's current lighting system has all but destroyed the original, carefully crafted mood of the room. The geometry of the colorful tiles, the grain of the marble, and the stepped arches may all be clearly seen in the bright light,

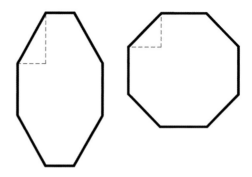

207. Rowland's eight-sided octowindow shape compared with a regular octagon. The octowindow has 30° and 60° angles and is derived from the root three rectangle. A regular octagon has 45° angles.

208. Each of the elevator alcoves contains a stained glass window. The winged figure holds aloft an eight-sided shield with the word "fidelity" in one window and "security" in the other.

209. The Union Trust Building's second basement—vault level. The root three rectangle shape (octowindow) appears here in the drinking fountain, in the deep arches above the walls, and in the colored tile designs. Even the banister—both in cross section and the shape of its termination—features the shape. The ceiling contains the root two rectangle design formed with darker stone.

but the feeling, emotion, or mood that might be sensed under lighting conditions intended by the building's designer is, unfortunately, no longer available.

The best option for experiencing the room may be during a power failure when the lights are off and the room is illuminated by the dim green cast of a passing thunderstorm. The colors will loom above in deep shades of ruby, emerald, and sapphire, perhaps rivaling the dark and mysterious northern lights.[26]

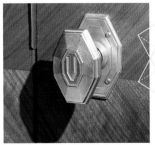

210. Door knobs are inscribed with the letters *U* and *T* (Union Trust) and have the same eight-sided octowindow shape as seen elsewhere on the building.

On the building's exterior, there is one prominent decorative feature inconsistent with the characteristic geometric theme seen throughout. Flanking the large window above the Congress Street entrance are two carved spiral designs that seemingly have no relationship

211. The lobby of the Union Trust Building. On the right side can be seen the large soffit containing spotlights; on the left, the soffit has been edited out of the photo, revealing the original appearance of the wall.

with the stepped and angled shapes seen elsewhere. It will be recalled from the previous chapter the manner in which a root rectangle may be divided by a diagonal and further divided into reciprocal rectangles by means of a second diagonal drawn at right angles to the first. This effect Jay Hambidge emphasized as second in importance only to the diagonal of a rectangle.[27] Each reciprocal rectangle can be further divided by a diagonal, resulting in a rectangular spiral figure. Hambidge repeatedly described and illustrated this rectangular spiral in his publications.

The rectangular spiral was well known to students of Hambidge's method. The resemblance of the spiral designs flanking the Congress Street window to the rectangular spiral raises the possibility that Rowland's intention was to memorialize Hambidge (who died in 1924), and perhaps to provide curious admirers of the building with a clue to aid them in understanding its geometric themes.

The actual stone carvings on the building differ somewhat from the design that appears on the original building plans; the alteration may have been due to the difficulty of

212. This photo of the lobby, taken shortly after the Union Trust Building was completed, gives some sense of the original lighting scheme. Four of the original wall fixtures may be seen here. They provided adequate illumination without compromising the effect of outside light; the reduced light level added a sense of mystery to the space and allowed the bright colors of the ceiling the subtle appearance intended by the building's designer. (Smith, Hinchman, and Grylls reproduced in *Michigan Architect and Engineer*, 1929)

rendering in stone the planned design. Whether the carving complies with the principles of dynamic symmetry can be evaluated only if accurate measurements are taken. The design of the original figure on the drawings, however, is consistent with Hambidge's principles of dynamic symmetry: it is a root two rectangular spiral.[28]

Rowland was fond of placing iconic representations on his buildings, some of which were quite subtle in their reference. The Palmer Park substation of the Detroit Public Lighting Commission, designed by Rowland and constructed in 1923, contains a shield with two carved images: a hand grasping a lightning bolt, and a skeleton key. The lightning bolt as a reference to electricity is rather obvious. The skeleton key, however, has nothing to do with electricity per se, except in the context of Benjamin Franklin's reputed experiment involving a thunderstorm, kite, and skeleton key. The key as an icon reaches beyond a simple reference to electricity and celebrates the pursuit of knowledge through experimentation, and scientist Ben Franklin in particular.

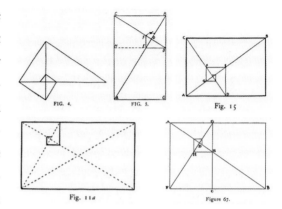

213. A sample of the many illustrations in Jay Hambidge's writing of the rectangular spiral formed from a diagonal to the reciprocal of a rectangle. From "Symmetry and Proportion in Greek Art" (*top left*); his journal *Diagonal*, 1919 (*top right*); from *Diagonal* (*bottom left*); and from *The Parthenon and Other Greek Temples*, 1924, "Figure 67" (*bottom right*). All illustrations by Jay Hambidge.

Depicted within the colored tile that surrounds the Congress Street window are three traditional images likely included at the request of Union Trust: "the beehive, symbolizing thrift and industry, the eagle, representing money, and the caduceus, symbol of authority and commerce."[29] These images are fairly literal and impersonal. The rectangular spiral, however, celebrates pursuit of knowledge in the arts and the pioneering efforts of Jay Hambidge in particular. The rectangular spiral was quite possibly Rowland's idea alone and was included on the building without explanation or specific approval from the Union Trust building committee. Rowland blended it into the surrounding scheme well enough that no one on the committee thought to question whether the decoration had some particular meaning.

On the exterior, the broad flanks of the building above the base, on Griswold Street and the alley, might have been left as a massive expanse of window and brick, but Rowland found this approach

214. The decorative carvings flanking the Union Trust Building's Congress Street window bring to mind Jay Hambidge's "rectangular spiral."

unacceptable. The base of a tall structure is viewed from a different perspective and distance than its top section, and the design of the two varied as a result. As a consequence, the midsection was often left starkly plain to avoid any conflict with the base or top, and to provide a neutral backdrop for those two important sections. This method is evident on the General Motors and First National Bank Buildings. With the Buhl Building, Rowland took a different approach, unifying the exterior by carrying the piers and pylons from bottom to top and de-emphasizing the distinctness of the base

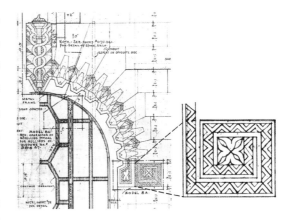

215. A section from the elevation for the Congress Street facade showing the original plans for the carved decorations flanking the window arch (sheet 43 of the building plans). This spiral design may be drawn by employing diagonals to the reciprocal of a root three rectangle.

and top. The Grand Rapids Trust Building continued the trend, relying on subtler vertical and horizontal features, and due to the building's shorter stature, the uninterrupted field of forty-two windows in its midsection is not objectionable. But the same treatment on the much larger Union Trust Building's midsection, with 368 windows, would have been uninteresting.

Rowland's solution involved a simple engineering innovation and a bit of tinkering with the spandrels between windows. The steel framing surrounding each pair of windows, instead of being attached along the centerline between steel structural piers, was placed alternately on the outside and inside. This resulted in a corduroy appearance to the building's exterior. Window pairs attached on the outside surface of the building's frame

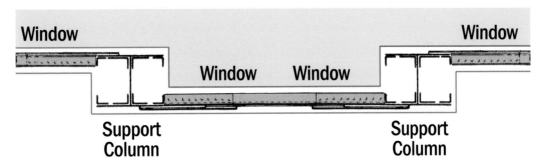

216. Instead of placing the steel framing for the Union Trust Building's walls through the center of the supporting piers, they were placed alternately outside and inside of the piers. This gave the exterior wall an undulating rather than flat appearance

protrude slightly and form an unbroken vertical column from the eighth floor to the roof. Windows on the inside of the support piers are separated vertically by pairs of gray metal spandrels or brick stepped-pattern spandrels. This small shift in placement breaks up an otherwise undifferentiated expanse of windows into a pleasing pattern of columns and rows. As the method was used consistently over the building's upper floors, the pattern formed by the groupings of windows and spandrels serves as a theme to further unify the structure's exterior.

217. To avoid a plain wall with an undifferentiated field of windows, Rowland placed spandrels between every other pair of windows vertically. Horizontally, two gray spandrels alternated with two spandrels of brick. As a result, windows are perceived in groups, rather than an undifferentiated mass.

Rowland faced a similar problem with the north wall (Fort Street) of the Greater Penobscot Building. From the fifth floor to the thirty-eighth, the massive face of the most visible side of the building was an unbroken expanse of more than five hundred windows. Rowland used two different spandrel styles to break the space into groups of windows in roughly the same way as he had with Union Trust. From the seventh floor to the twenty-eighth, each window is part of an identical twelve-window group—four wide by three high. Above the twenty-eighth floor, the pattern alters somewhat in the transition to setbacks that characterize the upper stories.

It's not surprising that Rowland would carry over methods from one building designed at the same time as another, particularly considering the similarities in purpose and location. Most striking, however, are the differences. Union Trust, as Rowland pointed out, "screams color," while Penobscot is conspicuously monochromatic, relying on its sculpted form to attract attention—March Phillipps's form and color embodied in two monumental structures.

Rowland's design for the Greater Penobscot Building was most likely constrained by time—it had to be developed on a rush basis while he was engaged on a number of other projects. But unlike the Union Trust, Penobscot was not a headquarters building and did not require the same attention-grabbing decorative treatment. The building was designed

to appeal to small businesses, professionals, and salespeople who generally rented
small- to medium-size offices in well-locat-
ed downtown buildings. Factors important to this clientele included a prestigious
address, preferably in the city's financial
district; convenience, in the form of a variety of retail services available within the
building; a well-appointed and dignified
business environment; and an upscale,
onsite restaurant or club—all available
in Penobscot.

While Rowland had only a relatively short amount of time to set forth
his plan for Penobscot, it is likely that he
had been considering for some time the
themes that found expression in the final
design. Among those ideas, certainly architectural developments in the American
West would have been of significant interest to Rowland.

During the early decades of the
twentieth century there was great interest
in the Pueblo Indians, particularly among
artists and architects. Artists traveled to
the pueblo cities and often remained on a

218. In this early photo of Penobscot Building
the pattern of windows created by Rowland's use
of dark and light spandrels is clearly visible. Instead of a massive field of over five hundred windows, the north (Fort Street) side of the building
appears to be built up from blocks containing
twelve windows each (four wide by three high).
The spandrels have since been painted a lighter
color, mitigating the effect. (Smith, Hinchman,
and Grylls and SmithGroupJJR, ca. 1928)

permanent or semipermanent basis. In 1915, the Taos Society of Artists was formed, and
among its prominent members was Detroit artist Julius Rolshoven, who in 1916 established
a studio in Santa Fe. Later that year, the Detroit Institute of Arts held an exhibition of
Rolshoven's paintings of New Mexico's Taos Pueblo, and in 1919, the museum hosted an
exhibition of paintings from the Taos Society of Artists.

Ties between Detroiters and the art and archaeology community of New Mexico
were well established by the end of World War I. The Santa Fe Archaeological Society/
Archaeological Institute of America had a number of Detroit members, including Roy
Chapin, chairman of Hudson Motor Company and a Union Trust board member. The

219. The Greater Penobscot Building.

220. Taos Pueblo in 1878 and 1936. (Photos: Byron H. Gurnsey and Arthur Rothstein, Library of Congress Prints and Photographs Division)

organization's journal, *El Palacio*, carried in its July 1920 edition an article on Detroit's *All the Arts* magazine, mentioning as well the magazine's coverage of Rolshoven's latest exhibit at the Detroit art museum.[30]

Architectural journals of the time published numerous articles highlighting the unique construction of the pueblos and the increasing popularity of Pueblo style through-out the Southwest and California. One of the foremost proponents of Pueblo Revival style was architect Richard Requa, who worked closely with Rowland as the local associate archi-tect on Rockwell Field in San Diego. Requa's flat-roofed Pueblo Revival style homes were featured in a number of publications, including the *Western Architect* in June 1920 and

House and Garden in November 1921.

In a 1923 *Los Angeles Times* article, Charles F. Lummis made the rather interesting claim that the pueblos, some reaching four or five stories in height, were "the first American sky-scrapers." Lummis described them as "unlike anything else in the world. They are terraced, so that the front of a building seems like a gigantic flight of steps."[31] The following year, in an article headlined "The New-Old Houses of Santa Fe," Omar Barker rebutted the commonly held notion that America "has no *native* architecture."[32] "Our own Southwest," wrote Barker, "offering its bit to the development of beautiful buildings in America, has evolved a style that is undeniably beautiful, practical and indigenous. It is the Santa-Fe-Pueblo type." The "only *true* American architecture," wrote Barker, was the pueblo type. Barker traced the origin of terraced, pueblo communities, such as Taos, to earlier cliff dweller communities of the American Southwest. Louise Cassidy, in a 1926 article from the *Architectural Record*, wrote: "It should be understood that 'pueblo' is an essentially Indian and not Spanish style."[33]

One notable building constructed in the Pueblo style during this period was the 1923 El Navajo Harvey House in Gallup, New Mexico, designed by Mary Jane Colter, architect for the Fred Harvey Company.[34] In an article on Colter, Claire Shepherd-Lanier describes El Navajo: "Colter borrowed elements freely from Pueblo and Navajo form, integrating them with modernist elements. The simple geometry of the facade is reminiscent of the patterns found in Navajo rugs, particularly the stair step, a familiar motif. The

221. The April 1917 issue of *Architect and Engineer* (later, *Western Architect*) featured on its cover the second-prize winner of the magazine's poster cover competition, "Pueblo Architecture," by Ernest E. Weihe. The height of this pueblo has been greatly exaggerated, giving it the appearance of a skyscraper. Note that the page corners are adorned with "whirling wind," or swastika, symbols.

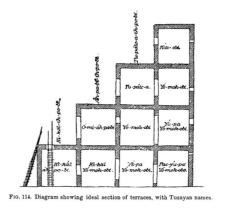

FIG. 114. Diagram showing ideal section of terraces, with Tusayan names.

222. An idealized cross section of a pueblo from *A Study of Pueblo Architecture in Tusayan and Cibola*, by Victor Mindeleff, US Government Printing Office, 1891.

building is composed of a series of rectangular masses that project and recede in the manner of traditional Pueblo architecture at Oraibi or Taos Indian Pueblo."[35]

Then, a new hotel in Albuquerque sparked a clamor within the architectural community. The Franciscan Hotel was financed by a group of Albuquerque businessmen who believed the fast-growing city could sustain a large hotel, despite the economic slowdown

223. El Navajo Harvey House in Gallup, New Mexico, designed by Mary Jane Colter and completed in 1923.

resulting from the Depression of 1920.[36] Trost and Trost, an architecture firm based in El Paso, Texas, was selected to design the building. The firm's head designer, Henry C. Trost (1860–1933), was one of the Southwest's early pioneers in the use of reinforced concrete, having built a number of such structures in El Paso between 1909 and 1916, including the twelve-story Mills Building.[37]

Trost set out to design a structure that was modern in every respect, yet drew on the architecture of the pueblos for its style—a building whose design was entirely American. Even before the Franciscan opened in late 1923, it was clear Trost had made an important contribution to American architecture. A *Los Angeles Times* article, announcing the hotel's opening, reported that "The Franciscan has been heralded in architectural trade journals."[38] Coverage and photos of the hotel appeared in the *American Architect*, the *Architectural Record*, and *Architecture*. Among the many periodicals mentioning the new hotel, the *Saturday Evening Post* in 1925 wrote: "The Franciscan Hotel [is] considered as among the most lovely of America's large buildings." Even in Europe the building had admirers; it was included in an exhibit at the 1926 Akademie der Kunste in Berlin—an unusual honor for an American hotel of modest size.[39]

George Edgell, in *The American Architecture of To-Day*, explained why the building was exceptional: "Trost & Trost have designed the Hotel Franciscan applying the principles of the pueblo style to hotel architecture on a large scale. This is modernism rampant, yet finely done. Angles are blunted, the mass of material is emphasized. Blocklike ornament

224. This photo of Albuquerque's Pueblo style Franciscan Hotel—taken shortly before the building's completion in 1923—appeared in dozens of publications.

with heavy cast shadows takes the place of the vocabulary of the historic past. The effort is cubistic, but cubism under definite intellectual control. It is closely related to the modernist productions of the German and Scandinavian peoples, by whom it has been acclaimed, but the ideas which it embodies, the forms which it displays, are taken from the pueblo style of the district in which it exists. It is thus a work of ultramodernism with an archeological basis and represents an original experiment in American architecture, as well."[40]

In appearance, the Franciscan Hotel looked less like a pueblo than previous Pueblo Revival buildings, and therein lies the reason for its recognition as a unique architectural experiment. The Franciscan was not a modern building dressed in a pueblo-like skin; Trost understood the characteristics that made pueblo buildings attractive, most importantly, the visual effect of simple cube-like forms stacked atop one another. He structured his design from the ground up, leveraging this characteristic in an artful and original manner. The large central tower of the structure had no cornice or other crowning feature, just the rounded top edges of the walls. In spite of this lack of ornament, the tower was imposing in its mass; the plain, unadorned sides presented a more striking appearance than expected from a building of only six stories.

Rowland would have, of course, followed these developments closely. His interest in the new architectural styles of the American West was evident in his 1911 plan for Hill Auditorium, described as incorporating the freedom from tradition of the Western school of architecture with the conservatism of the East.[41] His Spanish Mission style designs for Rockwell Field gave him practical experience working with architectural forms native to the Southwest. In his designs for major buildings, Rowland clearly sought to define a charac-

225. In this photo of the 1923 Franciscan Hotel and (to its left) the Neoclassical Masonic Temple—completed just four years earlier—the great contrast between the two styles is quite evident. Both buildings were designed by Henry C. Trost.

teristic American style, and, beginning with the Buhl, included overt references to Native Americans of the Southwest. With the Penobscot Building, idea and opportunity came together at the right moment.

By the standards of 1928, the Penobscot Building was, above the seventh floor, starkly devoid of exterior decoration. In spite of this lack of adornment—or, perhaps, because of it—the building's appearance is quietly powerful and imposing. Hawkins Ferry in his 1968 landmark tome, *Buildings of Detroit*, wrote of Penobscot: "it is devoid of archeological details . . . a series of setbacks ascend in a masterly cubistic composition to the apex."[42] Ferry, however, did not explain what Rowland was master of—what skills or principles did Rowland apply to achieve such a highly regarded masterpiece? What was it that made the "cubistic composition" "masterly"?

Considering the significance conferred upon the Franciscan Hotel by the architecture community, and the publicity it received, it is difficult to imagine it had no influence on Rowland, particularly as he had long reflected on a uniquely American architecture inspired by the American West. When Edgell and Ferry speak of "cubism" as applied to the Franciscan and Penobscot, they are describing appearance in a manner that implies no explanation. To describe a building, for example, as "neoclassical" implies not only its appearance—there are likely to be Greek or Roman columns and cornices—but its rationale—the principles and models employed by the architect. The key characteristic that differentiates Franciscan and Penobscot from other buildings and justifies "cubist" as a description is that they are *sculpted* works rather than frames dressed in a skin of a certain style. The *shape* of the building is the style, and little further decoration is necessary. More specifically, these two buildings were sculpted in accordance with a vision originating with the cubist appearance of the pueblos.

226. The cubist top section of the Greater Penobscot Building.

The upper section of Penobscot bears a resemblance to the Franciscan Hotel, in part due to Rowland's employment of the same design principles. It is possible that Rowland intended the similarity to serve the dual purpose of honoring the achievement of Henry Trost and displaying the next step in the evolution of Pueblo style—in this case, as applied to a much larger building. The similarities between Penobscot and the Franciscan, however, were not noted in the architectural press, an outcome that Rowland may have found puzzling.

On the other hand, a year after the building opened, the stock market crashed and demand for skyscrapers vanished, taking with it much of the interest in and discussion about their style.

Both Penobscot and Franciscan share with the pueblos a cubist appearance—flat roofs and terraced rectangular masses. Other Pueblo style characteristics tie the two buildings together as well. The top edges of walls on Pueblo Revival structures are rounded off, mimicking the pueblo's adobe walls. The Franciscan exhibited this feature, though the corners were carefully and consistently rounded, unlike the uneven edges of a pueblo. On Penobscot, the upper stories have beveled

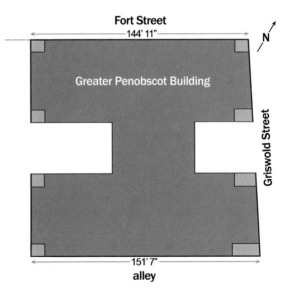

227. The plan of the Greater Penobscot Building is somewhat irregular, resulting in the south face being wider than the north. As a consequence, the setback on the southeast corner is deeper than the others.

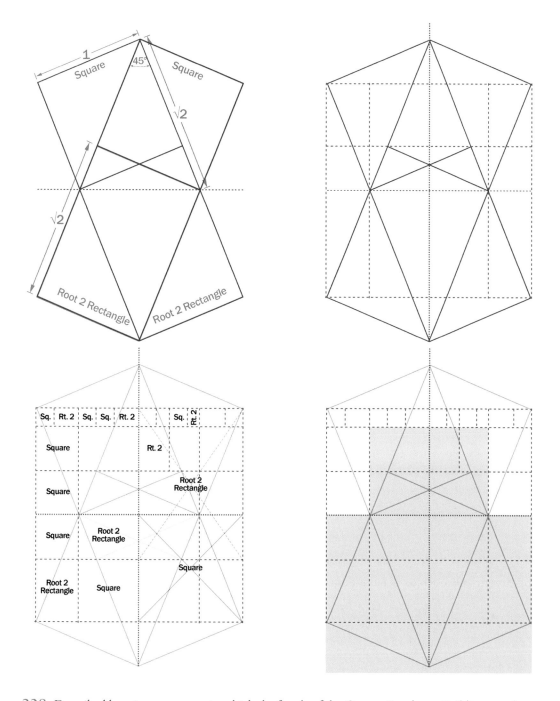

228. Described here is one manner in which the facade of the Greater Penobscot Building may have been developed employing root two rectangles. Begin with two figures, each comprised of one root two rectangle and one square. These are superimposed at a 45° angle (*top left*). The major intersection points of the figure are used to establish a grid (*top right*). The figure can be further subdivided into a multitude of squares and root two rectangles of various sizes (*lower left*), much as the bronze oinochoe example. With the lines of the grid guiding its location and size, the building's silhouette begins to take shape (*lower right*).

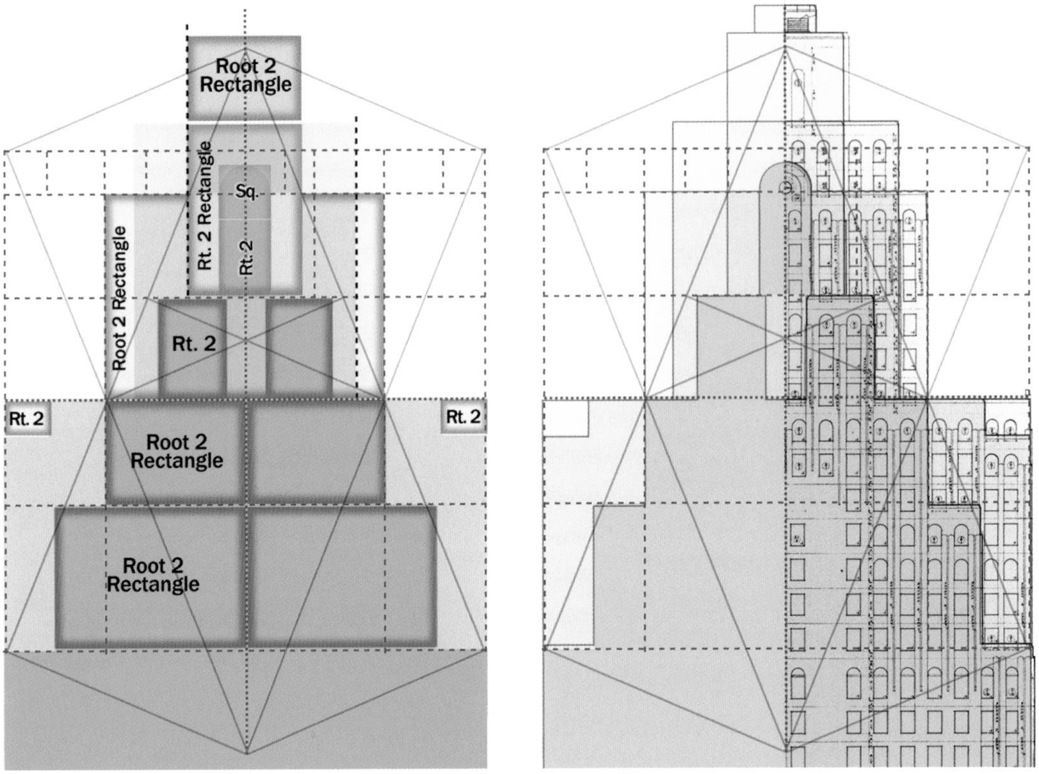

229. The design is further refined by adding multiple layers, accomplished by adding to or subtracting from the initial shape along lines that conform to the root two figure (*left*). Root two rectangles are combined to define the shape composing each layer of the building's face. When compared with the elevation drawing for the building's facade it may be seen the root two based shapes conform quite well to the original plan (*right*). Some deviation from an ideal root two based shape should be expected given that the dimensions of the building were constrained by standard heights for floors and standard widths for windows and bays. (All overlays by Michael G. Smith; the elevation drawing is adapted from sheet 42 of the Smith, Hinchman, and Grylls plans for the building)

coping topping the walls, presenting a similar appearance (some of this coping has since been removed). The tan color of Pueblo style is often replicated with adobe, plaster, or concrete, as with Franciscan. Penobscot's limestone skin is similar in color and was secured to the building in such a way as the seams between pieces are nearly invisible, so the structure appears as a solid mass. The beams supporting the roof of a pueblo typically project from the exterior wall; Pueblo Revival style buildings often copy this feature with decorative beam ends ("vigas"). This feature does not appear on Franciscan or Penobscot—Rowland was unlikely to use as decoration a phony version of a structural feature (for the same reason he wouldn't use a sham Greek column); perhaps Trost had the same aversion.

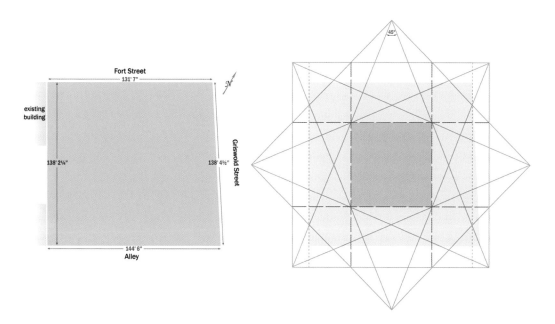

230. The Greater Penobscot Building's lot is nearly square, and the side along Griswold Street runs at an angle to the rest of the lot (*left*). A root two figure superimposed over the lot provides a starting point for shaping the tower of the building in much the same manner as with the Union Trust's north tower. Through the intersection points of the internal lines of the figure are drawn four (dashed) lines that divide the figure vertically and horizontally into five squares and four root two rectangles (*right*).

Aside from the general concept of pueblo-like sculpting of the building's top, what method did Rowland employ to arrive at a masterly composition? On the Union Trust Building, Rowland's opportunities to use geometric methods to determine the building's exterior form were limited, but on Penobscot, due to its height and shape, he had greater freedom to do so. The upper section of the building narrows through a series of setbacks beginning at the thirty-first floor and concluding with a small chamber atop the forty-seventh floor machinery penthouse (each floor is eleven feet high, except the penthouse, which is twenty-seven feet).

(The Greater Penobscot Building abuts and is connected to the 1905 Penobscot Building such that the corridors of the earlier structure continue seamlessly into the new building, as if they were a single structure. As a consequence of having to align the corridors, the inclusion of light courts in the new building was unavoidable.)

Of the four sides of the building's top section, the front (Griswold Street) and rear are nearly identical, as are the north and south faces. Due to the intersection of Griswold and Fort Streets being an angle greater than 90 degrees, the building's south face is wider than

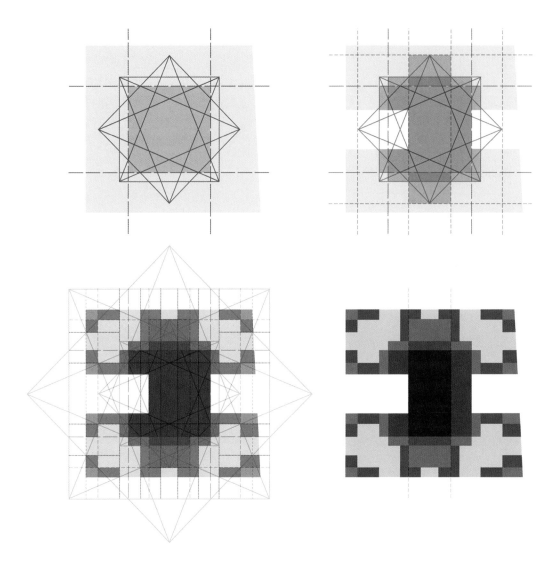

231. A second root two figure is drawn to align with the center square in the same manner as the larger figure aligns with the lot (*top left*). Vertical and horizontal lines (dashed) are added along points of the figure dividing it into smaller root two rectangles and squares. The light courts on the east and west have been added (*top right*). (The location and size of the interior corridors and light courts on the east and west of the structure were beyond Rowland's control as they were continuations of those in the adjacent, earlier Penobscot building.) Using the root two figures, lines are added through intersection points defining additional squares and root two rectangles (*lower left*). With the penthouse added in the center, the final form of the Greater Penobscot Building takes shape. The actual building varies in minor respects from the ideal form developed here due to construction considerations—standard structural dimensions, room sizes, and bay and window widths—and the thickness of walls (1¼ to almost 2½ feet) subtracted from or added to areas as small as 7 feet square.

the other three, so three of the minor setbacks on the building's corners facing Griswold are deeper than those on the west and north sides.

The major setbacks that form the "cubic" portion of the building on the north and south—from the thirty-first floor up—form a stepped shape similar to the stepped forms on the Union Trust Building. Like those on the Union Trust, these conform to a root two rectangle-based geometry.

Viewed from above, the Penobscot Building's east–west and north–south faces combine into a single, largely symmetrical design. The geometrical form for the root two rectangle that defines the north and south faces of the building also fits the top view of the building. This might have occurred naturally if all four faces of the building were identical, but they are not. Rowland had to arrange the setbacks on the east–west face to align with those of the north–south face, which he accomplished by conceiving the setbacks as a grid of rectangular shapes (as viewed from above), with corners aligned to the geometric form.

This approach entailed no difficulties or unusual building costs; in fact, Rowland's setbacks reflect the building's internal framework;

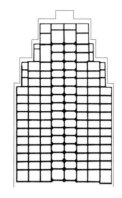

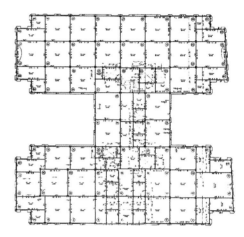

232. Steel framing plans for the thirty-fourth floor of the Penobscot Building (sheet S-21) (image is rotated upside down so north is up) and on the right, elevation of steel framing (sheet S-39) showing how the structure is composed of similarly sized rectangular sections. (Smith, Hinchman, and Grylls plans for the Greater Penobscot Building, May 16, 1927)

the dimensions of each setback are multiples or divisions of the building's framework modules: windows (width) and stories (height). Unlike the Buhl Building, where prominent piers and pylons were employed by Rowland as proxies to represent the building's internal frame, with the Penobscot Building, the innate shapes formed by the actual rectangular framing members are expressed directly. Arranged by Rowland according to geometric design principles, they are the most prominent feature of the building when viewed from a distance.

The setbacks in the building's upper section have, on occasion, been described as imitative of tall buildings in New York City. However, skyscrapers in New York adopted the terraced shape solely as a means of extracting the maximum amount of space permitted under the city's 1916 zoning law, enacted to prevent an unbroken wall of structures standing shoulder to shoulder, blocking the sun from reaching the streets below. The zoning law was spurred in part by the 1915 Equitable Building, which, with 1.2 million square feet, was the largest in the world at the time. Numerous buildings of that size, it was feared, would not only blot out the sun, but belch forth so many workers at lunch and quitting time, the sidewalks and transportation network would be overwhelmed. The zoning law permitted a building to fill the entire lot only to a certain height—determined by the width of the street. Each additional foot of height had to be set back from the street by a stipulated amount, except that a tower of unlimited height could be built if it did not cover more than 25 percent of the lot. The setbacks on Penobscot are much higher on the structure than those common in New York and differ in appearance as well.

Rowland wrote in 1921: "carved ornament of an appropriate character may add a human touch, a need often felt in buildings where the lines are otherwise rigid and geometrical."[43] For this reason, and others, Rowland included carved images of human figures within the building and on the lower floors of the exterior. This approach, however, was of little use with a very tall building viewed from a distance. Jay Hambidge devoted a great deal of his writing on dynamic symmetry to the human body, which is, like Greek art and architecture, dynamically symmetrical and best measured in terms of area rather than

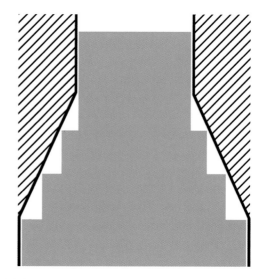

233. A depiction of the building envelope established under New York City's 1916 zoning law. Above a certain height, the law required buildings be set back from the lot line to avoid blocking sunlight, and to curb the number of building occupants. Buildings were often designed in stepped or ziggurat-like shapes to achieve the maximum square footage for a given number of stories.

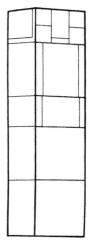

234. Jay Hambidge's three-dimensional representation of the human skeleton as measured by area. (Hambidge, "Dynamic Symmetry of the Human Figure for Advanced Students. Lesson IV," 1920 *Diagonal*, 74)

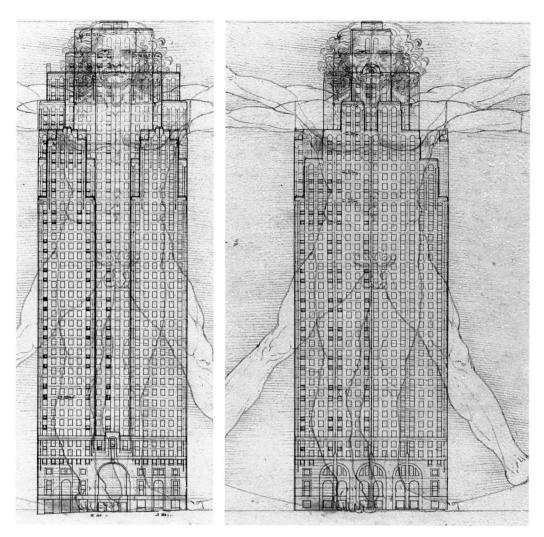

235. The Greater Penobscot Building aligns surprisingly well with the eyes, mouth, arms, and even body width of Leonardo da Vinci's "Vitruvian Man" sketch. (Building elevation from sheet 34 of the original Smith, Hinchman, and Grylls plans, Leonardo's sketch from Wikipedia)

line.[44] Hambidge also referenced Leonardo da Vinci and quoted extensively from a lecture by Robert Fletcher describing the Leonardo sketch popularly known as "Vitruvian Man."[45] Like Hambidge, Rowland also venerated the human body as a paradigm of function and beauty: "The most wonderful machine in the world is the human body, in spite of skeptical anatomists who wonder that it holds together. It was the chief inspiration in the days of Pericles and from it [the Greeks] may have achieved their high ideals of structural articulation."[46]

The Penobscot Building has dimensions (width and height) roughly similar to the human body, a fact that Rowland, a skilled artist who championed sketching the human body, would certainly have noticed. When the building is compared side by side with Leonardo's

236. Close examination of the drawn elevations of the Penobscot Building and Leonardo da Vinci's "Vitruvian Man" demonstrates that the major setbacks on the building align with significant features of the sketch. Shown are the Griswold and Fort Street elevations of Penobscot from the original Smith, Hinchman, and Grylls plans, sheet 34.

"Vitruvian Man" sketch, an astonishingly close resemblance may be seen. If the top of the head is aligned with the top of the building and the feet with the base, the tops of each of the major setbacks align exactly with the eyes, mouth, and top and bottom of the outstretched arms. Also remarkable, on the north and south elevations, the unusual half-round arch encircling a round opening aligns with the mouth of "Vitruvian Man." Even the width of the building matches up with the vertical lines indicating where the body ends and arms begin. This observation is clearly speculative and may represent an odd coincidence rather than conscious intent on Rowland's part, though the notion of proportioning a building according to the human body is not unprecedented.[47]

Rowland introduced a second theme to contrast with the building's cubist effect: the half-round arch, which may be seen in various sizes all over the building's exterior. The half-round is introduced at the building's entrance, where the front doors are framed by half-round granite columns, three of which are topped by carved downward-facing round features. Above the entrance is a massive half-round archway that frames individual

237. On the Penobscot Building, Rowland introduced a new ornamental feature: round vertical elements—presenting somewhat the appearance of organ pipes—seen here in a horizontal band and as a frame around the center window above the carved Indian figure.

windows, the uppermost in each grouping of six panes has a half-round top. This archway is echoed on the Fort Street facade by three large arches, each enclosing two smaller round arched windows.

Above the sixth floor, the building is encircled with a band of ornament comprised of convex vertical elements, similar in shape but varying in length. This same ornament encircles the center window above the entrance archway. These round elements appear to have sprung from Rowland's fertile mind; there was nothing similar in architecture. The zigzag, for example, that appears in another band was a common Romanesque decorative feature and appeared in Rowland's other buildings. If the idea for these round elements was inspired by something in Rowland's past, it may have been ranks of organ pipes, with which he was quite familiar, having played organ in church.

Beginning just below the band of carved zigzags are four vertical grooves cut into the stone, one on each corner of the protruding wings of the building. These grooves are inlaid with slate, the darker color of which helps these recessed features contrast with the lighter surrounding limestone. Extending upward, these grooves end just below the first setback at the thirty-first floor, where it becomes apparent the grooves are actually formed by the space between a pair of vertical panels ending in half-round shapes. Above and adjacent to these half-rounds, new pairs begin, extending upward until meeting the next setback. From the thirty-sixth floor up, a full row of these paired panels, terminating in half-rounds, appears below the roofline of each setback. Between the forty-third and forty-fourth floors, a band of these runs the full width of the building. Accompanying these paired half-rounds, beginning with the thirtieth floor, windows are topped with a half-round arch, becoming more numerous toward the top floors. (The windows are actually rectangular, the same as other windows on the building. The round arch is cut into the limestone cladding, which is superimposed over the window.) As the top of the building is approached, the cubist setbacks increase in number, and are joined by an increasing number of round-topped windows and paired half-round panels. Finally, on the north and south faces, an enormous half-round arch juts up above the roof of the forty-fourth floor. This large arch is visible from a great distance and contains nested circles, the innermost is an open oculus. The original building plans included a further round motif: a band of round "porthole" windows just above the arch at the highest (forty-fifth) floor.[48]

With the secondary theme of half-round shapes, Rowland created a

238. This photo, taken from the Penobscot Building's rooftop deck outside the thirty-eighth floor, shows the pairs of half-round topped panels (between the windows), each flanking a "groove" with an inlay of slate. The beveled coping atop the wall at the fortieth and forty-fourth floors is clearly visible. The spandrels are made of lead and painted.

239. Penobscot's cubist upper stories are softened by the addition of round-topped windows, paired half-round ornaments, and beveled coping.

counterpoint to the more dominant cubist theme of the building. The round shapes serve to soften the appearance of the angular cubes and give the upper section a more refined appearance. The darker grooves achieve the same result by providing finer detail to an otherwise homogenous surface. The contrast or tension between rectangular and round is not unlike contrasting themes in music. Beethoven's Grosse (great) Fugue, String Quartet op. 133, contains themes that appear to compete with each other—one is heavy and plodding, another, light and quick. They are heard alone and simultaneously, evolving the musical piece as well as the listener's understanding of each theme's role.

240. The Greater Penobscot Building under construction in 1928. The minor parapets at the thirty-eighth floor are clearly visible atop the two projecting wings on the western face of the building. (Courtesy of the Burton Historical Collection, Detroit Public Library)

The round-topped windows and paired half-round terminations of the vertical panels help define the setbacks of the upper stories, more effectively at times than the setbacks themselves. The uniform limestone surface of the building, under certain light conditions, lacks sufficient shadow for the setbacks to be clearly perceived. Windows, however, nearly always appear as dark voids; the round-topped windows stand out, accentuating the terraced exterior.

A subtle but significant alteration of the building's exterior occurred mysteriously, years after completion. Originally, a minor parapet was located at the thirty-eighth floor, on the peak of each of the building's four east- and west-facing wings. Although small—extending just three feet above the adjacent roofline—these pieces gave to the top of each protruding wing a well-defined stepped appearance that echoed the stepped setbacks. In addition, the beveled coping on the parapet around the large rooftop deck of the thirty-eighth floor, from which these pieces extended, was removed and replaced with railing—a minor alteration, but one at odds with the rhythmic appearance of the numerous beveled edges above and below.

It's not clear whether these parapets were removed due to some structural failure or as part of a plan related to the rooftop decks. It is not known, as well, when they were removed. A July 1942 photograph of the building shows the pieces still in place.[49] In a *Detroit*

News photograph from March 27, 1951, the pieces are missing.[50] An undated photograph in the Penobscot Building's archive shows one wing unaltered, with the parapet and coping in place, while on the second wing, both the minor parapet and coping are gone. Perhaps these pieces will turn up someday and be reinstated to their home on the thirty-eighth floor.

241. In this enlarged section of an undated photograph from the Penobscot Building archive, the building wing on the left is unaltered from its original appearance, while the wing on the right has lost its minor parapet and beveled coping.

The entire building is clad in limestone, except from the sidewalk to just beneath the second-floor windowsills; this section is covered in granite, very similar in color to the limestone. The cost of limestone declined in the 1920s due to improved mechanization of the quarrying process. The contract for Penobscot was filled by the Indiana Limestone Company of Bedford, Indiana, which had established a sales office in Detroit a few years earlier.

Above the building's entrance archway is a carved figure of a Native American. Although the figure is highly stylized—more abstract than those on the Buhl Building or Grand Rapids Trust—the headdress confirms its identity. Spandrels on the Griswold and Fort Street sides at the same level as the carved figure carry the whirling wind (swastika) symbol, while those higher up on the building do not. The spandrels between the windows of the second and third floors display sculpted Native American figures as well as symbols of commerce, industry, and prosperity.[51]

The main building entrance on Griswold Street is surrounded by polished mahogany-colored granite. The revolving doors are set behind deep columns that Rowland used to achieve a clever optical illusion. As Griswold Street intersects Fort Street at an angle somewhat larger than 90 degrees, the Griswold face of the building is at an angle to the remainder of the structure. Rowland, not wanting the lobby to have one wall at an angle to the other three, resolved the problem by increasing, from north to south, the depth of the passageway containing each of the four revolving doors. Consequently, the exterior of the entrance (at the columns) is parallel to Griswold, while the interior is square with the walls of the lobby.

Within the broad panel of granite above the doors of the Griswold Street entrance appear the words "Penobscot Building." However, the original granite panel contained an etched frieze depicting the signing of a treaty between settlers and Native Americans. In 1972, the building's name was changed to "City National Bank Building" and the panel was replaced by one carrying the new name. When City National Bank became First of America Bank around 1982, the original name of the building was reinstated and the words "Penobscot Building," in a typeface similar to the original, returned to the panel, but the frieze did not.

The root two rectangle theme employed by Rowland on the building's exterior is carried through to the interior in the large design on the lobby floor. The design is composed of cut marble in a variety of shades and shapes. The central starburst-like pattern is surrounded by four stylized whirling wind or swastika symbols. The entire design is derived from

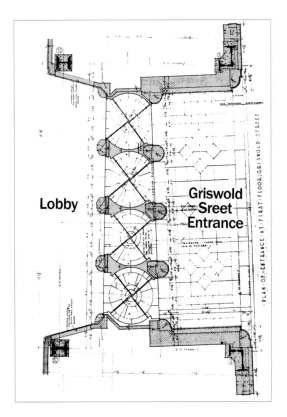

242. Rowland obscured the angle at which the Griswold Street face of the Penobscot Building runs relative to the rest of the structure. The outside of the entrance is parallel to Griswold, while the inside is square with the interior walls of the building. The angle is consumed within the four revolving doors by making them deeper from north to south. (Adapted from the original Smith, Hinchman, and Grylls building plans sheet 46)

243. Drawing for one-half of the frieze and lettering over the Griswold Street entrance. (From the original Smith, Hinchman, and Grylls plans, sheet 45)

a series of nested root two rectangles of various sizes.

In contrast to the Union Trust Building's dramatic public areas, those in Penobscot are subdued and modest in size. Marble covers nearly all surfaces, complemented by polished brass. The Native American theme is continued throughout the lobby with stylized bas-relief figures carved into the marble walls. These, as well as the figures on the exterior, were the work of Detroit sculptor Corrado Parducci.

244. Lobby of the Penobscot Building. The Griswold Street entrance is to the left; straight ahead is a passageway that leads to the elevator alcoves and then connects to the older Penobscot Building. Originally, a staircase to the right led up one story to the main banking hall of Guardian Detroit Bank.

The lobby, as originally constructed, had a grand stairway leading to the second-floor offices of Guardian Detroit Bank; the staircase faced the Griswold Street entrance. (The stairway was later removed.) The second-floor space once occupied by Guardian's main banking lobby is roughly forty feet high, forty feet wide, and 110 feet long. Teller cages lined both sides of the lobby, and banking offices on the north side of the second, mezzanine, and third floors extended to the Fort Street side of the building. Natural light entered through the large arched window on the Griswold Street side and from a matching window on the opposite end of the room. Large cross-shaped lighting fixtures located within the walls between the mezzanine and the third floor provided additional illumination. The offices on the north side of the banking lobby received light through the oversized windows along Fort Street.

The main banking lobby is characterized by a geometric theme of squares and regular octagons in the floor, ceiling, and woodwork. Rowland contrasted this with large half-round arches on all four sides of the room and segmental arches above the windows within the arches. The space is interesting in that it is more traditional in appearance than the Union Trust Building's banking lobby, yet was designed by Rowland a year later. This, of course, reflected the varied desires of the two firms involved. The Simon Murphy Company, owners of Penobscot, may have insisted that the decor of the banking lobby be suitable for use by other banks, should Guardian ever move out.

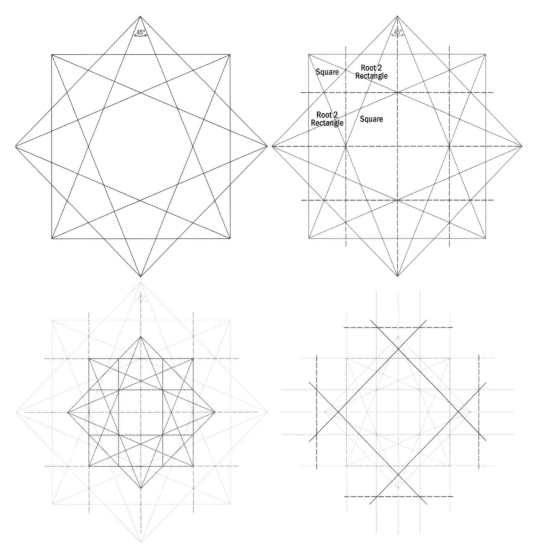

245. The marble design on the floor of the Penobscot Building's lobby is derived from root two rectangles and is a good example of dynamic symmetry applied to a design problem. The space may be divided with a root two rectangle figure (*top left*). The figure is divided into squares and root two rectangles by adding vertical and horizontal guidelines through intersection points within the figure (*top right*). The guidelines are used to add a second root two figure, which is divided into squares and root two rectangles in a similar manner as the larger figure (*lower left*). Angled lines (solid) are added that pass through intersection points within the root two figure and, where these lines intersect the guidelines, vertical and horizontal lines (dashed) are added (*lower right*).

Rowland was mindful of the context within which a building is viewed. Although the Penobscot and Union Trust differed in appearance from each other, and from the earlier Buhl Building, he employed visual themes to tie the three together. A prominent feature on the north and south sides of the Penobscot Building closely reflects a design appearing

246. Lines are drawn from the center to intersection points, creating triangular shapes (*left*). The resulting figure is overlaid on a graphic of the actual lobby design (*right*). By adding additional lines in the same manner, all the various shapes in the design can be developed.

247. The Guardian Group's banking lobby in the Greater Penobscot Building. (Private collection)

repeatedly on the Union Trust Building: angular steps topped by a half-round arch. This motif is found atop the large sixth floor windows of the Union Trust Building and again on its interior over the elevator alcoves, mural, and entrance.

The Union Trust Building reflects the appearance of the Penobscot as well. Penobscot's two protruding wings are its most characteristic feature when viewed from the front or rear. On the north and west sides of Union Trust, from the thirty-first to the thirty-sixth floors of the tower, the uniform pattern of the floors below evolves into two distinct protruding wings, mimicking Penobscot.

On the eastern face of the Union Trust Building, the windows in the top floors of the tower, and features in the parapet above, echo those of the Buhl Building—six windows wide, the middle pair set off by a contrasting background color and topped by an arch. The arch has a decorative feature at its apex and is flanked by piers that extend above the roofline.

248. In the center, from Penobscot Building plans, the north elevation showing the stepped facade topped by a half round arch. On the left is one of Union Trust's sixth-floor windows with a similar design. On the right, an elevation from the plans for Union Trust showing the same design over the Griswold Street entrance within the lobby. All are derived from the root two rectangle. (Drawings: Smith, Hinchman, and Grylls and SmithGroupJJR)

249. The northern face of the Union Trust (Guardian) Building's tower mimics the Penobscot Building's protruding wings and setbacks (seen here facing to the right). The eastern face echoes the Buhl Building across the street—on the tower, each of the top floors has six windows, the middle pair set off by a contrasting backgound color, as on the Buhl. The middle pair of windows is capped with an arch, which has a decorative feature at its apex, and the piers flanking these windows extend above the roofline.

8

END OF THE ROUND ARCH

The Romans brought the debasement of Greek detail as well as the much over-estimated circular arch forms, a reversion to fundamental barbaric clumsiness.

—Wirt Rowland, "Real Progress," 1931

The Union Trust and Penobscot Buildings represent Rowland's successful development of a modern American style of architecture, and positioned him at the forefront of his field. These were profoundly innovative creations and, though differing in appearance, were derived by Rowland through application of the same fundamental design principles. The Penobscot Building's dramatically sculpted upper section and smooth surface, free of piers and pylons, was pioneering. With the Union Trust, color was employed in a new and unprecedented manner (at least for such a large building), as was his use of stepped and angled arches. New materials and technologies were employed—instead of brass and bronze, hammered or cast as they had been for five thousand years, Rowland used Monel metal, cut and incised by machines, and welded together. The great size of the Union Trust and Penobscot Buildings afforded Rowland broad opportunities for developing themes—as does a symphony for a musical composer. The decorative treatment of each of these buildings is unified through themes on both the interior and exterior. Less obvious, but equally as significant, was Rowland's employment of dynamic symmetry as a geometric method to achieve harmony within these compositions.

Rowland was now fully confident in his ability to devise entirely new decorative schemes, inventing, rather than borrowing from the past. During the period from October 1926 to October 1930, Rowland turned out designs for a surprising number of smaller structures incorporating and evolving the design principles and motifs of his larger buildings, but with less complex themes. Michigan Bell was consistently the largest client during this time, requiring designs for central office buildings throughout the state and large buildings in Detroit and Saginaw. There were five schools, an office building, a printing plant, warehouse, and bridge. A number of branch banks rounded out Rowland's hefty workload. These structures may be roughly classified by Rowland's design approach to each. Most are modern ("modern" in this context as Rowland used the term, meaning not imitative of historic styles), decorated with elements he devised, and employing, most importantly, *angled and stepped arches* in preference to round arches; several of his designs mimic historic styles, and a number are (for Rowland) traditional in design.

Three buildings from 1928 and early 1929 best epitomize Rowland's application of concepts developed for the Union Trust and Penobscot Buildings—the further development of his version of modern architecture. The three vary widely in purpose, size, shape, and even appearance, yet are closely related by Rowland's approach to their design. The *Detroit Saturday Night* newspaper building at 1959 East Jefferson Avenue was completed in late 1929. Flint's 1930 Union Industrial Bank Building (now, the Mott Foundation Building) at 503 South Saginaw Street was built as a combination bank and office building, much like Second National in Saginaw and Grand Rapids Trust. At the corner of Oakman Boulevard and Woodrow Wilson in Detroit the former Michigan Bell and Western Electric Warehouse (now, the NSO Bell Building) was completed in 1930 as a storage and manufacturing facility.

Rowland's extensive use of stepped and angled arches on the Union Trust Building found further expression on these buildings. All have prominent decorative stepped or angled arches over windows and entrances, but no round arches. Rowland had previously employed the round arch as a contrasting feature to the many vertical and horizontal elements of a structure, but having discovered angled and stepped forms, he never again used the round arch on a modern building. The stepped and angled arches, being derived from dynamically symmetrical root two and root three rectangles, were readily transformed into new and different geometric themes. Yet as each variation was derived from the same root two or root three rectangle, a harmonious relationship of all the parts to the whole was maintained. Devising a distinctive angled arch or decorative design theme was as easy as rearranging geometric figures according to the principles of dynamic symmetry.

In Rowland's view, the effectiveness of the circular arch as a design feature was "overestimated."[1] He preferred angled arches for their "character, strength of contrast and a long range of visibility"; the round arch, by comparison, was "weaker and less definite."[2] Another reason for Rowland's rejection of the arch may have been its origin as a structural member (to support the wall above an opening); on modern buildings, walls were supported by the structure's frame and arches were unnecessary.

The building at 1959 East Jefferson was constructed for *Detroit Saturday Night*, a newspaper established in 1907 by Harry M. Nimmo and William R. Orr. In 1911, they had Smith, Hinchman, and Grylls design the building located at 550 West Fort Street as a home for the firm, but by 1928, *Saturday Night* had outgrown it and returned to Smith, Hinchman, and Grylls to design the new structure on East Jefferson. It was completed the following year. The heavy typesetting and printing equipment used by the newspaper dictated that the new building have high ceilings, a heavy-duty electrical system, and the capability of handling large floor loads. Although *Detroit Saturday Night* ceased publication in 1939, the parent firm continued on as a commercial printer: Saturday Night Press.

Detroit's leading role in the automotive industry brought many marketing and advertising firms to the city to produce the great amounts of promotional material used to market vehicles. These firms relied on vendors capable of setting type and producing printing plates—work that frequently required rapid turnaround. As a consequence, Detroit became a center for these types of businesses.[3] The Saturday Night Building was so well suited to typesetting, plate making, and printing operations that other such firms rented space in the building. Detroit Typesetting Company and Detroit Electrotype both relocated

250. The Detroit Saturday Night Building at 1959 East Jefferson was designed in 1928 and completed in 1930. Many of the decorative features of the building first appeared on the Penobscot Building.

there in the 1930s. In the 1940s, Michigan Typesetting moved to the building from West Fort Street, later absorbing Detroit Typesetting, making it the largest typographic firm in the Midwest.[4]

The city's second-largest type house was George Willens and Company. George Willens (1890–1973) was born in Chicago and moved to Detroit, establishing his typesetting firm in 1916. Willens was highly skilled in the typographic arts and focused his firm's efforts on newspaper and magazine ads, the most demanding and lucrative area of the business, and one that expanded greatly as automobile sales grew. Outside of Detroit, Willens is perhaps better known for having filmed the explosion of the Hindenburg as it attempted to land near Lakehurst, New Jersey, on May 6, 1937. Willens, and his sixteen-year-old son Harvey, had planned to travel to Europe on the Hindenburg's return flight.

In 1975, Willens and Company, headed then by Harvey Willens, merged with Michigan Typesetting, headed by Robert Levison, the new firm being called Willens+Michigan Company. Although Willens+Michigan was one of the first in the nation to adopt computerized, photographic typesetting, the development of the personal computer ultimately eliminated the need to purchase type from outside suppliers. Willens+Michigan faded slowly, closing its doors sometime in the early 1990s, bringing to an end 1959 East Jefferson's role as a home for Detroit's typesetting industry.

The Saturday Night Building presents a relatively smooth and monolithic face, devoid of the piers and pylons that characterized the Detroit News and Buhl Buildings. The Penobscot Building's smooth exterior also lacks these features, but its box-like masses reflect the modular arrangement of its steel framework. The Saturday Night Building lacks even these reflections of the structure's internal frame. Clearly, Rowland had concluded it was no longer necessary for the building's internal structure to be visually expressed on its exterior. Several factors likely contributed to Rowland's change in outlook, the first being that nearly thirty years had elapsed since the advent of steel reinforced concrete construction, and in that time, it had become the predominant method employed for nonresidential construction. The sight of steel and concrete buildings under construction was so common that providing visual clues to internal structure must, by 1928, have seemed superfluous.

A second influence may have been contemporary developments in transportation technology. Rowland was fond of comparisons between vehicles—the appearance of which was almost entirely determined by motive technology—and buildings. The locomotive, automobile, and airplane, Rowland claimed, are "the finest examples of architecture of this day."[5] Modern technology gave us the steel building frame, which, "cut away from the earth, become[s] dirigibles or aeroplanes." Rowland's point in comparing the frame of a vehicle with that of a building was to assert that, like a vehicle, there was no shame in a building having its essential technology exposed: "There is no disgrace in a frame," but the "frame has seemed so repugnant to the architect that he has dressed it over with more precious materials." In so thinking, Rowland was well ahead of his time; many years would pass before it became acceptable for the concrete or steel frame of a building to be visible. Although the underlying technology of automobiles, airplanes, and dirigibles did not fundamentally change during the 1920s, the outward appearance of these vehicles did. Automobiles evolved from open-topped wooden coaches mounted on frames to fully enclosed steel bodies, and in the process, much of the vehicle's structural frame was lost from sight. The Ford Trimotor, a large, all metal aircraft manufactured in Dearborn, Michigan, came along in 1926 and its aluminum skin gave no hint of the machine's internal frame, unlike the cloth-covered craft that preceded it. In 1922, a Detroit-based aircraft manufacturer received a US Navy contract to develop and build an entirely metal-clad dirigible with a smooth aluminum skin. A visionary like Rowland likely saw that machines were, for strength and performance, destined to cover their frame beneath a smooth surface. Why shouldn't buildings do the same?

An interesting comparison may be made between the Saturday Night Building and the Detroit Press Building (2751 East Jefferson, Detroit) as both were constructed to serve the same purpose and completed at the same time. George D. Mason and Company was the firm responsible for Detroit Press; the design was most likely the work of Rowland's good friend Herbert Wenzell. The building is clad in a light-colored brick with stone used on the first floor and for accents.[6] The general composition of the facade is a recessed central area flanked by two large, protruding pylons that extend above the roofline. Three piers in the center are topped by carved figures, and the pylons are adorned with a carved design scheme reminiscent of Ralph Walker's 1926 Barclay-Vesey Building (140 West Street, New York City). Detroit Press is an attractive building, with good lines, use of color, and subtle use of ornament. However, its prominent pylons and strong vertical piers belong to the earlier era of the Detroit

251. The Detroit Press Building at 2751 East Jefferson was constructed at the same time and for the same purpose as the Saturday Night Building. This building's design is based on the established formula of massive corner pylons and prominent piers; the Saturday Night Building, by contrast, emphasizes the central section of the facade.

News and Buhl Buildings. The Saturday Night Building points the way forward: a much flatter facade with emphasis on the central area (rather than corners) and geometric designs as decoration.[7]

The Saturday Night Building is an impressive structure. Close up or from a distance, the building soars and looms—its imposing appearance exceeds its actual size. To achieve this, Rowland incorporated into the design an effect he had employed previously on Hill Auditorium, Northern High School, and, in particular, the Detroit Savings Bank. The basic form is a relatively flat facade in the shape of an inverted U surrounding a recessed central area. This

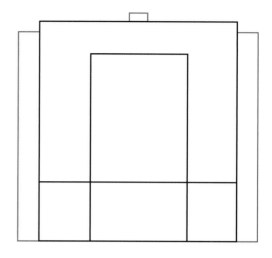

252. The Detroit Saturday Night Building shares a basic shape with the earlier Detroit Savings Bank: an inverted U surrounding a differentiated central area. Rowland found this composition gave the structure a more imposing appearance.

arrangement accentuates a structure's height and achieves a more commanding appearance. The Saturday Night Building is composed in the same manner—proportionally more similar to the Detroit Savings Bank, but set upon a base or pedestal as with Northern High School. Interestingly, Rowland reprised the layout of the building in the design on the six unusual spandrels.

Having settled on a layout for the facade, Rowland used a root two rectangle based geometric method to determine the exact location for all elements of the facade and assure the result would be properly proportioned. The factors over which Rowland had no control, building width and number and height of floors, resulted in an almost square facade, nearly ideal for a theme of root two rectangles and squares.

The decoration on the building's exterior consists of panels of round convex shapes similar to the "organ pipes" on the Penobscot Building. These shapes appear as a stepped design in the center of the parapet and above a window and door at ground level. They occupy the space between each window on the top floor, forming a horizontal band. The building's center is divided into three sections by two remarkable panels composed of three of these vertical rounds, which extend below the second-floor windowsills and then end in midair, so to speak, their ends cut at an oblique angle. The facade is capped by beveled coping in the same manner as the Penobscot Building.

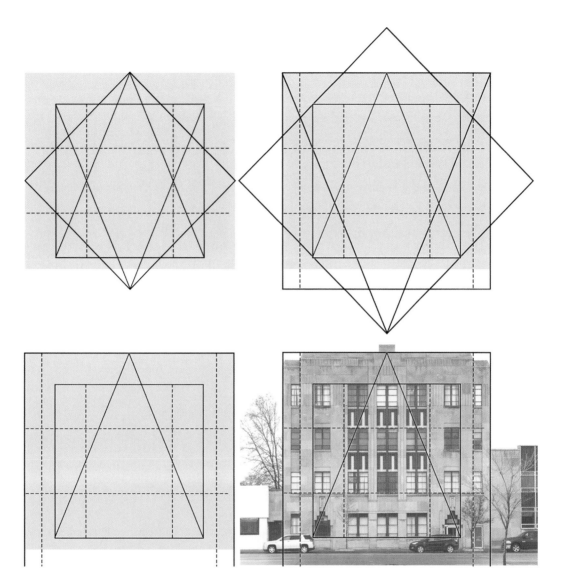

253. The composition of the Saturday Night Building is derived from nested root two rectangles. Beginning with the givens—lot width and approximate building height, shown in gray, upper left—a root two rectangle figure is inscribed equal in size to the building's width. Intersection points within this figure establish key vertical and horizontal locations for windows and decorative features (*upper left*). A larger root two rectangle figure is inscribed, its horizontal square equal to the building width (*upper right*). From this figure, the width of the narrow "wings" extending from each side of the building is established (*lower left*). All the design elements of the facade, including the stepped design in the center of the parapet and stepped arches on either side of the ground floor, are derived in this manner (*lower right*). The Saturday Night Building is a theme in root two rectangles and squares.

The sixteen-story Union Industrial Bank Building at 503 South Saginaw Street in Flint, Michigan, was designed by Rowland in 1928 as a combination bank headquarters and office building with a large banking lobby on the second floor. The bank came into existence in 1909 through the efforts of business and financial leaders in rapidly growing Flint; Charles S. Mott (1875–1973), head of a successful Flint-based axle manufacturing firm, was named president of the new bank. A short time later, Mott's company was acquired by General Motors, and Mott became one of GM's directors. Soon after, Walter P. Chrysler (1875–1940), president of GM's Flint-based Buick division, joined the bank as a director and became actively involved in the bank's management.[8] By 1928, the Industrial Savings Bank was the largest in Flint and had outgrown its 1923 headquarters building. Smith, Hinchman, and Grylls was selected to design a new building and construction began after the bank finalized its merger with Union Trust and Savings on May 1, 1929.[9]

When Rowland began work on the design of this new bank building, the Union Trust and Penobscot were nearly complete, giving him ample opportunity to evaluate how well the novel design ideas he developed for those buildings fared in practice prior to considering their further employment. The Union Industrial Bank Building primarily represented a fleshing out of possibilities and a more practiced application of concepts developed for the two earlier structures. Although Rowland could not have known at the time, this was to be his last skyscraper.

254. This design sketch of the Saturday Night Building shows clearly the layout of the facade. The ground floor, midsection, and parapet constitute three sections vertically; horizontally, the left side and mirror image right side flank the distinct center section. (Drawing: Smith, Hinchman, and Grylls and SmithGroupJJR)

255. The Detroit Saturday Night Building is clad in limestone and has a decorative treatment similar to the Penobscot Building. Convex round shapes—like organ pipes—adorn the building in stepped designs.

Rowland's most notable innovation for the building was an outgrowth of his use of Monel metal on Union Trust. By 1928, Nirosta, a stainless steel more easily worked and less expensive than Monel, had been introduced in the United States by Germany's Krupp Steel Works. Rowland selected Nirosta metal to be used throughout the structure's lobbies, banking hall, and other public spaces for decorative purposes. On the exterior of the building, instead of the painted steel used on earlier structures, Rowland specified aluminum for all exterior metal—window frames, storefronts, grilles, and spandrels.[10] The aluminum was finished in black enamel to contrast with the building's light-colored limestone cladding (aluminum was commonly used for spandrels at the time, but not for window frames and storefronts).

The building's second floor is entirely consumed by an expansive banking lobby, 66 feet wide with a clear space between columns of 38 feet, similar to the somewhat larger banking lobby of the Union Trust (80 feet wide with a clear space of 43 feet). To quiet the room, a new acoustical product from the Johns-Manville Company was used, consisting of a felt backing with a perforated canvas surface; the surface was painted in multiple colors. In the first-floor lobby and the basement safe deposit vault lobby a hexagon (root three rectangle figure) pattern was used for the ceilings. The surfaces were covered with aluminum and gold leaf metallic finishes accented by standard paint finishes.[11]

Angled arches based on root three rectangles are used throughout the building as the sole decorative theme. However, Rowland applied the geometric shapes here in a more direct manner than the Union Trust: instead of arranging small pieces to form a large (and often complex) geometric design, the geometric shapes formed by root three figures were employed directly. Rowland created a most interesting effect by combining two root three figures, one with the point up

256. Flint's Union Industrial Bank Building. To break up the massive expanse of windows on this face of the building, Rowland employed pairs of black enameled recessed aluminum spandrels to visually separate the windows into groups of twelve (four wide by three high), much the same as on the Penobscot Building.

257. The lobby of the Union Industrial Bank Building photographed just prior to completion in 1930. The aluminum and gold leaf metallic surface of the ceiling is evident. (Courtesy of the Charles Stewart Mott Foundation)

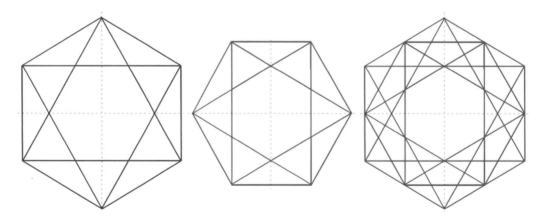

258. A root three rectangle figure (*left*) is combined with a second, root three rectangle figure turned on its side (*middle*) and sized so it is circumscribed by the first figure (*right*).

and a second with the flat side up, sized to fit just inside the first. There are no curved surfaces to be found; even the ceiling of the banking lobby is comprised of a series of angled panels.

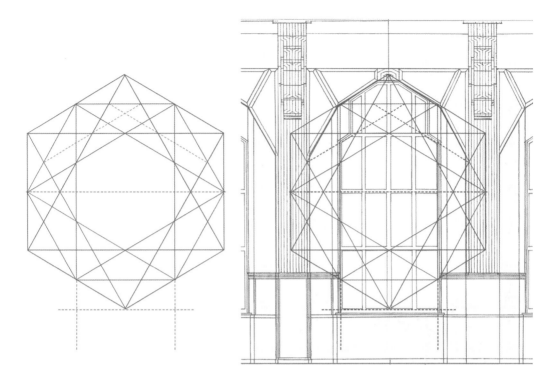

259. The shape, size, and location of the window and surrounding panels for the second floor banking lobby of the Union Industrial Bank Building are derived from the root three figure. The illustration on the right shows one of the large arches along the west side of the main banking room and the outside window framed by the arch. (Adapted from the original Smith, Hinchman, and Grylls drawing, sheet 26)

Variations of the root three figure are cut in the limestone exterior, much like the geometric designs incised in the Monel metal of the Union Trust Building. A similar geometric treatment appears within the building, cut into the stainless steel face of the elevator doors, wood paneling, wall and ceiling panels, banisters, and other hardware. Even the two large figures of eagles flanking the front entrance are comprised of these angles, resulting in a stylized carving that is quite modern in appearance.

Along the north-facing First Street side of the building, Rowland dealt with a potentially monotonous expanse of windows in the same manner as on the Union Trust and Penobscot Buildings, by separating windows visually into groups. From the sixth to the fourteenth floors, the windows are divided into groups of twelve—four wide by three high—by alternating light bands with dark spandrels. At the fifteenth and sixteenth floors, he employed much the same design as for the Union Trust Building: alternating recessed and projecting bays.

Although the design of the bank building was finalized prior to the end of 1928, little further work was carried out due to the pending merger of the firm with another

260. The second-floor banking lobby of Flint's Union Industrial Bank Building, taken just prior to completion. The ceiling is composed of facets, reflecting the angular arch shape used throughout the building. The hanging light fixtures are formed from the same faceted shape. (Courtesy of the Charles Stewart Mott Foundation)

Flint bank.[12] After the merger was executed in May 1929, work resumed, and in August, drawings for the sixteen-story building were completed. Shortly after, it was decided to add an additional floor, plans for which were completed on October 1, 1929. The seventeenth floor was to contain a dining room, a lounge, and a number of porches, and would connect via a circular stairway to the sixteenth floor, which was to have a dining room, lounge, and library instead of the previously planned rental space.[13] It is not known whether this club was intended solely for the bank's use or to serve some broader purpose, but in any case, the plan was short-lived.

On Thursday, October 24, the stock market crash began, bringing to light what the *New York Times* called "the most amazing bank swindle in history."[14] More than $3.6 million was embezzled from Flint's Union Industrial Bank by twelve employees in a conspiracy to profit from stock market trading. Among those involved were the bank's senior vice president, assistant cashier, discount manager, three vice presidents, and a number of tellers. The employees wrote fictitious notes to gain access to bank funds, with which they purchased stocks, repaying the ill-gotten loans after the stocks rose in price and were sold at a profit. They went so far as to pay informants at local hotels to provide a warning should a bank examiner arrive in town. The conspirators, however, were more skillful at thwarting bank safeguards than picking stocks, and losses began to mount. In the week prior

261. Front entrance of the Union Industrial Bank Building. All angles over the entry are derived from the root three figure. (The first-floor facade was altered and the chrome and black awning was added in the 1950s.)

to Tuesday, October 29, the stock market lost over 25 percent of its value; the conspirators realized they now had no hope of recouping their losses and repaying the covert loans. They met and decided to throw themselves at the mercy of the bank's board of directors. The fol-

lowing evening, Wednesday, October 30, the board heard the sorry tale of the embezzlers and, though there was a suggestion that the malfeasance be hushed up, bank president Charles Mott insisted the twelve be turned over to the authorities. Incredibly, Mott also announced that he would replace the stolen funds from his personal savings and had the money brought from Detroit the following day in armored trucks.[15]

Buffeted by the market crash and embezzlement scandal, the bank directors decided against adding the club to the building, and its plans were set aside. Demolition of the existing building on the property was begun that fall and, just over a year later, on December 15, 1930, the building opened.

262. Upper floors and equipment penthouse of the Union Industrial Bank Building, showing how the root three figure design was employed on the building's exterior.

Among the many Michigan Bell buildings designed by Rowland between 1926 and 1930, the largest, and one of the most interesting, is the Michigan Bell and Western Electric Warehouse, completed in 1930. As its name would suggest, the building was constructed to serve as a central warehouse for both Michigan Bell and its equipment supplier, Western Electric. It contained four functional areas: supplies storage, offices, vehicle garage, and phone equipment repair shops.[16] In addition to a large truck loading dock, the building was serviced by a spur of the Pennsylvania Railroad, and freight cars could be unloaded inside the building.

Western Electric had an efficient method of billing Michigan Bell for purchases. For each item shipped, a "tabulating card" was punched with holes, each of which recorded one detail of the transaction. Every month, the tabulating cards—about 100,000 in number—were run through tabulating machines to produce an itemized bill. The machines produced considerable noise, and so were housed in a special soundproof room within the building.[17]

In appearance, the Michigan Bell and Western Electric Warehouse is unusual, particularly considering its intended purpose as an industrial structure. The dominant feature is the extraordinary eleven-story central tower. For aesthetic reasons, it is taller than necessary, though it would have been somewhat less so had the planned addition of two stories to

263. The Michigan Bell and Western Electric Warehouse during its 2012 rehabilitation.

the main structure been carried out. The floors within the tower, above the main building, are 48 feet by 44 feet and originally housed phone company offices on the seventh through ninth floors, the building's PBX phone system on the tenth floor, and water tanks for the building's sprinkler system on the eleventh.[18]

Rowland was able to achieve, with little additional expense, an impressive appearance for the building, exemplifying a comment reported in the Michigan Bell company magazine: "the cost of erecting a building that adds dignity and beauty to a community is not greater than the cost of a plain structure."[19] This was accomplished in part by cladding the structure in bright orange bricks and the clever use of distinct vertical and horizontal lines within the brickwork to give the structure a more polished appearance. Most of Rowland's attention was focused on the tower—particularly its top, and around the entrance.

The tower is perceived as a distinct eleven-story unit, rather than as a five-story extension atop a six-story building. (In this respect, the Michigan Bell building may be compared to and contrasted with the Detroit Free Press Building [1925], which exhibits a somewhat similar arrangement and was designed by Albert Kahn's firm.) Rowland accomplished this primarily through his treatment of windows—the six-story main section of the building has bays of three windows each, while the tower has singles and pairs. The paired windows in the tower's center are separated vertically by black spandrels and provide a bold, unifying vertical element that begins with the entrance and ends in a prominent angled arch above the top floor. Flanking these paired windows are columns of single windows that rise between piers, adding another vertically unifying element. Rowland, however, wished

for the tower to appear—geometrically speaking—as a mass comprised of blocks, so the darker center strip of windows is divided every third floor by horizontal bands of brick. These bands create visual blocks comprised of twelve windows—three pairs flanked by six singles—much like those on the Penobscot Building.

The tower's top is finished in a manner that rivals the drama of Union Trust's crown and Penobscot's stepped cubes. From the tower's base, brick piers rise unbroken until terminating in a

264. The tower and rear sections of the Michigan Bell and Western Electric Warehouse Building.

265. In this 1930 photograph of the Michigan Bell and Western Electric Warehouse the octagonal superstructure on the tower and terra-cotta coping atop the walls on the main building (subsequently removed) may be seen. (Smith, Hinchman, and Grylls and SmithGroupJJR)

stepped arrangement above the top floor, where the eye is led to a conspicuous angled arch in the center. The arch is topped by a small, pier-like element echoing the larger piers. While this could be considered a keystone of sorts, it neither rests upon the arch below, or supports the arch as a keystone would. If this were a masonry wall building, with the arch supported by balanced stones, this unsupported assemblage would have fallen off. By placing this small pier and arch in such a way as they appear to defy gravity, Rowland flaunts the building's steel frame construction and demonstrates that a structure can appear strong and stable without having to mimic traditional methods of building.

The top of the tower is clad with a field of light-colored terra-cotta tiles, and similar tiles also cap the walls. A dimensional design on the face of the tiles is in the shape of the root three rectangle figure. The tiles capping the walls on the main, six-story building were removed at some point, but may still be seen on other sections of the structure. Also removed was an octagonal superstructure atop the tower.

The building's front entrance on Oakman Boulevard is set within a thirty-foot-high stone angled arch topped with a carved stone figure of a reel of phone cable. Recessed within the arch are the entrance and a large window. The space between is clad with aluminum

266. The Michigan Bell Niagara central office on the northwest corner of Mack Avenue and Cadieux Road was designed in 1928 and placed in service late in 1929. A third floor was added in the 1970s.

panels coated with a black enamel to contrast with the light stone. Above the doors, the panels are decorated with small lightning bolts on both the vertical surface and underside. The entire entrance, of course, was derived from the root two rectangle.

Rowland had freedom to experiment with new ideas and approaches on a number of Michigan Bell exchange buildings he designed from 1927 to 1929. One outstanding example is the Niagara central office in Detroit on Mack Avenue at Cadieux Road. This building was received by Rowland's design department early in 1928, construction began later that year, and the fully equipped building was placed in service in November 1929. (Once the building was complete, installation and testing of phone equipment could take up

267. Michigan Bell Niagara as it appeared as a two-story structure upon completion in 1929. Note the decorative carved limestone pieces along the parapet; when a third floor was added these were reused in place of some windows. (*Detroit News* collection, Walter P. Reuther Library, Archives of Labor and Urban Affairs, Wayne State University)

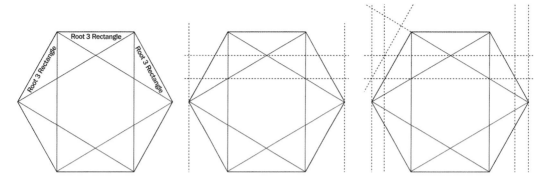

268. To design the arch for the Michigan Bell Niagara central office, Rowland may have begun with a root three rectangle figure turned flat side up (*left*). The full width of the window and frame is equal to the extreme width of the figure; horizontal lines through the intersections of the root three rectangles establish key points (*middle*). Lines parallel to the angled side of the figure are drawn through the points where vertical and horizontal lines intersect (*right*).

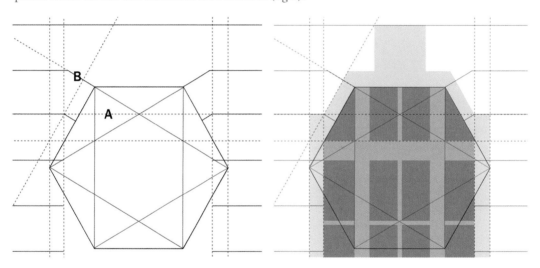

269. Lines indicating the location of the seams between each row of stone cladding are added. The baseline for the rows of stone facing is the dashed line "A." Seams between the stones atop the arch are angled (as at B) so they follow the extended internal lines of the figure (*left*). Using the lines of the figure and the rows of stone cladding, the entire arch takes shape as shown in the shaded area (*right*).

to a year.) Four massive angled arches dominate the facade, and, as with the Saturday Night Building, the height of the first floor is exaggerated by extending the arches nearly to the windowsills of the second floor. The bulk of the first story is clad in limestone, which gradually transitions to a pale yellow brick at the second floor.

The arch designed for this building provides an exceptional example of the flexibility of Rowland's geometric design system and the many variations it could produce. The main arch is derived from the root three rectangle figure, resulting in 60-degree angles, but, aside from sharing the 60-degree angle with other designs, the arch is unique in appearance.

Rowland could have arbitrarily altered the arch to achieve a different look, but his method of applying geometric design principles was certain to produce attractive and internally coherent results and was, in Rowland's hands, probably the fastest method as well—it may have taken him only minutes to design this arch (though in practice, he probably developed a number of alternatives and selected one).

To begin, Rowland likely took a figure comprised of three root three rectangles and rotated it so one of the flat sides was up. Vertical lines tangent to the extreme left and right points of the figure are equal to the full width of the window and surrounding frame. Horizontal lines drawn through the key intersection points of the three rectangles define additional elements of the design. The facing of the building is comprised of rows of stone blocks that figure in the design: the visible seams between the blocks align with the internal lines of the root three rectangle figure above the window.

Aside from the arches, Rowland

270. The completed arch on the Michigan Bell Niagara central office. Every aspect of the window and sash, stone facing blocks, and decorative design was derived from the root three figure. The structure's size is deceptive; the top of the window frame is twenty feet from the ground—the equivalent of a two-story commercial building.

dressed up the building with carved limestone designs. Above the second-floor windows are limestone spandrels containing a carved design in the form of angled lines. As originally constructed, the building had two floors; above the second was a parapet containing seven stone panels of carved limestone. When the third floor was added, these panels were moved and reused in pairs, set one on top of another, in lieu of windows on the third floor. These noteworthy panels have a deeply carved design comprised of layered, angular shapes closely resembling the diamond-shaped design in gold, black, and white terra-cotta atop the Union Trust Building. Decorative features were typically integrated into the structure in a permanent manner, but these deeply carved panels are a departure, installed more like a window frame and able to be removed without being demolished in the process.

In 1929, Rowland and his team designed the Michigan Bell Central Division Headquarters Building in Saginaw to house business offices and exchange equipment. The building has six full and two tower floors (constructed so that up to six more floors could be added), and was the largest Michigan Bell

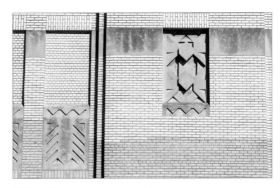

271. The unusual carved limestone spandrels and panels on Michigan Bell Niagara. The designs on the panels (*upper right*) are similar to those on the north tower of the Union Trust Building.

structure outside of the Detroit headquarters building. Clad in limestone with accents of enameled aluminum, the two-story-high angled arches on the base of the building present an imposing appearance. The treatment of the roofline on the sixth, seventh, and eighth floors is similar to that of the Union Industrial Bank Building, but is here much closer

272. The former Michigan Bell Saginaw office building at 309 South Washington Street.

to street level and so more a factor in the building's appearance. A layered design, angled and stepped, and derived from the root three rectangle, caps the piers between window pairs, the smaller intermediate piers, and even the area above the uppermost windows.

The root three rectangle theme is visible in many locations on the exterior of the building, particularly in the angled arches. Each large second-floor window is topped by an angled arch, and above is a second arch cut into the surface of the stone. The stone arch may appear at first glance to be inconsistent in shape with the arch of the windows; however, as both shapes are derived from the root three figure, they are, in fact, complementary.

Over the doors of the main entrance is an unusual arch comprised of thin slabs of bluish-green stone—a pleasing dab of color set within an otherwise monochromatic background. This feature, as well as the large, rectangular panels attached to the face of the arches over the second-floor windows, are examples of Rowland poking fun at our deeply embedded notion of the means by which modern buildings remain standing—not by blocks of stone carefully piled and balanced atop each other, but by means of a steel and concrete frame to which everything is securely attached.

While the exterior of the Saginaw building is conservative in its use of color,

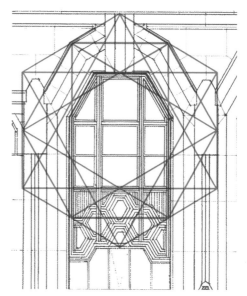

273. The double root three rectangle figure superimposed over the original building plans for the Michigan Bell Saginaw building. From the same figure, Rowland likely derived both of the arch shapes, as well as other features of the second-floor window area. Note that the figure is centered on the window vertically and the spandrel below is equal in height with the decorative stone piece above. (Smith, Hinchman, and Grylls original plans, sheet 11)

274. Michigan Bell employees enter the Saginaw building sometime in the 1940s. (Michigan Bell Telephone)

the interior is anything but. The lobbies are clad in green, taupe, and rose marble, and all metalwork is stainless steel. The public business office (now eliminated) on the north side of the first floor had an angled cove molding with hand-painted designs in bright colors ringing the room and each column. The walls were paneled in light and dark bands of walnut and cork (to reduce noise). The terrazzo floor had patterns of squares and diamonds in green, black, and white. The furniture was color coordinated in green leather, and even the operators' chairs had green wooden seats.

275. Above the dropped ceiling in the former business office of the Michigan Bell Saginaw Building the colorful hand-painted cove molding on the walls and piers can still be seen.

A large grille in the entrance to the front lobby is bordered by a frame with an inscribed design. The grille panels are custom made and have a pattern comprised of eight-sided root two figures.

The same root three figure served as the design basis for the Union Industrial Bank Building, Niagara central office, and Bell Saginaw office building. Rowland, however, extracted different geometric designs from the root three figure, giving each building a unique appearance. This flexibility is inherent in Rowland's geometric system—and dynamic symmetry—offering options unavailable with the round arch.

In Grand Rapids, another Michigan Bell building from 1929 was constructed as a warehouse and garage. Bell had the structure set well back from the street to leave room for an office building to be erected at a later time.[20] Despite this fact and the building's humble function, the facade was given an attractive brick skin and a large angled arch over the entrance, resulting in a building that Bell described as a "thing of beauty."[21] As the building approaches one hundred years of age, the design retains its freshness.

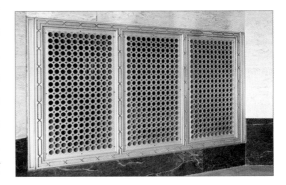

276. A large grille in the lobby of the Saginaw Michigan Bell building is made of stainless steel and has a pattern comprised of root two figures.

In 1927, work on the Ambassador Bridge was begun, and Smith, Hinchman, and Grylls was selected to design the terminal buildings, concrete piers, and the two massive cable anchorages, designed by Rowland and featuring the angled arch motif. While the cable anchorages support sections of the street approach to the bridge, their primary role is to anchor the two massive support cables from which the bridge is suspended. Each anchorage

277. The former Michigan Bell garage and warehouse at 1415 South Division Avenue in Grand Rapids. Except for the partially bricked-up windows, the building looks much like it did when completed in 1929.

278. The Ambassador Bridge was the world's longest suspension bridge upon its completion in 1929. It is supported by cables anchored within ten-story-high piers at each end of the span. The Canadian side is seen here.

rises over one hundred feet from ground level and extends 105 below the surface to rest on bedrock. Each anchorage is comprised of steel reinforced concrete and weighs 6,000 tons. The original terminal buildings are gone, but two roadway piers, which support the roadway approach over Fort Street on the American side, and two cable anchorages sporting Rowland's most colossal angled arch may still be admired.

279-1 & 279-2. Michigan Bell Pingree central office as it appeared in 1929 (*top*) (Photo from *Michigan Bell*, December 1929), and today, after numerous additions.

On a number of low-rise buildings from the period 1927 to 1930, Rowland relied on vibrant color as the chief decorative element. For Michigan Bell, he designed three central office buildings that exemplify this approach. The Pingree central office building, clad in bright orange brick, was constructed beginning in 1928 (simultaneously with Niagara) at the corner of Grenier Avenue and Grotto Court.[22] In its original incarnation, Pingree was two stories high and six bays wide; it has since been significantly enlarged in both directions. The first floor of the building is mostly stone with bands of brick; the stone bands give way to all brick in the middle of the second floor. Before the additions, the decorative treatment of the building's roofline consisted of stepped layers of brickwork over each of the second-floor windows.

Aside from the bright orange brick, the building's most interesting feature is Rowland's treatment of the first-floor windows, which are recessed within a frame of rounded stone, with corbels at the top. Over each window is a great stone lintel, twice as high as adjacent brick and stone bands.

Construction of the Madison central office on East Bethune Avenue at John R Street in Detroit's New Center area was begun in October 1928. The building's design and construction were handicapped by an unusual circumstance: Bell's existing two-story "Empire" exchange building on the property was to remain in operation and a new five-story building constructed around it. The new building was essentially an addition, but the property lacked adequate room for it, so a plan was devised to enclose the existing exchange building—a wall-bearing structure—within the new, reinforced concrete building. As a consequence, the Madison central office building presents an unorthodox appearance: the east side of the structure is U-shaped, due to the enclosed Empire building, while the west side is a simple rectangle. The western section later received a five-story addition.

Madison is clad in a vivid yellow-orange brick, giving the building a bright, sunny appearance even when the sun is not out. Limestone covers the area from the granite base to the middle of the second floor. Each pier is covered with a stone panel extending nearly to the top of the second-floor windows and topped with a prominent chevron-shaped design. These panels emphasize the vertical, while the crenellated underside of the second-floor windowsills adds a horizontal contrast—both the panels and crenellation serve as the outermost of several layers of framing for the large windows. The crenellation motif appears in miniature on the steel window frames.

280. Rowland's window design on the Michigan Bell Pingree central office is exceptional, combining the bright orange bricks with cool, gray stone. Rounded vertical corners contrast with sharp edges and terminate in corbels at the top.

The area above the windows of the five-story section of the structure bears some of the most interesting design work on the building. Although this section appears to be U-shaped with two wings flanking a central courtyard, the original design of the entire building was a large, rectangular western section with an L-shaped extension to the east. The five-floor addition did not, for some reason, cover the entire rectangular western section (and extend all the way to the courtyard), resulting in a five-story U-shaped section with unmatched wings on either side of the courtyard. The parapet on the eastern wing (along John R Street) has decorations capping the piers comprised of rounded stone piping of the sort Rowland used on the Penobscot Building, but here, single bands of stone trace more complex designs.

Between these, the space is filled with brick of a more reddish color than that of the rest of the building, contrasting in much the same manner as the band of red brick between the seventh and eighth floors of the Union Trust Building. The crenellation from the second floor is repeated here in an unusual double layer above the top-floor windows. In the courtyard, Rowland used a stepped motif on the parapet, reprised on the face of the penthouse above and behind.

281. Michigan Bell Madison central office at the corner of East Bethune and John R Street in Detroit's New Center area. The five-story addition on the west side of the building was not likely designed by Rowland.

In 1929, the design for Michigan Bell's Vinewood central office was produced by Rowland and his team. The building, located on Fort and Wheelock Streets in southwest Detroit, is exceptional in that its original appearance has not been altered by additions. (There have been minor modifications to the structure: bricking up of most of the windows, removal of the lanterns flanking the entrance, and replacement of the front door.)

Vinewood is clad in brick ranging in color from bright orange to medium red and, occasionally, deep bluish purple to give texture to the surface (Rowland nearly always

282. Michigan Bell Madison central office as it looked when completed in 1929, prior to the five-story addition. (Smith, Hinchman, and Grylls and SmithGroupJJR)

specified brick of varying shades, rather than all of the same color). The brick is sufficiently dark to contrast dramatically with the building's stone accents, yet bright enough to give the structure a distinctively colorful appearance. Some decorative features of the building may be seen as reminiscent of Romanesque or Gothic, and this is likely due to Rowland's desire to integrate Vinewood into the already well-established neighborhood of older storefront build-

283. The area above the fifth-floor windows of the Michigan Bell Madison central office contains the building's most interesting detail work. The designs continue on the mechanical penthouse, above the top floor.

ings and churches, particularly the nearby All Saints church (completed 1926), with which Vinewood shares a number of decorative elements.

The entrance is highlighted by a projecting frame of stone, within which is a round arch over the doorway. Flanking the doorway are two decorative buttresses that narrow

284. The Michigan Bell Vinewood central office building was completed in 1930 and placed in service July 10, 1931. It is noteworthy as one of the few central office buildings with its original roof and penthouse treatment still intact, as it was not modified by the addition of floors.

in steps as they rise. On the surface of these buttresses are decorations comprised of three vertical rods. The building's parapet is extended upward above the entrance in a stepped shape forming a decorative penthouse (essentially an extension of the actual penthouse located behind it). The stone face of this penthouse has four designs that mirror those flanking the entrance—three rods, the middle longer than the outer two—but cut in relief and with chevrons on either side. Stepped forms and chevrons appear elsewhere along the parapet and within the spandrels.

285. The Michigan Bell Vinewood central office was compatible in style with nearby structures, yet modern in design. The brick used is mostly red and orange with some bluish purple.

The Vinewood building is uncomplicated in its design. Only a small number of unique stone pieces were required to produce the rich-looking facade, a testament to Rowland's ability to wring a great deal of beauty from a small amount of material. An example of this may be seen on the face of each pier where a groove or recess in the brick extends from the decorative stone above to a small stone below. This decorative element required very little effort (or cost), yet it adds interest and variety to the facade, while helping to integrate the parapet with the lower stories.

A number of the Michigan Bell central office buildings from the period 1926 to 1930 were of a more traditional design. Buildings in Benton Harbor (West Wall Street, west of Pipestone), Jackson (South Jackson at West Washington Street), Pontiac (South Mill Street at East Huron Street), and Detroit's Columbia exchange (52 Seldon Street in Midtown) were all similar in size and design. All had prominent piers and large round arched windows at the first floor, much like the Detroit News Building. In fact, the first two floors of the Benton Harbor central office are nearly identical to Rowland's 1920 design for the United Savings Bank of Detroit on Griswold Street (figure 95, page 114). The most probable explanation for Rowland's use of a more traditional look was his desire to avoid an obvious clash with the older buildings in the immediate area (many of which are now

286. Michigan Bell Benton Harbor (*left*) and Detroit Columbia are both traditional designs, similar in many respects to the Detroit News and United Savings Bank of Detroit Buildings. (Compare the Bell Benton Harbor building with the United Savings Bank, completed in 1922; see chapter 4.) Prominent piers, corner pylons, and round arched windows on the first floor are characteristic of all four buildings.

gone), or perhaps the enormous workload faced by Rowland and his staff at this time necessitated reuse of proven designs with merely superficial changes. Nevertheless, it is interesting to note how Rowland's designs complement nearby traditional buildings and, at the same time, exhibit modern features.

In Holland, Michigan, is the Michigan Bell Holland central office (13 West Tenth Street), one of a number of structures designed by Rowland to evoke a historical style. The building recalls Dutch architecture of the seventeenth century (sometimes referred to as Flemish) and features a stepped gable, a common fea-

287. The Michigan Bell Flint central office, designed in early 1927, features decorative details similar to those on the Penobscot Building. The layout of its facade (in its original three-story configuration) with its simple cornice echoes older bank buildings one block east. (Courtesy of Kettering University Archives)

ture of the period. The appearance of the structure is further enhanced by superb brickwork and small decorative details. Another evocative central office, also designed in 1928, is

Michigan Bell University on Six Mile Road at Stoepel Street in Detroit's University District (which was enlarged in 1976, substantially altering the appearance of the building). Rowland designed this central office to complement the existing Spanish Mission style buildings in the area—Gesu School and the University of Detroit.

The close relationship between Smith, Hinchman, and Grylls and Michigan Bell may have resulted in an unusual design task for Rowland in 1928. It was at this time that the Bell System adopted a standard manhole cover for the entire country. The manhole frame and cover were developed by Bell Labs and supplied to the Bell operating companies by Western Electric Company.[23] According to a 1967 article in Western Electric's in-house journal, the company acquired more than 16,000 of the covers annually.[24] The design on the manhole cover, familiar to any pedestrian in the United States, consists of a center logo surrounded by rings of hexagons. While it is possible that Bell

288-1 & 288-2. The Michigan Bell University and Holland central offices were both designed in 1928 and placed in service in 1930. (*Top*, Smith, Hinchman, and Grylls and SmithGroupJJR, as published in *Michigan Manufacturer and Financial Record; bottom*, Brandon Bartoszek)

Labs came up with the art for the cover on their own, it seems more likely, given the marketing implications of hundreds of thousands of highly visible covers on streets and sidewalks, they would have procured the graphics from an experienced designer outside the company.

At the time, the Bell System's fastest-growing operating company was Michigan Bell, whose president, Burch Foraker (1872–1935), had strong national ties. Foraker started with New York Telephone in 1893, quickly working his way up through the ranks to division superintendent of the Manhattan area (in charge of plant construction and operation) and then general manager for New York State (excluding metro New York) until he was appointed head of Michigan Bell in 1926.[25] An article on Foraker's contribution to the development of New York City's phone system described how he learned the business:

"he had worked through the hard school of underground and overhead cable work in the streets and alleys of the metropolis and had become thoroughly acquainted with the problems and intricacies involved in building and operating a telephone plant."[26] The *New York Times* described Foraker as "one of the leading telephone operating and construction men in America . . . he originated many ideas and changes in telephone plants construction, operation and methods. Most of them are standard all over the world." "Many executives of the Bell System were trained in telephone work by Mr. Foraker."[27]

289. Over one million Bell System and AT&T manhole covers bearing a geometric design dating from 1928 grace the nation's streets and sidewalks.

After arriving at Michigan Bell, Foraker oversaw the massive construction program that added dozens of new central offices, the Saginaw building, the warehouse on Oakman Boulevard, and additions to the Detroit headquarters building—all designed by Rowland. Foraker was also a director of the Union Trust Company during the time the Union Trust Building was constructed. Foraker's familiarity with the technical side of the business and experience with plant construction would have placed him at the forefront of construction oversight and in direct contact with Smith, Hinchman, and Grylls, and likely with Rowland as well. Given Foraker's experience, it seems unlikely that Bell would have embarked on such a consequential project as designing a standardized manhole frame and cover without involving him. Having seen the endless variety of modern and interesting designs that Rowland was able to conjure, it is easy to imagine Foraker casually asking Rowland if he cared to try his hand at a small but interesting design challenge.

The geometric design for the manhole cover is easily derived from the same root three rectangle figure as Rowland used on his buildings. In fact, the root three rectangle permits the design to be drawn without measuring any lengths or calculating any angles. Rowland would have been familiar with this particular approach from having employed it to devise and draw the designs surrounding the exterior arches on the Union Trust Building, which are quite similar to those on the manhole cover.

A search of AT&T's historical records and Bell Labs publications failed to turn up documentation on the source of the design, and a search by Telephone Collectors

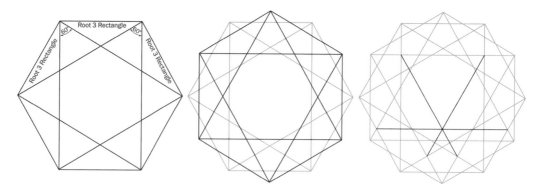

290. The geometric design on the Bell System manhole cover is derived from root three rectangles (*left*). Beginning with a figure comprised of three rotated root three rectangles, a second figure is overlaid and rotated (*middle*). Lines are added from intersection points and parallel to the sides of the root three rectangles (*right*).

291. A smaller root three figure may be drawn within the larger figure by connecting intersection points (*top left*). Drawing bisecting lines permits the addition of successively smaller root three figures within the first (*top right*). Continuing to add lines (and remove others) between intersection points results in a root three based pattern (*bottom left*). Once completed, the process results in precisely the same geometric design as found on the Bell System manhole cover (*bottom right*).

International also came up empty handed. The author of the design may never be confirmed, but the connections to Rowland and the similarity of the design with his other work of the time suggest he may have been responsible.

The Benjamin Nolan Intermediate School at 1150 East Lantz Street was designed by Rowland in 1926 for Detroit Public Schools. Nolan Intermediate is a striking two-story building on which Rowland made limited use of French Renaissance decorative features. The building faces north, so the facade is nearly always in shadow. To counteract the lessened contrast and absence of sunlight suffered by a north-facing wall, Rowland alternated vertical sections of light-colored stone with dark vertical bands of red brick. Where these sections meet, large quoins help blend them visually and add further vertical emphasis. Two pyramidal roofs highlight the entrances and add a bit of height to the structure.

292. The six-sided designs that appear on spandrels of the Michigan Bell Saginaw Building are similar to those on the manhole covers.

Nolan was the first of five schools designed for the Detroit system by Smith, Hinchman, and Grylls between 1926 and 1930. The second was David Mackenzie High School on Wyoming Avenue at West Point Street, designed in early 1927 and opened in September 1928.[28] As Detroit's population continued its rapid increase, the city was in desperate need of new school buildings; between 1921 and 1929, high school enrollment grew from 9,000 to over 25,500.[29] Mackenzie High was erected to meet this need—an otherwise typical and unexceptional building. Yet Rowland in no way shortchanged the school; it was stunning—he turned a plain-looking building into architectural art.

When Rowland set to work on Mackenzie, he was just completing the Union Trust Building, a fact that might be surmised from the school's appearance, as it sported a very similar decorative application of Pewabic tile. Rowland also brought to bear many of his clever brickwork techniques, such as those seen on buildings at Langley Airfield.

Mackenzie's Wyoming Avenue entrances had a spectacular surround of brick and terra-cotta tiles with angled and stepped arches that played out in three dimensions. The terra-cotta tiles were of different thicknesses, presenting a layered effect and, behind this frame, an entry alcove clad in bright orange tiles. Centered above the opening was a highly stylized human figure comprised of colored tile—very similar to the aviator over the Union Trust's Griswold entrance. Above the third-floor windows were eye-catching accents in blue, orange, and yellow terra-cotta set in stepped and diamond-shaped designs. The walls of the building were capped with an attractive band of polychrome tile coping (similar, except for color, to those on the Michigan Bell Madison building).

Mackenzie and other Detroit high schools during this period were constructed in phases, or units, beginning with a section of classrooms which could be quickly placed in service. The first unit of Mackenzie, consisting of six classrooms, was completed in 1928. The twelve classrooms of the second unit were ready in the fall of 1929, and the third unit, containing the library, cafeteria, offices, and specialized classrooms, was completed in 1931. The building's cornerstone was placed as part of the third unit and was, therefore, inscribed with the year 1931. Sadly, the building was abandoned in 2007 and demolished in 2012.

293-1 & 293-2. Although more complex, the design carved in stone surrounding the entrances to the Union Trust Building are derived in the same manner as the manhole cover design.

In 1929, the Detroit Board of Education contracted with Smith, Hinchman, and Grylls to design two more high schools: Pershing, on Ryan Road at Seven Mile Road, and Denby, on Kelly Road at Grayton Street. Except for cosmetic differences, the two buildings are essentially identical. Plans for Pershing were completed in June 1929, but construction was delayed due to problems acquiring land for the building.[30] Plans for Denby were completed in September 1929 and construction began prior to the end of the year.[31]

The first unit of each school (the southern wing of Pershing and northern wing of Denby) was opened to students in September 1930. As the completed portion of Pershing held only classrooms, the nearly 1,100 students ate in the corridor of the second

294. Detroit's Benjamin Nolan Intermediate School, completed in 1927, is located on East Lantz Street in the northern part of the city.

floor; hot food was brought in containers from the kitchen at Nolan Intermediate. The second unit of the building—with additional classrooms and cafeteria—was expected to open by the end of winter break, February 2, 1931, and so four hundred additional students were assigned to the school. Unfortunately, work on the addition was not completed in time and 1,500 students were jammed into the first unit for one week until the new section opened.[32]

Pershing High was named for General John J. Pershing, commander of US Army forces during World War I. The school was dedicated on September 23, 1931, but

295. Detroit's former David Mackenzie High School (demolished). (Timothy Boscarino, Historic Designation Advisory Board, City of Detroit)

General Pershing, who had been expected in Detroit at that time, was unable to attend due to illness. At 10:45 a.m., on an overcast but already unseasonably warm morning, two thousand students marched from the school onto the front lawn as the American Legion Band played "The Star-Spangled Banner." As the school was dedicated, a flight of twelve Boeing P-12 fighter aircraft from Selfridge Field conducted close formation aerobatics and mock dogfights to the delight of the crowd below.[33]

Edwin Denby was a well-regarded Detroiter whose death in February 1929 prompted a pledge by the Board of Education to name a school in his memory. Denby attended law school at the University of Michigan and later served six years in the US Congress. Denby was a cofounder of Bankers Trust Company and in 1914, with his brother Garvin Denby, founded the Denby Motor Truck Company. During the Spanish-American War, Denby served on the USS *Yosemite* and reenlisted in 1917 (at age forty-seven) as a private in the Marine Corps, working his way up to major by the end of World War I. In 1921, Denby was appointed secretary of the navy by President Warren G. Harding. Unfortunately, a decision made by Denby regarding disposition of the navy's oil reserves resulted in his unwittingly facilitating the Teapot Dome scandal, which ultimately led to his resignation.[34]

Both Denby and Pershing High Schools pay homage to their namesakes with inscriptions over the front entrances. Beneath the school name in each case appears the year "1929," another example of the whimsical nature of dates inscribed on buildings, as this was the year construction began, not when the building was completed or dedicated. Edwin Denby's name is flanked by two warships, a clear reference to Denby's service to his country.

The symbolism on Pershing High's similar stone panel is far less clear: on the left appears a row of large smokestacks of the type associated with a factory or power station, and on

296. Entrance to the former David Mackenzie High School. The figure over the door is similar to the tile figure over the Griswold entrance of the Union Trust (Guardian) Building. Although the school was opened in 1928, the section of the building seen here (unit 3) was completed in 1931, which is why the cornerstone bears that year.

the right, an oil lamp with a small flame—perhaps the lamp of knowledge. It turns out an explanatory inscription that appears on the building plans was not included on the completed stone panel: "Be strong in war and wise in peace." The quote provides context to the image of industrial might on the one hand and the light of wisdom on the other. As far as can be ascertained, the quote did not originate with Pershing, but rather from the 1894 article "Popular Government: Its Development and Failure in Antiquity" by Dr. Adolph Moses.[35] Born in 1840 in Poland, Moses became a rabbi and, in his twenties, immigrated to the United States in search of freedom and to escape the widespread persecution of Jews in Europe. He wrote and lectured on the American federal form of government, under which the American people enjoy, wrote Moses, "the greatest possible freedom of the individual."[36]

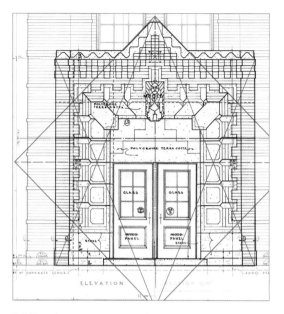

297. The proportions of the entrance to Mackenzie High School were likely derived from the root two rectangle figure. Note that the entrance actually built (see previous photo) was constructed several feet taller than the plan specifies. (The base drawing is from sheet 11 of the Smith, Hinchman, and Grylls plans for Mackenzie High School, dated June 27, 1927)

High school buildings were heated by radiators, the steam for which was produced by an onsite coal-fired boiler house. Denby, Pershing, and Mackenzie all shared the same unusual design for their boiler houses: a massive, stepped structure with a beveled smokestack topped with decorative brickwork. Mackenzie's boiler house was demolished with the school and Denby's was taken down in 2012. The boiler house for Pershing remains standing at this time, but has been partially absorbed into additions to the main building.

Denby and Pershing High Schools depart from the typical style for school buildings of the time. Both are clad in bright yellow-orange brick with restrained geometric ornamentation, rather than classical or Gothic decorations. There is very little in the appearance of these buildings to suggest their age; the designs remain fresh and appealing. The only significant alteration to the facade of either building is an entrance added to Denby High.

One of the strangest projects on which Rowland worked between 1926 and 1930 was the ill-fated Pontchartrain Club. Prior to the Great Depression, membership in social, service, arts, and professional clubs dominated urban social life. Clubs catering to the needs

298. Detroit's Pershing High School opened in 1930.

of business people—the Detroit Club and Detroit Athletic Club—were housed in buildings close to the city's financial center. During the 1920s, luncheon clubs located within large office buildings gained in popularity. Between 1923 and 1929, thirty-one new club buildings were constructed in Detroit, including the Players Club, League of Catholic Women, Scarab Club, and Women's City Club.[37] Another, the thirty-two-story Aviation Town and Country Club, was slated for the southwest corner of Washington Boulevard and Clifford Street,[38] and though the site was cleared, construction never commenced (In 1981, an apartment building [originally called Trolley Plaza] was constructed on the property.) The slightly less ambitious Union League Club of Michigan announced in April 1929 plans for a twenty-six-story home on the northwest corner of Fort Street and Washington Boulevard; club officers included Charles Mott and Frank Blair.[39] Construction of the first eleven stories of the clubhouse, designed by the Burnham Brothers of Chicago, began in November 1929—the additional stories were to be added later.[40] Over on East Jefferson Avenue, the Elks were constructing an eleven-story home on the shore of the Detroit River overlooking Belle Isle.

The Pontchartrain Club began as the Detroit chapter of the National Town and Country Club, an organization initiated in New York City with a plan to provide a national chain of membership clubs offering accommodations and facilities to members in major

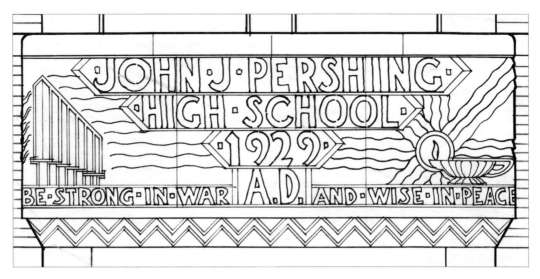

299. The original plan for the stone panel over the entrances to Pershing High School included an inscription, "Be strong in war and wise in peace," which provides context for the symbols of a lamp and industrial smokestacks. (Smith, Hinchman, and Grylls plans for Pershing High School—Unit 1, sheet 12, June 5, 1929)

cities and vacation destinations. The Detroit chapter was formed in 1924, and by the end of the year, life members included World War I ace and car manufacturer Eddie Rickenbacker and Smith, Hinchman, and Grylls partner Maxwell Grylls.[41] A sketch of the proposed home for the club showed a fanciful skyscraper of nearly forty stories.

In 1925, the New York City and Detroit branches of the club acquired sites in their respective cities for construction of clubhouses, New York for $1,250,000 at the corner of Forty-Eighth Street and Lexington Avenue,[42] and Detroit at the southwest corner of First Street and Bagley Avenue, at a cost of $525,000.[43] A revised sketch of the Detroit club was made public, and it showed the number of floors had been reduced to a more feasible eighteen, though the cost of the building had climbed from $2.5 million

300. Mackenzie High School's unusual boiler house and smokestack were nearly identical to those of Denby and Pershing High Schools.

to $4 million (nearly one-half the $8.5 million cost of the Greater Penobscot Building).[44] The sketch shows a Romanesque style building having arched windows on the first and top floors and a large penthouse capped by a tiled hip roof, features consistent with Rowland's other designs of the period.

The New York club, though it owned a site and was ready to begin construction, encountered difficulties enrolling the minimum of two thousand members required to make the enterprise financially viable. In spite of an aggressive recruiting effort, by the end of 1926, total membership stood at only 1,150 and a decision was made to abolish the New York chapter and sell the property.[45] This was, of course, a disappointment for members in Detroit, Cleveland, and other cities who had joined with the expectation there would be a New York City club at which they would be welcomed.

Nevertheless, planning continued on the Detroit club and in 1928 an updated design for the building was released to the press; the now ten-story building had a completely reworked exterior (the decrease in number of floors reduced the projected cost of the building from $4 million to $2.5 million). This version clearly reflected Rowland's post-1926 shift away from Romanesque to geometric design features; the earlier plan's round arches and ornamental balusters were replaced by stepped arches, stepped roofline elements, and windows grouped in pairs and singles.

A few months later, yet another iteration of the design appeared, this one far more flamboyant and glitzy than was typical of Rowland. Describing the building, the club's organizers explained: "economies could have been effected which would have cut the cost almost in two, they would also have detracted from the luxury and satisfaction."[46] Perhaps they felt Rowland's quietly distinctive design, though bolder and more modern than any existing club in town, needed to be "punched up" to aid

301. This sketch of the proposed National Town and Country Club was prepared by Smith, Hinchman, and Grylls and appeared in the Thumb Tack Club's Architectural Exhibition Catalog of November 1924.

in recruiting the additional one thousand members needed for the club to achieve financial solvency. Among the most noticeable differences between Rowland's 1928 design and the final version was the replacement of the angled arch motif (for window heads and ornamentation) with a theme based on circles. This circle-based motif appeared as well on the 1930 Michigan Bell Oregon central office in Dearborn, the one central office designed (prior to 1930) by Amedeo Leone; it is probable, therefore, that Leone, and not Rowland, was responsible for making the final revisions to the Pontchartrain Club.[47]

Ground was broken for the club building the first week in September 1928. Club chairman Edward Loveley jammed his spade in the soil to turn the first shovelful of dirt and a metallic clang was heard. Further investigation revealed he had struck

302. A Smith, Hinchman, and Grylls sketch from 1925 shows Detroit's proposed eighteen-story Town and Country Club. The building's decorative style is Romanesque, consistent with Rowland's other designs between 1922 and 1926.

a horseshoe buried just beneath the surface; when the cornerstone was placed in July 1929, the horseshoe was included among other memorabilia sealed within.[48] By this time, the club had terminated its affiliation with the National Town and Country Club and adopted a new name, the Pontchartrain Club, in memory of France's Count Pontchartrain.

At nearly the same time as the cornerstone was laid for the Pontchartrain Club, Union Trust's president, Frank Blair, was meeting with Guardian Group's president, Robert Lord, discussing a potentially momentous merger of their two banks. Lord had approached Blair earlier that summer, but Blair had little interest in a merger. A second entreaty in July found Blair more open, leading to a further series of discussions. In September, the men met again at Blair's country house and came to an agreement to merge the two firms.[49] Specifically, the merger combined the Union Commerce Corp (parent of Union Trust Company and National Bank of Commerce) with the Guardian Detroit Group (parent of Guardian Trust Company and the Guardian Detroit Bank) into two new companies. The two trust companies were merged under the name Union Guardian Trust Company and the two banks were combined into Guardian Detroit Bank. These two firms were owned by Guardian Detroit Union Group, a new parent company, of which the forty-three-year-old Lord was named president and chief executive officer and fifty-nine-year-old Blair, chairman of the board.

By turning management of the bank over to Lord, Blair could focus his energies on outside interests and pave the way for his retirement in 1932. Within months, Blair was elected president of the Ohio-Pennsylvania Joint Stock Land Bank—an institution engaged in meeting the specialized financial needs of farmers—and was chosen to serve on the American Bankers' Association economic policy commission. In January 1930, Blair was elected chairman of Detroit Aircraft Corporation—one of the country's largest aircraft manufacturers.[50]

Although the merger of Union Trust and Guardian was large by Detroit standards, it was eclipsed at the end of September when five of Detroit's largest banks determined to merge, creating the Detroit Bankers Company, the nation's eighth-largest banking firm. Detroit Bankers Company subsidiary banks now controlled 60 percent of the banking resources of Detroit (compared with 25 percent for the Guardian Detroit Union Group).[51] Statewide, Bankers controlled 29 percent and Guardian 17 percent of total resources.[52] It should be

303. Two 1928 versions of the ten-story Pontchartrain Club. The later design (*right*) shows the addition of ostentatious window treatments, particularly on the lower floors, and more prominent ornamentation throughout. This type of flamboyant decoration was uncharacteristic of Rowland. (Sketches: Smith, Hinchman, and Grylls and SmithGroupJJR)

recalled, however, that Michigan's bank consolidations were largely driven by the borrowing requirements of the state's rapidly growing industrial firms. As Julius Haas, president of Peoples Wayne County Bank, explained, the tendency toward bigness "first appeared in the industrial field, with the formation of billion-dollar corporations, the banks in the country found their capital structures too small in many cases to handle this larger business properly. That was probably the primary reason for the beginning of bank merging."[53]

Naturally, the merger of Union Trust and Guardian resulted in duplication of facilities. In April 1930, Guardian moved from its offices in the Penobscot

304. The Pontchartrain Club as it appeared when construction ceased. (Smith, Hinchman, and Grylls and SmithGroupJJR)

Building to the Union Trust Building. Although the distance was less than the length of a football field, one hundred armed guards were brought in to oversee the transfer of $100 million in cash from Guardian's vault to the vault in the Union Trust Building.[54] Guardian's former banking facilities within Penobscot were taken over by the Bank of Detroit, a still independent unit of the Guardian Detroit Union Group.[55]

During the last week of October 1929, Wall Street was roiled by a wave of selling that ultimately reduced stock values by 40 percent from their high point two months earlier. Although jaw-dropping news to the business community, it was of merely passing interest to most Americans, few of whom owned stocks. Detroit's business journals attributed the market "crash" to speculators whose incautious pursuit of easy riches had propelled a run-up in stock values. "The only ones hurt by the debacle in the market were speculators and those possessing small capital which prevented their covering margin calls," opined *Michigan Manufacturer and Financial Record* in a November 23, page one article headlined "See Business Unshaken by Stock Market Crash."

Despite the business community's forced happy face, the optimism with which affluent Detroiters viewed their economic prospects soured quickly—particularly for those reeling from losses in the stock market. Before the end of 1929, work on the Pontchartrain Club building came to a halt and the club was in financial distress. The shell of the building was erected at a cost of roughly $1 million, most of which was still owed to the contractors.[56] These bills went unpaid, and the contractors eventually foreclosed on the property. The building could not be sold or developed, so its shell remained for two decades as a distressing monument to the market crash and ensuing Great Depression. In 1940, the state seized the structure for nonpayment of taxes and then sold it at auction the following year for $34,600 (to the same owners from whom it had been seized).[57] Around 1950, the building was sold to a developer and the structure was converted to an apartment building;[58] the window openings were altered and much of the exterior stone ornamentation was removed and replaced by brick, though the north-facing side of the penthouse remains unchanged.

The Union League of Michigan began construction of their club building on November 11, 1929—too soon after the crash, perhaps, to anticipate the misfortune that would ensue. During 1930, the foundation, which included a parking garage, was completed, and by the spring of 1931, the steel frame of the building was up. However, in July 1931, workers were sent home and further construction was abandoned; the building corporation was declared bankrupt the following January.[59] Eventually, the steel building frame was scrapped and the remains of the foundation used as surface and below-ground parking. It was much the same with the Elks Club building, except that this shell remained an eyesore until the mid-1960s, when it was demolished and the land used to build the Shoreline East Apartments at 8200 East Jefferson (1966). One Town and Country Club was completed in Cleveland, Ohio, but closed almost immediately after opening. The building at 1983 East Twenty-Fourth Street was acquired in 1937 by Fenn College and renamed Fenn Tower; it is now part of Cleveland State University.

Abandonment and cancellation of projects spread financial distress to all corners of the community. Automobile production dropped from more than 5.4 million units in 1929 to 3.5 in 1930, hitting a low of 2 million in 1933.[60] The total value of construction in Detroit toppled from $100 million in 1929 to $48 million in 1930, finally bottoming out at an abysmal $4 million in 1933.[61] A telling indicator of the personal disruption engendered by the economic collapse was the decline in marriages: in 1929, 18,000 couples married in Wayne County; that number dropped to roughly 13,000 in 1930 and 1931 and then slid below 12,500 in 1932.[62]

There was a whiplash effect as economic activity dwindled in the wake of the crash. The Jefferson Avenue Presbyterian Church, completed in 1926 at a total cost of $1.25 million, was to be paid for in large part by proceeds from the sale of its former church building and that of the Bethany congregation.[63] The Bethany Church was sold to another congregation in 1926, with payments to be made over time to JAPC. Due to the economic distress, after 1930, payments to JAPC ceased.[64] The crash and ensuing depression caused a collapse in real estate values; many property owners wished to sell, but there were few buyers. (The old Jefferson Avenue Presbyterian Church, built at a cost of $50,000 in 1854, plus an additional $200,000 in 1893, was sold in 1940 to the Gregory Boat Works for only $10,000.) With no payments coming in from the Bethany sale, no opportunity to sell their old Jefferson Avenue building, and congregants unable to assist due to their own financial misery, JAPC could no longer make payments on the debt it owed for the new church building.[65]

JAPC's loan was held by Guardian Detroit Bank. Although loan payments from the congregation had ceased, the collapse of the real estate market made it pointless for the bank to foreclose on the loan and sell the church building. This scenario played out thousands of times as churches, stores, farms, dealerships, homeowners, and others fell behind—or ceased entirely—in their payments to the bank, setting the stage for worse financial repercussions.

Tall building construction came to a halt in Detroit and nearly every other American city after the crash. The eighty-one-story Book Tower on Washington Boulevard was canceled.[66] The second and third units of the Fisher Building were put on indefinite hold. Plans for smaller structures—offices, clubs, banks, and even schools—were canceled or scaled back. Even Michigan Bell, the largest client of Smith, Hinchman, and Grylls, experienced a precipitous decline in business and responded by nearly eliminating new construction.[67] The steady stream of work that had kept busy Smith, Hinchman, and Grylls's staff of nearly 250 dried up.[68] Employees were laid off, and in October 1930, fifty-two-year-old Wirt Rowland found himself unemployed.[69] By 1932, the once formidable firm had shrunk to just four officers and two employees.[70]

Might Rowland's situation have been different if he had become a partner in the firm? Given the extreme dearth of work, even officers and partners received paycheck envelopes that were empty, or nearly so, and unlike partners, employees who were let go at least had the option of seeking other work. Many did so by leaving Detroit for cities less profoundly affected by the crash. Herb Wenzell became a partner in George Mason's firm in 1920, along with Albert McDonald and David Williams, yet he was no better off financially as a consequence.[71] When the federal government instituted a work program in 1934 to help relieve the plight of architects nationally, Wenzell was one of twenty employed by the program in Michigan. So, even had Rowland been made a partner in his firm, it would not likely have benefited his financial situation. Today, it is common for large professional firms to encourage key employees to become partners, but in Rowland's day, many of these firms were still headed by founders. Mason was sixty-three years old when he reincorporated his firm with partners. Albert Kahn was seventy-one when he formed a new corporation to include as stockholders key employees who had been with the firm for at least twenty-five years.[72]

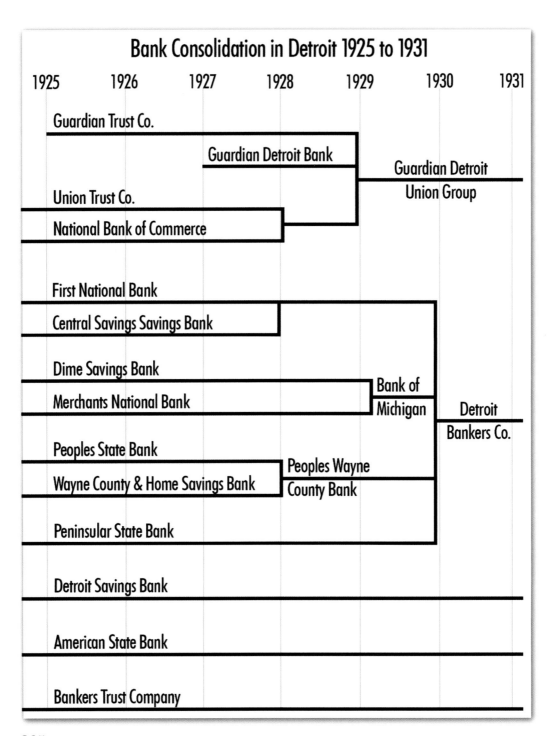

Bank Consolidation in Detroit 1925 to 1931

| 1925 | 1926 | 1927 | 1928 | 1929 | 1930 | 1931 |

Guardian Trust Co.

Guardian Detroit Bank

Guardian Detroit Union Group

Union Trust Co.

National Bank of Commerce

First National Bank

Central Savings Savings Bank

Dime Savings Bank

Merchants National Bank

Bank of Michigan

Detroit Bankers Co.

Peoples State Bank

Peoples Wayne County Bank

Wayne County & Home Savings Bank

Peninsular State Bank

Detroit Savings Bank

American State Bank

Bankers Trust Company

305.

9
AFTERSHOCKS

The accomplishment of good things in art, particularly architecture, by a nation at the end of a period of years, is not measured by the work of one or two of its geniuses. It is measured by the attainment of the group of men who by their training have been able to think straight, see clearly, and possess the will to carry out their convictions.

—Wirt Rowland, "The Making of an Architect," 1920

Rowland's designs for the Union Trust and Penobscot were widely influential, though determining the extent of his influence presents obvious difficulties. Perhaps the greatest being that so few buildings were constructed during the 1930s, the period when Rowland's influence would have been most visible.

In 1934, Talmage C. Hughes, an accomplished Detroit architect and founder and editor of the *Weekly Bulletin of the Michigan Society of Architects*, authored "Dynamic Detroit," an article intended to familiarize those outside the city with the great architecture and architects of Detroit. Hughes wrote: "Many of our architects are world famed for their contributions to contemporary art and architecture, but there is one designer who has been most intimately connected with our development whose name is not so well known to the public, perhaps, because for many years he did not practice under his own name. When the history of Detroit's present architecture is written, the name of Wirt C. Rowland will be near the top."[1] Hughes appears to credit Rowland, in part, for the development of fine architecture in Detroit, and though Rowland may not have been well known to the public, those within his own profession knew him well. Hughes continued: "In the Greater Penobscot Building, Rowland has departed from designing a mere elevation. He has discarded 'paper architecture' and designed a building from the standpoint of pure mass. In the Union Trust Building the use of color came prominently into play, and there are those who believe it is many years ahead of its time." In 1946, Hughes wrote, on behalf of the Detroit chapter of the American Institute of Architects, to the organization's national board of directors urging that Rowland be made a member emeritus, "because of Mr. Rowland's profound influence on the architecture of Detroit, the excellence of his design and because of his contributions to the profession of architecture."[2] (The letter was unusual in that Hughes informed the national organization that the executive committee of the Detroit chapter had voted to pay Rowland's membership dues, "as he is now incapacitated and unable to engage in any vocation" and requested that the national organization "take similar action by exempting Mr. Rowland from payment of institute dues.")

With these comments, Hughes suggested two means by which Rowland influenced other designers. First: Rowland trained and mentored many of the next generation of designers, some of whom worked under him, others learned from him through club activities; and second: his buildings provided examples and inspiration to others. Despite the limited construction of significant buildings during the 1930s, notable examples of Rowland's influence may be found among structures clearly imitative of his signature features: brightly colored exterior brick or terra-cotta, angled and stepped arches, and stainless steel or aluminum used in place of steel or brass.

Even before the Penobscot and Union Trust Buildings were completed, design innovations employed on them were picked up and used by other architects. The most prolific of Rowland's disciples was Charles Lewis Phelps (1884–1967), an independent architect whom Rowland had known since 1903, when both worked for George Mason. Phelps later worked for architect John Scott and Company and then, sometime prior to 1914, joined Albert Kahn, Architects and Engineers, as a designer, remaining there until starting his own firm in 1926.[3] Working under Rowland's tutelage, Phelps became a skilled designer of banks, small commercial buildings, and homes.

During 1929, Phelps designed two bank buildings that incorporated decorative elements of both the Union Trust and Penobscot Buildings. The large branch for the Detroit Savings Bank on the northwest corner of Grand River Avenue and Joy Road received an unusual degree of media attention, with a photo and caption appearing on the first page of the *Detroit News* business section and an article in the *Michigan Manufacturer and Financial Record* headlined: "Bank Is Masterpiece."[4] The building is clad in pink marble with granite trim around windows and entries. The overall appearance is modern and well balanced with subtle decoration; the dramatic focal point of the building is the large octowindow above the main entrance.

Each of the building's three doorways is topped with a stepped arch, similar to those on the Saturday Night Building. Windows are framed as a group, separated vertically by piers faced with convex vertical bands similar to those on the Penobscot Building. Large granite spandrels separate the windows vertically and contain insets of bronze with convex bands complementing those of the piers.

306. The former Detroit Savings Bank branch at Grand River and Joy Road, designed by Charles Phelps and completed in November 1929.

The second Phelps bank building was constructed as a headquarters for the Stephens State Bank and is located on the corner of Ethlyn Court and Gratiot Avenue in Eastpointe (formerly East Detroit). (Stephens State Bank became illiquid and in 1932 was closed by the state banking commissioner. The nearby First State Bank subsequently acquired the property and placed their name on the building.) This building is clad in limestone with marble spandrels; the only ornamentation consists of subtle designs carved in the limestone. On the front facade, three of the windows and the front door are flanked by curved panels with convex vertical bands. The fourth window, now closed in, was once a door and is topped by larger convex vertical bands. The first-floor windows near the corners are topped with stepped arches and those above on the second floor are standard rectangular windows set within an octowindow shaped frame. Beneath the second floor windowsills are bands of zigzag ornament nearly identical to that used decoratively throughout the main banking lobby of the Penobscot Building. Atop the piers, Phelps used convex vertical bands with equilateral triangles superimposed. The stepped or corbelled features on both bank buildings are rounded off, as are those flanking the main entranceway arch of the Penobscot Building.

On the eleven-story Capitol Park Building (southwest corner of Griswold and State Streets in downtown Detroit), Phelps employed the octowindow when remodeling the exterior. In 1938, Baumgartner's clothing store acquired the building and hired Phelps, by

307. The former First State Bank of East Detroit, designed by Charles Phelps and completed in 1929. The building is located on Gratiot Avenue, one block south of 9 Mile Road.

then a partner with Walter Bernardi in the firm of Phelps and Bernardi, to reface the first two floors.[5] Phelps replaced the existing triple window units with large octowindows set horizontally within a background of maroon porcelain enamel panels. Aside from the store's name in neon lights, the windows are the only feature on the second-floor facade—a simple and generally pleasing solution to an otherwise vexing design problem. (It was standard procedure at the time to disregard a building's style when refitting its retail facade.)

308. The Capitol Park Building facade was remodeled in 1938 by Charles Phelps. The second-floor triple windows were removed and replaced by horizontal octowindows on a field of maroon panels. (After an extended period of disuse, the building was again remodeled in 2015 and the facade seen here was removed.)

There are small buildings throughout the Detroit area that mimic Rowland's use of stepped and angled arches in a manner similar to these Charles Phelps designs. In some cases, the building has outlived any record of the architect responsible for the design; however, the decorative elements and date of construction suggest Rowland's influence.

309. Records indicate that this building at 2314 Gratiot Avenue (near Eastern Market) was built in 1910. The bright orange brick, stepped stone, and stone octowindow decorations suggest that it was remodeled around 1930 when the street was widened.

The angled arch and octowindow found their way onto at least two structures from the office of Albert Kahn, Architects and Engineers: the Miller-Judd auto dealership and New Center Building (now called the Albert Kahn Building). The Miller-Judd Company was a dealer of Nash automobiles and in 1929 had the building at 5454 Cass Avenue constructed as a sales and service facility. The two-story reinforced concrete structure is one of the most peculiar designs in the city, though oddly enjoyable to view. The plentiful profusion of pilasters across the facade feature convex vertical bands similar to those on Penobscot. (Classical Greek and Roman pilasters, like columns, have concave fluting.) The main entrance is surrounded by a prominent granite frame with an opening in the shape of an angled arch.

The ten-story New Center Building, on the northeast corner of Second and Lothrop, was designed by Albert Kahn, Architects and Engineers in 1930. All windows on the office floors are rectangular in shape, except for those on the ninth floor, which are topped with angled arches similar to those on the Union Trust Building. The building's bronze entrance is topped with a band of floral ornamentation of a style popular at the time. The doors, however, have decorative bronze pieces that create the octo-window shape within the glass door panel. Although it is not easily determined which designers in Kahn's office were responsible for these two buildings, it is likely that an active role was played by Joseph N. French, a founding member of the Thumb Tack Club who worked under Rowland from 1915 to 1922.

Detroiter Austin A. Howe (1885–1936) studied architecture for a year at Harvard and was active in the Michigan Society of Architects. He went into business on his own in 1920, initially as a contractor and later as an architect. In 1929, Howe designed for the Detroit board of education two schools: Anthony Wayne Elementary at 10633 Courville Avenue, and Frederick William Von Steuben Elementary at 12300 Linnhurst Street. The exteriors of the two are nearly identical, and the first units of both opened in 1930. The most prominent feature of the two buildings is the two-story angled arch over the entrance, quite similar to that of the Michigan Bell and Western Electric Warehouse. Howe framed this arch with stepped layers of bricks and employed creative brickwork elsewhere to add interest.

310. The Du Val Apartments at 741 West Euclid (near New Center) was built in 1929. There are prominent stepped designs above the top floor and smaller versions elsewhere. The bright orange bricks have been set in decorative patterns and, on the corners of the piers, are set in steps that increase in number toward the building's top—much like those on the tower of the Union Trust Building.

A similar approach was taken with Detroit's Henry Chaney School by Edward A. Schilling (1872–1952) of Van Leyen, Schilling, and Keough, a firm responsible for well over two hundred school buildings in Michigan (Fordson High School, Dearborn; Birmingham High School [demolished]; and River Rouge High School [demolished]), Ohio, and Ontario, as well as the Belle Isle Casino.[6] Schilling was an active member of the Thumb Tack Club and, at the time he designed Chaney School, served with Rowland on the Architect's Advisory Committee of the City Planning Commission. Chaney, at 2750

311. Another bright orange brick building, the Detroit Free Jewish Burial Association at 2995 Joy Road, was designed by Maurice H. Finkel and constructed in 1930. (Source: "Plans Are Prepared for Free Burial Home," *Detroit Free Press*, June 8, 1930, 10.) The stepped arches over the entrance and above the windows reflect similar designs on the Union Trust Building.

Selden Street, was completed in 1931 and combines a prominent angled arch above the entrance flanked by piers capped with colorful terra-cotta decorations.

The Logic of Modern Architecture, a 1929 book by Randolph W. Sexton, contains several photographs of the completed interior of the Union Trust Building. There is also a preliminary sketch (dated July 1929) by architect John Mead Howells for the entryway of the Title Guarantee and Trust Company Building in New York City (6 East Forty-Fifth Street, completed 1930). Howells employed the octowindow shape for the doors and an angled arch over the doorway, flanked by two prominent octowindow shaped openings, all in blue granite and Monel metal. Rowland was not in the habit of commenting negatively on the work of other architects, but for Howells—a favorite of the New York architectural press—he made an exception. Howells authored an article in 1930, "Vertical or Horizontal Design," in which he stated: "In designing a skyscraper, I believe in a composition of verticals. But I also believe in a composition of horizontal bands for long, low stores or apartment houses."[7] A number of months later, Rowland wrote sarcastically: "an expression of [the skyscraper's] vertical forces have now involved the architectural profession in a controversy over whether the direction of lines should be horizontal."[8]

The Winchester, Massachusetts, public library, constructed in 1931, was designed by architect Robert Coit (1861–1942) in collaboration with Kilham, Hopkins, and Greeley. Coit was a fairly prolific home designer in the Boston area and had served as a trustee for the library from 1914 to 1917.[9] He was a Harvard graduate[10] and, along with Langford Warren, active in the Boston Architectural Club and the Boston Society of Architects, which had awarded Rowland a prize in 1911 for his advanced design drawing. Rowland made frequent trips to Boston over the years to visit former professors and fellow architects, though it is uncertain what his relationship with Coit may have been. Nevertheless, the Winchester

312. Completed late in 1930 for the Crucible Steel Company, this building on Hubbard Street combines orange and yellow brick with stepped limestone trim in a manner quite similar to Rowland's Michigan Bell Madison central office. Over the entrance is a stepped arch resembling those on the Union Trust Building. This industrial building—mostly warehouse with office space overlooking the street—demonstrates that Rowland's decorative motifs were not limited to commercial and residential buildings.

313. The Miller-Judd auto dealership building at 5454 Cass Avenue was designed by Albert Kahn, Architects and Engineers, in 1929 and includes an angled arch entrance.

Public Library shows Rowland's influence in a number of ways, most notably in the octowindow that dominates the end of the main reading room. The window's frame was painted in gold and edged in red. The ceiling of this room is curved and, originally, had built-in light fixtures along its sides to reflect light into the room in much the same manner as in the lower banking lobby of the Union Trust Building. Inset between the front door and the exterior wall of the building is a band of decorative tile, similar to that over the entrance to the Buhl Building; the most noticeable design within the tile is the root two rectangle figure.

Two structures on opposite sides of the country may owe a bit of their distinctive styling to Rowland's influence: the Eastern Columbia Building in Los Angeles and New York City's Chrysler Building. Eastern Columbia is a thirteen-story office structure designed in 1929 by Claud Beelman (1883–1963), an Ohio native

314. The doors of the New Center Building have ornamental framing pieces that create the octowindow shape within the glass panel.

who relocated to Los Angeles in his thirties. The building is clad in a vibrant turquoise terra-cotta and sports a prominent penthouse, decorated with bright gold trim, much like the Union Trust. It appears that Beelman based his design for the Eastern Columbia Building on what he perceived to be the two most successful tall building designs of the previous decade: Eliel Saarinen's sketch for the Chicago Tribune Building (see the next chapter) and Rowland's colorful Union Trust Building.

The Chrysler Building began as the Reynolds Building, a project of Dreamland amusement park founder William H. Reynolds. Architect William Van Alen designed for Reynolds an imposing structure, crowned with a three-story observation dome trimmed in bronze.[11] Reynolds ran short of money and in October 1928 sold the entire project to automobile industrialist Walter P. Chrysler, who lived in Flint and whose Chrysler automobile

company was located in Detroit. A superbly competent engineer and business manager, Chrysler was already one of the automotive industry's wealthiest entrepreneurs
prior to founding Chrysler Corporation
in 1925.

After acquiring the skyscraper
project, Chrysler became deeply involved
in altering its design. He spent "hours
down on my hands and knees creeping
about the floor of my office carpeted with
the blueprints and the other drawings of
the architects; made the final choice for the
marbles in the corridors; chose the veneers
that make the interior of each elevator cab
seem to be the work of some extraordinari-
ly gifted cabinetmaker."[12] Construction of
the building's foundation began January
21, 1929,[13] and, as this was under way,

315. Detroit's Anthony Wayne Elementary
School was designed by Austin Howe and opened
in 1930. The massive angled arch reflects a number
of Rowland's buildings, as does the use of a carved
emblem above.

Chrysler had Van Alen redesign the crown of the building, eliminating the bronze dome
and replacing it with a larger crown clad in Nirosta metal, an alteration announced by
the press in March. Nirosta and aluminum were adopted for all metalwork throughout
the building's interior and exterior, which Van Alen described as "an innovation in metalwork. Practically all of the exposed metal window frames, copings, flashings, the finial and
tower decorations are of 'Nirosta' steel, a newly developed rust resisting non-corrosive alloy.
Aluminum is used for window sills and spandrels."[14]

It should be recalled that Nirosta stainless was used throughout the interior, and aluminum for all exterior metal, on the Union Industrial Bank Building, designed by Rowland
during 1928. By October 1928, the design of the Flint building was essentially complete,
but further progress was sidetracked due to the pending merger of Industrial Savings Bank
and Union Trust and Savings Bank. A front-page story in the December 11, 1928, *Flint
Daily Journal* reported that directors of the two banks voted in favor of consolidation and
intended to proceed with construction of the new headquarters building. The article also
noted: "Erection of this structure has been contemplated for some time by the officials of
the Union Trust Bank before the merger was considered" and the appended list of bank

316. Henry Chaney School was designed by Edward Schilling and completed in 1931. Rowland's influence may be seen in the building's large angled arch, orange brick, and colorful terra-cotta accents.

directors included Walter P. Chrysler. Adjacent to the story appeared a sketch of the proposed building, virtually identical in appearance to the completed building.

Did Chrysler, on his own, come up with the idea of using, in place of traditional materials, Nirosta steel and aluminum on his Chrysler Building? It seems far more likely that Chrysler, direc- tor of a bank that several months earlier had selected the very same materials for its headquarters—materials never before used on a building—brought the idea with him to his own skyscraper in New York City. Credit for initiating what rapidly became the widespread adoption of stain- less steel in place of brass for metalwork within buildings goes to Rowland, while Chrysler and Van Alen deserve credit for taking Rowland's idea to the next step and

317. A July 1929 sketch by architect John Mead Howells for the Title Guarantee and Trust Co. Building in New York City. A photo of the sketch appeared in the 1929 book *The Logic of Modern Architecture*.

318. The Winchester Massachusetts Public Library, designed by Robert Coit, as it looked upon completion in 1931. (*Winchester Public Library*)

employing stainless in unpainted form for decorative purposes on the exterior and as cladding on broad surfaces of a structure.[15]

Chrysler would have been familiar with the large banking lobbies of the Union Trust and Penobscot Buildings and the large banking room planned for the Union Industrial Bank, all unobstructed by supporting piers. One of the first alterations Chrysler insisted Van Alen make to the Chrysler Building was the removal of supporting piers in its lobby. Studying a plaster model of the building, Chrysler commented on the lobby: "It looks a little cramped to me . . . how about this?" and proceeded to pull out the offending columns.[16]

319. Front entrance of the Winchester Public Library showing the inset band of colored tile and the root two rectangle based design. (Daniel A. Smith)

Design sketches for the Chrysler Building show its evolution over time and reveal that Chrysler had the three-story round arch over the main entrance of the building changed to an angled arch. On the completed building, within this entryway arch is a decorative framework of glass and steel in the octowindow shape. (Additional angled arches are found near the top of the building.) While the entrance to the Chrysler Building has much in common with that of the Union Industrial Bank Building, it is strikingly similar to the Michigan Bell and Western Electric Warehouse, designed by Rowland at around the same time as the bank building. How much of a debt the iconic Chrysler Building owes to Rowland may never be known with certainty, but surely his ideas influenced Chrysler's important alterations to the design.

320. Eastern Columbia Building in Los Angeles. (Conrado Lopez of 2_L Studio Design and Architectural Photography)

One consequence of the 1929 market crash and ensuing Great Depression was that many architects relocated to areas where work could be found. One of those areas was Miami, Florida, which weathered the Great Depression of the 1930s better than many other communities.[17] During the early years of the twentieth century, Miami became a mecca for northerners seeking a respite from winter weather. Many Detroit automotive pioneers acquired second homes in the Miami area, often in the city of Miami Beach or within large, planned developments such as Coral Gables. By the 1920s, the railroads offered high-speed service between Detroit and Miami and, beginning in the late 1920s, small, inexpensively constructed hotels in Miami Beach along Collins Avenue and Ocean Drive began catering to the tourist trade. Construction in the Miami area totaled $16 million in 1929, but fell to $2.5 million in 1932. The area's economy recovered quickly, however, and by 1935, the value of construction in Miami Beach alone ranked it sixth among the nation's cities.[18]

Miami had fewer than two thousand inhabitants in 1900; by 1930 it had 110,000. Most of the architects practicing in the city during the 1930s came from New York, Chicago, and Detroit. Among the early arrivals were brothers John Llewellyn Skinner (1893–1972) and Coulton Skinner (1891–1963), who set up shop in 1925 as the architecture firm of Skinner and Skinner in Miami Beach.

321. Design sketches by architect William Van Alen for the Chrysler Building in New York City. The first two sketches were completed prior to October 1929. The second two were completed after Walter P. Chrysler acquired the project in October 1929. In the third sketch, the archway over the entrance is round; in the fourth sketch it appears in its final form, as an angled arch.

The Skinners were born in Cleveland, Ohio, and moved to Detroit as children, attending Central High School and earning degrees in architecture from the University of Toronto. John went to work for Albert Kahn, Architects and Engineers in 1916, remaining there for three years. Of this time, Skinner wrote that he "was under the personal supervision of Mr. Kahn and the chief designer Wirt Rowland."[19] (Skinner also wrote that "Mr. Kahn encouraged [Skinner] and loaned him sufficient funds to continue his education in Europe, at a time when it would have been impossible for him to undertake such a program at his own expense."[20]) In 1922, John Skinner left Detroit to head the Georgia Tech Department of Architecture, a position he held until 1925. Coulton Skinner, too, worked under Rowland in Albert Kahn's office and was active in the Thumb Tack Club from the beginning. After a brief stint as a designer for Malcomson, Higginbotham, and Palmer in 1921, he began working independently, designing apartment buildings and residences from an office on Linwood Avenue.[21]

322. The entrance to the Michigan Bell and Western Electric Warehouse (*left*) is very similar in design to the Chrysler Building's entrance. (Chrysler Building Norbert Nagel / Wikimedia Commons, License: Creative Commons Attribution—ShareAlike 3.0 Unported)

The two architects found immediate success in Miami, securing contracts for large industrial structures—an eight-story cold storage plant for White City Ice and Laundry in 1926—and numerous high-end homes, particularly in the Coral Gables development. Both men were quite active in professional organizations: Coulton was elected president of the Architectural League of Southern Florida in 1927,[22] the same year John was chosen to head the architecture department of the University of Florida, and in 1944, John was elected as president of the state board of architecture.[23]

A home designed by the Skinners for Eleanor Farrington in 1934 (6332 Alton Road) was featured in a 1935 *American Architect* article on Miami Beach. The home's unusual and modern appearance was a sharp departure from the prevailing colonial, Mediterranean, and

323. Architect John L. Skinner. (*Pencil Points* 1927)

Pueblo Revival styles of the area—and from the Skinner brother's previous home designs. The front facade is bilaterally symmetrical and dominated by a large window extending from the first floor nearly to the roof. On each side of this window is a doorway with an octowindow centered above. Both doors open into a large front room, two stories high and well-lit by the full-height window.

The house is a compilation of design elements often seen on Rowland's buildings, including a band of dentil molding surrounding the structure just below the roofline. Painted on the main windows are four small escutcheons (shields) at eye level bearing images of sea animals, in a style similar to the small images on windows of the Detroit News Building. The framed arrangement of windows—three columns of windows separated by minor piers—echoes the facades of the Detroit Saturday Night Building and Pershing High School.

John Skinner remained good friends with Rowland after moving from Detroit, and Rowland likely visited Skinner on his trips to Florida.[24] Some sense of the close relationship

324. This photo of the John and Coulton Skinner–designed Farrington house on Alton Road in Miami Beach appeared in the August 1935 issue of *American Architect*.

between the two men may be gleaned from a letter Skinner wrote to the editor of the *Weekly Bulletin* shortly after Rowland's death:

> I learned last week of the recent passing of Wirt C. Rowland. In view of his failing health in the past several years, this was no surprise. As far as I know, Wirt had no immediate family and so I am writing you, in a sense as being next of kin, to offer my humble tribute to his memory. In the days when I knew Wirt best, some twenty or twenty-five years ago, he was a great help and friend to the young architects and draftsmen in Detroit. His sincerity and complete integrity influenced us. His kindness and guidance encouraged us and his ability as a designer inspired us. He was a great friend and a fine architect.[25]

Considering the freshness and attractiveness of the Farrington house, its break with existing local style expectations, the use of Rowland's typical decorative elements, and the ongoing relationship between Rowland and John Skinner, it is easy to suspect that Rowland may have had some role in sketching out the home's design. Rowland's influence on the appearance of this home illustrates in part the process by which creative ideas become geographically dispersed: Rowland mentored and encouraged Skinner early in his career, and most likely advised him on occasion in later years. In many ways, Rowland's guiding principles are reflected in Skinner's designs.[26]

Two of Miami Beach's well-known art deco hotels were designed by the Skinner brothers, the Barbizon apartment hotel, completed in 1938,[27] and the Bentley Hotel, 1939. Both buildings are of concrete block construction with applied stucco—the most common method employed in the area. The Barbizon, at 530 Ocean Drive, originally had fifty-two units that could be combined to form larger suites. The Bentley, at 510 Ocean Drive, with an original complement of forty rooms was one of the first apartment hotels to have retail storefronts on the first floor. The building's front entrance is on the corner, set on an angle—much like that of the Bankers Trust Company Building. A band of stone wraps around the building at its base—a common feature in Detroit, but unusual on buildings in Miami Beach—and extends up and around the entrance. Flanking the entrance, and on the two floors above, are octagon-shaped windows (not octowindows). Another building at 1500 Alton Road with similar features—corner entrance, stone base, and stone entrance surround—was designed by the Skinners in 1939 and, upon completion, the offices of the firm were located on the second floor.[28]

The Skinners in 1940 added architect Harold Steward to the firm, and it was renamed Steward and Skinner Associates. In the following years, they designed the Miami

325-1 & 325-2. Details of the 1963 Pan Am Training Facility by Steward and Skinner. The exterior facade is a screen comprised of trapezoid shapes, and the same shape is repeated throughout the structure as seen here in the door handles (*right*). (Miami-Dade County Office of Historic Preservation)

Dade Public Library (1951, demolished 1986), Miami Dade Auditorium (1951), Miami Seaquarium (1955), Florida State University Main Library (1958), Miami International Airport 20th Street Terminal (1959); Pan Am Training Facility (1963, 5000 NW Thirty-Sixth Street), Claude Pepper Federal Building (1964), Eastern Airlines headquarters, and numerous other structures. By the 1950s, architectural styles had changed, and these buildings hardly resemble the earlier work of the Skinner brothers. Closer inspection reveals, perhaps, a link to the past: the Pan Am training facility is characterized throughout by a decorative theme of isosceles trapezoids—essentially an angled arch turned sideways. Trapezoid shapes were not an uncommon sight during the 1960s; however, on the Pan Am building they are employed as a unifying theme, appearing on various surfaces inside and out. Florida State's Robert Strozier Library is a midcentury modern version of Rowland's Hill Auditorium/Northern High School/Hatcher Library design, and, as with those buildings, the library has upgraded brickwork—English Bond—with thick mortar joints.

One of the most prolific architects practicing in Miami was Gerard Pitt (1885–1971), who moved to the area in 1930 from Detroit. Of Pitt, the National Register of Historic Places Designation Report for Miami Beach's Normandy Isles Historic District states: "Young architects like Gilbert M. Fein, Frank Wyatt Woods and Gerard Pitt dominated the new construction. . . . Together, these architects defined a new direction of mid-century modern design in Miami Beach."[29] Pitt was born and raised in New Rochelle, New York, graduated from Columbia University with a degree in architecture in 1909, and worked for a number of New York architectural firms. He accepted a position with Albert Kahn, Architects and Engineers in 1913 and continued with the firm until 1930, at which point he was likely laid off due to the Depression.

Pitt's father-in-law was Robert Henkel, head of Detroit's Henkel Flour Mill, also known as Commercial Milling Company, one of the largest in the Midwest and located on Detroit's riverfront where the Renaissance Center now stands. The Henkel family had a large winter home in Miami and enjoyed an active social life there, so for Pitt, relocating to Miami from Detroit would have entailed little difficulty. In a 1943 letter to Edgar Richardson, assistant director of the Detroit Institute of Arts, Emil Lorch, former director of the college of architecture at the University of Michigan, requested a Detroit Institute of Arts article on Detroit architecture (by Hawkins Ferry) be sent to Pitt. "His wife and he," Lorch wrote, "retain a real interest in Detroit."[30]

From 1934 until 1938,[31] Pitt partnered with George L. Pfeiffer, one of the area's most respected senior architects—Pfeiffer was president of the architectural league until 1927, when Coulton Skinner took over the position. One of the firm's most interesting designs is the Indian Creek Hotel, built in 1936.[32] Located at 2731 Indian Creek Drive, the hotel has a corner entrance set within a broad facade and, along the roofline, coping nearly identical to that on Detroit's Mackenzie High School. Pitt served as the supervising architect for the southeast district of the Florida Hotel Commission from 1935 until 1957.

A number of Detroit architects developed business in Miami, among them Louis Kamper, designer of the Book Building and Tower, Book Cadillac Hotel, Frank J. Hecker House, and David Broderick Building. In Miami, Kamper—with George Pfeiffer and Gerald O'Reilly as associate architects—designed the twelve-story Consolidated Bank Building (Huntington Building) completed in 1926[33] and the fifteen-story Roosevelt Hotel, constructed from 1925 to 1930 (demolished).[34] Rowland's former employer, George D. Mason, was licensed to practice in Florida and was hired in 1926 to design the Miami Masonic Temple, though the building was not constructed.[35]

The Michigan Society of Architects (MSA) had a counterpart in Florida, the Florida Association of Architects (FAA), both of which, by 1930, were quite active and included among their members a great majority of the leading local architects.[36] Both organizations conducted many educational and social activities that served to disseminate architectural knowledge and ideas throughout the professional community. Some sense of the increased number of architects in Florida and growth of the FAA may be had by considering that the organization's membership swelled from 28 in 1932 to 236 in 1938.[37] Among the FAA's prominent active members during the 1930s were the Skinner brothers, Gerard Pitt, Louis Kamper, L. Murray Dixon, Roy France, T. Hunter Henderson, Henry Hohauser, Russell Pancoast, and George Pfeiffer.[38]

In 1939, reflecting a trend toward national organizations, the Florida Association of Architects affiliated itself with the American Institute of Architects (AIA) and noted at that time in its monthly *Bulletin* the five other affiliated state associations, the largest of which was the Michigan Society of Architects with 415 voting members.[39] Shortly after, and at the suggestion of Detroit architect George J. Haas (1889–1956), the FAA and MSA began exchanging copies of their publications (FAA: *Bulletin*; MSA: *Weekly Bulletin*).[40] Increased interaction between the two groups followed, and in 1944, MSA president Emil Lorch was the guest of honor at the FAA's semiannual meeting.

In 1945, it appeared that Detroiters might seize control of the Florida South Chapter of the FAA as Coulton Skinner was elected president and George Haas, recently relocated from Michigan, was elected secretary treasurer. Haas was a dynamo of organizational activity his entire life: in addition to serving as president of the MSA (1924–25), he was elected mayor of Hamtramck for two terms (1919–21), and was a founding member and first vice president of Kiwanis Club. He was active in organizations as diverse as the Masons, Arts and Crafts Society, and NAACP.[41] As a practicing architect, he designed schools in Hamtramck and Grosse Pointe, including Defer Elementary School (1925) and Grosse Pointe High School (1928), and the thirteen-story Macomb County Building (1931–44),[42] which bears more than a passing resemblance to the Grand Rapids Trust Building. With the onset of the Great Depression, Haas found work as a district manager for Stran-Steel of Detroit, representing the company's products in Michigan and then Florida.

Architecture in the Miami area underwent a style transformation during the early 1930s from Mediterranean Revival, the dominant style of the 1920s, to a "modern" look that is now referred to as Art Deco. The terminology can be exasperating, but the Miami Design Preservation League has sorted the various styles (for Miami at least) into three categories: Mediterranean Revival, Art Deco, and Miami Modern (or MiMo). Mediterranean Revival is similar to the Mission style of California—a new interpretation of a historic style. Art Deco encompasses a great deal, but as it applies to southern Florida, it generally refers to Streamline Moderne, a genuinely new style that began as an attempt to apply to buildings the streamlined look of aircraft. The austere look of the style was well suited to Depression-era economic circumstances: Streamline Moderne buildings are typically devoid of costly materials—stone, wood, or metal—and exterior decoration is often fashioned from concrete—the material used to face the structure—and paint.

Many hotels and apartments built in Miami Beach during the 1930s and up to the start of World War II, particularly along Ocean Drive and Collins Avenue, were of similar design: three or four floors high, narrow in width, but deep. The facades of these buildings are often described as tripartite—a central decorative panel flanked by two side panels. The parapet above the top floor typically includes an extension of the central panel. Decorative features, particularly in the central panel, are frequently sections of convex round shapes that extend vertically across the second to the top floor. It so happens that this description, in addition to generally characterizing many of the Miami Beach hotels of the 1930s, also describes the Detroit Saturday Night Building, designed by Rowland in 1928. Although the tripartite facade was not unique, the Saturday Night Building, when completed in 1929, exhibited decorative features—both as to type and arrangement—that were unique. Why do buildings constructed in Miami Beach over the following decade bear such a strong resemblance to the Saturday Night Building?

Unlike the Union Trust Building, the Saturday Night Building did not receive widespread press coverage outside of Detroit. However, two Detroit journals, the *Detroiter* (monthly) and *Detroit Saturday Night* (weekly), published sketches and photos of the building on a regular basis throughout 1929 (see figure 254, for example, which appeared in the *Detroiter*, the *Detroit Free Press*, *Detroit Saturday Night*, and elsewhere). The population of Detroiters wintering in Miami, including more than a few Detroit architects, likely received copies of these periodicals by mail. Due to the widespread publicity surrounding the Union Trust Building, Rowland had become nationally recognized among architects as an innovative and pioneering building designer; sketches and photos of his most recent work would have been closely examined to discern his latest design ideas. Chicago architect Roy F. France (1888–1972), for example, a designer of homes and large apartment buildings, moved to Miami after vacationing there in 1931 and subsequently designed a number of the area's iconic hotels, including the 1936 Cavalier, which is similar in appearance to the Saturday Night Building. He would have been familiar with Rowland's work and was likely impressed to learn that John and Coulton Skinner and Gerard

326. Perhaps the first Streamline Moderne building design was this 1928 proposal for the clubhouse of the Long Island Aviation Country Club by architect Warren Shepard Matthews; it is aerodynamically shaped like an airplane. A more traditional looking structure was erected. (This photo was published in the *Detroit Free Press* on November 4, 1928, and other papers nationally around the same time.)

Pitt knew Rowland personally and apprenticed under him. France could have acquired sketches or photos of Rowland's less publicized designs through these men or from other Detroit architects vacationing in Miami; John Skinner may have even arranged for France and Rowland to meet during one of Rowland's visits to the city.

The effect of a single sketch can be quite substantial, as exemplified by the case of Finnish architect Eliel Saarinen (1873–1950). Saarinen's 1922 entry in the design contest for the Chicago Tribune Tower won second place, yet due to Saarinen's innovative approach, his design was far more influential within the architectural community than the winning entry. Over the following decade, dozens of tall buildings throughout the country incorporated features from Saarinen's perspective sketch, including Detroit's Fisher Building (Albert Kahn, Architects and Engineers, 1928) and David Stott Building (Donaldson and Meier, 1929). The influence of Saarinen's design may also be seen in Albert Kahn, Architects and

327. The three-story Cavalier Hotel at 1320 Ocean Drive in Miami Beach was designed by Roy France and completed in 1936. The two piers between the center windows have decorative panels comprised of convex vertical round shapes, much like those on the Detroit Saturday Night Building. (Larry Syverson)

Engineers low-rise buildings, such as the Detroit Free Press Building (1925), S. S. Kresge World Headquarters (1929), New Center Building (1931), and University of Michigan Burton Memorial Tower (1936).

Due to the positive reaction to Saarinen's sketch, Emil Lorch (1870–1963), director of the University of Michigan's College of Architecture, brought Saarinen to the school as a visiting professor in 1923; Lorch said of Saarinen: "He put us on the map internationally—and was important in establishing the name of the school."[43] One of Saarinen's students was Henry S. Booth, son of George Booth (Booth Newspapers and the *Detroit News*), who arranged for his father to meet Saarinen, with the result that the elder Booth hired Saarinen in 1925 as architect of the Cranbrook Foundation.[44] In this role, Saarinen designed the internationally acclaimed campus of the Cranbrook Educational Community in Bloomfield Hills.

Dayton, Ohio, is another city

328. Eliel Saarinen's entry in the 1922 Chicago Tribune Building design contest won second place. Saarinen's innovative approach to tall building design embodied in this sketch greatly influenced many architects.

with an architectural heritage influenced by Rowland. J. Douglas Lorenz (1900–1977), after graduating in 1923 with a degree in architecture from Cornell University, worked as a draftsman for Smith, Hinchman, and Grylls. He remained there two years before Detroit architect Robert O. Derrick hired him away to work as a designer.

Rowland recognized Lorenz had talent and ambition and continued to mentor the young man, partnering with him early in 1925 on an entry for a design contest sponsored by the architecture journal *Pencil Points*. Their design for a six-room suburban house was awarded an honorable mention and published in the journal's August 1925 issue. The judges wrote that the two men were to be "commended for an effort to avoid a conventional elevation," having "succeeded in striking out a novel arrangement."[45] The entry is interesting in that it makes use of an eight-sided window prominently featured over the front door and an eight-sided frame over the living room fireplace. This feature, however, drew the comment: "In the opinion of some of the judges, the eight sided window . . . was not wholly successful."

Lorenz remained in Derrick's office until 1926, when he returned to his hometown of Dayton and opened an office there. His work consisted mostly of large homes, including a mansion for Charles Kettering, founder of Delco and vice president of General Motors Research Corporation. In 1936, when his firm began to acquire more commercial commissions, Lorenz enticed Detroiter Milton R. Williams, a designer with whom he had worked in Robert Derrick's office, to join him in a partnership. Lorenz and Williams went on to design significant buildings in southwestern Ohio, including a laboratory for Monsanto

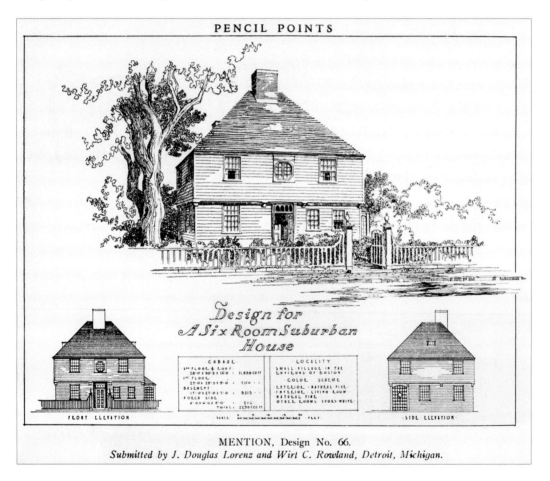

329. A contest design submitted by Rowland and Douglas Lorenz for a small suburban house was awarded a mention and published in the August 1925 issue of the architecture journal *Pencil Points.*

Chemical Company, featured in the May 1939 edition of *Architectural Record* for its innovative use of glass block and sash for exterior walls.[46] The firm designed Dayton's Talbott Tower, consisting of an expansive, three-story office and retail structure, completed in 1938, and an office tower, added in 1958. The structure, located at 100 West First Street, is noted for its curved corner entrance, much like the Bankers Trust Company Building, on which Lorenz would have worked with Rowland.[47] In the late 1960s, Dayton's tallest building, the thirty-story Kettering Tower, was designed by the firm.

Lorenz and Williams, now known as LWC Incorporated, is Dayton's oldest surviving architecture firm. A newspaper article on the company stated: "Doug Lorenz once told a son: 'The client, while not always understanding what constitutes beauty, will always recognize something which is beautiful.'"[48]

The extent to which Rowland's ideas, embodied in his designs of the late 1920s, influenced other architects is, of course, unlikely to be known with any certainty. However, given the large number of architects who trained under Rowland and the widespread publicity his buildings received, particularly the glowing reviews of the Union Trust Building, there can be no question that others learned and employed his principles and used decorative features pioneered in his designs.

10

A GREAT DEPRESSION

I am convinced that men, so inclined to write, as they grow older, leaving a
busy past behind them, do less and have more to say!

—Wirt Rowland, "Human—All too Human—Chapter II," 1939

As the decade of the 1930s began, so too did a new and markedly different phase of Rowland's life. The frenetic pace of design work that characterized the preceding years was at an end, and with more time on his hands, Rowland threw himself into other pursuits that served as an outlet for his creative energies. Although he produced many fewer buildings, Rowland's influence within the profession remained substantial by means of his writing, lecturing, professional leadership activities, and involvement with local architecture schools.

As far as is known, between June 1921, when Rowland's "Architecture and the Automobile Industry" was published in the *Architectural Forum,* and March 1929, when his "New Note in Architecture Struck" appeared in the *Detroit News*, he wrote no other articles for publication. However, as his busy years slipped into the past, Rowland did indeed "do less and have more to say";[1] in the nine years from 1931 to 1940, Rowland wrote at least twenty published articles, five of which are particularly formidable works addressing controversial issues of architectural philosophy or history. In addition, he authored a half dozen or so MSA committee reports published in the *Weekly Bulletin*, and gave numerous lectures. Rowland's writing from this period articulates his view of art in general and architecture in particular—at least to the extent it is possible to describe in words that which he acquired by long study and experience—and represents, perhaps, a greater gift to future generations than his buildings from the decade.

Fortunately for Rowland, his lack of employment was quickly resolved by joining in a partnership with his old friend Gus O'Dell, an opportunity made possible by George F. Diehl, O'Dell's former partner, electing to return to solo practice around the same time. The new firm, H. Augustus O'Dell and Wirt C. Rowland, Associated Architects, was established on January 1, 1931.[2] From the evidence available, at least in regard to the firm's significant projects, it appears O'Dell dealt with business matters and Rowland handled design work.

Drawings and letters from vendors suggest it was Rowland who oversaw design, selection of materials, and construction.

Both Rowland and O'Dell, having been relieved by the market crash of a large portion of their work obligations, took on leadership roles in each of the two professional organizations to which Michigan architects belonged. At the annual meeting of the Detroit chapter of the American Institute of Architects (AIA) in October 1930, Rowland was elected to a three-year term as a director of the organization,[3] and, shortly after, O'Dell was elected by the Michigan Society of Architects to serve as president—a position he held for three terms. (The two organizations were characterized by different membership policies; the MSA was open to all architectural professionals while the AIA was by invitation only. The two organizations unified in 1948 and the invitation-only policy was abandoned.)

A review of the minutes from meetings of the AIA during Rowland's tenure gives an idea of the vicissitudes faced by architects during the Great Depression. Those in the building profession contended not only with a dramatic falloff in business but in many cases were also unable to collect for work performed prior to the crash when the owner of an unfinished or recently completed building became insolvent. The head of the University of Michigan's College of Architecture reported to the college president in 1932: "The depression of the last two years is undoubtedly one of the most severe ever undergone by the architectural profession. Many offices have closed and the forces of large architectural organizations greatly reduced."[4] The troubled financial circumstances of most architects forced the Detroit AIA to reduce membership dues. To pay off debt incurred by a previous conference, directors Rowland, Herbert Wenzell, and Clair Ditchy were charged with devising a fund-raising plan.[5] Wenzell suggested that the organization take out a bank loan guaranteed by each of the directors. A note later appended to the minutes stated "The Detroit Savings Bank considered the Board of Directors as a hazardous risk and did not grant the loan, damn them." Another suggestion resulted in "a rather extended and prolific discussion of the project of a prize fight as a means of raising some much needed money for the treasury, the same idea being a generation of the mind of Mr. Palmer and bearing also the sympathy of Messrs. Rowland, and Wenzell, it was left that Mr. Palmer would gather the cold and clammy facts."[6]

The organization did not attempt to collect membership dues during 1932 and 1933, an outcome explained in the treasurer's report: "your Board of Directors and treasurer's office have realized that the strenuousness of the times would make it impossible for the large majority of the membership to pay any dues at all be the amount ever so reasonable."[7] The financial condition of the organization was at times a source of dark humor, as evidenced by the minutes of the August 1932 directors meeting: "The only other business placed before the Board was the matter of purchasing food for our evening meal. By motion unanimously approved, it was decided that the Treasurer be delegated to purchase the groceries with the funds of the treasury. Later it became known that, though the Treasurer was with us, there had been no treasury for many months; a fact we had tried hard to forget, only to have it brought painfully again to our attention."[8]

One project for which the AIA chapter held out high hopes as a source of work for architects was "Wider Woodward," an effort to widen Woodward Avenue and other major arteries into (and across) the city to better accommodate rapidly increasing auto traffic. Wider Woodward was part of a state effort begun in 1922 with reconstruction of Woodward from 8 Mile Road to Pontiac.[9] Subsequent to an agreement signed between the state and the city of Detroit in 1930, narrow sections of Michigan, Livernois, Gratiot, and Vernor Avenues were to be widened, as well as the remaining sections of Woodward.[10] In 1934, planning was begun for widening the section of Woodward south from Baltimore Avenue in New Center to Grand Circus Park. Although less than two and a half miles long, it was the most challenging stretch of the entire program due to the great number of substantial buildings lining both sides of the street. To reduce the demolition of buildings by half, Woodward was made wider by expanding one side of the street, allowing the other side to remain untouched. By widening the east side of Woodward from Grand Circus Park to Canfield Avenue, and the west side from Canfield to Farnsworth, demolition of major buildings was further reduced. This strategy resulted in the section of Woodward from Canfield to Farnsworth being somewhat offset to the west with slight jogs at both ends.

It was anticipated that the buildings situated on the side of Woodward to be widened would be demolished and replaced, thereby creating a great deal of work for the city's architects—all of which would be paid for by the city and state. Foremost in promoting Wider Woodward's potential to provide "Unemployment Relief" for Detroit's architects was Herbert Wenzell, who brought the idea to the attention of the Detroit AIA directors at a January 1933 meeting, resulting in the formation of a special committee—chaired by Wenzell—to pursue the idea.[11] An integral aspect of Wenzell's vision was replacing the discordant facades lining Woodward with well-planned structures of harmonious design. In February, sketches illustrating the concepts he had in mind were published in the *Detroit News* accompanied by an extensive article describing Wenzell's vision and the AIA's effort to bring it to life.[12]

The City Plan Commission was open to the idea of working with the architects and suggested that the AIA and MSA jointly appoint an Architectural Advisory Committee to

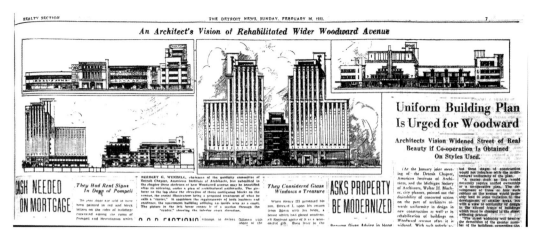

An Architect's Vision of Rehabilitated Wider Woodward Avenue

Uniform Building Plan Is Urged for Woodward

Architects Vision Widened Street of Real Beauty if Co-operation Is Obtained On Styles Used.

330. A group of drawings representing Herbert Wenzell's vision for a Wider Woodward from the *Detroit News*, February 26, 1933.

facilitate doing so. In March, the AIA established a committee consisting of Professor Emil Lorch, George D. Mason, Eliel Saarinen, Albert Kahn, Herbert Wenzell, Wirt Rowland, and William Palmer. By July, the makeup of the committee had been trimmed to just four: Rowland and Wenzell from the AIA, and Hugh T. Keyes and Amedeo Leone representing the MSA. (Rowland and Wenzell were both members of the MSA as well as AIA; Keyes and Leone were not members of the AIA at that time, but became members later.)

The committee developed a positive relationship with the City Plan Commission, and by April 1934, a plan submitted by the architects committee was approved by the commission. In early May, the committee met with property owners so as to secure their cooperation in implementing the approved plan. At this point, unfortunately, the superb efforts of both the committee and Planning Commission were derailed by an unforeseen obstacle: the large majority of building owners came to the realization that *moving* their existing building was far less costly than building anew—the settlement amount being fixed, moving would leave much more cash in their pockets. In the report on the work of the Advisory Committee, Wenzell wrote: "moving their front back to the established line represented a great saving. Thereby the architect lost a job, the Moving Contractor got one." "It was for this reason that a very laudable and workable scheme failed, the Depression being the answer."

In his 1933 year-end report to the AIA Detroit chapter, Secretary Arthur Hyde wrote with brutal frankness, "the activities of the Chapter this year have been not unlike those of the two preceding years. Continuation of inactivity in architects' offices during the past twelve months has again compelled the Chapter as a whole and many of its members to focus attention upon every known plan and cooperate with every agency designed to revive

331. Woodward Avenue before and after widening in photos taken from the Maccabees Building on Woodward Avenue in 1934 (*above*) and 1942 (*below*). North of Canfield Street, buildings on the west side of Woodward were moved or trimmed; south of Canfield, those on the east side were affected, resulting in a visible jog in Woodward. (Photos: "Woodward Avenue," Julius A. Clauss papers, 1908–1960, Bentley Historical Library, University of Michigan and Arthur Siegel, Library of Congress Prints and Photographs Division)

the building industry. Emergency efforts of various kinds have become so habitual that a sudden return, which we have no reason yet to fear, to the historic course of Chapter events would seem quite abnormal."[13]

Rowland's joining O'Dell in partnership salvaged for the firm an important commission that otherwise might have been lost. In 1930, O'Dell and Diehl were selected by the board of the Grosse Pointe school district to design a new elementary school on Cadieux Road. Diehl's departure from the firm would likely have triggered a reconsideration of the board's decision, but when the board learned that Diehl had been replaced by Rowland, they announced with pride: "The designer of the new Cadieux school is a Mr. Rowland who designed the new Union Trust building and the Penobscot building in Detroit."[14]

Although the commission for the school building was secure, the sour economy was causing serious financial problems for the school district. The approval in January 1931 of O'Dell and Rowland's plans for the new school by the school board was announced in the community paper, but the article was dwarfed by the full-page headline of another story: "SCHOOL TAXES UNPAID, BOARD FORCED TO BORROW IN CRISES; School District in Financial Troubles the Board Discloses."[15] School taxes were going unpaid, causing a shortfall in district revenue that was increasingly made up through bank loans. Funding for the new Cadieux Road school was to come from a bond issue that, given the economic circumstances, was unlikely to gain voter approval. Into this tumult, a note of absurdity was injected by a report in the same issue of the paper of a letter received by the school board from the federal government's Emergency Committee for Employment. The letter urged that contracts for construction of the Cadieux Road school be "let with the least possible delay," and "if there is any reason for delay, will you state these reasons and give your opinion as to how they may be overcome, in order that this Committee may assist you in any way possible in expediting the start of actual construction?" The school board, mindful that the chief obstacle was the doubtful prospect of passing a bond issue, suggested that the committee send "a regiment of militia to get a favorable vote out," or "a Tammany organization to swing the election."[16]

By April, it was official: construction on the proposed school would not be undertaken for some time. The president of the school board explained: "It would be folly to attempt to pass a bond issue at this time in view of the economic conditions."[17] Fortunately for O'Dell and Rowland, their design work on the school was largely complete, for which they were paid that year just over $9,000—a bit more than half of the eventual total fee.[18]

The American Civic Association, in October 1931, held its fifth annual national meeting in Detroit and selected Wirt Rowland, "specialist in skyscraper design,"[19] as one of its featured speakers. Rowland's comments were covered in newspapers throughout the country, many under the unintentionally cataclysmic headline "architect foresees end of cities." The *Frederick Post*, of Frederick, Maryland, for example, reported: "Great rural communities of the future, with every modern facility, will replace the densely populated metropolitan sections of today, Wirt C. Rowland, Detroit designer of skyscrapers, told the American Civic Association in session here."[20] *Detroit News* art critic Florence Davies provided more detail: "Science, said Mr. Rowland in discussing the dispersion of the cities, must master the traffic problem and bring about the movement of the cities out into the smaller communities as a means of increasing the joy of living." "Homes of the future will be planned from within . . . making the structure suit the human need rather than the human need fit itself willy-nilly into a boxlike structure." Rowland's most specific comments on building construction were directed not toward design, but materials: "We have many new materials," Davies quoted Rowland, "but we have only half learned how to use them."[21] The *New York Times* quoted Rowland: "Better buildings must come as a result of a more scientific knowledge of the function of the building and the proper use of materials. When science masters these fundamentals, beauty of design will take care of itself."[22]

Rowland's comment on the use of new materials was not idle speculation; at the time he was experimenting with an innovative application of porcelain enamel, a material comprised of a layer of glass fused to a metal base at high temperature, forming an exceptionally durable surface that may be of any color. Around 1890, the owner of an enameling plant in Germany used sheets of porcelain enamel as shingles on his own home, but little progress was made with architectural applications of the technology until the 1920s.[23] In 1924, the Wolverine Porcelain Enameling Company of Detroit began selling porcelain enamel roofing material, expanding in 1926 into additional interior and exterior surfaces under the trade name Glasiron.[24] White Castle in 1929 opened a restaurant in Wichita, Kansas,[25] employing white porcelain enamel panels on both the interior and exterior of the building (the chain first used porcelain enamel panels in 1925 on the interior of a restaurant in Saint Louis). The interior of the Detroit-Windsor Tunnel, constructed from 1928 to 1930, is surfaced with Glasiron panels, selected for their resistance to cracking and deterioration from exhaust fumes.[26]

Rowland aggressively pursued the use of new materials, particularly metals, in earlier buildings, and this experience fostered his relationships with the manufacturing firms that developed and produced them, giving Rowland an advantage in devising new architectural applications. In 1931, Rowland was designing a new storefront for an existing building to be occupied by L. Black Company, a Detroit jewelry and optical firm. He wished to use porcelain enamel panels as they were lightweight, low in cost, available in a wide range of colors, and exceptionally durable, but the panels had to be small in size in order to avoid damage from warping, expansion, and impact. Rowland realized that backing the panels with concrete would prevent them from moving, eliminating the warping problem and reducing the likelihood of damage, thereby allowing panels of a much larger size to be used. Concrete also provided much better fireproofing and insulation than the panels alone.[27]

In order to prevent the concrete backing from adding excessive weight to the facade, Rowland employed a recently developed concrete that was 50 percent lighter than standard concrete. In place of ordinary stone aggregate the concrete was comprised instead of burned and expanded clay called Haydite for its inventor, Kansas City contractor Stephen J. Hayde.[28] This lightweight concrete was

332. This photo of the L Black Company storefront at 1420 Woodward Avenue appeared in the July 1932 issue of *Pencil Points*. The facade was comprised of aluminum, glass, and porcelain enamel sheets backed with lightweight concrete.

first used as a substitute for steel to construct the hulls of cargo ships during World War I; the earliest significant architectural use was for a fourteen-story addition to a Kansas City building in 1928.[29]

The architectural publication *Pencil Points* carried a photo of the completed L. Black Company storefront and wrote that it "will be of interest because of its unusual construction," as "porcelain enamel is comparatively new in this sort of architectural application." The article lauded the concept of using "compound units" of enameled sheets backed with concrete, which afforded many advantages over the sheets used alone.[30]

Concrete-backed porcelain enamel sheets played a significant role in a widely publicized project on which O'Dell and Rowland were architects: the Good Housekeeping Stran-Steel House. The 1933 Chicago World's Fair, dubbed "A Century of Progress," had, within its housing section, eleven exhibit homes demonstrating technological and manufacturing advances employed to provide affordable small houses. Most of the structures were prefabricated, and steel figured prominently in the construction of at least four of them—a common view of this period held that housing costs could be greatly reduced if modern assembly line manufacturing processes could be applied to home building. If such a dramatic reduction in cost could be achieved, the ensuing increase in home buying might blunt the effects of the Depression.

Stran-Steel Corporation was founded in Detroit by Carl Strand (1883–1970) in 1933. Strand's first business venture, the Strand Lumber Company, begun in 1912, found success catering to the home-building market.[31] To prod renters into building a home, Strand had his lumber delivered on a truck trailer that looked like a house and had placards promoting low-cost "standardized homes and garages."[32] Strand foresaw that steel held the potential to replace wood in the construction of homes: steel did not burn, was vermin proof, could be manufactured in standard shapes and sizes, did not warp, and was comparable in cost to wood. The chief obstacle was onsite construction—carpenters had no experience working with steel. As a consequence, the handful of firms developing steel houses focused on prefabricated structures on which most of the construction was carried out by the manufacturer and only final assembly was performed on site. This worked, but resulted in standardized homes generally spurned by consumers.

Strand had the brilliant idea of manufacturing steel components into which standard nails could be driven, allowing carpenters to employ steel frame components in the same manner as wood. A Stran-Steel "2 x 4" was comprised of two U-shaped steel pieces riveted back to back with a narrow slot between them. The slot was just wide enough to admit a standard 8d common nail and grooved so as to tightly wedge a nail in place. A Stran-Steel House offered the advantages inherent in steel construction without the limitations of prefabrication.

Exhibit space in the housing section of the World's Fair was awarded based on a competitive design contest judged by the fair's organizers. As a typical Stran-Steel frame house was no different in outward appearance from a wood frame house, Strand likely opted to clad the World's Fair house in Glasiron porcelain enamel panels to give it a more futuristic appearance and justify a claim of having used two different advanced materials in its construction. Rowland's experience with Glasiron and reputation as a master of modern design made him the obvious choice for Strand's home. The fair's judges awarded Rowland's design entry first prize, securing for Strand not only exhibit space but also a sponsorship by *Good Housekeeping* magazine.[33]

333. The 1933 Chicago World's Fair Stran-Steel House, designed by O'Dell and Rowland. The taller man on the far left of the photo is likely Rowland. (*Good Housekeeping*)

The partnership with *Good Housekeeping* was a mixed blessing, as it came with input from two outsiders: a consulting architect, Dwight James Baum (awarded a gold medal by President Herbert Hoover in 1931 for the "best small-home design from 1926 to 1930"), and the director of Good Housekeeping Studio, Helen Koues. Moreover, the fair's design section, headed by Louis Skidmore (cofounder in 1936 of Skidmore, Owings, and Merrill, a large and influential international architecture firm), oversaw all exhibits, sometimes requiring alterations to bring a structure into conformance with the fair's design standards.[34]

The home included a single bathroom located within the master bedroom suite, the layout of which was attributed by Rowland to *Good Housekeeping*. It was proclaimed in promotional material as: "A bathroom with a new idea! It is divided into three sections, so that it can be used by three people at the same time."[35] This innovation was, apparently, not well received, for when the fair opened for its second year in 1934, the bathroom arrangement had been changed. After visiting the fair that year, Rowland lampooned the bathroom debacle in the *Weekly Bulletin*: "Last year, by virtue of *Good Housekeeping* [the bathroom] was called decentralized—in other words, a maze, through which an unsophisticated guest would need a guide for the general order of bath and other rites performed therein as prescribed by the host. Only the host himself, after several months training, could venture into this labyrinth of enameled porcelain and glitter of stainless steel without finding his wife or lady friend ensconced in precisely the same cella which he had so urgently desired to occupy himself. Ah! But this year I found it had been simplified—centralized in other words, into a nice, cozy one-man arrangement which would enable the owner to hold the fort by himself while the other members of his family bounce off the door trying to get in. Such does a year bring forth. What, indeed, could another 'Century of Progress' disclose?"[36]

Aside from the bathroom, the house had a very appealing plan, with a large living room, two bedrooms, dining alcove, laundry, and kitchen on the first floor. The second floor, smaller than the first, had a large recreation room and small sun room. As the home had a flat roof, the area over the first floor, not occupied by the two second-floor rooms, was enclosed by a three-foot-high parapet wall forming a sizable terrace, a feature well-liked by visitors to the home.[37] The house had no basement, though one could have been constructed.

The interior walls of the home were made up of drywall sheets nailed to the steel frame, covered with canvas and painted. The exterior was clad in Glasiron panels backed with 1¾ inches of lightweight concrete and nailed to the frame over a one-inch layer of composition board insulation.

For the second year of the fair, Stran-Steel added to its exhibit a second home constructed with traditional wood siding instead of Glasiron panels. This was likely an

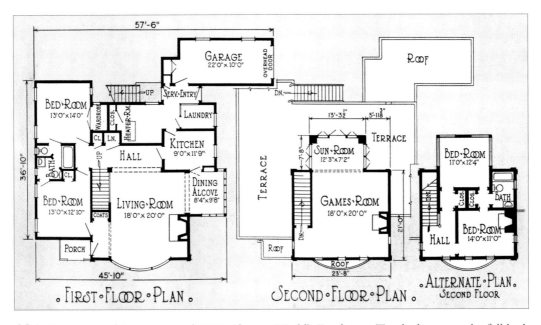

334. Floor plan of the Stran-Steel 1933 Chicago World's Fair house. Two bedrooms and a full bath could be built in place of the second floor recreation room. (*Stran-Steel House* brochure)

effort to demonstrate that Stran-Steel was in the business of selling steel frames for traditional home construction, a fact overshadowed by the unusual porcelain enamel exterior of the 1933 house. The sales brochure produced by Stran-Steel on the World's Fair house contains a first-page message from Strand stating: "Stran-Steel is not the pre-fabricated steel house of the visionary Technocrats. It is a simple and inexpensive system of steel members, which replaces wood joists and 2 x 4's." After the fair ended, the original Stran-Steel House was moved to a neighborhood in Wilmette, Illinois, and remains in use to this day.

335. The Ensign-Seelinger House, owned by Dr. Kathy Seelinger, in Huntington, West Virginia, was constructed from plans of the Stran-Steel House; brick was substituted for the Glasiron porcelain enamel exterior panels. (Dr. Monica Brooks)

Blueprints for the Stran-Steel House were available for sale, and a number of the homes were built, though there is no official record of how many. The most extensive research on this subject has been carried out by Dr. Monica Brooks of Marshall University, who lives in one of the Stran-Steel homes, the Ensign-Seelinger House in Huntington, West Virginia, which is listed on the National Register of Historic Places. According to Dr. Brooks, Darwin Ensign and his wife attended the fair, toured the home exhibit, and then purchased plans. They constructed the house, beginning in 1933, with minor modifications, including substitution of tan brick for Glasiron. "The home," said Dr. Brooks, "has great high ceilings and an interesting floor plan. At a time when art deco could have been very sterile and harsh, [Rowland] created a home that is uniquely elegant but still inviting and comfortable. Brilliant!"[38]

Annually in Detroit, a Builder's Show was held to showcase the latest home improvements and, in association with the show, an "Ideal Home" was constructed and held open to the public. O'Dell and Rowland's notoriety for designing the prize-winning, Stran-Steel *Good Housekeeping* World's Fair home secured for them the privilege of designing the Ideal Home for the 1933 Detroit Builder's Show. While the rationale for selecting O'Dell and Rowland was persuasive, the choice may have appeared peculiar to some, as the two architects had little experience in residential design.

Although the Detroit papers described the Ideal Home of 1933 as a duplicate of the house built for the World's Fair, it was, in fact, notably different. The two homes sought to achieve the same objectives: "low-priced housing for small families, yet designed to conform with the best quality standards of comfort and convenience, minimizing the work of housekeeping."[39] The Detroit house, however, was better aligned with the expectations of the average home buyer as to appearance and features, while including innovations not present in the World's Fair home. The floor plans of the two homes were similar, except that the Ideal Home's bathroom was entered directly from the hall, eliminating a circu-

336. This photo of O'Dell and Rowland's 1933 Detroit Builder's Show "Ideal Home" appeared in the brochure for the Stran-Steel World's Fair house.

itous route through one of the two bedrooms. The Ideal Home dispensed with the porcelain enamel exterior panels in preference for standard brick, though Glasiron was used on the exterior for windowsills, jambs, and the flower boxes along the top of parapet walls. The home had a less boxy shape than the World's Fair house, achieved in part through a slightly smaller second-floor recreation room, over which the flat roof projected well beyond the walls. The Detroit home had expansive floor-to-ceiling windows that were shaded by overhangs during the hottest time of day.

Inside, the home's floors were of concrete—poured over half-round forms that reduced the amount of concrete required—over which oak flooring was installed. The basement walls were of a new type, utilizing steel reinforcement, that permitted them to be made thinner. The home's built-in lighting fixtures were hidden from sight in aluminum ceiling moldings, so that lighting was indirect. As a safety feature, all interior and exterior lights could be turned on by a single switch in the master bedroom. Interior walls were of conventional plaster over metal lath nailed to the home's steel frame. As a consequence of the materials used, the Builder's Show manager claimed the house was nearly fireproof.[40] Nevertheless, the home was equipped with a fire alarm system having sensors and sirens in every room.

The Chicago Fair home's design was subject to a multitude of pressures and influences arising from its role as a heavily trafficked, commercial exhibit with a national audience.[41] The Ideal Home in Detroit, a local and lower-profile endeavor, may better represent Rowland's view of an attractive, low-cost, and practical dwelling tailored to the needs of midwesterners. An autograph book kept by Detroit architect Frank H. Wright (not to be confused with Frank Lloyd Wright, though Wright's autograph appears within the book) on behalf of the MSA indicates, perhaps, Rowland's view of the home's significance: beneath Rowland's late 1930s autograph is a sketch showing the Ideal Home flanked by the Union Trust and Penobscot Buildings.

337. Wirt Rowland's autograph, birth date, and sketch of the Union Trust Building, Ideal Home, and Greater Penobscot Building. This appeared as part of a ten-page section containing autographs of nearly four hundred architects in the May 9, 1939, issue of the *Weekly Bulletin of the Michigan Society of Architects*.

Ground was broken for the home September 20, 1932, and it was completed and furnished mid-February 1933. More than 30,000 toured the home during construction, and in the following week, another 8,000 passed through.[42] Yet in spite of excitement over new designs, features, and materials, the Depression's painful effects were plainly evident. In the Sunday *Detroit News* for April 30, 1933, a large headline announced, "Builder's Show Opens Next Friday"; far down the page appeared a two-paragraph article, "Architects Retrench to Meet Fiscal Crisis," reporting on an announcement by the American Institute of Architects president Ernest J. Russell. To meet the financial crisis faced by the seventy-six-year-old organization, its board adopted four measures: "Wide reduction in expenditures, remission of back dues conditional on full payment for 1933, renewed action to secure employment of private architects on Government building projects, and omission of the 1933 convention."[43]

The Ideal Home still stands on Prestwick Road, just off Mack Avenue, in Grosse Pointe Woods. It has been substantially altered, though, by expansion and efforts to conform its appearance to homes on the block through the addition of decorative shutters and a shingled, hip roof to cover its original flat roof.

Stran-Steel frames for home construction enjoyed limited success; in 1935, the company claimed it was selling material for one house per day.[44] The technology was more readily adopted for commercial structures, and Stran-Steel was employed to construct the Shrine of the Little Flower in Royal Oak, Michigan (1931–36).[45] Strand's greatest success was his redesign of the Quonset Hut in 1941, widely used by Allied armed forces from World War II on. The Stran-Steel Quonset was 60 percent less costly and 35 percent lighter than the Fuller Company's Nissen hut it replaced, the lighter weight and more compact unassembled structure facilitated shipping, and it was easily assembled with common nails driven into steel framing members much the same as those used on Stran-Steel houses.[46] In 1942, all production of Quonset Huts was shifted from the Fuller Company to the Stran-Steel Division of Great Lakes Steel Corporation in Detroit, which subsequently manufactured 120,000 of the total of 165,000 huts produced during the war.[47]

Strand, at the age of seventy-seven, invented a prefabricated doghouse of fiberboard that could be folded up to the size of a card table. The dog domicile could be used indoors and out and was easily transportable. In 1961, a steel version of the doghouse secured for Strand an appearance on the television game show *What's My Line*, where he explained the similarities in design between the doghouse and Quonset Hut.[48] Among Strand's many other inventions was the one-piece steel overhead garage door, in wide use beginning in 1940, and a lightweight fiberglass bathtub introduced in 1954.[49]

Another domestic project that received Rowland's attention in 1933 was the Free Press Institute of Home Economics' Tower Kitchen, located on the top floor of the tower of the Free Press Building. Within the test kitchen were developed recipes slated to appear in the newspaper's cooking section; students taking cooking classes in the adjacent Tower Auditorium practiced there as well. Prior to its opening in November 1933, the *Free Press* teased its readers for several months with descriptions of the labor-saving devices and efficient layout of the model kitchen, finally announcing in December 1933 that "Detroit's finest kitchen . . . was not designed by a woman, but a man."[50]

The report was accompanied by an article authored by Rowland describing the "common sense" approach taken in laying out the kitchen: "It is all in principle much like a Ford [assembly] line." "Food material is brought into the house through the service entrance, there must be a place to store it. Hence cupboards for that purpose and the refrigerator should be located adjacent to the rear kitchen door." Next in line are the counters and sink for food preparation, followed by the range and then a serving counter, so that "all is accomplished with as little as possible crossing or re-crossing the kitchen."[51] Rowland described how the cabinets were designed with rounded corners, both inside and out, to eliminate difficult to clean areas. Flanking the windows, small open shelves

Science Brings New Helps to Modern Home Makers

Architect Tells Story of Tower Kitchen

Detroit's finest kitchen, the model Tower Kitchen of the Free Press Institute of Home Economics, has attracted the attention and enthusiastic approval of hundreds of women. Yet it was not designed by a woman, but by a man. The Institute herewith presents him, Wirt C. Rowland, member of the Detroit firm of O'Dell and Rowland, designers of model homes.

By WIRT C. ROWLAND

Common sense is the foundation of all domestic planning. It sometimes goes under the name of science. But science is the means which enables us to use common sense to a further extent and the word "sensible" might almost be synonymous with "scientific." This especially applies to the modern kitchen in spite of the mystery which in some minds surrounds all of the gadgets which are provided to increase convenience and make the housekeeper happy by a reduction of her former slavery.

WIRT C. ROWLAND

338. This article by Rowland in the *Detroit Free Press* explained the common-sense approach taken to designing the newspaper's model kitchen.

were built into the ends of the upper cabinets so that "bits of china or a little greenery" could provide "points of interest."

Although the work done by O'Dell and Rowland was widely publicized, it did not generate a great deal of business. The partnership might have faced financial ruin, but Gus O'Dell seized on an idea that supplemented the company's revenue. Many of the firm's previous clients had insurance coverage on their structures based on pre-Depression values. To these clients, O'Dell offered the services of the firm to perform a reappraisal that typically arrived at a more realistic value for the structures, resulting in lower insurance premiums.[52]

The Michigan Society of Architects held its eighteenth annual convention in February 1932, and entertainment for the first evening was a "comedy in one act and a few gestures" presented by Wirt Rowland and Clair Ditchy. The play, "Bally Whose Who," begins with the architect, Joe Zilch, alone in his office examining a pencil: "2B or not 2B, it makes no difference. 2H with it!" Zilch nods off and dreams he is surrounded by merry revelers singing:

> We are the clients, bright and gay
> We have come your debts to pay
> We have money for your rent
> We will pay you ten percent
> Draw our drawings at your ease
> Draw our money as you please
> We won't say what style to use
> Follow any that you choose
> Fear from us no interference
> We don't care about the clearance
> We don't care about the prices
> We'll leave that to your devices
> You'll be building, we'll be billed
> And your trousers will be filled
> With cash to get yourself a car
> And buy yourself a good cigar
> Make our structures neat not gaudy
> Quite refined but never bawdy
> Like some lewd and flashy wimming
> Make them plain, give us the trimming.

The architect is awakened from his reverie by a rap at the door from a prospective client, Whyinell Tarrymore, who queries Zilch on the advisability of employing an architect. Zilch responds, "For bath-house or bridge, for horologium or hippodrome, for aquarium or armory, for excubitorium or auditorium, consult an architect. For mad-house or bad house, for bargello or bank, for light house or latrina, for kiosk or kimona."[53] Convinced of the need for an architect, the visitor sought information on several practicing in Michigan, including Rowland. "The other day," said Zilch, "I strolled into [Rowland's] office and was engaged in a friendly conversation when a fire-engine went tearing by. With that, Wirt jumped up, clapped on his hat and rushed out. I waited about an hour and was just about to leave, when Wirt came puffing in, all out of breath. He sank down in his chair and murmured, 'I am sorry to have kept you waiting so long. It was a larger fire than I anticipated. Three places burned. We got two of them, but Al Herman beat us out on the third.'"[54]

The March 31, 1930, merger of Guardian Group with Union Trust to form the Guardian Detroit Union Group relieved Frank Blair of day-to-day management duties as Robert Lord was appointed president of the new organization and Blair became chairman of the board (as well as chairman of the firm's trust subsidary, Union Guardian Trust). Blair made headlines on October 28, 1930—one year to the day after the market crash—for opposing a proposal to stimulate the economy by lowering interest rates and making credit available at lower cost. On the pages of the *Wall Street Journal*, Blair pointed out that in the preceding years manufacturers had built more production capacity than was required and businesses were, therefore, unlikely to borrow to further augment their capacity, regardless of how inexpensive the credit. The only real solution, argued Blair, was the "gradual utilization of present excess plant capacity" supplemented by "the development of new industries supplying new types of goods." "We believe that a normal working out of fundamental laws will be more helpful than attempts to apply artificial stimuli, which might cause a relapse at a later date."[55] Several months later, Blair was quoted in a front page *New York Times* article: "I favor the government's past policy of rapid debt reduction, economy in expenditures and continued reduction in taxes."[56]

Blair's views were in line with action taken by the federal government ten years earlier when the economy was roiled by the Depression of 1920–21. After World War I ended, federal spending declined from $18.5 billion in 1919 to $6.4 in 1920 and $3.3 in 1922, while at the same time the Federal Reserve raised interest rates to a record high of 7 percent in 1920. The unemployment rate rose to 11.7 percent in 1921, but then declined quickly to 6.7 percent in 1922 and 2.4 percent by 1923.[57] In effect, Blair was recommending the federal government do the same in 1930: get its own house in order by cutting spending and raising interest rates, and the economy would take care of itself—better to let nature take its course quickly than attempt to reinflate the bubble that had burst.

In January 1932, Blair retired as chairman of Guardian Detroit Union Group and its subsidiary, Union Guardian Trust, remaining only as a member of the board of directors.[58] Much of Blair's energy at this time centered on his role as president of the Joint Stock Land Bankers Association, an organization attempting to aid farmers during the Depression. In an address to the association in November 1932, Blair urged Congress to pass laws permitting banks to extend greater leniency to borrowers, so that farmers behind on payments, but still working the land, need not be foreclosed upon.[59] Blair explained that "the sad plight of agriculture was largely due to excessive taxation and extremely low prices of commodities." Property taxes in 1932, he said, "were approximately 266 percent of those for 1914," yet prices for agricultural products had fallen by 60 percent.[60]

By the beginning of 1933, economic calamity was raging through the country's financial system. On January 8, less than two months after Blair's plea for congressional action on farm foreclosures, farmers in one Iowa county averted foreclosure "with the threat of lynching," leading several large insurance companies to suspend foreclosures in that state; by the end of the month the suspension was extended to all owner-operated farms in the United States and Canada.[61] Fear that the banking system was on the verge of collapse led to hoarding of cash; bank failures and hoarding increased through the month of January.[62] On February 1, Detroit defaulted on its debt service, the first major US city to do so.[63]

At the time of Detroit's default, three years and three months had passed since the market crash in October 1929. At first, Detroit's banks and trust companies had suffered no difficulties, but by the beginning of 1931, the constant withdrawals of cash by depositors began to tell. From 1925 to 1928, Union Trust had increased its mortgage loans from $7 million to $18.5 million—a 300 percent increase—and the bank's customers had increased deposits of cash from $17 million to $42 million.[64] After the crash, depositors began to withdraw cash: $11 million total for 1929 and 1930, another $7 million in 1931, and $12 million more in 1932.[65] The trust company's cash reserves were vanishing, while at the same time, sources of revenue—mortgage payments, loan payments, city bonds—were vanishing as well. Henry and Edsel Ford, who had been instrumental in forming the Guardian Trust Company, sought to relieve the company's cash shortage by providing cash infusions, $4 million in 1931 and another $3.5 million in 1932.[66] The federal Reconstruction Finance Corporation (RFC) had loaned another $15 million.[67]

By January 1933, depositors were withdrawing cash from Detroit's banks at a rate of nearly $3 million per week.[68] To meet this continued drain, Union Guardian Trust sought further assistance from the RFC, which agreed to lend $22 million—sufficient to cover all the company's remaining liabilities—provided that Ford Motor was willing to subordinate the $7.5 million it had on deposit, a stipulation to which Ford agreed (subordinate in this case meant the cash could not be withdrawn and was, therefore, available to the bank to meet its needs and serve as collateral for the RFC loan). But then the RFC decided the value of assets put up by Union Guardian as collateral for the loan was inadequate; Union Guardian would be required to secure from Ford Motor an additional deposit of $5 million.[69] At this, Henry Ford balked, "he opposed being singled out to carry the burden, taking the position that he did not feel called upon to assume a responsibility of the government."[70]

To convince Ford to go along with the scheme, President Herbert Hoover arranged for Arthur Ballantine, undersecretary of the treasury, and Roy Chapin, former Hudson Motor chairman, now secretary of commerce, to meet with Henry and Edsel Ford in the company's offices in Dearborn on Monday, February 13 (Lincoln's birthday fell on a Sunday, so this was a legal holiday). Chapin and Ballantine made it clear to Henry that his failure to go along with the plan would likely cause the trust company to fail, and the ensuing financial mayhem might even bring down Ford Motor. Ford's view, however, was much like that of Frank Blair: the crash was unavoidable and the sooner problems were worked out of the system, the sooner people would get back to work. Even if his company was destroyed, said Ford, "he would proceed to start a new one and believed he could again build up a business, as he still felt young."[71]

Ford's rejection of the agreement and the RFC's unwillingness to offer an alternative loan arrangement meant the Union Guardian Trust could not open for business the following morning. The Guardian Detroit Bank, due to its close corporate connection with Union Guardian Trust, would be forced by federal authorities to remain closed as well. However, no action was to be taken to close the First National Bank, a subsidiary of the Detroit Bankers Company, despite the fact that it too was teetering on insolvency (and later failed).[72] Ford felt both banking organizations "should be treated alike in every instance."[73] At the time, Ford Motor had about $18 million on deposit at the First National Bank (and other Detroit Bankers Company subsidiaries), and Henry Ford declared he would withdraw these funds the following morning if Union Guardian Trust was closed.[74]

Ford may have believed this gambit would compel the RFC to reconfigure their assistance package; perhaps the RFC was certain that Roy Chapin or Senator James Couzens would ultimately prevail upon Ford to capitulate and accept the arrangement proposed by the RFC. Neither happened, and that night, faced with the prospect that Ford's Tuesday morning withdrawal would cause an immediate liquidity crisis for the First National Bank, federal banking authorities requested Michigan's governor declare an immediate banking holiday, ordering all banking institutions in the state to remain closed. The governor agreed, and the order went into effect at 1:32 a.m. on Tuesday, February 14, 1933.[75] Within two weeks, four more states closed their banks, and the first three days of March saw bank holidays declared in an additional seventeen states. On March 4, immediately following his inauguration, President Franklin Roosevelt instituted a nationwide banking moratorium. All commodity and security markets closed, gold payments and foreign exchange transactions were suspended, Congress outlawed hoarding and exporting of gold, life insurance companies ceased granting loans on policies, and steel output fell to 15 percent of capacity.[76] Meanwhile, in a classic case of government distraction, Congress decided that what Americans needed was a stiff drink: with the banking system collapsing around them, the Senate voted on February 16 to repeal Prohibition, followed by a similar vote in the House of Representatives on February 20.

Everyone involved in the negotiations to provide an RFC loan to Union Guardian Trust understood the stakes: if any of Detroit's major banks failed, or if a banking holiday was declared, panic would ensue, triggering a chain reaction of failures throughout the nation's banking system. It's puzzling that the RFC would allow a quibble over the estimated value of collateral to trigger a momentous banking failure.[77] That Ford Motor was singled out as the only possible savior of the bank when the RFC could have sought to make up the shortfall from other large depositors appears baffling as well.[78] At the February 13 meeting, Henry Ford said to Chapin and Ballantine that the "effort to talk him into the plan came from sources which they did not know about," intent on "harming or destroying his business."[79] The comment veers toward the paranoid, but the strange actions of the RFC suggest that Ford's theory was at least plausible. Recall too, that only eight years earlier, the opening of Guardian Trust's New York office was viewed in financial circles as an unwelcome "Ford invasion of Wall Street,"[80] heralding the entrance of Ford "into the banking field."[81] Although Senator James Couzens was among those who attempted to convince Ford to agree to the RFC's loan terms, he later denounced (through his personal attorney) the New York banks for their actions prior to the banking holiday as "cold-blooded." "The New York bankers preached leniency to the rest of the country," said Arthur J. Lacey, attorney for Couzens, "while they were being severe themselves."[82] According to Lacey, the New York banks had hoarded cash received from debtors as their loans matured, and then refused to refinance the debts. Without access to further financing, many of the debtors were ruined. Lacey characterized this behavior as "like a bank run. The first in line got theirs and left the rest holding the bag."[83]

Whatever the causes of the banking collapse, its sudden onset and extraordinary effects caught many by surprise. Wirt Rowland left home on Tuesday, February 14—the first day of the bank holiday—with nineteen cents in his pocket, more than enough to purchase a pack of cigarettes at the grocery and pay for a car to drive him to the office. He saw newspapers in the grocery, but so habituated was he to gloomy headlines that the dire message of that particular day went unnoticed. He arrived at work with just three cents remaining, but this was of no concern, as he had a customer's check that he intended to deposit at lunchtime, and from the proceeds would take his draw and replenish his wallet. Entering his office, Rowland was apprised by the firm's stenographer of the urgent implications of the bank holiday. Under the circumstances, three cents suddenly seemed woefully inadequate, so from O'Dell, Rowland secured the loan of a dollar, on which he lived the rest of the week.[84]

The banking holiday proved fatal for both Guardian Detroit Union Group and Detroit Bankers Group, which between them controlled more than 80 percent of Detroit's banking resources. However, by the end of March, order was restored as new banks replaced old with the establishment of the National Bank of Detroit, owned equally by General Motors and the RFC.[85] In July, a second new bank—Manufacturers National Bank—was formed by five former directors of the two failed Detroit bank groups: Edsel Ford, Wesson Seyburn, Fred Alger, John Ballantyne, and former president of the Union Guardian Trust, Clifford B. Longley.[86] Manufacturers National took Guardian's former space within the Greater Penobscot Building. These new institutions absorbed, with help from the RFC, assets and liabilities of the failed banks.

As dramatic and disruptive as the bank closures were, the economy fared no worse as a result. In fact, the bank holiday marked the deepest point of the Great Depression; employment began to rise in the spring of 1933 and continued rising through 1937, when employment and gross domestic product hit 1929 levels. This outcome lends credibility to Henry Ford's claim that banking failures were inevitable, but would purge problems from the system and then people could get back to work.

The Guardian Detroit Union Group's banking subsidiary, Guardian National Bank of Commerce, was placed in receivership and in 1935 was replaced by the Guardian Depositors' Corporation, which succeeded in returning to depositors and creditors over 90 percent of the money owed them by January 1939.[87] Under the supervision of the conservator of the Guardian Detroit Union Group, ownership of the Union Trust Building—known then as the Union Guardian Building—was turned over in late 1933 to a new corporation, the Union Building Company. The Union Guardian Trust Company was reorganized in 1934 as a nonbanking institution for the purpose of liquidating, over a period of six years, the assets owned by the firm, with proceeds used to pay off depositors and repay the loan to the RFC.

It was likely assumed that six years would allow adequate time for the economy to return to normal, and outstanding loans owed to Union Guardian Trust would be paid off or could be resold to other institutions. However, by 1939 the trust company still had loans outstanding, one of which was the loan to Jefferson Avenue Presbyterian Church. The trust company approached JAPC and offered to eliminate the remaining balance owed on the new church in exchange for an immediate payment of $50,000 and an additional $25,000 to be paid within three years.[88] While the offer was financially advantageous, the congregants had been in the grip of the Great Depression for ten years and were ill prepared to secure the necessary funds. Some money was raised by completing the sale of the old Bethany Church building through a cash settlement. Over several months, church trustees sought cash and pledges, and through "great sacrificial giving," the full amount was raised.[89]

The Thumb Tack Club, by 1933, had become as lifeless as the order books of the city's architecture firms. After a great deal of activity from 1920 to 1922, the club became focused primarily on holding annual exhibitions at the Detroit Institute of Arts, which it did from 1921 through 1925. After skipping 1926 and 1927, a renewed interest in the club resulted in a highly successful exhibition in December 1928, which included over four hundred sketches and photographs. Many of the leading architects from New York, Chicago, Boston, and Philadelphia exhibited their designs, an indication that Detroit's architectural community was held in high regard. Nevertheless, this was the last of the club's exhibitions. The chief purpose of the club had been to aid in the training of younger architects in a manner similar to the French atelier system, but by this time, university architecture schools had largely taken over the training process.[90] An attempt was made in 1934 to resurrect the club, spurred primarily by architect Robert O. Derrick (whose office served as a meeting place), but changes in the economy and the profession itself weighed against the effort.[91]

Rowland participated in Thumb Tack Club activities, though not as a central figure as he had previously. Nevertheless, he was actively involved in a wide range of other educational efforts, many of which were organized by the increasingly important architectural schools at the University of Michigan and Lawrence Institute of Technology (now known as Lawrence Technological University or LTU). It is noteworthy that both architecture schools rejected the Beaux-Arts model of architectural education on which other American schools were based.

The University of Michigan's College of Architecture was founded in 1906 under the direction of Emil Lorch. Born in Detroit in 1870, Lorch attended the Detroit School of

Art and the Massachusetts Institute of Technology, after which he worked one year for an architecture firm in Boston. In 1899, Lorch began teaching architecture at the Art Institute of Chicago, where he developed a teaching method based on "Pure Design," an approach to art education conceived by Harvard University professor Denman W. Ross.[92] During his two years in Chicago, Lorch gravitated toward Chicago School architects Louis Sullivan, Frank Lloyd Wright, and others, finding them receptive to his new teaching method. Lorch left Chicago in 1901 to earn a graduate degree from Harvard, followed by a teaching position in Philadelphia. In 1906 he was hired to head the University of Michigan's new architecture school, where he developed a curriculum based on Pure Design, rather than traditional methods. Lorch was quite active in the Detroit architecture community, serving as a director of the Michigan Society of Architects from 1931 through 1933, the same years that Gus O'Dell was president of the organization and Rowland was a director of the Detroit chapter of the AIA. He continued as a practicing architect, and among the structures designed by Lorch was the Belle Isle Bridge (MacArthur Bridge), completed in 1923.

Lawrence Tech was founded in 1932 by Russell E. Lawrence in a building adjacent to the Ford Highland Park plant on Woodward Avenue. The architecture department was established the same year and was headed by Earl Pellerin (1905–1994), a student of Lorch's and 1927 graduate of the University of Michigan's College of Architecture. During the summer of 1926, Pellerin worked for Albert Kahn, Architects and Engineers. The Marquette Building was, at the time, home to both Kahn's office and Smith, Hinchman, and Grylls, allowing Pellerin to become acquainted with Rowland. Pellerin said of Rowland, "Anyone in architecture at the time knew of him and admired him. He was friendly; and that year I got to know him quite well."[93] Pellerin worked again in Kahn's office during the years 1928 and 1929, and was an active member of the Thumb Tack Club.

For the architecture curriculum at Lawrence Tech, Pellerin, too, rejected Beaux-Arts methods in favor of the American architectural current of Henry Richardson, Louis Sullivan, Frank Lloyd Wright, and Rowland.[94] Pellerin, like Rowland, was focused on freeing American architecture from the grip of its European past. Describing the architecture of the 1920s, Pellerin said: "A great deal of good came out of those years, for American architecture [had] been too eclectic. We carelessly transplanted architecture from other countries here and there until much of it hardly seemed to be our own. It was during this period that a new theory of modern design developed which in time should make our buildings more American."[95]

Pellerin was deeply influenced by his participation in the Thumb Tack Club and appreciated that its role had to be taken up by architecture colleges. For working students, said Pellerin, "The evening segment of the Department of Architecture carries on in many ways the tradition of the Thumb Tack Club."[96] Rowland was often involved in the activities of Lawrence Technological University's architecture school; he served, along with Amedeo Leone, as judge of the school's first design contest in June 1933. In October, students led by Victor Basso and advised by Rowland formed an architecture club and named it the "Cliff Dwellers" to honor America's first architects, the pueblo city builders of the Southwest.[97] (In 1946, the club was renamed the Architects Club and later became a student chapter of the American Institute of Architects.)

In the early 1940s, at a time when Rowland felt he would have no further need for the architecture reference books kept in his home, he donated them to Lawrence Technological University's architecture department. These books formed the basis for the "Wirt C. Rowland Memorial Library," established in a room on the school's fourth floor in 1949. An article in the school paper that year described Rowland as "a close friend of the architectural department since its beginning in 1932."[98]

Pellerin maintained an architectural practice outside of his duties at Lawrence Tech and was an active member of the Michigan Society of Architects, where he served on a number of committees with Rowland. In 1934, Pellerin organized a regular drawing class, directed by architectural illustrator Frederick Crowther, that attracted Rowland, Clair Ditchy, Richard Marr, Herbert Wenzell, Corrado Parducci, and others. The class helped maintain the participants' creative energies during the depths of the Depression, served as an enjoyable social get-together, and provided employment for a model whose fee everyone chipped in to pay.[99]

The architecture club at the University of Michigan is the Iktinos chapter of the national architectural fraternity Alpha Rho Chi, and Rowland was inducted as an honorary member of the club in 1921. He was described in a newsletter as "one of our most popular honorary members," and frequently attended club meetings and events, often as a speaker. In spite of his busy work schedule in the latter part of 1926, for example, Rowland made several appearances at the club to give talks on his visit to Europe. For the 1930–31 and 1932–33 academic years,[100] Rowland served on the school's architectural design jury, along with Herb Wenzell, Robert Hubel, Amedeo Leone, and Clair Ditchy. This visiting jury, the school reported, "maintains a desirable contact between the profession and the School."[101] In 1933, Rowland was elected to serve as a director of the Iktinos alumni organization. When George D. Mason was inducted into Iktinos in 1935 as an honorary member, the group held a testimonial dinner for which Rowland served as toastmaster.[102]

Frank Lee Cochran (1913–2009) was a 1936 graduate of University of Michigan's architecture school and a member of Iktinos. Recalling his college years, he said of Rowland:

"Wirt was a source of inspiration to us. He loved music, was knowledgeable about art and literature and would also indulge in a few beers with us until all hours."[103] Cochran went on to a successful career with the large Chicago architecture firm of Perkins+Will, which he joined in 1945, eventually rising to senior partner and heading the firm's Washington, DC, office. During the 1940s and 1950s, Cochran specialized in the design of schools, noted for expansive windows that admit the maximum amount of natural light.[104]

Another member from the same period was Donald Wolbrink (1912–1997), who recalled "there was a modicum of music" in the Iktinos fraternity house. He played violin accompanied by members on piano and drums while Rowland sang.[105] Wolbrink became a highly regarded landscape architect and city planner, instrumental in establishing Hawaii as a tropical paradise tourist destination in the 1960s.[106]

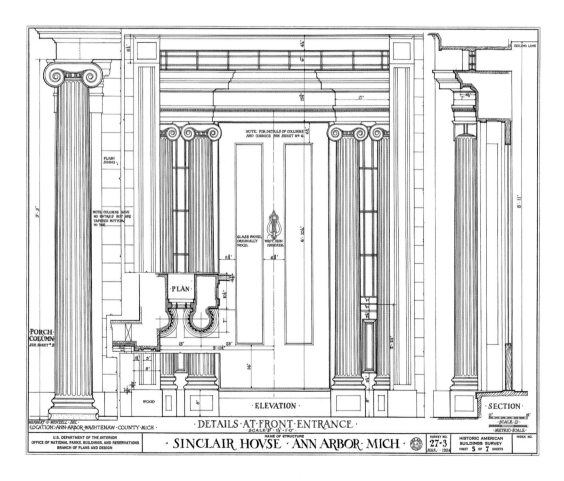

339. A typical drawing from a set of plans created for the Historic American Buildings Survey in 1934; this one is of the Sinclair House in Ann Arbor, drawn by Herb Wenzell. (Historic American Buildings Survey, Library of Congress)

In 1933, as a result of prodding from the American Institute of Architects, the federal government's Civil Works Administration authorized funds to establish the Historic American Buildings Survey (HABS).[107] The twofold purpose of the program was to provide employment for architects and create a record of historically important structures, accessible to any interested party through the Library of Congress. HABS continues to this day (as most government programs do) providing a valuable source of documentation and, in particular, photographs of structures, most of which are accessible online. Architect Branson V. Gamber was district HABS officer for the state of Michigan, and in January 1934, he established a committee directed by Emil Lorch and comprised of two architects, Rowland and Marcus R. Burrows, and two nonarchitects, George Booth and J. Bell Moran. The committee was responsible for selecting buildings to be included in the HABS survey.[108]

Beginning January 11, the twenty or so architects deployed in teams of two throughout the state.[109] To create an accurate set of architectural plans, the exterior of each structure was carefully measured, including such details as column fluting and hardware. Although it was one of Michigan's coldest winters, the participants were thankful for the paid employment. Originally the ten-week program focused on the small number of structures selected by the committee, but near the end, the National Park Service ordered the architects to comb the state and create a detailed card file on other buildings worthy of attention in the future.[110]

11
CHURCH AND STATE

Literature can never penetrate to the sources of art—the subconscious mind. From that proceeds by imagination the ideas which become tangible in architecture, painting and music; they must be grasped through their own language.

—Wirt Rowland, letter to Edwin George, July 28, 1944

Occasionally the poetic intellect—that intellect which we now feel to have been the most exalted of all—since those truths which to us were of the most enduring importance could only be reached by that analogy which speaks in proof-tones to the imagination alone, and to the unaided reason bears no weight.

—Edgar Allan Poe, "The Colloquy of Monos and Unos," 1850

For O'Dell and Rowland, 1934 saw a distinct increase in architectural work over prior years, with projects coming from throughout the state. The firm was hired to remodel the Blake Building in Grand Rapids, design a single-story store in Bad Axe, and prepare plans for a rustic resort. The resort building was located within the Canada Creek Ranch near Onaway, Michigan, and was a two-story structure with kitchen and dining facilities, capable of accommodating 125 guests in thirty-eight bedrooms. The land for Canada Creek Ranch was acquired that year by Detroiter Almond C. Monteith of the Monteith Land Company from a nonprofit land holding organization founded by another Detroiter, Edwin S. George (1873–1951).[1] Around this time, George and Rowland had become acquainted through what George later described as "our incidental meeting."[2] It is possible that the two met as a result of George's involvement with the Canada Creek Ranch, or at Cranbrook, as George served on the board of directors of the Cranbrook Institute of Science, and Cranbrook had become a popular meeting venue for Detroit's architects.

340. The rustic Canada Creek Ranch lodge building designed by Rowland in 1934. (Uncredited photo postcard)

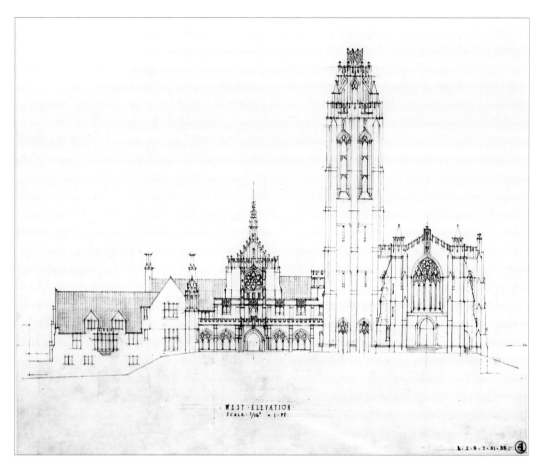

341. This sketch by Rowland shows the front of Edwin George's church. The church and tower on the right side differ little from the completed building. In the lower right corner appear George's initials, "E. S. G," and the date, "7-21-1935." (From the collection of Kirk in the Hills)

Shortly after meeting, George sought out Rowland for input on George's dream of building a Gothic style church. He provided Rowland with sketches and photos of Melrose Abbey, a partially demolished Scottish monastery built in the twelfth century, on which George wished to base the church's design. Rowland sensed George's deep desire to serve God through beautiful works of architecture and art, an ambition with parallels to the church builders of the Middle Ages. Rowland prepared preliminary sketches in 1935, which greatly impressed George as "beautifully conceived and executed."[3] By the end of summer that year, the form of the church and tower had been worked out, differing only in minor detail from the building that was ultimately constructed. Rowland continued to provide George with charcoal and pencil detail sketches, some of which were speculative in nature, though most expressed Rowland's specific vision of the church's windows, tracery, and interior rib designs.

These sketches served a purpose beyond refining details and securing George's approval for the design. Construction of the church was to take place on land owned by George adjacent to his home on West Long Lake Road in Bloomfield Hills, and be paid for by the Edwin S. George Foundation (established by George in 1935). The adequacy of these foundation funds for such an ambitious project was uncertain; George was in his sixties and appreciated that he may not live to see the structure, or even its plans, completed. To assure the church would be built according to the plans and detail sketches provided by Rowland, George signed and dated each sketch and stored them in the trust's safe deposit box with the understanding that they represented the "accepted church plans."[4]

George initially sought to name the church "All Souls Church," in part, due to his desire that the building be open to all who wished to pray and meditate within.[5] He later chose the name "Kirk in the Hills," "kirk" being the Scottish word for church, and "hills," short for Bloomfield Hills, the location of the church.

In 1934, Wider Woodward was finally getting under way as monetary awards were made to property owners whose buildings were to be demolished or moved. O'Dell and Rowland profited from this project, securing at least a half dozen jobs involving either removal of fifty to sixty feet of the front of a structure and constructing a new facade, or demolishing the middle of a building to make room for moving the facade back from the street. In 1934, the firm handled such alterations to 3408 Woodward Avenue (Peninsular Engraving), 3922 (now demolished), 4112 (Garden Bowl), and 4454 (Standard Auto Company/Museum of Contemporary Art) Woodward Avenue.[6] (3408 Woodward is sometimes referred to as the "Kahn Print Shop," but was actually built in 1912 for the Peninsular Engraving Company. It is now occupied by Michigan State University.)

Despite the surge of work for O'Dell and Rowland in 1934, the following year was quite lean, and by its end, Rowland was two years behind in his membership dues to the American Institute of Architects. The number of members in arrears at that time was so large that the organization extended by one month the deadline for payment of dues to January 31. Nevertheless, in February 1936, letters were sent to Rowland and hundreds of others who were more than two years in arrears notifying them of the termination of their membership.[7] The organization, having already significantly reduced dues and severely reduced spending, was in no position to waive the dues requirement. AIA's archive manager, Nancy Hadley, has reviewed many individual member files from the era and attests to the "widespread" and "genuine hardship" experienced. "There are letters about having had no jobs for two years and no prospect of work; about clients unable to pay for work that was

342. Grosse Pointe's Lewis E. Maire Elementary School on Cadieux Road opened in October 1936.

completed around the time of the crash; and one especially sad letter where the architect had no work coming in plus the bank in which the firm kept its accounts had failed so all the assets of the firm were lost."[8] Fortunately for Rowland, by early 1938, business had improved sufficiently for him to pay off his back dues and have his membership reinstated.

Late in 1935, Grosse Pointe's Cadieux Road elementary school project awoke from hibernation, spurred by a federal Public Works Administration project grant covering 45 percent of the cost.[9] A bond issue authorizing construction of the school was passed in December 1935, though only 396 of the district's ten thousand eligible voters cast ballots, provoking a reprimand from the local paper for the other 9,604.[10] Ground was broken the first week in January 1936 and Rowland predicted the three-story school would be ready for occupancy by February the following year.[11] Incredibly, the Lewis E. Maire School on Cadieux Road opened to students October 20, 1936.[12]

The advisability of federal subsidies for Grosse Pointe aside, Washington and Grosse Pointe certainly received their money's worth from Rowland. In spite of a limited budget, Rowland crafted an astonishingly attractive and unique building.

Large in size for an elementary school, Rowland sought to make the school appear smaller and more inviting by visually breaking it up into sections—an approach that in some ways was the opposite of his approach for tall office buildings. Bay windows and the entrance porch project from the building's front and, along with the visible gabled roof, add depth to the building, to avoid the appearance of a massive sheer face. The section of the building in which the entrance is located resembles in shape the traditional one-room schoolhouse, and the entrance porch echoes this shape. The building's front is characterized by a variety of window sizes, arranged symmetrically, and brick surfaces set in multiple layers, adding interest to the facade. A variety of brick colors were used in facing the building, which, along with string courses of bricks set on end, provide texture to the surface.

As was typical with Rowland, a great deal of design effort was focused on the entrance and the result is quite remarkable. The doors to the building are set deep within the projecting porch, which is of a scale more like a home than a large building. The porch is constructed of both standard brick and Roman brick, which is half as thick. The Roman brick is set in assorted patterns and angles that dazzle the eye. Inside the porch are openings, all the faces of which are set at an angle, including the walls and limestone sills. The 45-degree angles of these surfaces are reflected in an exceptionally clever design in brick on the floor, the windows within the doors, and the ceiling of the porch. In fact, the 45-degree angle characterizes nearly every aspect of the porch and appears elsewhere on the exterior of the building, serving as a unifying motif.

343. The entrance to Marie Elementary is an exceptional example of Rowland's design skills.

Directly above the entrance is a carved image by Corrado Parducci of a robed individual holding a quill pen and scroll. The figure is roughly carved—not smooth and refined—yet the face is highly expressive. Within the porch, over the double doors, is a panel of colorful Pewabic tiles set in a diamond pattern to complement the 45-degree angles surrounding it. Pewabic also supplied tiles for drinking fountains, aquariums, and fireplaces.[13]

In the spring of 1936, O'Dell and Rowland was hired to plan and oversee one of the last Wider Woodward projects: moving Saint John's Church, the oldest church building on Woodward Avenue (built 1860–61) and, according to Emil Lorch, one of the best examples of ecclesiastical architecture in the Midwest.[14] (It became the oldest church on Woodward in 1955 when Mariner's Church was moved from Woodward Avenue to a new location to make way for construction of the Civic Center and Hart Plaza.) The church, on the east side of Woodward at Vernor Highway (now Fisher Freeway), needed to be demolished or moved to

344. Rowland (*center*) at his fifty-year grade school reunion in 1936. (Historical Society of Clinton)

make way for the widening project. The decision to widen the east or west side of the street was purely economic; the west side of Woodward in this block held the Fyfe and Palms Buildings and the Fox and State Theaters, the combined value of which was much greater than that of the buildings on the east side.

Moving the 2,000-ton church presented certain challenges, some of which had been addressed by advocates of a Wider Woodward in 1925, when representatives from three building moving firms in other states were brought to Detroit. After examining the churches on Woodward, these experts gave assurances that the buildings "can be moved back to the new line of the avenue without even so much as cracking plaster." One of the firms had been responsible for moving the Hyatt Roller Bearing building, which it cited as an example of the firm's capabilities.[15]

Church members had been aware since 1928 that a decision was required to either move the church building or demolish it. The congregation at the time was shrinking due to an exodus of members from the downtown area. Reasoning that the 1,300-seat church was simply too big for the community being served, some favored using the condemnation award to relocate the congregation to one of the city's growing areas. However, by the time a decision was forced upon them in 1936, sentiment had swung toward remaining at the present location.[16]

It was determined that moving the building would be facilitated by first disassembling and removing the tower. A typical wall-bearing structure, the tower had walls nearly four feet thick. It was rebuilt around a new steel reinforced concrete frame, resulting in a stronger structure with much thinner walls. Its original exterior stones were carefully removed and numbered so they could be reassembled on the new frame as they were before.[17] A less visible, but important, alteration was made to the tower due to a severe storm that struck downtown Detroit on June 3, 1936, killing two and injuring at least five others. Wind gusts of sixty miles per hour sent roofs sailing, scattered the press box at Tiger Stadium across the infield, and toppled a crane. As the storm moved west across the city, lightning struck the tower of Saint John's, causing extensive damage. To prevent a repeat, a modern lightning rod and grounding system were added to the roof and belfry.[18]

345. Saint John's Episcopal Church at Woodward and Vernor around 1905, prior to the move. Just to the right of the church is the rectory, demolished in 1937. (Detroit Publishing Company Photograph Collection, Library of Congress Prints and Photographs Division)

To reinforce the old building and alleviate any possibility the roof would collapse when it was moved, steel supports were installed, and remain to this day hidden within the piers that line the nave. The engineering challenges of the job were beyond the capabilities of O'Dell and Rowland, so Smith, Hinchman, and Grylls was contracted to handle that aspect of the work under Rowland's supervision.[19] The entire project took just under two years to complete, winding up around Easter of 1937, though only twenty-four hours were required for the movers to roll the building sixty feet east—about one-half inch each minute.[20]

Moving and reconstructing the church provided an opportunity for Rowland to make minor changes and improve the building's interior appearance. A church history from 1939 says of Rowland's efforts: "the interior of the Church was made so beautiful that it is today generally recognized as one of the most churchly in the diocese, and so modified that the work of the clergy, organist, Altar Society and Sunday Schools has been made much easier and more efficient."[21] Reverend Irwin C. Johnson, rector of the church from 1934 to 1962, was also pleased with the outcome: "Special tribute at this point should be paid to the architect, Mr. Wirt C. Rowland and the building committee of the

346. Saint John's Church, with its tower removed, being moved 60 feet back from Woodward Avenue. Directly behind the church entrance is the parish house (1888), and to its right, the large excavation was the former location of the eight-story Berlin Building. When this photo was taken, the widening of Woodward south of this block was already complete. (*Detroit News* collection, Walter P. Reuther Library, Archives of Labor and Urban Affairs, Wayne State University)

vestry who labored so long and so diligently that the task of moving and reconstruction might be carried through while at the same time preserving the charm and the traditions of the beautiful old church."[22]

Rowland's attention to detail and conscientious oversight of the project gained him favor with Johnson and the church leaders, resulting in additional commissions, the first of which being plans for a new parish house. The church's existing three-story parish house, built in 1888, was unaffected by the widening as it was located on Montcalm Street. The church rectory on Woodward, dating from 1858, however, was demolished instead of moved. The condemnation award Saint John's received exceeded the amount required to move the church and Rev. Johnson strongly favored spending some of the excess funds to construct a new parish building adjacent to the rear of the church. Johnson and William Zabriskie, chairman of the special building committee, had Rowland prepare preliminary sketches, and at the annual parish meeting of January 18, 1937, Rowland presented the proposal to the group of one hundred congregants, using his detailed sketches of the building's exterior and floor plans (these sketches were retained by the church and may be Rowland's only surviving original architectural sketches).[23] In spite of Johnson's support for the idea, it was ultimately decided to instead roll the remaining $150,000 into the church's endowment fund as a hedge against future financial shortfalls.[24]

Several months later, Johnson arranged for Rowland to meet with Mrs. Frederic B. Stevens, a church member who wished to make a gift to Saint John's in memory of her late husband (he had established a highly successful foundry in Detroit). Attached to the church building's rear and fronting on the side street is the congregation's original chapel, built 1858–59. Mrs. Stevens wished to have constructed in the chapel a new altar and reredos (screen behind the altar) of a design consistent with the Gothic style of the church.

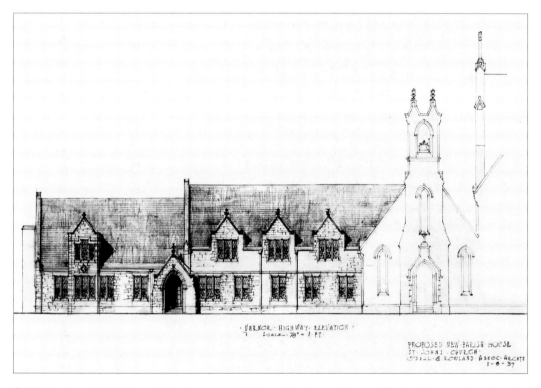

347. Rowland's 1937 sketch for the proposed Saint John's parish house. The building outlined on the right is the existing chapel, and to its right, the rear of the main church building. This is one of four parish house sketches that are the only known surviving original architectural drawings by Rowland. (Collection of Saint John's Episcopal Church, Detroit)

Although Rowland's forte was Modern design, he approached this project with enthusiasm; his deep understanding of medieval art and architecture permitted him to produce a plan with which Mrs. Stevens was in complete accord.[25] Rowland's sketches for the memorial were displayed at a church meeting on June 7, 1937, and approved, with the additional stipulation, suggested by Johnson, that, as the cost of the project had grown "considerably greater than originally contemplated" by Stevens, the church pay the architect's fee.[26]

Thus began one of Rowland's most unusual and extraordinary design efforts. When completed, the Stevens Memorial was selected (by a jury) to be displayed at the Fifty-Second Annual Exhibition of the Architectural League of New York in 1938—the only design of Rowland's to be recognized in this way during his lifetime. The memorial was also the subject of a Sunday, December 18, 1938, *Detroit News* article, "In the Gothic Spirit," by art critic Florence Davies. "The week of Christmas," wrote Davies, "is a peculiarly fitting time to consider a Gothic altar of rare beauty." "The altar was designed by Architect Wirt C. Rowland, and exemplifies in a marked degree the true spirit of Gothic Art."[27]

By the time of its completion, in addition to the altar and reredos, the Stevens Memorial included a chancel, lectern, litany desk, two sedilia (seats), and an organ screen,

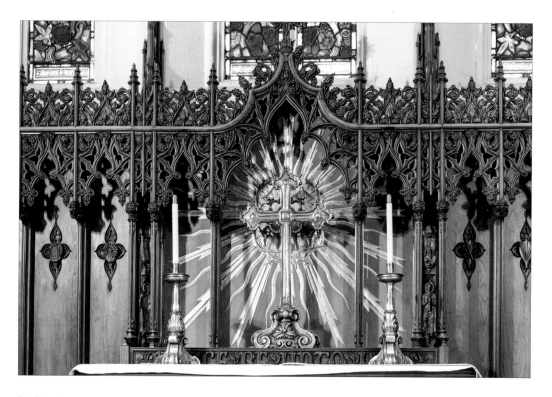

348. The Stevens Memorial within the old chapel of Saint John's Episcopal Church, completed in 1938. The woodwork was carved by Alois Lang according to a detailed plan by Wirt Rowland.

superbly executed in American walnut by Alois Lang (1872–1954), a skilled Bavarian woodcarver who worked for American Seating Company in Grand Rapids.[28] This was not merely an exercise in Old World craftsmanship and quality materials, as Rowland explained to Davies: "The design of such an altar is a major responsibility in the field of architectural design." "Modern usage has tended to debase the true spirit of Ecclesiastical art and orna-

349. A close-up look at the wood carving of the Stevens Memorial.

ment. Because of modern industrial practice such ornament has often been standardized and rendered sterile."[29] Applying Gothic ornaments as decoration with little regard for the context and purpose, and without an informed appreciation of the "true spirit of the Gothic age," was, in Rowland's view, insincere and "dishonorable for the high purpose of a place of worship."[30]

Frank B. Thompson's *Eighty Years: A Brief History of St. John's Church* (1939) contains an excellent description of the Stevens Memorial written with Rowland's assistance.[31] In addition to explaining the importance and meaning of the many symbols contained within the carved wood, Thompson provides the following description: "As one sits in the Chapel during the day there is a surprising pulsation and glow of light on the gold of the center panel. The recessed position of the altar with comparatively little light from the sides of the Chapel allow the center gold part to catch the reflection of light through the entrance doors from the street. Passing objects obscure the reflection which comes on again as the object passes and adds an ever changing and surprising glow to the background—a play of light and shade on the altar which is unusual and fascinating to watch."[32]

The same June meeting at which plans for the Stevens Memorial were approved, a suggestion—raised at the previous meeting—to install an electric clock in the church tower was revisited. The building committee chairman had sought Rowland's opinion on the idea and reported to those assembled, "Mr. Rowland advised that we do not install such a clock."[33] Rowland opined publicly on the propriety of such features some months later when describing a new church building in New York City: "The interior lacks interest and that interest is hardly awakened by the modern lighting proudly shown by the verger in charge," wrote Rowland. "It is modern, clever and somewhat concealed, and can be dimmed or increased till the entire interior is flooded with light. To me, this is theatrical and thereby contrary to the purposes of the church as a place in which to worship. It is entirely on the same plane as the floodlighting of church towers which is a descent into rank commercialism. I am not a strict medievalist, but obviously there must be a fairly firm line drawn where end those things which pertain to buying and selling, and where begins that which pertains to the spirit and has no price."[34]

Another proposal requested of Rowland was for a large, painted tapestry to be hung on the south wall of the chancel depicting the story of Saint John's vision of new Jerusalem descending from heaven.[35] A detailed sketch was prepared by artist Angelo Lanzini, according to a design by Rowland; however, no donor stepped forward with an offer to purchase the piece.

It has been suggested that Rowland's favorite architectural style was Gothic, perhaps because of the highly visible work he did on Saint John's and Kirk in the Hills. To understand Rowland's view of Gothic, it is important to appreciate that he disliked categorizing styles according to external

350. A proposed tapestry designed by Rowland and executed by artist Angelo Lanzini. The prominent elements of the work are arranged according to the lines of root three rectangle figures. (Collection of Saint John's Episcopal Church)

characteristics, preferring to view them as a reflection of the technology and culture of the era. "Ordinary parlance calls anything Gothic that has a pointed arch, and I guess we might as well give in to the vulgar public," wrote Rowland in a 1939 letter to *Detroit News* art critic Florence Davies. "But Gothic, fairly unrelated to the Goths, themselves, but some way, by accident, bearing their name, is derived from a certain structural principle of thrust and counter-thrust—for example, the vaulting of a nave which thrusts outward and was met by the flying buttresses which thrust inward and thus keeps the vaults from collapsing. That principle may be traced all through Gothic work, the tracery, ornament, and even its sculpture."[36]

The pointed arches and flying buttresses arose from a desire to construct tall buildings with ever larger windows—the large, stained glass windows being the vital element of these religious structures (as explained in detail by Rowland in a 1938 article, "An Influence of Glass on Architecture"). The building was "a vehicle—a frame upon which the craftsman expressed his ideas and molded that frame according to his will consistently with what would *stand up*."[37]

That Rowland was engaged in work on several Gothic designs during the 1930s and 1940s was a reflection of the work he was able to get, not necessarily the work he preferred to do. It was during this time he also did most of his writing, much of it critical of Gothic. In his 1931 article "Real Progress" Rowland wrote:

351. In December 1937, O. W. Burke Company, the firm responsible for reassembling the church, sent out Christmas cards that bore this sketch made by Rowland. (Collection of the Detroit Historical Society)

Romanesque followed (Roman), its broad surfaces creating a certain repose which the Gothic afterward lacked and could have attained by proper development. The Romanesque also attained a plan development and consistency with its idea of unity which the exterior expression of the Gothic churches never reached.

The Gothic cathedral is not much more than emotionally stimulating. Its impression is that of confusion; not so much from the different periods of its construction as from a chaos of conception. Its interior was the only part which reached a partial expression of an ethical building idea. Its tracery forms were boyishly crude and lacking in real form articulation until the flamboyant period. The thrust and counter-thrust of its section and its flexible system of vaulting were the result of rude experiment and remain to us as the one significant precursor of the steel truss of our day which now solves a similar problem so much better and more simply. I have no hesitation in saying that the importance of Gothic architecture has been hugely over-estimated. I do not see why it should be selected as inspiration, nor why it should contain any especial lesson for us who are now so admirably equipped with a more flexible means of modern construction for our expression.

Nevertheless, Rowland was in awe of that which he viewed as the significant achievement of the Gothic period: the artistry incorporated within the structures in the form of colored glass:

> In the great church of Chartres, to us, the wonder here is accomplished which so far outstrips any color before or since that period. Light, through windows of minute units made up of different shades and densities of glass wrought into symbolism and biblical story, transforms the very atmosphere of the interior, wrapping the worshippers in a glowing and mystical nimbus. . . . The color and glow of the Medieval windows have that quality of great music—transcendent, intangible and unearthly—a sublime emotion.[38]

Rowland considered himself a "modernist," meaning that his architecture was *of the time in which he lived*. When the client's desire was for a building having the appearance of a historic construction technology (such as the Jefferson Avenue Presbyterian Church or Kirk in the Hills), Rowland was well prepared to deliver. Otherwise, Rowland's preference was for designs that frankly incorporated the best available technology and materials, arranged in a design that optimally met the need for which it was constructed. He was critical of designers seemingly compelled to wrap a new building in an old skin: "Architects who quail and rebel at the vast paraphernalia of practical requirements in these days do not belong in this age, especially when they try to disguise [buildings] by the precious relics of antiquity."[39] On the other hand, he disdained architects who violated convention purely for the sake of doing so, such as those "who go out of their way to fling rows of pipes in one's face," or "for the sake of exterior effect puts the light in the wrong end of the room."[40] "We must follow the age. My plea is not for the individualist but for the man who can rightly see the signs of his times and cooperate."[41]

O'Dell and Rowland were hired for a small project around 1938 that brought Rowland's design skills back to Detroit's Financial District: the Murphy Building at 151 West Congress Street was given a facelift. Updating the ground floor facade of a building such that it complements, rather than clashes with, the floors above is challenging. Rowland succeeded by designing an exceedingly uncomplicated treatment, the chief feature being an impressive angled arch comprised of dark stone surrounding the main entrance. The focal point above the center of the arch was highlighted by a simple banded ornament. The result was so successful that the manufacturer of the dark stone, Virginia Green Tremolite, featured the building in a full-page ad in the December 1939 issue of the *Architectural Forum.*

352. This photo of the new facade of the Murphy Building appeared in a full-page ad for Virginia Green Tremolite in the *Architectural Forum.*

Again in 1938, O'Dell and Rowland were the beneficiaries of federal government largesse when the Public Works Administration (PWA) approved funds for two projects, a library in Detroit and a dormitory at the University of Michigan in Ann Arbor. As with Maire Elementary, the taxpayers paid 45 percent of the cost of these buildings.

The University of Michigan in 1938 had an on-campus enrollment of roughly 12,000 (8,400 men and 3,600 women), all of whom were required to reside in dorms, fraternity or sorority houses, or university approved private homes. Housing for men was insufficient and overcrowding was a concern, particularly as a number of students had died in house fires the previous year. The university embarked on a program in 1936 to build additional "fireproof" dorms, completing the first unit in 1937, with two more planned for 1938, contingent on receiving $2,100,000 in grant money from the PWA.[42] Approval of grants for the two dorms, West Quadrangle (housing 850 students) and Victor Vaughan House, a medical school dormitory (140 students), was received in August 1938, by which time the architects were already engaged in drawing plans.

O'Dell and Rowland were selected to design Vaughan House, situated on the crest of a small rise with its rear facing what is now called West Medical Center Drive, at the corner of Catherine Street. At the time, it was assumed Vaughan House would be the first of three buildings arranged in a "U" around a central courtyard, a plan that dictated the building's long and narrow shape.[43] (The additional structures were never built; in their place, several massive medical buildings were constructed just far enough east of Vaughan House to allow pedestrians to pass between the structures. Connecting these medical buildings with a distant garage is an enormous "hamster tube" that protects commuters from the elements, but the tube and a strategically placed supporting trestle almost completely block the south facade of Vaughan House.)

Rowland was concerned to avoid a long, unbroken corridor running the full length of each floor, fearing that it would conduct noise and serve as a temptation "to become a race track or a bowling alley."[44] By offsetting by six feet the central portion of the building from its wings, a slight jog was introduced into the corridor at two points.

Rowland placed projecting windowed bays along the building for much the same reason as he had in his structures dating back to the Hotel Pontchartrain: to facilitate the admission of light and air and add interest to an otherwise plain exterior wall. As with Maire Elementary, Vaughan House is clad in brick with limestone accents. String courses of brick and a modest corbelled brick cornice constitute the decorative treatment. Entrances are surrounded by contrasting stone with an angled arch above the opening modeled on the root three rectangle. The building was described in 1940 as "very modern . . . the only dormitory on campus which is strictly modern in its treatment."[45] Interestingly, the building is of reinforced concrete construction with the exception of the exterior walls, which are self-supporting, rather than hung from the frame of the structure.

In Detroit, the widening of Gratiot Avenue resulted in the demolition of the Osius branch of the Detroit Public Library, and in late 1938, the PWA approved funds for a replacement building on a larger site at the same location. Construction was overseen by the public library's administration committee, headed by Edwin George, who was likely responsible for steering the contract to his good friend Wirt Rowland. The building, a "regional library," was larger than a typical branch and offered many of the same services as the main branch. Its interior was of a new type, "an informal

353. Victor C. Vaughan House on the campus of the University of Michigan was completed in 1939.

public reading clubhouse," equipped with sofas, easy chairs, fireplaces, and wood paneled walls to create a "clubby" atmosphere.[46] The new building, named Mark Twain Library, was opened in February 1940 and dedicated on April 20, 1940, at a ceremony in which Rowland handed the key to the building to Edwin George.[47]

The middle section of the building, housing the entrance, was flanked by two large wings containing reading rooms with ceilings more than thirty feet high. These enormous rooms might have presented a bulky appearance, inconsistent with the surrounding residential neighborhood, but Rowland carefully disguised them behind the building's rambling Gratiot Avenue facade. The larger of the two rooms was set perpendicular to the street, and the roof angled back from the two-story-high front window. The second room had a single gabled dormer flanked by a gambrel roof—parallel with the street—that extended down to the height of the first floor, resulting in a small-scale facade masking the bulk of the nearly three-story structure behind.

Three arches framed in stone marked the front entrance. These arches as well as those on the inside of the building were pointed, nominally characterizing them as Gothic in style. Other Detroit Public Library buildings of the period were similarly designed, suggesting Gothic style may have been selected by the library's administration committee, perhaps by Edwin George, whose personal preference was Gothic. In any case, the building exhibited a restrained application of English Gothic inspired elements judiciously applied to convey the informal appearance sought. Nevertheless, the design exemplified Rowland's

354. The Mark Twain Library on Gratiot Avenue around the time of its completion in 1940. (Detroit Public Library)

disdain for copying historic styles: the pointed arches of the interior's vaulted ceiling rested upon piers topped by fanciful capitals of Rowland's own design. Looking somewhat like an upside down Ionic capital with four faces, this feature would have outraged both Gothic and classical traditionalists. On occasion, Rowland employed elements inspired by decorative features of the past to solve a current design problem, as in this case, to achieve an intimate and clubby atmosphere, and not for the purpose of creating a historically styled building.

A similar approach was taken by Rowland when selecting materials; the building's exterior combined old and new: traditional copper gutters and slate roof, and a bare aluminum front door. Had Rowland intended to design an authentic Gothic style building, he certainly would not have chosen aluminum for such a prominent feature. The building plans called for a slate roof, as on Maire Elementary, but it appears from photos of Mark Twain Library that asphalt shingles were used instead, likely due to cost considerations. Had the roof been built as planned, the building might still be standing, as deterioration of the roof resulted in the library being closed for repairs in the late 1990s. The damage was subsequently discovered to be more extensive than thought and the cash-starved city repeatedly put off repairs until the damage to the interior became irreparable. The building was razed in 2011.

In January 1938, Frederick Meyer, vice president of the American Institute of Architects, claimed that homebuilding "is now on the upgrade and will experience increasing

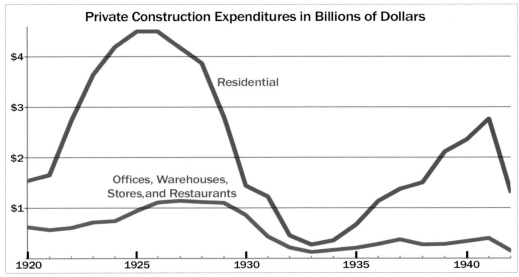

355. The total value of private construction for the years 1920 through 1942, residential and nonresidential-nonindustrial. (Source: *Historical Statistics of the United States 1789–1945, Supplement to the Statistical Abstract, 1949,* page H 1-26)

prosperity until 1944."[48] As it turned out, home construction did continue to increase, peaking at $2.8 billion in 1941 from a Great Depression low of $278 million in 1933, and a pre-Depression high of $4.5 billion in 1925.[49] However, non-residential private construction of offices, warehouses, restaurants, and stores continued to stagger, dropping from $378 million in 1937 to $279 million in 1938, down from $1.12 billion ten years earlier.[50] With work nearly complete on the two PWA projects and little else in the offing, O'Dell and Rowland ended their business partnership in the latter part of 1938 (though Rowland continued to oversee completion of Vaughan House and Mark Twain Library).[51]

356. Architect Herbert Wenzell. (Collection of the Detroit chapter of the American Institute of Architects)

Rowland moved in April 1940 from O'Dell's office into unused space within the office of architect Andrew Morison (1889–1951) at 616 Murphy Building, and practiced as "Wirt C. Rowland, Architect" offering "consultation, free lance—plan, design, and detail."[52] Andy Morison was born in Scotland where he attended architecture school, and in 1909 joined Walter Painter's architecture firm in Toronto, Canada.[53] (Painter was George D. Mason's associate partner during Rowland's first year with the firm in 1903. Working with Morison in Painter's office from 1911 to 1913 was Victor Nellenbogen, who later became a noted Miami Beach architect.[54]) Morison moved to Detroit in 1916 to join Smith, Hinchman, and Grylls and continued there until starting his own firm in 1923. He served as president of the AIA Detroit chapter from 1936 to 1937 and was a director of the Michigan Society of Architects at the time Rowland came looking to share office space.

In May 1939, Rowland suffered a personal blow when his good friend of forty years, Herb Wenzell, died of a heart attack at the age of fifty-five. Rowland and Wenzell were at the time debating the merits of modern and traditional architecture in the pages of the *Weekly Bulletin*; Wenzell's final installment was published the day following his death. Funeral services were held at the Central Woodward Christian Church, designed by Wenzell in 1926. He also designed Detroit's Masonic Temple (the world's largest) and the Detroit Yacht Club.[55] In the two months prior to Wenzell's death, Rowland wrote five articles for the *Weekly Bulletin*. "Since then," he said, "it had not seemed to me that I could resume my comments."[56]

After a hiatus of eight months, Rowland penned for the *Weekly Bulletin* "Music and the Architect," revisiting a topic on which he had written twenty years earlier. This time he approached the subject in a deeply introspective manner, evidence that Rowland, grieving the loss of his friend, found solace in music—the same source that earlier provided inspiration for his designs. Great music makes its impression upon the "subconscious mind," explained Rowland in this article, "And all we can know or say about its real essence is

357. This January 23, 1940, issue of the *Weekly Bulletin of the Michigan Society of Architects* was mailed to architect and nationally recognized watercolor artist Louis Bruyere.

that, if we let it, it will carry us into realms uncharted by the intellect. It will reveal to us the reasons for a pestered existence about which we are completely inarticulate." This was not the first time Rowland had commented on the inadequacy of prose to convey certain ideas or experiences. His *Detroit News* article on the Union Trust Building began: "Architecture, like music, is difficult to discuss."[57] Explaining his views on medieval art and architecture, Rowland wrote "words and language were the most inadequate means of expressing ideas. Art—architecture, painting, sculpture, and music were the ample vehicles of expression."[58] In this article on music, Rowland goes beyond citing the inadequacy of prose and reveals the role of great art: to affect those portions of the mind not directly accessible by intellect. These domains of the mind, when stirred by art, reveal to us an understanding of both the wonders and ordeals of life. By creating or appreciating great art, we participate in that common element of humanity that may be experienced, but not easily described.

This article also offers an interesting insight into Rowland's influence. In 2014, nearly seventy-five years after it was published, a copy of the article, carefully cut from the *Weekly Bulletin*, appeared on a popular online auction site. An "X" in the margin drew attention to Rowland's first paragraph, underlined in blue pencil: "a man's knowledge, experience and wisdom is not fully rounded out without a vital appreciation of design in all other arts, a love for *nature's* materials which you will use in building—a high regard for the masters of painting and sculpture—and more than a passive receptivity—a positive comprehension." The subscriber's name and address is stamped on the issue: "Louis U. Bruyere, Toledo, Ohio." Louis Bruyere (1884–1962) was a member of the Michigan Society of Architects (though he lived in Ohio) and a practicing architect who designed numerous schools in the Toledo area. He was also

358. This photo of Rowland often accompanied his articles and committee reports in the *Weekly Bulletin*.

a highly regarded watercolor artist with a national reputation; his pictures were displayed throughout the country and remain popular.

Bruyere was not the only recipient of the *Weekly Bulletin* living outside of Michigan; of all the 727 dues-paying members (as of 1940) of the Michigan Society of Architects who received the journal, 215 of them lived in other states—primarily New York and Illinois.[59] Although the *Weekly Bulletin* was a state publication, due to the quality of its articles and the prominence of Detroit architects at the time, many leading architects throughout the country purchased subscriptions, including Frank Lloyd Wright and Ralph Walker. Its popularity was such that in 1945, the *Bulletin* became a national publication.[60]

In addition to "Music and the Architect," Rowland turned out more than twenty profound (and often humorous) articles during the 1930s, most of them published in the *Weekly Bulletin* and some later republished in national journals. Rowland's contributions were often accompanied by his photo. However, in a 1940 letter to editor Talmage Hughes, accompanying his latest manuscript, Rowland asked that the photo be dropped, as Ada May "always raises a terrible row when she sees that and is not reconciled to my appearing so old as I did when the picture was taken."[61]

A less public enterprise occupied Rowland's time during these years, one that merged music and art: a series of unusual monochrome charcoal, pencil, and wash sketches illustrating musical works. Most of the nineteen extant pieces depict individual movements of the four symphonies of Brahms. The striking characteristic of these works is their darkness,

Symphony IV 1st Movem't. Brahms

359. Rowland's sketch representing the first movement of Symphony no. 4 by Johannes Brahms. (From the collection of Genevieve Burroughs Baker)

nearly all seemingly taking place at night, the scenes faintly lit by torches, fire, moonbeams, or the figures themselves. In mood and even subject matter they resemble Francisco Goya's early nineteenth-century series *The Proverbs*.

In 1940, the public information committee of the Michigan Society of Architects conducted a successful outreach effort, presenting four lectures on architecture during October at the Detroit Institute of Arts. Rowland's lecture, "History and Modern Architecture," was reported as inclining toward the philosophical, "as only Rowland can do."[62] Rowland said that, though architecture "had become an integral part of him, he was beginning to find the more he thought of architecture, the less he had to say about it."[63] Whether he was becoming less inclined to speak about the topic or finding it more difficult to put his ideas into words is not clear, but other than a letter to the editor, nothing more appeared in print from Rowland after his article the following month, aptly titled "A Vacation from Architecture."

The successful Detroit Institute of Arts lectures notwithstanding, MSA committees were not always effective, despite the prominence of committee members. An architectural

Symphony II 3rd Movement Brahms

360. Rowland's sketch representing the third movement of Symphony no. 2 by Brahms. (From the collection of Genevieve Burroughs Baker)

guidance committee report submitted by Rowland in 1936 on behalf of the three committee members stated: "Without a meeting of this Committee the opinions of all three members is united by the Chairman with his own well known clairvoyant methods and in the same characteristic manner discarding all dissenting opinions."[64] A 1939 synopsis for the education committee written by Rowland declared: "It inevitably seems to be my lot each year to report on what has not been done and what should have been done. This report is no exception and no excuse can be offered."[65] Nevertheless, Rowland took the opportunity of the committee report to expound on the topics under consideration and make well-considered suggestions for future action.

Although less than twenty-one years had elapsed since the end of World War I, on September 1, 1939, Europe was again plunged into bloody conflict when Germany invaded Poland. Americans, appalled by the horrific loss of life and futility of the earlier war, were far less enthusiastic about becoming involved in the latest European conflict. Congress made nonintervention the official policy of the United States with passage of the Neutrality Acts in the late 1930s. President Franklin Roosevelt, however, heeding the lessons of America's lack of preparedness for World War I, spoke out against the Nazis and aggressively pressed to prepare the American military for war. In April 1940, Germany invaded Denmark and Norway, followed a month later with offensives into France, Belgium, Luxembourg, and the Netherlands. On May 16, President Roosevelt called on Congress to immediately authorize funds for expansion of the nation's armed forces, which Congress approved on June 26. Included was funding to increase the number of US Navy aircraft from three thousand to ten thousand, upped to fifteen thousand the following month when Congress ordered the navy to build a "two-ocean" capable force.[66]

A significant amount of the navy's budget was allocated to the Naval Air Station in Norfolk, Virginia. Already the navy's largest and most important air base, it grew in size several times during the course of World War II and provided training to nearly every naval air squadron that saw action. From just over two thousand personnel in December 1940, the base became home to nearly twenty-nine thousand by war's end, including facilities at nine outlying airfields and a seaplane base.[67] The Naval Supply Depot located on the base, which provisioned fleets and distant military installations, grew over the course of the war from under two million square feet to over seven million.

The unprecedented expansion of facilities required the armed services to seek outside vendors to perform much of the architectural and engineering work. One of the significant contributors was the Detroit firm of Giffels and Vallet, Inc., Engineers and Architects, L. Rossetti, Associate, formed in 1925 by two civil engineers, Raymond Giffels and Victor Vallet, from the office of Albert Kahn, Architects and Engineers.[68] In 1929, the two men recruited from Kahn's office French-born architectural engineer Louis Rossetti, and by 1930, the company employed 150 in two Detroit area offices.[69] Much of the firm's work consisted of large, industrial structures, often for Ford Motor's enormous River Rouge plant in Dearborn, Michigan.

By early 1941, the firm was operating an office at the Norfolk Naval Air Station to design and oversee construction of buildings on the rapidly expanding base. Rowland was ideally suited to aid this effort due to his extensive work with large, steel reinforced concrete buildings and experience during World War I designing structures that could be rapidly constructed with readily available materials and labor. Rowland was hired by Giffels and Vallet and relocated to the firm's Norfolk office in early 1941. Working with Rowland were fellow architects Tony Buczkowski, Charles M. Valentine, and John R. Valentine from Detroit and Edward X. Tuttle of Battle Creek.[70] Prior to joining Giffels and Vallet, Buczkowski and Charles Valentine worked in George Mason's office, and John Valentine in Kahn's office. Tuttle was in a partnership with Harold Peterson and a director of the Michigan Association of Architects.

361. Tony Buczkowski and Wirt Rowland in Williamsburg, Virginia, around 1943. (David Brent)

Rowland was particularly close with Buczkowski and his wife, Clara, who were fortunate to own a car—a 1941 Packard sedan—allowing them to explore the area and dine at many of the better restaurants.

In July 1941, Rowland was visited by Bud Cullen, a serviceman and son of one of Rowland's friends in Michigan. Rowland and Buczkowski gave Cullen a tour of the area by car and wished to include the naval base, but security was very tight and Cullen had no pass. Approaching the guardhouse with all three sitting in the front seat, Rowland and Buczkowski held out their passes while Cullen held out his good conduct card and furlough pass. Incredibly, the guards waved them through and Cullen was treated to views of the battleship USS *Wyoming* and two British carriers, HMS *Illustrious* and HMS *Formidable*, both of which had been badly damaged in battles with the German navy and were undergoing extensive repairs at Norfolk.[71]

That evening, Rowland treated Cullen and the Buczkowskis to dinner at one of the area's finest restaurants: Thalia Acres Inn. Rowland bought Clara a corsage of seven roses, prompting Cullen to say, "When [Rowland] does things, he does them right and he certainly knows how to entertain."[72] After a steak dinner, the four strolled on the boardwalk at Virginia Beach. The following morning, they attended mass at the Basilica of Saint Mary, and Cullen was surprised that Rowland "acted just like a Catholic and seemed quite

362. The Giffels and Vallet office at the Norfolk Naval Air Station where Rowland worked. Tony Buczkowski is in the center, crouched low over his drafting table. (David Brent)

at home. He really is a remarkable fellow even though Len Gray saw him tight once." (By "tight" Cullen may have meant "drunk" or possibly "tense" as the word was in use for both at the time.) In a letter to his parents, Cullen wrote: "Before I left at 11:30, Wirt tried to force $5.00 on me. Can you imagine that? I would look a long time before I could find anyone, outside of my family, who would treat me more royally than he did. Nothing was too good, nothing was enough; and through it all made you feel so comfortable. I will never forget it."[73]

Rowland and his fellow architects designed structures at the base ranging from enormous hangars and warehouses to guardhouses and barracks. Rowland was good humored about the nature of his work, noting that his coworkers "point out 'how the mighty have fallen' when they see me sawing away on various latrines and other similar convenient structures," yet he found work on these buildings satisfying, "because they are simple and meet the purpose in a direct way."[74] Rowland's self-deprecating comments aside, he skillfully designed structures in such a way as they could be erected quickly and economically. There were also projects for which Rowland's expertise in design made him ideally suited, such as the base's chapel on the southeast corner of Gilbert Street and Maryland Avenue. This E-shaped building contains several houses of worship designed by Rowland, including two beautifully detailed altars of carved wood for Our Lady of Victory Chapel (Roman Catholic) and David Adams Memorial Chapel (Protestant).[75]

In 1942, the Union Trust Building—at the time called the Union Guardian Building—was taken over by the Tank-Automotive Center (TAC), the vehicle division of the Ordnance Department of the US Department of War. TAC was responsible for building and operating the Detroit Tank Arsenal. When this development was announced in the Detroit papers in August 1942, Talmage Hughes clipped the articles and sent them to Rowland. "I would be curious to know," responded Rowland, "if they will use the main banking room for a parade ground with a band marching up and down it."[76] Although his comment was lighthearted, it also revealed a disappointment over the humble fate of the building's large open space, the creation of which had required so much effort.

The quality of work performed for the Navy by Giffels and Vallet was recog-

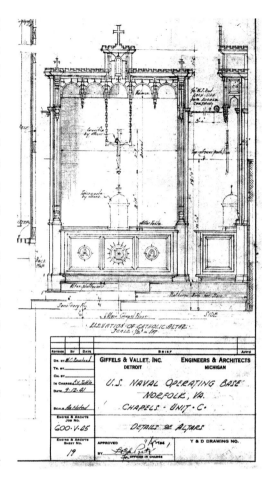

363. Elevation of the altar for Our Lady of Victory Chapel at Naval Station Norfolk, drawn by Rowland in September 1942. The "In Charge" signature is of Ed Tuttle of Battle Creek, Michigan.

nized by the government in 1944: the firm received a commendation from the Bureau of Yards and Docks "For Outstanding Service in furthering of the Navy's War Construction Program." The work benefited Rowland's health as well. After rising at five thirty each morning, he would walk two miles to the east gate of the Air Station, catching a bus there that took him to the office. The extensive walking permitted him to dispense with his arch supports.[77]

Rowland returned to Detroit in the spring of 1944 and continued working for Giffels and Vallet in their Detroit office. His design for Edwin George's church was essentially complete in 1940, yet the project was no closer to beginning construction. Funded in part by George's foundation, the balance was to be acquired by selling off much of the land surrounding the church—a process expected to take years. George hoped that he might live to see the church completed, but at age seventy, he wished to provide the foundation's trustees with specific direction as to the design of the building in the event of his death. To this end, Rowland wrote descriptions to accompany the design sketches he had made and George combined them in an album with photographic copies of the sketches and floor plans.[78] The album represented George's final word on the church's design, and each trustee was provided with a copy.[79] George also asked Rowland to begin work on detailed plans for the building, which he did in his spare time in space provided by Giffels and Vallet in their office.[80]

In these written descriptions, Rowland took pains to explain his understanding of Gothic style, dismissing the popular notion that the interior of a cathedral is "derived from nature in the form of vertical rocks or the forests with arching

364. An early sketch by Rowland of a design for the tower of Kirk in the Hills. The stepped arrangement shown here is much closer in style to Rowland's skyscrapers than the more traditionally Gothic tower that Edwin George ultimately approved. (Kirk in the Hills collection)

limbs the inspiration for vaulted interiors. The building of Gothic cathedrals during the Middle Ages was a far more serious thing in development than such romantic ideas."[81]

Rowland did not elaborate for the trustees on the "serious thing in development" that Gothic represented, but he had done so many times previously. In a 1938 article, "An Influence of Glass on Architecture," Rowland noted that the ancient Greeks and Romans conducted their activities within buildings illuminated by an open roof. Later, as church buildings evolved from Roman basilicas, small openings within the thick supporting walls of these roofed-over structures provided what little light was required. The desire to build structures with thinner walls into which larger windows could be placed resulted in the invention of arched ribs resting on buttressed piers. "Gradually," explained Rowland, "as the light began to dawn from the dark ages, all crafts were quickened," pouring their efforts into the beautiful sculpture, colored glass, and architecture that we see in the great cathedrals of Europe. "From the small colored window, which by increasing skill and intuitive artistry had been made to convey symbols and stories and figures pertaining to the Christian religion, it was conceived that whole walls of churches could be made to cover an entire range of symbolism."[82] "It is astounding to observe what the craftsman of the Middle Ages accomplished."[83] "The color and glow of the Medieval windows have that quality of great music—transcendent, intangible and unearthly—a sublime emotion."[84] It is clear from Rowland's sketches and accompanying descriptions that his focus in the design of Kirk in the Hills was not to re-create Melrose Abbey or imitate any other Gothic cathedral, but to create a building in which architecture, color, and light could be combined so the "sublime emotion" might be experienced.

That the Kirk in the Hills Presbyterian Church is nominally Gothic in architectural style was more the result of George's prodding than Rowland's choice. An early sketch that does not bear George's initials of approval shows a stepped tower, similar to Rowland's earlier skyscraper towers, adorned with narrow, pointed arch windows and prominent piers. Rowland would likely have preferred to approach the church's design unencumbered by the

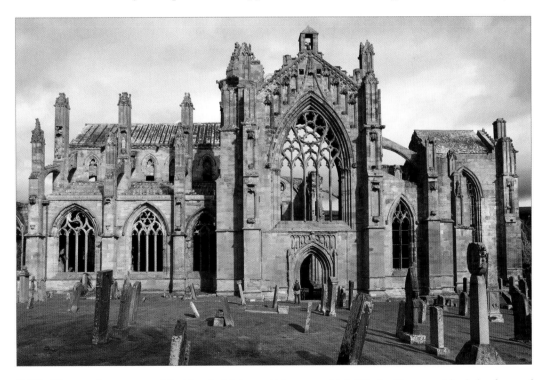

365. The south transept of Scotland's Melrose Abbey on which Edwin George wished the front of Kirk in the Hills to be modeled. (Daniel Wilson)

366. On the left is Rowland's 1940 sketch illustrating his vision for the entrance to the lower level of Kirk in the Hills with the large baptistery window above. On the right, the same location as it appears on the completed building. The arches of the lower level were executed in a more ornate design than the original Norman English style, and the baptistery window is simpler than the planned English Perpendicular style design. (Drawing from the collection of Kirk in the Hills)

Gothic style requirement. (In the early 1930s, the Shrine of the Little Flower was construct-ed in Royal Oak, Michigan; a church of modern design, it incorporated stepped arches, quite possibly inspired by the Union Trust Building.) Rowland, however, conceded in his description that for the average churchgoer, "seemingly by habit of association, and the memory of Old World examples, no type of architecture seems to suit [worship] like some form of Gothic."[85]

Edwin George wished the entrance to the church to be modeled on the south transept of Melrose Abbey, and though this section of the old abbey is largely intact, much of the window detail was missing. Rowland's solution was to base the window on a similar intact window in the nearby Carlisle Cathedral.

English Gothic cathedrals were typically built on ruins or foundations of earlier Norman (Romanesque) churches, so they retained the architecture of the earlier building's lower level. Windows on the lower level of Kirk in the Hills reflect this characteristic as they are "Roman in character without being too inconsistent with the Gothic detail above."[86] This may be seen on the exterior of the Kirk beneath the east end of the transept at the entrance to the lower level, though in Rowland's original plan, these arches were to have a less ornate appearance more characteristic of Norman architecture.

367. An early drawing of the tower for Kirk in the Hills. Above the tower (behind the spire) may be seen the planform of the structure in the root two rectangle shape. (Kirk in the Hills collection)

The west arm of the Kirk's transept ends in the "Melrose Chapel," designed by Rowland with proportions "in more of a French tradition,"[87] recalling cathedrals of the continent. The interior of the chapel, inspired by Early English Gothic, is high and narrow, with the roof supported by ribbed vaulting, a method that allowed windows to extend higher into the ceiling. As the chapel reflects a later form of Gothic, "Everything in detail," wrote Rowland, is "kept delicate and refined and the window tracery more fine than in any other part of the building."[88] The stained glass windows illustrate stories from the Old Testament.

The church's tower is topped by a striking crown, which Rowland described as "a stone lantern topped by a spire . . . though in this case not a steeple."[89] The crown is similar to that of the late Gothic Saint Giles' Cathedral in Edinburgh and is comprised of flying buttresses extending toward the center of the tower from beneath pinnacles on four of its corners.

Beneath the open crown, the mass of the tower is more substantial in construction with an unusual planform. Most Gothic church towers are square or, occasionally, octagonal (in plan, as if viewed from above); the Kirk's tower, however, has the same root two rectangle shape as the north tower of the Union Trust Building. This shape may be seen sketched above the tower in one of Rowland's early drawings, perhaps added as he was explaining the concept to Edwin George.

368. Sketch by Rowland, completed in 1940, showing the original design for the front of Kirk in the Hills, which at this point in the planning faced west. (Kirk in the Hills collection)

With the presentation of the album to the trustees of George's foundation in August 1944, nothing further could be accomplished on the church until the sale of lots generated sufficient funds to proceed with construction. War raged in Europe, and the following year marked the beginning of the atomic age and the jet age.

Shortly after Germany's surrender in May 1945, Rowland received a letter from Frank Burroughs Jr., who was in the army serving in Germany. Frank graduated in 1942 from the University of Michigan's Reserve Officers Training Corps as a medical corps officer with an MD degree and was at the time caring for two thousand Russian soldiers released from a German prisoner of war camp. "Both France and Germany have been terribly damaged," wrote Burroughs, "scarcely a town but what has been blasted—most of the large ones—well, they're just like the pictures of ruins in the newspapers. The most awful part of it is the way the Germans treated their forced laborers and prisoners of war. These comprise our patients and besides the many dead already, many more are dying every day and will die because of the diseases contracted in stalags and labor camps. Tuberculosis is widespread as well as other diseases. Starvation was the chief cause of hospitalization but these people are recovering on American food."[90]

In September, Rowland's work on Kirk in the Hills was interrupted when illness—most likely diabetes—forced him to quit work and remain at home. In October, he was admitted by his doctor to Jennings Hospital for "rest"; he remained there through the end of December, when his condition improved sufficiently to return home.[91]

Too ill to return to work, Rowland spent time writing letters to his many friends and fellow architects across the country. In a letter from Birmingham, Alabama, a young and recently wed friend apologized for not writing sooner: "Marriage is a very wonderful state of affairs but I had no idea how much it cuts into one's spare time." "I trust your health continues to improve. I frequently think of the days at Mrs. Ritchie's and many pleasant memories always return. I wonder if you are continuing your work on the beautiful memorial church you had sketches of when I was there."[92]

A particularly poignant exchange took place between Rowland and Lester F. "Andy" Anderson, a designer with whom Rowland had worked at Smith, Hinchman, and Grylls. Anderson had relocated to the Washington, DC, area early in the Depression and maintained his friendship with Rowland. Responding to Rowland's expression of regret over having no children, "In your next life," Anderson wrote, "you can correct the error by becoming an architect of men, rather than an architect of monumental buildings." "It was perhaps just a detail you overlooked in your busy years. Or did you? One could ponder over that, knowing of your sojourns in remote lands, you a robust person in full possession of all such faculties, far from censorious eyes and tongues. NO! That just couldn't be you. It would be so unethical. Stop! Tittering girls."[93]

Anderson mentioned Rowland's "Gothic Project" and, referring to his incapacitating illness, noted, "How wonderful it is that the mind can continue solving architectural problems in the absence of any physical application. I recall AL's [Amedeo Leone most likely] potent remark, 'Less drawing and more thinking.'"[94]

Reflecting on the controversy over the Union Trust Building that raged within Detroit's architect community, Anderson wrote, "Never mind the opinions of the 'Detroit Architects,' or Architects anywhere else. Most of them are just business persons and very few are great designers like yourself. The design of the Union Guardian Building was terrific . . . a cascade of architectural eloquence, it lives in moving color. . . . What's more it's unforgettable because it leaves such a deep impression. It's just too exciting for those timid little souls who call themselves architects. I am glad I was at SH&G when you designed it and was able to witness your bold resourceful accomplishment as well as your disdainful disregard of all the dissenters. I'll say you have had an important part in the shaping of the physical aspect of Detroit." "Most of the present day architects and designers hope to succeed, but you do not need to bother, you have succeeded. You can fail from now on, none of them will ever surpass you."[95]

Anderson closed saying, "Dorothy and I send our deepest regard, our hopes for a great and permanent return to health." But Rowland's health was not improving and his longtime friends in Detroit's AIA chapter feared the worst. In June, the executive committee of the chapter wrote to the national organization's board of directors asking that Rowland be elected Member Emeritus and nominated him for Fellowship,[96] which recognizes "those architects who have made a significant contribution to architecture and society and who have achieved a standard of excellence in the profession."[97] However, under AIA rules fellowship could be granted only after ten years of continuous membership; though Rowland had been a member since 1933, his lapse in dues payments from 1936 to 1938 had reset the clock. Deeply concerned over the state of Rowland's health, Talmage Hughes wrote to the AIA board asking if there was "any way to overcome the requirement of ten years' continuous service. It is not believed that we should wait until 1948."[98] The organization's director responded that Rowland's fellowship nomination would be considered at its next meeting in the spring of 1947.[99] The title Member Emeritus was conferred by the organization on Rowland on August 27, 1946.

In October, Rowland was visited by his longtime friend Leander Kimball, who, forty-five years earlier, had secured for Rowland his first architecture job in Detroit. In the ensuing years, Kimball's bank had become the State Savings Bank of Clinton and Kimball was now chairman of its board. Although Rowland was confined to Mrs. Ritchie's

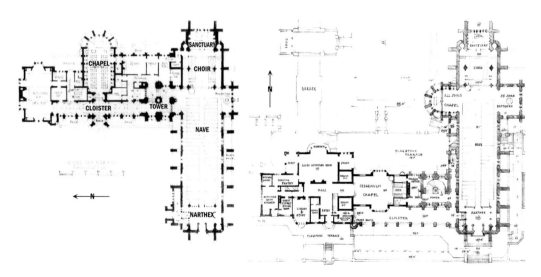

369. The 1940 floor plan of Kirk in the Hills drawn by Rowland (on the left) and the 1947 plan by George Mason's office incorporating Cedarholm. (Kirk in the Hills collection)

boarding house, this environment, Kimball noted, was pleasant, comfortable, and convenient. Kimball mentioned to Rowland that his granddaughter had returned home to Los Angeles after a visit, leaving Grand Rapids by plane at 10:00 p.m. and arriving at eight the next morning. "When you think of the old days," Kimball said, "in 1849 (or thereabouts) when your father and the Richmond crowd made the journey over land?"[100] Both men must have thought as well of the great changes wrought by technology on the skylines of Detroit and other cities, and the important role played by Rowland in giving shape to that technology. They likely wondered, once again, what might have been had Kimball not secured for Rowland that first architecture job.

The land around Edwin George's country estate on Long Lake Road—Cedarholm House—was platted into subdivisions, and the sale of home sites picked up after the war, though the amount raised by 1946, $70,000, was far short of the building's anticipated cost in excess of one million dollars. Although Rowland's work on detailed drawings of the building was "well advanced," the funds were not adequate to begin construction. As George sat one morning stewing over this dilemma, he had a sudden revelation: "Why not have Cedarholm House become a part of the church structure?"[101] Perhaps George's large home could be converted to accommodate the church offices, activity rooms, kitchen, library, and a small chapel, significantly reducing the cost of the project. George visited Rowland and carefully reviewed the idea, to which Rowland gave his enthusiastic approval.[102]

George's new plan involved moving the church about five hundred feet south from its planned location between Island Lake and Kirkway Road to a spot adjacent to George's house. More

370. The original small chapel (unbuilt) of Kirk in the Hills included a small roundel window to catch the final rays of the setting sun. This 1940 sketch by Rowland shows the effect. (Kirk in the Hills collection)

371. Kirk in the Hills as seen from the front. Just left of the tower is Cedarholm, the former country house of Edwin George, in which the church's administrative offices, chapel, and library are located.

significantly, the church would face south instead of west and the west side of the structure required reworking to integrate it into the side of Cedarholm. Rowland hoped to revise the drawings to accommodate the alterations, but would need access to architecture reference books—he had previously donated his personal volumes to Lawrence Tech. He wrote to George Mason, who at ninety years of age was still working half days in his architecture office downtown, arriving by taxi at noon and catching a ride home with Albert McDonald at five. Mason was pleased to hear from Rowland and replied warmly: "We have plenty of room in our office and I know Dave Williams would be glad to have you." "Our library is always open to you."[103]

Several days later, on November 21, Rowland jotted a quick note on a postcard to the Detroit AIA chapter: "I wish to extend my kindest greetings to all in the Detroit Chapter. I have resumed work on the Edwin S. George Foundation project in my home."[104] Rowland was determined to complete the project, but his declining health did not permit it; within days, he suffered a cerebral hemorrhage and was admitted to the hospital. There was little the doctors could do for Rowland, yet he was too ill to return home, so on November 27, he was taken by ambulance to Frank Burroughs's house in Grand Rapids. Although ailing,

Rowland retained his eye for color: when Burroughs's daughter Genevieve entered the room wearing a reddish-purple dress, Rowland expressed his disapproval. After changing into a blue dress, she reentered the room and was greeted by Rowland with the comment, "Thank heaven; don't ever wear that color again."[105] She didn't.

The next day was Thanksgiving, which Rowland spent at home with the Burroughs family, under the care of Dr. Frank Burroughs Jr. On Friday, Rowland's condition worsened and he was taken to Saint Mary's Hospital, where he died the following day, November 30, 1946—one day short of his sixty-eighth birthday. Rowland was buried in Riverside Cemetery in his hometown of Clinton, within sight of the Mortuary Chapel he designed in 1912.

Rowland's passing was heralded in the *Detroit News* by art critic Florence Davies, who wrote that he "probably contributed more to the beauty of Detroit's skyline than any other one person." She

372. The passageway or cloister between the church and functional areas of Kirk in the Hills. Rowland described it as having "been kept low and intimate as though it could be open to the weather,—vines and plants growing into it from the outside. This is not practical in this climate but the floor of the cloister is kept only a step higher than this entering level so that planting may be plainly visible from its windows." (Rowland, "To The Trustees of The Edwin S. George Foundation," description for "The Cloister and Main Entrance to the Chapel")

noted that Rowland's use of color in the Union Trust Building was achieved, "not by the use of applied color, but by the selection of such materials as brick, marble and Pewabic tile in which the color was inherent and hence permanent." The Greater Penobscot Building was designed by Rowland at about the same time, she said, "but in a wholly different spirit." "While the Penobscot Building is a perfect example of the use of pure form without applied ornament, the Union Trust Building achieves the effect of ornament wholly through the pattern employed in the use of vari-colored substances, both sound contemporary practices."[106]

Rowland was gone, yet his work remained unfinished. To complete plans for Kirk in the Hills, the Edwin George Foundation hired George Mason's architectural firm in 1947—the firm that designed Cedarholm—and architect Eugene T. Cleland was placed in charge.

Revising the plans to allow for Cedarholm to substitute for new construction was straightforward and had little effect on the church. The most notable alteration was elimination of the separate small chapel, while retaining its apse, which was moved to the west transept, becoming Melrose Chapel. The original small chapel would have been a dramatic space as it was designed to take maximum advantage of its west-facing facade: "at the apex of the vaulting," wrote Rowland, is "a roundel window to catch the last rays of the west sun."[107]

373. Among the portraits created by Corrado Parducci that surround the entrance to the lower level of Kirk in the Hills is this one of Rowland. He is depicted using a compass and triangle, the only tools required to work in dynamic symmetry.

The first services of the newly established church were held September 21, 1947, in Cedarholm, and in September of the following year, ground was broken for the new church. Initially, only the cloister (the windowed passage leading from Cedarholm to the church) and the base of the tower were constructed.

Edwin George died on January 25, 1951, and was buried in the narthex of the unfinished building. In 1954, after George's remaining assets were transferred to the trust, contracts were signed to construct the building. With both Rowland and George out of the picture, much of the day-to-day oversight of the project fell first to Reverend Dr. Leslie Bechtel, who headed the church from 1948 to 1953, and then Reverend Dr. Harold C. DeWindt. As a result of this succession of guiding hands, the final form of the Kirk expresses the influence of each. Corrado Parducci, who produced most of the architectural sculpture for the building, was frustrated by the change in direction imposed when DeWindt took over. Parducci began his work on the church sculptures under George's direction and produced modern interpretations of medieval craft—"expressing the mood" of the original rather than exactly copying it.[108] When DeWindt took over, he criticized Parducci's work as too modern and asked that he change to a more rigidly authentic Gothic style.[109] Parducci became angry with DeWindt and architect Cleland (who Parducci felt had allowed the situation to arise) and wrote to the trustees asking to be relieved from any further work on the job.[110]

374. Like the medieval cathedrals that inspired it, the interior of Kirk in the Hills is awash in colored light from the stained glass windows, creating a sublime and mysterious atmosphere.

DeWindt also criticized Parducci's sculptures of four biblical insects on the building's exterior as too large. Parducci responded that it was the size and shape of the wall, not "Gothic predilections," that determined the nature of the sculptures—he wanted observers to be able to see them from a reasonable distance. Parducci, in turn, criticized the illustrations on the stained glass windows (constructed under DeWindt's supervision) as too small to be clearly seen.[111] Rowland's original 1944 description of the baptistery window in the trustee's album noted, "It is nearer the congregation than the other large windows, hence the incidents it may portray . . . are more readable,"[112] lending support to Parducci's view of the matter.

In June 1957, as the new church neared completion, the roof was struck by lightning, igniting a terrific fire that required two hundred firefighters from ten communities to quell. Destroyed along with the building's roof were the oak ceiling beams, three stained glass windows, and, due to water damage, much of the undercroft. More than four thousand square feet of stone had to be replaced.[113] Finally, in September 1958—twenty-three years after Rowland delivered the first sketch to Edwin George—Kirk in the Hills was completed.

To what extent does Kirk in the Hills represent Rowland's vision? The designer's freedom is always subject, more or less, to the client's predispositions, and in this case,

Edwin George sought a Gothic church rather than modern. Nevertheless, he gave Rowland a great deal of latitude, and the resulting 1944 plan was a modern interpretation of Gothic. Rowland's design respected the Gothic structural system that permitted large, stained glass windows illustrating symbolic religious stories. These windows illuminate the interior of the church with colored light, the means by which Rowland sought to achieve George's objective that worshippers "feel the very spiritual presence of God."[114] That the windows may not have been executed precisely as Rowland would have preferred is a less important point.

The church's tower, a wholly original design crafted by Rowland, combines nominally Gothic elements in a graceful, striking structure. The cloister—carried over with little alteration from the 1944 design to the later plan—with its expansively windowed outside wall provides a stimulating contrast to the dark and mysterious interior of the church. Finally, the exterior of the church—little changed from Rowland's plan—when viewed from the open, lower ground behind, presents an extraordinary and impressive sight. These are just a few of the exceptional design elements devised by Rowland and carried through to the completed building essentially unchanged.

Rowland's career began in 1899 with his design for the belfry of the First Congregational Church of Clinton, and his final work, completed in 1958—twelve years after his death—was also a church. The intervening years saw the introduction of a revolutionary new building technology in the form of steel and concrete, and it fell to Rowland, and other innovators, to devise designs appropriate to the new methods, particularly for skyscrapers, as nothing in the history of architecture could serve as a guide for the design of such tall buildings. Rowland dug deeply into the history of architecture to expose and understand the principles underlying the greatest designs of the past and, working from those principles, he built up a new system, suitable to a new age with new technology and requirements, and created buildings that are astonishing and beautiful.

375. Kirk in the Hills (rear view). Melrose Chapel projects from the church just to the left of the tower.

ACKNOWLEDGMENTS

I am deeply appreciative to many individuals who made this book possible, beginning with Thomas Holleman. While an employee of Smith, Hinchman, and Grylls, he cowrote with James Gallagher in 1978 *Smith, Hinchman & Grylls: 125 Years of Architecture and Engineering, 1853–1978*, the most important source of information on Rowland's work with the firm. Tom returned to the subject in 2004, working with Sharon Scott, Rebecca Binno Savage, and Matt Hubbard to further research Rowland for the Historical Society of Clinton's "Wirt C. Rowland Exhibit." Out of this project came the *Wirt C. Rowland Catalog*, a biographical sketch of Rowland. The *Catalog* formed the outline and starting point for this book. Tom, Rebecca, and Sharon encouraged my efforts along the way, and Sharon was kind enough to read my first draft and provide a great deal of constructive feedback.

Geometer Rachel Fletcher provided insights into dynamic symmetry for which I am indebted. Without her input, Rowland's specific application of Hambidge's system would not have appeared in this book. Robert Benson, former architecture critic for the *Detroit News* and professor (emeritus) of architecture at Miami University, encouraged me to "go for it" and write the book.

Jeff Hausman and Paul Tonti of SmithGroupJJR (formerly Smith, Hinchman, and Grylls) were more than generous with their time and facilitated my access to plan sets and photos essential to understanding Rowland's work. Don Bauman of Albert Kahn Associates, Inc. was equally accommodating, giving me access to vitally important plan sets and documentation.

Managers of the large buildings designed by Rowland were very cooperative, sharing photos and blueprints and touring me through their buildings. Attarah Paglia of HDC Partners arranged a terrific walk through of the Buhl Building led by Bob Kunz. Kim Farmer, manager of the Penobscot Building, provided me with similar access to her structure. Dan Kleiner gave me an extraordinary tour of the Guardian Building, from which I gained insight into its unusual construction. Elizabeth Slane, regional property manager for Roger Hinman and the Hinman Company, owners of 77 Monroe Center (Grand Rapids Trust Building), was generous with her time and shared with me rare detail sketches made by Rowland. Janet Stevens led me through the bowels of the First National Bank Building. Glen Birdsall and Debra Bullen of the Mott Foundation were very helpful, providing photos, documents, and access to the building. Peter C. Smith, pastor of the Jefferson Avenue Presbyterian Church, made an enormous amount of archival material available to me, as did Father Steven Kelly of Saint John's Episcopal Church. Crystal Thomas and Jayne Zellers of Kirk in the Hills were wonderfully supportive. Larry Golicz, owner of a former Michigan Bell building, assisted me in securing a plan set. Fred

Czerewko, of AT&T Saginaw, led me on a great tour of his building in the final days prior to his retirement. In the last week of the *Detroit News*'s occupancy of their building on Lafayette, Michael Hodges showed me the building's highlights.

The Historical Society of Clinton, primarily through the efforts of Sharon Scott, has accumulated a phenomenal cache of essential Rowland material, including artwork, photos, and letters from Genevieve Burroughs Baker and other Rowland relatives. Important contributions came as well from Grace Ritchie's grandnephew, Dr. Kenneth Olson.

From David Brent, son of Tony Buczkowski, came fantastic color photos of Rowland taken during World War II and an important blueprint. Lanie Tobin, daughter of Detroit architect Clair Ditchy, provided back issues of the *Weekly Bulletin* and postcards from Rowland. Dr. Monica Brooks helped with information on the Rowland designed Stran-Steel houses. Architect Allan Machielse shared background on Rowland's school buildings.

The American Institute of Architects has a phenomenal archive on American architects of the twentieth century, curated by Nancy Hadley, who was terrifically helpful. Evelyn Dougherty of AIA Michigan generously assisted my access to important records on local architects.

Pewabic Pottery played a significant role in many of Rowland's buildings, and archivist Hanne Nielsen was fantastic at digging out relevant material. Jennie Morton of Stamats Communications bent over backward to secure long-forgotten articles from *Buildings* magazine. Thomas Trombley, deputy director of the splendid Castle Museum of Saginaw History, provided documents related to the Second National Bank of Saginaw. Timothy Boscarino, historic preservation planner for the city of Detroit, shared photos of Detroit schools that no longer exist. William Caughlin, archivist for AT&T, copied many articles from the Michigan Bell company magazine.

My friends Dale Carlson, Elliott Milstein, Ted Held, and David Warren all made significant contributions to advancing this book from idea to reality. Chris Casteel and Larry Golicz went out of their way to provide me with plan sets for buildings.

Documents and journals held by the Bentley Historical Library, University of Michigan's Buhr Shelving Facility, Detroit Public Library's Burton Historical Collection, and Detroit Historical Museum were indispensable to this book. I offer a sincere thank you to the knowledgeable and friendly staff at each who assisted me, and to those whose generous donations (and tax money) have made these institutions possible.

Finally, this Rowland biography would not have come to be without the encouragement and attentiveness of Kathryn Wildfong of Wayne State University Press and all the talented individuals whose hands and minds transformed it from manuscript to book: Kristin Harpster, Dawn Hall, Jamie Jones, Emily Nowak, Rachel Ross, and Kristina Stonehill.

APPENDIX 1

PUBLISHED WORKS BY WIRT ROWLAND

"The Thumb Tack Club," January 1920, *All the Arts*

"The Making of an Architect," February 1920, *All the Arts*

"An Architect's Attitude Towards Music," March 1920, *All the Arts*

"The Architect as a Builder of Homes," September 1920, *All the Arts*

"Architecture and the Automobile Industry," June 1921, *Architectural Forum*

"New Note in Architecture Struck," March 31, 1929, *Detroit News*

"Real Progress," August 1931, *Architectural Progress*

"What Do People Need?" August 1931, *Architectural Forum*

"Mr. Wirt C. Rowland on Modernism," June 14, 1932, *Weekly Bulletin of the Michigan Society of Architects*

"Science Brings New Helps to Modern Homemakers," December 19, 1933, *Detroit Free Press*

"An Architect Writes a Student," January 2, 1934, *Weekly Bulletin of the Michigan Society of Architects*

"The Architecture of Your Church," June 19, 1934, *Weekly Bulletin of the Michigan Society of Architects*

"Heigho! I Go to 'The Fair!'" October 23, 1934, *Weekly Bulletin of the Michigan Society of Architects*

"Architectural Guidance" (MSA Committee Report), 1936, *Weekly Bulletin of the Michigan Society of Architects*

"Architectural Guidance" (MSA Committee Report), 1936, *Weekly Bulletin of the Michigan Society of Architects*

"[To Be or] 'Not to Be,'" November 9, 1937, *Weekly Bulletin of the Michigan Society of Architects* and December 1937, *Architect and Engineer*

"New York, Old and New," February 22, 1938, *Weekly Bulletin of the Michigan Society of Architects*

"An Influence of Glass on Architecture," March 8, 1938, *Weekly Bulletin of the Michigan Society of Architects*

"Sunday's Child," January 17, 1939, *Weekly Bulletin of the Michigan Society of Architects*

"Committee on Education" (MSA Committee Report), March 14, 1939, *Weekly Bulletin of the Michigan Society of Architects*

"State Registration Examination" (MSA Committee Report), February 13, 1934, *Weekly Bulletin of the Michigan Society of Architects*

"State Registration Examination" (MSA Committee Report), January 22, 1935, *Weekly Bulletin of the Michigan Society of Architects*

"On Gothic Architecture," March 1939, *Weekly Bulletin of the Michigan Society of Architects*

"Human—All too Human–Chapter I," April 18, 1939, *Weekly Bulletin of the Michigan Society of Architects*

"Human—All too Human–Chapter II," April 25, 1939, *Weekly Bulletin of the Michigan Society of Architects*

"An Event," May 2, 1939, *Weekly Bulletin of the Michigan Society of Architects*

"Another Event," May 16, 1939, *Weekly Bulletin of the Michigan Society of Architects*

"Human—All too Human, Chapter III," May 22, 1939, *Weekly Bulletin of the Michigan Society of Architects*

"Human—All too Human, Chapter IV," April 23, 1940, *Weekly Bulletin of the Michigan Society of Architects* (erroneously published with the title "Chapter III")

"Human—All too Human, Chapter V," November 5, 1940, *Weekly Bulletin of the Michigan Society of Architects* (erroneously published with the title "Chapter IV")

"Music and the Architect," January 23, 1940, *Weekly Bulletin of the Michigan Society of Architects*

"Committee on Education" (MSA Committee Report), March 12, 1940, *Weekly Bulletin of the Michigan Society of Architects*

"A Vacation from Architecture," November 12, 1940, *Weekly Bulletin of the Michigan Society of Architects*, republished February 1941 in *Western Architect and Engineer* as "Eastern Architect is Thrilled by the West"

"Letter to the Editor," August 25, 1942, *Weekly Bulletin of the Michigan Society of Architects*

APPENDIX 2

ESSENTIAL READING

John C. Breiby: "Design in the Drafting Room," *Pencil Points*, June 1925.

Jay Hambidge:

"Symmetry and Proportion in Greek Art," *American Architect*, November 12, 1919.

Diagonal (journal, 12 issues), Yale University Press, New Haven, CT, 1919–20.

Dynamic Symmetry: The Greek Vase, Yale University Press, New Haven, CT, 1920.

"Dynamic Symmetry and Modern Architecture," *Architecture*, November 1921.

Dynamic Symmetry in Composition as Used by the Artists, Cambridge, MA, 1923.

The Parthenon and Other Greek Temples: Their Dynamic Symmetry, Yale University Press, New Haven, CT, 1924.

Lisle March Phillipps:

The Works of Man, Duckworth, London, 1911 (an exceptional explication of the meaning of architecture in the broadest sense).

Form and Colour, Charles Scribner and Sons, New York, 1915 (specifically recommended by Rowland, this book analyzes the use of color in architecture and art and provided the foundational concepts on which Rowland based his design for the Union Trust Guardian Building).

Denman Ross: *A Theory of Pure Design*, Houghton, Mifflin, Boston, 1909.

Thomas Whitney Surette: "Music" (chapter 10), *The Significance of the Fine Arts*, American Institute of Architects, Marshall Jones, Boston, 1923.

Langford Warren:

"Dante Rossetti as a Religious Artist," *New World: A Quarterly Review of Religion, Ethics and Theology*, March 1897.

"The Influence of France upon American Architecture," *American Architect and Building News*, November 25, 1899.

"Report of the Committee on Education of the American Institute of Architects," *American Architect and Building News*, December 9, 1899.

"Architecture: Renaissance and Modern," *Progress, for the Promotion of the Fine Arts: Architecture, Sculpture, Painting, Decoration in Their Development and History*, International Art Association, Chicago, 1900.

"Recent Progress in Architectural Design," *American Architect and Building News*, January 26, 1901.

"What May the Schools Do to Advance the Appreciation of Art?" *New England Magazine*, February 1908.

"The Study of Architectural History and Its Place in the Professional Curriculum," *Architectural Quarterly of Harvard University*, June 1912.

The Foundations of Classic Architecture, Macmillan, New York, 1919.

Eugene Emmanuel Viollet-le-Duc:

Discourses on Architecture, translated by Henry Van Brunt, James R. Osgood, Boston, 1875 (particular attention to "Ninth Discourse").

Annals of a Fortress: Twenty-Two Centuries of Siege Warfare, 1875.

Herbert G. Wenzell: "Symposium on Modernism," *Weekly Bulletin of the Michigan Society of Architects*, June 21, 1932.

Ernest Wilby: "The Mystery and Philosophy of Architecture," *Weekly Bulletin of the Michigan Society of Architects*, March 11, 1941.

APPENDIX 3

FURTHER READING

"Ancient and Modern Architecture in Santa Fe, N.M.," *American Architect and Architectural Review*, May 7, 1924.

Henry H. "Hap" Arnold: *The History of Rockwell Field*, US Army Air Service, 1923 (unpublished).

Francis G. Awalt: "Recollections of the Banking Crisis in 1933," *Business History Review*, autumn 1969.

S. Omar Barker: "The New-Old Houses of Santa Fe," *Overland Monthly and Out West Magazine*, September 1924.

George Bellows: "The Relation of Painting to Architecture," *American Architect*, December 29, 1920.

Arnold Berke: *Mary Colter: Architect of the Southwest*, Princeton Architectural Press, 2001.

Oleh Bodnar: "Dynamic Symmetry in Nature and Architecture," Mathematical Institute of the Serbian Academy of Sciences and Arts, 2010.

Carla Breeze: *Pueblo Deco*, Rizzoli International Publications, 1990.

Wilford S. Conrow: "What Next in Art and Architecture?" *New York Times*, February 3, 1924.

Louise Lowber Cassidy: "The Southwest Develops Native Architecture," *Architectural Record*, March 1926.

Paul Cret: "A Recent Aspect of an Old Conflict," *Octagon*, October 1938 (recommended by Rowland).

George H. Edgell: *The American Architecture of To-Day*, Charles Scribner's Sons, New York, 1928.

Rachel Fletcher: *Infinite Measure: Learning to Design in Geometric Harmony with Art, Architecture, and Nature*, George F. Thompson Publishing, 2013.

Forty Stories from Bedrock: A Handbook for Visitors to the Union Trust Building, Detroit, Michigan, Union Trust Company, 1929.

Samuel Gardner: *A Guide to English Gothic Architecture*, Cambridge University Press, 1922.

Rose Henderson: "A Primitive Basis for Modern Architecture," *Architectural Record*, August 1923.

William Henry Goodyear: *Greek Refinements: Studies in Temperamental Architecture*, Yale University Press, London, 1912.

"Dynamic Symmetry and the Greek Vase," *American Architect*, November 24, 1920.

Thomas J. Holleman and **James P. Gallagher**: *Smith, Hinchman & Grylls: 125 Years of Architecture and Engineering, 1853–1978*, Wayne State University Press, 1978.

Talmage Hughes: "Dynamic Detroit," *Architectural Progress*, May 1931.

Michel Jacobs: *The Art of Composition: A Simple Application of Dynamic Symmetry*, Doubleday, Page, 1926.

Edward G. Longacre: "A Place Like No Other, The Origins of Langley Field," *Air Power History*, winter 1997.

Charles F. Lummis: "Ancient Homes That Were Used as Forts," *Los Angeles Times*, September 30, 1923.

Sylvanus G. Morley: "Development of the Santa Fe Style of Architecture," *Santa Fe Magazine*, June 1915.

Amos R. Morris: "When Science Comes of Age," *Michigan Technic*, November 1931.

Rexford Newcomb: "Santa Fe, The Historic and Modern," *Western Architect*, January 1924.

Francis S. Onderdonk Jr.: *The Ferro-Concrete Style*, Architectural Book Publishing, New York, 1928.

Michael G. Smith and **Rachel Fletcher**: "Proportioning Systems in Wirt C. Rowland's Union Trust Guardian Building," *Nexus Network Journal: Architecture and Mathematics*, April 2015, vol. 17, issue 1, 207–29.

Albert A. Southwick: "Dynamic Symmetry," *American Architect and Architectural Review*, January 18, 1922.

Mary Taschner: "Richard Requa; Southern California Architect," master's thesis, University of San Diego, 1982 (unpublished).

Union Trust Building, Special Supplement, *Michigan Manufacturer and Financial Record*, March 30, 1929.

TABLE 1. Selected Jobs, 1912–17: Malcomson and Higginbotham

DESCRIPTION	DATE OPENED	DESIGNER	LOCATION	STATUS
Bennett Elementary School—Detroit	February 1913	M&H	2111 Mullane St., Detroit	extant
Northwestern High School—Detroit	January 26, 1914	M&H	6300 W. Grand River, Detroit	demolished
Burton Elementary School—Detroit	January 1914	M&H	3420 Cass Ave., Detroit	extant
Hillger Elementary School—Detroit	January 1914	M&H	8411 E. Forest Ave., Detroit	demolished
Homedale Elementary School—Flint	September 1914	Rowland	1501 Davison Rd., Flint	demolished
Parkland Elementary School—Flint	September 1914	Rowland	North St. at Pasadena, Flint	demolished
Lynch Elementary School—Hamtramck	September 1914	Rowland	7575 Palmetto St., Detroit	extant
Thirkell Elementary School—Detroit	September 1915	Rowland	7724 14th St., Detroit	extant
Joyce Elementary School—Detroit	January 3, 1916	Rowland	8411 Sylvester St., Detroit	extant
Northeastern High School—Detroit	January 31, 1916	Rowland	4830 Gandy St., Detroit	demolished
Ellis Elementary School—Detroit	January 31, 1916	Rowland	4443 Junction, Detroit	demolished
Marxhausen Elementary School—Detroit	January 31, 1916	Rowland	5082 Cadillac, Detroit	demolished
Fairview Elementary School—Flint	September 1916	Rowland	1243 Central Ave., Flint	demolished
Nordstrum School—Detroit	September 11, 1916	Rowland	6920 W. Fort St., Detroit	extant
Carstens School—Detroit	November 1916	likely Rowland	2592 Coplin Ave., Detroit	derelict
Southeastern High School—Detroit	January 3, 1917	Rowland	3066 Fairview Ave., Detroit	extant
Northern High School—Detroit	January 29, 1917	Rowland	9026 Woodward Ave., Detroit	extant
Breitmeyer Elementary School—Detroit	February 1917	Rowland	8210 Cameron St., Detroit	demolished
Harms Elementary School—Detroit	March 29, 1917	Rowland	2400 Central Ave., Detroit	extant

TABLE 1. SELECTED JOBS, 1912–17   413

TABLE 2. Selected Jobs, 1910–22: Albert Kahn, Architects and Engineers

JOB[1]	DESCRIPTION	DATE[2]	DESIGNER[3]	SOURCE[4]	LOCATION	STATUS[5]
450	Hudson Motor Car Co.	1910	Rowland/Wilby	plans	E. Jefferson Ave., Detroit	demolished
451	San Telmo Cigar Co.	1910			5716 Michigan Ave., Detroit	extant
462	Ford Motor Office Building	1910			7310 Woodward, Detroit	altered
474	Dollar Savings & Trust Co.	1910	Rowland	plans	Wheeling, West Virginia	demolished
478	National Theater	1910			116 Monroe St., Detroit	extant
494	Hill Auditorium, U of M	1910	Rowland/Wilby	plans	825 N. University, Ann Arbor	extant
502	Dearborn State Bank	1910	Rowland	plans	(approx.) 1040 Mason St., Dearborn	extant
548	Peninsular Engraving Co. Building	1913			3408 Woodward Ave., Detroit	moved
593	Detroit Athletic Club	1913	Amedeo Leone	AIA file	251 Madison Ave., Detroit	extant
637	Detroit Trust Company Building	1914	Wilby	plans	201 W. Fort St., Detroit	extant / NRHP-HD
641	Detroit News	1914	Rowland/Wilby	Rowland	615 W. Lafayette, Detroit	extant
652	Grosse Pointe Shores Town Hall	1914	possibly Rowland		795 Lake Shore, Grosse Pointe Shores	extant
689	Detroit Savings Bank	1915	Rowland/Hugh Keyes	plans	6438 Woodward, Detroit	extant
702	Store building for C. G. Edgar	1915			Milwaukee Ave., Detroit	
663	U of M Library (Hatcher)	1916	Rowland/Wilby	plans	913 S. University Ave., Ann Arbor	extant
770	Vinton Building	1916	Wilby/Henry Janssen	plans	600 Woodward Ave., Detroit	extant / NRHP-HD
796	US Signal Corps, Langley Field	1917	Rowland	Rowland	Hampton, Virginia	extant
809	US Signal Corps, Joy (Selfridge) Field	1917			Mt. Clemens, Michigan	demolished
842	US Signal Corps, Rockwell Field	1917	Rowland		North Island, San Diego, California	some extant / NRHP-HD
610	First National Bank Building	1919	Rowland	Rowland	660 Woodward Ave., Detroit	extant / NRHP-HD
863	Detroit News Warehouse	1918	Rowland	Rowland	NE corner 3rd & Fort St., Detroit	extant
897	Detroit Savings Bank	1919	Rowland		5705 W. Fort St., Detroit	extant / NRHP

JOB[1]	DESCRIPTION	DATE[2]	DESIGNER[3]	SOURCE[4]	LOCATION	STATUS[5]
902	General Motors Headquarters	1919	Rowland	Rowland	3044 W. Grand Blvd., Detroit	extant / NRHP / NHL
900	Cadillac Motor Car Sales and Service	1920	Rowland		6001 Cass Ave., Detroit	extant
952	Standard Accident Insurance Co. Building	1920			640 Temple, Detroit	extant
959	Detroit Savings Bank	1920			4800 Michigan Ave., Detroit	extant
990	City of Detroit Police Headquarters	1920			1300 Beaubien St., Detroit	
991	United Savings Bank	1920	Rowland/ Robert Hubel	plans	1133 Griswold, Detroit	refaced
1001	Clements Library, U of M	1921	Rowland/ Robert Hubel/ Wayne Yates	plans	909 S. University Ave., Ann Arbor	extant
1058	Park Avenue Building	1922			2001 Park Ave., Detroit	extant

NOTES

1. Albert Kahn, Architects and Engineers job number
2. Date from Albert Kahn, Architects and Engineers job listing (in most cases, year the job was begun)
3. Principal designer (if known) as well as other principal designers whose names appear on drawings
4. Source for principal designer information (if available); "Rowland" indicates the building was listed by Rowland on his 1932 application to Harvard Alumni Assoc.
5. NRHP = National Register of Historic Properties; NHL = National Historic Landmark; NRHP-HD = National Register of Historic Places Historic District contributing building

TABLE 2. SELECTED JOBS, 1910-22   415

TABLE 3. Selected Jobs, 1922–30: Smith, Hinchman, and Grylls

JOB[1]	DESCRIPTION	DATE[2]	DESIGNER[3]	SOURCE[4]	LOCATION	STATUS[5]
	Mistersky Power Plant DPLC	1922 job start	Leone	AIA file	5425 W. Jefferson Ave., Detroit	extant
	Palmer Park DPLC	1922 job start	Rowland		17551 Woodward Ave., Detroit	extant
4873	Jefferson Ave. Presbyterian Church	11/2/1922 plans	ext: Rowland, int: Kapp		8625 E. Jefferson Ave., Detroit	extant
4877	Buhl Building	11/1/1923 plans	ext: Rowland	plans	535 Griswold St., Detroit	extant NRHP-HD
4944	Yost Field House	5/31/1922 plans	likely Leone		1116 S. State St., Ann Arbor	extant
5165	J L Hudson Farmer St. Building	1923 plans	likely Leone		Farmer St. N of Gratiot, Detroit	demolished
	Kales Realty/ Jefferson Terminal Warehouse	1923 job start	likely Rowland		1900 E. Jefferson Ave., Detroit	extant
	Harold Palmer store building	1923 job start	likely Rowland		18 W. Adams Ave., Detroit	extant
	MI Bell Ann Arbor CO	1923 job start	Rowland		315 E. Washington St., Ann Arbor	extant
	MI Bell Grand Rapids CO	1923 job start	Rowland		114 Division Ave. North, Grand Rapids	floors added
5283	Second National Bank of Saginaw	6/2/1924 plans	Rowland	plans	101 N. Washington Ave., Saginaw	extant
5498	George H Phelps Building	7/15/1925 plans	Rowland	plans	2761 E. Jefferson Ave., Detroit	extant
	MI Bell Lenox CO	1924 job start	Rowland		11640 Kercheval Ave., Detroit	1 floor added
5642	Bankers Trust Company Building	1924 job start	Rowland		205 W. Congress, Detroit	extant NRHP-HD
	Parke, Davis & Co. Admin. Building	1924 job start	Leone	AIA file	River Pl. or 100 Talon Centre Dr., Detroit	extant
	The Players	1924 job start	Kapp		3321 E. Jefferson Ave., Detroit	extant / NRHP
	Burnham, Stoepel & Co. Warehouse	1924 job start			441 E. Jefferson Ave., Detroit	altered
5521	Grand Rapids Trust Building	8/31/1925 plans	Rowland	plans	77 Monroe Center St. NW, Grand Rapids	extant
	Pontchartrain Club	1925 job start	Rowland/Leone		1511 First St., Detroit	extent
	MI Bell Headquarters addition	1925 job start	Rowland		1365 Cass Ave., Detroit	extant

JOB[1]	DESCRIPTION	DATE[2]	DESIGNER[3]	SOURCE[4]	LOCATION	STATUS[5]
	MI Bell Hogarth CO	8/1926 const. start	Rowland		10515 Northlawn St., Detroit	1 floor added
	MI Bell Longfellow CO	6/1926 const. start	Rowland		70 Highland St., Highland Park	extant
	MI Bell Royal Oak CO	6/1926 const. start	Rowland		421 S. Williams St., Royal Oak	floors added
5585	MI Bell Redford CO	10/7/1925 plans	Rowland		21543 Grand River Ave., Detroit	extant
	Country Club of Detroit	1925 job start			220 Country Club Dr., Grosse Pointe Farms	extant
	Trombly School	1926 job start			820 Beaconsfield Ave., Grosse Pointe Park	extant
5756	Benjamin Nolan School	1926 job start	Rowland		1150 E. Lantz St., Detroit	extant
5776	Union Trust (Guardian) Building	8/15/1927 plans	Rowland		500 Griswold St., Detroit	extant / NRHP / NHL
5782	C F Smith Warehouse Building	1926 job start	Rowland		2410 Vinewood St. Detroit	extant
5783	Dime/Detroit Savings Bank Branch	8/7/1926			E. Jefferson Ave. at Piper, Detroit	demolished
5786	Kelvinator Headquarters	9/30/1926	Leone	AIA file	14250 Plymouth Rd., Detroit	abandoned
5851	Guardian Group Bank (in Greater Penobscot)	3/22/1928 plans	Rowland	plans	645 Griswold St., Detroit	extent
5865	Greater Penobscot Building	5/16/1927	Rowland		645 Griswold St., Detroit	extent / NRHP-HD
5924	Mackenzie High School	6/27/1927 plans	Rowland	plans	Wyoming Ave. at West Point Ave., Detroit	demolished
	MI Bell Madison CO	10/1928 const. start	Rowland		105 E. Bethune Ave., Detroit	extant
	MI Bell Flint CO	1927 const. start	Rowland		502 Beach St., Flint	floors added
	MI Bell Traverse City CO	1927 job start	Rowland		142 E. State St., Traverse City	extant
	MI Bell Pontiac CO	1927 job start	Rowland		54 N. Mill St., Pontiac	altered
	MI Bell Jackson CO	1927 job start	Rowland		304 S. Jackson St., Jackson	floors added
	MI Bell Columbia CO	1927 job start	Rowland		52 Seldon St., Detroit	extant / NRHP
	MI Bell Pingree CO	1927 job start	Rowland		13635 Greiner St., Detroit	altered

TABLE 3. SELECTED JOBS, 1922–30   417

JOB[1]	DESCRIPTION	DATE[2]	DESIGNER[3]	SOURCE[4]	LOCATION	STATUS[5]
	MI Bell St. Joseph	1928 const. start	Rowland		415 Main St., St. Joseph	extant
	MI Bell Grand Rapids Garage	1927 job start	Rowland		1415 S. Division Ave., Grand Rapids	extant
6012	Mt. Clemens Savings Bank	1927 job start			Gratiot Ave. & Cass Ave., Mt. Clemens	demolished
6022	Ambassador Bridge: buildings and piers	1927 job start	Rowland		W. Jefferson Ave. at 21st St., Detroit	piers extant
6110	Industrial Mutual Auditorium	11/16/1928	likely Leone		E. Second St., Flint	demolished
6134	Charles Oakman School	1928 job start			12920 Wadsworth St., Detroit	extant
6148	Dime Savings Bank Branch	1928 job start	Rowland		9980 Gratiot Ave., Detroit	derelict
	Dime Savings Bank Branch	1928 job start	Rowland		10001 Puritan St., Detroit	extant
	Dime Savings Bank Branch	1928 job start	Rowland		4101 Fenkell, Detroit	extant
6166	Detroit Saturday Night Building	1928 job start	Rowland		1959 E. Jefferson Ave., Detroit	extant
	Women's Colony Club	1928 job start			2310 Park Ave., Detroit	extant
	Cunningham Drug Building	12/6/1928 const. start	Rowland		1134 Griswold (also fronts on State St.), Detroit	extant / NRHP-HD
	MI Bell & Western Electric Warehouse	7/1929 const. start	Rowland		82 Oakman Blvd., Detroit	extant / NRHP
6217	MI Bell Saginaw Office Building	8/26/1929	Rowland		309 S. Washington Ave., Saginaw	extant / NRHP
	MI Bell Niagara CO	1928 job start	Rowland		17045 Mack Ave., Detroit	1 floor added
	MI Bell University CO	1928 job start	Rowland		7000 W. McNichols Rd., Detroit	altered
	MI Bell Benton Harbor CO	1928 job start	Rowland		58 Wall St., Benton Harbor	extant
	MI Bell Holland CO	1928 job start	Rowland		13 W. 10th St., Holland	extant
	MI Bell Port Huron CO	1928 const. start	Rowland		919 6th St., Port Huron	1 floor added
	MI Bell Oregon CO	7/1929 const. start	Leone	AIA files	13905 Ford Rd., Dearborn	1 floor added
6223	Union Industrial Bank Building	8/10/1929	Rowland	plans	503 Saginaw St., Flint	extant

JOB[1]	DESCRIPTION	DATE[2]	DESIGNER[3]	SOURCE[4]	LOCATION	STATUS[5]
6354	Pershing High School	6/5/1929 plans	Rowland	plans	18875 Ryan Rd., Detroit	extant
6423	Denby High School	9/20/1929 plans	Rowland	plans	12800 Kelly Rd., Detroit	extant / NRHP
6465	Detroit Ball Bearing	1929 job start			110 W. Alexandrine Ave., Detroit	demolished
	University Club	9/1930 plans	Kapp	AIA files	1411 E. Jefferson Ave., Detroit	demolished
	YMCA Northeastern Branch	9/1930 plans			10100 Harper Ave., Detroit	extant
	Downtown Branch Library (Skillman)	1930 job start	Kapp	AIA files	121 Gratiot	extant

NOTES

1. Smith, Hinchman, and Grylls job number, if known
2. Date of plans if known; otherwise, the year design work by SH&G commenced (job start) or year construction began
3. Designer of the building if known
4. Source for principal designer information (if available); "ext." = exterior and "int." = interior
5. NRHP = National Register of Historic Properties; NHL = National Historic Landmark; NRHP-HD = National Register of Historic Places Historic District contributing building

TABLE 3. SELECTED JOBS, 1922–30   419

NOTES

INTRODUCTION

1. Davies, "Wait and See."

2. "New Bank Home in Detroit Ready," *Wall Street Journal*, April 1, 1929, 4.

3. Kahn, "Color in Bank Buildings."

4. "Put the Orange Brick in Union Trust," *Michigan Manufacturer and Financial Record*, July 28, 1928.

5. Letter from Lester Francis "Andy" Anderson to Wirt Rowland, October 13, 1946, 3 (in the archives of the Historical Society of Clinton).

6. Ibid., 3.

7. Perry, *Adventures in Ceramics*, 140.

8. Barrie, Interview with Corrado Parducci.

9. Wirt Rowland: First National Bank Building, Buhl Building, Michigan Bell (AT&T) Headquarters, Union Trust (Guardian) Building, Greater Penobscot Building; Louis Kamper: Washington Blvd. Building (1923), Book Cadillac Hotel (1924), Book Tower (1926), David Broderick Tower (1928), Industrial Building (1928), Real Estate Exchange Building (1919), Water Board Building (1928); John Donaldson: Penobscot Building (1905) and Penobscot Building Annex (1913), David Stott Building (1929). The Cadillac Tower Building (1927) was designed by Bonnah and Chaffee. The Dime Building (Chrysler House) and Ford Building were excluded as they were not designed by a local architect. (Twenty-three stories, or equivalent, in height.)

10. Alastair Duncan, *American Art Deco* (New York: Harry N. Abrams, 1986), 195.

11. Talmage C. Hughes, "Dynamic Detroit," *Weekly Bulletin of the Michigan Society of Architects* 8, no. 50 (December 11, 1934): 1, republished in *Architectural Progress*, May 1931.

12. *Western Architect* 24, no. 4 (October 1916): 125.

13. Binno-Savage and Kowalski, *Art Deco in Detroit*, 7: "Detroiters take it for granted, and don't always think of their city as being on the cutting edge of design . . . but in the late 1920s it was."

14. *Historical Statistics of the United States, 1789–1945*, US Department of Commerce, 1949, "Series K 225–235—Motor Vehicles—Production, Registrations, and Motor Fuel Usage: 1900 to 1945," p. 223.

15. The Penobscot, Union Trust (Guardian), First National Bank, Union Industrial Bank (Flint), Grand Rapids Trust, and Second National Bank of Saginaw were bank headquarters buildings; though the Buhl Building was headquarters to the Guardian Trust Company, the bank was incidental, not essential, to the construction of the building. (The Michigan Bell headquarters building was excluded due to its being a private, single-use structure.)

16. "Short Talks with the Trade," *Cement World* 1, no. 5 (August 15, 1907): 299.

17. Aymar Embury III, "Impressions of Three Cities," *Architecture* 31, no. 3 (March 1915): 80.

18. *Western Architect* 24, no. 4 (October 1916): 125.

19. Rowland, "Making of an Architect," 39.

20. *History of the First Congregational Church of Clinton, 1844–1923*, 1923.

21. Sharon Scott, "Clinton: Greatest Trading Point West of Detroit," Historical Society of Clinton website.

22. "A Great Calamity at Clinton," *Manchester Enterprise*, December 6, 1889 (in the archives of the Historical Society of Clinton).

23. *The Advance* 61, no. 2361 (February 2, 1911), p. (155) 27.

24. Rowland, "Sunday's Child"; Holleman, *Wirt C. Rowland Exhibition Catalog*, 7.

25. Rowland, "An Architect Writes a Student," 3.

26. Rowland, "Sunday's Child."

27. "A Great Calamity at Clinton," *Manchester Enterprise*, December 6, 1889 (in the archives of the Historical Society of Clinton).

28. A copy of the Rowland family Bible is in the archives of the Historical Society of Clinton.

29. Rowland, "Sunday's Child."

30. Ibid.

31. Ibid.

32. *History of the First Congregational Church of Clinton, 1844–1923*, 1923.

33. "Leander W. Kimball, Clinton Banker, Dies," *Adrian Daily Telegram*, March 17, 1955, and letters from Leander Kimball to Wirt Rowland, September, October, and November 1946, in the archives of the Historical Society of Clinton.

CHAPTER 1

1. "Fifty-Five Million Dollars Worth of Tires," *Michigan Manufacturer and Financial Record*, January 19, 1918, 104 and 106.

2. 1957 AIA biography of Gus O'Dell, Detroit AIA chapter architect file for O'Dell; and Rowland, "Sunday's Child," 1.

3. Clarence M. Burton, editor in chief, *The City of Detroit, Michigan, 1701–1922*, 1922, 696.

4. "News of the Architects," *Detroit Free Press*, March 23, 1902, A6.

5. In his personal diary, George D. Mason wrote on August 16, 1902: "Kahn—settled partnership interests" (Burton Collection, Detroit Public Library).

6. George D. Mason diary from March 1902.

7. "Real Estate Market, Usual Midsummer Dullness Prevails," *Detroit Free Press*, August 3, 1902, B8.

8. "Partners Had Falling Out," *Detroit Free Press*, June 10, 1903, 11.

9. Rowland, "Sunday's Child," 1.

10. Baldwin Memorial Archive of American Architects, draft biographical information for George D. Mason, compiled by Emil Lorch, based on talks with Mason, dated April 4, 1950, p. 5, stored with the Emil Lorch papers at the Bentley Library in Ann Arbor, Michigan.

11. Letter from George Mason to Wallace Sabine, Harvard University, September 14, 1910, Harvard University, Records of the Faculty of Arts and Science (UA III 15.88.10).

12. "Detroit's New Hotel Will Be a Delight to the Traveling Public," *Detroit Free Press*, August 20, 1905, A10.

13. "Building News," *American Architect and Building News* 88, no. 1549 (September 2, 1905), viii.

14. "One Blames Weather Another the Wall," *Detroit Free Press*, October 17, 1902, 2.

15. *Detroit Free Press*, October 17, 1902, p. 2.

16. Hyde, "Assembly-Line Architecture," 7.

17. Kahn, "Industrial Architecture," 6; "Work Done by the Cleveland Silex Stone Co." (advertisement), *Detroit Free Press*, July 4, 1902, 18

18. Moritz Kahn, "A Reinforced Concrete System with Rigid Shear Members," *Concrete and Constructional Engineering* 1, no. 1 (March 1906): 69.

19. As the use of steel reinforced concrete construction developed over time, the type and extent of steel employed for reinforcement varied depending on the strength required, type of structure, and preferences of the architectural engineer. "Value of Concrete as a Reinforcement for Structural Steel Columns," an article in the June 1912 issue of *Cement Age*, noted: "Sometimes the structural steel shapes form a relatively small proportion of the column section and are considered as reinforcement for the concrete. In other designs the amount of steel is much larger and the structural shapes will carry a large proportion of the load so that the column instead of being a reinforced concrete column is really a steel column reinforced with the concrete in which it is embedded."

20. *Cement Age*, August 1906, 206.

21. "Concrete Building Construction," *Engineering News* 48, no. 6 (December 18, 1902): 521; "Concrete Construction," letter to the editor from George Keller, *New York Times*, September 8, 1905, 6.

22. "Four Stories Too High: Cleveland's Building Code in Way of Big Hotel," *Detroit Free Press*, November 3, 1907, A10.

23. "Building News," *American Architect and Building News*, September 2, 1905, viii; and George Mason personal diary entry for March 1, 1905, and others.

24. Mason, anticipating the great potential of steel reinforced concrete buildings, took a course in higher mathematics in order to perform the engineering calculations required by the method. (Mason biography in *City of Detroit, Michigan, 1701–1922* by Clarence M. Burton.) Much of the engineering was likely carried out by Julius Kahn's Trussed Concrete Steel Company, provider of the steel reinforcement for the structure.

25. "New Apartment Building," *Detroit Free Press*, May 14, 1905, 16

26. "One Man Burned in Hotel Fire," *Detroit Free Press*, December 23, 1903, 2.

27. "Four Met with Death," *Detroit Free Press*, April 30, 1904, 1.

28. "Hero of Hotel Fire," *Detroit Free Press*, December 29, 1905, 2.

29. The death rate from fire in 1905 was about 8.3 people per 100,000 (*Mortality Statistics 1905*, Bureau of the Census, 1907, 166). By 2005, the rate had dropped to 1.1 per 100,000 (*National Vital Statistics Reports*, 56, no. 10 [April 24, 2008], 55).

30. "Hero of Hotel Fire," *Detroit Free Press*, December 29, 1905, 3.

31. "Detroit Will Have Magnificent Hotel," *Detroit Free Press*, May 19, 1905, 1.

32. George D. Mason diary (Burton Collection, Detroit Public Library) for September 7, 1905.

33. George D. Mason diary (Burton Collection, Detroit Public Library) for December 19 and 22, 1905, and January 1 and 2, 1906.

34. "Excavating Is Finished," *Detroit Free Press*, July 10, 1906, 5; "Now Watch It Grow," *Detroit Free Press*, August 19, 1906, 4; "The Foundations of the Hotel Pontchartrain," *American Architect*, August 17, 1921, 127–31; "Concrete-Piling vs. Concrete Pillars for Foundation Work," *Concrete* 6, no. 5 (November 1906): 21–22.

35. *Report on Proposed Belle Isle Bridge*, by the Consulting Board, Belle Isle Bridge Division of Engineering and Construction, Department of Public Works, City of Detroit, 1918, 53–56 and 69–70; W. S. Wolfe and D. R. Martin, "Foundation Plans Changed after Water Enters Excavation," *Engineering News Record* 99, no. 26 (December 29, 1927): 1034–35.

36. "Concrete-Piling vs. Concrete Pillars for Foundation Work," 21–22.

37. "Excavating Is Finished," 5; "Now Watch It Grow," 4.

38. "Pontchartrain Thrown Open," *Detroit Free Press*, October 30, 1907, 1.

39. Letter from George Mason to Wallace Sabine, Harvard University, September 14, 1910, Harvard University, Records of the Faculty of Arts and Science (UA III 15.88.10).

40. Baldwin Memorial Archive of American Architects, draft biographical information for George D. Mason, compiled by Emil Lorch, based on talks with Mason, dated April 4, 1950, p. 1, stored with the Emil Lorch papers at the Bentley Library in Ann Arbor, Michigan.

41. "The Board of Health Hospital Buildings," *Detroit Free Press*, June 26, 1909, 9; George D. Mason diary for June 17, 1909; and "Last Addition Now to Go Up," *Detroit Free Press*, August 10, 1910, 5.

42. Plate 48 of *The Four Books of Architecture* by Andrea Palladio, 1570, Dover Publications edition, 1965.

43. There is no direct evidence that Rowland was responsible for the design of the administration building; however, it is reasonable to infer based on the quality of the design, Rowland's position as Mason's chief designer, and a comparison with Mason's other work. The two flanking ward buildings are of a different style, featuring (in their original configuration) a portico supported by round columns and large modillions beneath the eaves, decorative elements not characteristically employed by Rowland. It is possible that Rowland designed the administration building and Mason (or Herbert Wenzell) the wards.

44. *Course of Study, Art Education, Elementary Schools, Grades One to Eight*, Detroit Public Schools, Board of Education, City of Detroit, 1925, 45–46 and 56–57.

45. *Detroit Free Press*, November 16, 1902, A5, and December 22, 1902, 5.

46. *Detroit Free Press*, June 28, 1903, 5, and December 19, 1904, 5.

47. *Detroit Free Press*, January 9, 1905, 5; Detroit's Philharmonic Hall was located on the corner of Lafayette and Shelby Streets and was demolished after Orchestra Hall was built.

48. *Detroit Free Press*, December 29, 1905, 3.

49. *Detroit Free Press*, April 27, 1906, 3.

50. *Detroit Free Press*, September 9, 1900, 25.

51. *Detroit Free Press*, September 25, 1910, 8.

52. "In Selecting the Mikado," *Detroit Free Press*, January 31, 1909, 20.

53. "'Mikado' Cast Full of Stars," *Detroit Free Press*, February 12, 1909, 14.

CHAPTER 2

1. "Wilby Made Fellow of Architects' Institute," *Weekly Bulletin of the Michigan Society of Architects* (May 20, 1941).

2. Albert Kahn, Architects and Engineers job list.

3. Originally called the Metzger Building, the structure was financed by Joy for an independent auto dealership run by William E. Metzger: "Metzger Is Climbing," *Detroit Free Press*, June 11, 1905, D8.

4. Hyde, "Assembly-Line Architecture," 7 and 9; Albert Kahn, Architects and Engineers job list.

5. Albert Kahn, Architects and Engineers job list; *American Architect and Building News*, July 14, 1906, v11.

6. Rowland, "Sunday's Child."

7. Ibid.

8. Albert Kahn, speech to the American Concrete Institute, "Reinforced Concrete Architecture these past Twenty Years," 1924, transcript in the Albert Kahn papers collection of the Bentley Historical Library.

9. *Architecture* 24, no. 4, 147, plates CII and CIV.

10. *Reading Architect's Blueprints (Part 1)* (Scranton, PA: International Textbook Company), 38–39.

11. "University Scholarships of the Architectural League of America for 1908–1909," *Architectural Record* 23, no. 4 (April 1908): 333.

12. Letter from Albert Kahn to Wallace C. Sabine, Harvard University, September 9, 1910 (from the Historical Society of the Village of Clinton, Michigan).

13. Letter from Wirt Rowland to Wallace C. Sabine, Harvard University, August 27, 1910 (from the Historical Society of the Village of Clinton, Michigan).

14. Unsigned letter from Harvard to Wirt Rowland advising him of acceptance as a special student, September 20, 1910 (from the Historical Society of the Village of Clinton, Michigan).

15. Charles A. Coolidge, "Herbert Langford Warren (1857–1917)," *Proceedings of the American Academy of Arts and Sciences* 68, no. 13 (1933): 689–91; and William S. Parker, "Herbert Langford Warren," *Harvard Graduates Magazine* 26 (1917–18): 45–47. Published by: American Academy of Arts and Sciences.

16. Warren, "Department of Architecture of Harvard University," 138.

17. Ibid., 138.

18. Viollet-le-Duc, *Discourses on Architecture*, 431–32.

19. Ibid., 456.

20. Ibid., 413.

21. Ibid., 426.

22. Rowland, "Real Progress," 15.

23. Rowland, "Mr. Wirt C. Rowland on Modernism," 4.

24. Ibid.

25. Rowland, "Architecture and the Automobile Industry," 201.

26. Viollet-le-Duc, *Discourses on Architecture*, 419–20.

27. Ibid., 433.

28. "Architectural Design," *Architecture and Building* 44, no. 5 (1912): 201–2.

29. Lewis Mumford, "The Sky Line, Two Theaters," January 14, 1933, *New Yorker*, 94.

30. Emily Ann Thompson, *The Soundscape of Modernity: Architectural Acoustics and the Culture of Listening in America* (Cambridge, MA: MIT Press, 2004), 74.

31. Tallant, "Acoustic Design in the Hill Memorial Auditorium," 169.

32. In a March 24, 1932, letter to the Harvard Architectural School Alumni Association, Rowland attached a detailed list of buildings the design of which was in part or solely his responsibility. Hill Auditorium is listed with the comment "in design collaboration with Mr. Ernest Wilby." Wilby's February 24, 1938, application to the American Institute of Architects under "Nominee's Achievement in Architectural Design" lists twelve buildings of various types, including Hill Auditorium, Detroit News Building, and Detroit Athletic Club. Wilby is known to have collaborated with Rowland on the first two and Amedeo Leone on the third. Rowland's initials appear on the following drawings for Hill Auditorium: Attic and Ceiling Plan, sheet 6; Front Elevation, sheet 8; Longitudinal Section, sheet 12; and Transverse Section, sheet 13.

33. "The Arthur Hill Memorial Hall," *Michigan Alumnus*, February 1912, 191.

34. "Public School Architecture at Chicago, the Work of Dwight Perkins," *Architectural Record* 27, no. 6 (June 1910): 507.

35. A variety of factors affect the accuracy of overlay analysis of plan sheets. The original architectural drawing was traced (copied) onto drafting linen; the technology in use at the time was ink pen and straightedge, so drawings were less exact than today's, produced by computer-aided design systems. Scanning can introduce small amounts of distortion, though this has been corrected to the extent possible. The use of geometric figures may involve measures that are irrational; an isosceles triangle, for example, has one side equal to the square root of two. These must be rounded to a rational number for use on the building plan. The most significant source of inaccuracy between overlay lines and original drawings is likely the deviation from the architect's ideal intent to avoid unnecessary expense in construction. Many building components come in standard sizes; a geometrically ideal size, shape, or location may be slightly adjusted to avoid additional cost, but without noticeably affecting the appearance of the building.

36. John C. Breiby, "Design in the Drafting Room, III," figure 6, "Suggestive Sketch Study for an Office Building," *Pencil Points* 6, no. 6 (June 1925): 72.

37. Irma Bronimau, *The Village of Clinton, Michigan: A History, 1829–1979*, Clinton Women's Club, 1979, 30 and 86–87; "Ceremony of Laying Cornerstone of the Mortuary Chapel," and "Clinton Citizens Witness and Partake in Interesting Ceremony Saturday," September 30, 1912, newspaper articles in the archives of the Historical Society of Clinton.

38. "Dedications at Clinton of Mortuary Chapel," August 18, 1913, newspaper articles in the archives of the Historical Society of Clinton; Bronimau, *Village of Clinton*, 87; "Mr. and Mrs. William Uhr Mark 60th Anniversary," *Ann Arbor News*, June 24, 1937; and Betty Cummings, "Manchester: A Look Back; Stone Masons Made Good Progress on St. Mary Church," *Manchester Enterprise*, August 10, 2011.

39. Dr. Eugene Duquesne, "Report for the Jury and Criticism," *Brickbuilder* 21, no. 2 (February 1912): 4; Rowland and Wenzell's entry appeared on p. 13. The judges for the competition included

Rowland's Harvard professors H. Langdon Warren and Eugene Duquesne.

40. Interview by Margaret Brown of her father, Dr. Kenneth Olson, nephew of Grace Ritchie, August 14, 2004, reported to Sharon Scott of the Historical Society of Clinton by e-mail, August 16, 2004 (in the archives of the Historical Society of Clinton).

41. Ibid.

42. Charles L. Spain, assistant superintendent of schools, "The Detroit Public Schools," *School Board Journal* 52, no. 2 (February 1916): 11.

43. Ibid.

44. *Seventy-First Annual Report of the Board of Education of the City of Detroit*, for the year ending June 30, 1914, 9.

45. "Six Schools Are Needed," *Detroit Free Press*, November 24, 1911, 2.

46. "Near Eruption on School Board," *Detroit Free Press*, April 26, 1912, 6.

47. "Architects to Be Reappointed," *Detroit Free Press*, April 26, 1912, 5.

48. "Among the Architects," *Construction News*, November 2, 1912, 16.

49. School planning and completion timelines were established based on articles in the *Detroit Free Press*, school board minutes, school board annual reports, and construction announcements in *Construction News* and the *American Contractor*. Schools were often dedicated at a later time than when they first opened for use.

50. "New High School to Open Monday," *Detroit Free Press*, January 28, 1917, 1.

51. William B. Stratton, "The Growth of Detroit," *Western Architect* 24, no. 4 (October 1916): plate section.

52. *American Architect* 121, no. 2385 (January 18, 1922): plate section.

53. "Education Board, Despite Protest, Buys Goethe Site," *Detroit Free Press*, August 14, 1914, 6.

54. *Journal Proceedings of the Board of Education of the City of Detroit, for the year 1914–1915*, July 23, 1914, 47.

55. "Estimators View School Buildings," *Detroit Free Press*, January 6, 1914, 5.

56. "Says City Should Have More Ornate School Buildings," *Detroit News*, January 7, 1914.

57. "Five New Schools to Open Monday," *Detroit News*, January 24, 1914.

58. According to the "List and Description of Buildings" charts in the *Seventy-Second Annual Report of the Board of Education, City of Detroit* (1914–1915), Condon Elementary, a sixteen-room school, cost $85,000 to build in 1914, and Joyce Elementary, a twenty-room school, cost $100,000 the same year.

59. *Construction News*, November 2, 1912, 32; December 7, 1912, 29; and *American Contractor*, March 1, 1913, 85 and 96.

60. Attributing responsibility for the design of schools from this period is challenging, in part because building plans are not available or no longer exist and many of the buildings have been demolished. Even establishing the months during which a school was designed is difficult as the minutes of school board meetings often indicate votes taken by the board, but not actions of the real estate and school buildings committee, which was directly responsible for overseeing the architects in real time. The attributions made here are based on careful analysis of buildings known to have been designed

by Malcomson and Higginbotham prior to Rowland's employment with the firm, those designed during his tenure, and those begun well after his departure.

In addition to the twenty-room school buildings, a number of sixteen-room schools were begun while Rowland was with the firm and, though the basic pre-1913 design remained unchanged, certain cosmetic elements show his influence. The stone bands flanking the doors and bright-colored brick on Hillger School, for example, and on Burton School, the brickwork designs, inset spandrels, and dormer/parapet with two finials extending above the roofline over the door appear to be Rowland's handiwork. Carstens School, though it differed from the twenty-room school buildings that shared a common design, appears to have been Rowland's design—the exterior at least. Rowland's own estimate of the number of elementary schools he designed during this period was "approximately twelve grade schools." In Detroit, there were eight, twenty-room schools (including Carstens); three schools in Flint, plus Hamtramck's Lynch School, brings the total to twelve.

61. *Program of Competition for the Selection of an Architect to Design and to Supervise the Construction of a Main Building for the Public Library of Detroit*, the Detroit Library Commission, February 15, 1913.

62. "Announce Winners in Architectural Library Contest," *Detroit Free Press*, April 5, 1913, 6.

63. Lisa B. Mausolf, *Edward Lippincott Tilton, A Monograph on His Architectural Practice*, 2007, 2.

64. Certificate of Death for Ruth Melissa Rowland, State of Michigan, Lenawee County, May 25, 1915.

65. It is possible that Rowland performed work for Kahn's office on a contract basis as early as 1914. Plans for the Grosse Pointe Shores Town Hall—Albert Kahn, Architects and Engineers job number 652—were drawn on plain paper (rather than the standard: drafting linen), are unsigned, undated, and have a nonstandard title block appearing on only the first page of the seven-page set. Most striking, however, is that the design is nearly identical in style to Rowland's design for the Detroit Public Library.

66. "Building for Speed with Reinforced Concrete," *Michigan Manufacturer and Financial Record*, February 26, 1916, 34.

67. Ferry, *Buildings of Detroit*, 185.

68. Rebecca Binno Savage, "Lower Woodward Avenue Historic District, Final Report," 1998, 25.

69. Eric J. Hill and John Gallagher, AIA Detroit, *American Institute of Architects Guide to Detroit Architecture*, 2003, 66.

70. Edwin V. Wight and M. Marallyn, "Wight House History" (Rowland House), undated, unpublished, in the archives of the Historical Society of Clinton, p. 2.

71. Undated typewritten draft of obituary for Wirt C. Rowland, copy from the files of the American Institute of Architects, Washington, DC.

72. Hughes worked for Albert Kahn, Architects and Engineers, from 1920 to 1921 according to 1956 AIA *American Architects Directory* bio for Talmage Coates Hughes.

73. "Wirt C. Rowland," *Weekly Bulletin of the Michigan Society of Architects* (December 10, 1946). Two other lines, referencing well-known facts of Rowland's work on the Guardian and Penobscot Buildings, and Jefferson Avenue Presbyterian Church, were also omitted: "The two office buildings mentioned were done about the same time and are of contemporary design, the church of Gothic. All are from the office of Smith, Hinchman & Grylls."

74. "Building for Speed with Reinforced Concrete"

75. "T. B. Rayl Company Will Have Block of Seven Stories," *Detroit Free Press*, July 11, 1915, real estate section, p. 1.

CHAPTER 3

1. "Wall St. Men to Go into Military Camp," *New York Times*, June 30, 1915.

2. Donald M. Kington, "The Plattsburg Movement and Its Legacy," *Relevance* 6, no. 4 (Autumn 1997), www.worldwar1.com/tgws/rel011.htm, accessed September 8, 2014.

3. Rowland, "Sunday's Child," 4.

4. Kahn, "Thirty Minutes with American Architects and Architecture," 11.

5. "The Detroit Evening News, a Milestone in the History of its Progress," *Linotype Bulletin*, January 1918, 84.

6. White, *Detroit News: 1873–1917*, 26.

7. "The Detroit News Building, an Imposing Example of Commercial Architecture and an Efficient Newspaper Plant," *Architectural Forum* 28, no. 1 (January 1918): 27.

8. Edgell, *American Architecture of To-Day*, 293–94.

9. "The Detroit Evening News," *Michigan Alumnus* 25, no. 241 (February 1919): 240.

10. Viollet-le-Duc, *Discourses on Architecture*, 177.

11. Ibid., 182.

12. Rowland, "Mr. Wirt C. Rowland on Modernism," 8.

13. Although installed in all commercial and industrial buildings, incandescent bulbs provided inadequate light, particularly in open areas with high ceilings. Designing structures to admit natural light became unnecessary after the introduction in 1938 of the fluorescent tube light. Around-the-clock production during World War II spurred the rapid adoption of fluorescent lights for industrial and commercial applications.

14. "$2,000,000 Building Completed," *Building Management* 18, no. 2 (February 1918): 11.

15. *Architectural Forum* (January 1918): 27.

16. The practice of disguising new technology or materials to appear as that which was being replaced was not limited to architecture. As iron and steel were replacing wood as the primary material used in passenger railroad cars, their metal surfaces were often painted to look like wood.

17. Wilby, "Mystery and Philosophy of Architecture," 4.

18. Warren, "Department of Architecture of Harvard University," 138.

19. Rowland, "Mr. Wirt C. Rowland on Modernism," 8.

20. Rowland, "Real Progress," 16.

21. "Mirror of the public mind . . . Interpreter of the public intent . . . Troubler of the public conscience" "Reflector of every human interest . . . Friend of every righteous cause . . . Encourager of every generous act" "Bearer of intelligence . . . Dispeller of ignorance and prejudice . . . A light shining into all dark places" "Promoter of civic welfare and civic pride . . . Bond of civic unity . . . Protector of civic rights" "Scourge of evil doers . . . Exposer of secret iniquities . . . Unrelenting foe of privilege and corruption" "Voice of the lowly and oppressed . . . Advocate of the friendless . . . Righter of

public and private wrongs" "Chronicler of facts . . . Sifter of rumors and opinions . . . Minister of the truth that makes men free" "Reporter of the new . . . Remembrancer of the old and tried . . . Herald of what is to come" "Defender of civil liberty . . . Strengthener of loyalty . . . Pillar and stay of democratic government" "Upbuilder of the home . . . Nourisher of the community spirit . . . Art, letters, and science of the common people."

22. Reinhard Beck, Johann Besicken, John Byddell, Robert Copeland, Albrecht Dürer, Richard Grafton, Gregorius, F de Guinta, Urbanus Kaym, Philippe Le Noir, Johannes Muer, Oswalt, Michael Otter, Jacobus de Pfortzheim, Philippe Pigouchet, Jean du Pre, Henry Pepwell, John Rastell, John Reynes, John Siberch, Hugh Singleton, Jacobi Thanner, Michelet Topie, Wendelius Winter.

23. Rowland, "Architecture and the Automobile Industry," 201.

24. White, *Detroit News: 1873–1917*, 26.

25. Rowland, "Architecture of Your Church," 1.

26. Rowland, "Mr. Wirt C. Rowland on Modernism," 4.

27. Rowland, "On Gothic Architecture," 4.

28. Romanesque was a European building method employed during the sixth through twelfth centuries, at which point it was superseded by Gothic architecture. (Romanesque in England is sometimes referred to as Norman, and in Italy, as Lombard.)

29. Rowland, "Mr. Wirt C. Rowland on Modernism," 5.

30. Rowland, "An Influence of Glass on Architecture," 1.

31. Rowland, "Mr. Wirt C. Rowland on Modernism," 1.

32. Viollet-le-Duc, *Discourses on Architecture*, 182.

33. C. Howard Walker, "The Development of Wrought Iron," *American Architect* 113, no. 2196 (January 23, 1918): 82.

34. Albert Kahn, Architects and Engineers job number 641, dated 9-18-15: sheet number 20, sections through stairs; sheet number 21, elevations and details for lobbies, wood carved doors in lobby; and sheet number 28, interior details of stairway no. 3 (northeast corner, adjacent vice president's office, from 2nd to 3rd floor).

35. "Detroit Savings Bank Opens Branch at Woodward and Milwaukee Aves.," *Detroit Free Press*, March 4, 1917, 27.

36. The Detroit Savings Bank on Woodward at Milwaukee served as a bank for many years. It is now the home of Anew Life Prosthetics and Orthotics and co-owner Chris Casteel has done a remarkable job preserving and restoring the building's original fittings. Chris provided the author with a high-quality scanned copy of the original plans, without which the analysis included here would not have been possible.

37. "U. of M. Gets New Library through Work of Its Head," *Detroit Free Press*, May 2, 1915, C7.

38. William Warner Bishop (head librarian of the building), "New Library Building of the University of Michigan," *Library Journal* 44, no. 10 (October 1919): 633–37; "Opening of the New General Library of the University of Michigan," *Library Journal* 45, no. 3 (February 1, 1920): 107–9; and "The New Library Building of the University of Michigan," *Public Libraries* 25, no. 2 (February 1920): 78.

39. "Opening of the New General Library of the University of Michigan," *Library Journal*, 108. The cost

of "the building and equipment" is stated as $615,000 in the article by William Bishop and on the University of Michigan's website. Kahn is quoted in this article saying the cost per cubic foot was "25 cents." The cost divided by the square footage equals $0.29 per cubic foot. Kahn's figure may have been for the building alone, excluding equipment included in the $615,000 total.

40. In a March 24, 1932, letter to the Harvard Architectural School Alumni Association, Rowland attached a detailed list of buildings the design of which was in part or solely his responsibility. The University of Michigan Library he lists as "in collaboration with Ernest Wilby."

41. Kellie Woodhouse, "Eight Great Places to Study on University of Michigan's Campus," *Ann Arbor News*, December 13, 2011, online at www.annarbor.com/news/eight-great-places-to-study-on-university-of-michigans-campus/, retrieved September 18, 2014.

42. "Campus Tour (part 1)," So Midwestern at http://somidwestern.blogspot.com/2012/03/campus-tour-part-1.html, March 27, 2012, retrieved September 18, 2014.

43. Letter from Ernest Wilby to the secretary of the American Institute of Architects, Washington, DC, dated March 7, 1918. It reads in part: "Two years ago failing health compelled me to give up my practice of architecture in Detroit."

44. Letter from Ernest Wilby to E. L. Brant, executive secretary, Detroit chapter, American Institute of Architects, dated January 18th, 1938.

45. Letter from Ernest Wilby to Charles Ingham, secretary, American Institute of Architects, dated March 2nd, 1941.

46. "Wilby Made Fellow of Architects' Institute," *Weekly Bulletin of the Michigan Society of Architects* (May 20, 1941).

47. Letter from Wirt Rowland to Ernest Russell, chairman of the American Institute of Architects Jury of Fellows, received May 9, 1940.

48. Wilby, "Mystery and Philosophy of Architecture," 4.

49. Ibid., 1.

50. Ibid., 4.

51. Rowland, "Sunday's Child," 1; "Chapter Hears Wilby," *Weekly Bulletin of the Michigan Society of Architects* (March 4, 1941): 4.

52. Fiske Kimball, *American Architecture* (New York: Bobbs-Merrill, 1928), 197–98; Hyde, "Assembly-Line Architecture," 14.

53. Kimball, *American Architecture*, 197–98.

54. Ernest Wilby Application for Fellowship, American Institute of Architects, dated January 18, 1938, 3 and 4.

55. Letter to the Editor from Ernest Wilby, *Weekly Bulletin of the Michigan Society of Architects* (June 27, 1950): 8.

56. "Wayne Yates, Detroit Architect Dies," *Michigan Architect and Engineer* 10, no. 10 (October 1928); Plans for New Center Development Corporation Building [Fisher Building], Albert Kahn, Architects and Engineers, job 1378, sheets 28 and 30, dated 10-27-1927, "In Charge: Wayne Yates."

57. Plans for the Vinton Building, Albert Kahn, Architects and Engineers, job 0770, sheets 5, 6, 10, 11, 12, 18, and 21, dated 10-21-1916.

58. Cameron, *Training to Fly*, quoted from General George Pershing, p. 102.

59. Henry B. Joy, "Joy Field Not an Aviation School," letter to the editor, *Detroit Free Press*, April 30, 1917, 7.

60. Ibid.

61. Cameron, *Training to Fly*, 121.

62. Kennelly, "Biographical Memoir of George Owen Squier," 153.

63. Ibid., 152.

64. Winfield Scott Downs, editor, *Encyclopedia of American Biography*, "Edgar, Brigadier General Clinton Goodloe" (New York: American Historical Society, 1936), 13–15.

65. Aircraft Production Hearings before the Subcommittee of the Committee on Military Affairs, United States Senate, 65th Congress, 2nd Session, 1918, p. 5.

66. Albert Kahn, Architects and Engineers, list of jobs, job number 0693, C. G. Edgar residence, 1915; job number 0702, C. G. Edgar store building on Milwaukee Avenue, 1915.

67. Ibid.

68. The other fields—named for aviation pioneers, military personnel killed in aviation accidents, and a prominent military figure—are as follows: *Nonmilitary aviation pioneers*: Octave Chanute (Chanute Field, Rantoul, Illinois); Samuel Pierpont Langley (Langley Field, Hampton, Virginia); John Wise (Camp John Wise, near San Antonio, Texas); and Wilbur Wright (Wilbur Wright Field, Riverside/Dayton, Ohio); *Military personnel killed in aviation accidents*: Raynal C. Bolling (Bolling Field, Anacostia, Washington, DC); Private Sidney Johnson Brooks Jr. (Brooks Field, San Antonio, Texas); First Lieutenant Loren H. Call (Call Field, Wichita Falls, Texas); First Lieutenant Victor Carlstrom (Carlstrom Field, Arcadia, Florida); Cadet W. K. Carruthers (Carruthers Field, Benbrook, Texas—later renamed Benbrook Field); Second Lieutenant Rex Chandler (Chandler Field, Essington, Pennsylvania); Sergeant Victor Chapman (Chapman Field, Miami, Florida); Private Stephen H. Dorr (Dorr Field, Arcadia, Florida); Lieutenant Melchior McEwan Eberts (Eberts Field, Lonoke, Arkansas); Second Lieutenant E. L. Ellington (Ellington Field, Houston, Texas); Second Lieutenant Fredrick J. Gerstner (drowned while swimming ashore from a seaplane) (Gerstner Field, Lake Charles, Louisiana); Lieutenant Leighton Wilson Hazelhurst Jr. (Hazelhurst Field, Mineola, New York); Second Lieutenant George E. M. Kelly (Kelly Field, San Antonio, Texas); First Lieutenant Moss Lee Love (Love Field, Dallas, Texas); Second Lieutenant Peyton C. March Jr. (March Field, Riverside, California); Second Lieutenant Carl Spencer Mather (Mather Field, Sacramento, California); First Lieutenant Joseph D. Park (Park Field, Millington, Tennessee); Captain Dewitt J. Payne (Payne Field, West Point, Mississippi); Cadet Eugene Doak Penn (Penn Field, Austin, Texas); Second Lieutenant Henry Burnet Post (Post Field, Fort Sill, Lawton, Oklahoma); Second Lieutenant Perry C. Rich (Rich Field, near Waco, Texas); Second Lieutenant Lewis G. Rockwell (Rockwell Field, San Diego, California); First Lieutenant Cleo Jepson Ross (Ross Field, Arcadia, California); Corporal Frank S. Scott (Scott Field, Belleville, Illinois): Major Henry Souther (died of illness while acting director of Langley Field) (Souther Field, Americus, Georgia); First Lieutenant Walter R. Taliaferro (Camp Taliaferro, Fort Worth, Texas); Captain Ralph L. Taylor (Taylor Field, Montgomery, Alabama). *Prominent military figure*: Major General Alexander McDowell McCook (McCook Field, Dayton, Ohio).

This list was compiled from various sources, in particular, "Location of U.S. Aviation Fields," *New York Times*, July 21, 1918, 42. Where sources contemporary with construction of the fields were in disagreement with more recent sources, the contemporary information was used.

69. "Joy Field, Near Mt. Clemens, Chosen for U.S. Aero School," *Michigan Manufacturer and Financial Record* 19, no. 23 (June 2, 1917): 19; Plot Plan Signal Corps Mobilization Camps, U.S.A., job No. 809, Sheet 1A, Albert Kahn Architect, Detroit, May 19, 1917.

70. "Airfield to Be Opened July 11," *Detroit Free Press*, July 8, 1917, 4.

71. "Training at Selfridge Begins," *Air Service Journal*, July 19, 1917, 59.

72. Aircraft Production Hearings before the Subcommittee of the Committee on Military Affairs, United States Senate, 65th Congress, 2nd Session, 1918, 8.

73. Daniel B. Niederlander, "United States Aeronautical School, Kelly Field No. 2, South San Antonio, Texas," *Architectural Record* 45, no. 5 (May 1919): 444.

74. Ibid., 45.

75. "American and German Air Fleets," *Washington Post*, July 23, 1917, 6.

76. *American Contractor*, April 7, 1917, 75 and 77; "War Plans Outlined," *Washington Post*, May 27, 1917, 9.

77. In a March 21, 1917, letter from Albert Kahn to John H. DeKlyn, chief engineer for NACA, Kahn responded to a question from DeKlyn regarding electrical service in Detroit auto plants: "Practically all are run on a three-wire direct system 115 and 230 volts, the 230 volts being used for power and the 115 for lighting. Our engineers here advise the use of direct current for your problem."

78. Letter from Albert Kahn to Captain C. T. Waring, August 11, 1917, 2 (National Archives).

79. *Decisions of the War Department Board of Contract Adjustment*, vol. 3, part 1, 1920, GPO, 282.

80. Albert Kahn, Architects and Engineers, wartime contributions job list, Langley Field, project #0796, 1917–18; "Plan of Langley Field Aeronautical Experimental Station," Hampton, Virginia, Albert Kahn Architect, job 796, sheet 4, August 2, 1917.

81. Jody Cook, "A Place Called Langley Field," *Cultural Resource Management*, National Park Service, Washington, DC, vol. 23, no. 2 (2000): 30.

82. Arnold., "Evolution of Modern Office Buildings and Air Conditioning," 66–67.

83. Ibid., 68.

84. Ibid., 68–69.

85. National Register of Historic Places, Registration Form for US Army Rockwell Field Historic District, continuation sheet, section 8, page 10, dated May 1, 1990.

86. Sylvanus Griswold Morley, "Development of the Santa Fe Style of Architecture," *Santa Fe Magazine* 9, no. 7 (June 1915). Morely (1883–1948), of the School for American Archaeology in Santa Fe, was instrumental in promoting Santa Fe Style within New Mexico and distinguishing it from California Mission style.

87. Albert Kahn, Architects and Engineers, wartime contributions job list, Rockwell Field, project #0824, 1917.

88. Ibid., 81.

89. General Henry "Hap" Arnold's history of Rockwell Field, written in 1923, makes no mention of the

guard house being completed, while the National Register of Historic Places Registration Form for Rockwell Field lists the guard house/meter house as an original Kahn designed structure, little altered from its original form. Arnold may have overlooked this building as it served both Rockwell Field and the navy's base.

CHAPTER 4

1. Marc Braun, "What the GMC Building Plans Mean to Business," *Michigan Manufacturer and Financial Record*, April 12, 1919, 12.

2. "Keeping Track of Progress on General Motors Building Excavation," *Engineering News-Record*, April 8, 1920, 737.

3. Ibid.

4. Kahn, "Conserving Labor and Material," 731–34.

5. Kahn, "Architects Problems in Designing Office Buildings," 268.

6. "The Proposed Buhl Building, Detroit," *Buildings and Building Management* 23, no. 19 (September 17, 1923): 20, Chart III, columns E, F, G, and H.

7. A light court is generally defined as a courtyard that is deeper than it is wide. Each wing of the General Motors Building is separated by what would commonly be thought of as a courtyard, however, as these courtyards are square, the depth is no greater than the width, and so they are not considered light courts.

8. "General Motors Building Fills Up," *Detroit Free Press*, August 1, 1921, 14; Braun, "What the GMC Building Plans Mean to Business," *Michigan Manufacturer and Financial Record*, April 12, 1919, 13.

9. "GMC Occupies New Building," *Detroit Free Press*, November 25, 1920, 15.

10. Joseph Matte Jr., "Construction Details of General Motors Office Building," *Engineering News-Record* 86, no. 15 (April 14, 1921): 624–30.

11. Ibid.

12. "General Motors Building, Detroit, Mich.," *American Architect* 120, no. 2381 (November 23, 1921): 393–98 (plans), 401, and plates.

13. Edgell, *American Architecture of To-Day*, 348.

14. Rowland, "Architecture and the Automobile Industry," 203.

15. Ibid., 204.

16. Ibid.

17. Barrie, *Interview with Corrado Parducci*.

18. *Detroit Times*, November 17, 1929, as quoted in C. Monroe Burton, *History of Wayne County and the City of Detroit, Michigan* (Chicago: S. J. Clarke, 1930), 895.

19. The General Motors Building was originally named the Durant Building in honor of company president William C. Durant, which is why there are large emblems on the corners of the building containing the letter "D." Durant was ousted as president in February 1921 when the building was nearly complete; the name "Durant" was dropped, but the emblems were left in place.

20. "3 Groups Seek Hotel Building," *Detroit Free Press*, January 28, 1920, 5.

21. "Hotel Is Sold; Big Bank Goes to Woodward," *Detroit Free Press*, March 26, 1919, 1. At the time,

the bank was known as "First and Old Detroit National Bank," the name taken when Old Detroit National Bank merged with First National Bank in 1914. In January 1920, the bank merged with Central Savings Bank, and in January 1922, shortened its name to First National Bank of Detroit.

22. "First and Old Buys Pontchartrain," *Michigan Manufacturer and Financial Record*, March 29, 1919, 40.

23. "The Foundations of the Hotel Pontchartrain, Detroit," *American Architect* 120, no. 2374 (August 17, 1921): 127–31.

24. "Man, 33, 'Built' First National Bank," *Detroit Free Press*, March 12, 1922, 2; *Yale Alumni Weekly* 29, no. 1 (September 26, 1919): 17, and 29; no. 8 (November 14, 1919): 186; and *Sausalito News* 34, no. 11 (March 16, 1918): 2.

25. March 24, 1932, letter from Rowland to the Harvard Architectural School Alumni Association includes a detailed list of buildings the design of which was in part or solely his responsibility: "As Chief Designer, Preliminary Work & Exterior Design, First Unit of First National Bank Building, Detroit."

26. "Banks New Home Is Lofty Monument to Faith in the City," *Detroit Free Press*, March 12, 1922, 2.

27. "Announcement," advertisement by First National Bank, March 17, 1922.

28. "New Architectural Club of Michigan," *Michigan Architect and Engineer* 1, no. 9 (December 1919): 163.

29. "Michigan Architects Form Thumb Tack Club of Detroit," *American Architect* 116, no. 2291 (November 19, 1919): 639.

30. Ibid.

31. Under the numbering system in place at the time, the address was 83 Fort. After 1920, the address became 253 West Fort.

32. "Detroit's Thumb Tack Club is Booming," *Michigan Architect and Engineer* 2, no. 1 (January 1920): 9.

33. "Thumb Tack's House Warming Party," *Michigan Architect and Engineer* 2, no. 2 (February 1920): 35.

34. "Another Thumb Tack Party Scheduled," *Michigan Architect and Engineer* 2, no. 2 (February 1920): 41.

35. "Educational Work of the Thumb Tack Club," *Michigan Architect and Engineer* 2, no. 5 (May 1920): 87.

36. "Thumb Tack Club Notes," *Michigan Architect and Engineer* 2, no. 5 (May 1920): 91.

37. "New Thumb Tack Club Quarters Opened," *Michigan Architect and Engineer* 3, no. 2 (February 1921): 30.

38. "Thumb Tack Club's New Officers," *Michigan Architect and Engineer* 3, no. 12 (December 1921): 171.

39. "Personal Notes," *Michigan Architect and Engineer* 1, no. 9 (December 1919): 170.

40. "The Chamber Music Society," *All the Arts*, January 1920, 31; Clarence Monroe Burton, *City of Detroit Michigan, 1701–1922*, vol. 3, p. 148; Crathern, *Courage Was the Fashion*.

41. "Thomas Whitney Surette," *Bulletin of the Detroit Institute of Arts* 13, no. 3 (January 1919): 26.

42. "Surette Defends Glee Club Stand," *Harvard Crimson*, February 2, 1926, online at www.thecrimson.

com/article/1926/2/2/surette-defends-glee-club-stand-pthomas/.

43. Surette, "Music," 423–24.

44. Ibid., 425.

45. "Music Notes," *Detroit Free Press*, September 25, 1910.

46. "Music Notes," *Detroit Free Press*, October 28, 1917, C2.

47. Surette, "Music," 426.

48. Ibid., 427.

49. Ibid., 427–28.

50. Ibid., 431.

51. Ibid., 434–35.

52. "Musical Activities of the Chamber Music Society," *Bulletin of the Detroit Institute of Arts* 1, no. 8 (May 1920): 136.

53. In a postscript to Rowland's Thumb Tack Club article in *All the Arts*, Corey states Rowland "at one time occupied one of the organ positions of the city." An organist himself for the Fort Street Presbyterian Church, organ instructor and former dean of the American Guild of Organists, Corey was certainly in a position to know, but no further confirmation of Rowland's role as an organist in Detroit has surfaced.

54. Rowland, "An Architect's Attitude Towards Music," 5.

55. Ibid.

56. Edmund D. Fisher, "Result of Competition for Small City Bank," *Michigan Architect and Engineer* 3, no. 1 (January 1921): 5–7.

57. Just south of the United Savings Bank, at 751 Griswold (southwest corner of West Lafayette Boulevard and Griswold Street), is the former First State Bank, designed by Albert Kahn's office in 1924, after Rowland's departure from the firm. This bank features massive classical columns, ornate stone cornice, and parapet.

CHAPTER 5

1. Barrie, *Interview with Corrado Parducci*. Parducci states Rowland "was Albert Kahn's designer at one time, then went with [Smith, Hinchman, and Grylls] in order to free himself from the restrictions that Kahn imposed on his designers."

2. Smith, Hinchman, and Grylls presently operates under the name SmithGroupJJR.

3. Holleman and Gallagher, *Smith, Hinchman, and Grylls: 125 Years of Architecture and Engineering*, 61.

4. Ibid., 210–11.

5. Ibid., 95.

6. "Buhl Block Yields to Progress," *Michigan Manufacturer and Financial Record*, November 24, 1923, 4.

7. "Detroit's 'Wall Street' Sees $30,000,000 Improvement," *Michigan Manufacturer and Financial Record*, November 3, 1928, 1.

8. *Statistical Abstract of the United States, 1929*, "No. 829—Index Numbers of Building Material Prices and Construction Costs," 846.

9. Letter from Arthur Buhl to T. H. Hinchman, May 11, 1922.

10. Ibid., 265.

11. Amedeo Leone's Application for Membership in the American Institute of Architects, January 7, 1942.

12. Holleman, *Wirt C. Rowland Exhibition Catalog*, 13, references Thomas Holleman's interview of Amedeo Leone.

13. Holleman, *Wirt C. Rowland Exhibition Catalog*, 15.

14. "Personal Notes," *Michigan Architect and Engineer*, July 1922, 108.

15. Letter from Clair Ditchy to Jury of Fellows, American Institute of Architects, August 2, 1956, and letter from Earl G. Meyer to same, September 19, 1956, Amedeo Leone 1956 Fellowship Application.

16. Original Smith, Hinchman, and Grylls building plan for Fyfe building, job 3476. March 9, 1918, and Amedeo Leone 1965 Fellowship Application, "Nominee's Achievement in Architectural Design."

17. Holleman and Gallagher, *Smith, Hinchman, and Grylls: 125 Years of Architecture and Engineering*, 106.

18. *The Buhl Building*, section "Advantages of the Latin Cross Plan," Buhl Land Co., Detroit, 1925.

19. "The Proposed Buhl Building, Detroit," *Buildings and Building Management* 23, no. 19 (September 17, 1923): 20.

20. *The Buhl Building*, section "Something about Rentals," Buhl Land Co., Detroit, 1925.

21. John C. Breiby, "Design in the Drafting Room, III," *Pencil Points*, June 1925, 67.

22. Ibid., 72.

23. Approximately 5,000 sq. ft. compared with 2,600 sq. ft. as per measurements taken from the "Plan of 4th to 16th Floors," sheet 10 of the original Smith, Hinchman, and Grylls November 1, 1923, drawings for the Buhl Building.

24. Kahn, "Thirty Minutes with American Architects and Architecture," 5.

25. A six-foot-high band of granite clad the structure from the sidewalk up to the point where the terra-cotta began.

26. The ad appeared in *Pencil Points* and others in 1927; in fairness, the Fyfe Shoe Store Building, designed several years earlier by Amedeo Leone, used a very similar terra-cotta throughout.

27. *Indian and Mexican Handicraft*, 55.

28. Among these were *The Cliff Dwellers and Pueblos* by Rev. Stephen Denison Peet, 1899 (shelved in the architecture section of the Detroit Public Library); *The Swastika* by Thomas Wilson, Smithsonian Institution, 1896 (454 pages!), which was the subject of a book review in the *American Architect and Building News* of February 26, 1898, p. 70; *A Study of Pueblo Pottery as Illustrative of Zuni Culture-Growth*, by Frank Hamilton Cushing, US Bureau of Ethnology, 1886; and *The Cliff Dwellers of the Mesa Verde Southwestern Colorado*, by G. Nordenskiold, Mesa Verde Museum Association, 1893.

29. It's puzzling that Hitler chose the swastika as an emblem for the Third Reich, considering that it was closely associated with a non-Aryan race and, by the 1930s, commonly appeared on "cheap, plated, factory-made" jewelry.

30. Rowland, "Vacation from Architecture," 1.

31. Meier, "Eight Years of Planning for Profit, The Stott Building, Detroit,"45–47.

32. "Building Planning Service," *Buildings and Building Management*, September 3, 1923; and "The Proposed Buhl Building, Detroit," *Buildings and Building Management*, September 17, 1923, 13.

33. Buhl Building sheets 39, 39A, and 40 through 46. All architectural drawings for the Buhl Building were checked by team leader Joseph Leinweber and countersigned by William Kapp.

34. "Artist's Work Is Widespread," *Detroit Free Press*, May 10, 1931, 18.

35. *Atlantic Terra Cotta* 8, no. 6 (March 1926); though this article refers specifically to the Second National Bank of Saginaw Building, constructed six months later, there is no question Rowland would have provided at least the same degree of oversight for the Buhl Building.

36. Letter from T. H. Hinchman, Smith, Hinchman, and Grylls, "Comparison—Original & Revised Bids, Buhl Land Company," job #4877, 1-8-1924.

37. "Contracts Let for Buhl Bldg.," *Detroit Free Press*, January 16, 1924; and "Award Buhl Contract," *Michigan Manufacturer and Financial Record*, January 20, 1924.

38. "Building Completed without a Strike by American Plan Firm," *Detroit Saturday Night*, May 2, 1925, section 3.

39. Ibid.

40. "New Buhl Building, Detroit's Tallest Skyscraper, Opens Doors," *Detroiter*, May 4, 1925, 32.

41. Letter from W. F. Austin, President of W. E. Wood Company, to R. P. Shorts of Second National Bank of Saginaw, July 29, 1925: "Office buildings are usually 30% to 35% rented when completed."

42. Holleman and Gallagher, *Smith, Hinchman, and Grylls: 125 Years of Architecture and Engineering*, 105.

43. "Management Policies in the Buhl Building, Detroit," *Buildings and Building Management*, May 6, 1929, 52–66.

44. "Detroit Chapter Awards Medals," *Michigan Architect and Engineer*.

45. "Fiftieth Annual Report of the Public Lighting Commission, City of Detroit," 1945, 24 and 32.

46. Ibid., 29.

47. Attribution of the Palmer Park substation to Rowland: Holleman, *Wirt C. Rowland Exhibition Catalog*, 31n52.

48. Substations designed by Smith, Hinchman, and Grylls (but not necessarily Rowland) between 1923 and 1931 include: 1923—Palmer Park; 1925—Townsend, Walton, Woodward Terminal, and Wyoming; 1926—Connor, Custer, LaBelle, Ludden and Porter; 1927—Joy Rd. (1), Mullet, and Schaefer; 1928—Riopelle and Trombley; 1929—Leesville and Montrose; 1930—Greenfield, Mt. Elliott, and Turner; 1931—Joy Rd. (2), and Philip.

49. "History of the Michigan Bell Telephone Company," online at www.fundinguniverse.com/company-histories/michigan-bell-telephone-co-history/.

50. Michigan Bell figures from *Detroit Free Press*, "Michigan Bell Telephone Company Congratulates the *Detroit Free Press*," May 10, 1931, 3.

51. "Michigan Bell Telephone, Company to Spend $2,000,000 in Detroit for Extensions to Meet Enlarged Demand," *Wall Street Journal*, June 12, 1925, 2.

52. Central offices might house one or more "exchanges" and were usually named after one of the exchanges hosted. The first two letters of the exchange's name were included in the phone numbers of connected subscribers. For example, the exchanges *HOgarth, LEnox, MAdison, NIagara, PIngree, UNiversity,* and *VInewood* were each housed in central offices bearing the name of the exchange.

CAdillac, *CHerry*, and *RAndolf* were all located in the main Michigan Bell building on Cass Avenue at State Street.

53. "Our Thirty-Four Buildings in Detroit Would Make a Fair Sized City," *Michigan Bell*, February 1929, 28.

54. "Our Niagara and Pingree Offices Differ from Other Installations," *Michigan Bell*, December 1929, 17.

55. "Royal Oak versus Greece," *Mouthpiece* (*Michigan Bell*), April 1928.

56. Rowland, "Real Progress," 15.

57. A biforate arch contains beneath it two smaller arches, and all three begin at (or "spring" from) the same level. This arrangement was a common feature of Romanesque architecture and came into vogue again during the Renaissance (see the Palazzo Medici-Riccardi in Florence, Italy).

58. Weary and Alford later designed the Fifth Third Bank Building (1930) at 136 East Michigan Avenue in Kalamazoo and the Heritage Tower (1931) at 25 West Michigan Mall in Battle Creek.

59. The original firm named D. H. Burnham and Company was founded in 1891 by noted Chicago architect Daniel Hudson Burnham, designer of the Ford Building and Dime Savings Bank (Chrysler House) Building in Detroit. After Burnham's death in 1912, the firm continued under surviving partner, Ernest R. Graham, and Burnham's sons, Hubert and Daniel Jr.; the name was changed to Graham, Burnham and Company (the firm that designed Detroit's David Whitney Building). The Burnham brothers left the firm around 1917 and founded D. H. Burnham and Company.

60. The Second National Bank of Saginaw, Building Committee Minutes, September 21, 1923, through July 30, 1925, on file at the Castle Museum of Saginaw, Michigan.

61. Ibid.

62. Ibid.

63. Sketch submitted by Fred Smith to the building committee meeting of February 1, 1924; in the collection of the Castle Museum, Saginaw, Michigan.

64. Undated sketch showing the Washington Avenue and Genesee Avenue corner; in the collection of the Castle Museum, Saginaw, Michigan.

65. The Second National Bank of Saginaw was Corrado Parducci's second job as a self-employed sculptor working in Michigan; Barrie, *Interview with Corrado Parducci*.

66. "Modern Romanesque, Second National Bank Building, Saginaw, Michigan," *Atlantic Terra Cotta* 8, no. 6 (March 1926): 1, 11, with plates.

67. Ibid.

68. *Architectural Forum*, June 1928, 855–56.

69. Smith, Hinchman, and Grylls memo from L. L. Smith and W. E. Kapp to Fred Smith, September 10, 1924, p. 1, included within building committee minutes.

70. The Peninsular State Bank at 132 West Fort, by Donaldson and Meier (*American Bankers Assoc. 38th Annual Convention*, 1912, 54); National Bank of Commerce at 144 West Fort, by Albert Kahn, Architects and Engineers; and Bank of Detroit at 241 West Fort, by Giaver, Dinkelberg, and Ellington (*Michigan Architect and Engineer*, January 1921, 17) have been demolished.

71. Edmund D. Fisher, "Result of Competition for Small City Bank," *Michigan Architect and Engineer* 3, no. 1 (January 1921): 5.

72. Leo D. Heaphey, "Branch State Banks in Detroit," *Michigan Manufacturer and Financial Record*, June 17, 1922, 7 and 8.

73. *Baist's Real Estate Atlas of Detroit*, 1923.

74. Architectural historian Thomas Holleman, in his book *Smith, Hinchman, and Grylls: 125 Years of Architecture and Engineering* (1978), attributes the George Harrison Phelps building to William Kapp. Holleman is an exceptional researcher and, as an employee of Smith, Hinchman, and Grylls at the time his book was written, had access to certain material that no longer exists. The original drawings for the building are countersigned—authorizing them for use in construction—by William Kapp. Kapp frequently countersigned drawings for buildings designed by Rowland, but it seems unlikely he would countersign his own work. Kapp's 1946 fellowship application to the American Institute of Architects lists twelve buildings designed by him under "Works," including three during Rowland's tenure at Smith, Hinchman, and Grylls: Jefferson Avenue Presbyterian Church (1921 version), University Club (1930), and Skillman Library (1930). The George Phelps Building was not listed. The design of the building is exceptionally sophisticated and entirely consistent with Rowland's work at the time. Given the importance and complexity of the project, it would almost certainly have been entrusted to Rowland. In any event, the working relationship between the two men was so close that the distinction is likely moot.

75. Smith, Hinchman, and Grylls plans for the Studio and Office Building for George Harrison Phelps, Inc., job 5498, July 15, 1925, sheets 8, 12 and 13.

76. Kahn, "Color in Bank Buildings," 8.

77. Rowland, "Mr. Wirt C. Rowland on Modernism."

78. "Builds Model Banking Home," *Michigan Manufacturer and Financial Record*, December 25, 1926, 6.

79. *Mouthpiece* (*Michigan Bell*), various articles dating from 1925 through 1931; Holleman and Gallagher, *Smith, Hinchman, and Grylls: 125 Years of Architecture and Engineering*, 212–13; *Detroiter* and *Michigan Manufacturer and Financial Record*, multiple articles 1926, 1928 through 1930.

80. "12 Stories to Be Added to Telephone Co. Building," *Detroit Free Press*, March 27, 1927, pt. 4, p. 1.

81. *Journal of the Electrical Workers and Operators* printed a letter in its October 1919 issue from a Bell worker in Grand Rapids, Michigan, who referred to the company as "Ma Bell" (144–45); Michigan Bell's official journal *The Mouthpiece* ran an article in 1922 that referred to the company as "Ma Bell."

82. Jefferson Avenue Presbyterian Church, *One Hundred Years of Service: 1854–1954: A Review of the Historical Background and Development of the Jefferson Avenue Presbyterian Church* (Detroit, 1954).

83. "Church, Where Many First Families Worshiped, Sold," *Detroit Free Press*, December 29, 1921, 22.

84. JAPC Building fund pledges, sheets 45 and 61.

85. Minutes of the Jefferson Avenue Presbyterian Church, 88.

86. *Michigan Architect and Engineer*, 2, no. 11 (November 1920): plates 71–74.

87. Letter from Raymond Dykema to James T. Shaw, July 18, 1922.

88. William E. Kapp, American Institute of Architects Nomination for Fellowship by Chapter, October 24, 1946, Nominee's Achievement in Architectural Design.

89. The continued haggling was too much for Hinchman, who, as a trustee of the church and principal of Smith, Hinchman, and Grylls, had to represent interests that, on occasion, were opposed. In

November, Hinchman wrote to James Shaw, chairman of the trustees: "Dear Jim, I do not write to shirk my responsibilities, but this dual personality business gets on my nerves. Is there any way in which you could get a good trustee in place of myself" (letter from Theodore Hinchman to James Shaw, November 5, 1924). The situation was resolved by having Maxwell Grylls—the only partner of Smith, Hinchman, and Grylls not a member of Jefferson Avenue Presbyterian Church—represent the architectural firm in its dealings with the church (from the JAPC corporation minutes for meeting held May 5, 1925, and letter from John Russel to James Shaw dated June 26, 1925).

90. *Michigan Architect and Engineer*, July 1931, 87–88.

91. Statement of charges, Smith, Hinchman, and Grylls #4873, May 28, 1925.

92. *Through the Ages*, National Association of Marble Dealers, vol. 7, no. 3, July 1929, 21.

93. Holleman and Gallagher, *Smith, Hinchman, and Grylls: 125 Years of Architecture and Engineering*, 120.

94. Rowland, "Human—All Too Human, Chapter II," 4.

95. W. E. Kapp, "The Jefferson Avenue Presbyterian Church," March 19, 1926.

96. *American Architect* (December 31, 1924); *Architect and Engineer* (1927); *Architecture* (September 1927); and *The Architectural Forum* (March 1929).

97. March 20, 1926.

98. Architectural Book Publishing Company, New York.

99. Florence Davies, "In the Gothic Spirit," *Detroit News*, December 18, 1938.

100. "Specifications for Building Work for Church and Parish House, Northeast Corner of Jefferson & Burns Avenue," Smith, Hinchman, and Grylls Order number 4873, February 5, 1923, p. 4-B.

101. Ibid., 23-A.

102. Jefferson Avenue Presbyterian Church, *One Hundred Years of Service,* 35.

103. Rowland, "Architecture of Your Church," 4.

104. Holleman and Gallagher, *Smith, Hinchman, and Grylls: 125 Years of Architecture and Engineering*, 108; Barrie, *Interview with Corrado Parducci*.

CHAPTER 6

1. Viollet-le-Duc, *Discourses on Architecture*, 411–12.

2. Hambidge, "Symmetry and Proportion in Greek Art," 599.

3. Ibid., 597.

4. William H. Goodyear, "Dynamic Symmetry and the Greek Vase, a Communication from Professor William H. Goodyear of the Department of Fine Arts, Brooklyn Museum," *American Architect* 118, no. 2344 (November 24, 1920): 669.

5. "Jay Hambidge Dies," *American Architect*, January 30, 1924, 22.

6. "The Relation of Painting to Architecture," *American Architect* 118, no. 2349 (December 29, 1920): 847.

7. Ibid.

8. Ibid.

9. Hambidge, "Dynamic Symmetry and Modern Architecture," 343–45.

10. "Art: Re-Discovered Principles of Greek Design," *New York Times*, July 4, 1920, 43.

11. Eleanor Jewett, "Columbus of New Key to Art—Square Root of 5—Is Here," April 5, 1921, 25; and

Jewett, "Square Root of 5 Root of All Art, Says Jay Hambidge," April 10, G10.

12. "Dynamic Symmetry: The Rediscovery of the Basic Principles of Greek Art," *Scientific American* 4, no. 1 (July 1921).

13. "University of Michigan News," *Michigan Architect and Engineer* 3, no. 5 (May 1921): 68.

14. Oscar L. McMurry, George Eggers, and Charles A. McMurry, *Teaching of Industrial Arts in the Elementary School* (New York: Macmillan, 1923), plate 4.

15. An article in the July 8, 1928, *Free Press* quoted J. W. Fraser, Chrysler sales manager, describing how the vehicles were "scientifically designed": "careful study has been devoted to the Greek theory of dynamic symmetry which is, in part, that all lines should be placed in sympathetic and harmonious relationship with one another" ("New '65' and '75' Models Announced by Chrysler," 56).

16. *Life*, April 15, 1926, 27.

17. "Chiffon Hose Has New Heel; Novel Lines Achieve a Flattering Effect for All Ankles," *New York Times*, March 21, 1926, X12.

18. Detroit Public Schools, *Course of Study, Art Education, Elementary Schools, Grades One to Eight*, Detroit Board of Education, 1925, 405.

19. *University of Michigan, Colleges of Engineering and Architecture, General Announcement, 1926–1927*, Ann Arbor, 1926, 76.

20. Wilford S. Conrow, "What Next in Art and Architecture?" 11.

21. Leo D. Heaphey, "Branch State Banking in Detroit," *Michigan Manufacturer and Financial Record*, June 17, 1922, 7.

22. "New Trust Company Here Backed by Ford," *New York Times*, May 19, 1925, 1.

23. "Ford Banks in Gotham," *Los Angeles Times*, May 19, 1925, 1.

24. "New Trust Company Here Backed by Ford," *New York Times*, May 19, 1925, 1.

25. "Guardian Trust Will Open in July," *Detroiter*, June 15, 1925, 9.

26. Ibid., 9, 19.

27. Ibid.

28. "The Fourth Important Commission within Nine Months for the Building Planning Service," *Buildings and Building Management*, January 7, 1924, 18–19.

29. "Why Frank Blair Grins," *Michigan Manufacturer and Financial Record*, April 23, 1927, 6.

30. Stock exchange practices: hearings before the Committee on Banking and Currency, United States Senate, Seventy-Third Congress, second session, on S. Res. 84 (72d Congress), 1934, p. 4766.

31. Ibid.

32. Carlyle Van Dyke, "Wings Enlarge Scope of Business," *Brooklyn Daily Eagle*, August 7, 1927, 81.

33. Ibid.; and "From the President," Union Trust Company, Detroit, 1927, Detroit *Saturday Night Press*, 9.

34. Cassidy, "The Southwest Develops Native Architecture," 24; and "American Life Buys Union Trust Building," *Detroiter*, October 11, 1926, 18.

35. While banking facilities in Detroit grew faster than those of any other leading city in the country between 1911 and 1925, Detroit's banks were merely attempting to keep up with the extraordinary growth of the area's industrial production. According to the US Census Bureau, the value of products manufactured within Detroit more than tripled between 1914 and 1925. The increase in value of

building permits between 1910 and 1925 was 959 percent and wages paid to workers increased 300 percent from 1914 to 1923. "Detroit's Banks Lead Country in Growth," *Michigan Manufacturer and Financial Record*, March 5, 1927, 5.

36. Charles D. Kelley, "Union Trust Interests to Organize New Bank," *Detroit News*, November 15, 1925, pt. 2, p. 1.

37. "Michigan Business Personified," *Michigan Manufacturer and Financial Record*, June 6, 1928, 14.

38. "Banking House to be 40 Stories," *Michigan Manufacturer and Financial Record*, April 9, 1927, 25.

39. Minutes of the Special Congregational Meeting, November 28, 1918, 87–90; and minutes of a meeting of the members of Jefferson Avenue Church Corporation, January 31, 1924, 3.

40. Richards, "Trust Building Opens Tuesday," 3.

41. According to the *Detroiter*, there were thirty-three office buildings with a value of just over $8 million constructed in Detroit in 1924. In 1925, there were twenty buildings valued at just over $7 million, and in 1926: seventeen buildings, $7 million ("Detroit Third in Building," February 11, 1929, 9).

42. Rowland's application to the Harvard University Department of Architecture Alumni Association, March 24, 1932.

43. Rowland, "Mr. Wirt C. Rowland on Modernism," 6.

44. Perry, *Adventures in Ceramics*, 122.

45. Ibid., 121–27.

46. Viollet-le-Duc, *Discourses on Architecture*, 453.

47. Ibid., 454 and 458.

48. Ibid., 454.

49. W. C. Richards, "Trust Building Opens Tuesday," *Detroit Free Press*, March 31, 1929, 1 and 3.

50. Rowland, "Real Progress," 15. The quote from Rowland within context: "From two authors of the present day, divergent in some of their opinions, we may find something of interest and profit, because they deal with underlying motives of thought.

"Babbit of Harvard deals with romanticism versus classicism. It was from his various writings that I achieved my rudimentary understanding of the Greek idea of humanism. It has helped me to appreciate Greek architecture toward which my sympathies have always leaned. March Phillips [*sic*], an English author, has contributed to a view of the essential difference between the emotional Orient and the intellectual West, making the point that color in its essential sense is the product of emotion, and that form and the satisfaction of its combination is intellectual.

"Be it far from me to dispute either of them. I can see that from the Middle Ages down architecture has been much dominated by romanticism; that the only discipline exerted upon the imagination was comprised of the rudest ideas of construction; that any order which was brought about resulted from sheer necessity. But with regard to the undoubted difference between eastern emotionalism and the western intellectualism of form, the latter may still be sub-divided into both intellect and emotion, and thus prove the presence of romanticism in all architecturally creative work since the time of Pericles, and an absence of the ethical attitude."

51. Phillipps, *Form and Colour*, 60.

52. Ibid., 83.

53. Rowland, "New Note in Architecture Struck."

54. See Kingston Forbes, *The Principles of Automobile Body Design* (Philadelphia: Ware Bros., 1922), 324; and Hearn, *Exotics and Retrospectives*, 163.

55. Kahn, "Color in Bank Buildings."

56. On his first trip to the West in 1940, Rowland visited the Grand Canyon and commented, "The color of the walls is less vivid than often pictured," revealing, perhaps, that printed representations exaggerated its colorfulness. Color postcards were produced from black-and-white photographs to which color was artificially added.

57. W. C. Richards, "Trust Building Opens Tuesday," *Detroit Free Press*, March 31, 1929, 3.

58. Ibid.

59. "Form $12,500,000 Bank Group to Serve Michigan Business," *Michigan Manufacturer and Financial Record*, February 12, 1927, 1.

60. "Detroit Guardian Group Forms New Bank," *Banker's Magazine* 114, no. 3 (March 1927): 503.

61. "Lord Heads New Bank," *Detroiter*, May 9, 1927; and Report No. 1455: Stock Exchange Practices; Hearings before the Committee on Banking and Currency, United States Senate, Seventy-Third Congress, second session, on Senate Res. 84, 73d Congress, 1934, 233.

62. The Smith, Hinchman, and Grylls job number for the Guardian Group Bank (5851) was earlier than that of the Greater Penobscot Building (5865). This is likely due to the fact that Smith, Hinchman, and Grylls was asked first to provide a rough design for the large banking lobby to secure approval from Guardian Group. Once this approval was secured, the Murphy Company removed the entire job from Donaldson and Meier and turned it over to Smith, Hinchman, and Grylls. The plan set for the Greater Penobscot Building was completed and dated May 16, 1927, and the set for the Guardian Group Bank was dated March 22, 1928.

63. "Union Trust to Build Magnificent New Home," *Detroit News*, April 10, 1927, pt. 2, p. 1. The description "a cathedral devoted to finance" was used later that year as a caption beneath a sketch of the proposed building appearing in the Union Trust Company's thirty-sixth anniversary booklet. The quote was attributed there to the *Detroit News*.

64. "Union Trust Co. Will Add Banking Facilities," *Michigan Manufacturer and Financial Record*, April 16, 1927, 12.

65. Ibid.

66. Blair's fascination with aviation was sparked in 1925 when an employee of the bank, former army captain Ray Collins, took him for a short ride. Frank W. Blair, "How I Became Interested in Aviation," *Detroiter*, July 4, 1927, 12.

67. "Union Trust Gets Plane," *Detroiter*, November 7, 1927.

68. Blair had known Sanger for some time, as the two men in 1923 organized in Detroit a joint stock land bank under the Federal Farm Loan Act. "Detroit Joint Stock Land Bank," *Wall Street Journal*, April 23, 1923, 4.

69. Stock Exchange Practices: Hearings before the Committee on Banking and Currency, United States Senate, Seventy-Third Congress, second session, on S. Res. 84, 72d Congress, 1934,4780.

70. "Union Commerce Investment Co., later known as Union Commerce Corporation, created to unify

the management of the Union Trust Co. and the National Bank of Commerce was organized under the laws of the State of Delaware on May 17, 1928, as a holding company." "Delaware was selected as the State of incorporation since the Michigan law did not permit of incorporation for the purposes desired." Report No. 1455: Stock Exchange Practices: Hearings before the Committee on Banking and Currency, United States Senate, Seventy-Third Congress, second session, on Senate Res. 84, 73d Congress, 1934, 234.

71. As a consequence of its merger with Union Trust, the National Bank of Commerce planned to move into the new Union Trust Building and sell the Albert Kahn–designed building on Fort Street that had been its headquarters since 1917.

72. William S. Wolfe, "Foundation Plans Changed after Water Enters Excavation," *Engineering News-Record* 99, no. 26 (December 29, 1927): 1034.

73. Ibid., 1035.

74. "Two Men Die on Construction Job," *Niagara Falls Gazette*, May 3, 1927, 1; "Gas Traps Two Men in Shaft," May 3, 1927, unidentified newspaper clipping in the archives of the Penobscot Building.

75. Robert M. Baughey, "Penobscot 'Sand Hogs' Risk Lives in Earth," 1927, undated and unidentified newspaper clipping in the archives of the Penobscot Building.

76. William S. Wolfe, "Simultaneous Steel Erection and Basement Excavation on 40-Story Building," *Engineering News-Record*, July 4, 1929, 4–8.

77. Edmund D. Fisher, "Result of Competition for Small City Bank," *Michigan Architect and Engineer* 3, no. 1 (January 1921), 5.

78. Wolfe, "Simultaneous Steel Erection and Basement Excavation on 40-Story Building," 8.

79. Rowland, "New Note in Architecture Struck."

80. "Ten Thousand Tons of Steel," *Michigan Manufacturer and Financial Record*, December 17, 1927, advertisement, unnumbered page.

81. Ibid.

82. Wolfe, "Simultaneous Steel Erection and Basement Excavation on 40-Story Building," 6.

83. Tom L. Munger, "Working on Top of the World," *Detroit Saturday Night*, February 25, 1928, 1–2 and 11.

84. Ibid.

85. Loren T. Baker, "New Penobscot Building Is Formally Dedicated," *Detroiter*, April 9, 1928, 6.

86. Ibid.

87. Davies, "Wait and See."

88. Ibid.

89. "The Penobscot Building Opens," *Detroit News*, October 22, 1928, 1 and 2.

90. "Union Trust Building is Ready," *Detroit News*, March 31, 1929, Union Trust Section, 2.

91. "30,000 Inspect New Union Trust Building," *Michigan Manufacturer and Financial Record*, April 6, 1929.

92. "New Structural Methods and Materials Distinguish the Union Trust Building," *Buildings and Building Management* 29, no. 12 (June 17, 1929): 29.

93. "Drafting for Metal Work, Part III," *Metal Arts*, January 1929, 11.

94. "Founded on Principles of Faith," *Through the Ages* 7, no. 3 (July 1929): 15.

95. "The Modern Bank Dresses Up," *Bankers' Magazine* 120, no. 1 (January 1930): 151.

96. Kahn, "Color in Bank Buildings."

97. Ibid.

98. Ibid.

99. Perry, *Adventures in Ceramics*, 140.

100. "Recognizing Good Craftsmanship," *American Architect*, December 5, 1928, 14.

101. Perry, *Adventures in Ceramics,* 140–41.

102. Davies, "Wait and See."

103. A. E. Hanson, "The Daring Break from Bronze to Monel Metal," *Michigan Manufacturer and Financial Record*, supplement, 43, no.13, March 30, 1929, 32.

104. Rowland, *Metal Work, Union Guardian Building*, unpublished two-page memo included in correspondence from Rowland to Edward Hensen, Taliesin, Spring Green, Wisconsin, July 7, 1931.

105. "Drafting for Metal Work, Part III," *Metal Arts*, January 1929, 14.

106. *Michigan Manufacturer and Financial Record*, supplement, 43, no.13, March 30, 1929, 34.

107. Rowland, *Metal Work, Union Guardian Building*.

108. "Drafting for Metal Work, Part IV," *Metal Arts*, 1929, 235–36.

109. Ibid., 237.

110. The claim of first air-conditioned skyscraper is based on the Union Trust Building's height of forty stories. The American Society of Engineers lists the first United States air-conditioned high-rise office building as the Milam Building in San Antonio, Texas. It opened in January 1928, but is only twenty-one stories tall, which does not meet most definitions of "skyscraper." On the other hand, the Union Trust was not fully air-conditioned, so another building holds the title of first fully air-conditioned skyscraper.

111. Al Chase, "Detroit Grows Air Minded in Its Building," *Chicago Daily Tribune*, October 6, 1929, B9.

112. Ibid.

113. *Michigan Manufacturer and Financial Record*, supplement, 43, no.13, March 30, 1929, 74.

114. Ibid.

115. Rowland, *Metal Work, Union Guardian Building*.

CHAPTER 7

1. Legend has it that in order to secure the red Numidian marble for the building's lobby, Rowland traveled to Africa to reopen a mine that had been closed for thirty years. There is no evidence that this actually occurred and, in fact, Kleber Quarries in Algeria provided Numidian red marble for other buildings during the same time period. The marble floor of the Crypt Church (Our Lady of the Catacombs) in the National Shrine of the Immaculate Conception in Washington, DC, contains red Numidian marble (and walls and ceiling of Pewabic tile); it was completed in 1928. The wainscoting on the sanctuary walls of Saint James Roman Catholic Church in Lakewood (Cleveland), Ohio, are of red Numidian. The church was constructed between 1929 and 1936.

Red Numidian was used in the Retiring Rooms for both the Senate and House chambers of the

Minnesota capitol, built from 1896 to 1905; in numerous mansions built around the turn of the century; and in Detroit's Wayne County Building, completed in 1902. A May 20, 1916, article, "Marble as Used in Modern Building," which appeared in *Michigan Manufacturer and Financial Record*, refers to brecciated marbles, stating: "Breccia Violet and Red Numidian are familiar varieties of the marble."

A half-page article on "North African Marble" in the November 1922 issue of the journal *Stone* notes the use in ancient Rome "of North African or Numidian marble produced in the French Colonies of Algeria and Tunis, and in Morocco." "The colors of the marbles range from warm yellow of the Gialla Antico, or Juane Antique so popular in ancient Rome, to the brilliant red of Breche Sanguine for which Kleber and Kristel (Algeria) are noted." Describing quarries from which these varieties were then available, the article stated: "Breche Sanguine is a very handsome dark red marble, with pale red fragments, shading off into the dark red ground. It is quarried at Kleber and Kristel (Algeria), and was employed in parts of the interior trim of Westminster Cathedral and in the Trocadero."

The July issue of the same journal contains a brief description of red Numidian used in the Searles Castle, built in 1893, with a story oddly similar to the Rowland legend about the quarry being reopened: "There was a special shipment of Numidian marble blocks quarried for this work, among the first taken from the famous classical quarries reopened after being lost and forgotten for nearly two thousand years."

Rowland's overseas travel is well documented. He visited Algeria in 1908 and again in 1930 during his extensive tours of Europe. There is no record, however, of his having traveled there during the planning and construction of the Union Trust Building.

2. Rowland, "New Note in Architecture Struck."

3. Surette, "Music," 427.

4. Rowland, "Music and the Architect," 1.

5. Hambidge, *Dynamic Symmetry and the Greek Vase*, 52.

6. The figures illustrating the use of dynamic symmetry in the design of the Union Trust Building (as well as subsequent illustrations for later buildings) are intended to provide evidence that Rowland's designs are consistent with the use of dynamic symmetry. There is no direct evidence of Rowland's use of the method in the form of, say, preliminary sketches or drawings showing compass lines or specific notes, as these have all been lost or discarded. Consequently, his method must be inferred from surviving building plans. There are two obstacles to this approach, the first being the lack of precision in hand-drawn plans (as compared with drawings executed by computer), and the second being compromises made by the designer to vary proportions from the ideal due to cost considerations.

Hand-drawn plans were carefully prepared to present an accurate portrayal of the structure to be built, but actual construction was based on the dimensions noted on the plans, not the drawing per se. The accuracy of drawings varied greatly with scale. An elevation depicting the entire facade of a building would accurately portray the height and width of the structure, but inaccuracies in the location and dimensions of small features might be quite significant. It was for this reason that plan sets included detail drawings of individual features.

Regardless of the method employed, designers were constantly faced with making compromises for practical or cost reasons. Building components, from steel beams to floor tiles, were manufactured in standard sizes and a designer would reasonably be expected to alter "ideal" dimensions suggested by a geometric figure to the nearest standard size as a practical expedient, particularly if the difference would not be noticeable to the eye.

These two issues, inaccuracy and expediency, complicate the ability to demonstrate that a drawn plan matches perfectly with a geometric figure. In many cases with Rowland's designs, the match between the ideal and the plan as drawn is exceedingly good; in other cases, the fit is quite close, but arguably off in certain minor respects. It is impossible to know if the mismatch is a drawing error, a compromise for expediency, or an indication that dynamic symmetry was not employed.

On the other hand, there is abundant evidence Rowland used dynamic symmetry as the basis for his designs (after 1926); to prove otherwise would require that each and every example of his having used the method be shown to be in error.

7. Niagara Falls info website, "Illumination of the Falls," at www.niagarafallsinfo.com/history-item. php?entry_id=1517&current_category_id=128, accessed February 12, 2015.

8. "Union Trust to Make Sky a Kaleidoscope of Color," *Detroit News*, May 19, 1929 (Burton Collection).

9. Phillipps, *Form and Colour*, 86.

10. Ibid., 65–66.

11. Ibid., 83.

12. Justice has not been done here to the analysis of color in art and architecture by March Phillipps. A deeper understanding of the principles elaborated by Phillipps and employed by Rowland on the Union Trust Building may be had by reading *Form and Colour*.

13. *Loan Exhibition of Tapestries*, Detroit Institute of Arts, 1919, 4.

14. Interview with Marilyn Ward Hewlett by Sharon Scott, 2004 and 2015. Hewlett's parents rented Rowland's house in Clinton from the mid-1930s until 1940. Rowland constructed an addition to the house in 1927 in which he stayed when visiting Clinton. This addition included a studio.

15. "Dvořák on His New Work," *New York Herald*, December 15, 1893, quoted in Aborn, "Influence on American Musical Culture of Dvořák's Sojourn in America," 190.

16. Stair, *Lighting Book*.

17. Ibid., figure 80.

18. Marsh's submission is in the collection of the Wolfsonian at Florida International University, Miami Beach.

19. Rowland, "New Note in Architecture Struck."

20. Phillipps, *Form and Colour*, 85.

21. Rowland, "Influence of Glass on Architecture," 5.

22. Ibid.

23. Phillipps, *Form and Colour*, 73.

24. Ibid.

25. *Forty Stories from Bedrock*, 21.

26. An interesting discussion and critical analysis of the alterations made to the building in the 1950s and 1960s and the extensive restoration carried out by Michigan Consolidated Gas Company beginning in 1977 may be found in the article "Regilding the Guardian," by Robert A. Benson. Originally

published in the January/February 1988 edition of *Inland Architect*, the article was reprinted in a collected works: *Essays on Architecture in the Midwest*.

27. Hambidge, "Root Rectangles," 20.

28. The method employed to develop this design is discussed in greater detail in the article "Proportioning Systems in Wirt C. Rowland's Union Trust Guardian Building," by Michael G. Smith and Rachel Fletcher, in *Nexus Network Journal*, April 2015, vol. 17, issue 1, Springer Science+Business Media, 207–29. Also recommended is Fletcher's book *Infinite Measure: Learning to Design in Geometric Harmony with Art, Architecture, and Nature* (2013, Thompson Publishing).

29. *Forty Stories from Bedrock*, 12.

30. "Detroit's Art Magazine," *El Palacio* 8, no. 7/8 (July 1920): 187.

31. Charles F. Lummis, "Ancient Homes That Were Used as Forts," *Los Angeles Times*, September 30, 1923, X15.

32. Omar Barker, "The New-Old House of Santa Fe," *Overland Monthly and Out West Magazine* 82, no. 9 (September 1924): 403.

33. Cassidy, "Southwest Develops Native Architecture," 396.

34. El Navajo was originally built as a train depot (in 1918) with a small hotel, enlarged in 1923 with the Colter-designed "El Navajo" addition. In 1957, most of the structure was demolished to make way for an enlarged Route 66. A portion of the original train station remains and has been restored.

35. Claire Shepherd-Lanier, "Trading on Tradition: Mary Jane Colter and the Romantic Appeal of Harvey House Architecture," *Journal of the Southwest* 38, no. 2 (Summer 1996): 182.

36. "New Hotel to Open in September," *Los Angeles Times*, August 12, 1923, V3.

37. Henry, *Architecture in Texas*, 47.

38. "New Hotel to Open in September," V3.

39. Lloyd C. Engelbrecht and June F. Engelbrecht, "Franciscan Hotel, Albuquerque, New Mexico," online article, accessed February 26, 2015, www.henrytrost.org/buildings/franciscan-hotel/.

40. Edgell, *American Architecture of To-Day*, 340.

41. "The Arthur Hill Memorial Hall," *Michigan Alumnus*, February 1912, 191.

42. Ferry, *Buildings of Detroit*, 329.

43. Rowland, "Architecture and the Automobile Industry," 201.

44. Jay Hambidge, "The Dynamic Symmetry of the Human Figure for Advanced Students: Lesson II," in the *Diagonal*.

45. Jay Hambidge, "Dynamic Symmetry of Man for Advanced Students," in the *Diagonal*.

46. Rowland, "Mr. Wirt C. Rowland on Modernism," 7–8.

47. The claim of meaningful alignment of the setbacks on Penobscot with features of the human body depicted in Leonardo da Vinci's sketch may be met—not unreasonably—with skepticism. It could be argued that Leonardo's sketch might be found to align with points on many buildings. Rowland's use of dynamic symmetry appears repeatedly in his buildings, strongly reinforcing the case for his having used the method, but there is no evidence that Leonardo's sketch, or any similar inspiration, played a role elsewhere in Rowland's designs. Nevertheless, building designs based directly on hu-

man proportions are well documented. Surviving sketches from Renaissance architect Francesco di Giorgio Martini (1439–1501) show buildings and building details superimposed over drawings of the human body or face with features of one aligned with features of the other.

48. Sheets #40 "North Elevation" and #43 "West Elevation," Smith, Hinchman, and Grylls job 5865, May 16, 1927, and Sheet #67 "Revision at 45th Floor," January 9, 1928.

49. "Detroit, Michigan. Top of Detroit's city hall dwarfed by the modern Penobscot Building in the background," Arthur S. Siegel, photographer, Library of Congress call number LC-USF34-110169-C.

50. "Penobscot Building; New," number 50506_2, *Detroit News*, Wayne State University Virtual Motor City Collection.

51. "The Greater Penobscot Building," marketing booklet produced by the Simon J. Murphy Company, 1928, 15.

CHAPTER 8

1. Rowland, "Real Progress," 16.

2. Rowland, "New Note in Architecture Struck."

3. A 1925 survey by the Adcraft Club of Detroit found that Detroit ranked third in the amount of money expended by local firms on advertising in the thirty-two leading national magazines (*Detroiter*, February 2, 1925, 43).

4. "Michigan Typesetting Completes Expansion," *Michigan Purchasing Management* 45 (1964): 84.

5. Rowland, "Real Progress," 23.

6. "New Home for the Detroit Press," *Detroiter*, May 27, 1929, 13.

7. The windows of the Detroit Press Building are notably larger than those of the Saturday Night Building, which were intentionally designed smaller due to concern over excessive heat and glare from direct sun on a south-facing building. As an added precaution, venetian blinds were installed—an early application of a product just then coming back into commercial use.

8. Pound, *Building on Faith in Flint*, 18–19.

9. Ibid., 20–22.

10. "Aluminum, Bronze Steel, Stainless Steel, Benedict Nickel, Cast Iron: Union Industrial Bank," *Metalcraft*, April 1931, 175.

11. "First Floor of Bank Building Has Many Modern Features," *Flint Sunday Journal*, December 14, 1930, Union Industrial Bank edition, 1.

12. "New Flint Bank and Office Building," *Flint Daily Journal*, December 11, 1928, 1.

13. Sheet #1, Smith, Hinchman, and Grylls job 6403, October 1, 1929, "Club for Union Industrial Bank."

14. "A Bank Swindle Linked with the Market Break," *New York Times*, February 2, 1930, 127.

15. Ibid.

16. "New Supply, Garage and Shops Building in Detroit Marvel of Efficiency," *Michigan Bell*, October 1930, 1.

17. Ibid., 4.

18. Ibid., 1, 2.

19. "Final Report: Proposed Michigan Bell and Western Electric Warehouse Historic District," prepared by the Historic Designation Advisory Board of the City of Detroit from the National Register nomination of the Michigan Bell and Western Electric Warehouse by Kristine Kidorf, 2009, quoting from the *Michigan Bell*, August 1931.

20. "Our New Grand Rapids Garage and Supplies Building Occupied," *Michigan Bell*, September 1930, 8.

21. Ibid.

22. A. S. Fetters, "Our Niagara and Pingree Offices Differ from Other Installations," *Michigan Bell*, December 1929, 17.

23. Jim Barner, "Under Cover," *P.T.M. Pacific Telephone Magazine*, March 1964, San Francisco, California, 1.

24. "Top Art for the Bell System," *Western Electric News Features*, June 1967, 4.

25. "Burch Foraker, New York Alpa '91, Heads Michigan Bell Telephone Co.," *Shield of Phi Kappa Psi* 51, no. 1 (November 1930): 96–98.

26. "Foraker, Noted Telephone Man, Dies in Detroit," *Schenectady Gazette*, March 30, 1935, 8.

27. "Burch Foraker, 63, Phone Chief, Dead," *New York Times*, March 30, 1935, 15.

28. Smith, Hinchman, and Grylls plans for David Mackenzie High School, Unit 1, job number 5924, dated June 27, 1927; and *Histories of the Public Schools of Detroit, Volume II*, Board of Education of the City of Detroit, January 1967, 1515.

29. Edwin Denby High School National Park Service Nominating Form, by Dr. Charles K. Hyde, item number 04001581, 2005, section 8, page 8.

30. Ibid., section 8, page 5.

31. Ibid.; and Smith, Hinchman, and Grylls building plans for Denby High School, job 6423.

32. *Histories of the Public Schools of Detroit, Volume II*, Board of Education of the City of Detroit, January 1967, 1576–77.

33. Ibid., 1578, in part quoting from a letter to the school from First Lieutenant Frank J. Coleman, Army Air Corps, Selfridge Field.

34. Clarence M. Burton, editor in chief, *City of Detroit Michigan, 1701–1922*, Detroit 1922, vol. 4, p. 596, and vol. 5, p. 961; *Automobile Trade Journal* 19, no. 2 (August 1, 1914): 189; and "Secretary of Navy Leader in Industry," *Automotive Industries*, March 3, 1921, 532.

35. Dr. Adolph Moses, "Popular Government: Its Development and Failure in Antiquity," *American Journal of Politics* 5, no 4 (October 1894): 381–91.

36. Ibid., 391.

37. "Five Years Building Construction (From Reports of Department of Building and Safety Engineering)," *Detroiter*, February 6, 1928, 11, and March 10, 1930, 12.

38. "How Downtown Detroit Has Changed," *Detroiter*, January 28, 1924, 17.

39. "Union League, Michigan Plans $3,200,000 Home," *Michigan Manufacturer and Financial Record*, April 13, 1929.

40. "Starts $1,500,000 Club House," *Michigan Manufacturer and Financial Record*, November 9, 1929, 4.

41. "Local Chapter of National Town and Country Club Is Being Organized—$2,500,000 Home Planned," *Detroiter*, December 1, 1924, 17.

42. "New Club Buys Site for 26-Story Home," *New York Times*, September 18, 1925, 4.

43. "National Town & Country Club Banquet," *Detroiter*, April 26, 1926, 14.

44. Ibid.; and "The Penobscot Building Opens," *Detroit News*, October 22, 1928, 1.

45. "Club Will Discuss Plan to Disband," *New York Times*, January 6, 1927, 5.

46. *The Pontchartrain Club, Detroit, Michigan*, limited edition booklet, ca. 1929, section: "Conclusion" (unnumbered), in the collection of the Detroit Historical Society.

47. Amedeo Leone's 1952 AIA nomination for fellowship form, page 3, lists Michigan Bell Telephone Co., Dearborn, 1930 under "Nominee's Achievement in Architectural Design."

48. "Corner Stone of Club Laid," *Detroiter*, July 22, 1929, 14.

49. Report No. 1455: Stock Exchange Practices; Hearings before the Committee on Banking and Currency, United States Senate, Seventy-Third Congress, second session, on Senate Res. 84, 73d Congress, 1934, 4685.

50. "Motor Car Executive Quits Job," *Los Angeles Times*, November 2, 1930, E2.

51. "New Detroit Bank Merger Eighth Largest in Nation," *Michigan Manufacturer and Financial Record*, September 28, 1929.

52. "Two Banks Control Half of State's Banking Resources," *Michigan Manufacturer and Financial Record* 44, no. 14 (October 5, 1929): 1.

53. Ibid.

54. "Guards Move 100 Millions," *Detroit Free Press*, April 14, 1930, 1.

55. "Guardian Units in New Lineup," *Detroit Free Press*, June 13, 1930, 23.

56. "4 Intervene in Club Suit," *Detroit Free Press*, August 1, 1931, 9.

57. Sidney Gorman v. Commissioner, Myron A. Keys v. Commissioner, Docket Nos. 7508, 7509, United States Tax Court, 1947 Tax Ct. Memo Lexis 330; 6 T.C.M. (CCH) 52; T.C.M. (RIA) 47008, January 23, 1947.

58. Report of the Detroit Department of Buildings and Safety Engineering for 1951, 23.

59. In re Union League Bldg. Corporation; Union League of Michigan v. Union Guardian Trust Co., No. 7006, Circuit Court of Appeals, Sixth Circuit, 84 F.2d 183; 1936 U.S. App. Lexis 4425, June 5, 1936.

60. "Direct Mail Advertising Exhibition," *Detroiter*, February 3, 1936, 8.

61. "Detroit Building Industry Shows Gain," *Detroiter*, February 3, 1936, 4.

62. Ibid.

63. Pledge letter from Charles M. Pigott to the JAPC congregation, distributed Easter 1922.

64. *One Hundred Years of Service, 1854–1954*, a review of the historical background and development of the Jefferson Avenue Presbyterian Church, Detroit, Michigan, January, 1954, 51.

65. Ibid.

66. The eighty-one-story Book Tower was announced in 1925 by James B. Book (see "81-Story Book Tower Under Way," *Detroiter*, December 21, 1925, 12). Land was cleared on the northwest corner of Washington Boulevard and State Street and some construction of the foundation may have been completed, but no further work on the enormous Louis Kamper–designed structure was carried out.

67. In 1929, Michigan Bell had 352,000 phones in service and averaged 1.6 million daily calls. In 1933,

there were 239,000 phones and less than one million daily calls (*Detroiter*, February 3, 1936, 8).

68. Holleman and Gallagher, *Smith, Hinchman, and Grylls: 125 Years of Architecture and Engineering*, 129.

69. Ibid., 131.

70. Ibid., 137.

71. "Detroit Architects to Combine," *Michigan Manufacturer and Financial Record* 25, no. 7 (February 14, 1920): 10.

72. "New Corporation for A. K.," *Weekly Bulletin of the Michigan Society of Architects* 14, no. 31 (July 30, 1940): 1.

CHAPTER 9

1. Talmage C. Hughes, "Dynamic Detroit," *Weekly Bulletin of the Michigan Society of Architects* 8, no. 50 (December 11, 1934): 1, republished in *Architectural Progress*, May 1931.

2. Letter from Talmage Hughes, executive secretary of the Detroit chapter of the American Institute of Architects, to the Board of Directors of the American Institute of Architects, Washington, DC, June 20, 1946.

3. Original drawing for Detroit Trust Company, sheet 12-R, drawn by C. L. P. and E. W. (Ernest Wilby), and sheet 13 by C. L. P., Job 637, dated 12-15-14, Albert Kahn, Architects and Engineers, in the collection of the Bentley Library; blueprint for Bay County National Bank, Sheet no. 6, dated 4-14-15, drawn by C. L. P., Job 610, Albert Kahn, Architects and Engineers, in the collection of Ball State University; Polk's Detroit Directory for 1906, 1917, and 1925–26; "Of Interest to Salesmen," Detroit Savings Bank at Hillger and Jefferson, *Michigan Manufacturer and Financial Record*, August 14, 1926; Application for Membership, the American Institute of Architects for Charles L. Phelps, dated March 3, 1930; and "Architects Registered in Michigan, Corrected to March 1, 1939," *Weekly Bulletin of the Michigan Society of Architects*, 85.

4. "New Quarters for Bank Branch," *Detroit News*, March 31, 1929, 1, pt. 10; and "Bank Is Masterpiece," *Michigan Manufacturer and Financial Record*, November 9, 1929.

5. *Ice and Refrigeration*, Detroit, Michigan, construction news, 1938, vol. 94.

6. Edward Arthur Schilling entry in *The City of Detroit, Michigan, 1701–1922*, vol. 4, edited by Clarence Monroe Burton, William Stocking, and Gordon K. Miller, Detroit, 1922, 113.

7. John Mead Howells, "Vertical or Horizontal Design?" *Architectural Forum*, June 1930, 782.

8. Rowland, "Real Progress," 16.

9. "Report of the Trustees of the Winchester Public Library," 1915–16, 3–4.

10. *Harvard College, Class of 1883*, June 1903, 7.

11. "Proposed Chrysler Building in N.Y.," *Detroit News*, October 28, 1928.

12. Walter P. Chrysler with Boyden Sparkes, *Life of an American Workman* (New York: Dodd, Mead, 1937), via Project Gutenberg Canada.

13. Cobb, *History of Stainless Steel*, 109.

14. Chrysler Building, National Register of Historic Places Inventory—Nomination Form, p. 137, quoting from Willian Van Alen, *Architecture and Building* 62, no. 8 (August 1930): 223–24.

15. The only prior extensive use of silver metal as decoration on a significant building was the Monel met-

al used on the Union Trust Building. A 1980 book published by the National Park Service, *Metals in America's Historic Buildings*, took an exhaustive look at the use of metal in architecture. The book's introduction carries a photo of the Union Trust Building's Monel metal gates and cites the structure as an example of the early use of "white metal" as a decorative feature. In the section on white metals, the Union Trust Building is prominently featured and no earlier example of the use of stainless, nickel silver, or Monel for decorative purposes is cited.

16. Chrysler, *Life of an American Workman*.

17. Paul S. George, PhD, "Miami: One Hundred Years of History," *South Florida History* 24, no. 2 (Summer 1996): 30.

18. "Story of a Mangrove Swamp," *American Architect* 147, no. 2636 (August 1935): 14. (Ranking is based on numbers for the first six months of 1935.)

19. John Llewellyn Skinner's Nomination for Fellowship in the American Institute of Architects, dated received February 20, 1948, 2.

20. Ibid.

21. "Architect Combines with Realty Firm," *Detroit Free Press*, May 14, 1922, A6; *American Contractor*, August 12, 1922, 25; "Building Permits," *Michigan Manufacturer and Financial Record*, September 9, 1922, 21; and *American Contractor*, November 11, 1922, 55, and December 16, 1922, 55.

22. *Miami News*, November 2, 1927, N3.

23. "John L. Skinner Heads Architects," *Sarasota Herald-Tribune*, January 18, 1944, 2.

24. The *Weekly Bulletin* of April 15, 1942, included a notice that Rowland recently returned from a vacation in Florida. Many of Detroit's architects vacationed in Florida during the winter. Rowland was an inveterate traveler; it is reasonable to assume he made many other trips there.

25. "Letter to Mr. Ditchy," sent by John L. Skinner, *Weekly Bulletin of the Michigan Society of Architects* (December 31, 1946).

26. While researching this section of the book, I learned an application was pending before the Review Board of Miami Beach to permit demolition of the home and replacement with a new structure. I forwarded a copy of the *American Architect* article to the Miami Design Preservation League, which used it to rally support for saving the home. The board subsequently denied the application for demolition, its decision largely influenced by the 1935 article. A short time later, the home was sold for substantially more than the owner had paid. These developments were the subject of two postings on the popular *Curbed Miami* website: "Great Art Deco House on Alton Saved from Wrecking Ball" and "Almost Demo-ed Art Deco Gem on Alton Coming Back to Life."

27. Preservation sources give the "construction date" as 1937. The building permit is dated October 9, 1937. An article in the *Miami Daily News* on February 27, 1938, reported, "The Barbizon apartment hotel at Sixth St. and Ocean drive, Miami Beach has been completed," 2-F.

28. *Daily Bulletin of the Manufacturers Record*, 1939, vol. 82, p. 189 (retrieved through Google Books).

29. Normandy Isles Historic District introduction summary downloaded from http://web.miamibeachfl.gov/WorkArea/DownloadAsset.aspx?id=55056.

30. Letter from Emil Lorch to Edgar P. Richardson, undated but marked with the note "sent 4-28-43 M.K.," likely indicating when the article was forwarded to Pitt. The letterhead is "Michigan Society

of Architects, Committee on Michigan Architecture, Emil Lorch, F.A.I.A., Chairman, 1023 Forest Avenue, Ann Arbor, Mich."

31. Many sources give the dates of Pitt's association with George L. Pfeiffer as 1940 to 1941. This is almost certainly incorrect as Pfeiffer died on June 15, 1938, thereby ending the partnership.

32. Collins Waterfront Historic District Designation Report, City of Miami Planning Department, August 10, 2000, 37.

33. National Register of Historic Places Inventory—Nomination Form for the Huntington Building, October 1988.

34. Ibid.; and Emporis.com entry for the Roosevelt Hotel/Dade County Vocational Education Building.

35. License issued by the State Board of Architecture of the State of Florida, #684, dated January 16, 1926; George D. Mason job list, "Design for Masonic Temple—Miami, 1926"; design sketch for "Miami Masonic Temple, Geo. D. Mason & Co., Architects, Detroit," published in *Thumb Tack Club of Detroit 1928 Architectural Exhibition*, Detroit, Michigan (unnumbered).

36. In its September 1945 *Bulletin*, the FAA stated that the membership of its three AIA chapters in Florida included 148 of 338 architects resident in the state, or 44 percent (4). In the April 1945 FAA *Bulletin* it was reported that more than 80 percent of Michigan architects were members of the state's chapter of the AIA (2).

37. FAA *Bulletin*, December 1938, 4.

38. Based on lists of paid members published in the FAA *Bulletin*, 1938 to 1946.

39. FAA *Bulletin*, February 1939, 5.

40. FAA *Bulletin*, March 1940, 5.

41. George B. Catlin, *Local History of Detroit and Wayne County*, National History Association, Dayton, Ohio, 1928, 329–30.

42. *American Architects Directory*, 1st edition, R. R. Bowker, 1956, listing for George J. Haas.

43. "MSA's Oldest Living Member, Emil Lorch—Architect and Educator," manuscript for MSA April 1963 *Bulletin*, author unknown, but probably Lorch. Held by the AIA Detroit chapter; in the Emil Lorch file.

44. "College of Architecture News," *Michigan Architect and Engineer* 4, no. 11 (November 1922): 166; Hawkins Ferry, "Representative Detroit Buildings, a Cross Section of Architecture, 1823–1943," *Bulletin of the Detroit Institute of Arts* 22, no. 6 (March 1943): 60.

45. "Small House Competition Drawings," *Pencil Points* 6, no. 8 (August 1925): 69.

46. "Glass Block and Sash Combined in Exterior Walls of Building: Laboratory of Monsanto Chemical Company, Dayton, Ohio," *Architectural Record*, May 1939, 48–49.

47. Emporis online building directory listing for Talbott Tower, accessed February 26, 2016, www.emporis.com/buildings/128314/talbott-tower-dayton-oh-usa.

48. "Architecture Firm Has Helped Form Dayton's Skyline," *Dayton Daily News*, October 27, 2002.

CHAPTER 10

1. Rowland, "Human—All Too Human, Chapter II."

2. Letter from H. A. O'Dell to Talmage Hughes, January 27, 1931.

3. Minutes of the annual meeting of the Detroit chapter of the AIA, October 15, 1930, Arthur K. Hyde, secretary, p. 3.

4. "The Presidents Report to the Board of Regents for the academic year 1932–1933," August 20, 1933, vol. 34, no. 10, University of Michigan, Ann Arbor, p. 75.

5. Minutes of the directors meeting, Detroit chapter of the AIA, November 18, 1931.

6. Minutes of the directors meeting, Detroit chapter of the AIA, December 16, 1931, Aloys Frank Herman, secretary pro tem.

7. Report of the treasurer, Detroit chapter of the AIA, for the year ending October 26, 1933, Aloys Frank Herman, treasurer.

8. Minutes of the directors meeting, Detroit chapter of the AIA, August 26, 1932, Arthur K. Hyde, secretary.

9. Nineteenth Annual Biennial Report of the Michigan State Highway Commissioner, 1941–42, 31.

10. Ibid., 36–38; and Stanley N. Oates, Proposed System of Trafficways, Detroit City Plan Commission, 1946, section "Bank in '25."

11. Minutes of the directors meeting of the Detroit chapter of the AIA, January 10, 1933, Arthur K. Hyde, secretary, 3.

12. "Uniform Building Plan Is Urged for Woodward," *Detroit News*, February 26, 1933, 7, realty section.

13. Report of the Secretary, Detroit Chapter AIA, for the year ending October 26, 1933, Arthur K. Hyde, secretary, 1.

14. "Preliminary Plans for Cadieux School Approved by Board," *Grosse Pointe Review* 5, no. 8 (January 22, 1931): 1.

15. Ibid.

16. Ibid., 1, 4.

17. "Delay Hinted on New School on Cadieux by School Board Head," *Grosse Pointe Review* 5, no. 21 (April 23, 1931): 1.

18. Grosse Pointe school district financial report, Schedule 8, "Others," *Grosse Pointe Review* (August 6, 1931): 8.

19. "Detroit Traveling Annual Meeting in Retrospect," *Civic Comment*, January–February 1932, 17.

20. "Forsees [sic] End of Cities," *Frederick Post*, October 23, 1931, 1.

21. Florence Davies, "Designer of Skyscrapers Sees Trend to Suburbs," *Detroit News*, October 8, 1931, arts section, 1.

22. "For Dispersion of Cities," *New York Times*, October 8, 1931, 43.

23. Jester, *Twentieth-Century Building Materials*, 255.

24. "Glasiron" trademark, serial number 71300847, registration number 0275807; *Porcelain Enamel in the Building Industry: Conference Proceedings, November 12 and 13, 1953*, 77–78.

25. Jester, *Twentieth-Century Building Materials*, 256.

26. "Iron Tiles Line Interior of Great Tunnel That Connects Detroit and Windsor," *Metalcraft*, October 1930, 180–81.

27. A patent for concrete backed porcelain enamel panels was filed by Peter J. Maul of Detroit in May 1933 and granted May 1934. It is not clear why the patent was filed after the L. Black Company

facade was completed and its construction details revealed in a national publication, unless Maul perceived a patent opportunity overlooked by others.

28. "Prominent Clay Men Organize to Make New Building Material," *Brick and Clay Record*, September 9, 1919, 484–85.

29. Website of Buildex Inc., producer of Haydite, at www.buildex.com/haydite.html, accessed May 22, 2015. The lightweight concrete permitted more floors to be added to the building than would have been possible with standard concrete.

30. "An Unusual Shopfront Construction," *Pencil Points*, July 1932, 502 and 508.

31. *Lumber World Review*, December 25, 1912, 38.

32. *American Lumberman*, August 14, 1920, 57.

33. The award of "first prize" to Rowland's design by the fair is reported in numerous places, including "Work on Ideal Home Rushed by Builders," in the November 27, 1932, *Detroit News* (real estate section). That *Good Housekeeping* sponsored the Stran-Steel home as a result of its winning first prize is speculation.

34. Jennifer L. Strayer-Jones, "No Place Like Home: Domestic Models in Chicago's Public Places, 1919–1938," PhD thesis, University of Iowa, 1996, 285–86.

35. "Stran-Steel House at A Century of Progress, Exhibited in Co-Operation with Good Housekeeping," booklet, 4.

36. Rowland, "Heigho! I Go to 'The Fair,'" 4–5.

37. Dorothy Raley, ed., *A Century of Progress Homes and Furnishings* (Chicago: M. A. Ring, 1934), 101.

38. Interview with Dr. Monica Brooks via e-mail, October 7–9, 2013.

39. "Builders Show Opens in March," *Detroit Free Press*, September 25, 1932, 10, sports.

40. "'33 Ideal Home Is Open Today," *Detroit News*, January 15, 1933, 7, real estate.

41. Typically, between five and seven thousand visitors passed through the house each day of the fair in 1933, according to *Good Housekeeping*, September 1933, 52. The *Free Press* of March 12, 1933, reported the number of visitors to the Ideal Home the previous Sunday was estimated at more than 10,000. The Ideal Home was only held open for three months, from February 12 to May 14, 1933.

42. The foregoing was extracted from a series of articles in the *Detroit Free Press* and the *Detroit News* covering construction of the Ideal Home: "Builders Show Opens in March," *FP*, 9-25-1932, p. 10 sports; "Work Started on Ideal Home," *FP*, 10-2-1932, p. 10 sports; "Work Pushed on Ideal Home," *FP*, 10-16-1932, p. 10 sports; "Show's Home Awaits Steel," *FP*, 10-23-1932, p. 10 sports; "Ideal Home's Frame Ready," *FP*, 11-6-1932, p. 10 sports; "Work on Ideal Home Rushed by Builders," 11-27-1932, *News* real estate; "Light Feature of Ideal Home," 12-11-1932, *News* real estate; "'33 Ideal Home Is Open Today," 1-15-1933, *News* real estate; "Work Finished on Ideal Home," 2-12-1933, *News* real estate; and "Interest High in Ideal Home," 2-19-1933, *News* real estate.

43. *Detroit News*, 7, real estate.

44. Bemis, *Evolving House*, 531.

45. Stran-Steel 4-panel sales brochure, "A New Time-Proved Method of Framing," undated.

46. US Navy Quonset Hut, "Morphology," at http://quonset-hut.blogspot.com/p/morphology.html, accessed June 3, 2015.

47. Seabee Museum and Memorial Park, "Quonset Huts" website, at www.seabeemuseum.com/quon-set_huts.html, accessed June 3, 2015.

48. *What's My Line*, episode 575 (season 12, episode 48), aired on July 30, 1961.

49. Garage door: *American Builder and Building Age*, February 1940, 4; "Steel Windows Feature of Davis-Leonard Firm," *Miami Daily News*, June 15, 1941, building page; and Bathtub: Stacy V. Jones, "Lightweight Bathtub Is Patented, Made of Glass Fibers and Plastic," *New York Times*, November 17, 1954, 19.

50. Rowland, "Science Brings New Helps to Modern Home Makers," 13.

51. Ibid.

52. "H. Augustus O'Dell, FAIA," two-page biographical sketch, circa 1957, on file at the office of the Detroit chapter of the American Institute of Architects.

53. Horologium: a time-keeping machine; hippodrome: an ancient or modern sport venue; excubitorium: gallery in a church occupied throughout the night; bargello: bordello, brothel; latrina: communal toilet; kiosk: Turkish summer house or small structure open on one or more sides; kimona: embroidered blouse with extended sleeves.

54. Wirt C. Rowland, with Clair W. Ditchy, "Bally Whose Who, A Comedy in one Act and a Few Gestures," *Weekly Bulletin of the Michigan Society of Architects* 6, no. 10 (March 8, 1932): 1 and 4–7 (part 1), and 6, no. 11 (March 15, 1932): 4–7 (part 2). Aloys Frank Herman was a Detroit architect.

55. "Bankers Oppose Macaulay Plan," *Wall Street Journal*, October 28, 1930, 8.

56. "Bonus Plan Fought by Banking Leaders," *New York Times*, February 2, 1931, 1 and 3.

57. Robert P. Murphy, "The Depression You've Never Heard of: 1920–1921," *Freeman*, Foundation for Economic Education, November 18, 2009, online at http://fee.org/freeman/detail/the-depression-youve-never-heard-of-1920-1921, accessed June 4, 2015.

58. "Detroit Guardian Union," *Wall Street Journal*, January 18, 1932, 5; and Report No. 1455: Stock Exchange Practices: Hearings before the Committee on Banking and Currency, United States Senate, Seventy-Third Congress, second session, on Senate Res. 84, 73d Congress, 1934, 4813.

59. "Joint Land Bankers See Aid for Farmer," *Washington Post*, November 22, 1932, 14.

60. Ibid.

61. "Chronological Survey of Outstanding Financial Events of the Last Year," *New York Times*, January 2, 1934, 30.

62. Ibid.

63. In 2013, Detroit was again unable to pay its debts and declared bankruptcy. In another example of consistency over time, according to a 1928 study, Detroit had the highest per capita murder rate in the nation at 16.5 per 100,000, followed by Chicago (15.8), Cleveland (13.3), Philadelphia (8.8), and New York (6.7). Figures from the *Detroiter*, April 29, 1929, 10.

64. Report No. 1455: Stock Exchange Practices: Hearings before the Committee on Banking and Currency, United States Senate, Seventy-Third Congress, second session, on Senate Res. 84, 73d Congress, 1934, 4806.

65. Ibid., 4803 and 4818.

66. "Ford Helped Bank Twice," *Wall Street Journal*, June 17, 1933, 6.

67. Banks operate by taking in deposits from customers and lending that money to others. Although the bank may hold customer deposits, deposits are considered a "liability," as the money is owed by the bank to its customer. A loan made by the bank is considered an "asset" because the unpaid amount of the loan (plus interest) is owed to the bank by the borrower. Under normal circumstances, a bank can safely lend out a large percentage of the cash deposited by its customers, keeping on hand only enough to satisfy the small number who seek to make withdrawals. During the first three years of the Great Depression, customer withdrawals far outstripped deposits. Although the banks still owned the loans (and the underlying collateral), most of these loans were for real estate, which had declined in value and become difficult to sell. In theory, the assets owned by the bank were worth more than what the bank owed to depositors, but there was no way to convert the assets to cash to meet the demand for customer withdrawals. Without loans (from investors, other banks, or the RFC), the banks did not have adequate cash available to distribute to customers seeking to withdraw money from their accounts. The particular loan Union Guardian Trust was seeking from the RFC would have covered all of the bank's liabilities—sufficient to cash out all of the bank's depositors.

68. Awalt, "Recollections of the Banking Crisis in 1933," 350.

69. Ibid., 350–51; and Report No. 1455: Stock Exchange Practices: Hearings before the Committee on Banking and Currency, United States Senate, Seventy-Third Congress, second session, on Senate Res. 84, 73d Congress, 1934, 4692.

70. "Michigan Crisis Is Not General," *Wall Street Journal*, February 17, 1933, 6.

71. Awalt, "Recollections of the Banking Crisis in 1933," 353–54.

72. Report No. 1455: Stock Exchange Practices: Hearings before the Committee on Banking and Currency, United States Senate, Seventy-Third Congress, second session, on Senate Res. 84, 73d Congress, 1934, 294.

73. Testimony of Edsel Ford, Report No. 1455: Stock Exchange Practices: Hearings before the Committee on Banking and Currency, United States Senate, Seventy-Third Congress, second session, on Senate Res. 84, 73d Congress, 1934, 4695.

74. Report No. 1455: Stock Exchange Practices: Hearings before the Committee on Banking and Currency, United States Senate, Seventy-Third Congress, second session, on Senate Res. 84, 73d Congress, 1934, 4696.

75. Awalt, "Recollections of the Banking Crisis in 1933," 356–57.

76. "Chronological Survey of the Outstanding Financial Events of the Past Year," *New York Times*, January 2, 1934, 30.

77. According to the testimony of John K. McKee, examiner in charge of bank reorganization at the Reconstruction Finance Corporation: "The Reconstruction Finance Corporation, empowered to make loans only on full and adequate security, refused to increase the loan [to Union Guardian Trust], which it considered very liberal on the collateral offered, or permit other lenders to participate in this collateral. An analysis of the liquidating value allocated by the Reconstruction Finance Corporation to the proffered collateral demonstrates the helpful and liberal attitude assumed by the Reconstruction Finance Corporation." Report No. 1455: Stock Exchange Practices: Hearings before

the Committee on Banking and Currency, United States Senate, Seventy-Third Congress, second session, on Senate Res. 84, 73d Congress, 1934, 4736.

78. After the Michigan bank holiday was declared, newspaper articles claimed that, except for Ford, the major auto companies had agreed to subordinate their Union Guardian Trust deposits, and it was Ford, therefore, who scuttled the RFC loan. It later came to light that just the opposite was the case: Henry Ford was willing to subordinate his deposits, while General Motors, Chrysler Corporation, and others had refused to do so. Testimony of John K. McKee, "Stock Exchange Practices," January 15, 1934, hearings before the US Senate, Subcommittee of the Committee on Banking and Currency, vol. 10, p. 4737.

79. Awalt, "Recollections of the Banking Crisis in 1933," 353.

80. "New Trust Company Here Backed by Ford," *New York Times*, May 19, 1925, 1.

81. "Ford Banks in Gotham," *Los Angeles Times*, May 19, 1925, 1.

82. "Calls in Records of New York Banks," *New York Times*, August 29, 1933, 14.

83. Ibid.

84. Letter from Wirt Rowland to the Burroughs Family, February 19, 1933.

85. "RFC to Match Dollars with Bank Stockholders," *Wall Street Journal*, March 22, 1933, 1. The new bank was owned by the RFC and Ford's chief competitor, General Motors, raising further questions about the RFC's motivations for its earlier treatment of Ford and Guardian Detroit Union Group.

86. "Charter Is Asked by Detroit Bank," *Wall Street Journal*, July 15, 1933, 8.

87. "Guardian Depositors Reach 92% Recovery Point," *Michigan Manufacturer and Financial Record* 62, no. 26 (December 24, 1938): 1.

88. *One Hundred Years of Service, 1854–1954*, a review of the historical background and development of the Jefferson Avenue Presbyterian Church, Detroit, Michigan, January, 1954, 49.

89. Ibid., 49, 51.

90. Lilian Jackson Braun, "The Story of AIA Michigan," 1977, available online at www.aiami.com/Resources/Leadershp%20Retreat/AIA%20MI%20History.pdf.

91. Report on the Organization of the Thumb Tack Club of Detroit, submitted at the meeting of the Detroit Chapter of the AIA by Malcolm R. Stirton, October 1934, Minutes of Regular and Directors Meetings, AIA Detroit Chapter.

92. Ross explains his approach in *A Theory of Pure Design: Harmony, Balance, Rhythm*.

93. Donaldson, Hubbard, and Hurtienne, "Interview," 14.

94. "History of the School of Architecture at Lawrence Institute of Technology," unpublished report, 1972, 2, Statement of History.

95. "Pellerin Discusses Trends in American Architecture," *Lawrence Tech News*, November 5, 1934, 4.

96. Dr. Earl W. Pellerin, "Reflections on Life in Architecture and Education—Thoughts and Works," *Monthly Bulletin of the Michigan Society of Architects*, December 1974, 4.

97. "Students Form Architectural Club with Pellerin as Critic," *Lawrence Tech News*, October 13, 1933, 3; "History of the School of Architecture at Lawrence Institute of Technology," unpublished report, 1972, 1, Tech News Index; and "Architectural Club Has Varied History," *Lawrence Tech News*, March 25, 1959, 11.

98. "Architects Procure Room for Research," *Lawrence Tech News*, October 19, 1949, 4.

99. Barrie, *Interview with Corrado Parducci*; and "Thumb Tack Club Atelier," *Weekly Bulletin of the Michigan Society of Architects* 9, no. 4 (January 22, 1935): 1.

100. It appears the jury was discontinued after the 1932–33 school year, quite possibly due to strains on the school imposed by the economy, which caused rapidly declining enrollment, staff reductions, and even the loss of the important George G. Booth Fellowship in Architecture.

101. "The President's Report to the Board of Regents for the academic year 1930–1931," August 15, 1931, vol. 33, no. 14, University of Michigan, Ann Arbor, 88; and August 20, 1932, vol. 34, no. 10, 59.

102. From various issues of *The Archi*, newsletter of Alpha Rho Chi.

103. Reineri, *Iktinos: This Is Our History*, V-1.

104. "Death Notice: F. Lee Cochran," *Chicago Tribune*, February 21, 2009; Perkins+Will history, online at http://history.perkinswill.com/; *American Architects Directory*, 1st edition, 1956, R. R. Bowker, entry for Frank Lee Cochran, 100; and "Start to Build Gary Grade School," *Chicago Daily Tribune*, January 1, 1950, S2.

105. Reineri, *Iktinos: This Is Our History*, V-3.

106. "Obituaries, Donald Wolbrink, 85, helped plan Waialae-Kahala," *Star-Bulletin*, Honolulu, Hawaii, March 4, 1997; and Don Hibbard, *Designing Paradise: The Allure of the Hawaiian Resort* (New York: Princeton Architectural Press, 2006), 88–89.

107. American Institute of Architects website, page "The Historic American Buildings Survey." Interview with Nancy Hadley, Assoc. AIA, CA, Manager, Archives and Records, American Institute of Architects, Washington, DC (July 20, 2013): "The AIA pushed for the creation of the Historic American Buildings Survey (HABS) program and endorsed the PWA programs as ways for architects to get work and contribute to the public good."

108. "Historic American Buildings Survey," *Weekly Bulletin of the Michigan Society of Architects* 8, no. 7 (February 13, 1934).

109. Time sheets maintained by Emil Lorch begin with the period January 11–31, 1934. Michigan architects and draftsmen listed on the time sheets: Lilly M. Roberts, J. Philip McDonnell, Frank Eurich, Earl Pellerin, Howard Simons, Talmage C. Hughes (editor of the *Weekly Bulletin of the Michigan Society of Architects*), Frank H. Wright, Sylvester Lucas, George A. Golchert, Herbert G. Wenzell, F. Orla Varney, Andrew Lindsay, Warren L. Rindge, Charles Norton Jr., George Singers, Robert B. Frantz, Frederick Crowther, Ralph D. VerValin, Lewis W. Simpson, and Carl F. Kresbach. The time sheets are part of the Emil Lorch collection of papers at the Bentley Historical Museum in Ann Arbor, Michigan.

110. "HABS Comes to a Close," *Weekly Bulletin of the Michigan Society of Architects* 8, no. 20 (May 15, 1934): 1.

CHAPTER 11

1. "Our Early History and Beginnings," Canada Creek Ranch website, at www.canadacreekranch.com/About_Us/History.aspx, accessed June 15, 2015.

2. Letter from Edwin S. George to Wirt C. Rowland, July 28, 1944, archives of Kirk in the Hills, Bloomfield Hills, Michigan.

3. Ibid.

4. Ibid., the text of the relevant section of the letter is as follows: "Further drawings duly materialized into the general exterior and floor plans, that have been placed in the Foundation safety deposit box as the accepted church plans on the part of the donor, and for the knowledge of the trustees of The Edwin S. George Foundation. (Each trustee is being given an album containing photo copies of these exterior and interior drawings and the floor plans.)"

5. Letter from Edwin George to Wirt Rowland, July 28, 1944, 3.

6. "Architect's Reports," *Weekly Bulletin of the Michigan Society of Architects*, various during 1934.

7. Letter from the executive secretary, American Institute of Architects, to Wirt Rowland, February 20, 1936, from Rowland, Wirt (ahd1038448), Membership files, The American Institute of Architects Archives, held within the archives of the organization.

8. Interview with Nancy Hadley, Assoc. AIA, CA, Manager, Archives and Records, American Institute of Architects, Washington, DC (July 20, 2013).

9. "Pierce Is Community Achievement," *Grosse Pointe Review*, March 28, 1940, 3.

10. "Attention Again Please, Voters," *Grosse Pointe Review*, October 29, 1936, 1.

11. "Construction of New G. P. School Started," *Grosse Pointe Review*, January 9, 1936, 1.

12. "Pierce Is Community Achievement," 3.

13. Letter from Pewabic Pottery to James Sharp, April 27, 1936. This letter states, "all as approved by Mr. Rowland," confirming Rowland's chief role in designing the building. Pewabic Pottery archives.

14. Johnson, *St. John's Centennial Book*, 47.

15. John W. Chandler, "Widening Project in Final Phase," *Detroiter*, 8 and 25.

16. Johnson, *St. John's Centennial Book*, 39 and 47.

17. "Craftsmen in Distant States Help Revamp City Churches," *Detroit Free Press*, November 7, 1936, 10.

18. "Severe Storm in Detroit Area Kills 2 Persons," *Washington Post*, June 3, 1936, X3; original plans for St. John's Episcopal Church, electrical and mechanical alterations, prepared by O'Dell and Rowland, Associate Architects, Smith, Hinchman, and Grylls, Engineers, Job No. 192, Nov. 2, 1936, File No. 6998.

19. Original plans St. John's Episcopal Church, electrical and mechanical alterations, prepared by O'Dell and Rowland, Associate Architects, Smith, Hinchman, and Grylls, Engineers, Job No. 192, Nov. 2, 1936, File No. 6998.

20. Thompson, *Eighty Years: A Brief History of St. John's Church*, 31.

21. Ibid., 32.

22. Johnson, *St. John's Centennial Book*, 52.

23. St. John's Church, minutes of the Annual Parish Meeting, January 18, 1937, 107, 109, 111.

24. Johnson, *St. John's Centennial Book*, 52.

25. Thompson, *Eighty Years: A Brief History of St. John's Church*, 33.

26. St. John's Church, minutes of the Parish Meeting, January 18, 1937, 145 and 147.

27. Florence Davies, "In the Gothic Spirit," *Detroit News*, December 18, 1938, art and music section.

28. Thompson, *Eighty Years: A Brief History of St. John's Church*, 33; Johnson, *St. John's Centennial Book*, 53; and St. John's Church, minutes of the Parish Meeting, January 18, 1937, 145.

29. Davies, "In the Gothic Spirit."

30. Ibid.

31. Thompson's forty-page book is available online at Hathitrust.org, and his description of the Stevens Memorial is well worth reading (pages 33 and 34).

32. Thompson, *Eighty Years: A Brief History of St. John's Church*, 34.

33. St. John's Church, minutes of the Parish Meeting, January 18, 1937, 147.

34. Rowland, "New York, Old and New," 6.

35. Description attached to the back side of the original proposal sketch in the collection of St. John's Episcopal Church.

36. Rowland, "On Gothic Architecture."

37. Ibid.

38. Rowland, "Influence of Glass on Architecture," 5.

39. Rowland, "Mr. Wirt C. Rowland on Modernism," 6.

40. Ibid., 7.

41. Ibid.

42. "$2,100,000 for Dorms Submitted by University as PWA Building Project," *Michigan Daily*, August 6, 1938.

43. Andrews, "Victor C. Vaughan House and East Quadrangle," 2.

44. Ibid., 6. George Andrews, the student author of this report, played no role in designing the building; his comments came directly from Rowland, who provided "valuable information on how these dormitories were planned."

45. Andrews, "Victor C. Vaughan House and East Quadrangle," 16.

46. "Atmosphere of Club to Mark New Detroit Branch Library," *Detroit Free Press*, February 18, 1940 (from the collection of the Historical Society of the Village of Clinton, Michigan, Wirt Rowland archives).

47. "Dedication Is Set for New Library," *Detroit Free Press*, April 13, 1940; and "Third Regional Library Will Be Opened Thursday," *Detroit News*, February 18, 1940 (from the collection of the Historical Society of the Village of Clinton, Michigan, Wirt Rowland archives).

48. "Building Upswing to Last until 1944, Says A.I.A. Official," *Weekly Bulletin of the Michigan Society of Architects* (January 4, 1938): 3.

49. *Historical Statistics of the United States 1789–1945, A Supplement to the Statistical Abstract of the United States*, Bureau of the Census, US Department of Commerce, USGPO, Washington, DC, 1949, p. H 1-26.

50. Ibid.

51. Several sources list 1938 as the end date of the partnership. "O'Dell and Rowland" appears in *Weekly Bulletin* architect reports until June 28, 1938, then in the December 13, 1938, issue, a listing for

"O'Dell, H. Augustus" suggests the partnership had broken up and O'Dell was operating on his own.

52. Announcement appearing in the *Weekly Bulletin of the Michigan Society of Architects* (April 2, 1940): 5; and Letter from Wirt Rowland to Talmage Hughes, October 30, 1940, on letterhead "Wirt C. Rowland, Architect, 616 Murphy Bldg., Detroit."

53. "Architects Registered in Michigan," *Weekly Bulletin of the Michigan Society of Architects* (March 14, 1939): 76.

54. *American Architects Directory*, 1st edition, R.R. Bowker, 1956, listing for Victor Hugo Nellenbogen.

55. Obituary, *Detroit Free Press*, May 29, 1939.

56. Rowland, "Human—All Too Human, Chapter V," 1.

57. Rowland, "New Note in Architecture Struck."

58. Rowland, "On Gothic Architecture."

59. "Membership Committee Report," John C. Thornton, chairman, *Weekly Bulletin of the Michigan Society of Architects* (March 12, 1940): 76 and 78.

60. Letter from Clair Ditchy, president of the American Institute of Architects, to Talmage Hughes, editor, MSA *Weekly Bulletin of the Michigan Society of Architects* (February 14, 1945), in the archives of the AIA Detroit chapter.

61. Letter to Talmage Hughes from Wirt Rowland, October 30, 1940, in the archives of the AIA Detroit chapter.

62. "History and Modern Architecture," *Weekly Bulletin of the Michigan Society of Architects* (November 5, 1940).

63. Ibid.

64. Architectural Guidance committee report, submitted by Wirt Rowland, chairman, published in the *Weekly Bulletin of the Michigan Society of Architects*, 1936.

65. Committee on Education report, submitted by Wirt Rowland, chairman, published in the *Weekly Bulletin of the Michigan Society of Architects* (March 14, 1939).

66. *Building the Navy's Bases in World War II: History of the Bureau of Yards and Docks and the Civil Engineer Corps, 1940–1946*, Department of the Navy, Bureau of Yards and Docks, Volume I, Chapter 10, USGPO, 1947 (available online through the HyperWar Foundation at www.ibiblio.org/hyperwar/, an exceedingly useful project initiated by the late Patrick W. Clancy).

67. Ibid.

68. Both men had degrees in civil engineering, Giffels from Michigan State, class of 1915, and Vallet from University of Colorado, class of 1916; *Michigan Manufacturer and Financial Record*, August 31, 1929, 100.

69. Ibid.

70. Buczkowski: information from his son David Brent; Charles Valentine: AIA membership application, December 21, 1943, question 13. Professional Training; John Valentine: *American Architects Directory*, 1st edition, R. R. Bowker, 1956, listing for John Robert Valentine; Tuttle: "Architects Registered in Michigan," *Weekly Bulletin of the Michigan Society of Architects* (March 14, 1939): 100, and *Weekly Bulletin of the Michigan Society of Architects* (August 25, 1942): letter from Wirt Rowland, 3.

71. Letter to his parents from Edward "Bud" Cullen, July 7, 1941, in the Wirt Rowland archives of the

Historical Society of the Village of Clinton.

72. Ibid.

73. Ibid.

74. Ibid.

75. Plan sheet number 19, "U.S. Naval Operating Base, Norfolk, VA, Chapels, Unit C," Details of Altars, drawn by W. C. Rowland, 9-12-1941, Giffels and Vallet job number 600-V-45.

76. Letter to Talmage Hughes from Wirt Rowland published in the *Weekly Bulletin of the Michigan Society of Architects* (August 25, 1942): 3.

77. Ibid.

78. A full-size set of photographic copies of Rowland's sketches are displayed in Kirk in the Hills lower level, and constitutes the largest and most significant collection of Rowland's drawings.

79. The original album given to trustee Henry A. Fielding (George's son-in-law) is in the archives of Kirk in the Hills.

80. Letter to Wirt Rowland from Edwin George, July 28, 1944 (copied in the trustee album); and Donaldson, Hubbard, and Hurtienne, "Interview," 14.

81. Rowland, "To The Trustees of The Edwin S. George Foundation," 1.

82. Rowland, "Influence of Glass on Architecture," 4.

83. Rowland, "To The Trustees of The Edwin S. George Foundation," 2.

84. Rowland, "Influence of Glass on Architecture," 5.

85. Rowland, "To The Trustees of The Edwin S. George Foundation," 2.

86. Rowland, "To The Trustees of The Edwin S. George Foundation," description for "East End of Nave" (the building as constructed faces south, while Rowland's plans were for a building facing east).

87. Rowland, "To The Trustees of The Edwin S. George Foundation," description for "The East End of the Chapel" (as constructed, this chapel is on the west end of the transept; in the original plan it was independent of the main cathedral).

88. Rowland, "To The Trustees of The Edwin S. George Foundation," description for "The West End of the Chapel Interior 1947."

89. Rowland, "To The Trustees of The Edwin S. George Foundation," description for "The Tower from the West."

90. Letter from Frank Burroughs Jr. to Wirt Rowland, May 23, 1945, in the archives of the Historical Society of Clinton, Michigan.

91. Wirt C. Rowland obituary, *Weekly Bulletin of the Michigan Society of Architects* (December 10, 1946); "Wirt C. Rowland, AIA, is confined to Jennings Hospital," *Weekly Bulletin of the Michigan Society of Architects* (October 23, 1945): 1; and "Detroit Chapter Hears Boase," *Weekly Bulletin of the Michigan Society of Architects* (December 11, 1945).

92. Letter from David Matthews to Wirt Rowland, November 3, 1946, copy in the archives of the Historical Society of Clinton.

93. Letter from Lester F. Anderson to Wirt Rowland, October 13, 1949, copy in the archives of the Historical Society of Clinton.

94. Ibid.

95. Ibid.

96. Letter from Talmage Hughes to Board of Directors, the American Institute of Architects, June 30, 1946, copy in the Wirt C. Rowland file of the AIA archives.

97. "Fellowship," from the American Institute of Architects website.

98. Letter from Talmage Hughes to Board of Directors, the American Institute of Architects, June 30, 1946, copy in the Wirt C. Rowland file of the AIA archives.

99. Letter to Talmage Hughes from Executive Director of AIA, June 26, 1946, copy in the Wirt C. Rowland file of the AIA archives.

100. Letter from Leander Kimball to Wirt Rowland, October 19, 1946, in the archives of the Historical Society of Clinton.

101. Letter from Edwin George to the trustees of the Edwin S. George Foundation, December 27, 1946, copy in the archives of Kirk in the Hills.

102. Ibid.

103. Letter from George D. Mason to Wirt Rowland, November 17, 1946, copy in the archives of the Historical Society of Clinton.

104. Postcard from Wirt Rowland addressed to Detroit Chapter, AIA, postmarked November 21, 1946.

105. Sharon Scott of the Historical Society of Clinton interview with Genevieve Burroughs Baker, April 22, 2003.

106. Florence Davies, "Death Calls Wirt Rowland," *Detroit News*, December 2, 1946.

107. Rowland, "To The Trustees of The Edwin S. George Foundation," description for "The West End of the Chapel Interior (1937)."

108. Barrie, *Interview with Corrado Parducci*.

109. Gregg Sutter, *Oakland Press*, July 5, 1981, 13, supplement, in the archives of Kirk in the Hills.

110. Barrie, *Interview with Corrado Parducci*.

111. Sutter, *Oakland Press*.

112. Rowland, "To The Trustees of The Edwin S. George Foundation," description of "St. John the Baptist Bay and Baptismal Alcove."

113. *Dreams and Visions: Kirk in the Hills, the First 50 Years*, Bloomfield Hills, Kirk in the Hills, 1997 (unnumbered).

114. Ibid.

BIBLIOGRAPHY

"A City's Beauty." *Art Digest* (mid-December 1927), 6.

Aborn, Merton Robert. "The Influence on American Musical Culture of Dvořák's Sojourn in America." PhD diss. Ann Arbor, MI: University Microfilms, 1965.

Aircraft Production Hearings before the Committee on Military Affairs, Vol 1. United States Senate. Washington, DC: Government Printing Office, 1918.

Aircraft Production Hearings before the Subcommittee of the Committee on Military Affairs, United States Senate, 65th Congress, 2nd Session. United States Congress. Washington, DC: Government Printing Office, 1918.

"Airman's View and Plan of the Typical New Army Flying Field." July 12, 1917. *Air Service Journal*, 20–21.

Albert Kahn, Architect, Detroit Michigan. 1921. New York: Architectural Catalog Company, 1921.

Albert Kahn Associates, Inc. list of jobs through 1942. Detroit: unpublished, 2013.

Albert Kahn Associates, Inc. list of wartime contributions. Detroit: unpublished, 2013.

Andrews, George F. "Victor C. Vaughan House and East Quadrangle Men's Dormitories, University of Michigan." Ann Arbor: University of Michigan, College of Architecture, 1940.

Annual Report of the Board of Education of the City of Detroit. Detroit: City of Detroit, 1911–12, 1912–13, 1914–15, 1915–16.

"Appropriateness." *Art Digest* 1, no. 13 (1927): 4.

Architecture: A List of Books in the Detroit Public Library. Detroit: Detroit Public Library, 1925.

Arnold, D. "The Evolution of Modern Office Buildings and Air Conditioning." *ASHRAE Journal*, June 1999, 40–54.

Arnold, Henry H. *The History of Rockwell Field.* US Army Air Service, 1923.

"Aviation Hospitals." In *Medical Department of the U.S. Army in the World War, Vol. V: Military Hospitals in the U.S.* Vol. 5. US Army Medical Department Office of Medical History, n.d. Retrieved from http://history.amedd.army.mil/booksdocs/wwi/MilitaryHospitalsintheUS/chapter20.htm.

Awalt, F. G. "Recollections of the Banking Crisis in 1933." *Business History Review* 43, no. 3 (1969): 347–71.

Baldwin, G. C. "The Offices of Albert Kahn, Architect." *Architectural Forum* 29, no. 5 (1918): 125–30.

Barclay-Vesey Building, NYCLPC Landmark Designation Report. New York: Landmarks Preservation Committee, 1991.

Barrie, D. *Interview with Corrado Parducci*, March 17, 1975. Retrieved from Archives of American Art,

Smithsonian Institution, www.aaa.si.edu/collections/interviews/oral-history-interview-corrado-parducci-12608#transcript.

Bell, N. R. *Architecture*. London: T. C. and E. C. Jack, 1914.

Bemis, Albert F. *The Evolving House*. Vol. 3, *Rational Design*. Cambridge, MA: Massachusetts Institute of Technology, 1936.

Benson, Robert A. *Essays on Architecture in the Midwest*. Oxford, Ohio: Interalia/Design Books, 1992.

Berke, Arnold. *Mary Colter: Architect of the Southwest*. New York: Princeton Architectural Press, 2002.

Binno-Savage, Rebecca. *Lower Woodward Avenue Historic District Final Report*. Detroit: Detroit City Council Historic Designation Advisory Board, 1998.

Binno-Savage, Rebecca, and Greg Kowalski. *Art Deco in Detroit*. Charleston, SC: Arcadia Publishing, 2004.

Boyd, Thomas M. *Worship in Wood*. Chicago: American Seating Company, 1927.

Bragdon, Claude. *The Beautiful Necessity*. Rochester, NY: Manas Press, 1910.

Braun, Lilian J. *The Story of AIA Michigan*. Detroit: American Institute of Architects Michigan Chapter, 1976.

Breeze, Carla. *American Art Deco*. New York: W. W. Norton, 2003.

———. *Pueblo Deco*. New York: Rizzoli International, 1990.

Brick and Mortar: Tallest Buildings of Each U.S. City, 1950, February 4, 2010. Retrieved March 5, 2012, from SkyscraperPage: http://forum.skyscraperpage.com/showthread.php?p=4681187.

The Buhl Building (marketing brochure). Detroit: Buhl Land Company, 1924.

"Building of Arts and Crafts Society of Detroit." *American Architect* 111, no. 2145 (1917): 78–80.

"Buildings of the Murphy Power Co." *American Architect and Building News* 92, no. 1660 (1907): 127.

Buildings: A Selection of Representative Construction Work. Detroit: Bryant and Detwiler, 1921.

"Built and Proposed Skyscrapers." *Architectural Forum* (June 1930): plate section.

Business and Finance: "Deals: Sep. 23, 1929." *Time*, September 23, 1929.

Calvert, A. F. *The Alhambra*. 2nd ed. New York: John Lane, 1907.

Cameron, R. H. *Training to Fly: Military Flight Training, 1907–1945*. Air Force History and Museums Program, 1999.

Carlson, D. A., and M. G. Smith. *Albert Kahn: 400 Buildings in Metro Detroit*, June 14, 2013. Retrieved 2015, from I Love Detroit Michigan: http://ilovedetroitmichigan.com/detroit-architecture/albert-kahn-400-buildings-in-metro-detroit/.

Cary, E. L. "New Skyscraper Modes." *New York Times*, February 12, 1928, 122.

Cassidy, L. L. "The Southwest Develops Native Architecture." *Architectural Record* (March 1926): 395–96.

Causey, E. H. "New Billion Dollar War Industry." *Rotarian* 11, no. 6 (1917): 503–7.

Chase, A. "Detroit Grows Air Minded in Its Building." *Chicago Daily Tribune*, October 6, 1929, B9.

Chrysler, Walter P. *Life of an American Workman.* 2nd ed. New York: Dodd, Mead, 1950.

Clapsadel, E. E. Letter to Smith, Hinchman and Grylls, Re: Union Industrial Bank Building, July 11, 1931.

Clark, William C., and John L. Kingston. *The Skyscraper: A Study in the Economic Height of Modern Office Buildings.* New York: American Institute of Steel Construction, 1930.

Cobb, Harold M. *The History of Stainless Steel.* Materials Park, Ohio: ASM International, 2010.

Collins, Rodney S. "9th Street West Historic District—Huntington, WV, National Register of Historic Places, Nomination Form." Charleston, WV: National Park Service, 1980.

"Color Dominates New Skyscrapers." *Washington Post*, August 4, 1929, R2.

"Color Dominant in Design of the Union Trust Building." *American Architect* (November 1929): 32–39.

"Concrete-Piling vs. Concrete Pillars for Foundation Work." *Concrete* 6, no. 5 (1906): 21–22.

Connick, Charles J. *Adventures in Light and Color.* New York: Random House, 1939.

Cook, J. "A Place Called Langley Field." *Cultural Resource Management* 23, no. 2 (2000): 27–31.

Cram, Ralph A. *American Church Building of Today.* New York: Architectural Book Publishing, 1929.

Crathern, Alice T. *Courage Was the Fashion: The Contribution of Women to the Development of Detroit.* Detroit: Wayne State University Press, 1953.

Cret, Paul P. "A Recent Aspect of an Old Conflict." *Octagon* 10, no. 10 (1938): 3–6.

Cushing, Frank H. *A Study of Pueblo Pottery as Illustrative of Zuni Culture Growth.* Washington, DC: Smithsonian Institution, Bureau of Ethnology, 1886.

Cyclopedia of Architecture, Carpentry, and Building. Vol. 4. Chicago: American Technical Society, 1912.

Davies, F. "In the Gothic Spirit." *Detroit News*, December 18, 1938, Art and Music, 1.

———. "Stone and Steel." *Detroit News*, May 14, 1939, Art and Music, 1.

———. "Wait and See." *Detroit News*, July 8, 1928, Arts, 1.

Le Detroit des Grandes Aventures (The Straits of High Adventure). Detroit: Guardian Group, 1928.

Detroit Financial District National Register of Historic Places Registration Form. Washington, DC: National Park Service, 2009.

"Detroit: Its Progress in Industry, Commerce and Banking." *Bankers Magazine* 92, no. 1 (1916): 39–61.

"The Detroit News Building; An Imposing Example of Commercial Architecture." *Architectural Forum* 28, no. 1 (1918): 27–28 and plates.

Detroit News, Union Trust Building, special supplement, March 31, 1929, 15.

"The Detroit Saturday Night Building." *Detroit Saturday Night*, September 21, 1929, section 3.

Donaldson, D., M. Hubbard, and B. Hurtienne. "Interview with Dr. Earl Pellerin." *Architext* 3, no. 2 (1985): 14–17.

Draft Final Report Capitol Park Local Historic District. Detroit: Detroit City Council Historic Designation Advisory Board, 2012.

Duffus, R. L. "The Metropolis of the Future." *New York Times*, December 8, 1929, BR6.

Edgell, George H. *The American Architecture of To-Day*. New York: Charles Scribner's Sons, 1928.

Edwards, Edward B. *Dynamarhythmic Design: A Book of Structural Patterns*. New York: Century, 1932.

"Effect of the New York Zoning Resolution on Commercial Buildings." *American Architect* 125, no. 2448 (1924): 546–50.

"The Era of Tall Buildings." *Michigan Manufacturer and Financial Record*, July 17, 1929, 113–15.

Ferry, W. Hawkins. *Buildings of Detroit*. Detroit: Wayne State University Press, 1968.

"Fifty-Third Annual Convention—The American Institute of Architects." *American Architect* 117, no. 2318 (1920): 633.

"First National Bank in Detroit, Mich." *Bankers Magazine* 105, no. 1 (July 1922): 137–49.

"Flamingo Waterway Historic District Designation Report." Miami Beach: City of Miami Beach Planning Department, 2004.

Fletcher, B. *A History of Architecture on the Comparative Method*. 17th ed. New York: Charles Scribner's Sons, 1967.

Fletcher, Rachel. *Infinite Measure: Learning to Design in Geometric Harmony with Art, Architecture, and Nature*. Staunton, VA: George F. Thompson, 2013.

Forty Stories from Bedrock: A Handbook for Visitors to the Union Trust Building. Detroit: Union Commerce Group, 1929.

Fowler, H. A. *Modern Creative Design and Its Application*. Ann Arbor, MI: George Wahr Publishing, 1951.

Frank, M. "Emil Lorch: Pure Design and American Architectural Education." *Journal of Architectural Education* 57, no. 4 (2004): 28–40. Retrieved September 7, 2013, from www.jstor.org/stable/40480508.

Gardner, S. *A Guide to English Gothic Architecture*. Cambridge: Cambridge University Press, 1922.

Gayle, M., D. W. Look, and J. G. Waite. *Metals in America's Historic Buildings*. Washington, DC: US Department of the Interior National Park Service, 1992.

"George Harrison Phelps, Inc., Building, Detroit." *Architectural Forum* (August 1926): 79–.

Goodyear, W. H. *Greek Refinements: Studies in Temperamental Architecture*. London: Henry Frowde, Oxford University Press, 1912.

"The Great Enterprises Originated by the Late Simon J. Murphy." *Detroit Free Press*, April 19, 1908, 7.

The Greater Penobscot Building (marketing brochure). Detroit: Simon J. Murphy Co., 1928.

Grinyer, C. E. *A Guide to St. John's Episcopal Church*. Detroit, 1959.

Hambidge, Jay. "Dynamic Symmetry and Modern Architecture." *Architecture* 44, no. 5 (1921): 333–35.

———. *Dynamic Symmetry and the Greek Vase*. New Haven, CT: Yale University Press, 1920.

———. *Dynamic Symmetry in Composition as Used by the Artists*. Cambridge, MA: Jay Hambidge, 1923.

———. *The Parthenon and Other Greek Temples: Their Dynamic Symmetry*. New Haven, CT: Yale University Press, 1924.

———. "The Root Rectangles." *Diagonal* 1, no. 1 (1919): 18–20.

———. "Symmetry and Proportion in Greek Art." *American Architect* 116, no. 2290 (1919): 597–605.

Hambidge, Jay, ed. *The Diagonal*. New Haven, CT: Yale University Press, 1920.

Hamlin, Alfred D. *A Text-Book of the History of Architecture*. New York: Longmans, Green, 1918.

Hearn, Lafcadio. *Exotics and Retrospectives and in Ghostly Japan*. Boston: Houghton Mifflin, 1922.

Henderson, R. "A Primative Basis for Modern Architecture." *Architectural Record* 54, no. 2 (1923): 188–96.

Henry, J. C. *Architecture in Texas*. Austin: University of Texas Press, 1993.

Histories of the Public Schools of Detroit. Detroit: Board of Education of the City of Detroit, 1967.

History of Architecture and Ornament. Scranton, PA: International Textbook Company, 1922.

History of Architecture: Architectural Design; Specifications. Scranton, PA: International Textbook Company, 1903.

History of the School of Architecture at Lawrence Institute of Technology. Southfield: unpublished, 1972.

Holleman, T. J. *Wirt C. Rowland Exhibition Catalog*. Edited by R. B. Scott. Clinton, MI: Wirt C. Rowland Exhibition Committee, Historical Society of Clinton, Michigan, 2004.

Holleman, T. J., and J. P. Gallagher. *Smith, Hinchman, and Grylls: 125 Years of Architecture and Engineering*. Detroit: Wayne State University Press, 1978.

Houghton, M. *Pioneers in Preservation: Biographical Sketches of Architects Prominent in the Field before WWII*. Washington, DC: American Institute of Architects, 1990.

"The Housing Problem in Detroit." *American Architect* 111, no. 2142 (1917): 29.

"How Automobiles Hold up Building." *Architect and Engineer* 62, no. 3 (1920): 74.

Hughes, T. C., ed. "Architects Registered in Michigan." *Weekly Bulletin of the Michigan Society of Architects* (March 14, 1939): 23–103.

Hyde, Arthur K. "Is Architecture a Skin." *Weekly Bulletin of the Michigan Society of Architects* 6, no. 23 (1932): 1, 4–8.

Hyde, Arthur K., ed. *Detroit Chapter AIA Minutes of Regular Meetings, Directors Meetings, Special Meetings.* Detroit: unpublished, 1930–33.

Hyde, Charles K. "Assembly-Line Architecture: Albert Kahn and the Evolution of the U.S. Auto Factory, 1905–1940." *Journal for the Society of Industrial Archeology* 22, no. 2 (1996).

———. *Edwin Denby High School National Register of Historic Places Nominating Form.* Washington, DC: National Park Service, 2004.

An Illustrated Story of the First Half Century of Public Lighting in Detroit 1895–1945. Detroit: Public Lighting Commission, City of Detroit, 1945.

Indian and Mexican Handicraft, Wholesale and Retail. Mesilla Park, NM: Francis E. Lester Company, 1907.

Jacobs, Michel. *The Art of Composition: A Simple Application of Dynamic Symmetry.* New York: Doubleday, Page, 1926.

Jefferson Avenue Presbyterian Church. *100 Years of Service, 1854–1954: A Review of the Historical Background and Development of Jefferson Avenue Presbyterian Church.* Detroit, 1954.

Jester, T. C. *Twentieth-Century Building Materials: History and Conservation.* New York: Technical Preservation Services, National Park Service, US Department of the Interior, 1995.

Johnson, Irwin C. *St. John's Centennial Book, 1858–1958.* Detroit: Saint John's Church, 1958.

Johnson, I. E. "A Study of Characteristic Work of Certain Contemporary Architects in the U.S." PhD diss. University of Southern California, Department of Fine Arts. Ann Arbor: ProQuest, 1939.

Journal Proceedings of the Board of Education of the City of Detroit. Detroit, 1911–12, 1912–13, 1913–14, 1914–15, 1915–16.

Kahn, Albert. "The Approach to Design." *Pencil Points* 13, no. 5 (1932): 299–301.

———. "The Architect in Industrial Building." *Architect and Engineer of California* 54, no. 3 (1918): 101–9.

———. "The Architects Problems in Designing Office Buildings." In *Proceedings of the Twentieth Annual Convention of the National Association of Building Owners and Managers*, 264–79. National Association of Building Owners and Managers, 1927.

———. "Conserving Labor and Material." *American Architect* 116, no. 2294 (1919): 731–.

———. "Designing Modern Office Building." *Architectural Forum* (1930): 775–78.

———. "Industrial Architecture." *Weekly Bulletin of the Michigan Society of Architects* (December 27, 1939): 5–10.

———. "Thirty Minutes with American Architects and Architecture." *Weekly Bulletin of the Michigan Society of Architects* (February 9, 1937): 1, 3–5, 8–10.

Kahn, Dorothea. "Color in Bank Buildings." *Christian Science Monitor*, June 20, 1929, 8.

Keep, Helen E., and Margaret A. Burton. *Guide to Detroit*. Detroit: Conover Press, 1916.

Kennelly, A. E. "Biographical Memoir of George Owen Squier." In *National Academy Biogrpahical Memoirs—Vol. XX*. National Academy of Sciences, 1938, 150–59.

Kimball, Fiske M. *American Architecture*. Indianapolis: Bobbs-Merrill, 1928.

———. "The Development of American Architecture, III: Eclecticism and Functionalism." *Architectural Forum* (July 1918): 21–25.

———. "The Family Tree of the Skyscraper." *Forum* 79, no. 3 (1928): 390–.

Kimball, Fiske M., and George H. Edgell. *A History of Architecture*. New York: Harper and Brothers, 1918.

Korom, Joseph J., Jr. *The American Skyscraper, 1850–1940: A Celebration of Height*. Boston: Branden Books, 2008.

Koyl, G. S., ed. *The AIA Historical Directory of American Architects: 1956 American Architects Directory*. 1st ed. New York: R. R. Bowker, 1955. Retrieved from http://public.aia.org/sites/hdoaa/ wiki/Wiki%20Pages/1956%20American%20Architects%20Directory.aspx.

Langley Air Force Base Historic Walking Tour, Heavier-Than-Air Area. Air Combat Command Office of History, 2010.

Lethaby, William R. *Architecture: An Introduction to the History and Theory of the Art of Building*. New York: Henry Holt, 1912.

Lowndes, William S. *Reading Architects' Blueprints*. Scranton, PA: International Textbook Company, 1922.

Longacre, E. G. "A Place Like No Other: The Origins of Langley Field, 1916–1921." *Air Power History* 44, no. 4 (1997): 4–17.

Lorch, E. Emil Lorch Papers, 1891–2004. Ann Arbor, MI: Bentley Historical Library, University of Michigan.

Mason, George D. Personal diary for the years 1902–1909. Burton Historical Collection of the Detroit Public Library.

McClelland, L. F., D. L. Ames, and S. D. Pope. *Historic Residential Suburbs in the United States, 1830– 1960*. Washington, DC: National Park Service, US Department of the Interior, National Register of Historic Places, 2002.

McMurry, O. L., G. W. Eggers, and C. A. McMurry. *Teaching of Industrial Arts in the Elementary School*. New York: Macmillan, 1923.

Meier, W. R. "Planning for Profit: The Stott Building, Detroit." *American Architect* (September 1930): 44–47, 110.

Michigan Bell and Western Electric Warehouse Historic District Final Report. Detroit: Detroit City Council Historic Designation Advisory Board, 2009.

Michigan Manufacturer and Financial Record. Union Trust Building. Special supplement, 43, no. 13, March 30, 1929, 1–94.

Mindeleff, Victor. *A Study of Pueblo Architecture in Tusayan and Cibola*. Washington, DC: Bureau of Ethnology and Smithsonian Institution, 1891.

Miscall, Leonard. *Erection of Steel Building Frames*. Scranton, PA: International Textbook Company, 1938.

Moore, C. J. "Some Essentials of the Modern Manufacturing Building." *American Architect* 99, no. 1851 (1911): 219–.

Morgan, J. "Story of the Dollar Savings." *National Magazine*, December 1913, 531–32.

Morphology. US Navy Quonset Hut, Weapons of Mass Construction, December 2012, http://quonset-hut.blogspot.com/p/morphology.html, retrieved October 7, 2013.

The Mouthpiece (through 1928); The Michigan Bell (beginning in 1928). Detroit: Michigan Bell Telephone Company, 1922–31.

Mumford, L. "American Architecture To-Day." *Architecture* 57, no. 4 (1928): 181–88.

Newcomb, Rexford. *Outlines of the History of Architecture*. Part IV, *Modern Architecture*. New York: John Wiley and Sons, 1939.

"New York Again in Skyscraper Race." *New York Times*, February 20, 1927, RE13.

Niederlander, D. B. "United States Aeronautical Schools." *Architectural Record* 45, no. 248 (1919): 441–49.

"Office Building and Studio, George Harrison Phelps, Inc., Detroit, Mich." *American Architect* 130 (July 20, 1926).

Onderdonk, F. S. *The Ferro-Concrete Style: Reinforced Concrete in Modern Architecture*. New York: Architectural Book Publishing, 1928.

Our Early Beginnings and Traditions . . . Canada Creek Ranch, n.d.. www.canadacreekranch.com/About_Us/History.aspx, retrieved 2014.

Paris, W. F. "Italian Renaissance in Detroit." *American Architect and Architectural Review* 123, no. 2410 (1923): 15–19, 21.

Part I: The Age of Propellers; Chapter 3: The Lean Years, 1918–26. Quest for Performance: The Evolution of Modern Aircraft (NASA), n.d., http://history.nasa.gov/SP-468/ch3–3.htm, retrieved December 4, 2014.

Peet, Stephen Denison, Rev. *The Cliff Dwellers and Pueblos*. Chicago: Office of the American Antiquarian, 1899.

Pellerin, E. W. "Reflections on Life in Architecture and Education." *Monthly Bulletin of the Michigan Society of Architects* (December 1974): 3–5.

Perry, M. C. *Adventures in Ceramics: The Story of Mary Chase Perry and the Pewabic Pottery*. Detroit: Unpublished, ca. 1930.

"Pewabic Tiles to Decorate Crypt in Beautiful Shrine in Washington." *Detroit News*, April 19, 1925, 9.

Phillipps, Lisle March. *Form and Colour*. New York: Charles Scribner's Sons, 1915.

———. *The Works of Man*. London: Duckworth, 1911.

The Pontchartrain Club (promotional brochure). Detroit: Pontchartrain Club, ca. 1929.

Poore, C. G. "108-Story Building Focuses Skyscraper Issue." *New York Times*, December 26, 1926, XX5.

Pound, A. *Building on Faith in Flint*. Flint, MI: Union Industrial Trust and Savings Bank, 1930.

Quonset Huts. Seabee Museum and Memorial Park, 2014, www.seabeesmuseum.com/quonset_huts.html.

Reineri, A. B. *Iktinos: This Is Our History*. Ann Arbor, MI: Alpha Rho Chi, 1992.

Report No. 1455: Stock Exchange Practices: Hearings before the Committee on Banking and Currency, United States Senate, Seventy-Third Congress, Second Session, on Senate Res. 84 73d Congress. United States Congress, Senate, Committee on Banking and Currency. Washington, DC: US Government Printing Office, 1934.

Rice, W. G. *Carillon Music and Singing Towers of the Old World and New*. New York: Dodd, Mead, 1925.

Richards, W. C. "Trust Building Opens Tuesday." *Detroit Free Press*, March 31, 1929, 1 and 3.

Ross, Denman W. *A Theory of Pure Design: Harmony, Balance, Rhythm*. Boston: Houghton, Mifflin, 1907.

Rowland, Wirt Clinton. "An Architect's Attitude Towards Music." *All the Arts* 3, no. 1 (1920): 3, 5.

———. "An Architect Writes a Student." *Weekly Bulletin of the Michigan Society of Architects* 8, no. 1 (January 2, 1934): 1, 3–4.

———. "Architecture and the Automobile Industry." *Architectural Forum* (1921): 199–206.

———. "The Architecture of Your Church." *Weekly Bulletin of the Michigan Society of Architects* 8, no. 25 (June 19, 1934): 1, 4.

———. "Heigho! I Go to 'The Fair.'" *Weekly Bulletin of the Michigan Society of Architects* 8, no. 43 (October 23, 1934): 1, 4–6.

———. "Human—All Too Human, Chapter II." *Weekly Bulletin of the Michigan Society of Architects* (April 25, 1939): 7.

———. "Human—All Too Human, Chapter IV." *Weekly Bulletin of the Michigan Society of Architects* 14, no. 17 (April 23, 1940): 1, 4.

———. "Human—All Too Human, Chapter V." *Weekly Bulletin of the Michigan Society of Architects* 14, no. 45 (November 5, 1940): 1, 4.

———. "An Influence of Glass on Architecture," edited by T. Hughes, *Weekly Bulletin of the Michigan Society of Architects* 12, no. 10 (March 8, 1938): 1, 4–5.

———. "The Making of an Architect," edited by N. J. Corey, *All the Arts* 3, no. 2 (1920): 39, 41.

———. *Metal Work, Union Guardian Building*. Personal correspondence, Detroit, July 1931.

———. "Mr. Wirt C. Rowland on Modernism." *Weekly Bulletin of the Michigan Society of Architects* (June

14, 1932): 1, 4–8.

———. "Music and the Architect." *Weekly Bulletin of the Michigan Society of Architects* 14, no. 4 (January 23, 1940): 1, 5.

———. "New Note in Architecture Struck." *Detroit News*, March 31, 1929, special section, 3.

———. "New York, Old and New." *Weekly Bulletin of the Michigan Society of Architects* 12, no. 8 (February 22, 1938): 1, 6, 7.

———. "On Gothic Architecture," edited by T. Hughes, *Weekly Bulletin of the Michigan Society of Architects* 13 (March 1939): 4.

———. "Real Progress." *Architectural Progress* (August 1931): 15, 16, 23.

———. "Science Brings New Help to Modern Home Makers." *Detroit Free Press*, December 1933, 13.

———. "Sunday's Child." *Weekly Bulletin of the Michigan Society of Architects* (January 17, 1939): 1, 4.

———. "To The Trustees of The Edwin S. George Foundation." In *Trustee Album*, by E. S. George. Bloomfield Hills, MI, 1944.

———. "A Vacation from Architecture." *Weekly Bulletin of the Michigan Society of Architects* 14, no. 46 (November 12, 1940): 1, 4–6.

Saarinen, E. "Foreign Architect on $100,000 Tribune Contest." *Michigan Architect and Engineer* 5 (April 1923): 54–55.

Schnitz, J. L. "Moving Reinforced Concrete Building to a New Site." *Concrete* (August 1919): 60–62.

Secord, Paul R. *Albuquerque Deco and Pueblo*. Charleston, SC: Arcadia Publishing, 2012.

Selfridge Field, Historic American Engineering Record. Library of Congress, n.d.

"The 'Set-Back' Runs through the Ages." *New York Times*, February 27, 1929, SM6.

Sexton, R. W. *American Commercial Buildings of Today*. New York: Architectural Book Publishing, 1928.

———. *The Logic of Modern Architecture*. New York: Architectural Book Publishing, 1929.

Sharpe, Edmund. *The Seven Periods of English Architecture*. New York: E. and F. N. Spon, 1888.

Shedd, C. L. "Steel Construction." *Architectural Forum* (April, May, and June 1921): 129–32, 183–86, 207–11.

Smith, M. G., and R. Fletcher. "Proportioning Systems in Wirt C. Rowland's Union Trust Guardian Building." *Nexus Network Journal: Architecture and Mathematics* 17, no. 1 (2015): 207–29.

Spain, C. L. "The Detroit Public Schools." *School Board Journal* 52, no. 2 (1916): 11–15, 86–88.

Squier, George O. *Aeronautics in the United States at the Signing of the Armistice 1918*. American Institute of Electrical Engineers, 1919.

Stair, J. L. *The Lighting Book*. Chicago: Curtis Lighting, 1930.

Stock Exchange Practices: Hearings before the Committee on Banking and Currency, United States Senate, Seventy-Third Congress, Second Session, on S. Res. 84 (72d Congress). United States Congress. Washington, DC: Government Printing Office, 1934.

Stran-Steel House at A Century of Progress (promotional brochure). Detroit: Stran-Steel Corporation, 1933.

"The Studio Presents The Good Houskeeping—Stran-Steel House." *Good Housekeeping*, July 1933, 52–55, 109–10.

Sturgis, Russel. *A Dictionary of Architecture and Building*. New York: Macmillan, 1905.

———. *A History of Architecture*. Vol. 2, *Romanesque and Oriental*. New York: Baker and Taylor, 1909.

Sullivan, Louis H. *The Autobiography of an Idea*. New York: Press of the American Institute of Architects, 1924.

Surette, T. W. "Music." In *The Significance of the Fine Arts*, by American Institue of Architects. Boston: Marshall Jones, 1923.

Tallant, H. "Acoustic Design in the Hill Memorial Auditorium, University of Michigan." *Brickbuilder* 22, no. 8 (1913): 169–73, and plates.

Tallmadge, Thomas E. *The Story of Architecture in America*. New York: W. W. Norton, 1936.

Taschner, Mary. "Richard Requa: Southern California Architect, 1881–1941." Master's thesis, University of San Diego, Department of History, 1982.

Thompson, Frank B. *Eighty Years: A Brief History of St. John's Church, Detroit*. Detroit, 1939.

Tottis, James W. *The Guardian Building: Cathedral of Finance*. Detroit: Wayne State University Press, 2008.

Truscon Floretyle Construction (marketing booklet). Youngstown, OH: Truscon Steel Company, 1923.

Union Trust Company Detroit, 36th Anniversary Booklet. Detroit: Union Trust Company, 1927.

"Value of Concrete as Reinforcement for Structural Steel Columns." *Cement Age* (June 1929): 282–83.

Various. 1919–64. *The Archi of Alpha Rho Chi*.

Various. 1926–55. *Weekly Bulletin of the Michigan Society of Architects*. Detroit: Michigan Society of Architects.

Viollet-le-Duc, E. E. *Discourses on Architecture*. Translated by H. V. Brunt. Boston: J. R. Osgood, 1875.

Walker, Ralph T. "Architecture." *North American Review* 231, no. 6 (1931): 528–31.

———. "Selecting Materials for the New York Telephone Building." *Architecture* (January 1928): 59–60.

Ware, William R. *The American Vignola, Part 2: Arches and Vaults, Roofs and Domes, Doors and Windows*. Scranton, PA: International Textbook Company, 1906.

Warren, H. L. "Architecture: Renaissance and Modern." *Progress for the Promotion of the Fine Arts* (1900): 190–232.

———. "The Department of Architecture of Harvard University." *Architectural Record* 22, no. 2 (1907).

Wenzell, Herbert G. "Symposium on Modernism." *Weekly Bulletin of the Michigan Society of Architects* 6, no. 25 (1932): 1, 4–5.

———. "Architect Predicts Short Life for Streamlined Buildings." *Architect and Engineer* 137 (June 1939): 46, 61.

White, L. H. *The Detroit News 1873–1917: A Record of Progress*. Detroit: Evening News Association, 1918.

Wilby, E. "The Mystery and Philosophy of Architecture," edited by T. C. Hughes. *Weekly Bulletin of the Michigan Society of Architects* 15, no. 10 (March 11, 1941): 1, 4–5.

William G. Malcomson Scrapbook of Newspaper Clippings Related to Detroit Public School Work. Detroit: unpublished, 1913–21.

Withey, Henry F., and Elsie Rathburn Withey. *Biographical Dictionary of American Architects (deceased)*. Los Angeles: New Age Publishing, 1956.

"Work Progresses on New Saturday Night Building." *Detroiter*, March 25, 1929, 6.

Yatsko, A. U.S. Army Rockwell Field Historic District, National Register of Historic Places Registration Form. National Park Service, 1990.

Year Book of the Thumb Tack Club of Detroit and Catalogue of the Annual Exhibition. Detroit: Thumb Tack Club, 1921, 1922, 1923, 1924, 1925, and 1928.

INDEX

Page numbers in italics refer to images.

A

H

Murphy, Fred T., 172

Murphy, Simon J., 172

Murphy, William H., 172, 191

music and design, 5, 38, 111–15, 201, 259, 384

N

National Advisory Committee for Aeronautics (NACA), 90, 433n77

National Town and Country Club, 304–7, *306–7. See also* Pontchartrain Club

Native Americans, 94, 127–29, 145, 151, *150–51*, 221–22, 226, *229–30*, 241, 247, 260–62, *261*, 362

Nellenbogen, Victor, 383

neoclassical architecture, 101, 116, *247*, 248. *See also* classical architecture; First National Bank Building; General Motors Building; United Savings Bank Building

Netzorg, Rose, 169

New Center area of Detroit, 78, 97, 290, *292*, 317, *321*

New Center Building (Albert Kahn Building), 317, *321*, 335

Nirosta stainless steel, 274, 323–24

Norfolk Naval Air Station (Virginia), 388–91, *390–91*

Norman architecture. *See* Romanesque architecture

Numidian marble, 201; quarry in Africa, 446–47n1

O

Octowindow shape, *218*, 230–31, *234–35*, 314–19, *315–17*, 321, *321*, *323–24*, 325, *327*, 328, *328*

O'Dell, H. Augustus "Gus," 11, 63–64, 339–40, 344, *351*, 354, 359, 383

O'Dell and Rowland, 339–40, 344, 346, *348*, 350–51, *351*, 354, 365, 367, 369, 371, 378, 383

office buildings, design considerations, 98–100, 118, 120–23, *120–21*, 129–31, 179, *180*, 181–82, 187–89

office space, rental of, 99, 120–21, *120–21*

Olson, Dr. Kenneth, 50

ornamentation (on buildings), 1–2, 40, 44, 50, 62, 68, 74–76, 80, 103, 123, 126, 116, 141–43, *141–42*, 144–45, *144*, *147*, 150–51, 155–56, *156*, 165, 176–78, 270–72, 285, 293–94, 303

Our Lady of Victory Chapel, 391, *391*

P

Painter, Walter S., 11–12, 383

Palladio, Andrea, 24, *25*

Palmer, Clarence W., *33*

Rookwood Pottery, *214*

root rectangles. *See* dynamic symmetry; geometric design methods: root rectangles

Rosetti, Louis, 388

Ross, Denman W., 361

Rowland, Wirt C.: and AIA, 107, 133, 313–14, 340–42; and MSA, 107, 339, 386–87; architects' opinions of, 3, 313, 329, 363; architectural drawings, *43*, *49*, *63*, *131*, 366, *366*, 373, *373*, *391–92*, *394–96*, *399*, 465n78; artwork, 8, *163*, *377*, 385–86, *386–87*; autograph, *352*; contest entries, 40, *43*, 49, *50*, 60–61, 335–36, *336*; death, 329, 401; described by Albert Kahn, 35; described by George Mason, 23; education, 7–8, *7*, 37, 40; effect of bank holiday on, 359; employment, 4, 8, 11, 23, 30, 40, 53, 61–62, 68, 119, 311, 383, 388; family home, 5–6, *6*, 63, 222; foreign travel, 26, 116, 176, 178; freelance work, 63, 383; illness, 397, 400–401; independence as a designer, 103, 117, 119; lectures at DIA, 113, 386; lifestyle, 5, *163*; marriage, 5; memorial library, 362; military career, 67–68; on architectural sculpture, 74; on architectural themes, 202; on church design, 232–33, *401*; on Classical architecture, 39, 74–75, 102–3; on color, 176, 180, 196, 201–2, 232–33, 444n56; Gothic architecture, 102, 163, 375–78, 392–93; on home design, 345, 348–49; on kitchen design, 353–54; on music, 113, 116, 384–85, 202; on music and architectural design, 202; on propriety of church architecture, 375–76; on Romanesque architecture, 74, 102; on round arch, 267; on understanding architecture, 165; organist, 436n53; personality, 2, *163*, 390; residences, 26, 50–51, *51*; school design, attribution of, 427–28n60; singing, 25–26, *27*, 48; speaker American Civic Association, 344–45; Thumb Tack Club president, 107, 111; two reinforced concrete buildings on the same location, 106; types of buildings designed, 4; writing, 113, 339, 384–87, *385*, 392

Rowland, Wirt C., family of: Clinton Charles (father), 5, 7; Grace Gail (sister), 6–7, *8*; Ruth Melissa Willis (mother), 5, 61. *See also* Burroughs family

Russel, Henry, 173, 184

Russell House Hotel, 19, 20

Ryan Automatic Electric Scintillator, 215–18

S

Saarinen, Eliel, 125, 321, 334–35, *335*, 342

Sabine, Wallace C., 42

Saginaw, Michigan. *See* Michigan Bell office buildings: Saginaw; Second National Bank of Saginaw Building

Santa Fe style, 94–95, 244

Saturday Night Building. *See* Detroit Saturday Night Building

Schilling, Edward A., 318

school buildings, design of, 53–59, *58*, 300–301, 303, 368–69

school buildings, Detroit public: Anthony Wayne, 318, *322*; Bennett, 53, 57, 413; Breitmeyer, 57, *61*, 413; Burton, 53, 413; Capitol High (destroyed by fire), 51, *52*; Carstens, *61*, 413; Chaney, 318–19, *323*; Denby High, 300, 302–3, 419; Ellis, 57, 413; Harms, 57, *61*, 413; Hillger, 53, 413;

Tuller Hotel (Detroit), 12, 18–19, *19*

Tuller, Lew Whiting, 18

Tuttle, Edward X., 388, *391*